CHAPTER 5: Biological and Psychological Theories

THEORY	MAJOR THEORISTS	WHAT THE THEORY EXPLAINS	POLICY IMPLICATIONS	INFLUENTIAL ACTORS
BIO-CRIMINOLOGY		Searches for the causes of antisocial behavior within the brain or body.	Head Start programs; youth programs that develop the brain and provide nutrition; drug and alcohol rehabilitation programs; parenting classes.	researchers, scientists, doctors, social workers, nutritionists, teachers
Genes and behavior	Adrian Raine, Guang Guo	The idea that both genes and environment are responsible for behavior.		
Evolution, aggression, and survival		Antisocial behavior influences human evolution.		
Neurological perspectives		Neurological conditions affect antisocial behavior.		
Environmental perspectives		The substances most commonly connected to antisocial behavior and criminal offending are drugs and alcohol.		
PSYCHO-LOGICAL AND PSYCHIATRIC PERSPECTIVES			School and after-school programs; parenting classes; recreational programs; Head Start programs; psychological counseling.	researchers, scientists, doctors, social workers, nutritionists, teachers
Behaviorism	B. F. Skinner	Environment and learning mainly determine behavior.		
Social learning theory		People learn behavior from watching others, then develop their own thoughts and attitudes about that behavior.		
Cognitive theory	Lawrence Kohlberg	Used to learn more about the mental processes that precede the decision to break the law.		
Language impairment and IQ		IQ and language ability affect delinquency and adult offending.		
Antisocial personality disorder, psychopathy, and insanity	Robert Hare	Mental disorders affect the propensity of individuals to break the law.		

INTRODUCTION TO

Criminology

A BRIEF EDITION

INTRODUCTION TO

Criminology

A BRIEF EDITION

John Randolph Fuller
Professor Emeritus, University of West Georgia

New York Oxford
Oxford University Press

Oxford University Press is a department of the University of Oxford.
It furthers the University's objective of excellence in research, scholarship,
and education by publishing worldwide. Oxford is a registered trade mark of
Oxford University Press in the UK and certain other countries.

Published in the United States of America by Oxford University Press
198 Madison Avenue, New York, NY 10016, United States of America.

For titles covered by Section 112 of the US Higher Education
Opportunity Act, please visit www.oup.com/us/he for the
latest information about pricing and alternate formats.

Cataloging-in-Publication data is on file at the Library of Congress
ISBN: 978-0-19-064169-6

9 8 7 6 5 4 3 2 1
Printed by LSC Communications, United States of America

For Amy
For Everything

Brief Contents

Contents

PART II THEORIES OF CRIME

FEATURES

FEATURES

Preface

Criminology is a rapidly changing discipline, and it is changing in many directions. This text, *Introduction to Criminology: A Brief Edition* puts the changes into context so that the student will be able to appreciate the history of criminology, the forces that are compelling it to change, and how those transformations affect criminology and the criminal justice system's response to crime. The text should inspire the reader to think critically about the study of crime as it presents the field in an organized and innovative way.

Criminal offenses are varied in the motivations of offenders and the harm they do to individuals and society. Thus, criminology has evolved in many ways. *Introduction to Criminology: A Brief Edition* illustrates the emerging changes in the relationship between society and its attempts to control deviant and unlawful behavior.

The changes in criminology are envisioned in the following concerns:

- ***Maturation and innovation in criminological theory.*** Theories devoted to the explanation of why people break the law have been evolving over the past 40 years. Theories have been developed by the application of new empirical studies and the introduction of new technologies to ascertain the reasons why people break the law. This text includes consideration of these changes in criminological theory in part by focusing on advances in biological explanations of crime, emphasizing life-course and integrated theories, and covering critical theories that emphasize the influence of variables such as sex, gender, social class, and race.
- ***Tension between security and privacy.*** Although individual rights and the protection of society have long been a concern in criminology, this tension has been heightened by the problems of terrorism. The protections afforded by the U.S. Constitution, international law, and the Geneva Convention are all now subject to reinterpretation in light of the threat of terrorism. Of particular concern to some scholars is the way in which concern for terrorism has fueled significant changes in how traditional crime is addressed.
- ***A blending of domestic and international crime control.*** Terrorism has caused sweeping and often confusing changes in the missions of its criminal justice agencies. These changes are most evident in the creation of the Department of Homeland Security which reorganized the federal portion of the criminal justice system and demanded a new relationship between local, state, and federal agencies. It is not yet clear exactly how crime will be addressed in the future, but it is clear that an expanded vision of criminal activity has introduced new political and structural changes in how the United States responds to crime.
- ***The introduction of new types of crime.*** Technology has enabled many types of criminal offenses that did not exist only a few years ago. Additionally, technology has made it possible for lawbreakers to become more sophisticated in committing old offenses in new ways. Variations on offenses such as stalking, identity theft, larceny, child pornography, and the threat of biological, chemical, and nuclear terrorism all have emerged or become more serious in recent years. The discipline of criminology is struggling to develop theories and responses to these nascent forms of crime.

Introduction to Criminology: A Brief Edition does not neglect consideration of how the discipline has fared to this point. The text is grounded in the history of crime and criminology, traditional theories, and traditional crime control efforts, but it aims to extend the consideration of these issues to incorporate recent changes in the political, social, and economic concerns of the new century. Criminology is an exciting discipline that is affected by technology, nationalism, global concerns, and identity politics. Only by considering these developments can criminology explain antisocial behavior to students, suggest policy implications to decision-makers, and keep current with new and different criminal threats to society. *Introduction to Criminology: A Brief Edition* provides a balanced context while remaining faithful to the important and substantial work of previous scholars.

Organization of the Text

This book is 14 chapters long and divided into four parts.

1. **Part I** helps the student develop an understanding of the definition of crime and the scope of the discipline. Chapter 1 presents a brief history of criminology as an academic discipline and an overview of social control. It differentiates criminology from criminal justice and demonstrates how criminology is an interdisciplinary endeavor. Chapter 1 discusses what criminologists do and how they inform the criminal justice system. Chapter 2 presents the challenges and difficulties inherent in measuring crime. It covers the major techniques of measuring crime and points out their strengths and shortcomings. Chapter 3 considers the discipline from the victim's viewpoint. Often the forgotten party in crime, the victim is being welcomed back into the criminal justice decision-making process. This book gives them a prominent role in the first part of the text.
2. **Part II** covers the important criminological theories and features a separate chapter on the classical and positivist schools of criminology. These perspectives are at the heart of the discipline, and some texts cover them in a superficial manner. This text covers the major figures in each school and also provides sections that explain how these schools still influence crime-control policy. Four additional chapters cover the theories that professors expect from a criminology text. Of special note here is the expanded coverage given to critical and political theories of crime and how they are related to the new challenges posed by terrorism. By relating traditional theories of crime to new issues, students can appreciate how central the study of criminology is to becoming an informed citizen.
3. **Part III** deals with crime typologies. Its four chapters cover the range of criminal offenses and are organized by offenses against people; offenses against property; organized, corporate, and political crime; and, finally, public-order offenses. Each chapter attends to the traditional problems associated with these offenses and the challenges posed by globalism, terrorism, and technology. The themes underlying these chapters are that the nature and threat of many criminal offenses are changing, and public policy is lagging behind.
4. In **Part IV**, Chapter 13 covers terrorism's effect on the criminal justice system. This is important to the study of criminology because everyone has to reorient the roles, mandates, and boundaries of each type and level of criminal justice agency. Additionally, this chapter discusses hate crime. Much like terrorism, hate crime is not a unique offense, but rather is an enhancer of

crime. For instance, a murder committed during a terrorist or hate crime incident is still a murder, but the political nature of the offense makes it different, thus demanding a bolstered response from society. Chapter 14 focuses on the issue of balancing the rights of individuals with concerns for safety and security. This promises to be a continuing concern in criminology and deserves a full chapter to explore its many dimensions. It is hoped that the students who are alerted to these issues in this text will be the ones who develop the vision to construct the future of criminology in a way that is fair, just, and humane.

Pedagogical Features

These features should excite the interest of students while showing them how criminology affects individuals and society, how theories have implications for the way society responds to crime, and how ethical decision-making in the criminal justice system is often difficult.

- **Opening vignettes.** Each chapter begins with an opening vignette that presents real-life incidents drawn from media coverage. These cases relate to the chapter material and illustrate how human behavior may harm others. The intent of the vignettes is not to sensationalize crime, but rather to show the range of violations of the law and how the study of criminology can help make sense of deviant behavior. Students will recognize many of these vignettes, whereas other scenarios will be new to them. All of the vignettes will help students comprehend the materials in the chapter.
- **Policy Implications.** Policy Implications emphasize real-world implications of criminological theory. This feature is especially important in Part II which deals with criminological theory. The intent is to alert students to how theory relates to criminology and criminal justice.
- **Focus on Ethics.** Focus on Ethics presents students with scenarios in which they must make decisions in situations in which the right answer is not always clear. These scenarios often challenge students to choose between preserving their self-interest, remaining loyal to friends, enforcing the law, or preventing harm to someone else. The scenarios demonstrate that dealing ethically with challenges in the criminal justice system is not easy. Focus on Ethics stimulates class discussions and allows students to compare how their reasoning compares with the reasoning of others.
- **Critical thinking.** In addition to the Critical Reflections questions at the end of each chapter, questions are included in every figure, feature, photograph, and at the end of each section. These questions consistently encourage the students to reflect on the material they have read. In addition, many of the questions require the students to apply the knowledge they have gained from the book to broader issues.

Supplements

Oxford University Press offers a complete and authoritative supplements package for both instructors and students. When you adopt *Introduction to Criminology: A Brief Edition*, you will have access to an exemplary set of learning resources to enhance teaching and support student learning.

Ancillary Resource Center (ARC)

A convenient, instructor-focused destination for resources accompanies *Introduction to Criminology: A Brief Edition*. Accessed online through individual user accounts (https://arc2.oup-arc.com/), the ARC provides instructors with access to up-to-date ancillaries at any time, while guaranteeing the security of grade-significant resources. In addition, it allows Oxford University Press to keep instructors informed when new content becomes available. The ARC for *Introduction to Criminology: A Brief Edition* includes:

- **Instructor's Manual:** For each chapter of the textbook, the instructor's manual includes the following:
    - **Learning Objectives:** The learning objectives are based on the content of the book and expressed in a manner that makes assessment possible.
    - **Chapter Summaries:** Full summaries of each chapter provide a thorough review of the important facts and concepts covered.
    - **Chapter Outlines:** Detailed outlines give an overview of each chapter.
    - **Key Terms:** Key terms are defined in the instructor's manual as well as in the margins of the book and in the glossary.
- **Textbook Figures and Tables:** All of the textbook's illustrations and tables are provided for instructor use.
- **PowerPoint Resources:** Complete lecture outlines are presented, ready for use in class.
- **Computerized Test Bank:** A complete test bank provides instructors with a wide range of test items (approximately 40 multiple-choice and five essay questions per chapter).
- **Focus on Ethics Videos:** Designed to enhance the educational value of the Focus on Ethics features at the end of each chapter, these videos and accompanying exercises help students connect the scenarios presented in the chapters to real-world situations. Available on the text companion website, the exercises guide students through a series of questions expanding the analysis of the ethical and practical implications of each Focus on Ethics scenario. They are ideal for use as lecture starters or as assignments.
- **Complementary Lecture Topics:** A list of topics that relate to specific issues raised in the text.
- **Careers in Criminal Justice:** An annotated list of 50 criminal justice agencies' websites allows students to learn what each of these agencies require for employment and what benefits they provide to their employees.
- **Interactive Media Activities:** Designed to reinforce key concepts with real-world situations, each activity:
    - Takes approximately 10 minutes to complete and produces unique results for each student.
    - Enable students to see how criminal justice works, experiencing the decision-making required of the job.
    - Is optimized to work on any mobile device or computer.
    - Ends with assessments to connect the activity to classroom discussions.

Student Companion Website

The free and open access companion website for *Introduction to Criminology: A Brief Edition* helps students to review what they have learned from the textbook as well as explore other resources online.

- **Chapter Summaries:** Full summaries in each chapter provide a thorough review of the important facts and concepts covered.
- **Learning Objectives:** The learning objectives are based on the content of the book and expressed in a manner that makes assessment possible.
- **Self Quizzes:** Self quizzes provide sessions that are separate from the test bank. Approximately 15 questions per chapter.
- **Find It Online:** An exercise designed to enhance students' research expertise by finding related criminology concepts online.
- **Chapter Outlines:** Detailed outlines give an overview of each chapter.
- **Key Term Flashcards:** An interactive study feature where students click on key terms and reveal definitions.
- **Crossword Puzzles:** Each chapter as a crossword puzzle that utilizes the key terms.
- **Careers in Criminal Justice:** An annotated list of 50 criminal justice agencies' websites allows students to learn what each of these agencies require for employment and what benefits they provide to their employees.
- **Focus on Ethics Videos:** Designed to enhance the educational value of the Focus on Ethics features at the end of each chapter, these videos and accompanying exercises help students connect the scenarios presented in the chapters to real-world situations. Available on the text companion website, the exercises guide students through a series of questions expanding the analysis of the ethical and practical implications of each Focus on Ethics scenario. They are ideal for use as lecture starters or as assignments.
- **Interactive Media Activities:** Designed to reinforce key concepts with real-world situations, each activity:
  - Takes approximately 10 minutes to complete and produces unique results for each student.
  - Enables students to see how criminal justice works, experiencing the decision-making required of the job.
  - Is optimized to work on any mobile device or computer.
  - Ends with assessments to connect the activity to classroom discussions.

  Interactive Media Activities will cover topics such as discretion criminal justice system, prosecutor misconduct, prison contraband, job application dilemmas, and probation internship.

Dashboard

Dashboard is Oxford University Press's nationally hosted learning management system. It features a streamlined interface that connects instructors and students with the functions they perform most often, simplifying the learning experience to save instructors time and put student's progress first. Dashboard's prebuilt assessments were created specifically to accompany *Introduction to Criminology: A Brief Edition* and are automatically graded so that instructors can see student progress instantly.

- **Practice Questions:** There are 20 questions per chapter (10 multiple-choice, 10 true/false), distinct from what is offered in the ARC and student companion website.
- **Interactive Media Activities:** Designed to reinforce key concepts with real-world situations, each activity:
    - Takes approximately 10 minutes to complete and produces unique results for each student.
    - Enables students to see how criminal justice works, experiencing the decision-making required of the job.
    - Is optimized to work on any mobile device or computer.
    - Ends with assessments to connect the activity to classroom discussions.
- **Careers in Criminal Justice:** An annotated list of 50 criminal justice agencies' websites allows students to learn what each of these agencies require for employment and what benefits they provide to their employees.
- **Focus on Ethics Videos:** Designed to enhance the educational value of the Focus on Ethics features at the end of each chapter, these videos and accompanying exercises help students connect the scenarios presented in the chapters to real-world situations. Available on the text companion website, the exercises guide students through a series of questions expanding the analysis of the ethical and practical implications of each Focus on Ethics scenario. They are ideal for use as lecture starters or as assignments.
- **Chapter Summaries:** Full summaries in each chapter provide a thorough review of the important facts and concepts covered.
- **Learning Objectives:** The learning objectives are based on the content of the book and expressed in a manner that makes assessment possible.
- **Self Quizzes:** Self quizzes provide sessions that are separate from the test bank. Approximately 15 questions per chapter.
- **Find It Online:** An exercise designed to enhance students' research expertise by finding related criminology concepts online.
- **Chapter Outlines:** Detailed outlines give an overview of each chapter.
- **Key Term Flashcards:** An interactive study feature where students click on key terms and reveal definitions.
- **Crossword Puzzles:** Each chapter as a crossword puzzle that utilizes the key terms.

Course Cartridges

For instructors who wish to use their campus learning management system, a course cartridge containing all of the ARC and Dashboard resources is available for a variety of e-learning environments.

eBook

Introduction to Criminology: A Brief Edition is available as an eBook via Redshelf, Vitalsource, and Chegg.

Introduction to Criminology: A Brief Edition strives to spark the interest of students in the fascinating and rapidly changing field of criminology. The text is written in a style that will maintain the students' interest and impart the necessary information to master the subject. Finally, it convinces the reader that the study of criminology is a story that is still unfolding. By equipping the student with the critical-thinking skills to ascertain the changing nature of the discipline, *Introduction to Criminology: A Brief Edition* entices students to engage in the further study of crime.

Acknowledgments

I wish to thank the following reviewers for their many insightful comments and suggestions. This text has benefited greatly from their constructive input.

Amin Asfari, Wake Technical Community College
Abigail R. Ellis, University of North Florida
Jacqueline M. Mullany, Triton College
Anne L. Strouth, North Central State College
Carl S. Taylor, Michigan State University
Prabha Unnithan, Colorado State University
Dr. Harold A Wells, Texas Southern University/Tennessee State University
Bonnie Black, Mesa Community College/Arizona State University/ Yavapai College
James C. Brown, Utica College
Samantha L. Carlo, Miami Dade College
Michael Costelloe, Northern Arizona University
Tina Freiburger, University of Wisconsin-Milwaukee
Joel Maatman, Lansing Community College
Maria Tcherni-Buzzeo, University of New Haven
Shonda Whetstone, Blinn College
Lauren Barrow, Chestnut Hill College
S. Marlon Gayadeen, SUNY Buffalo State
Amy Grau, Shawnee State University
Tim Robicheaux, Pennsylvania State University
Robert A. Sarver III, USC Upstate
David Scott, University of Texas at Tyler
Clayton Steenberg, Copper Mountain College
Jason S. Ulsperger, Arkansas Tech University
Joachim Kibirige, Missouri Western State University
Patrick McGrain, Gwynedd Mercy University
Nicole Doctor, Ivy Tech Community College
Glen Ishoy, Indiana University of Pennsylvania

Furthermore, I wish to thank the wonderful individuals at Oxford University Press for their expertise and support. Steve Helba is a treasure to have as an editor. His wise counsel has improved this book, and his friendship enhanced my writing experience. Tony Mathias, Kora Fillet, William Murray, and Sandy Cooke all deserve credit for their contributions. Finally, Amy Hembree, to whom this book is dedicated, has my everlasting love and respect for all the many ways she contributed to this project.

John Randolph Fuller
University of West Georgia

About the Author

Dr. John Randolph Fuller brings both an applied and theoretical background to his scholarship. He served as a probation and parole officer for the Florida Probation and Parole Commission in Broward County, Florida, where he managed a caseload of more than 100 felons. In addition, he served as a criminal justice planner for the Palm Beach Metropolitan Criminal Justice Planning Unit. In this capacity, he worked with every criminal justice agency in a three-county area writing and supervising grants for the Law Enforcement Assistance Administration.

Dr. Fuller received his Bachelor of University Studies (BUS) degree from the University of New Mexico and his Master of Science (MS) and Doctor of Philosophy (Ph.D.) degrees from the School of Criminology at Florida State University. Dr. Fuller taught at the University of West Georgia from 1981 to 2014 and has been recognized by students as a superior teacher and advisor. In 1991 he was awarded the College of Arts and Sciences Faculty Member of the Year, and in 2001 he was given Professor of the Year Award by the Honors College. In 2006, the Institute of Higher Education and the Center for Teaching and Learning at the University of Georgia named Dr. Fuller a Governor's Teaching Fellow.

In addition to numerous journal articles and book chapters, Dr. Fuller has published nine books on topics ranging from juvenile delinquency to peacemaking criminology to global crime and justice. He is a frequent presenter at meetings of both the American Society of Criminology and the Academy of Criminal Justice Sciences. Additionally, he served as the Faculty Ombuds at the University of West Georgia where he worked to resolve conflicts for faculty, students, and administrators.

Recognized as an accomplished scholar, teacher, adviser, and mentor, Dr. Fuller is committed to the ideals of fairness and justice for all for victims, offenders, and practitioners in the juvenile and criminal justice systems. In addition to reading widely, Dr. Fuller enjoys playing golf and painting.

PART I

The Scope of Crime

Thinking Critically about Crime

FEATURES

Shining new light on the problem of crime requires critical thinking. Which academic disciplines contribute to the manner in which criminologists look at crime?

Steve W. Stephens posted a video on Facebook of him shooting a man. He later killed himself when confronted by police. What would have happened to Stephens if the police had been successful in arresting him?

In 2017, Steve W. Stephens of Cleveland, Ohio, posted to Facebook a video of himself shooting and killing 74-year-old Robert Godwin Sr., a man Stephens apparently had picked at random. The video remained on Facebook for more than two hours before it was removed. Stephens, 37, fled Cleveland after the murder. He was soon identified, and his face and name appeared on billboards across the country.[1]

After two days, an employee in an Erie, Pennsylvania, McDonald's spotted Stephens in the drive-through lane and notified police. Stephens sped from the restaurant but was stopped after a short police pursuit. As police prepared to arrest Stephens, he pulled a pistol and shot himself in the head.[2]

Stephens, who had worked at a behavioral health agency since 2008, had not exhibited any problems on the job. However, he had been a gambler who struggled with debt and recently had been evicted from his apartment for failure to pay rent. On his video, Stephens said he had lost everything. He demanded that Godwin say the name of Stephens's girlfriend, saying, "She's the reason this is about to happen to you." Unlike many offenders who are on the run, he did not dispose of his cell phone, switch cars, or travel far from the crime scene.[3]

One of the victim's daughters said, "We are not happy about the outcome because we would have preferred that he turned himself in and paid the penalty for taking my father's life. We forgave him, but even the Bible says the law is the law. Him dying serves us no purpose."[4]

What Is Criminology?

LEARNING OBJECTIVE | 1

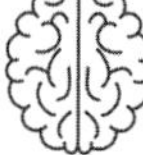

State Sutherland's definition of criminology.

The classic definition of **criminology** was hammered out by sociologist Edwin Sutherland, who stated that "[c]riminology is the study of the making of laws, breaking of laws, and society's reaction to the breaking of laws." To understand the purpose of criminology, let's break this definition down using the opening scenario.[5]

The Making of Laws

Laws are written by legislatures to ensure that society runs in an orderly fashion and does not succumb to **crime**, or behavior that is prohibited by laws and has prescribed punishments. Legislatures comprise elected individuals who spend a great deal of money campaigning and building their influence. Once elected, they work with other legislators to create law. This is a simplified explanation, but it is basically how lawmaking in the United States works.

We divide law into **criminal law**, which guides the definition and prosecution of crime, and **civil law**, which governs private rights and disputes between citizens (see Table 1.1 for more on the difference between the two). In this text, we are concerned with criminal law from a criminological perspective.

The criminal law is perhaps most important to ensuring an orderly society. For a society to be orderly, its citizens must feel safe. Most of the offenses defined as crime are those that threaten other people in some way: murder, rape, assault, robbery, and so on. Although crime is **deviance**, or behaviors that violate cultural norms, rules, or laws, it is also more serious than most deviant acts (see Figure 1.1). The offense perpetrated by Steve W. Stephens is of the sort that society deems most heinous. Thus, many laws have been created to specify exactly what actions constitute these and similar offenses, how the criminal justice system will deal with them, and what will be done with the perpetrators. In this text, we will encounter some theories that critique the criminal law and how

TABLE 1.1 The Major Differences Between Criminal Law and Civil Law

	CRIMINAL LAW	CIVIL LAW
What it does . . .	The criminal law enforces the laws that keep society safe. It is composed of the rules that define criminal offenses and how these offenses are prosecuted by the state.	The civil law is for the settlement of disputes between private citizens and other entities, such as businesses.
An offense is called . . .	A "crime" or "criminal offense"	A "tort"
Examples	Murder, robbery, rape, burglary	Contested divorces, property ownership disputes, contract disputes
Who brings the action . . .	The state prosecutes criminal offenses in the name of the state (not the victim), which also has the only right of enforcement.	An individual or group
A case is won when . . .	The guilt of accused defendants is proven beyond a reasonable doubt	A preponderance of evidence favors one party over another
Possible punishments . . .	Restitution, probation, incarceration, death	The party who loses the case must pay a specified amount of money

it is written and applied. From a broad perspective, however, the basic social rules that prohibit offenses such as Stephens's are required for people to feel safe enough to go about the business of making a society work. Law, then, is what makes a society rather than just a collection of people, many of whom are violent, doing what they please.

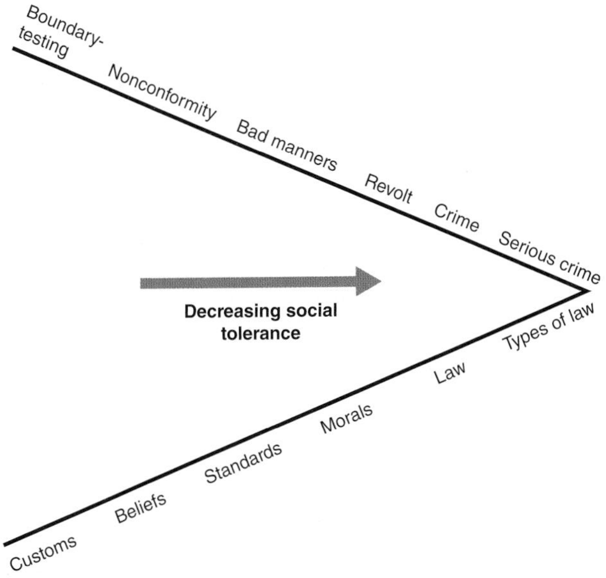

FIGURE 1.1 Continuum of Deviance

The Breaking of Laws

Why laws are made is pretty obvious. The mystery begins with why they are broken. Some say laws are made to be broken. Laws are not *made* to be broken, but they are *certain* to be broken. Human beings are not perfect, and neither is society. The reasons people give for breaking the law are many, the most common ones being necessity, choice, mental or physical defect, or somehow a means of making up for their own victimization by an individual or society. Often, the offender just does not know.[6]

---

criminology—The study of the making of laws, the breaking of laws, and the social reaction to the breaking of laws.

crime—Behavior that is prohibited by laws and has prescribed punishments.

criminal law—Law that deals with the prosecution and definition of crime.

civil law—Law that is related to private rights and disputes between citizens.

deviance—Behaviors that violate cultural norms, rules, or laws.

Local residents pray near the apartment complex outside Tokyo where nine bodies were found the previous week at the home of murder suspect Takahiro Shiraishi. Crime in Japan occurs at a much lower rate than in the United States. Can you think of some reasons why?

Society's Reaction to the Breaking of Laws

This issue is not as clear as you may think. Society's reaction to the breaking of laws includes fear, anger, and even disgust. However, this is not always the case. Society's reaction to the breaking of laws may be as varied as the reasons people break them, and these reactions vary among individuals, regions, and societies.

One common reaction you may not expect is fascination. The breaking of laws is fascinating. This is probably why you are reading this text right now. Maybe you or someone you know has been a crime victim, and you are angry or at least determined to study criminology and perhaps even become a criminologist or criminal justice professional so that you can go out and do something about it.[11] It is more likely, however, that you have never been a victim of serious crime, and you may not even know anyone who has. Given the proliferation of crime-related media—true-crime books, novels, serial-killer biographies, television dramas, talk shows, films, and websites—it is clear that the more gory and outrageous the offense, the more people want to know about it. Specific aspects of crime come into vogue. Murder mysteries have always been popular. Your parents or grandparents probably watched television shows about private eyes and tough police investigators. As a child, you may have watched "cop shows" replete with car chases. A few years ago, serial murderers were all the rage. Now everyone seems to be interested in forensic investigation.[12]

Society's reaction to crime, then, is complex. When we learn of especially heinous offenses, we are outraged. When crime hits close to home, we are aggrieved and incensed. If it hits too close to home, we are devastated or perhaps even the victim. When it happens to a stranger, we are often interested.

It has been said that a single death is a tragedy, but a million deaths are a statistic.[13] This holds true for crime. The media will often spend a lot of time on

Much of criminological **theory**—perhaps the bulk of it—is devoted to understanding why people break the law so that we can control the amount of offending. Basic criminal laws are similar across most industrialized countries, but societies have different rates of offending. For example, Japan's crime rate is quite low compared with that in the United States, although both countries have similar criminal laws.[7] A murder in Japan is just as illegal as it is in the United States. A person who murders randomly, such as Steve W. Stephens, provokes the same amount of fear and official concern in both countries.[8] So why does the crime rate between the two societies differ so widely?[9] The answer lies in how and why people break the criminal law. The reasons differ not only among individuals, but also among neighborhoods, towns, cities, and whole societies.[10] However, if we can understand the causes of crime and address them, then we can better control crime. These are the answers criminology seeks.

---

theory—A statement or set of statements that explains a concept and that has withstood repeated tests and can be used to make inferences about other concepts.

serial murder—The killing of a sequence of victims committed in three or more separate events over an extended period of time.

DOUBLETAKE

Serial Murder and the Media

When we think critically about crime, we must recognize that **serial murders**—the killing of a sequence of victims committed in three or more separate events over an extended period of time—are actually rare. They have become part of the national conversation because of intense media scrutiny which has created a distorted picture of the danger posed by serial murderers, their prevalence, and the amount of attention law enforcement gives them. This bias occurs for three main reasons:

- All criminal offenses are local. Because of the availability of a variety of communication devices, especially television and the Internet, events that occur thousands of miles away now seem local. When a serial killer strikes in a distant state, it becomes news on our local and cable television stations. This gives the impression that the killer is right around the corner and that we must protect our loved ones. In actuality, the chances of being harmed by a serial killer are extremely small.
- Serial killings are sensational. Crime news must compete with other news and other media to get attention, so the most sensational cases get the most coverage. Although a gruesome murder may make news for a short period of time, a series of murders that appear linked can generate coverage for weeks or months. Many people become fascinated by these unsolved murders and speculation about the predators, but they also become anxious about the possibility of future victims.
- Our culture fosters the creation of celebrity. Media attention makes instant celebrities of both perpetrators and victims. Covering these sensational cases has also made celebrities of some television hosts, who specialize in picking apart the minutest details of such offenses and making entertainment of them.

Most criminal offenses do not get the level of attention that serial murder attracts. This does not mean serial murder is not serious or does not do great physical and psychological harm. However, it does mean that criminology students must be vigilant about the media's effect on our understanding of crime. We must remember that crime is not entertainment but rather a serious social problem that requires not only critical thinking, but also mature judgment and compassion for all involved.

THINK ABOUT IT

1. Give some possible reasons why the media are so interested in serial murder and other sensational offenses.
2. Show how innovations in communications have allowed sensational crime from other states and countries to become treated as local crime.

the disappearance or murder of an attractive or interesting person. However, few people beyond criminologists and criminal justice professionals are interested in crime statistics. Many people believe that crime is always rising (it isn't) and that we were safer in the "good old days" (not necessarily).[14] The funding for much criminological research, which comes from public coffers as well as programs directed at rehabilitation and criminal justice reform, is endangered, and the public often seems little concerned except to demand tougher laws and more prisons.[15] Few people know what the crime rate is in their city, state, or region. Even fewer know any criminological theories. Society's reaction to the breaking of laws from a statistical and theoretical perspective—that is, a *criminological* perspective—is poorly informed. Crime stories, however, get the public's attention, which is evidenced by the large number of crime-related dramas and talk shows.[16] The story of a serial murderer is always welcome (see Doubletake).

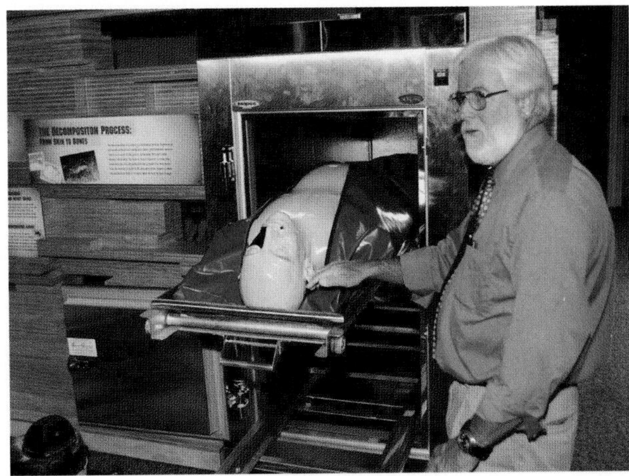

Forensic entomology, or the study of insect evidence, has only within the last 30 years been adopted as an integral part of crime scene investigation. The types of insects on a body and their stages of development can help determine how much time has elapsed since death. Shown here is an exhibit at the Science Museum of Minnesota called CSI: Crime Scene Insects. How has media attention to crime made forensic investigation more popular?

Bob George looks through a notebook with his first letters from Charles Manson. George began corresponding with Manson in 1997 and continued until Manson's death in 2018. Why are people so fascinated with sensational criminal offenses?

Many incarcerated serial murderers get fan mail. In the mid-1990s, Charles Manson—who received quite a bit of mail—had a website administered by a devotee.[17] John Wayne Gacy, convicted of the murders of 33 young men and boys, sold enough of his paintings in prison to leave $100,000 to his heirs.[18] On the one hand, many people are repulsed by a murderer making millions from a book or film. On the other hand, many people pay to read such books and see the films. There is even a bustling trade in so-called murderabilia in which anything belonging to an offender, from writings to mementoes to nail and hair clippings, is sold over the Internet.[19]

As we can see, the public's reaction to crime is a multifaceted mixture of fear, disgust, and fascination. We expect the first two reactions, especially from anyone who has ever been or known a crime victim. Many people who have never been victims of crime are afraid of becoming victims, even if the chances are unlikely, and they take extra precautions such as installing home security alarms and extra locks. The last reaction, fascination, is one many people have but may not admit to. However, a degree of fascination with crime is not only natural—after all, crime is social in nature and we are social creatures—but desirable. A healthy interest in crime is at the root of criminology.

PAUSE AND REVIEW

1. **Explain the three components of Sutherland's definition of criminology.**
2. **Critique the public's perception of the frequency of serial murder.**
3. **What is the difference between criminal law and civil law?**

The Interdisciplinary Nature of Criminology

LEARNING OBJECTIVE | 2

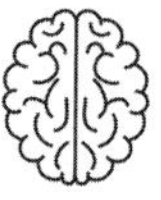

Demonstrate how political science, economics, psychology, law, biology, and sociology contribute to criminology.

On Sunday morning, July 30, 1995, Duane Buck went to the Houston, Texas, home of his former girlfriend, Debra Gardner. Carrying a rifle and a shotgun, Buck, 32, entered the house and shot his stepsister Phyllis Taylor and Gardner's friend Kenneth Butler. Gardner ran out of the house with her young children, and Buck followed. While Gardner's son and daughter begged Buck not to kill their mother, Buck shot Gardner in the chest. Gardner and Butler died, and Taylor survived. One of the police officers who arrested Buck later testified that Buck was laughing and remained "happy" and "upbeat" as he was driven to the police station.[20]

At his 1997 trial, Buck was convicted of the murders of Gardner and Butler. During the trial's penalty phase, the jury was instructed to impose the death penalty only if it found—unanimously and beyond a reasonable doubt—"a probability that the defendant would commit criminal acts of violence that would constitute a continuing threat to society."[21]

Among other witnesses, defense counsel called two psychologists to testify as experts. The first, Dr. Patrick Lawrence, said that Buck had served a previous prison sentence in minimum custody with no problems. The second expert called by Buck's defense was Dr. Walter Quijano. Dr. Quijano considered seven "statistical factors" in determining whether Buck was likely to be violent in prison. Of the fourth factor, "race," Dr. Quijano's report

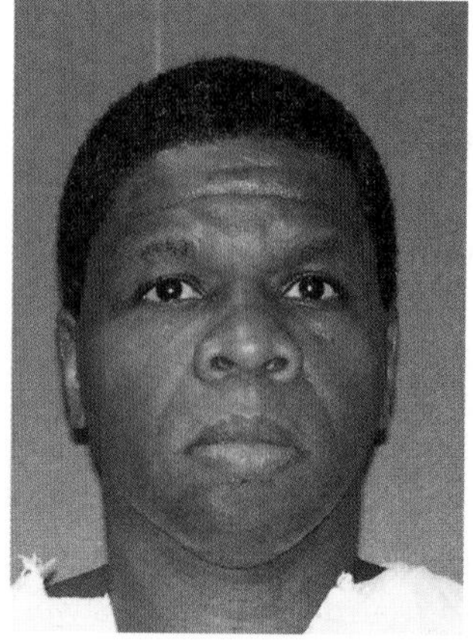

Nearly two decades after a Texas jury sent Duane Buck to death row for killing two people, including his ex-girlfriend, the U.S. Supreme Court reduced his death sentence to life in prison after it determined that his case had been tainted by ineffective counsel. How did the prosecution use race to obtain a death sentence?

read: "Race. Black: Increased probability. There is an overrepresentation of blacks among the violent offenders." The prosecutor then questioned Dr. Quijano about the role of race: "You have determined . . . that the race factor, black, increases the future dangerousness for various complicated reasons; is that correct?" Dr. Quijano replied, "Yes."[22]

After two days of deliberation, which included studying Dr. Quijano's report, the jury returned a death sentence. Buck's conviction and sentence were affirmed on appeal. His case wound through the legal system until 2017, when the U.S. Supreme Court held that Buck had demonstrated ineffective assistance of counsel. Buck's sentence was reduced to life in prison.[23]

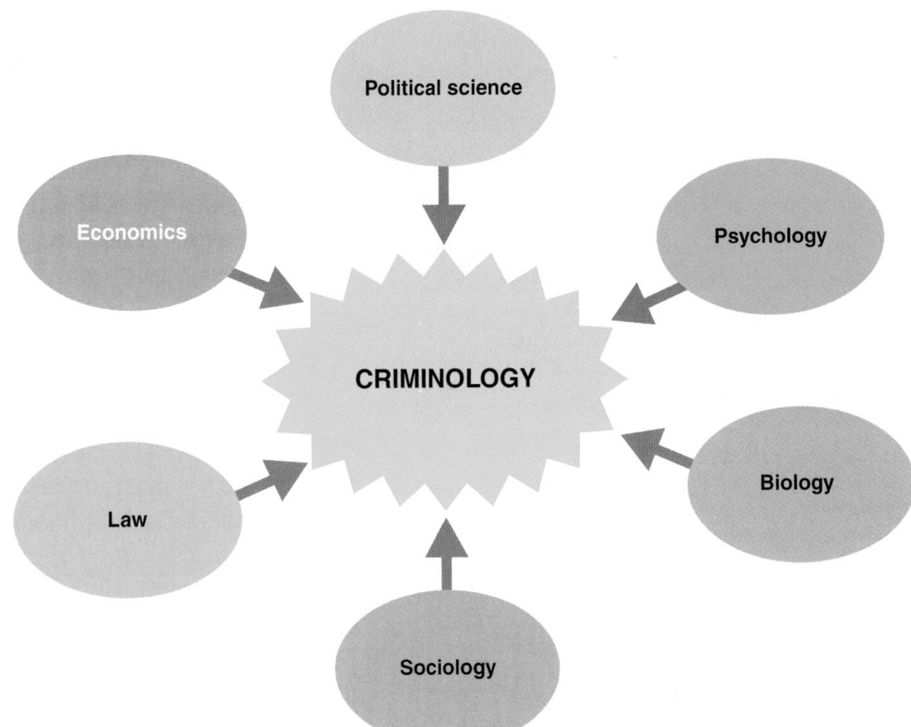

FIGURE 1.2 The Interdisciplinary Nature of Criminology

As a relatively new field of study, criminology is interdisciplinary. This means that it draws upon other academic disciplines, including political science, economics, psychology, law, biology, and sociology (see Figure 1.2). Understanding the problems of crime and criminal justice requires knowledge of many areas of study, and experts from all these fields contribute knowledge and research. Using the case of Duane Buck, let's see how this works.

Political Science

As we will see later, political forces control how crime is defined and how criminal law works, so some political scientists contribute to criminology by studying the role of political power in social control.[24] People of color, despite composing a lower percentage of the U.S. population, are more likely to be sentenced to death. Although only 13 percent of the U.S. population is black, as of the beginning of 2014, 42 percent of inmates sentenced to death were black, and 56 percent were white.[25] Studies have shown that juries are more likely to sentence black defendants to death than white defendants.[26] Black potential jurors are also excluded from juries at a higher rate than white potential jurors. One study found that prosecutors struck black potential jurors at about 2.5 times the rate they struck potential jurors who were not black.[27]

Economics

Economic principles are at the heart of many of the transactions defined as crime.[28] For instance, some economists have mathematically modeled the cost-benefit analysis some offenders use. It is a truism in criminology that, although every offender does a calculus to determine if the offense is "worth it," many offenders are just bad at math. Sometimes the costs and benefits of a criminal offense make no sense to anyone but the offender. According to the officers who arrested Buck, he was laughing and upbeat throughout the entire arrest, stating that Gardner got what she deserved. For his offense, Buck paid the price of his freedom and almost his life. Buck is in his 50s now, but it is unknown today what he thinks of his transaction.

Psychology

Criminologists rely on many psychological perspectives. Psychologists often treat inmates to determine why they have broken the law as well as to provide rehabilitation to help prevent further

Two inmates meditate at the Utah County Jail in Spanish Fork, Utah. The inmates are part of the Chain Breakers program, which teaches inmates mindfulness, including skills such as meditation. In what ways is psychology an important component of criminological practice?

antisocial behavior, that is, behavior intended to harm society and individuals.[29] For example, a psychologist would look into the reasons that Buck committed the murders, especially in the context of testimony from a former girlfriend that he routinely struck her and pointed a gun at her, as well as his prior convictions of delivery of cocaine and unlawfully carrying a weapon.[30]

Law

The study of law is integral to criminology. Laws specify which actions should be punished and how justice is dispensed. Because laws are made by people to control other people, criminologists are interested in how laws are made, what activities they control, and, in turn, who they control. In the case of Duane Buck, Texas law stated that Buck could be sentenced to death if a jury determined that he would be violent in prison. Psychologist Walter Quijano told a jury that Buck was likely to be violent because of the color of his skin, and so the jury condemned him to death. It was not the first time Quijano had provided such testimony in a trial. In six death penalty cases, Quijano testified that Hispanic and black men were likely to be dangerous in prison.[31] If the U.S. Supreme Court had not issued its ruling, it is likely that Buck would still be on death row.

antisocial—Following standards of behavior intended to harm society and individuals.

recidivism—Repeat offending. *Also* recidivate.

Biology

Many criminologists and biologists are looking for the roots of antisocial behavior within the human body.[32] Is there a biological reason that Buck committed his offense? Why did Buck continue to be violent toward women? Why was he so happy that he had murdered his former girlfriend? A criminologist working from a biological perspective may look for answers in brain chemistry, hormones, or other physical factors that affect mood or personality.

Sociology

Of all the academic disciplines, sociology has contributed the most to the field of criminology.[33] The United States has a long history of applying sociological analysis to the study of crime, and sociologists did much of the pioneering work in criminology. As a result, sociological theories can offer reasonable explanations for the actions of Duane Buck as well as critiques of his treatment by the criminal justice system. As we can see, criminology borrows from many different academic disciplines to give us a fuller and more comprehensive view of crime. This will become apparent in future chapters as we see how these various academic perspectives are used to construct criminological theories.

PAUSE AND REVIEW

1. **Choose two of the disciplines that criminology draws on and compare and contrast how they approach the Duane Buck case.**

The Difference Between Criminology and Criminal Justice

LEARNING OBJECTIVE | 3

Differentiate between criminology and criminal justice.

Richard Powell, 57, has been arrested 344 times. The homeless Florida man has been charged with offenses including drinking alcohol in public, theft, robbery, and sexual battery. Powell's latest arrest was for trespassing in a Miami Beach area from which he had been banned, yelling in public, carrying alcohol, and possessing marijuana, which was stuffed into his shoes. Powell, who has been convicted five times in the last 12 months, pleaded guilty and was sentenced to 90 days in jail.[34]

Apparently, Powell is not the only repeat offender who continues to return to the area. An organization called the Miami Beach Crime Prevention and Awareness Group attends court hearings in an effort to ensure that repeat offenders receive longer sentences and are kept in custody. Group members record videos of people they believe are acting suspiciously and encourage area residents to report anything that seems illegal or peculiar. The group also supported the City of Miami Beach's proposal to hire its own prosecutor to press minor offenses that might otherwise be dropped. However, the American Civil Liberties Union has warned that the group's activities could lead to racial profiling and the harassment of homeless people.[35]

What is the difference between criminology and criminal justice? Criminology emerged from sociology because social scientists wanted to understand a major social problem: crime. Criminal justice, in turn, emerged from criminology because practitioners wanted to understand the social mechanisms for dealing with crime.[36]

To better understand the differences between criminology and criminal justice, let's consider the case of Richard Powell. The criminal justice system has three branches: police, courts, and corrections. The police "keep the peace," which may mean different things depending on the community and the style of policing in the jurisdiction. Police officers use their discretion to answer calls for service, ensure public safety, see that laws are followed, and sometimes make arrests. The courts enforce the law by dealing with those whom the police charge with criminal offenses and by attempting to see that defendants receive due process. The corrections system carries out the sentences handed down by the courts by restricting the freedom of offenders while ideally also seeing to their rehabilitation and the eventual return of most offenders to society. A criminal justice practitioner, then, is interested in why Powell keeps getting arrested (various street crimes), what happens to him in court (a trial or a plea bargain), and how he is treated by the correctional system (typically, he is released or is jailed for a while, then released). Also of interest to the criminal justice practitioner is the reaction of the community: Local residents have formed a group to try to ensure that offenders like Powell are convicted and sentenced as harshly as possible so that they will not return to the community and continue to break the law. By doing so, is the group violating Powell's civil rights?

A sign is displayed on the site where a homeless resource center is expected to be built in South Salt Lake, Utah. Why do many citizens believe the homeless are likely to break the law?

(For more on **recidivism**, or repeat offending, see Theory to Practice.)

A criminologist will be more interested than the criminal justice practitioner in how and why Powell began to engage in antisocial behavior to the point that he repeatedly enters the criminal justice system. Are the roots of such behavior social or psychological, or are they a bit of both? What is the long-term future like for a repeat, minor offender like Powell? Could he be encouraged through therapy or rehabilitation to "get his life together," or will he eventually die behind bars? Does Powell's behavior have its roots in drugs, alcohol, or childhood abuse? It is possible that Powell is as much a victim as he is an offender. Will the community's reaction of forming an anticrime group have any effect on local street crime?

As we can see, criminology and criminal justice overlap considerably. Although criminology explores several criminal justice areas, the focus of this text will be limited to theories of crime causation, types of crime, victimization, and special topics such as terrorism and individual rights.

PAUSE AND REVIEW

1. **Describe the reasons you are interested in either criminology or criminal justice.**
2. **Compare and contrast criminology and criminal justice.**
3. **What are the major distinctions between criminal justice and criminology?**

THEORY TO PRACTICE

Recidivism and Criminological Theory

Recidivism, or repeat offending, is frustrating to both criminologists and criminal justice practitioners. Many offenders tend to repeat their offenses or commit entirely new ones and get arrested again. The so-called revolving door of the criminal justice system speaks to the failure of society to positively change offenders. Depending on how we measure recidivism—by rate of re-arrest, reconviction, or re-incarceration—more than half of offenders recidivate.[37] Several criminological theories can guide policies for reducing recidivism. Let's look at three theories that feature policies aimed at reducing the number of recidivists. We will discuss each of these in detail in later chapters, but here they are useful to illustrate how theory can guide the formulation of laws, rehabilitation efforts, and criminal justice policies.

- Deterrence theory. Deterrence theory suggests that if the consequences of breaking the law are unattractive enough, people will not do it anymore. Policies derived from deterrence theory involved hiring more police officers, specifying severe and harsh punishments, and developing special initiatives to discourage certain types of offending. Examples include increasing penalties for driving while under the influence of alcohol, the war on drugs, and "three-strikes" penalties that prescribe harsh sentences for those convicted of a third offense, even minor ones. The idea is that potential recidivists will think twice about breaking the law again because they understand that the benefits of doing so do not outweigh the consequences if they are caught. We will cover deterrence theory in detail in Chapter 4.
- Labeling theory. Criminal offenders may be identified as felons, swindlers, convicts, sex offenders, and so on according to their offense. These labels can damage an ex-offender's prospects for employment, educational funding, and emotional relationships. Some criminal justice policies attempt to mitigate the negative effects of the "criminal" label, such as programs in which defendants who successfully complete treatment have their criminal record expunged. Just as important, these "first-offender policies" may prevent the offender from internalizing the label and making it a self-fulfilling prophecy. Chapter 8 will explain more about labeling theory.
- Social disorganization theory. This theory suggests that neighborhoods with transient, low-skilled, and alienated residents tend to have more crime. Policies aimed at increasing these communities' social support could significantly reduce the crime rate. Social disorganization theory suggests that residents who have sufficient schools, good jobs, and strong community networks are likely to be more invested in their communities and to behave in a pro-social manner. (See Chapter 6 for a discussion of social disorganization theory.)

These are just three theories dealing with the potential to reduce recidivism. Each focuses on a different aspect of why people break the law, and each suggests different policy alternatives. The lesson here is that there is no single solution to the problems of crime, and we can apply a variety of theories to different types of factors that may be responsible for the development of crime.

THINK ABOUT IT

1. Summarize the arguments that two of the three theories would use to explain recidivism.
2. In your opinion, what is the most accurate measure of recidivism: re-arrest, re-conviction, or re-incarceration?

Criminological Theories

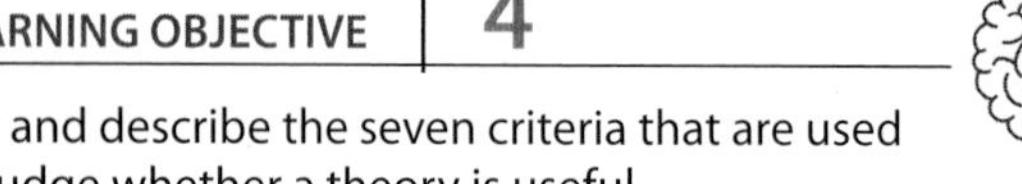

List and describe the seven criteria that are used to judge whether a theory is useful.

In 2017, most members of the Galanis family were behind bars. John Peter Galanis, 74, who has been in and out of federal prison, is known as "one of the 10 biggest white-collar criminals in America."[38] He was sentenced to another six years in federal prison in 2017 for a stock manipulation scheme.[39] Also pleading guilty to the scheme were his son Derek Galanis, 44, who was sentenced to six years, and his son Jared Galanis, 37, who was sentenced to 150 days. Finally, his son Jason Galanis, 47, who was already serving 11 years for the stock scheme, was sentenced to another five years in a separate scam that defrauded one of the most impoverished American Indian tribes, the Oglala Sioux Nation, of \$60 million.[40] In 2007, Jason Galanis had been fined \$60,000 by the U.S. Securities and Exchange Commission in an accounting fraud case.[41]

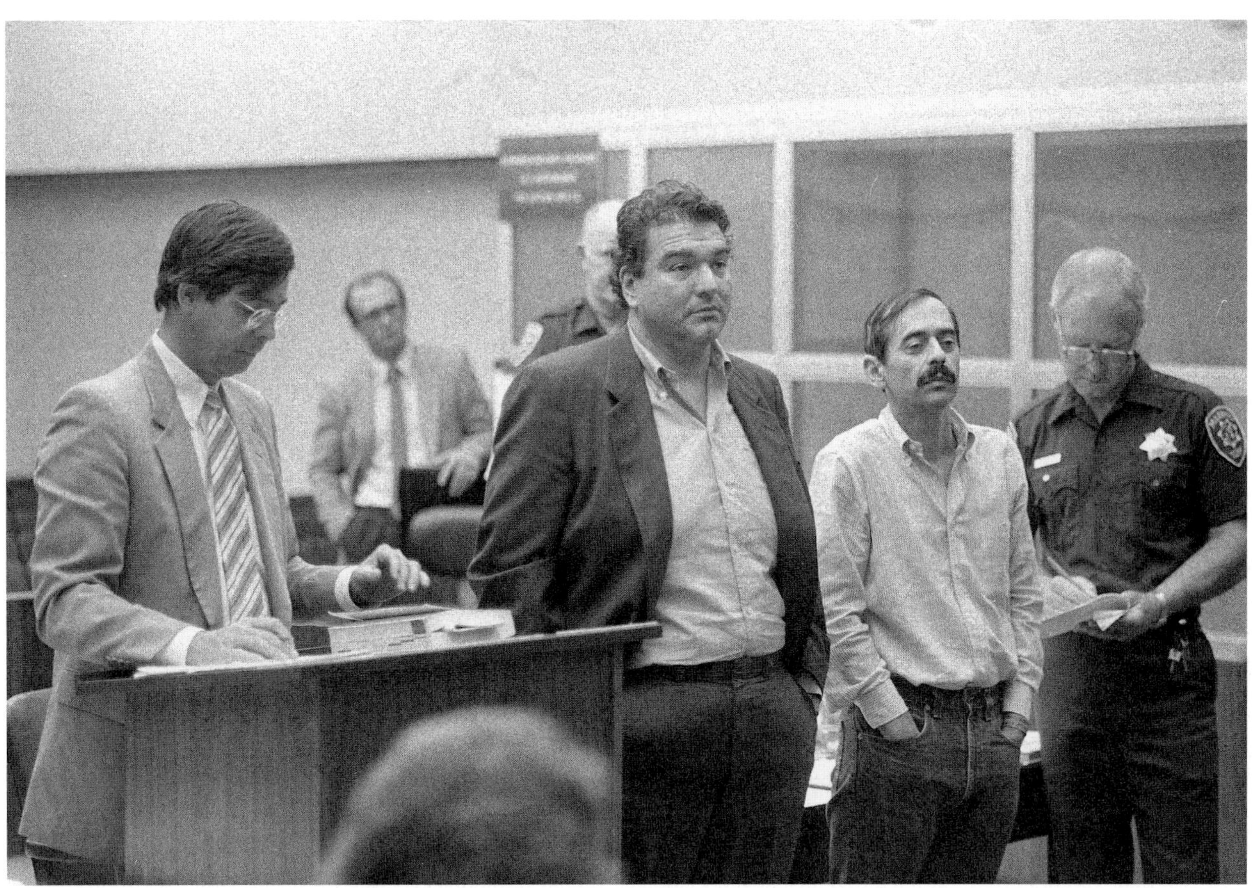

John Peter Galanis, left, and his associate, Laurence Klusky, appear in municipal court in San Diego, California, in 1987. Galanis and Klusky waived extradition to New York to face charges in an investment swindle. How are white-collar offenders treated differently from those who commit street crimes?

John Galanis has been involved with the federal criminal justice system since the early 1970s, and his sons have seemingly been determined to follow his lead. Part of Jason Galanis's defense in the Oglala Sioux Nation case was the claim that his father's influence had been "toxic" to young Jason.[42] However, when John Galanis was not in prison, he showered his sons with luxuries. Jason received a Ferrari for his 16th birthday. The family had a ranch in Utah, mansions in Greenwich, Connecticut, and Del Mar, California, a yacht, and a Learjet.[43] As remarkable as this story sounds, it has received little coverage outside business media. If the Galanis family had been as committed to perpetrating violent crime as they were to **white-collar crimes**, the reaction by the public, the media, and the criminal justice system would likely have been far more dramatic.

Until recently, white-collar crime—financially motivated criminal offenses committed by way of deceit and without violence, usually involving the offender's place of employment or business—has not been considered to be as serious as violent crime. A major criminological finding is that most offenders in the United States are young white males. Although they typically start breaking the law early in life, usually during childhood, most stop in young adulthood and go on to lead lives that are **pro-social**—that is, following standards of behavior intended to facilitate society and individuals. However, some offenders, such as Steve W. Stephens and John Peter Galanis, continue to engage in antisocial behavior well into adulthood. The reasons for this and other criminological phenomena are not clear, which is why criminologists construct theories to help explain why some offenders behave as they do. Remember, although theory

white-collar crime—Financially motivated criminal offenses committed by way of deceit and without violence, usually involving the offender's place of employment or business.

pro-social—Following standards of behavior intended to facilitate society and individuals.

POLICY IMPLICATIONS

Constructing a Response to Crime

The discipline of criminology has policy implications. This means that the development of criminological theory and research on how the criminal justice system works can be used to develop policies to prevent crime, diminish its effect on victims, and construct a just, fair response to crime. Not all disciplines have this potential. For instance, astronomers discover new galaxies light-years away from Earth, and although this is fascinating and adds to the knowledge of astronomy, nothing can be done in terms of policies for altering the universe. Criminology deals with tangible, real-world problems that can be addressed.

This is why measuring crime is important. By understanding the frequency, location, seriousness, and effects of crime, policymakers can develop new laws, hire more police, or hand out more severe sentences as ways of trying to prevent crime. In fact, almost everything the criminal justice system does is an attempt to enact policies to deal with crime.

- Three strikes. Some states have laws specifying that repeat offenders are subject to more severe sanctions. It is believed that when potential lawbreakers realize that getting caught committing a third offense will result in a life sentence, they will decide against breaking the law further. Additionally, after three offenses, it is reasoned that the individual is not amenable to deterrence or treatment and should be incapacitated in a secure environment in order to protect society.
- Hotspots. Crime is not evenly distributed over a jurisdiction. Some places have more crime than others, and the police, recognizing this fact, array their resources accordingly. Only by measuring where and when crime occurs can the police deploy their efforts effectively.
- Victim programs. Many critics of the criminal justice system believe that victims are neglected. Research has shown that victims of rape and violent offenses feel doubly victimized when the criminal justice system does not respond in an effective and sympathetic manner. By considering the feelings and problems of crime victims, the criminal justice system has been able to develop programs that not only help individual victims, but also ensure their cooperation in the prosecution of their perpetrators. Additionally, victim-witness programs have been able to educate the public on ways to prevent victimization.

Throughout this text, we will highlight the policy implications of each chapter to demonstrate that criminological theories, as well as the workings of the criminal justice system, are not abstract or purely academic. Rather, they are susceptible to intentional change by policymakers who rely on research.

THINK ABOUT IT

1. Why is measuring crime important?
2. Can you think of other ways the criminal justice system enacts policies to deal with crime?

is complicated, it is not just academic hot air. By better understanding antisocial behavior, we can improve criminal justice response, offender rehabilitation, medical and psychological treatments, and victim assistance. See Policy Implications for a more detailed discussion of how theories relate to the real world of crime.

How to Study Theory

Everyone uses theory, and criminologists are no exception. It is important to understand, however, that not all theories are equal. Theories must be evaluated according to several criteria. Figure 1.3 specifies the seven criteria that are used to judge whether a theory is useful. As we will see later, each theory that is discussed can be assessed by asking how it measures up to these seven criteria.

1. Usefulness and policy implications. A good criminological theory should be able to direct real-world policy and be useful in dealing with crime.
2. Empirical validity. This means that a tool is measuring what it is designed to measure. A good theory can stand up under strong empirical validity or the use of effective measuring tools.
3. Scope. Good theories seek to explain a range of behavior.
4. Testability. A good theory is stated so that all its elements and propositions can be tested.

5. Parsimony. In reference to theory, "parsimony" is the economical use of words. Good theories explain complicated ideas in simple language.
6. Ideology. Some theories are based in specific ideologies, which can affect the objectivity of the theory. It is always best to know if the theory is based on an ideology.
7. Logical consistency. The theory must make sense.

To better illustrate the importance of criminological theory, let's take a look at how three specific theories can be applied to the case of the Galanis family. We will address these theories in detail later in the text. For now, just use these examples to get a feel for how theory is used.

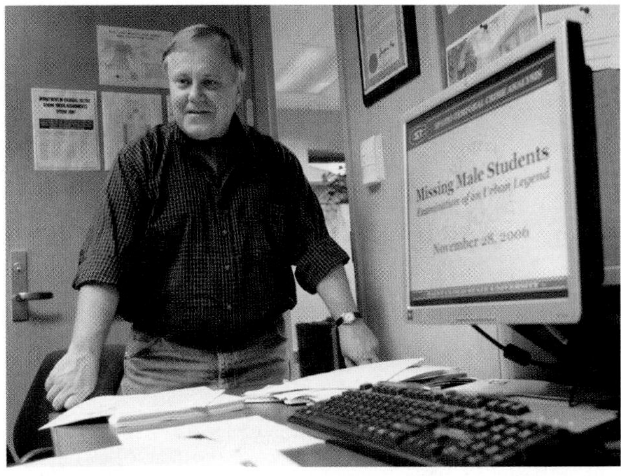

A criminology professor explains his theories on college student drownings across the Midwest. What elements make a good theory of crime?

Social Learning Theory

One explanation of criminal behavior is that it is learned. Sociologist Edwin Sutherland's differential association theory can be applied to the Galanis family to explain why John Galanis's three sons perpetrated white-collar crime much as their father did. Sutherland argued that criminal behavior is learned by interacting with others, especially intimate others. He states that "when criminal behavior is learned, the learning includes (a) techniques of committing the crime, which are sometimes very complicated, sometimes very simple; and (b) the specific direction of motives, drives, rationalizations, and attitudes."[44] Because John Galanis enriched his family with his ill-gotten gains, his sons learned that committing fraud would enrich them as well. It is possible that living an honest life and working a regular job never even occurred to Galanis's sons because their father never behaved in that way.

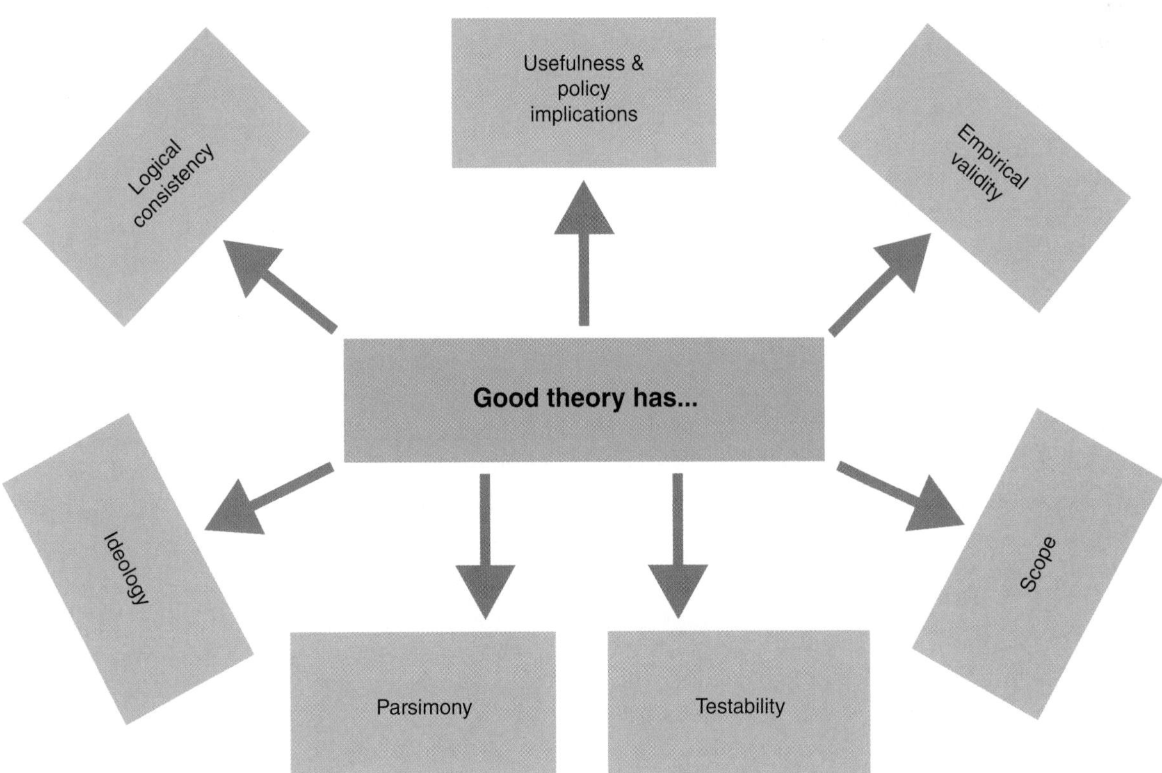

FIGURE 1.3 Elements of Good Theory

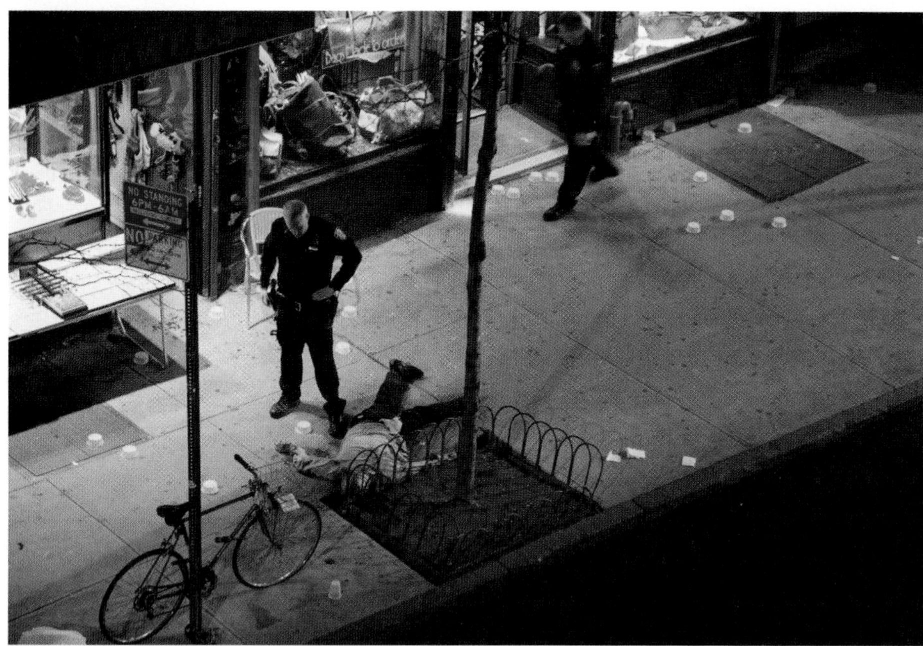

A policeman looks at the body of an unidentified gunman in the street in New York's Greenwich Village. The man shot and killed a restaurant employee and two unarmed volunteer police officers who pursued him. He was then shot to death by other police officers. Why is violent street crime generally considered to be more harmful than white-collar crime?

White-collar crime is a complicated type of crime, and only those who have exposure to the methods and motivations of this type of crime are able to engage in it effectively. A major proposition of differential association is that crime is learned through the frequency, duration, priority, and intensity of interactions with significant people (such as parents) who provide definitions favorable to the violation of law. In this case, the Galanis sons were provided with early (priority) examples of the father's deviant behavior, multiple (frequency) arrests of the father, and significant financial gain (intensity), which the family enjoyed for many years (duration). It is easy to see how this family learned the complicated techniques of perpetrating white-collar crime.

Merton's Strain Theory

Strain theory is a broad concept that has a few different versions. In general, criminologist Robert Merton's strain theory proposes that Americans value material wealth and success and have several ways of reaching that goal. Strain is much like stress; being unable to reach the goal of wealth and success creates strain with social mores, personal strain, strain with family members, and so on. Merton's version of strain theory—covered in detail in Chapter 6—states that people deal with strain using one of five methods. The method the Galanis family uses is called "innovation." The Galanises accepted the cultural goal of attaining wealth and success but rejected the legal, pro-social means of reaching that goal, having been convicted of using illegal, shortcut methods of amassing wealth.

Merton's strain theory may be more useful as a critique of society and as a way of recognizing the social reasons some people behave as they do. According to Merton, attaining wealth is such a pervasive goal in American society that some crime may be traced to the fact that many people feel worthless if they cannot meet this goal and so they believe they must break the law in order to do so.

Conflict Theory

According to conflict theory, covered in detail in Chapter 8, crime stems mainly from social-economic imbalance rather than from individuals. Conflict theorists consider most crime to be rooted in impoverishment and maintain that the powerful perpetuate the social imbalances leading to impoverishment and crime. One view is that the law is created by those who have power to favor themselves and their peers. A conflict perspective of the Galanis case, then, would focus not on their individual behavior but on their treatment by the criminal justice system.

The law deals most harshly with **street crime**—materially destructive or violent criminal offenses that are often interpersonal and represent those for which the police are most often called. Street crime consists of violent offenses and common property-related offenses such as theft, vandalism, and arson. In fact, the work of local police revolves around street crime: They investigate offenses, make arrests, detain suspects, defuse violent situations,

---

street crime—Materially destructive or violent criminal offenses that are often interpersonal and represent those for which the police are most often called.

and generally enforce the laws against rape, murder, assault, robbery, and so on. Street crime is mainly the realm of the lower and middle classes, ranging from the impoverished to the moderately well-off. White-collar crime, however, tends to be the realm of the wealthy.

Traditionally, the criminal justice system, from legislators to the courts, has treated white-collar crime much more gingerly than street crime. For example, a white-collar offender—if incarcerated at all—may be sent to a medium- or low-security institution and serve a few years. A street-crime offender, depending on how violent, is typically sent to a high-security institution. The stated reason is that white-collar offenders are rarely, if ever, violent. In fact, there are no violent white-collar offenses: They are all related to fraud and finance. The street-crime category contains all the violent offenses. A conflict theorist sees the situation differently, however.

A street offender may be more violent than a white-collar offender, but this is not always the case. Many street offenders are thieves, shoplifters, burglars, prostitutes, con artists, and drug sellers who are not violent. The prisons, in fact, are full of inmates who are not violent. Violence, the conflict theorist would say, is not the defining difference between the treatment of street offenders and white-collar offenders. Rather, the lifestyle and social class of white-collar offenders, especially the successful ones, match those of legislators, judges, prosecutors, attorneys, and law enforcement administrators. On the one hand, some of those individuals may even aspire to the white-collar offender's lifestyle (without the crime). On the other hand, how often does a police officer admire an impoverished murder suspect she is arresting and want to imitate his lifestyle?

The practical aspects of the conflict perspective have only recently begun to make themselves felt. In recent years, the economic recession, the apparent irresponsibility of financial and corporate professionals, and the revelation that several white-collar offenders became wealthy by victimizing others for decades have finally led to some harsher penalties for white-collar offenses.[45]

These examples show us how criminologists use theory to explore criminal behavior in a systematic way. Without clearly stated and testable theories, criminology would be reduced to competing opinions based on biases, political agendas, stereotypes, and unexplored assumptions. Criminological theory is a work in progress, and the popularity of various theories waxes and wanes as new evidence is presented, new social conditions appear, and scholars improve their research.

As we think critically about criminological theory, we will see that criminology has offered many different explanations of why people break the criminal law and has given us ideas about how society should respond. The challenge for criminology students and scholars is to appreciate the subtle differences between these theories, examine the evidence supporting each, and apply the theories to real-life problems of crime.

PAUSE AND REVIEW

1. **List and describe three criminological theories that can be applied to real-life examples of crime.**
2. **Explain how criminologists use theory.**

The Making of Laws

One of the central features of criminology is the making of laws. Law-making is a difficult process and requires lawmakers to examine their motivations and aspirations for achieving a just and peaceful society. Imagine that you are a state senator who must vote on upcoming regulations concerning the regulation of marijuana. Although you have never used marijuana yourself, you are conflicted about how to vote on a pending bill that would legalize recreational marijuana in your state. You are being lobbied by several people who have varying interests in this legislation, and you must decide how you are going to vote. Here are some of the issues that are complicating that decision.

- Two of your three adult children presently use marijuana illegally. They are constantly asking you to vote for legalization. They contend that using marijuana is a personal decision that every individual should be allowed to make and that conservative politicians should embrace legalization because it keeps the government out of people's lives.

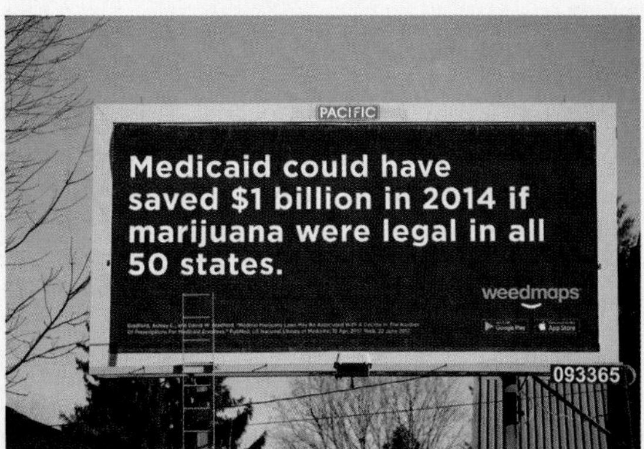

This billboard in Portland, Oregon, states that Medicaid could have saved money in 2014 if marijuana had been legal in all 50 states. What effect would the national legalization of recreational marijuana have on the country's criminal justice system?

- Your friend, who is a physician, has told you that she believes that marijuana is less harmful to the human body and to society than alcohol. Additionally, she argues that marijuana has some useful outcomes: Notably, it helps deal with chronic pain, which makes it an alternative to opioid painkillers.
- Police executives in your jurisdiction insist that marijuana should remain illegal because it is a health and safety hazard. Because there is no way to determine how impaired someone who uses marijuana is while driving, legalizing it would cause an increase in fatal accidents.
- Deacons in your church say that any kind of intoxicants are against God's law. They argue against the use of alcohol, nicotine, caffeine, and any other substance that alters one's perceptions or behavior.
- Your colleagues in the state senate explain that the revenue expected from taxing the legalization of marijuana would produce enormous benefits for the state. The money could be used to support educational initiatives and badly needed infrastructure projects, as well as relieve the need to raise property and sales taxes to finance the city's responsibilities. Your political party has traditionally been against any type of leniency for drug laws, but several of your colleagues have approached you with a proposal that could be financially rewarding to anyone who is given permission to open a recreational marijuana dispensary. They suggest that they could write the laws to ensure that friends and relatives could be first in line in getting these dispensary licenses.

What Do You Do?

1. Vote to legalize recreational marijuana because it would make your children happy, increase tax revenue for the state, and be consistent with your views that the government should stay out of people's lives.
2. Vote to keep recreational marijuana illegal because you fear the consequences of drug use not only for the human body but also for society.
3. Work with colleagues in your party to take advantage of the legalization of marijuana by ensuring that those who get dispensary licenses include members of your family and close friends, thus ensuring financial benefits to yourself.
4. Vote to allow only medical marijuana that would be available by a prescription from a licensed physician. Preventing recreational use would benefit society, while people with illnesses that are improved by marijuana use can get the help they need.

Summary

LEARNING OBJECTIVE 1 State Sutherland's definition of criminology.	Sutherland created the classic definition of criminology. It states: "Criminology is the study of the making of laws, breaking of laws, and society's reaction to the breaking of laws."
LEARNING OBJECTIVE 2 Demonstrate how political science, economics, psychology, law, biology, and sociology contribute to criminology.	Criminology is interdisciplinary, meaning that it draws upon other academic disciplines. Understanding the problems of crime and criminal justice requires knowledge of many areas of study.

LEARNING OBJECTIVE 3 — Differentiate between criminology and criminal justice.	Criminology and criminal justice are not interchangeable. Criminology emerged from sociology to focus on the social issue of crime. Criminal justice emerged from criminology to focus on the social mechanisms for dealing with crime.
LEARNING OBJECTIVE 4 — List and describe the seven criteria that are used to judge whether a theory is useful.	(1) Usefulness and policy implications: A good criminological theory should be able to direct real-world policy and be useful in dealing with crime. (2) Empirical validity: A good theory can stand up under the use of effective measuring tools. (3) Scope: Good theories seek to explain a range of behavior. (4) Testability: A good theory is stated so that all its elements and propositions can be tested. (5) Parsimony: Good theories explain complicated ideas in simple language. (6) Ideology: Some theories are based in specific ideologies, which can affect the objectivity of the theory. (7) Logical consistency: The theory must make logical sense.

Critical Reflections

1. **Does criminology focus on why people break the law or on what society does about it?**
2. **In what ways is criminology interdisciplinary?**
3. **Describe how strain theory and conflict theory offer different explanations of the same offense.**
4. **Do you think criminologists have created all possible theories of crime causation? Why or why not?**

Key Terms

antisocial p. 10
civil law p. 4
crime p. 4
criminal law p. 4
criminology p. 4
deviance p. 4
pro-social p. 13
recidivism p. 11
serial murder p. 7
street crime p. 16
theory p. 6
white-collar crime p. 13

Notes

1 Mike Isaac and Christopher Mele, "A Murder Posted on Facebook Prompts Outrage and Questions over Responsibility," *New York Times*, April 17, 2017, https://www.nytimes.com/2017/04/17/technology/facebook-live-murder-broadcast.html. Richard Pérez-Peña, Christopher Mele, and Serge F. Kovaleski, "Hunt for Facebook Killer Ends with McDonald's Sighting and a Suicide," *New York Times*, April 18, 2017, https://www.nytimes.com/2017/04/18/us/facebook-killer-suicide-erie.html. Accessed April 2018.

2 Ibid.

3 Ibid.

4 Ibid.

5 Edwin H. Sutherland, *Principles of Criminology* (Philadelphia: Lippincott, 1939), 2.

6 Melanie A. Taylor, "A Comprehensive Study of Mass Murder Precipitants and Motivations of Offenders," *International Journal of Offender Therapy and Comparative Criminology* 62, no. 2 (2018): 427–449.

7 Komiya Nobuo, "A Cultural Study of the Low Crime Rate in Japan," *British Journal of Criminology*, no. 3 (1999): 369.

8 CNN, "Japan Executes Serial Killer," June 17, 2008, http://edition.cnn.com/2008/WORLD/asiapcf/06/17/japan.executions/index.html. Accessed August 2018.

9 David E. Kaplan, "More Stressed, but Still Safer," *U.S. News & World Report* 142, no. 11 (March 26, 2007): 66.

10 Nobuo, "A Cultural Study of the Low Crime Rate in Japan," 369.

11 Megan J. O'Toole and Mark R. Fondacaro, "When School-Shooting Media Fuels a Retributive Public: An Examination of Psychological Mediators," *Youth Violence and Juvenile Justice* 15, no. 2 (2017): 154–171.

12 Andreas Baranowski, Anne Burkhardt, Elisabeth Czernik, and Heiko Hecht, "The CSI-Education Effect: Do Potential Criminals Benefit from Forensic TV Series?" *International Journal of Law, Crime and Justice* (October 2017).

13 Josef Stalin is credited with this statement, although Russian historians apparently have no record of it. Julia Solovyova, "Mustering Most Memorable Quips," *Moscow Times*, October 28, 1997.

14 Mark Dolliver, "In Our Minds, at Least, Crime Is Coming Back," *Adweek* 50, no. 38 (October 26, 2009): 17.

15 James D. Unnever and Francis T. Cullen, "The Social Sources of Americans' Punitiveness: A Test of Three Competing Models," *Criminology* 48, no. 1 (2010): 99–129; Michael T. Costelloe, Ted Chiricos, and Marc Gertz, "Punitive Attitudes Toward Criminals," *Punishment & Society* 11, no. 1 (January 2009): 25–49; Monica Williams, "Beyond the Punitive Public: Governance and Public Opinion on Penal Policy," Conference Papers—Law and Society (Annual Meeting 2009): 1. Lydia Saad, "Americans Hold Firm to Support for Death Penalty," *Gallup Poll Briefing* (November 17, 2008): 1.

16 Diana C. Mutz and Lilach Nir," Not Necessarily the News: Does Fictional Television Influence Real-World Policy Preferences?" *Mass Communication and Society* 13, no. 2 (April 2010): 196–217.

17 Dan Mitchell, "Manson's Family Affair Living in Cyberspace," *Wired*, April 16, 1997, https://www.wired.com/1997/04/mansons-family-affair-living-in-cyberspace. Ted Rowlands, "Charles Manson Spends Most of His Time Alone," CNN, March 20, 2009, http://www.cnn.com/2009/CRIME/03/20/charles.manson.prison/index.html. Accessed April 2018.

18 "Execution Date Only Hours Off for John Gacy," *New York Times*, May 9, 1994, http://www.nytimes.com/1994/05/09/us/execution-date-only-hours-off-for-john-gacy.html. Accessed August 2018.

19 Bonnie L. Cook, "Web 'Murderabilia' Sales Spark Outrage," *Philadelphia Inquirer*, June 17, 2009.

20 *Buck v. Davis*, 580 U.S. (2017). Available at http://www.scotusblog.com/case-files/cases/buck-v-stephens. Accessed January 2018.

21 Ibid.

22 Ibid.

23 Ibid.

24 Megan Moore and Meghan Brenna Morris, "Political Science Theories of Crime and Delinquency," *Journal of Human Behavior in the Social Environment* 21, no. 3 (2011): 284–296.

25 Tracy L. Snell, Capital Punishment, 2013–Statistical Tables (Washington, DC: U.S. Department of Justice Office of Justice Programs Bureau of Justice Statistics, 2014), 1. Available at http://www.bjs.gov/index.cfm?ty=pbdetail&iid=5156. Accessed April 2018.

26 Jack Glaser, Karin D. Martin, and Kimberly B. Kahn, "Possibility of Death Sentence Has Divergent Effect on Verdicts for Black and White Defendants," *Law & Human Behavior* 39, no. 6 (2015): 539–546. Justin D. Levinson, Robert J. Smith, and Danielle M. Young, "Devaluing Death: An Empirical Study of Implicit Racial Bias on Jury-Eligible Citizens in Six Death Penalty States," *New York University Law Review* 89, no. 2 (2014): 513–581.

27 Catherine M. Grosso and Barbara O'Brien, "A Stubborn Legacy: The Overwhelming Importance of Race in Jury Selection in 173 Post-Batson North Carolina Capital Trials," *Iowa Law Review* 97, no. 5 (2012): 1531–1559.

28 Peter-Jan Engelen, Michel W. Lander, and Marc van Essen, "What Determines Crime Rates? An Empirical Test of Integrated Economic and Sociological Theories of Criminal Behavior," *Social Science Journal* 53, no. 2 (June 2016): 247–262.

29 Alex R. Dopp, Charles M. Borduin, Emily C. Willroth, and Amelia A. Sorg, "Long-term Economic Benefits of Psychological Interventions for Criminality: Comparing and Integrating Estimation Methods," *Psychology, Public Policy, and Law* 23, no. 3: (2017): 312–323.

30 *Buck v. Davis*, 580 U.S. (2017). Available at http://www.scotusblog.com/case-files/cases/buck-v-stephens. Accessed January 2018.

31 Brandi Grissom, "TYC Ends Contract With Doctor Who Gave Race Testimony in Court," *Texas Tribune*, October 31, 2011, https://www.texastribune.org/2011/10/31/tyc-ends-contract-doctor-who-gave-race-testimony. Accessed April 2018.

32 Bryanna Fox, "It's Nature and Nurture: Integrating Biology and Genetics into the Social Learning Theory of Criminal Behavior," *Journal of Criminal Justice* 49 (March 1, 2017): 22–31.

33 Jeffery T. Ulmer, *Sociology of Crime, Law and Deviance* (Amsterdam: JAI Press, 2000).

34 Brittany Shammas, "Vigilantes Mount a Controversial Effort to Take Back South Beach," *Miami New Times*, January 9, 2018, http://www.miaminewtimes.com/news/miami-beach-vigilantes-harass-the-poor-and-homeless-9974172. Susan Askew, "Public Defender vs Citizens Crime Group," RE:MiamiBeach, November 16, 2017, http://www.remiamibeach.com/citywide/public-defender-vs-citizens-crime-group. Liane Morejon, "Arrested 344 Times, Miami Beach Man Heads Back to Jail," Local10.com, January 23, 2018, https://www.local10.com/news/florida/miami-beach/arrested-344-times-miami-beach-man-heads-back-to-jail. Madeleine Marr, "He's Been Arrested 344 Times. One Group Is Working to Make Sure 345 Doesn't Happen," *Miami Herald*, January 24, 2018, http://www.miamiherald.com/news/local/community/miami-dade/miami-beach/article196532144.html. Accessed April 2018.

35 Ibid.

36 Brendan D. Dooley and Jason Rydberg, "Irreconcilable Differences? Examining Divergences in the Orientations of Criminology and Criminal Justice Scholarship, 1951–2008," *Journal of Criminal Justice Education* 25, no. 1 (2014): 84.

37 National Institute of Justice, Office of Justice Programs, Recidivism, https://www.nij.gov/topics/corrections/recidivism/pages/welcome.aspx. Accessed January 2018.

38 Erik Larson, "A Prisoner Seeks Court Mercy for Being Born into a White-Collar Crime Family," *Bloomberg*, July 28, 2017, https://www.bloomberg.com/news/articles/2017-07-28/born-into-life-of-white-collar-crime-convict-seeks-court-mercy. Erik Larson, "White Collar Crook's Son Gets 14 Years in Native Bond Scam," Bloomberg, August 11, 2017, https://www.bloomberg.com/news/articles/2017-08-11/son-of-white-collar-crook-gets-15-years-in-native-american-scam. Accessed August 2018.

39 U.S. Department of Justice, Father and Son Sentenced in Manhattan Federal Court for Market Manipulation Scheme, February 16, 2016, https://www.justice.gov/usao-sdny/pr/father-and-son-sentenced-manhattan-federal-court-market-manipulation-scheme. Accessed April 2018.

40 Jonathan Stempel, "Father, Son in Gerova Stock Scam Get Six Years Prison," *Reuters*, February 16, 2017, https://www.reuters.com/article/us-gerova-financial-fraud/father-son-in-gerova-stock-scam-get-six-years-prison-idUSKBN15V2YV. U.S. Department of Justice, Jason Galanis Sentenced to More Than 14 Years in Prison for Defrauding Tribal Entity and Pension Funds of Tens of Millions of Dollars, August 22, 2017, https://www.justice.gov/usao-sdny/pr/jason-galanis-sentenced-more-14-years-prison-defrauding-tribal-

entity-and-pension-funds. Accessed April 2018.

41 Larson, "A Prisoner Seeks Court Mercy for Being Born into a White-Collar Crime Family." Larson, "White Collar Crook's Son Gets 14 Years in Native Bond Scam."

42 Ibid.

43 Ibid.

44 Francis T. Cullen, Robert Agnew, and Pamela Wilcox, *Criminological Theory: Past to Present*, 5th ed. (New York: Oxford University Press, 2014), 137.

45 Kristy Holtfreter, Shanna Van Slyke, Jason Bratton, and Marc Gertz, "Public Perceptions of White-collar Crime and Punishment," *Journal of Criminal Justice* 36, (2008): 50–60.

J. Edgar Hoover FBI Building
BUSINESS APPOINTMENTS

Measuring Crime

FEATURES

The FBI Headquarters building in Washington, D.C. Who uses the crime statistics collected by the FBI?

Frank Reyos, right, sits with his defense team as he is sentenced to life in prison without parole. Prosecutors said Reyos killed 16-year-old Kenyatta Winston as retribution after Winston left him behind during a gunfight. Why is it important for the FBI to report the data on the characteristics of arrests for gang and drug-related homicides?

Each year, the FBI releases a report titled *Crime in the United States* that is a collection of crime statistics gathered from most of the country's law enforcement agencies. This report, which is part of the Uniform Crime Reports, is the most comprehensive database of crime and police activity in the United States and is used by researchers, journalists, policymakers, and public interest groups to get a picture of the level and trends of crime and the activities of the criminal justice system.

When the 2016 report was released in September 2017, observers quickly noted that much of the data was missing. The website FiveThirtyEight has reported that the 2016 report contained close to 70 percent fewer data tables than did the 2015 report.[1] The changes in the report's format were made without the consultation of its Advisory Policy Board, which is responsible for reviewing operational issues for several FBI programs.[2] Instead, it is reported that the staff of the Office of Public Affairs reviewed the number of times the tables were viewed on the Internet and decided not to include much of the data from the report.[3]

Most of the missing data is related to arrests. Arrest data reveal if there are differences between arrests by jurisdiction, race, sex, age, gender, offense, or circumstance. Knowing who is being arrested and why is necessary for understanding the nature of crime in a jurisdiction, as well as how the police operate.[4] The data also include information such as the relationship between homicide victims, their killers, and the circumstances of the offense. In the absence of these data, it is more difficult for researchers to understand family and intimate partner violence, as well as gang- and drug-related homicide.[5] As of May 2018, the FBI published an amendment including some of the missing data.

Researchers and criminal justice agencies need an accurate, uniform, and comprehensive measurement of crime. In this chapter, we will see how the measurement of crime is not straightforward and how many issues, including political factors, influence the measurement and reporting of crime.

The Importance of Measuring Crime

LEARNING OBJECTIVE | 1

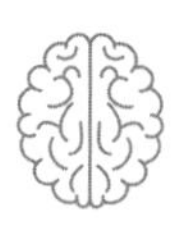

Identify some reasons that jurisdictions or criminal justice officials might alter crime statistics.

It is difficult to study the breaking of criminal law and develop theories to explain it without knowing which laws are being broken, who is breaking them, why, and how often. Although measuring crime might seem a relatively straightforward activity in which criminologists record the type and frequency of criminal offenses across jurisdictions, in reality it is an extremely complex task.

This chapter covers the four major sources of crime statistics: the Federal Bureau of Investigation's **Uniform Crime Reports** (the subject of the opening scenario), the **National Incident-Based Reporting System**, the **National Crime Victimization Survey**, and **self-report studies**. In this text, we illustrate their strengths and shortcomings, and discuss the political dimension of crime measurement. Because crime statistics affect law enforcement agencies and communities, criminal justice officials and administrators sometimes attempt to control the collection and dissemination of crime data. The following examples illustrate why.

- A criminal justice official may wish to acquire more police officers and other resources, such as weapons, vehicles, or communication equipment. By showing a rising crime rate and an agency ill equipped to deal with new challenges, law enforcement officials may try to convince local government that more resources are needed.

- A criminal justice official may be criticized because of a high crime rate and fear that he or she could be fired or lose an election.
- A jurisdiction competing for federal anti-crime funds may need to show that a significant crime problem exists. By emphasizing a problem with illegal drugs or gangs, the community may become eligible for funds it can use for a variety of purposes.
- A jurisdiction that derives substantial income from the tourism and convention industries must project itself as safe. A sharp increase in crime statistics is bad for business. Other jurisdictions trying to attract business and residents may see their efforts rendered useless by a high crime rate or even the public perception that the area is not as safe as others.

These examples illustrate the concerns of law enforcement officials and city administrators about how crime statistics portray their jurisdiction. Although measuring crime is a serious business fraught with political and economic concerns, substantial efforts have been made to measure it in an accurate, scientific manner. Although each method of crime measurement has its strengths and weaknesses, together they provide different perspectives on crime. Another point about the measurement of crime—and one that may surprise you—is that all of the methods are flawed. The statistics of the Uniform Crime Reports, the National Incident-Based Reporting System, and the National Victimization Survey are not exact counts of how many offenses have occurred. Because of the problems of reporting and recording criminal offenses, the crime data that we are all familiar with and that are reported by the government and trumpeted by the media are only a vague representation of the actual amount of crime. Furthermore, counting the actual number of criminal offenses is impossible.

Finally, we will look at how these methods of measuring crime affect criminology itself. In addition to conducting their own studies, criminological researchers use statistics to build theories and hypotheses as well as suggest and help implement public programs. Because researchers are using the same flawed statistics as everyone else, as well as conducting their own flawed surveys, we will learn how they try to work around these imperfections to get closer to the true amount of crime. First, we must comprehend the most significant obstacle to achieving an accurate count: the dark figure of crime.[6]

PAUSE AND REVIEW

1. **Why might some jurisdictions or criminal justice officials try to alter crime statistics?**

The Dark Figure of Crime

LEARNING OBJECTIVE | 2

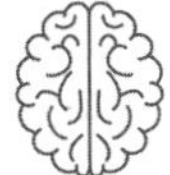

Define the dark figure of crime.

Much more crime occurs than we know. The offenses recorded in government statistics are only a representation of the true amount of crime. The unknown amount is called the **dark figure of crime**, a term that describes criminal offenses that are unreported to law enforcement officials and are never recorded.[7] Two types of offenses feed the dark figure of crime: the vast number that are not reported and those that are reported but not recorded (see Figure 2.1).

For offenses to enter the measures of crime, they must be reported to the proper authorities who define it as a criminal offense and must be recorded in the appropriate category. This presents two decision points critical to accurate reporting: whether to bring the activity to the attention of the official record-keeper (in most cases the police) and whether to identify the activity as a criminal offense. Between these two decisions, a large amount of crime goes unreported and unrecorded.[8] We will get into the reasons that offenses go unrecorded later in this chapter. First, let's look at reporting. A criminal offense may not be reported for a number of reasons.

Uniform Crime Reports—A Federal Bureau of Investigation program that collects law enforcement statistics from voluntarily participating agencies throughout the United States.

National Incident-Based Reporting System (NIBRS)—The Federal Bureau of Investigation's incident-based reporting system in which data are collected on every single offense.

National Crime Victimization Survey (NCVS)—A survey of a nationally representative sample of residences that collects information about crime from victims.

self-report study—Research based on data offered by respondents about themselves.

dark figure of crime—A term that describes criminal offenses that are unreported to law enforcement officials and never recorded.

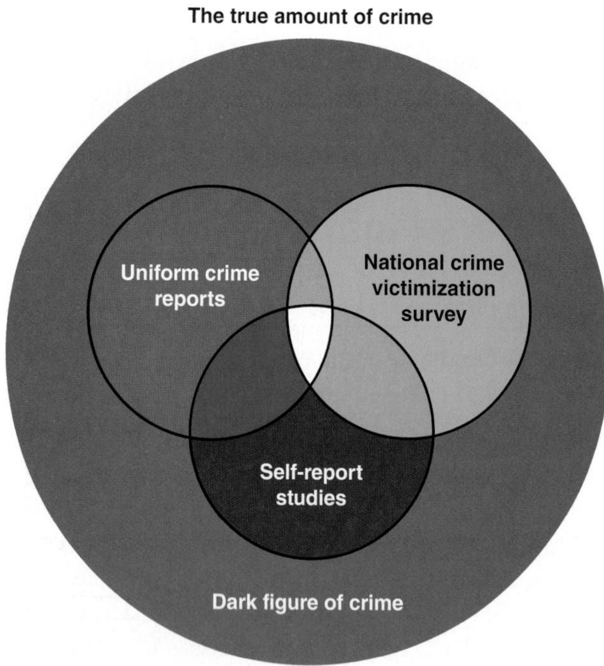

FIGURE 2.1 The Dark Figure of Crime

The Uniform Crime Reports, the National Crime Victimization Survey, and self-report studies shed some light on the dark figure of crime. Although it is possible that crime reported in one measure may have been reported in one or both of the other measures, we cannot know this for certain.

THINK ABOUT IT

In your estimate, about how much crime goes unreported?

- Failure to recognize it as an offense. An offense may occur, and witnesses and/or victims may not actually realize it is a criminal offense. For instance, someone passes counterfeit money at a bank, and the bank teller does not recognize that the bills are not legal tender. If a $20 bill is exchanged hundreds of times before it is recognized as bogus, it will be recorded as a criminal offense only the final time it is exchanged.
- Fear of retaliation. A victim or witness may fear the possible consequences of reporting an offense. This is especially true in cases of domestic assault in which a spouse or children are routinely beaten. Neighborhood residents may also hesitate to report drug sales because they are afraid of the dealers.
- Fear of legal consequences. A crime victim may not be totally blameless. A person cheated in a transaction of illegal drugs is not likely to report it to the police.
- Lack of faith in the system. Individuals may not believe that police are able to make an arrest or that judges will impose a significant sentence. On occasion, a victim may attempt to seek justice in his or her own way by engaging in vigilante activities. In neighborhoods where the police are not trusted, victims may not report offenses because they do not want to "snitch" or cooperate with police.[9]
- Lack of insurance. Victims who do not have insurance cannot be compensated for the theft of their property, so they may see no reason to report the offense.

These are but a few of the reasons that people may not report a criminal offense. This failure to report can be observed by comparing the statistics in the Uniform Crime Reports with those in the National Crime Victimization Survey, which asks participants if they have been crime victims (we will discuss both these measures in detail later in the chapter). The number of reported offenses, especially violent ones, is traditionally higher in the National Crime Victimization Survey than in the Uniform Crime Reports. A comparison of the 2016 versions of both reports found that the Uniform Crime Reports recorded 7.9 million property offenses and 1.25 million violent offenses, whereas the National Crime Victimization Survey recorded 15.9 million property victimizations and 5.7 million violent victimizations.[10] Clearly, more criminal offenses are occurring than are being reported to police.

The non-reporting of crime is also closely related to social class, sex, and race. One example is related to the reputation of the police in unstable neighborhoods or among minorities. The police may not be trusted, or victims of earlier offenses may have had what they considered to be unjust experiences with the criminal justice system. These victims may feel safer dealing with their victimization in some other way, such as vigilantism, than in calling the police. None of the criminal offenses committed in these common examples would be reported to the police, and they would remain unrecorded. If the level of non-reporting in these cases is as high as many researchers believe, then much of recorded crime is the product of reports by victims who are relatively affluent, white, male, residents of stable neighborhoods, or all these. This bias distorts the picture of crime and can lead policymakers to misallocate crime-control resources to protect those who already have privileged status in society.[11]

Although a lot of crime goes unreported, the major sources of crime data still generally agree with one another. Even if these sources cannot be matched number for number, scholars point out that they show similar broad patterns and distributions of crime. The crime statistics recorded by the Uniform Crime Reports tend to agree in pattern, if not in volume, with those recorded by the National Crime Victimization Survey. Until the recent convergence of these surveys—which we will discuss later—researchers considered these two measures of crime to complement rather than contradict each other. The same goes for self-report studies, which show some agreement—again, in patterns of offending, if not in number of offenses reported—with both the Uniform Crime Reports and the National Crime Victimization Survey. For example, in juvenile self-report studies, the groups of juveniles whom the justice system most often designates as "delinquent"—that is, boys, minorities, poor students, and youths with delinquent peers and family issues—self-report more delinquent activities than groups of juveniles who have no records of delinquency and do not fall into those categories.[12] That juvenile delinquents admit to committing more delinquent acts seems to be a common-sense observation, but it is relevant when it confirms other independent surveys.

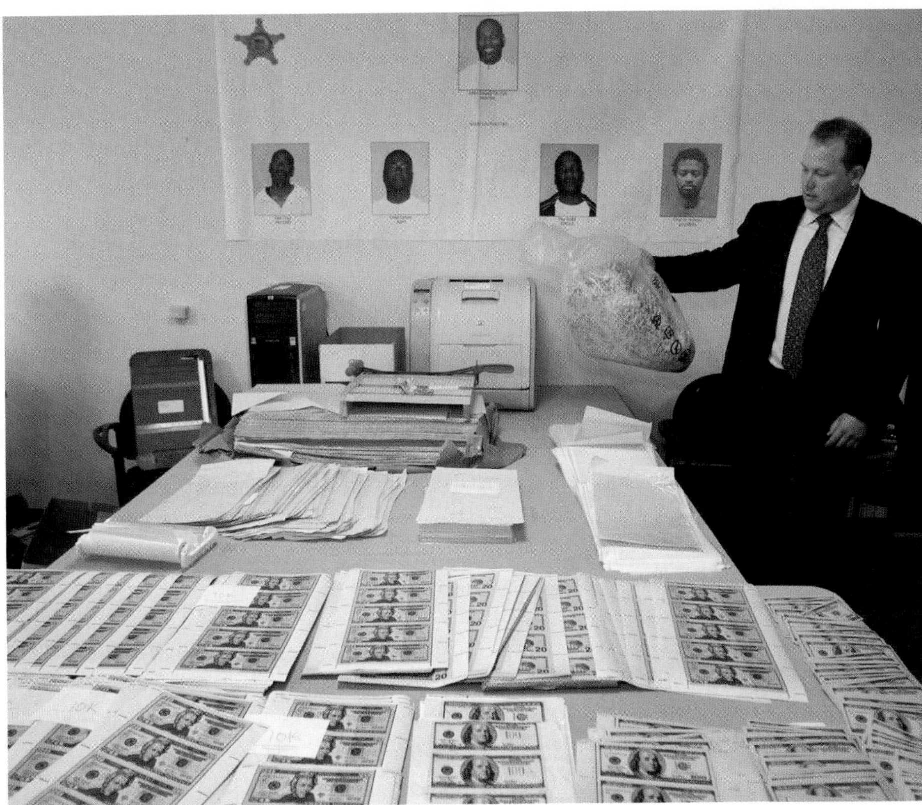

A Secret Service agent holds a bag of shredded counterfeit $100 and $20 notes displayed along with other evidence. Offenses involving counterfeit money are not reported in crime statistics. Can you think of reasons why?

Protesters march in response to the verdict in the trial of former St. Louis police officer Jason Stockley who was acquitted in the 2011 shooting death of black driver Anthony Lamar Smith. Why are many citizens of minority communities reluctant to report crime to the police?

Despite law enforcement's best efforts to collect accurate crime data, the dark figure of crime remains large and significant. We have discussed many reasons people do not report crime, but some issues remain that affect the level of reporting. One has to do with public confidence in the police. In some neighborhoods or jurisdictions, the police have a rapport with citizens that encourages the reporting of crime. In others, the police are viewed as ineffective or, worse, as working against citizens.[13] For instance, in some minority communities, the police are considered to be an invading army or even a rival street gang. Although the police may be only doing their job, their presence and paramilitary demeanor discourage some citizens from cooperating.[14]

Scholars have suggested that race and social-class biases are inherent in policing. This has been a consistent criticism of law enforcement for many years. Even with racial and gender integration of law enforcement agencies, the perception remains that laws are disproportionately enforced against the impoverished and people of color.[15] Criminologist John Irwin argues that the criminal justice system disproportionately incarcerates impoverished individuals as a method of managing the underclass. He refers to these individuals as the "rabble" who find themselves detained and arrested with little provocation. Instead of concentrating on controlling crime, the police are performing a sort of public-order maintenance that results in the overrepresentation of impoverished people in criminal justice statistics.[16]

Another problem with these reporting systems is methodological—that is, how the crime rate is calculated. The crime rate may be reasonably accurate in years recent to the last census, but by the time eight or nine years have passed, the population may have grown significantly larger or even shrunk. The population of some jurisdictions in the Southeast and Southwest grew tremendously in a few years, and crime significantly increased. However, because of the outdated population estimate, it appeared to be a less serious problem than it actually was.[17]

Perhaps most important for criminologists and criminology students to understand is that no crime-measurement technique is perfect. All have their flaws and drawbacks, and pulling something useful out of them is more difficult than the media would have us believe. Although headlines shouting that crime trends are headed up or down are indeed based on government statistics, with quotes from criminologists to boot, the reality is far less clear.

For example, according to the Uniform Crime Reports, the violent crime rate increased sharply between 1960 and 1990, then began to decline in the mid-1990s. However, victimization surveys showed stable violent victimization rates between the 1970s and mid-1990s, followed by a decline similar to that described by the Uniform Crime Reports.[18] How could the Uniform Crime Reports show a steady increase in violent crime for 30 years while victimization surveys showed a flat rate? Irregularities such as these keep researchers looking for the source of the discrepancies. Before we get to that issue, however, let's first learn a bit more about these sources of statistics.

methodology—The rules and principles that govern how research is performed.

PAUSE AND REVIEW

1. **List the reasons why someone would not report a criminal offense.**
2. **Show how the major methods of measuring crime attempt to shed light on the dark figure of crime.**

Government Statistical Efforts

LEARNING OBJECTIVE | 3

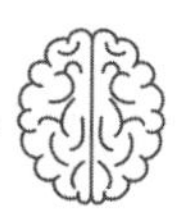

Summarize the advantages and limitations of the Uniform Crime Reports.

LEARNING OBJECTIVE | 4

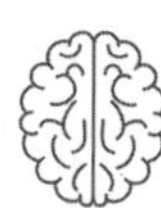

Compare and contrast the National Incident-Based Reporting System and the Uniform Crime Reports.

LEARNING OBJECTIVE | 5

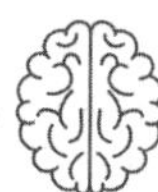

Discuss the reasons for the creation of the National Crime Victimization Survey.

The three major government efforts to measure crime in the United States come from the Federal Bureau of Investigation (FBI). They are the Uniform Crime Reports (UCR), its offshoot the National Incident-Based Reporting System (NIBRS), and the National Crime Victimization Survey (NCVS). The UCR has been around the longest and is the workhorse of crime statistical reports. Its purpose is to provide statistics for the administration of the criminal justice system. Without the UCR, we would have little idea of the actual incidence of crime. Its numbers are freely available, and anyone from researchers to criminal justice professionals to the general public can use them to study crime. The NIBRS is like the UCR in that it follows many of the same rules for collecting statistics, scoring items, and reporting data; however, it is far more detailed. Finally, the purpose of the NCVS is to provide information about victims, offenders, and unreported crime. Let's look at the UCR first.

The Uniform Crime Reports

The FBI collects and publishes data from more than 17,000 jurisdictions with the objective of providing reliable statistics to assist law enforcement in operations and management.[19] The federal government makes participation in the UCR program voluntary, but about 38 states require police departments to send data either to a state program or directly to the FBI.[20] This makes the UCR the most comprehensive crime-data collection effort in the country. Since the UCR has continued for 80 years, some of the **methodology**—the rules and principles that govern how research is performed—that makes reporting crime such a difficult endeavor has been worked out. Currently, the UCR represents one of the most reliable measures of certain types of violent and property offenses.

Getting every agency to use standard definitions of crime and record offenses in consistent ways is an ongoing challenge for the UCR program. Before 1929, when the International Association of Chiefs of Police began to standardize crime reporting, crime statistics were not systematically collected. Although some large cities recorded arrests and offenses, the definitions of offenses and standards for recording them varied widely. For instance, the attitude of the police and the public toward lynching, abortion, domestic violence, drug and alcohol use, and dueling depended on the jurisdiction. Some jurisdictions abhorred some of these activities and made them offenses, while tolerating others. A jurisdiction that supported dueling was less likely to define a resulting death as a homicide. And until recent decades, chances were good that assaulting a spouse, domestic partner, or children would not be recorded as an offense.[21]

Developing crime statistics is difficult because U.S. law enforcement is decentralized; each state and municipality has its own police force. In countries like England, where the police force is highly centralized, it is much easier to define and record offenses in a consistent manner. In the UCR's early years, some jurisdictions were dropped because the numbers they reported diverged so widely from those of other jurisdictions of the same size and demographic composition. The Department of Justice could not guarantee the accuracy of crime statistics from many jurisdictions and cautioned readers about making comparative judgments. The 1930 Wickersham Commission offered the following caveat: "It takes but little experience of such criminal statistics as we have in order to convince that a serious abuse exists in compiling them as a basis for requesting appropriations or for justifying the existence of or urging expanded powers and equipment for the agencies in question."[22]

The early UCR measured seven offenses which, in 1960, became the Crime Index: murder and non-negligent manslaughter, rape, robbery, aggravated assault, burglary, larceny, and motor vehicle theft. These offenses were selected for five reasons.

- They were the most likely to be reported to police.
- Police could easily establish that an offense had occurred.
- The offenses occurred in all geographic areas of the United States.
- They occurred with sufficient frequency to provide an adequate basis for comparison between jurisdictions.
- They were serious in nature and volume.[23]

Although the FBI tinkered somewhat with the definitions and types of offenses included in the Crime Index (arson was added in 1979 to create the Modified Crime Index), it remained substantially unchanged until 2004 when the Crime Index and the Modified Crime Index were discontinued in favor of a simple violent crime total and property crime total. (See Figure 2.2 for the levels of violent and property crime in the United States from 2011 to 2016.) The Crime Index and the Modified Crime Index were determined to inaccurately represent the degree of crime because they were inflated by the most frequently committed offense, which is usually larceny/theft. Therefore, a jurisdiction that

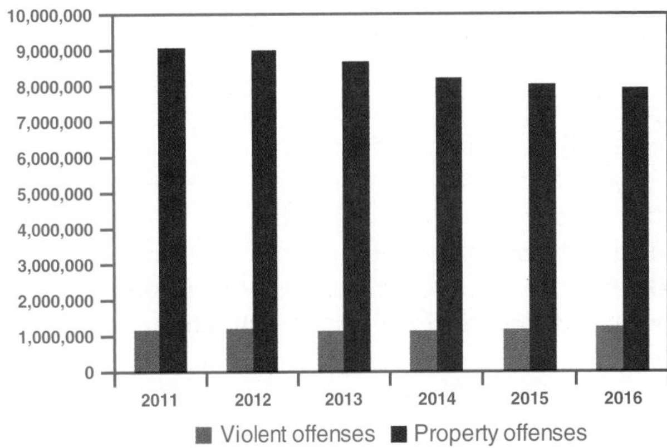

FIGURE 2.2 Number of Recorded Violent and Property Offenses in the United States, 2011–2016

THINK ABOUT IT

Compare the number of property offenses to the number of violent offenses. Can you think of reasons why so many more property offenses are recorded?

Source: Federal Bureau of Investigation, Uniform Crime Reports, Crime in the United States, *2016, Table 1, https://ucr.fbi.gov/crime-in-the-u.s/2016/crime-in-the-u.s.-2016/topic-pages/tables/table-1.*

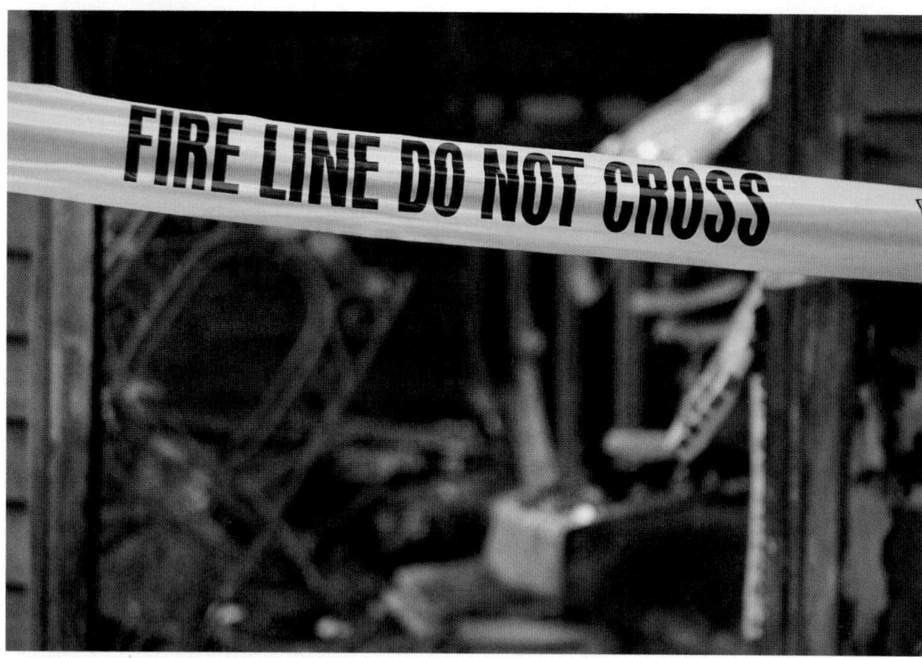

Arson is one of the property crimes recorded in the FBI *Uniform Crime Reports*. What other property crimes are recorded by the UCR?

appeared to be dangerous because of a high crime index may simply have had a large number of larceny/thefts and not necessarily a large number of more serious offenses.

Today, the UCR counts four types of violent offenses and four types of property offenses (see Table 2.1).[24] Violent offenses use force or threat of force. The property offenses—burglary, larceny/theft, and motor vehicle theft—include the taking of money or property, but victims suffer no force or threat of force. Although arson victims may experience force, arson is a property offense because property is destroyed.

Currently, the UCR publishes several reports and publications. *Crime in the United States*, the publication that is most frequently used to describe the extent of crime in the United States, includes three major data collections: Offenses Known to Law Enforcement, Persons Arrested, and Police Employee Data. All data are based on records that state and local police agencies submit to the FBI either directly or through state UCR programs. The FBI defines each collection as follows.

TABLE 2.1 Uniform Crime Reports Violent and Property Offenses

The Uniform Crime Reporting program records information about four violent offenses and four property offenses. Violent offenses are those that involve force or threat of force. As for the property offenses, burglary, larceny/theft, and motor vehicle theft involve the taking of money or property, but victims suffer no force or threat of force. Although arson victims may experience force, arson is included in this category because the offense involves the destruction of property.

VIOLENT OFFENSES	PROPERTY OFFENSES
Murder	Burglary
Rape	Larceny/Theft
Robbery	Motor Vehicle Theft
Aggravated Assault	Arson

Federal Bureau of Investigation, Uniform Crime Reports, Crime in the United States, Offenses Known to Law Enforcement, 2016, https://ucr.fbi.gov/crime-in-the-u.s/2016/crime-in-the-u.s.-2016/topic-pages/offenses-known-to-law-enforcement.

- Offenses Known to Law Enforcement. The UCR collects data on violent and property offenses known to law enforcement, as well as data regarding **clearances**, the closure of an offense by either arrest or "exceptional means." Exceptional means refers to situations beyond a police department's control that prevent it from arresting and formally charging a suspect, such as the suspect's death. (For the reporting system, the UCR does not distinguish between offenses cleared by arrest and those cleared by exceptional means.) In 2016, about 46 percent of known violent offenses were cleared by arrest.[25]
- Persons Arrested. Arrest data are collected for 28 offenses. The UCR counts one arrest for each separate instance in which a person is arrested, cited, or summoned for an offense. Because the same person may be arrested several times a year, the data do not reflect the number of individuals arrested, just the number of arrests.[26]
- Police Employee Data. The UCR defines "law enforcement officers" as individuals who carry a

firearm and a badge, have full arrest powers, and are paid from government funds allotted specifically for sworn law enforcement representatives ("sworn" means having full arrest powers granted by a state or local government). The data provide a count of existing staff levels of law enforcement officers, including totals for patrol officers, officers assigned to administrative and investigative positions, and officers assigned to special teams.[27]

New York City has a population of over 8 million people. How do researchers compensate for population when they are calculating crime rates?

One of the UCR's most controversial reporting techniques is the **hierarchy rule**, which states that in any incident involving more than one offense, the most serious offense is the only one officially recorded. For instance, if your house is broken into (burglary), you are beaten (aggravated assault and battery), your spouse is killed (murder), and your car is stolen (motor vehicle theft), the UCR records only the most serious of these offenses, murder. The exception is arson, which is always reported regardless of what other offenses have occurred. The hierarchy rule means the actual number of offenses is under-reported by design. (A deeper discussion of this rule appears in Chapter 9.)

The UCR includes not only the total number of specific offenses, but also the crime rate. The **crime rate** is not the actual number of offenses but a rate of occurrence calculated by dividing the number of offenses in a given jurisdiction by its population and multiplying by 100,000. For instance, the total number of offenses in a large city such as New York or Los Angeles will be far greater than that in a smaller city, but it is possible for the smaller city to have the higher crime rate, that is, more offenses per 100,000 people (see Figure 2.3). By compensating for population size, the crime rate makes it easy to compare crime across jurisdictions.

This ease of comparing crime rates has led to what many criminologists believe is a misuse of the

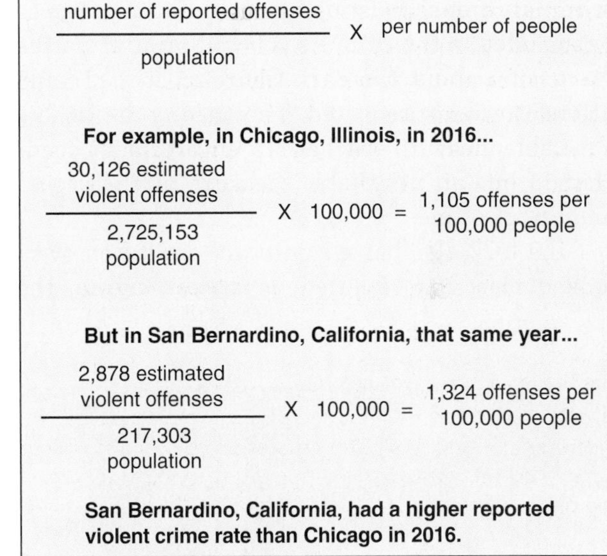

number of reported offenses / population X per number of people
For example, in Chicago, Illinois, in 2016...
30,126 estimated violent offenses / 2,725,153 population X 100,000 = 1,105 offenses per 100,000 people
But in San Bernardino, California, that same year...
2,878 estimated violent offenses / 217,303 population X 100,000 = 1,324 offenses per 100,000 people
San Bernardino, California, had a higher reported violent crime rate than Chicago in 2016.

FIGURE 2.3 How to Calculate Crime Rates

THINK ABOUT IT
Go to the most recent Uniform Crime Reports, *Crime in the United States*, on the FBI website and use the statistics there to calculate the violent crime rate for your jurisdiction.

Source: Federal Bureau of Investigation, Uniform Crime Reports, Crime in the United States, 2016, Table 4, https://ucr.fbi.gov/crime-in-the-u.s/2016/crime-in-the-u.s.-2016/topic-pages/tables/table-4.

---

clearance—The closure of an offense by arrest or other means.

hierarchy rule—The Federal Bureau of Investigation's practice of recording in the *Uniform Crime Reports* only the most serious offense in a set of offenses.

crime rate—The number of offenses divided by the population, usually expressed as a rate of offenses per 100,000 people.

UCR: The media and other organizations that rank "best places to live" often use the UCR's figures to compare the safety of jurisdictions. However, the UCR strongly cautions against making such comparisons.[28] That the UCR can be misused in this way points to one of its major shortcomings: its statistics give a vague, simplistic picture that shows the outlines of the crime problem but not the details.

PROBLEMS WITH THE UCR

Because of the concentrated effort to train personnel and law enforcement agencies to define and record offenses in a consistent manner, the UCR provides valuable data for policymakers and law enforcement administrators. However, along with the hierarchy rule, the UCR has three other significant limitations.

- It records only offenses reported to the police.
- It is focused on street crime.
- Its data are incomplete.

Let's explore these limitations a bit further. A criminal offense must be reported to the police to be included in the UCR. As you will recall from the discussion about the dark figure of crime, many offenses are not reported. This means the UCR is a reliable measure of what law enforcement agencies do but an unreliable measure of the actual amount of crime.

The UCR also has a significant and often overlooked bias: it is focused on **street crime**, the offenses that typically represent those for which the police are most often called. The UCR does not provide a good picture of white-collar, corporate, organized, or environmental crime because these offenses are far more difficult to capture and measure. Remember, the UCR was designed by the FBI, a federal law enforcement agency, to measure what the police do and to help them do it better. Police departments are concerned with curtailing street crime, so those are the statistics recorded in the UCR. A major, complicated corporate financial offense investigated by the Securities and Exchange Commission will not be recorded in the UCR, although such an offense may involve more money and may harm the public more than a series of robberies or burglaries. Much of criminological theory is focused on street crime. If white-collar, corporate, environmental, and organized offenses were counted in the same manner as street crime, perhaps more criminological theories would be developed to explain them, and they would draw more public and media attention.[29]

Despite the improvement in developing consistent definitions of criminal offenses, police departments, as we saw in the Introduction, have political motivations to provide data that support their agency agenda (see Doubletake). A law enforcement agency may under-report offenses to present a better crime rate and to improve the picture of the work it does. An agency may over-report crime to procure more funding or resources. Finally, an agency may report no crime data at all. In fact, a significant amount of data is missing from Offenses Known to the Police, and more apparently goes missing every year.[30]

Recall that UCR participation is voluntary; federal law does not require agencies to participate. The FBI notes in its UCR publication *Crime in the United States, 2016*, that in 2016 of the 18,481 law enforcement agencies eligible to participate in the UCR program, 16,782 submitted data, meaning that 90 percent of agencies participated.[31] Some agencies will report offenses in a time or place

This stripped bike frame is still locked to a pole. Why is street crime reported more than white-collar crime?

DOUBLETAKE

Bad Numbers

Police misreporting of crime statistics is a serious problem. Regardless of the reasons for misreporting, bad numbers mean criminologists, the media, criminal justice officials, and the public cannot make accurate assumptions about crime. How much misreporting actually occurs? Like the dark figure of crime, the true amount of crime misreporting can never be known. Often, it is only when police officers admit to altering statistics that misreporting is discovered.

- According to a *Los Angeles Times* analysis, the Los Angeles Police Department from 2005 to 2012 misclassified about 14,000 serious assaults as minor offenses. Violent crime was actually 7 percent higher than first reported, and the number of serious assaults was 16 percent higher.[32]
- A retired police officer who served 20 years with the Geneva, New York, Police Department described to *Police Magazine* how statistics were misrepresented at the department. "Burglaries would be reclassified to trespasses. Even attempted burglaries with smashed windows and damaged doors would be changed to criminal mischief. This prevented corresponding stats for the Uniform Crime Report and gave wiggle-room for the chief to tell the public that property crime was down across the city." In another case, there were several reports of rape at a local college. "With the first two, the victims reported their rapes to campus security, [but] the college never reported the rapes to the police department. The third victim actually came to the [police] after her rape and the investigation led to the other two . . . [it was] another classic case of the colleges not wanting those crime stats known."[33]
- A 2014 *Chicago Magazine* investigation revealed that the Chicago Police Department under-reported homicides in 2013 by misclassifying at least 10 homicides, and downgrading other violent felonies and serious property offenses. The magazine also found that the city's murder totals in 2014 were also likely under-reported, with at least 21 homicides that should have been counted as murders. Current and former police officers told the magazine that the misclassifications occurred because police supervisors pressured officers to lower the statistics.[34]

THINK ABOUT IT

1. What is harmful about the misreporting of crime statistics?
2. Should police departments that are caught misreporting crime be penalized?

other than when or where they occurred, report the year's offenses in December rather than when they became known to the police, or not report anything. Some agencies send reports for only one month.[35]

Although this may not sound problematic, nearly three-quarters of law enforcement agencies in states with statewide UCR programs submit complete reports, but in states without UCR programs, just over half do so.[36] Thus, the UCR does not include data from every police department in the country for every month.[37] This means that some data are missing. Although data are considered missing when law enforcement agencies do not properly report offenses or arrests, most of the missing data can be attributed to agencies that do not report at all. If the missing data were randomly distributed across the country, its absence might not be so troubling. However, it appears that data are missing in chunks from specific places, which can compromise the UCR's effectiveness. Imagine a fishing net with a few holes scattered evenly throughout it. If the holes are far enough apart, the net will still be strong enough to catch fish. But what about a net with gaping holes in the corners? This net may be missing as many links as the first net, but it is weaker because the holes are grouped in specific places where fish slip through, so fewer are caught. The missing data in the UCR are much like the missing links in the second, more compromised net; agencies that do not submit data tend to be grouped into specific types and geographic areas:

- small agencies;
- agencies from rural and suburban counties;
- agencies from the New England and South Atlantic regions; and
- agencies in states without UCR programs.[38]

street crime—Usually materially destructive or violent criminal offenses that are often interpersonal and represent those for which the police are most often called.

Because the missing data are so concentrated, the UCR cannot afford to ignore them. The holes must be accounted for somehow. The FBI has two ways to estimate missing data in order to compute annual state and national crime rates. First, for an agency that has reported at least three months of crime data, the FBI will apply the crime rate for those months to the entire year. Second, for an agency that has submitted two or fewer reports, the FBI will throw out the data and instead use the crime rate from a similar agency and jurisdiction. These methods are adequate for providing large-scale estimates of crime but not for estimating county-level crime rates or seasonal crime-rate variations.[39]

What this means is that the UCR contains a large, unknown amount of error, and researchers are still uncertain how this error affects our understanding of the actual amount of crime. One study found that not only is classification error present in the UCR, it varies by offense type, with some offenses being under-counted and others being over-counted. One reason for this kind of error is the difference between the FBI's definitions of offenses and individual police departments' definitions. For example, a police department's definition of simple assault may be different from the FBI's version. So, to record simple assaults for the UCR, the department must translate its version of the offense to the FBI's version, which results in recording errors; simple assaults may be recorded as aggravated assaults and vice versa. Generally, the study found that police over-counted larceny and under-counted aggravated assault, burglary, and robbery.[40] We can therefore draw three conclusions.

- The UCR records most offenses known to law enforcement.
- The UCR does not record every single offense known to law enforcement.
- The exact error rate is unknown.

So, although the UCR is the most reliable method of measuring crime in the United States, it does not give a complete, reliable picture of crime. That is why researchers and criminal justice administrators try to complete the picture with two other measures: the FBI's National Incident-Based Reporting System and the Bureau of Justice Statistics' National Crime Victimization Survey.[41]

The National Incident-Based Reporting System

The National Incident-Based Reporting System (NIBRS) is run in much the same way as the UCR, but it includes more information about offenses reported to police. The NIBRS collects data on each single incident and arrest within 46 specific offenses, which are called Group A offenses. There are also 11 Group B offenses for which only arrest data are reported (see Table 2.2). Compare this classification to that of the UCR, which collects extensive data on four violent offenses and four property offenses and arrest data on 29 offenses. In addition to collecting more detailed data about crime, the NIBRS is considered a more accurate reflection of crime because it does not use the hierarchy rule. In a multi-offense incident, each offense is recorded. This increases statistical accuracy and better reflects the overall level of crime. For this reason, NIBRS and UCR statistics are not comparable.[42]

Administered by the FBI, the NIBRS began collecting data in the late 1980s and has been under development since that time. Currently, the FBI's aim is to implement the NIBRS as the

Rep. John Lewis of Georgia speaks at an event on the steps of the U.S. Capitol Building for an evening of remembrance honoring the victims and survivors of the mass shooting at Pulse nightclub in Orlando in 2016. How would the UCR report of this crime differ from the NIBRS report?

TABLE 2.2 National Incident-Based Reporting System Offenses

Extensive crime data are collected for the Group A offenses. Only arrest data are reported for the Group B offenses. In 2016, the Group A categories of animal cruelty, identity theft, and hacking/computer invasion were added.

GROUP A OFFENSES

- Animal cruelty
- Arson
- Assault: aggravated assault, simple assault, intimidation
- Bribery
- Burglary/breaking and entering
- Counterfeiting/forgery
- Destruction/damage/vandalism of property
- Drug/narcotic offenses: drug/narcotic violations, drug equipment violations
- Embezzlement
- Extortion/blackmail
- Fraud: false pretenses/swindle/confidence game, credit card/automatic teller machine fraud, hacking computer invasion, identity theft, impersonation, welfare fraud, wire fraud
- Gambling offenses: betting/wagering, operating/ promoting/assisting gambling, gambling equipment violations, sports tampering
- Murder and non-negligent manslaughter
- Negligent manslaughter
- Justifiable homicide
- Human trafficking: commercial sex acts, involuntary servitude
- Kidnapping/abduction
- Larceny/theft offenses: pocket-picking, purse-snatching, shoplifting, theft from building, theft from coin-operated machines or devices, theft from motor vehicle, theft of motor vehicle parts or accessories, all other larceny
- Motor vehicle theft
- Pornography/obscene material
- Prostitution offenses: prostitution, assisting or promoting prostitution, purchasing prostitution
- Robbery
- Sex offenses: rape, sodomy, sexual assault with an object, fondling
- Sex offenses, non-forcible: incest, statutory rape
- Stolen property offenses
- Weapon law violations

GROUP B OFFENSES

- Bad checks
- Curfew, loitering, and vagrancy violations
- Disorderly conduct
- Driving under the influence
- Drunkenness
- Non-violent family offenses
- Liquor law violations
- Peeping tom
- Runaway
- Trespass of real property
- All other offenses

Source: Federal Bureau of Investigation, NIBRS Offense Definitions, Crimes Against Persons, Property, and Society, https://ucr.fbi.gov/nibrs/2016. Accessed July 2018.

exclusive national crime data collection method by January 2021.[43] Authorities hoped many more agencies and jurisdictions would be participating in the NIBRS by now, but due to funding limitations and low participation rates among police agencies, its use is not as widespread as planned.[44] The NIBRS covers about 29 percent of the U.S. population, and the crime rates in jurisdictions participating in the NIBRS are lower than rates in jurisdictions that do not participate. Thus, the NIBRS data are not a good indicator of U.S. crime counts or crime rates.[45] Currently, the NIBRS remains ill-funded and underdeveloped. The system also has a few other drawbacks.

- The complexity of the coding schemes, the number of categories, and other definitional issues. The increased complexity of the NIBRS over the UCR makes the system cumbersome for law enforcement officials.
- Lack of incentives for agency participation. Although the NIBRS provides good data collection, it requires time that some police agencies view as better spent responding to the public.

- Fear of the perception of an increase in crime. By eliminating the hierarchy rule, the NIBRS may show an artificial increase in a jurisdiction's crime rate. Given that police agencies are often evaluated on their ability to keep crime low, police agencies may be threatened by the change in reporting systems.[46]

The National Crime Victimization Survey

Conducted annually by the Bureau of Justice Statistics (BJS), the National Crime Victimization Survey (NCVS) is the primary source of criminal victimization data in the United States.[47] Census Bureau interviewers working with the BJS collect information from about 225,000 individuals age 12 and older in about 135,000 households about the frequency, characteristics, and consequences of crime.[48] This information allows researchers to estimate the likelihood of rape, sexual assault, robbery, assault, theft, household burglary, and motor vehicle theft for the entire U.S. population, as well as for groups, including women, the elderly, minorities, and urban residents.[49] Over the past decade, the NCVS has also begun to record details about hate crimes and identity theft as well as respondents' disabilities in order to estimate the amount of victimization of the developmentally disabled.[50] Because it depends on self-reporting, the NCVS, unlike the UCR, excludes homicide, arson, commercial criminal offenses, and offenses against children under age 12 because victims cannot report or reliably report their experiences.[51]

The purpose of the NCVS has changed since 1967 when President Lyndon Johnson's Commission on Crime and the Administration of Justice declared a need for a national victimization survey. At a time that was beset with demonstrations, riots, and civil unrest, the country had also suffered an explosion of street crime. To many, criminals seemed to be running rampant, victimizing innocent citizens at will. The first victimization survey, called the National Crime Survey, was designed to inform the public about the nature and extent of crime victimization as well as to check the efficacy of the UCR.

Today, after several major revisions, the NCVS still performs this task, but crime and the public response to it have changed. For example, although people still fear offenses committed by strangers, **intimate-partner violence** (IPV)—abuse that occurs between two people in a spousal, domestic, or romantic relationship—and offenses perpetrated by acquaintances or relatives compose a significant amount of crime. Also, financial and information-related offenses have become more visible, especially identity theft, which did not exist in any significant fashion in the late 1960s.[52] Therefore, survey researchers have recently developed supplements to measure stalking, fraud, and identity theft.[53]

The value of the NCVS is that it gathers information about offenses regardless of whether they are reported to the police and thus captures valuable information about the dark figure of crime. In questioning a respondent about an incident, the interviewer does not ask whether the respondent was a victim of a specific offense. Instead, the interviewer asks about the details of the offense. Only later are these details analyzed and coded as a specific offense, such as "assault."[54] NCVS researchers do not want respondents to speculate about offenders' motives, only to report the incident as accurately as possible. This means the NCVS defines some offenses slightly differently from the UCR. For example, the UCR defines burglary as the unlawful entry of a structure to commit a felony or theft, but the NCVS defines it as the entry or attempted entry of a residence by a person who has no right to be there. The UCR's definition requires the respondent to assume that the offender was there to commit a felony or theft.[55]

A pickpocket lifts a wallet of an unsuspecting victim. How do victim surveys differ from the Uniform Crime Reports in recording crime?

intimate-partner violence—Abuse that occurs between two people in a spousal, domestic, or romantic relationship.

PROBLEMS WITH THE NCVS

As useful as the NCVS is, it has a persistent problem related to time. Respondents are asked to report only the incidents that occurred within the last six months. So respondents must not only recall the incidents and many of the details, but also place the event within the last six months. This is more difficult than it sounds. Respondents may erroneously include incidents that did not happen within the last six months and omit incidents that did. They may completely forget important details or entire incidents, especially victimizations they deem trivial. They may also lie out of embarrassment, the desire to give what they believe is a socially acceptable response, distrust of the interviewer, a desire to protect the perpetrator, or lack of interest in answering questions.[56]

Most of the problems are related to the under-reporting of victimization; however, some respondents may over-report victimization. Interviewers can discover under-reporting fairly easily by questioning respondents who have reported offenses to the police. Therefore, if the respondent is on record with the police for having reported an incident but does not report that incident to the victimization survey, researchers can safely assume that the respondent is under-reporting victimization. Over-reporting is a different matter, however. If a respondent tells the NCVS interviewer about victimizations that have not been reported to the police, the interviewer cannot know whether the respondent is lying. An Oregon study found that only 48 percent of the offenses that respondents claimed to have reported to police were actually listed in police records.[57]

Some NCVS observers point to another issue: "series incidents." Crime occurs more often in some places than in others, and some people are victimized more often than others, often repeatedly. If an NCVS respondent reports six or more similar victimizations in a six-month period without providing details about each incident, NCVS interviewers record this as a "series incident" and collect information on only the most recent incident. Sorting out and recording details for what might be dozens of intermittent victimizations can be difficult for both the respondent and interviewer. Unfortunately, the NCVS is designed to record separate victimizations, such as a one-time burglary, and not intermittent victimizations that continue for months and years. Therefore, series incidents are excluded from the BJS's published annual victimization rates. According to some researchers, this is problematic for two reasons.

1. The national crime tally is severely underestimated. In 1993, for example, about three of every five violent victimizations were excluded from published figures. Integration of these series incidents into the 1993 count would have raised victimization estimates by more than 30 percent.
2. Some groups are more likely to experience series victimization than others. If females are more likely to report series incidents, such as those related to intimate-partner violence, the level of crime among this population will be underestimated because not all the victimizations will be counted. Routinized victimizations that are often related to sex, age, or impoverishment are omitted from the crime tally and compose a large portion of the dark figure of crime.[58]

A significant amount of research shows that relatively few people experience much of the crime that occurs.[59] Therefore, it is possible that a considerable amount of crime could be addressed if policies or programs helped groups of repeat victims early in their victimizations.[60]

The UCR and the NCVS: Divergence, Convergence, and the Future

The UCR and NCVS do not produce matching crime statistics. As we have discussed, victims have always reported far more offenses in the NCVS than police recorded in the UCR. Criminologists grudgingly accepted this phenomenon and attributed the divergence largely to differences in procedures, definitions, counting rules, and population. For example, the UCR represents a flat count of offenses reported to the police; it is not a sample, so the error is supposedly slight. However, NCVS statistics are based on a sample of offenses reported by a set of randomly selected households from the last six months. Sampling errors, then, are inherent in the NCVS method.[61]

Despite the fact that the NCVS has sampling errors and the UCR has none, the surveys' findings began to converge in 1992. In other words, the number of offenses police recorded in the UCR began to more closely match the number of offenses victims reported to the NCVS. This convergence has continued, although some researchers say the surveys are now beginning to diverge again. The phenomena of convergence and divergence puzzle many criminologists, who are of three opinions about the situation.

- Divergence is to be expected, and it is good. The UCR and NCVS complement one another. They are conducted in different ways and define crime differently. They take different pictures of crime much as two photographers standing in different places would take different pictures of an elephant. The pictures would be different, but both would represent the animal correctly.

- Divergence is to be expected, and it is bad. The UCR and NCVS compete. They measure the same thing—the amount of crime in the United States—and it should be possible for both to do so objectively. If the UCR records 101 burglaries in Wabasha, Minnesota, but the NCVS reports 945, then one (or both) of the surveys is flawed and must be corrected. The surveys cannot diverge by that much and both be correct. Some criminologists believe that consistency among the UCR, victimization studies, and self-report studies (discussed later in this chapter) means social phenomena have been successfully measured, and too much divergence is a sign of something wrong.[62]
- Convergence is interesting, but why is it occurring now? That the UCR and the NCVS are showing more similar statistics makes a bit more sense—citizens, the media, and policymakers certainly prefer it—but why did convergence begin when it did in the 1990s? Is it an artifact of changes in the surveys? Does this mean that the surveys no longer complement each other or that they never did?[63]

One study attributes much of the convergence to changes in police reporting and in the social perception of crime, especially aggravated assault. The police and the courts, driven by public opinion, are treating aggravated assault far more seriously than they did in previous decades by upgrading some offenses to aggravated assault and recording others as aggravated assault that, before the 1990s, were not recorded at all. For instance, although victim reporting of aggravated assault to the NCVS has increased 5 percent since 1973, police recording of the offense in the UCR increased 116 percent from 1973 to 1995.[64]

One of the main reasons given for increased UCR reporting is intimate-partner violence legislation. What the public once considered to be a private matter between a husband and wife is today a criminal matter of assault or aggravated assault, and the definition of intimate partner has broadened to include unmarried and same-sex couples. It is probable that the police are now acting on and recording IPV incidents that they used to handle informally or not at all.[65] Other offenses are also likely contributing to increased recording of aggravated assault through simple "upgrade." Offenses such as fights, arguments, and threats with firearms that once may have been recorded as simple assault are now often recorded as aggravated assault. This increased response to both IPV and other street violence is indicative of changes in the way the police operate and, therefore, in what they record.

Aggravated assault is a crime against persons that is recorded by the Uniform Crime Reports. Give reasons why the police are treating aggravated assault more seriously than in previous decades.

Finally, the study goes on to caution that convergence between the UCR and NCVS has occurred at the same time as a general drop in crime and thus may be an artifact of that drop. The number of offenses reported to police fell a little, whereas the number of offenses not reported to police (as evidenced by NCVS data) fell a lot. It is possible that if, or when, crime begins to rise again, the UCR and NCVS will once again diverge.[66] Currently, however, analysis confirms that the differences between the UCR and the

NCVS crime rates are decreasing significantly and that the reports are continuing to converge.[67]

PAUSE AND REVIEW

1. **Who is responsible for gathering and disseminating the UCR?**
2. **Compare and contrast the strengths and weaknesses of the UCR and the NIBRS.**
3. **Why might NCVS respondents under-report a victimization?**
4. **How may the UCR's limitations be addressed?**
5. **Why does the FBI caution against using the UCR to compare the frequency of crime between jurisdictions?**
6. **How is the NIBRS an improvement over the UCR?**

Self-Report Studies

LEARNING OBJECTIVE | 6

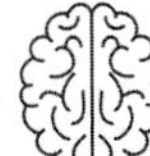

Outline the advantages and disadvantages of self-report studies as tools to measure crime.

Self-report studies—research based on data that respondents offer about themselves—have evolved into a useful alternative to government crime reports, though they have their own limitations and do not give us a comprehensive and clear picture of crime. However, in conjunction with other measures, they play a meaningful role in helping us understand the frequency and seriousness of crime.[68]

Self-report studies ask individuals about any illegal activities they have committed within a given time period, typically the past six months, year, or two years. The primary goals are:

- to establish the prevalence and incidence of crime and delinquency within specific populations that better represent the actual incidence of crime and delinquency than government measures;
- to find out what activities or attitudes correlate with lawbreaking;
- to test theories about the causes of crime.[69]

One of the reasons criminologists developed self-report studies was to provide an alternative look at the crime picture and reduce reliance on government statistics. Researchers decided that reliance on government statistics would limit what they could learn about crime and its causes.[70]

Self-report studies are considered to be better, more adaptable tools for researchers to discover exactly what they need to know, especially if the government data skirt a particular issue. For example, self-report data are considered to be better than police or victimization data for gathering information about so-called victimless crimes such as substance abuse.[71] Self-report studies have greatly contributed to our understanding of what makes people break the law, such as versatility (committing different types of offenses), intermittency (starting and stopping criminal activity), escalation (committing increasingly serious offenses), and age of onset.[72] Self-report studies provide a better picture than the UCR and the NCVS of the demographics and personal characteristics of offenders, which makes self-report studies suitable for testing and developing criminological theory. In particular, Hirschi's social bond theory (which we meet in Chapter 6) was developed on the basis of self-report data.[73]

The first problem to tackle when conducting a self-report study is deciding whom to include. On one hand, it makes sense that those who have been incarcerated would be good sources for self-report studies. On the other hand, if we surveyed only the incarcerated, we would miss collecting data from those who broke the law without detection. Researchers survey several different types of populations to ascertain self-reported criminality. Asking questions of each has its own concerns and issues. But taken together, self-report studies are a useful tool in developing an accurate picture of crime. In

A young girl injects heroin. Why are self-report studies better than other forms of measuring crime in detecting so-called victimless crimes?

criminology, many if not most self-report studies are carried out with youths, very young adults, and juvenile delinquents. The first reason for choosing this population is that it is easier to find groups of young people than groups of adults. Once adults enter the workforce, it is difficult to find groups of them to test. Most non-delinquent youths are in school, and delinquent youths can be found in training schools, group homes, or other youth correctional facilities. The second reason is that youths are more likely to tell the truth about themselves on self-report studies than adults. Adults are more concerned about their social standing, more aware of how they appear to the interviewers, and more cautious about admitting to serious criminal offenses.[74] However, self-reports are still used to estimate the prevalence and frequency of offending among groups such as incarcerated adults.[75]

Self-report studies have been used in criminology since the mid-20th century. The first published results appeared in the 1940s, when sociologist Austin Porterfield isolated 55 offenses committed by a group of juvenile delinquents and administered a self-report study to a group of college students asking if they had committed any of the offenses. Porterfield's study uncovered what became a recurring theme in self-report studies on juvenile delinquency: the relationship between social class and delinquency. The college students had committed all of the 55 offenses the delinquents had but not as frequently, and few had come into contact with law enforcement.[76] In the 1950s, sociologists James F. Short Jr. and F. Ivan Nye produced another set of landmark studies that also focused on delinquency. Short and Nye's studies were distinguished by their sophistication and, like Porterfield's, examined the relationship between social class and delinquency. Both Porterfield's and Short and Nye's studies, along with many later studies, challenged prevailing criminological theory that assumed a relationship between low social class and delinquency.[77] From a practical standpoint, their studies suggested that the juvenile justice system tended to make determinations of delinquency based partly on class.[78]

reliability—The ability of research to be successfully repeated and to provide similar results.

validity—A statistical property that describes how well a study is measuring what it is designed to measure.

longitudinal—A type of survey that follows respondents throughout their lives or a significant proportion of their lives.

Criminologists expect some level of convergence between self-report studies and government statistics. For example, the demographic characteristics recorded in self-report studies are consistent with the UCR measures, as are the rank order of offenses committed by youths. However, criminologists also expect absolute estimates of crime to be much higher in self-report studies than in government measures. Like government measures, self-report studies also show more commission of property offenses. Finally, they have been known to predict government measures to some extent. In one particular instance, self-report studies reported an increase in juvenile violence before it was recorded in police data, which means that juveniles were self-reporting violent offending before their activities were reflected by increased arrests.[79]

Problems with Self-Report Studies

Self-report studies are designed and executed by academics for research purposes; for the most part, researchers seem satisfied with their performance. However, like government crime measures, self-report studies have some inherent weaknesses that prevent complete accuracy. The first and perhaps most glaring weakness is that like the NCVS, self-report studies rely on samples and not on exact counts. A delinquency self-report study will not include every youth in the United States. Researchers sample a group of youths, then extrapolate data from that sample. Whenever a sample is used, sampling errors are likely.

Two properties important to all research studies are reliability and validity. Briefly, **reliability** is the consistency of a study, or how successfully it can be repeated and still provide similar results. For example, a self-report study that gets similar answers from several similar groups of youths about the amount of vandalism they have perpetrated in the last six months is considered reliable. **Validity** describes whether a study is measuring what it is designed to measure. If most of the youths decide to lie about how often they commit vandalism, then the study is not valid. Criminologists have decided that although the reliability of self-report studies is generally acceptable, validity is more difficult to ascertain because there is nothing to measure respondents' answers against.[80] As in victimization studies, researchers must trust participants to tell the truth.[81]

Self-report studies are also problematic when quantifying some types of offending and offenders. The studies have been criticized for excluding or under-representing repeat offenders and youths who tend to commit serious delinquency, as well as for measuring little more than non-serious delinquency and property offenses.[82] Trivial and frequent offending tends to be over-reported—imagine the teen who wants to appear tough to the interviewers—but serious offending, such as homicide, is under-reported, presumably because respondents fear being caught.[83]

The methodology of, or procedures of researching, self-report studies has grown increasingly sophisticated. In the next section, we review three of the more developed studies that have the state-of-the-art resources necessary to assess the frequency and seriousness of crime as reported by those who commit it.

The National Youth Survey Family Study

Initiated in 1976, the National Youth Survey was one of the first and most impressive self-report studies to assess delinquency. Between 1977 and 1981, researchers interviewed 1,725 adolescents 11 to 17 years of age and one parent in their homes on an annual basis and, between 1981 and 1995, on a two- or three-year basis. The study continues to this day; although some of the participants have become unavailable for various reasons, more than 90 percent remain in the sample.

The National Youth Survey has evolved into a more comprehensive data-collection effort called the National Youth Survey Family Study. One interesting aspect of the study is the addition of a genetic component. In addition to asking questions about delinquent and criminal involvement, researchers collected the participants' DNA to see whether there was any interaction of genes, the environment, and antisocial behavior. Specifically, they were looking for a connection between the monoamine oxidase A (MAOA) gene (see Chapter 5 for details about this gene) and aggressive behavior, which had previously been shown in both mice and humans. In this study, the MAOA gene did not show a correlation with aggressive behavior, but researchers continue to use this expansive database to look for other measures of a genetic influence on behavior.

Several other studies using the National Youth Survey database have provided a wealth of information about the conditions under which delinquency occurs. Researchers have looked at the relationships between crime and gender, race, and social class, as well as the influence of drug use on antisocial behavior.[84] The strengths of this study are twofold. First, because it used a scientific and systematic sampling procedure, it allows for generalization to the entire country based on interviews with only 1,725 respondents. Second, the study is a **longitudinal** research effort; that is, it has followed the respondents throughout their adult lives or a significant proportion of their lives. This allows researchers to ascertain the stability of their respondents' antisocial behavior in ways that are not possible when looking at interview data based on only one year.

Monitoring the Future

The Monitoring the Future study is an ambitious effort to assess youths' values, attitudes, and behaviors. Each year, researchers survey approximately 50,000 students in the 8th, 10th, and 12th grades and follow up on a sample of those who were studied in previous years. The results are useful to government policymakers (e.g., to monitor progress toward

High school can be a perplexing and dangerous time for many teenagers. What are the advantages of measuring substance abuse using longitudinal studies?

national health goals and to assess trends in substance use and abuse among adolescents and young adults) and are used routinely in the White House Strategy on Drug Abuse.[85]

The study has a number of advantages over previous self-report studies in that it is both longitudinal and repeated each year with new respondents. This feature allows researchers to assess trends in two ways. First, as the youths move through 12th grade and beyond, it is reasonable to expect that their delinquent and criminal behavior patterns will change. By doing follow-up studies on those who were previously surveyed, researchers are able to track such changes. Second, the survey's methodology allows researchers to see whether new **cohorts**—groups of people who share statistical or demographic characteristics—of youngsters are reporting different levels of delinquency and crime than previous cohorts. In this way, the study is able to look at four levels of change:

- Changes in particular years reflected across all age groups. Changes in the economy, such as a recession, could affect all young people across the country regardless of what grade they are in. When jobs are scarce, parents are unemployed, and recreational programs are denied funding, youngsters feel the economic effects regardless of their age or location.
- Developmental changes that show up consistently for all panels. Moving through the life course can affect delinquency and crime. Although these developmental changes may not be identical for each age group, a longitudinal study can reveal the pressures to commit or desist from crime.
- Consistent differences among class cohorts through the life cycle. One of the reasons for selecting youngsters of different ages for this type of research is to reveal how self-reported delinquency can differ by age cohort. For instance, in any particular year when 12th graders are graduating from high school, they may have a better chance of getting a job if the unemployment rate is low. Contrasting this opportunity with years when the unemployment rate is high helps correct for the economic environments into which adolescents graduate, which can affect their rate of delinquency and later criminal offending.
- Changes linked to different types of environments (high school, college, employment) or role transitions (leaving home, marriage, parenthood). Making the transition from high school to college or the work environment can affect the propensity for breaking the law. By tracking the youths as they move through their high school years, researchers can discern how changes in their status as well as in their age are reflected in their self-reported delinquency.[86]

---

cohort—A group of people who share statistical or demographic characteristics.

cross-sectional survey—Research in which different individuals are studied during each research period.

The Monitoring the Future study has continued for more than 30 years, periodically adding questions that reflect changes in both society and delinquency. Perhaps the most important and significant feature of the Monitoring the Future surveys is the way researchers have refined their questionnaires to make self-reported delinquency a more robust and valid way of measuring crime.

The National Survey on Drug Use and Health

Since 1971, the National Survey on Drug Use and Health has conducted annual interviews with more than 70,000 randomly selected individuals age 12 and older.[87] Some might legitimately question the expense of doing so many interviews each year. This survey is an example of how technology has allowed researchers to focus on a large sample scattered throughout the United States. It uses a combination of computer-assisted personal interviewing in which interviewers ask questions of respondents in their homes and audio computer-assisted self-interviewing for confidential questions regarding admitted drug use. This latter technique is believed to elicit more honest answers about drug use because there is no personal interaction.

The National Survey on Drug Use and Health is a **cross-sectional survey**—research in which different individuals are studied during each research period—as opposed to a longitudinal survey. This means it surveys different individuals each year and makes no effort to track specific individuals from year to year. The cross-sectional method allows the survey of a larger number of individuals, though without being able to track changes in their behavior.

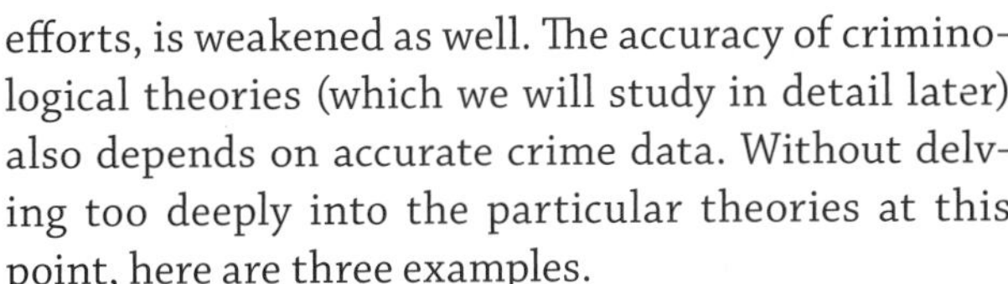

PAUSE AND REVIEW

1. **How can self-report studies that use longitudinal data answer different questions than cross-sectional studies?**
2. **How might researchers use self-report studies to develop criminological theories?**
3. **Critique the methodology of self-report studies in terms of reliability and validity.**
4. **Why are some individuals included in self-report studies, whereas others are not?**

Putting It All Together

LEARNING OBJECTIVE | 7

Explain how the reporting and measuring of crime can affect the development of criminological theory and public policy.

Criminological theory is not developed in a vacuum. Theorists do not just come up with ideas from their armchairs and send them out into the world for other criminologists to think about and students to memorize. To be useful, theories must accurately describe some aspect of how and why the law is constructed and broken, or who is breaking it, or how society reacts to these activities. The development of sound criminological theory depends on the accurate reporting and measurement of crime. The four major sources of crime data discussed in this chapter—the UCR, the NIBRS, the NCVS, and self-report studies—provide a complementary picture of crime.[88] Each data-collection effort offers a particular view of crime. Taken together, these studies provide a more coherent view of the nature and extent of crime. The UCR and the NIBRS represent police records of offenses and arrests; the NCVS utilizes victims' experiences; and researchers' self-report studies look closely at the offending patterns of individuals and groups by asking them to describe their personal experiences in breaking the law.

Just as good crime data help criminal justice administrators plan budgets and programs, they also help criminologists develop and test hypotheses and theories (see Policy Implications). This is important because many programs are based on criminological theories and are implemented to utilize and test their ideas.[89] However, if the crime data are not accurate, then everything based on the data, including programs and criminal justice administrative efforts, is weakened as well. The accuracy of criminological theories (which we will study in detail later) also depends on accurate crime data. Without delving too deeply into the particular theories at this point, here are three examples.

- Opportunity theories of victimization. According to opportunity theories, the chances of victimization are related to an individual's lifestyle, amount of routine exposure to offenders, attractiveness as a crime target, and availability of those who can protect the individual from victimization. The correct assessment of these attributes and their frequency depends on accurate data from demographic and victimization surveys. However, if the victimization surveys are inaccurate—which can be caused by anything from respondents' faulty memories to the survey's rules for counting victimizations—then the validity of opportunity theories of victimization must be questioned.[90]
- Biological theories of sex differences in violent crime. Some theories seek biological reasons to explain why most crime, especially most violent crime, is committed by males. However, for this search to be valid, sex differences in the commission of violent and antisocial behavior must be consistent across time, culture, and geography. In other words, to assert that males are more violent and commit the most crime, similar statistics showing this must be collected from different years, places, and cultures. Although some countries have highly developed statistical collection efforts, others do not, so wide-ranging, accurate numbers on sex differences in violent offending are not available.[91]
- Social disorganization theories. These theories consider crime as the product of neighborhoods or jurisdictions that are impoverished and have transient populations, poor social and physical infrastructure, and lack of economic opportunity. Data that show more arrests of people of low socioeconomic status could certainly be explained by social disorganization theories, but what if the police are simply biased toward the arrest of impoverished, disadvantaged people? If people from higher socioeconomic classes are arrested less often because of police bias, even if they commit the same amount of crime, then it is faulty to blame disadvantaged neighborhoods for a high crime rate. For the sake of argument, if collection of crime data focused

POLICY IMPLICATIONS

Why Measuring Crime Matters

The measurement of crime is more than an academic activity. A great deal of money and many resources are put into trying to ascertain the frequency of crime, as well as the seriousness of individual offenses because important decisions by politicians, criminal justice administrators, and the public are based on the perceived level of crime. Mistakes in crime measurement can lead to the improper allocation of resources. The policy implications of measuring crime include the following:

- Lawmakers. Legislators are responsible for developing laws that reduce crime. Unless crime is measured accurately, policymakers are working in the dark, or worse, working with misconceived ideas about who breaks the law and where crime happens. Without an accurate measure of crime, personal biases, discrimination, and stereotypes seep into the crafting of laws. For instance, the relative harm of various drugs is not reflected in the criminal penalties applied to them. Although some harmful drugs such as alcohol and tobacco are legal, other less harmful ones, such as marijuana, remain federally illegal (and illegal in most states) and have criminal penalties attached. When lawmakers understand the issues, they are better able to develop effective laws.
- Law enforcement officials. How do police chiefs and sheriffs allocate their patrol officers? Are some areas of the city experiencing more crime than others? Is crime more prevalent at certain times of the day or week? Accurate crime measurement can address all such questions.
- The media. The accurate measurement of crime also has implications for how the media report it. For instance, in order to suggest that the criminal justice system engages in racial profiling, it is necessary to have a database that captures the race of individuals who come in contact with the criminal justice system. Although anecdotal information may suggest racial profiling, it cannot be proven without statistics.
- The public. Citizens need to know the level of crime in order to fully participate in the democratic process. If an elected sheriff is successfully addressing crime, he or she may be re-elected based on the public's understanding of how law enforcement initiatives actually address the jurisdiction's crime problems. Additionally, the public relies on measures of crime to help them decide what measures to take to avoid becoming crime victims.

As we have seen in this chapter, crime measurement is an inexact science that is best addressed by multiple methods of inquiry. Although imperfect, the measurement methods have policy implications, and agencies make decisions about crime and justice based on their knowledge of the level and seriousness of crime.

THINK ABOUT IT

1. Can you think of some other policy implications of the mismeasurement of crime? Should the government allocate more resources to measuring crime or less?
2. If you had to move out of your present jurisdiction, would you use crime statistics to determine the best place to move to?

on white-collar or corporate offenses, then advantaged neighborhoods could just as well be considered a major source of crime. Thus, the focus of crime-data collection on street crime is a major problem for sociological theories that depend heavily on police data sources.[92]

So, how do researchers deal with flaws they know are likely to occur in their data? In some cases, researchers just do not use the data. One researcher suggested that county-level UCR data, which tend to be weak and inaccurate, are so small and difficult to work with that they do not produce a quality study, even though statistical techniques could correct some disadvantages.[93]

In a self-report study, gang members were asked to answer questions about their recent drug use. This study posed two major validity issues: First, were the self-selected "gang members" actually members of gangs, and second, were they telling the truth about their drug use? The second issue was easy to check with urinalysis tests. The first item, however, was impossible to confirm. There is no scientific test that can prove an individual's gang membership. So what did the researchers do? They used the educated guess. One-fourth of the juvenile arrestees self-reported past or current gang membership, a number the researchers decided was too high to be entirely inaccurate. Certainly, some of the respondents would lie about being in a gang in order to seem tough but not as many as one-fourth. The researchers also found that two other studies reported 18 percent and 28 percent of respondents admitting to gang membership. So, although they allowed for the likelihood of error in their survey, on the whole it appeared to draw a fairly accurate picture of the amount of drug usage in gangs.[94]

In yet another self-report study, this time on the effect of abusive families on delinquency, nearly half the youths who had been arrested during the interview period did not report any arrests, and nearly one-quarter who had no arrest records reported being arrested. How could these data, so much of which was poorly recalled and falsely reported, be useful? The researchers admitted that if the survey had set out to learn about delinquent patterns within individuals, the data would have been problematic because so many individuals were incorrectly reporting their arrests or lack of arrests. However, the researchers were looking for information about delinquent patterns among a group of individuals. In this case, the data confirmed that abusive families in impoverished neighborhoods produce more juvenile arrestees.[95]

PAUSE AND REVIEW

1. **How do researchers deal with flaws in their data?**
2. **How does criminological theory depend on the accurate measurement of crime?**

The Measure and Mismeasure of Crime

As the elected sheriff of a large metropolitan county, you are coming under increasing pressure from local businesses to show that the city is a safe place for tourism, industry, and family life. Recently, your city has developed a national reputation as a dangerous place for conventions and nightlife. The downtown hotel area has fallen into disrepair, and one national publication has described it as "decorated by broken glass and scented by urine." The crime rate is one of the highest in the country, and everyone from the mayor to the chamber of commerce has complained about the effectiveness of your officers in deterring and responding to crime.

You are up for re-election in two years, and you realize that you must develop new strategies to reduce the crime rate, or you may find yourself out of office. Also, a new problem has come to your attention. A juvenile gang in the downtown convention area is breaking into cars, robbing tourists on the street, and spray-painting gang graffiti on every wall, sidewalk, lamp post, and mailbox they can reach. Additionally, a large homeless population congregates downtown and makes the streets appear to be unsafe. The city council is demanding that you clean up the gang activity and the homeless problem and once again make the city a haven for convention and tourist activity.

Although you have consistently argued that you need more officers and more resources, you understand that these resources will not be forthcoming. Here are some options that you are considering.

- Encourage homeless individuals to leave town. By providing them with a bus ticket, you can ship them to neighboring cities along with the criminal offenses that they may be committing.
- Impose a juvenile curfew in the downtown area. Any juveniles who are on the streets after 10 PM will be stopped, detained, searched, and otherwise harassed. You will instruct your officers to find pretenses for taking juveniles into custody for at least 48 hours. If the downtown area is unattractive enough to juveniles, maybe they will take their activities somewhere else.
- Instruct your officers not to report criminal activity. Instead of recording interactions with the juveniles, your officers are told to use a little "street justice" to discourage them from gathering on the street.
- Instruct your officers to attach as many criminal offenses as possible to each arrest. For example, if someone is arrested for larceny, the officers are to add many other related incidents of larceny, even if it is not clear that the arrestee committed them. The idea is to give the impression that more offenses are solved by each individual larceny arrest.
- Have your officers charge arrestees with as minor an offense as possible. Therefore, an aggravated assault should be reduced to a simple assault. A murder is reduced to manslaughter. By manipulating the charges for each offense, you hope to make your city appear to be less dangerous.

What Do You Do?

1. Which of these activities might be illegal?
2. Which of these activities might be unethical?
3. Which of these activities are you willing to pursue in order to ensure your re-election?
4. Will any of these activities make your city safer?
5. Can you think of any other solutions to your city's crime problem?

Summary

LEARNING OBJECTIVE 1 Identify some reasons that jurisdictions or criminal justice officials might alter crime statistics.	A criminal justice official may wish to acquire more police officers and other resources, such as weapons, vehicles, or communication equipment. A criminal justice official may be criticized because of a high crime rate and fear that he or she could be fired or lose an election. A jurisdiction competing for federal anti-crime funds may need to show a significant crime problem. A jurisdiction that derives substantial income from the tourism and convention industries must project itself as safe. Other jurisdictions trying to attract business and residents may see their efforts rendered useless by a high crime rate or even the public perception that the area is not as safe as others.
LEARNING OBJECTIVE 2 Define the dark figure of crime.	A term that describes criminal offenses that are unreported to law enforcement officials and never recorded.
LEARNING OBJECTIVE 3 Summarize the advantages and limitations of the Uniform Crime Reports.	The most comprehensive crime data-collection effort in the country, the Uniform Crime Reports has four significant limitations: It applies the hierarchy rule (reporting only the most serious offense if more than one is committed); it records only offenses reported to the police; it focuses on street crime; and its data are incomplete.
LEARNING OBJECTIVE 4 Compare and contrast the National Incident-Based Reporting System and the Uniform Crime Reports.	The NIBRS was designed as an improvement upon the UCR and follows many of the same rules but is far more detailed. Unlike the UCR, the NIBRS does not follow the hierarchy rule, but collects data on each single incident and arrest for 46 specific offenses.
LEARNING OBJECTIVE 5 Discuss the reasons for creation of the National Crime Victimization Survey.	The National Crime Victimization Survey is conducted annually by the Bureau of Justice Statistics and provides information about victims, offenders, and otherwise unreported crime within the past six months. It is the primary source of criminal victimization data in the United States. The survey was designed to inform the public about the nature and extent of crime victimization as well as to check the efficacy of the UCR. The NCVS gathers information about offenses regardless of whether they are reported to the police and thus captures valuable information about the dark figure of crime.
LEARNING OBJECTIVE 6 Outline the advantages and disadvantages of self-report studies as tools to measure crime.	Self-report studies (1) establish the prevalence and incidence of crime and delinquency within specific populations, (2) find out what correlates with crime, and (3) test theories about the causation of crime. Self-report studies do not use absolute counts, which makes sampling errors likely. Researchers must trust participants to tell the truth. Self-report studies have been criticized for excluding or under-representing repeat offenders and youths who commit serious delinquency. Trivial and frequent offending tends to be over-reported.

LEARNING OBJECTIVE 7	
Explain how the reporting and measuring of crime can affect the development of criminological theory and public policy.	Good crime data help criminal justice administrators plan budgets and programs, and help criminologists develop and test hypotheses and theories. Many programs are based on criminological theories and are implemented to utilize and test their ideas. If the crime data are not accurate, then everything based on the data—hypotheses, theories, programs, and criminal justice administrative efforts—is also weakened.

Critical Reflections

1. **Is it reasonable to expect individuals to accurately report the offenses they have committed?**
2. **In your opinion, do the Uniform Crime Reports provide enough accurate information to make criminal justice system policy?**
3. **What can be done to encourage more citizens to report crime?**
4. **How do self-report studies provide a useful addition to more traditional methods to measure crime?**
5. **If you had unlimited funds, how would you design a crime measurement system?**

Key Terms

Notes

1 Clare Malone and Jeff Asher, "The First FBI Crime Report Issued under Trump Is Missing a Ton of Info," *FiveThirtyEight*, October 27, 2017, https://fivethirtyeight.com/features/the-first-fbi-crime-report-issued-under-trump-is-missing-a-ton-of-info. Accessed April 2018.

2 Federal Bureau of Investigation, The CJIS Advisory Process, https://www.fbi.gov/services/cjis/the-cjis-advisory-process. Accessed January 2018.

3 Malone and Asher, "The First FBI Crime Report."

4 Brian Root, "New FBI Report on US Crime Notable for What's Missing," *Human Rights Watch*, October 31, 2017, https://www.hrw.org/news/2017/10/31/new-fbi-report-us-crime-notable-whats-missing. Accessed April 2018.

5 C. J. Ciaramella, "Critical Data Is Missing from the FBI's Annual Crime Report and Researchers Want It Back," *Reason*, November 30, 2017, http://reason.com/blog/2017/11/30/critical-data-is-missing-from-the-fbis-a. Accessed April 2018.

6 Mark T. Berg and Ethan M. Rogers, "The Mobilization of Criminal Law," *Annual Review of Law and Social Science* 13, no. 1 (2017): 451.

7 Cecili Doorewaard, "The Dark Figure of Crime and Its Impact on the Criminal Justice System," *Acta Criminologica* 27, no. 2 (July 2014): 1.

8 Patrick Q. Brady and Matt R. Nobles, "The Dark Figure of Stalking: Examining Law Enforcement Response," *Journal of Interpersonal Violence* 32, no. 20 (2017): 3149–3173.

9 Ryan Thorneycroft and Nicole L. Asquith, "The Dark Figure of Disablist Violence," *Howard Journal of Criminal Justice* 54, no. 5 (2015): 489–507.

10 Rachel E. Morgan and Grace Kena, *Criminal Victimization, 2016* (U.S. Department of Justice Office of Justice Programs Bureau of Justice Statistics, 2017), 1. Available at https://www.bjs.gov/index.cfm?ty=pbdetail&iid=6166. Federal Bureau of Investigation, Uniform Crime Reports, *Crime in the United States, 2016*, Violent Crime, https://ucr.fbi.gov/crime-in-the-u.s/2016/crime-in-the-u.s.-2016/topic-pages/violent-crime and Property Crime, https://ucr.fbi.gov/crime-in-the-u.s/2016/crime-in-the-u.s.-2016/topic-pages/property-crime. Accessed January 2018. Douglas Clement, "Beware of Data," *Fedgazette* 21, no. 2 (March 2009): 8.

11 Jason T. Eastman, "The Wild (White) Ones: Comparing Frames of White and Black Deviance," *Contemporary Justice Review* 18, no. 2 (2015): 231.

12 Josine Junger-Tas and Ineke Haen, "The Self-Report Methodology in Crime Research," *Crime and Justice* 25 (1999): 291–367.

13 Jose Alexis Torres, "Predicting Perceived Police Effectiveness in Public Housing: Police Contact, Police Trust, and Police

Responsiveness," *Policing and Society* 27, no. 4 (2017): 439–459.

14 Desmond Matthew, Andrew Papachristos, and David Kirk, "Police Violence and Citizen Crime Reporting in the Black Community," *American Sociological Review* 81, no. 5 (2016): 857–876.

15 Sean Nicholson-Crotty, Jill Nicholson-Crotty, and Sergio Fernandez, "Will More Black Cops Matter? Officer Race and Police-Involved Homicides of Black Citizens," *Public Administration Review* 77, no. 2 (2017): 206–216.

16 Junger-Tas and Haen, "The Self-Report Methodology in Crime Research," 86.

17 Ibid., 87–92.

18 Clayton J. Mosher, Terance D. Miethe, and Dretha M. Phillips, *The Mismeasure of Crime* (Thousand Oaks, Calif.: Sage Publications, 2002), 173.

19 Stephen Woods, "By the Numbers," *Documents to the People* 34, no. 1 (Spring 2006): 11–14.

20 James P. Lynch and John P. Jarvis, "Missing Data and Imputation in the Uniform Crime Reports and the Effects on National Estimates," *Journal of Contemporary Criminal Justice* 24, no. 1 (2008): 69–85.

21 Mosher, Miethe, and Phillips, *The Mismeasure of Crime*, 60.

22 Ibid., 36.

23 Ibid., 37.

24 Federal Bureau of Investigation, Uniform Crime Reports, *Crime in the United States, 2017*, Offenses Known to Law Enforcement, https://ucr.fbi.gov/crime-in-the-u.s/2017/crime-in-the-u.s.-2017/topic-pages/offenses-known-to-law-enforcement. Accessed October 2018. The Uniform Crime Reports used to break down crime by Part I and Part II offenses. This practice was discontinued in 2004 (see Suspension of the Crime Index and Modified Crime Index at https://www2.fbi.gov/ucr/cius_04/summary/index.html). Accessed April 2018.

25 Federal Bureau of Investigation, Uniform Crime Reports, *Crime in the United States, 2017*, Clearances, https://ucr.fbi.gov/crime-in-the-u.s/2017/crime-in-the-u.s.-2017/topic-pages/clearances. Accessed October 2018.

26 Federal Bureau of Investigation, Uniform Crime Reports, *Crime in the United States, 2017*, Persons Arrested, https://ucr.fbi.gov/crime-in-the-u.s/2017/crime-in-the-u.s.-2017/topic-pages/persons-arrested. Accessed October 2018.

27 Federal Bureau of Investigation, Uniform Crime Reports, *Crime in the United States, 2017*, Police Employee Data, https://ucr.fbi.gov/crime-in-the-u.s/2017/crime-in-the-u.s.-2017/topic-pages/police-employee-data. Accessed October 2018.

28 Federal Bureau of Investigation, Uniform Crime Reports, *Crime in the United States, 2017*, UCR Statistics: Their Proper Use, https://www.fbi.gov/file-repository/ucr/ucr-statistics-their-proper-use.pdf/view. Accessed October 2018.

29 Zachary Bookman, "Convergences and Omissions in Reporting Corporate and White Collar Crime," *DePaul Business and Commercial Law Journal* 6, no. 3 (Spring 2008): 347–392.

30 Lynch and Jarvis, "Missing Data," 69–85.

31 Federal Bureau of Investigation, Uniform Crime Reports, *Crime in the United States, 2017*, CIUS Summary, https://ucr.fbi.gov/crime-in-the-u.s/2017/crime-in-the-u.s.-2017/topic-pages/cius-summary. Accessed October 2018.

32 Ben Poston, Joel Rubin, and Anthony Pesce, "LAPD Underreported Serious Assaults, Skewing Crime Stats for 8 Years," *Los Angeles Times*, October 15, 2015, http://www.latimes.com/local/cityhall/la-me-crime-stats-20151015-story.html. Accessed April 2018.

33 Dean Scoville, "What's Really Going On with Crime Rates," *Police Magazine*, October 9, 2013, http://www.policemag.com/channel/patrol/articles/2013/10/what-s-really-going-on-with-crime-rates.aspx. Accessed April 2018.

34 David Bernstein and Noah Isackson, "New Tricks," *Chicago Magazine*, May 11, 2015, http://www.chicagomag.com/Chicago-Magazine/June-2015/Chicago-crime-stats. Accessed April 2018.

35 Lynch and Jarvis, "Missing Data," 69–85.

36 Ibid.

37 Ibid.

38 Ibid.

39 Michael D. Maltz, "Missing UCR Data and Divergence," in *Understanding Crime Statistics*, ed. James P. Lynch and Lynn A. Addington (New York: Cambridge University Press, 2007), 269–294.

40 James Nolan, Stephen Haas, and Jessica Napier, "Estimating the Impact of Classification Error on the 'Statistical Accuracy' of Uniform Crime Reports," *Journal of Quantitative Criminology* 27, no. 4 (December 2011): 497–519.

41 Maltz, "Missing UCR Data," 269–294.

42 Philip D. McCormack, April Pattavina, and Paul E. Tracy, "Assessing the Coverage and Representativeness of the National Incident-Based Reporting System," *Crime & Delinquency* 63, no. 4 (2017): 493–516.

43 Federal Bureau of Investigation, Uniform Crime Reports, *Crime in the United States, 2017*, Recent Developments in the UCR Program, https://www.fbi.gov/file-repository/ucr/recent-developments-in-the-ucr-program.pdf/view. Accessed October 2018.

44 David M. Bierie, "Enhancing the National Incident–Based Reporting System," *International Journal of Offender Therapy and Comparative Criminology* 59, no. 10 (September 2015): 1125–1143.

45 Philip D. McCormack, April Pattavina, and Paul E. Tracy, "Assessing the Coverage and Representativeness of the National Incident-Based Reporting System," *Crime & Delinquency* 63, no. 4 (2017): 493–516.

46 Mosher, Miethe, and Phillips, *The Mismeasure of Crime*, 72.

47 Lynn Langton, Michael Planty, and James P. Lynch, "Second Major Redesign of the National Crime Victimization Survey (NCVS)," *Criminology & Public Policy* 16 (2017): 1049–1074.

48 Bureau of Justice Statistics, Data Collection: National Crime Victimization Survey (NCVS), https://www.bjs.gov/index.cfm?ty=dcdetail&iid=245. Accessed February 2018.

49 Janet L. Lauritsen, "Social and Scientific Influences on the Measurement of Criminal Victimization," *Journal of Quantitative Criminology* 21, no. 3 (September 2005): 245–266.

50 Lauritsen, "Measurement of Criminal Victimization," 245–266. Rand, "The National Crime Victimization Survey," 289–301.

51 Rand, "The National Crime Victimization Survey," 289–301.

52 Ibid.

53 Langton, Planty, and Lynch, "Second Major Redesign of the National Crime Victimization Survey (NCVS)."

54 Lauritsen, "Measurement of Criminal Victimization," 245–266.

55 Stephen Woods, "By the Numbers," *Documents to the People* 34, no. 1 (Spring 2006): 11–14.

56 Mosher, Miethe, and Phillips, *The Mismeasure of Crime*, 168.

57 Ibid., 163, 168.

58 Michael Planty and Kevin Strom, "Understanding the Role of Repeat Victims in the Production of Annual US Victimization Rates," *Journal of Quantitative Criminology* 23, no. 3 (September 2007): 179–200.

59 Jody Clay-Warner, Jackson M. Bunch, and Jennifer McMahon-Howard, "Differential Vulnerability: Disentangling the Effects of State Dependence and Population Heterogeneity on Repeat Victimization," *Criminal Justice and Behavior* 43, no. 10 (October 2016): 1406–1429.

60 Planty and Strom, "Understanding the Role of Repeat Victims in the Production of Annual US Victimization Rates."

61 Maltz, "Missing UCR Data," 269–294.

62 Junger-Tas and Haen, "The Self-Report Methodology," 291–367.

63 James P. Lynch and Lynn A. Addington, eds., *Understanding Crime Statistics* (New York: Cambridge University Press, 2007). See the introduction.

64 Shannan M. Catalano, *The Measurement of Crime* (New York: LFB Scholarly Publishing, 2006). See Chapter 6.

65 Ibid.

66 Ibid.

67 Sami Ansari and Ni He, "Convergence Revisited: A Multi-Definition,

Multi-Method Analysis of the UCR and the NCVS Crime Series (1973–2008)," *JQ: Justice Quarterly* 32, no. 1 (February 2015): 1–31.

68 Julie Baldwin et al., "The Development and Impact of Self-Report Measures of Crime and Delinquency," *Journal of Quantitative Criminology* 26, no. 4 (December 2010): 509–525.

69 Junger-Tas and Haen, "The Self-Report Methodology," 291–367.

70 Alex R. Piquero, Carol A. Schubert, and Robert Brame, "Comparing Official and Self-report Records of Offending across Gender and Race/Ethnicity in a Longitudinal Study of Serious Youthful Offenders," *Journal of Research in Crime and Delinquency* 51, no. 4 (2014): 526–556.

71 Junger-Tas and Haen, "The Self-Report Methodology," 291–367.

72 Ibid.

73 Ibid.

74 Ibid.

75 Ibid.

76 Terence P. Thornberry and Marvin D. Krohn, "The Self-Report Method for Measuring Delinquency and Crime," *Criminal Justice 2000* 4: 33–83, https://www.ncjrs.gov/App/Publications/abstract.aspx?ID=185538. Accessed April 2018.

77 Ibid.

78 Ibid.

79 Junger-Tas and Haen, "The Self-Report Methodology," 291–367.

80 Thomas Loughran, Ray Paternoster, and Kyle Thomas, "Incentivizing Responses to Self-Report Questions in Perceptual Deterrence Studies: An Investigation of the Validity of Deterrence Theory Using Bayesian Truth Serum," *Journal of Quantitative Criminology* 30, no. 4 (2014): 677–707.

81 Thornberry and Krohn, "The Self-Report Method," 33–83.

82 Junger-Tas and Haen, "The Self-Report Methodology," 291–367.

83 Ibid.

84 David Huizinga, Scott Menard, and Delbert S. Elliott, "Delinquency and Drug Use: Temporal and Developmental Patterns," *Justice Quarterly* 6 (1989): 419–455. Suzanne S. Ageton, *Sexual Assault Among Adolescents* (Lexington, Mass.: Lexington Books, 1983). Delbert S. Elliott, David Huizinga, and Suzanne S. Ageton, *Explaining Delinquency and Drug Use* (Beverly Hills, Calif.: Sage Publications, 1985). Delbert S. Elliott, David Huizinga, and Scott Menard, *Multiple Problem Youth: Delinquency, Drugs and Mental Health Problems* (New York: Springer, 1989).

85 Monitoring the Future: A Continuing Study of American Youth, http://monitoringthefuture.org/purpose.html. Accessed February 2018.

86 Ibid.

87 National Survey on Drug Use and Health, nsduhweb.rti.org. Prior to 2002, this survey was called the National Household Survey on Drug Abuse.

88 April Pattavina, Danielle Marie Carkin, and Paul E. Tracy, "Assessing the Representativeness of NIBRS Arrest Data," *Crime & Delinquency* 63, no. 12 (2017): 1626–1652.

89 James Byrne and Don Hummer, "An Examination of the Impact of Criminological Theory on Community Corrections Practice," *Federal Probation* 80, no. 3 (2016): 15–25.

90 Mosher, Miethe, and Phillips, *The Mismeasure of Crime*, 41.

91 Ibid.

92 Ibid.

93 William Alex Pridemore, "A Cautionary Note on Using County-Level Crime and Homicide Data," *Homicide Studies* 9, no. 3 (August 2005): 256–268.

94 Vincent J. Webb, Charles M. Katz, and Scott H. Decker, "Assessing the Validity of Self-Reports by Gang Members: Results from the Arrestee Drug Abuse Monitoring Program," *Crime & Delinquency* 52, no. 2 (April 2006): 232–252.

95 David Kirk, "Examining the Divergence Across Self-Report and Official Data Sources on Inferences about the Adolescent Life-Course of Crime," *Journal of Quantitative Criminology* 22, no. 2 (June 2006): 107–129.

Victims of Crime

FEATURES

Recent school shootings have highlighted the problems faced by victims of violence. What role do crime victims play in the criminal justice system?

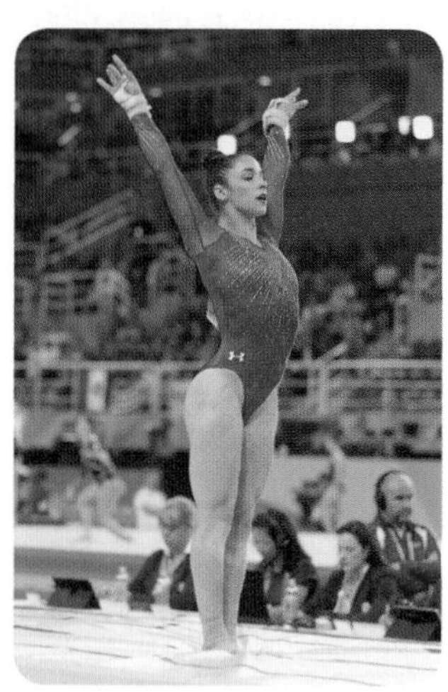

Aly Raisman reacts to news of her silver medal at the 2016 Summer Olympics. Why did it take so long for the allegations against Larry Nassar to come to light?

"The supervisor dismissed my complaints and basically treated me as though I were crazy. She indicated that Dr. Nassar used this procedure with many female athletes."[1]—Tiffany Thomas-Lopez

"My parents, who had my best interest at heart, will forever have to live with the fact that they continually brought their daughter to a sexual predator, and were in the room as he assaulted me."[2]—Marie Anderson

"He was always that person who would stick up for me and make me feel like he had my back. The more I think about it, the more I realize how twisted he was, how he manipulated me to make me think that he had my back when he didn't."[3]—Aly Raisman

"He's the type of person who knows how to make you want to trust him."[4]—Rachael Denhollander

In August 2016, Rachael Denhollander filed a complaint with Michigan State University police against Dr. Larry Nassar. Denhollander told police that she was sexually assaulted by Nassar in 2000 when she was a 15-year-old gymnast.[5]

Denhollander's accusations of sexual assault eventually resulted in more than 160 young women claiming that Nassar had assaulted them, too. These athletes included gymnasts, dancers, rowers, runners, softball players, soccer players, volleyball players, swimmers, and figure skaters.[6] At Nassar's trial, 156 young women, including at least five Olympic gymnasts, testified about Nassar's sexual abuse.[7]

Nassar was a renowned sports medicine doctor who began his career as an athletic trainer for USA Gymnastics in 1986. In a 2017 lawsuit, a former gymnast made the earliest known allegation against Nassar, which she states occurred in 1992 when Nassar was still a medical student.[8] Over the next 23 years, Nassar continued to build his career and reputation, treating hundreds of athletes for sports injuries.

Olympic medalist Jamie Dantzscher stated that Nassar began abusing her when she was 12 years old in 1994 and continued the abuse over the next six years. In 1996, Nassar became the national medical coordinator for USA Gymnastics, and in 1997 he took positions as the gymnastics team physician and as an assistant professor at Michigan State University. That year, in separate incidents, a 16-year-old gymnast and a parent complained about Nassar's treatments.[9] Nassar's career continued apace even as many of his young patients continued to assert that he was abusing them. According to a 2016 federal indictment, it was in 2004 that Nassar acquired child pornography.[10] In 2000 and 2008, Nassar attended the Olympic Games as a gymnastics team physician. Another complaint against Nassar was made in 2014, but he continued to treat patients during the police investigation. In December 2015, a prosecutor told police that Nassar would not be charged. In early August 2016, the ***Indianapolis Star*** reported on sexual abuse inside USA Gymnastics, and later that month, Denhollander filed her complaint.[11] Finally, in September 2016, Michigan State University fired Nassar, and USA Gymnastics reported that Nassar had been "relieved of his duties" the year before.[12]

In 2018, Nassar, 54, pleaded guilty to a host of charges and was sentenced to 40 to 125 years in prison in Eaton County, Michigan, and 40 to 175 years in prison in Ingham County, Michigan. However, he must first complete his first prison sentence, 60 years in federal prison for possessing child pornography.[13]

The Study of Victimology

LEARNING OBJECTIVE | 1

Define victimology.

The origin of the word "victim" is the Latin *victima*, which refers to an animal destined for sacrifice. This ancient definition puts the plight of crime victims in sharp perspective. The picture of a **victim**—a person who suffers a criminal offense—as an innocent with no control over his or her past, present, or future and whose fate is predetermined, has best matched the criminological and criminal justice treatment of victims, at least until recently.

Until the Middle Ages, victims (or their families) were expected to deal with their victimizers themselves. The philosophy of *lex talionis*, or an eye for an eye, is a legacy of this practice. Gradually, as Western systems of criminal justice matured, the state became the aggrieved party, and the victim, who was cut out of the justice process, became merely an element of the criminal act, much like evidence or witnesses.[14] In the United States, the role of the victim in crime was ignored for decades until the 1940s. Then criminologists, seeking to understand what early researcher Hans von Hentig called the "criminal–victim dyad," began looking to victims as much as to offenders in order to understand crime.

Victimology, the study of the various types of harm people suffer as a result of crime, began when researchers realized that half of the victim–offender dyad was being overlooked. Victimology research began with the study of rape victims, those who contributed to their victimization, the socially weak such as the very young or old, recent immigrants, and the mentally ill. As the crime rate rose throughout the 1960s, the President's Commission on Law Enforcement and the Administration of Justice asked criminologists to study victimization more thoroughly to help law enforcement catch offenders and prevent crime. Since then, other goals have come to include reducing victims' suffering, improving the criminal justice system's responses, and restoring victims' mental and physical health and financial resources. Some criminologists assert that offenders themselves are often victims of class and economic differences. However, victimology has lately concentrated on direct victims of crime who through little or no fault of their own have been targeted by an offender.[15]

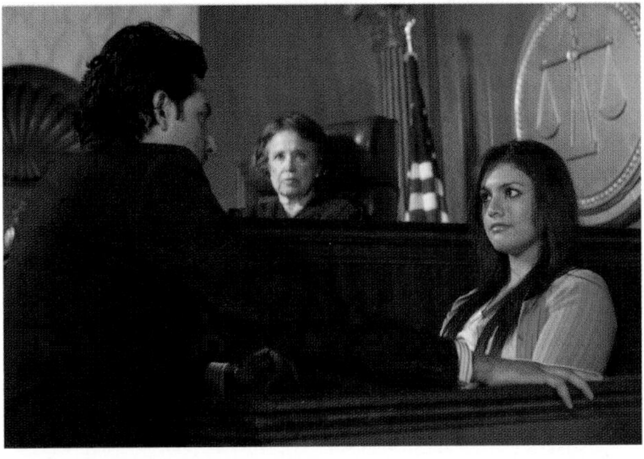

Testifying in court can be a traumatic experience for crime victims. Why has the criminal justice system only recently paid appropriate attention to the concerns of victims of crime?

Victimologists study the effects of crime on victims. They do not directly assist victims, which is the task of legal and criminal justice professionals, as well as physical and mental health professionals. Instead, victimologists research:

- victims' plight;
- the effects of physical and psychological injuries and financial losses;
- public reaction to victims; and
- the way criminal justice professionals deal with victims.[16]

The study of victimization has its critics. Some scholars point to a growing culture of victimhood in which everyone is a victim of everything: themselves, others, and society. One critique points to the creation of a "victim industry" in which an expanding mental health field continues to identify classes of victims that society responds to because identifying victims is an easy way to deal with broad social injustices.[17] The merits and criticisms of this search for victims are subject to debate. However, in this chapter, we will adhere to the basic motivations of victimology: to understand the effects of crime on its immediate victims.

PAUSE AND REVIEW

1. **What is victimology?**
2. **What do victimologists research?**

---

victim—In criminology, a person who suffers a criminal offense.

victimology—The study of the harm that people suffer as a result of crime.

The Extent of Victimization

LEARNING OBJECTIVE 2

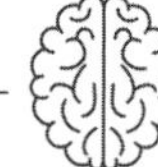

Compare macro-victimization and micro-victimization.

One of the first things we must know in the study of victims is who the victims are, how they are victimized, who victimizes them, and what they lose. The Uniform Crime Reports from the Federal Bureau of Investigation (FBI) records information about criminal offenses, arrestees, and clearances, but it records less about the victims besides what is reflected in the offense statistics. We will not find statistics describing victims' families, the physical and psychological effects of victimization, or how the criminal justice system processes the cases. As we learned in Chapter 2, the National Crime Victimization Survey (NCVS) captures deeper victimization statistics.

The NCVS collects statistics on non-fatal violent and property victimizations against people age 12 and older and measures rape, sexual assault, robbery, aggravated assault, simple assault, household burglary, motor vehicle theft, and personal theft. Unlike the UCR, the NCVS records offenses that are both reported and not reported to police and looks at only a sample of the U.S. population. In 2016, the NCVS interviewed about 135,000 households and nearly 225,000 individuals. Households remain in the study for three years, and eligible residents in those households are interviewed every six months either in person or over the phone for a total of seven interviews.[18]

In 2016, U.S. residents age 12 or older were victims of about 5.7 million violent offenses and 15.9 million property offenses.[19] Males had a higher rate of violent victimization than females, and people age 35 and older experienced less violent victimization than younger people.[20]

- Age. As you can see in Figure 3.1, the risk of violent victimization drops steadily after age 34. Although the elderly are perhaps the most afraid of victimization, they are the least likely to be victimized, as opposed to the very young, who tend to be the least afraid but are the most likely to be victimized. In 2016, 1.3 percent of all people age 12 or older, 3.6 million people, experienced at least one violent victimization.[21]
- Property offenses. In 2016, 119 property offenses were committed per 1,000 households. Motor vehicle thefts were the property offense most likely to be reported to police.[22]
- Firearms. About 481,000 non-fatal firearm victimizations occurred in 2016. Sixty percent of all serious violent offenses that involved a firearm were reported to police.[23]

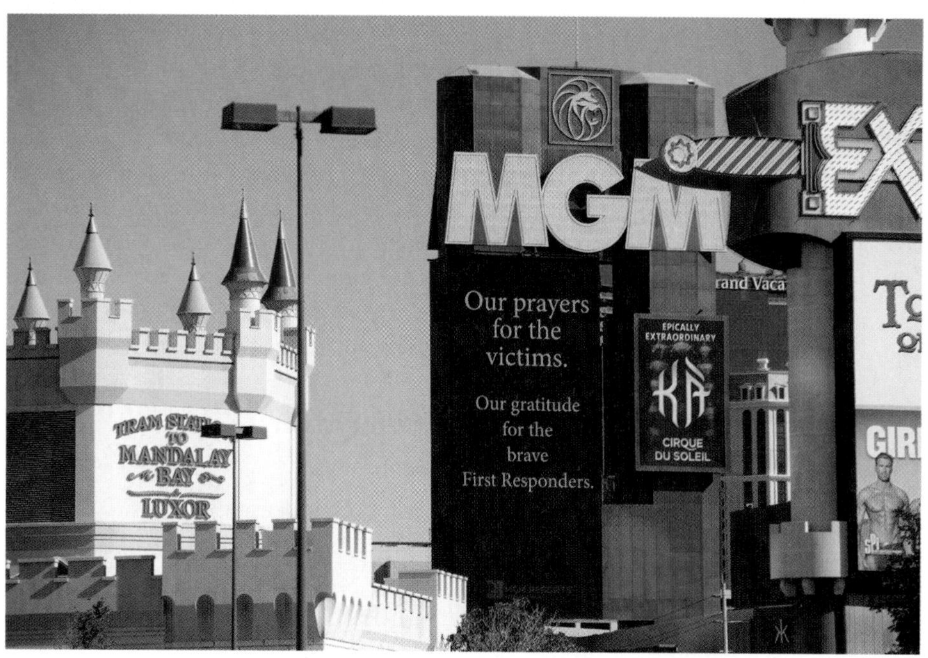

A sign asking for prayers is displayed at the MGM hotel in Las Vegas. In 2017, a gunman opened fire on an outdoor concert killing dozens of people and injuring hundreds. Why are there so many victims of firearms in the United States?

Micro-Victimization

Micro-victimization describes the type of victimization we are most familiar with: individual street-crime victimization—that is, the harm caused to small groups of people or individuals by small-scale criminal offenses. It is easier to measure than macro-victimization, and victims probably receive more productive assistance as well. It is simply a matter of numbers. An individual robbery victim in a politically stable country can get faster, better help than the families of a thousand genocide victims in a civil war.

The federal government has tried to recognize the plight of crime victims and to better integrate them within the criminal justice process. The Justice for All Act establishes and enforces the rights of crime victims in federal criminal proceedings by allowing victims to be heard at public proceedings about offender release, pleas, or sentencing. The U.S. Department of Justice Office of Community Oriented Policing Services suggests that several factors be considered in creating a more satisfactory criminal justice response to victims.

- Victims are key participants in the immediate response to an offense, the investigation of the incident, and efforts to prevent further crime.
- Victim service organizations have unique knowledge and capabilities that may enhance efforts to investigate and control crime.
- Better communication between police and victims leads to more productive investigations and crime-control efforts.
- An effective response to crime reduces the risk of repeat victimization. The police should develop community partnerships to improve their response to victims. Victim service organizations should also help victims who are at risk of further victimization to better plan for their safety.[24]

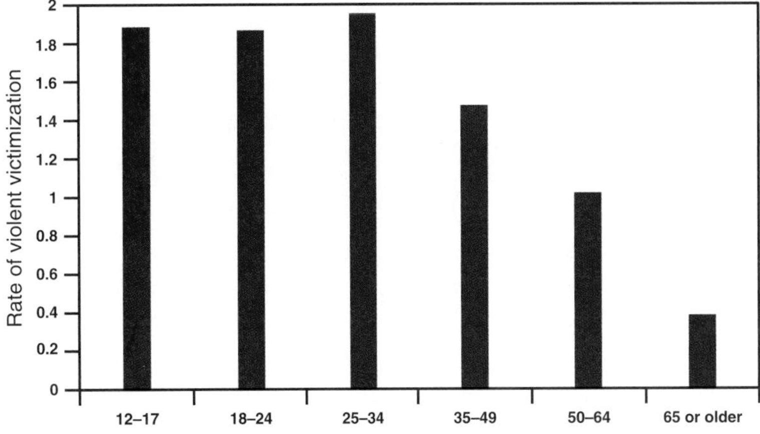

FIGURE 3.1 Rate of Violent Victimization by Age

Note the drastic decrease in victimization for people age 65 or older. Why do the elderly fear criminal victimization more than younger people if they are actually at a lower risk of victimization?

Source: Rachel E. Morgan and Grace Kena, Criminal Victimization, 2016, *Table 11 (Washington, D.C.: U.S. Department of Justice Office of Justice Programs Bureau of Justice Statistics, 2017), 13. Available at https://www.bjs.gov/index.cfm?ty=pbdetail&iid=6166.*

Now let's look at the victims of the major types of crime in the United States. The four major violent victimizations as typified by the FBI—murder, rape, robbery, and assault—are discussed individually because they are so serious. The four major property victimizations—burglary, larceny-theft, motor vehicle theft, and arson—are discussed as a unit.

MURDER VICTIMS

Murder is willful homicide, that is, the killing of another person on purpose with forethought. Accidental homicides, even those committed because of recklessness or assault, are not usually considered first-degree murder; instead, they are typically labeled as manslaughter or a lesser degree of murder (discussed in Chapter 10). Because the legal definition of murder requires purposeful action and motive on the offender's part, the offender–victim relationship is important. Usually, they know each other.[25]

In 2017, the FBI estimated 17,284 murders in the United States.[26] Most murder weapons were firearms (10,982).[27] Of murder victims, 7,851 were black, 6,579 were white, and 2,354 were Hispanic or Latino. Male murder victims (11,862) far outnumbered female victims (3,222).[28] Black offenders typically murdered black victims, and white offenders typically murdered white victims (see Figure 3.2).[29] When the victims' race and sex were combined, black males were the most likely murder victims, followed by white males, Hispanic/Latino males, white females, black females, and, finally, Hispanic/Latino females.[30]

RAPE VICTIMS

Historically, rape is the only violent offense in which the victim has also been a suspect. Feminists, scholars, researchers, and criminal justice professionals have worked for decades to ensure that rape victims are treated as victims and not as willing participants or, at best, as parties in some poorly understood physical altercation.

In 2012, the federal government changed its definition of rape. Until 2012, the government defined its term "forcible rape" as "the carnal knowledge of a female forcibly and against her will."[31] This definition was criticized because it did not count males and various forms of rape. The word

---

micro-victimization—The harm caused to small groups of people or individuals by small-scale criminal offenses.

murder—Willful homicide.

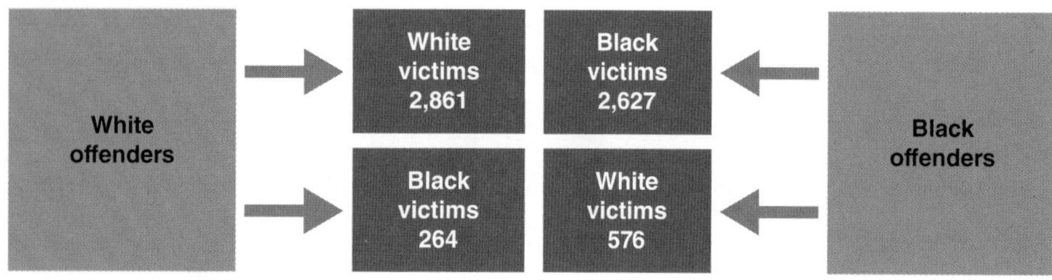

FIGURE 3.2 Races of Murder Victims and Offenders in the United States, 2017

In 2017, 264 black murder victims were killed by white offenders and 2,627 by black offenders. Of white victims, 2,861 were killed by white offenders and 576 by black offenders. Why might the victims and offenders of most of these murders be of the same race?

Source: Federal Bureau of Investigation, Uniform Crime Reports: Crime in the United States, 2017, *Expanded Homicide Data Table 6: Murder Race, Sex, and Ethnicity of Victim by Race, Sex, and Ethnicity of Offender, https://ucr.fbi.gov/crime-in-the-u.s/2017/crime-in-the-u.s.-2017/topic-pages/tables/expanded-homicide-data-table-6.xls.*

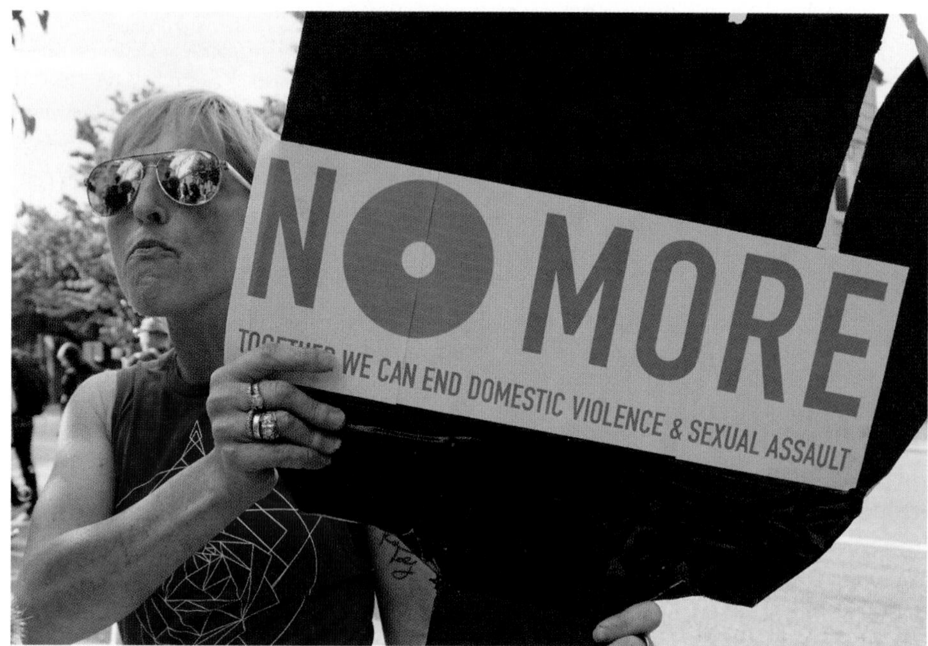

A woman protests as Bill Cosby departs after the fourth day of his 2017 sexual assault trial. Why has it been difficult for women to get their accusations of sexual assault taken seriously by the criminal justice system?

"forcible" has now been removed, and the new definition of **rape** is as follows "The penetration, no matter how slight, of the vagina or anus with any body part or object, or oral penetration by a sex organ of another person, without the consent of the victim."[32] The rape totals in the 2017 UCR are presented using both the legacy and revised definitions of rape.[33] In 2016, the NCVS recorded 323,450 rape and sexual assault victimizations.[34] The 2017 UCR estimated 135,755 rapes under the revised definition.[35]

History and Prejudice in Rape Victimization. Because women play a vital role in family lineages, female sexuality historically has been tightly controlled. In many ancient cultures, a woman's value was directly related to her ability to produce healthy children for a male who was sure that the children were his. A man whose wife was raped could not be sure that the child she bore, if any, was his. A victimized girl lost her value for the same reason and would remain a burden to her father, who could not marry her off. For these reasons, although the traditional object of rape has been women, the traditional victims were men, and the women merely property. This is one source of the paradox in which women were never considered true victims of rape and yet were the focus of rape laws.

Rape occurs in some form in all societies, but some condone it more than others and others use it for social control. In some hunter–gatherer societies, rape is less about controlling women for their reproductive value than it is about simply controlling them. In *Against Our Will,* feminist author Susan Brownmiller discusses gang rape as a means of social control among several South American tribes. Females who did not "toe the line" were gang raped to keep all females under control.

> Institutionalized gang rape . . . had been observed . . . among the Tapirapé Indians of Brazil in the case of an independent young woman who refused to join the other females in manioc processing. The woman in this case was unmarried and she was turned over to the village men for punishment by her brother. The action of the Tapirapé brother suggests that the deviation of a female constitutes a crisis that requires direct and immediate action regardless of bonds of kinship.[36]

The ancient laws that led to English common law—the basis of U.S. law—were likewise concerned with control of females. Because males are not controlled in this way, it was long considered that they cannot be raped. An echo of these ancient prejudices can be seen in the FBI's old definition of rape, which did not specify the rape of men. Until 2012, according to the FBI, "Sexual attacks on males [were] counted as aggravated assaults or sex offenses, depending on the circumstances and the extent of any injuries."[37]

Historical prejudices concerning rape have wronged male victims as much as female victims. Presumably because male–male rape did not present reproductive issues, the assault was deemed to be not important, a loss of honor, the spoils of war, just punishment for a crime, or merely homosexual play. The stigmatization of homosexuality has added a dimension to the plight of male victims. The idea that a heterosexual male can be raped by another heterosexual male (outside prison) is only beginning to be officially accepted. Too often, a male who does not fight off his attacker is considered to have consented to the rape. For this and other reasons, males often wait years to report an attack, and many never do.[38]

Child Rape and Sexual Abuse. The proscription on sex with children, specifically prepubescent children, is recent in the West. It is possible that modern laws and social attitudes have made child sexual abuse and rape less prevalent now than in prior centuries. In ancient Greece and Rome, sex between men and boys was common. Throughout the Middle Ages in Europe, sexual activity between adults and children was almost a social norm. What we now call "statutory" rape—sex with a person under a specific age, usually 18—was not prosecuted at all, and prostitution of girls under age 15 was common. Not until the 19th century did France and England adopt modern attitudes and laws concerning child–adult sex.[39]

Although child rape and sexual abuse are among the most highly publicized serious offenses, it is difficult to estimate how often they occur. One reason is that they simply go unreported. The victim is often too young to understand what happened or is afraid or unable to tell anyone. According to the American Academy of Child and Adolescent Psychiatry (AACAP), children age 5 or older may feel trapped between love or affection for their abusers, who may be relatives or adult friends of the family, and the feeling that the sexual activities are wrong. Children who try to end the abuse may be threatened with violence or loss of their abusers' love. Federal statistics, then, probably underestimate the actual occurrence of child rape and sexual abuse.

According to AACAP, child sexual abuse is reported almost 80,000 times a year.[40] One study found that 9.8 percent of the children in its sample of children aged 0 to 17 had experienced sexual victimization during their lifetimes. Girls experienced more sexual victimizations than boys, and these were concentrated among 14- to 17-year-olds.[41] In another study of a large, nationally representative sample of adults in the United States, about 1 in 10 adults had experienced sexual abuse before age 18, with child sexual abuse occurring more among women than men.[42] These findings agree with a study of 841 cases at a child advocacy center, where 73 percent of the children at the center were girls. For girls, the frequency of sexual abuse increased with age: 2- to 5-year-olds were the least frequently abused (18 percent); 6- to 10-year-olds the next most frequently abused (38 percent); and 11- to 17-year-olds the most frequently abused (45 percent). Of boys, those aged 6–10 were the most frequently abused (56 percent), with the frequency of abuse decreasing at later ages.[43]

In June 2008, the U.S. Supreme Court ruled the death penalty unconstitutional for the rape of a child. In a controversial 5–4 decision, the Court overturned laws in Louisiana and five other states, but it did not overturn federal military law, which Congress amended in 2006 to allow capital punishment in child-rape cases.[44]

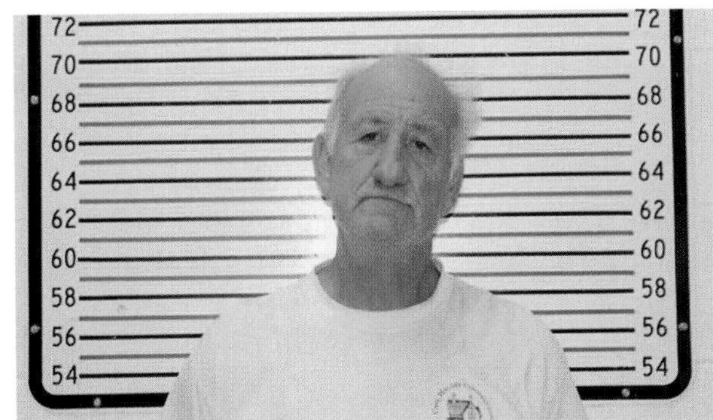

Carl Axel Hagnas, known as the "Candyman" for handing out sweets to children, was arrested on multiple counts of child sexual abuse dating back more than 20 years. What can be done to prevent child sexual abuse?

rape—As defined in the Uniform Crime Reports, "The penetration, no matter how slight, of the vagina or anus with any body part or object, or oral penetration by a sex organ of another person, without the consent of the victim."

ROBBERY AND ASSAULT VICTIMS

Robbery is the taking or attempting to take anything from another person or persons by violence or the threat of violence. In 2017, 74,340 robbery suspects were arrested, with 18-year-olds posting the highest number of arrests (5,171).[45] One study found that robbers' main motivation is to get cash or valuable items, but their secondary motivation is to gain control over their victims and experience the excitement of the offense. The robbers in the study did not plan their offenses and committed robbery so casually that they could not keep up with how many people they had robbed.[46] The study found that robbers preferred white victims because they were less likely to fight back than black victims. White victims usually carried only credit cards and checkbooks, though, if they had cash, the amount was substantial. The robbers also preferred drug dealers or drug buyers as targets, although drug dealers were more likely to be armed and connected with others who could take revenge. Preferred victims were white drug users who entered the robbers' neighborhood to buy drugs. Such victims were likely to carry large amounts of cash and unlikely to call the police.[47] Another study revealed that at the initial stages of a robbery, the amount of physical force the offender uses is influenced by how tough and streetwise they believe the victim to be. Robbers are more likely to use force against a defiant victim than against a submissive victim.[48] Another study found that robbers are less likely to be violent toward victims if they are committing the robbery alone rather than with a partner (although most robbers, who are overwhelmingly male, are more likely to act in pairs or groups).[49] However, the likelihood of a robbery leading to arrest significantly increased with the number of offenders.[50]

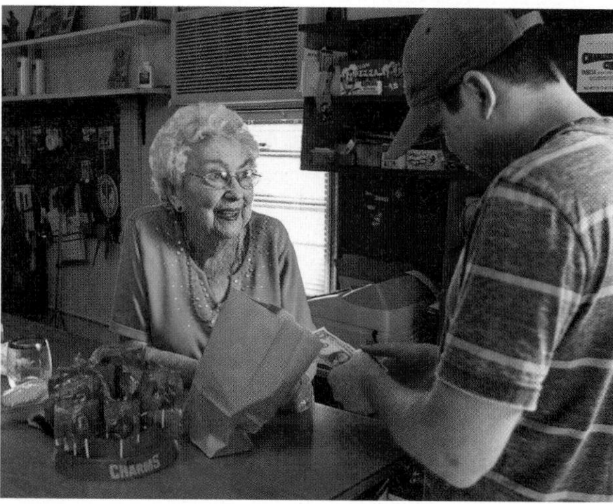

Marge Wolf, 96, makes a sale at her grocery store in Marshfield, Wisconsin, the day after a masked man attempted to rob her at knifepoint. The man ordered Wolf to open the cash register, but she refused. The frustrated robber spotted a security camera in the corner and fled on foot. Are female victims likely to resist a robber's demands?

Robbery victimization also has some significant gender dimensions. Although it is generally assumed that female victims will resist less in a robbery attempt, the NCVS suggests that female victims often resist robbery attempts regardless of the offender's sex. Also, female victims are no more or no less likely than male victims to be injured by either male or female robbery perpetrators. Although, there are no differences between male and female victims in reporting perpetrators' race or age, male robbery victims are much more likely than female victims to omit the perpetrator's sex in their reports.[51]

Assault Victims. Assault is the criminal offense of attempting to inflict immediate bodily harm or making another person fear that such harm is imminent. Assaults are generally divided into two categories: aggravated and simple. According to the FBI, aggravated assault is "an unlawful attack by one person upon another for the purpose of inflicting severe or aggravated bodily injury. . . . this type of assault is usually accompanied by the use of a weapon or by other means likely to produce death or great bodily harm." Simple assault as defined by the FBI refers to those offenses "that do not involve the use of a firearm, knife or cutting instrument, or other dangerous weapon and in which the victim did not sustain serious or aggravated injuries."[52] In 2017, there were nearly 250 aggravated assaults per 100,000 people.[53] Age is an important factor in assault, with simple assault being the most frequently committed violent offense by arrestees 18 and under.[54] Typically, most simple assaults perpetrated by youths victimize other adolescents. Youths who commit serious violent victimizations usually commit aggravated assaults rather than rape, robbery, or murder.[55]

Victims of Intimate-Partner Violence. Females are more likely than males to suffer **intimate-partner violence** (IPV), which occurs between two people in a spousal, domestic, or romantic relationship. Of all murders in 2017 (15,129), 3.6 percent were of wives, 3.2 percent were of girlfriends, 1.2 percent were of boyfriends, and .72 percent were of husbands.[56] In the United States, more than 1 in 3 women and more than 1 in 4 men have experienced rape, physical violence, and/or stalking by an intimate partner during their lifetime.[57] Intimate-partner violence has a particularly strong connection to economic hardship. On average, women living in households with lower annual incomes suffered the highest rates of nonfatal IPV. Victims risk losing their jobs because they miss work while finding new housing, separating from their victimizers, and getting medical attention, and because employers fear the perpetrator may cause problems at the workplace. A third to one-half of employed domestic violence victims lose their jobs. As a result, several states and jurisdictions have passed legislation prohibiting employers from firing employees for problems related to domestic abuse.[58]

A woman holds a cutout that represents a woman who died from intimate partner violence during the "Walk a Mile in Her Shoes" event at the University of Southern Indiana. Participants walked in women's high-heeled shoes on the campus to protest rape, sexual assault, and gender violence. What are some economic problems that victims of domestic violence suffer?

PROPERTY OFFENSE VICTIMS

The UCR records four property offenses:

- **burglary**—the unlawful entry of a structure with the intent to commit a felony or theft
- **larceny/theft**—the unlawful taking of money or property from another person
- motor-vehicle theft
- **arson**—the deliberate setting of fires

During larceny/theft, there is no force or threat of force against victims (as with the offense of shoplifting). The other three offenses may include physical harm to victims, threat of harm, or intent to inflict harm. In 2017, larceny/theft offenses accounted for 72 percent of all property offenses.[59]

About 7,694,086 property offenses occurred in the United States in 2017.[60] In addition:

- Burglary victims lost an estimated $3.4 billion worth of property, with the average loss per offense totaling $2,416.
- Larceny/theft victims lost an estimated $5.6 billion.
- Six billion dollars' worth of motor vehicles was stolen at an average cost of about $7,708 per vehicle.[61]

One effort to help victims that presents an alternative to the traditional criminal justice process is victim–offender mediation. Because property offenses are less serious than violent offenses, victim–offender meetings are a realistic scenario. The object is to allow the victim to confront the offender in a safe, structured setting and to help develop a satisfactory restitution plan for the victim. Victim–offender mediation emphasizes dialogue, victim healing, offender accountability, and restoration of losses.[62] We will discuss this subject in more detail later in the chapter.

VICTIM PRECIPITATION

Victim precipitation occurs when the victim plays an active role in initiating or escalating the offense. Precipitation is different from provocation, a legal concept used to focus on the offender for the purposes of establishing guilt and deciding sentencing.[63] Victim precipitation is concerned with the victim's behavior for the purpose of analysis and not to establish fault. It is important to clarify this concept because it is often mistaken for "blaming the victim." Victim precipitation merely considers the victim's actions and the role he or she played in a violent event.[64]

---

robbery—The taking or attempting to take anything from another person or persons by violence or the threat of violence.

assault— The criminal offense of attempting to inflict immediate bodily harm or making another person fear that such harm is imminent.

burglary—The unlawful entry of a structure with the intent to commit a felony or theft.

larceny/theft—The unlawful taking of property from another person.

arson— The deliberate setting of fires.

victim precipitation—An offense in which the victim plays an active role in initiating or escalating the offense.

Instant Recall from Chapter 2 **intimate-partner violence** — Abuse that occurs between two people in a spousal, domestic, or romantic relationship.

There are two broad types of victim precipitation: active and passive. Passive victimization occurs when a victim unknowingly provokes an attack or fails to protect against an attack. Active victimization occurs when the victim threatens or somehow actively provokes an assailant, or even attacks first. For example, a passive victim may be someone who acquires something someone else wants or feels like he or she deserved, such as winning a competition, getting a job promotion, or inheriting money. The victim has no idea that someone else is coveting his or her success or possessions and is caught off-guard by an attack. The majority of bullied children are excellent examples of passive victims: they have no idea why or how they are being attacked and bullied, but they continue to be harassed.[65]

As an example of active precipitation, consider two groups of inebriated people walking home from a bar. A man in Group I makes a disparaging comment about a woman in Group II, and the men in Group II demand a fight. Group II loses badly after a short brawl, and one member dies. From a criminal justice perspective, the key questions are who threw the first punch and who was fighting in self-defense. The Group I men might be charged with some lesser degree of murder. The victim precipitation perspective, however, would study the actions of Group II and its members' role in the incident. Some criminology scholars look at long-term victim precipitations, such as when a person kills an abusive spouse. In this case, the victim's actions that contributed to the homicide took place over several years and not just in an isolated incident.

Related to victim precipitation is criminologist David Luckenbill's concept of murder as a **situated transaction**, or the idea that a scenario is the result of agreed-upon norms, interactions, and roles played by those involved. In Luckenbill's study of 70 cases, the following pattern emerged.

1. The victim made a move the offender thought offensive.
2. The offender retaliated with a verbal or physical challenge.
3. The victim's response typically cemented an "agreement" to use violence to settle the situation.
4. The victim lay dead or dying after a fight.
5. The offender ended the scene in a manner related to the relationship with the victim and any observers.

If the victim was a family member or other intimate, the offender would usually remain on the scene and notify the police; if the offender and victim were acquaintances, the offender would try to destroy evidence, dispose of the body, and then flee. If observers were present, their relationship to the offender would determine the offender's actions: Victim-supportive observers would direct the offender to remain; victim-hostile observers would encourage the offender to flee; and neutral observers would do nothing, leaving the offender to act.[66]

The idea of situated transactions has helped clarify criminologists' understanding of both intimate-partner violence and some neighborhood street violence since both develop between parties familiar with one another and can include some concept of saving face or honor.[67]

Macro-Victimization

When we think of crime victims, we tend to think of individuals. **Macro-victimization**, in contrast to micro-victimization, considers large masses of people as victims of large-scale criminal offenses. We can divide this new field into three broad categories: terrorism, large-scale corporate and environmental crime, and crimes against humanity.

Macro-victimization is different from street-crime victimization. Two of the categories, crimes against humanity and terrorism, are related to war. The other, corporate and environmental victimization, represents offenses so large and complicated that they are difficult to imagine as traditional crime. It is easy to imagine a robber pointing a gun at another person as victimization. It is not easy to read hundreds of pages of financial documents or to ferret out who on the board of directors knew what and when so that it can be understood who was victimized and how. However, the size and complexity of a destructive event does not make it any less of a criminal offense. Sometimes it is not useful to imagine a victim as a single person victimized by a street crime as defined by the FBI. Victims may be groups of unrelated people, children, the elderly, the disabled, civilians living with the horrors of war, and their families.

TERRORISM VICTIMIZATION

Author William Gibson wrote, "Terrorism as we ordinarily understand it is innately media-related."[68] Because terrorists seek to produce panic and gain media notice for their cause, their victims are typically civilians and occupy an especially critical position in the offender–victim dyad. Early on, adult victims of terrorism and political violence suffer shock, anxiety, confusion, sorrow, grief, survivors' guilt, and other forms of psychological distress. Later, they suffer increased anxiety, depression, phobias, reduced sense of safety, post-traumatic stress, and increased tobacco, alcohol, and drug usage.[69] Experts are still studying how best to help them, although trauma counseling seems no more therapeutic than simply talking to friends and family.[70] Some governments have set up legal means for victims to recover financially, even if all their psychological wounds cannot be addressed. The United Nations has recommended eight steps for providing effective support to victims of terrorism:

1. Provide an Internet-based communication and information center for terrorism victims, government officials, experts, and service providers.
2. Strengthen the law at the national and international levels, providing victims with legal status and protecting their rights.
3. Establish short- and long-term health services for victims.
4. Create an international rapid response team to support victims.
5. Provide financial support to victims.
6. Improve the capacity of the United Nations to assist survivors and families of U.N. staff killed or injured in terrorist attacks.
7. Engage in global awareness supporting terrorism victims.
8. Improve media coverage of terrorism victims.[71]

Victimization in the United States. The United States is new to providing for victims of domestic and international terrorism primarily because such attacks are relatively recent. U.S. government agencies have set up special offices and victims' funds.

- The U.S. Justice Department's International Terrorism Victim Expense Reimbursement Program allows U.S. citizens who are victims of terrorism outside the United States to apply to a single federal office for compensation.[72]
- The FBI's Office for Victim Assistance provides emergency assistance to injured victims and families of victims killed in domestic and international attacks.[73]
- The U.S. Victims of State Sponsored Terrorism Fund provides compensation to some international terrorism victims harmed by state-sponsored terrorism. The fund compensates victims of international terror attacks who have secured final judgments in a U.S. district court against a state sponsor of terrorism, or who were held hostage at the U.S. Embassy in Tehran, Iran, from 1979 to 1981 (this includes their spouses and children).[74]

A family member of one of the victims of the crash of United Flight 93 walks along a section of the National Memorial following its dedication near the crash site of Flight 93 in Shanksville, Pennsylvania. The names of the crash victims are inscribed on the marble panels. In what ways are family members of victims of terrorism also victims?

Often, charitable compensation funds are created for victims of terrorism. For example, such funds were created for the victims of the 2013 Boston Marathon bombing and the 2016 Orlando, Florida, Pulse Nightclub shootings. The September 11th Victim Compensation Fund, created to compensate those who suffered harm and the families of those who were killed in the terrorist attacks of September 11, 2001, was reactivated from 2011 to 2016. The original fund operated from 2001 to 2004.[75]

Victimization in Other Countries. In 2016, 11,072 terrorist attacks happened worldwide, resulting in 25,621 people killed, 33,814 injured, and 15,543 people kidnapped or taken hostage.[76] Outside the United States, children and civilians are disproportionately

---

situated transaction—The idea that a scenario is the result of agreed-upon norms, interactions, and roles played by those involved.

macro-victimization—The harm caused to masses of people by large-scale criminal offenses.

victims of terrorism. Some countries have been politically unstable for so long that few of their citizens can remember a stable government, and terrorism has become a fact of life. In this section, we will briefly consider how victimization occurs, characteristics of the victims, and forms of victim assistance, if any.

Council of Europe guidelines for the treatment of terrorism victims basically hold that European states should ensure that victims and their families receive emergency assistance; medical, psychological, social, and material assistance; access to the law; fair, appropriate, and timely compensation; protection of privacy and family life; and protection of dignity and security. Finally, the granting of services should not depend on whether the terrorists are identified, captured, or convicted.[77]

The reality of assistance to terrorism victims in many non-European countries is not as systematic or fair. Depending on the country, terrorism victims may receive anything from good assistance to no assistance. Victims in Western countries may receive money from public and private organizations as well as counseling and other assistance. Unfortunately, in countries where terrorism occurs almost daily, international organizations such as the Red Cross may offer counseling, but financial reparations or legal redress is unlikely.

CORPORATE AND ENVIRONMENTAL VICTIMIZATION

The true number and characteristics of victims of corporate and environmental offenses cannot be known because some of the offenses are so wide-ranging in terms of geography and time that they may affect whole countries, or even continents or hemispheres, for decades. A particularly serious oil spill affects not only the health of the local people, animals, and plants, but also industries such as fishing, tourism, and anything else that depends on a healthy environment. To generate an accurate picture of this type of victimization, we will consider two modern examples of environmental and corporate offenses: the BP-*Deepwater Horizon* disaster and the conspiracy by automaker Volkswagen to cheat on U.S. emissions tests.

The BP-*Deepwater Horizon* Disaster. On April 20, 2010, the BP oil drilling platform *Deepwater Horizon* exploded and sank, killing 11 men and causing the largest ocean oil spill in U.S. history.[78] The Macondo oil well the rig was attached to released at least four million barrels of oil into the Gulf of Mexico and required 87 days to plug.[79]

The accident was the result of a cascade of events. The explosions on the rig were caused by a blowout—a buildup of oil and gas inside the well—that followed a pressure test inside the sealed well. The conditions in the well spun out of control, and gas, oil, and mud rushed up the pipe connecting the rig to the well.[80] The rig's 126 crew members struggled to control the blowout and ensuing explosions but finally had to abandon ship. Thirty-six hours later, the *Deepwater Horizon* sank.[81]

BP began cleanup immediately, but its efforts were not successful. As of 2014, the blowout site, an area on the ocean floor "the size of Rhode Island," was still coated in oil.[82] In the year after the spill, more than 6,000 birds, 600 sea turtles, and 150 marine mammals, including dolphins and sperm whales, were found dead.[83] Currently, in eight of the region's most important fishing zones, commercial catches of shrimp, crab, and yellowfin tuna are greatly reduced.[84]

In 2013, BP pleaded guilty to 14 criminal charges and agreed to pay $4 billion in penalties.[85] Two years later, BP agreed to pay $18.7 billion and another $20 billion to settle federal, state, and local civil and environmental claims.[86]

Five workers connected with the companies that ran the rig were criminally charged. The U.S. Department of Justice accused former BP supervisors Donald Vidrine and Robert Kaluza of failing to properly conduct the pressure tests before the blowout. Vidrine pleaded guilty and was sentenced to 10 months of probation on a misdemeanor pollution charge. Kaluza, who went to trial, was acquitted. Former BP vice president David Rainey was acquitted of lying to investigators about how much oil was spilled. Former BP engineer Kurt Mix pleaded guilty to obstruction of justice after deleting text messages he had sent while trying to stop the spill, but that conviction was overturned owing to juror misconduct. Later, Mix pleaded guilty to a misdemeanor charge of damaging a computer and received six months of probation.[87] Anthony Badalamenti, a manager at Halliburton Energy Services, which serviced the rig, pleaded guilty to destroying evidence and received one year of probation.[88]

Two companies other than BP were also criminally charged. In 2013, Halliburton, which had originally sealed the well, pleaded guilty to a misdemeanor charge of destroying evidence and was fined the maximum allowable amount of $200,000.[89] The owner of the *Deepwater Horizon*, Transocean, agreed to a criminal misdemeanor violation of the Clean Water Act and was fined $100 million. The company also paid the National Academy of Sciences and the National Fish and Wildlife Foundation $150 million each.[90]

The Volkswagen Conspiracy. In September 2015, the U.S. Environmental Protection Agency (EPA) discovered that, for the last decade, Volkswagen had been fitting some of its diesel cars sold in the United States with software that could detect when the cars were being tested and change their performance to improve environmental results.[91]

A typical test involved the cars being put into a stationary test rig. The software would then detect that it was being tested and run the engine below normal power and performance. The software could sense test scenarios by monitoring speed, engine operation, air pressure, and steering wheel position. During regular driving, the engines would return to normal mode, emitting nitrogen oxide pollutants up to 40 times above what is allowed in the United States.[92] Volkswagen admitted that the software was present on about 482,000 cars manufactured in the United States and on about 11 million cars sold throughout the world.[93]

In March 2017, Volkswagen pleaded guilty to three **felony** counts of conspiracy to defraud the United States, engage in wire fraud, and violate the Clean Air Act; obstruction of justice; and importation of merchandise by means of false statements. Volkswagen's plea agreement required the company to pay a $2.8 billion penalty. The company also agreed to pay an additional $1.5 billion to settle civil penalties in connection with the importation and sale of the cars, as well as a U.S. Customs and Border Protection claim for customs fraud.[94]

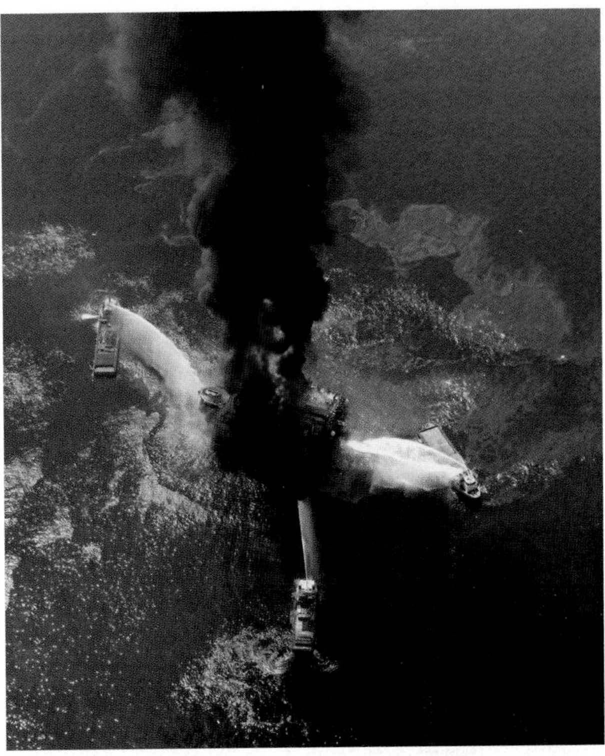

The *Deepwater Horizon* oil rig burns after it exploded in the Gulf of Mexico. What are the effects on victims of environmental crime?

VICTIMS OF CRIMES AGAINST HUMANITY

A look at any ancient text will confirm that human beings can justify any cruelty for political, religious, or social gain. However, it was only in the 20th century during the Nuremberg Trials of Nazi officers that the term "crimes against humanity" was coined to describe such activities. Crimes against humanity include "murder, extermination, enslavement, deportation, imprisonment, torture, rape, or other inhumane acts committed against any civilian population."[95] In 2002, the Rome Statute of the International Criminal Court revised this definition to include "enforced prostitution, forced pregnancy, enforced sterilization, other comparably severe forms of sexual violence of comparable gravity, the enforced disappearance of persons, apartheid and other inhumane acts intentionally causing great suffering or serious injury, when such acts are knowingly committed as part of a widespread or systematic attack directed against any civilian population, with knowledge of the attack."[96]

Crimes against humanity are typically state sponsored; that is, they are committed by some form of government against a civilian population. Modern criminal court jurisdiction is firmly established not only by the Nuremberg Trials, but also by several more recent international statutes, including the Geneva Convention, the Universal Declaration of Human Rights, and the International Criminal Court.[97]

Given growing populations, declining resources, unstable world and national politics, and advanced weaponry that simplifies the control

felony—A serious offense usually punishable by a prison sentence of more than one year or sometimes by life imprisonment or death.

and extermination of large numbers of people, a crime against humanity probably occurs somewhere in the world every day and probably always has. With better and increased communications, however, including media coverage, these offenses are now better and more frequently known. We will now turn to some examples of crimes against humanity in an effort to better understand the issues.

Nazi War Atrocities. The isolation, imprisonment, sterilization, torture, and murder of 6 million European Jews and at least 11 million political and religious dissenters, Polish, Soviet, and Romani civilians, and German homosexual and handicapped individuals first helped define the term "crimes against humanity."[98] From 1945 to 1946, Allied prosecutors tried the 22 German officials deemed most responsible for Nazi atrocities, including party leaders, military officers, and government bureaucrats. Most were found guilty and hanged, although some were sentenced to prison. Three defendants were acquitted, and Hermann Goering, Adolf Hitler's second-in-command, committed suicide.[99]

Helping the victims has been a monumental task that has continued since World War II ended. The offenses included not only imprisonment, torture, and murder, but also the theft of untold amounts of wealth, much of which was never returned. It was not until the end of the 20th century that Swiss banks, which handled much of the wealth that the Nazis took, agreed to a financial settlement with some survivors of Nazi atrocities.[100]

As we will explore in the next two sections, one of the problems of assisting victims of crimes against humanity is the scale of the offense. Often, there are too many victims for each individual to be helped effectively. Even after Allied soldiers liberated the Nazi concentration camps, thousands of sick, weak survivors still died despite efforts to help them. In some cases, the vast number of corpses made pestilence and disease such a serious threat that bulldozers were used to push heaps of bodies into the mass graves.[101] Whole families who perished in the camps were buried this way. Even the most valiant efforts to assist victims shrivel in the wake of this kind of offense.

ISIL. ISIL (also called ISIS or Daesh) began in 2004 as the group Al-Qaeda in Iraq. In 2006, it merged with other Iraqi jihadist groups and began calling itself the Islamic State of Iraq (ISI), then Islamic State in Iraq and al-Sham (ISIL). After the U.S. counterterrorism efforts in Iraq from 2006 to 2011, ISIL took advantage of the region's instability to recruit and organize. After the outbreak of the Syrian civil war in 2011, ISIL joined local militants in Syria to fight Syrian government forces. By April 2013, ISIL was a well-organized force that controlled large, significant populated areas in Syria and Iraq. ISIL's resources were bolstered by victories in Iraq in July 2014, and it consolidated its power in areas it controlled by killing community leaders, other armed-group commanders, and activists.[102] By 2018, however, ISIL was largely defeated and had lost all its territories and most of its fighters.[103]

In areas it controlled, ISIL maintained a rigid administration that utilized morality police, a general police force, courts, and groups that managed recruitment, tribal relations, education, and basic services. According to the United Nations, ISIL's control over territory and populations obliged the group to treat the people who live in those areas humanely.[104] Regardless, the group used torture, rape, murder, and forced displacement to control entire regions of people.

The treatment of females was of particular concern. ISIL imposed an onerous dress code, requiring females over the age of about 7 to be completely covered in public.[105] ISIL considered all unmarried females past puberty—including those as young as age 9—as marriageable. Many parents married their daughters off as soon as possible so that they would not be forced to marry ISIL fighters, who kidnapped and married females as young as 13. ISIL executed both women and men for unapproved contact with the opposite sex. In 2014, ISIL executed eight women in Raqqah, Syria, for this reason, with most being stoned to death. The group also beheaded a female dentist in Al-Mayadin who continued to treat patients of both sexes.[106]

By its regular usage of violence, torture, and mutilation, ISIL violated international humanitarian law. Thus, its commanders could be held individually responsible for war crimes. These crimes include, but are not limited to:

- kidnapping, murder, sexual violence, and torture;
- training and using children in combat;

- slavery;
- forced pregnancy;
- forced displacement;
- mutilating, permanently disfiguring and/or disabling individuals;
- displaying dead, mutilated bodies in order to humiliate and degrade the victims and their families.[107]

Transnational Victimization

Although countries define and handle crime differently, most define the same behaviors as criminal offenses: murder, rape, assault, theft, robbery, and so on. The major differences lie in the details of how the offenses are handled. The same goes for victim assistance. Some countries offer little or no help for victims, whereas others have special laws and networks of government and private agencies. Most countries probably fall between these two extremes.

In this section, we focus on crime that involves victims and offenders in more than one country. The 21st century's instant communications, global economy, and ability to move large amounts of goods vast distances cheaply, though convenient, is a growing problem. Not only is it easier than ever to break the laws of several countries at once, it is increasingly profitable. But what happens to the victims of these offenses? To answer this question, we will look at transnational crime and how it affects individual victims.

Transnational crime involves offenses that originate in one country, cross one or several national borders (or oceans), and find victims in still other nations. Credit card theft is an example: People in one country access an online database, steal the credit card numbers of people in another country, and either sell the numbers or use them to purchase items. Transnational crime often depends on exploiting the differences and distances between national borders. Because doing this successfully requires a certain amount of resources and sophistication, criminal organizations often perpetrate transnational crime. Common transnational offenses are trafficking in some banned material such as intellectual property, wildlife, drugs, body parts, human beings, stolen goods, oil, food, precious metals and stones, and medicine. Corruption, bribery, money laundering, environmental offenses, and some forms of terrorism and sea piracy may also be perpetrated transnationally.

A common form of the transnational crime of **human trafficking**, the buying and selling of human beings, is prostitution. Women from countries in Africa, Asia, and some eastern European countries are taken to countries with booming tourist economies where their captors confiscate their documents, passports, and other means of communication with their families and force them to work as prostitutes. Other forms of human trafficking involve taking shiploads of people to work in foreign sweatshops (including some in the United States), kidnapping for ransom, and even harvesting vital organs from unwilling donors.[108]

Often, transnational crime resembles domestic organized crime. For example, automobile thieves often steal cars in the United States to sell overseas. The cars are shipped across the world to countries where they can bring handsome black-market profits. For the victim, the only difference between international and domestic theft is that the victim has no chance of getting the car back if it has gone overseas.[109]

Finally, transnational crime can include environmental offenses, such as illegal logging and timber smuggling, wildlife smuggling, illegal dumping of hazardous waste, and illegal trade in environmentally harmful chemicals. Without the assistance of the host country (which may be profiting from some offenses), these offenses are difficult to control. Victims can include individuals, groups, countries, or, in the case of wildlife smuggling, other species.[110] Unfortunately, unstable global politics and shaky economies can make obtaining justice dangerous, which leads governments to consider the issue not worth pursuing.

PAUSE AND REVIEW

1. **Show how corporate and environmental victimization are difficult to measure.**
2. **Distinguish between micro-victimization and macro-victimization.**
3. **What is transnational victimization? Give an example.**

---

transnational crime—Criminal offenses that originate in one country and cross one or many several national borders.

human trafficking—The buying and selling of human beings.

The Problems of Victimization

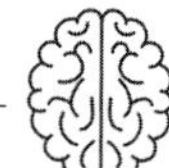

LEARNING OBJECTIVE | 3

List the problems of victimization.

LEARNING OBJECTIVE | 4

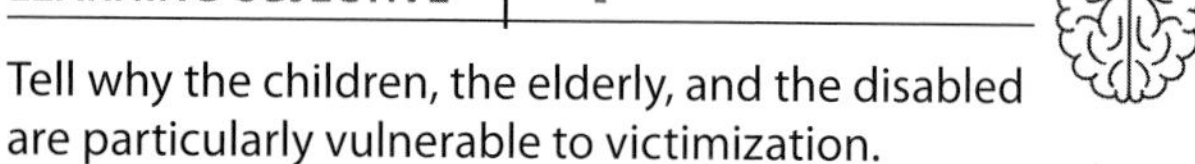

Tell why the children, the elderly, and the disabled are particularly vulnerable to victimization.

Criminal victimization, especially violent victimization, involves far more than a brief event for the victim. After the offense, the victim, and often his or her family and friends, try to resolve a series of physical, psychological, financial, and legal problems. Even the simplest questions may seem monumental: Do I call the police? Seek medical care? Get counseling?[111] The experiences of victimized children can affect their adult lives, and elderly victims tend to be more vulnerable to physical injury. (For a look at the unusual manner in which one victim dealt with her victimization, see Doubletake.)

Generally, the problems crime victims experience are physical, emotional, family related, economic, or a product of the criminal justice system itself. It is indicative of victimization that police officers are instructed to understand the "three major needs" of crime victims: the need to feel safe; the need to express emotions; and the need to know what comes next in terms of the criminal justice system, the victim's worries for his or her family, and economic costs of the offense.[112] In this section, we will consider each of these problems.

Physical Trauma

Physical injury, usually the first type of trauma we associate with being a crime victim, is more obvious than psychological or financial injury. Physical injury is easier than psychological injury for police, judges, and juries to empathize with and for doctors to treat or at least define. Generally, injury rates

DOUBLETAKE

A Victim with a Twist

An 80-year-old woman was getting into her car in a Baltimore parking garage when two teenage boys attacked her. A 13-year-old boy blocked the car door, and a 15-year-old boy hit her in the face hard enough to give her a black eye. She screamed as they pulled her from the car and threw her into a concrete pillar.[113]

What the teens did not know is that Councilwoman Rochelle "Ricky" Spector was not an ordinary 80-year-old woman. Instead of seeking vengeance, Spector decided to help them by becoming their advocate. With the help of a team of non-profit workers, mentors, and coaches, Spector worked with the teens during and after their house arrest to improve their school attendance, grades, and peer relationships. Both teens were placed under house arrest, and the 13-year-old spent two months in a juvenile rehabilitation facility.[114]

The non-profit organization UEmpower of Maryland was instrumental in forging a relationship between Spector and the two teens. UEmpower's programs provide food, job training, and work opportunities to the youths of southwest Baltimore.[115] In the neighborhood where the teens come from, nearly half the families live below the poverty line. The 13-year-old lived in a house without electricity and seldom attended school.[116]

In working with Spector and the two teens, Michelle Suazo, the co-founder and vice president of UEmpower, said, "We went to court not to say they shouldn't be punished, but to see if there was some way we could find a solution. They need to stay busy. They need to stay engaged. Our goal was to be louder than the streets. If you're not there every day, the streets just call the kids in at a very early age."[117]

The change in the youths' behavior has been noticeable. By showing them that the system is not just trying to punish them but also to improve their lives, the two teens have exhibited a new attitude toward the future. The older one has said, "I just started busting my school work out. My grades started going up and up and up. I don't hang around the people I was doing that dumb stuff with. I hang around with whole new people who don't even live on this side of town. So my life, it just turned around."[118]

THINK ABOUT IT

1. Do you believe that you could forgive your attackers and spend your time and energy attempting to turn their lives around?
2. How might the juvenile justice system better engage victims of crime and ensure that they understand the problems that plague our cities?

are higher among the young, the impoverished, city dwellers, blacks, Hispanics, and American Indians. Injury rates tend to be lower among the elderly, the wealthy, the educated, and people who are married or widowed. Victims of intimate-partner violence are more likely to be injured than people victimized by acquaintances or strangers.[119]

Victims may sustain physical injury from abuse inflicted by the offender or from resisting the offense. Some research has shown that resistance reduces both the chance and severity of injury, with forceful tactics being the most successful.[120] Relatively few victims fight off their attackers with a weapon. According to one government study, only 1.3 percent of victims who took self-protective measures counter-attacked with a weapon. Most simply resisted or somehow captured the offender (22.3 percent), talked the offender out of the attack (12.7 percent), or ran away or hid (16.2 percent).[121]

Psychological Trauma and Fear of Crime

It is normal for victims, especially those of violent offenses, to experience psychological and emotional problems. The four indicators of psychological issues are depression, posttraumatic stress disorder (PTSD), anger, and anxiety; violent crime victims typically experience higher levels of these symptoms. Such trauma is usually increased by subsequent victimizations.[122] Victims of even minor offenses can experience psychological trauma. One study of identity theft victims, especially those whose cases were unresolved, showed that they experienced increased psychological and even physical distress. The longer the case went unresolved, the more stress the victim experienced.[123]

Some criminological literature differentiates between "concrete" and "abstract" fear of crime. Concrete fear of crime is an individual's personal fear that he or she may be the victim of a criminal offense. Abstract fear of crime is concerned with the effect crime is having on communities and society in general. Research has found that heightened concrete and abstract fear of crime following victimization was more likely after recent, direct victimization, repeat direct victimizations (for instance, a second burglary occurring weeks after an initial burglary), and multiple victimizations. Indirect victimization—the victimization of friends, family, co-workers, neighbors, and so on—influenced concrete, but not abstract, fear of crime.[124]

Julie Dombo celebrates her first full day with her new electronic hands with her husband, John. Julie's hands and feet had to be amputated after she was shot during a robbery. Can robbery victims do anything to prevent being hurt or killed?

Still other research has found that not only victimization, but also high social disorder (imagine a run-down neighborhood) predicted fear of crime. A factor that affected this fear of crime, however, was perceived risk or how safe individuals feel. A person who feels safe in his or her neighborhood fears crime less. This relationship is not as simple as it sounds. *Feeling* safe and *being* safe are two different things. Someone may feel safe but not actually be safe. Alternatively, a person may be quite safe but not feel safe. For example, one study found that females tend to be more afraid of crime than males because they feel they are at greater risk of victimization. The study suggested that fear of crime can be reduced by community initiatives that increase social trust and improve neighborhood ties. Neighbors who know and trust one another are likely to have less fear of crime.[125]

Family Trauma

Victims' families may be distressed about the event and the victim's feelings, or about his or her being unable to work, being injured, or suffering posttraumatic stress or depression. Distress may also arise from significant loss of possessions or money through, for example, arson or fraud. The ultimate trauma occurs when a family member is murdered.

In the last 30 years, more than 500,000 people have been murdered in the United States, which makes the number of affected families and friends quite a bit larger than half a million. It is difficult, if not impossible, to completely move on after such an event. Two-thirds of survivors still felt significant distress five years later and were more likely than the direct victims of less serious offenses to exhibit post-traumatic stress symptoms for the rest of their lives.[126]

Survivors typically describe their grief as "intense, persistent, and inescapable," which increases with the perceived intentionality and viciousness of the murder. They are more anxious about their own safety and that of relatives and friends.[127] Appetite and sleep problems, gastrointestinal and cardiovascular disorders, and poor immune response are all symptomatic of survivors' distress. It is not uncommon for immediate relatives to die within a few years of the murder: men tend to suffer heart disease and early death, and women become anxious and depressed.[128] Ethnically or socially marginal families, or those engaged in antisocial activities themselves, receive little or no support from their communities, which may feel that the victim "deserved it" and the families should "get over it."[129]

Economic Trauma

Victimization can be expensive. Aside from economic losses stemming directly from the offense, such as in a robbery or burglary, the victim may also have to pay for medical care, mental health care, property repair, and some types of legal proceedings. Medical bills, even with insurance, can be crushing, and some injuries are permanent and can result in job loss. Property and money are often unrecoverable.[130] Identity theft victims not only are victims but may also be mistaken for offenders. One identity thief wrote checks on a bank account opened in the victim's name. The victim was arrested when the checks bounced and had to pay $1,500 bail and $5,000 for a lawyer.[131]

Generally, the less money a victim has, the more likely it is that he or she will be victimized and the more difficult it is to recover economically. Crime can also wreak indirect economic damage by affecting property values in neighborhoods where crime rates are highest. Although we can ask which came first—the impoverished neighborhood or the crime—the result is the same. Everyone who can afford to leave a crime-affected neighborhood does, and property values plummet for those who remain.[132]

Legal Trauma

The legal proceedings that sometimes follow victimization, such as a suspect's trial, have often been described as "secondary victimization" because of stress the victim (or victim's family) endures during the process. The most common victim reaction to secondary victimization is bewilderment and frustration. Some victims have reported that the legal proceedings harmed them more than the offense.[133] The mere expectation of secondary victimization keeps many victims from reporting offenses because the legal proceedings are not "worth it." Other research has found that innovations like victim-impact statements, compensation, and counseling have not improved victims' satisfaction with the criminal justice process.[134]

Secondary victimization is perhaps most associated with rape trials. Before the passage of rape shield laws (statutes that limit the introduction of evidence about a victim's sexual conduct), victims were often subjected to intense and humiliating personal inquiries by the defense. Sometimes, victims suffered insensitive treatment by the criminal justice system. In one case, a sexual assault victim was waiting in a large, crowded room in a courthouse to give testimony. As the bailiff retrieved witnesses, the woman realized that her suspected assailant was sitting next to her.[135]

The police are an especially important element in the prevention of secondary victimization. A study of rape victims found that when police were courteous and showed interest, victims were less likely to be traumatized by further criminal justice proceedings.[136] Still, statistics indicate that only about half of violent offenses and a little less than half of property offenses are reported. This is unfortunate because some research shows that participation in the criminal justice process helps some victims by encouraging their sense of "justice being done."[137]

Many victims feel the criminal justice system will not deal with the offenders harshly enough. After the stress of a trial, many victims find out that the rapist sentenced to 10 years was out in 7, the robber sentenced to 8 years was released in 4, and the murderer sentenced to 16 years got out in 8.[138] Murder cases present especially heartbreaking problems for victims. A registered nurse writing about helping homicide survivors details the problem eloquently:

> Where sufficient evidence permits charges to be filed against the alleged killer, family members find that the 'state' is the victim, not their loved one; in fact, their loved one's name is rarely used during the proceedings. Family members often are excluded from the courtroom, either on the pretext they may be called as witnesses or because of the fear their emotional reactions might somehow

influence the jury. In cases where there is insufficient evidence for the jury to find the defendant guilty, the family may feel even more anguish, helplessness, and rage that their loved one's killer was not brought to justice. Plea bargaining may bring additional frustration to family members. Even if the perpetrator is found guilty, surviving family members may find the sentence wasn't long enough or that the sentence given was not the sentence actually served.[139]

SPECIAL VICTIMS: CHILDREN, THE ELDERLY, AND THE DISABLED

Children, the elderly, and the disabled are typically mentally and physically dependent and provide easy targets for abuse and financial exploitation by caregivers as well as strangers. Because they may have limited communication skills and ability to travel, they may be cut off from anyone who can intervene, report the victimization, or get help.

Children. The risk of violent victimization is greatest during youth, especially from late adolescence to early adulthood.[140] Routine or extreme victimization can interfere with the maturation process, damaging the child's socialization and psychological development, eventually producing an adult who is paranoid, anxious, and unable to cope. Violent victimization in particular undermines the child's confidence, educational and future socioeconomic achievement, and perceptions of how society is supposed to work. It also increases the child's risk of later involvement in crime and antisocial activities.[141]

Much of the literature on child victimization addresses child abuse, which is defined as victimization or neglect by adults. However, because of the increase in fatal school violence since the 1990s, the subject of bullying—the victimization of children by other children—has received more attention. Still, most child victimizations, whether abuse or bullying, are not reported to police, and many are not reported to any authority, including parents. There are several basic reasons for this.

1. The child or parent may not define the offense as serious or as a criminal offense.
2. The child may not want to involve parents or school officials, or the parent may not want to involve police.
3. The child may not want his or her autonomy infringed.
4. The child or parent may have emotional issues or antisocial attitudes.
5. The parent may not want to spend time or money dealing with the issue.[142]

Finally, it is difficult to prosecute cases in which children are victims or witnesses. Sometimes adults have difficulty testifying and facing an alleged victimizer; the task is much more difficult for children, who may suffer lasting effects. Courts can help by shielding children behind screens, having them testify via closed-circuit television or videotape, or excluding from the courtroom anyone without a direct interest in the case.[143]

The Elderly. Of all age groups, the elderly are the least likely to be victimized by street crime, although they fear it the most. It is possible that because the elderly probably take greater precautions against it, they are the least victimized. When it does happen, victimization is much more serious than it is for younger people. An elderly person who is assaulted and robbed is much more likely to need medical care, end up in a nursing home or other institutionalized care, or even die.[144] Unfortunately, the elderly may have the most to fear from their own families and caretakers.

In the past 20 years, the number of reported cases of domestic elder abuse has greatly increased. Physical victimization most commonly occurs at the hands of an adult child, spouse, or sibling. The typical victim is a woman over 70 and in poor health. Abusive sons are more likely to commit assault and financial victimization; abusive daughters are more likely to commit neglect or emotional

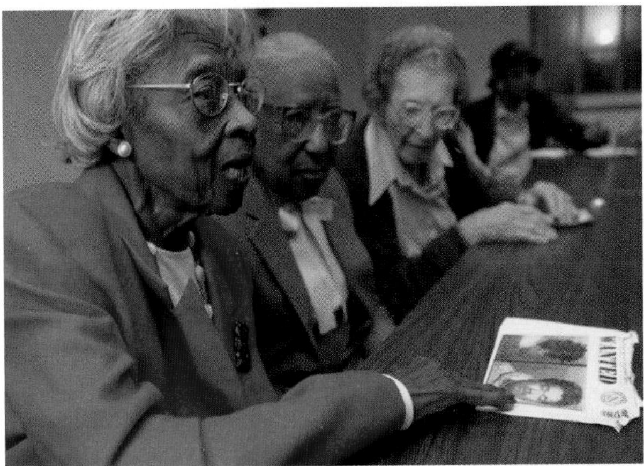

Nellie, 80, speaks to fellow support group members in Philadelphia. Nellie was a victim of a scam that she reported to the Crimes Against Elderly and Retired Unit, a police unit that focuses on criminal offenses committed against elderly persons. Why are the elderly not only more vulnerable to crime but also more affected by it than younger citizens?

abuse.[145] Home health aides or nursing home staff may also be abusive.

Financial victimization often goes uninvestigated because no one reports it. Victims may not know or understand what is happening, or they may fear the perpetrator, who is often someone they know.[146] Elders exploited by a stranger may not report it because they do not want family members to find out for fear of losing financial independence. Finally, elderly victims may think nothing can be done and thus may be willing to let the offense go.[147]

The Disabled. Like the elderly and children, disabled people are often under the care of others who may be family or staff in an institution, and the abuse can take many forms. In one incident, a woman who was responsible for the care of her developmentally disabled sister, including receiving her sister's Social Security checks, forced her sister into prostitution. The perpetrator solicited customers online and told her sister that if she did not cooperate, she would be returned to a group home. The victimization was revealed only when the perpetrator called police to complain about harassment by neighbors who complained about the prostitution.[148]

This example is typical of the victimization the developmentally disabled face: They may fear their caretakers, who threaten them with institutionalization; they may be exploited financially and physically; and they may be unable or afraid to report the abuse. The victimizer may be the victim's sole caretaker, so if the victimizer is incarcerated, the victim's situation may worsen with transfer to an institution or group home. An Australian study found that although all disabled adults were as likely as non-disabled adults to report victimization, intellectually disabled adults often reported victimization to a caregiver who did not report it to police.[149]

Like the elderly, the developmentally disabled are in more danger from relatives and caretakers than from strangers. Victimization may occur at any age and via any type of offense. However, there is somewhat less risk of property offenses, possibly because the developmentally disabled own so little property.[150] Disabled children were more likely than other children to suffer physical abuse resulting in injury, as well as severe sexual abuse, with the risks of sexual abuse increasing with higher levels of disability.[151] One study of developmentally disabled murder victims found that of those who could be identified by age and sex, the typical victim was a boy less than four years of age, with more than half being age 14 or younger. Generally, such murders were carried out by simple neglect, followed by burning, beating, shooting, or asphyxia.[152]

PAUSE AND REVIEW

1. **List the five types of trauma that crime victims may experience.**
2. **Discuss how special victims of crimes such as children, the elderly, and the disabled are differently affected by victimization.**

Getting Help for Victims

LEARNING OBJECTIVE | 5

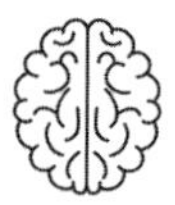

Identify the reasons for rendering better assistance to victims.

LEARNING OBJECTIVE | 6

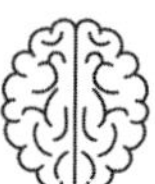

Describe three ways in which the criminal justice system tries to satisfy victims' need for justice.

The benefits to society of assisting crime victims are as great as they are for rehabilitating offenders (see Policy Implications). Unfortunately, both initiatives tend to be neglected in favor of prosecuting and punishing offenders. Victimology seeks to focus attention on an overlooked but important element of the crime equation: rendering better assistance to victims. There are a few practical reasons for this.

- Recovery is costly and time consuming. Violent-crime victims have an increased risk for physical and mental health problems. Receiving help soon after an offense reduces this risk and the intensity of any problems that do develop. With better help, victims can continue to provide for their families and be active in society.
- The criminal justice system needs victims' help. Victims often have valuable information that can help police catch suspects, help courts deal with defendants, and help the corrections system control convicted offenders. It is difficult, sometimes impossible, for prosecutors to prepare cases without victim cooperation. Parole boards also need information from victims to decide which offenders may be released.
- Helping victims increases public confidence in the criminal justice system. Victims who return to their communities with "horror stories" about

POLICY IMPLICATIONS

Putting Victims First

Considering victims as primary actors in the criminal justice process allows for the development of more effective policy. The emphasis on victims' concerns is both desirable and necessary because it addresses some of the imbalances in the amount of resources devoted to victims as opposed to offenders. Specifically, the following concerns may be addressed after the criminal justice system focuses on the harm done to victims.

- Restoring faith in the criminal justice system. Victims of crime, particularly violent crime, who are kept in the dark about the progress of the case, who see offenders sent to treatment programs, and who have little input into sentencing tend to lose faith in the criminal justice process. This loss of faith can have cascading effects. Some victims may no longer report crime, thus leaving offenders free to victimize others.
- Reducing vigilante activity. Some victims may try to take justice into their own hands. Instead of calling the police to deal with crime, victims may attempt to enact their own street justice. They may kill the burglars who break into their houses, beat up the teenagers who bully their children, or attack the drug dealers who conduct business near the playground. Although some people might see these actions as justifiable efforts to deal with crime, they are actually criminal offenses that reduce the effectiveness of the police and the courts.
- Restoring the relationship between victims and offenders. Often, the victim has a relationship with the offender, who may be a neighbor, a family member, or a schoolmate. If such relationships are to continue, it is desirable not only to ensure that the offender is corrected and the victim receives justice, but also that their relationship is repaired. Sometimes this means a parent going to family therapy to learn effective parenting skills or schoolmates resolving their differences through structured mediation. By focusing on victims' concerns in this way, future victimization can be averted.
- Developing more victim programs. A range of victim programs may be introduced into most jurisdictions. Common programs are rape crisis centers and victim-witness programs that help victims deal with the bureaucracies of the court system. Other services try to recover restitution from the offenders in the forms of community service or fines.

Policies that recognize the victim as an important part of the criminal justice process can go a long way toward restoring community to crime-ravaged areas. Victims are more than statistics. They are at the heart of what the criminal justice system should be concerned with. Their voices need to be heard, their injuries addressed, and their faith in the criminal justice system restored.

THINK ABOUT IT

1. What are some possible results of the criminal justice system addressing the harm done to victims?
2. Why is it important to recognize the victim as an important part of the criminal justice process?

the criminal justice system make other victims less likely to report offenses and follow through with prosecutions. Poor treatment of victims can even breed contempt for the law if the community believes the system does not care.[153]

Victims' Rights

The Crime Victims' Rights Act states that the federal government will try to accord victims of federal offenses the following rights:

- The right to be reasonably protected from the accused.
- The right to reasonable, accurate, and timely notice of any public court or parole proceeding about the offense or any release or escape of the accused.
- The right not to be excluded from any such public court proceeding, unless the court, after receiving clear and convincing evidence, determines that victim testimony would be materially altered if the victim heard other testimony.
- The right to be reasonably heard at any public proceeding in the district court concerning release, plea, or sentencing, or any parole proceeding.
- The reasonable right to confer with the attorney for the government in the case.
- The right to full and timely restitution as provided by law.

- The right to proceedings free of unreasonable delay.
- The right to be treated with fairness and respect for the victim's dignity and privacy.[154]

All states provide victims some variation of these rights, although they differ in who is eligible and what rights are provided. All states provide for compensation rights, notification of court appearances, and submission of a pre-sentencing **victim-impact statement**, a communication to the court by those directly affected by an offense that states the personal effects of the offense. About 40 percent of the states extend these, and sometimes other, rights to all victims; some states extend these and other rights only to victims of violent offenses. Most states provide the right to restitution, to attend sentencing hearings, and to consult with officials before offers of pleas or release of defendants.[155]

To educate criminal justice agencies and the public, victims' rights compliance programs in more than a dozen states conduct training seminars, provide information and referrals to other victim services, and take complaints from victims who believe their rights have been violated.[156]

All states have a crime victim compensation program. Programs that accept federal funding must follow federal guidelines. This makes victim compensation programs uniform from state to state. According to the National Center for Victims of Crime, violent offense victims who report in a timely fashion and cooperate with investigation and prosecution may have some offense-related expenses paid, such as uninsured medical and counseling expenses, some lost wages, and funeral costs.[157]

Offender Punishment, Restorative Justice, and Victim-Impact Statements

Punishment, restorative justice, and victim-impact statements are three ways in which the criminal justice system attempts to satisfy victims' need for justice. One motive for punishing offenders is to satisfy victims' and society's urge for **retribution**, or "just deserts"—the idea that any punishment proportional to the offense is just. **Restorative justice**, a fairly new practice, seeks to resolve some types of offenses through cooperation of the victim, offender, and justice system. Finally, as discussed above, victim-impact statements are declarations of how an offense has affected the victim.

OFFENDER PUNISHMENT

One motive for punishment is **deterrence**—the idea that punishment will prevent offenders and others from further lawbreaking. Victims often want their victimizers to be incarcerated or, if the offense is particularly violent, executed "so they can't do this to anyone else." A new trend in punishment is the payment of **restitution** to victims to compensate for loss or injury. Before the advent of criminal justice systems, the offender was often under social pressure to repay his or her offense to the victim. As such systems developed, victims were excluded in part to ensure they did not overly influence punishments. Economic penalties, such as fines, then became payable to the state and not the victim.[158] Modern restitution has been criticized for not being severe enough for the wealthy, who can usually easily afford it, and too severe on the impoverished, who typically cannot pay. Regardless, courts sometimes use economic sanctions because they are quantifiable. Restitution in general is becoming more popular for three reasons.

1. Justice is expensive. Law enforcement, incarceration, and the legal process are becoming so expensive that offenders are now expected to bear some costs in the form of fines and fees.
2. Concern for victims is increasing. When restitution is paid, victims at least get some material relief for their suffering.
3. Restitution is an alternative to incarceration. High costs and space shortages are making it impractical to impose long periods of incarceration, especially for nonviolent offenders.[159]

Finally, some victims may never collect. The court can order restitution, but it is difficult for an offender serving years in prison to earn the hundreds or thousands of dollars he or she is often ordered to pay. Many victims are satisfied, however, if the offender was at least held accountable in this way.

---

victim-impact statement—A communication by those directly affected by an offense to the court stating the personal effects of the offense.

restorative justice—A form of resolving offenses that emphasizes repairing the harm done by crime through cooperation of the victim, offender, and justice system.

deterrence—The idea that punishment for an offense will prevent that offender and others from further breaking the law.

restitution—Money paid to compensate for loss or injury.

At the other end of the punishment spectrum is execution. Most victims are happy to see offenders go to prison. In the case of murder, however, some families want the offenders and their families to suffer as much as they have. Studies have noted that in some capital cases, victims' families say they forgive the offenders and have empathy for the offenders' families and for the offenders' life troubles, but still support the offenders' execution.[160] There is wide debate about whether witnessing an offender's execution can help families deal with the loss of a relative. One study found that no families who witnessed the execution of their loved ones' killers regretted it.[161]

RESTORATIVE JUSTICE

Restorative justice was developed in New Zealand and Canada in an effort to deal with the overwhelming number of indigenous youths in the criminal justice system. The idea was that the youths might respond better to their families and tribal leaders than to the legal system. Having the youths directly face their victims and the consequences of their offenses has meant that fewer go to prison as adults.[162]

Good results have led to the spread of restorative justice practices to other legal systems around the world, and victims have benefited (see Theory to Practice). A study conducted in the Czech Republic found that compensation, acknowledgment, punishment, and forgiveness tend to ameliorate victims' desire for retribution.[163] In 2009, Canada enacted the "Apology Act," which holds that apologies cannot be used as an admission of fault, guilt, or legal responsibility.[164] Research has shown that offenders are more likely to admit their wrongs, apologize, and reaffirm their moral obligations to the community if they are not held legally responsible.[165] Other evidence suggests that offenders often want to apologize, and victims want to hear that apology. The apology directly addresses the offense, which may reduce recidivism and help victims feel empowered in the criminal justice process.[166]

VICTIM-IMPACT STATEMENTS

Commonly heard at sentencing, the victim-impact statement is a way for victims to participate in the criminal justice process. If the victim is unable to make the statement, the victim's survivors, the parent

THEORY TO PRACTICE
Who Owns a Crime?

Crime victims often feel left out of the criminal justice system. Although victims are the ones who suffer, the state, working through the prosecutor, can "take the crime away" from the victim. The prosecutor must make several decisions based on the strength of the case, the workload of the office, and the court system's punishment philosophy. The prosecutor changes the nature of the case to one in which society is the victim, and society decides what will happen to the accused. However, criminologist Nils Christie has argued that victims should be brought back into the system because they are part owners of the conflict that resulted in their victimization.

This perspective, practiced by the restorative justice movement, seeks to allow victims and offenders to work out their differences in a less formal arena than court. According to Christie, this personalized encounter with the offender has been taken away from victims:

> The victim is so totally out of the case that he has no chance, ever, to come to know the offender. We leave them outside, angry, maybe humiliated through a cross-examination in court, without any contact with the offender. He will need all the classical stereotypes around "the criminal" to get a grasp on the whole thing. Of course, he will go away more frightened than ever, more in need than ever of an explanation of criminals as non-human.[167]

The idea of a conflict as something that victims partly own returns the victim to the justice equation. The case is no longer the offender versus the state but rather the offender versus the victim, the state, and the community. When all parties are included in the resolution, it is more likely that not only will everyone be satisfied, but also that the underlying causes of the conflict can be addressed and harm repaired.

THINK ABOUT IT

1. What do we mean by the idea of conflict as something that victims partly own?
2. How does the traditional criminal justice process leave out the victim?

Kathy Branson, mother of murder victim Kianna Jackson, stands with Jackson's grandmother, Diane Menzies, as she delivers a victim-impact statement during the sentencing of Steven Dean Gordon. Gordon was sentenced to death for the murders of Kianna Jackson, 20, Josephine Vargas, 34, Martha Anaya, 28, and Jarrae Estepp, 21. Authorities say Gordon and another sex offender, Franc Cano, abducted four women with ties to prostitution and had sex with their victims before killing them. Why are victim-impact statements allowed in the sentencing phase of court cases?

or guardian of a juvenile victim, or the guardian of an incompetent, incapacitated, or disabled victim may do so. Every state and federal court allows victim-impact statements at sentencing, and most require that the information be included in the **pre-sentence report**, a report about an offender that is prepared by a probation officer to assist a judge in sentencing.

Victim-impact statements typically detail the effects of the offense on the victim and the victim's family, descriptions of the treatments the victim has required to recover, and the need for restitution. Some states list what information a victim-impact statement must include, and some allow the victim to state what sentence he or she believes is appropriate for the offender. Most states also allow defendants to contest the veracity of the victim-impact statement information, and a few states allow cross-examination of victims.[168]

Some states allow victim-impact statements in capital cases, which are typically introduced in the sentencing phase. Some critics argue that the emotional content of victim-impact statements in this context leads to harsher sentencing (capital punishment versus life in prison), a concern that some research has confirmed. In one study, test subjects who heard victim-impact statements were more likely to feel anger, hostility, and vengeance and to have unfavorable perceptions of the offender. They were also more likely to feel sympathy and empathy for the victim and to have favorable perceptions of the victim and victim's family, feelings that were related to a greater chance of them imposing the death penalty.[169] An earlier study, however, found that victim-impact statements did not substantially affect the court's acceptance of either aggravating or mitigating factors that may affect sentencing. Indeed, sentencing in cases with victim-impact statements was more likely to be lenient if the offender was intellectually disabled, had been hospitalized for mental illness, was schizophrenic, or had been sexually abused as a child.[170]

pre-sentence report—A report about an offender's personal details and history that is prepared by a probation officer to assist a judge in sentencing.

PAUSE AND REVIEW

1. **Describe how victim-impact statements give crime victims a voice in criminal justice proceedings.**
2. **Show how restorative justice is an alternative to the usual criminal justice process.**
3. **Discuss the provisions of the Crime Victims' Rights Act.**
4. **Construct a list of reasons why restitution is a popular remedy for crime victims.**

FOCUS ON ETHICS Protecting the Victim

You and your two brothers grew up in an abusive household. Your father had chronic problems with drugs and alcohol, which resulted in long periods of unemployment and shorter periods in and out of jail and prison. He would come home drunk and assault your mother, beat up your brothers, and occasionally sexually abuse you. You hated your father, and your sexual victimization only stopped when you were 13, when your oldest brother intervened and punched your father in the mouth and broke his jaw. Your father returned to prison for violating his parole by assaulting you, and you were able to turn your life around, graduate from a good university, and find a job in publishing where you quickly rose to the position of executive editor.

You now have a dilemma. Your older brother and protector is now exhibiting many of the same behaviors as your father. He drinks too much, dabbles in hard drugs, and is verbally abusive toward his wife. He barely graduated from high school and entered the military where he became a decorated combat veteran, but he was eventually discharged under less-than-honorable conditions because of substance abuse and fighting. You are convinced that he suffers from PTSD, but he refuses to seek help.

Yesterday, his wife came to you pleading for your assistance. She claims your brother is constantly intoxicated and that he is now physically abusing her. She claims he has threatened to kill both her and himself. You believe her, but you are torn about to what to do.

You love your brother and feel greatly indebted to him for protecting you in your time of need. You feel an obligation to protect him now. But you know you also need to help your sister-in-law.

What Do You Do?

1. Tell your sister-in-law to be nice to your brother and not provoke him in the hope that he will stop his abusive behavior.
2. Talk to your brother and try to convince him that his abusive behavior toward his wife is similar to the behavior your father exhibited.
3. Encourage your sister-in-law to go to the police and take out a restraining order against your brother.
4. Contract the Veterans' Administration to see if there is a counseling program to help with veterans who are experiencing PTSD.
5. Call the police yourself and try to have him arrested.

Summary

LEARNING OBJECTIVE 1 Define victimology.	Victimology is the study of the harm that people suffer as a result of crime.
LEARNING OBJECTIVE 2 Compare macro-victimization and micro-victimization.	Macro-victimization is the consideration of large masses of people as victims of singular, large-scale criminal offenses. The types of groups responsible for civilian victimization during civil wars and some types of domestic terrorism can be classified as organized armies, paramilitary forces, and criminal groups. Corporate and environmental offenses can be wide ranging in terms of geography and time, and some offenses may affect whole nations, or even continents or hemispheres, for decades. Crimes against humanity typically stem from some form of government against a civilian population. Micro-victimization best describes individual street-crime victimization. Victims of street and small-scale crime in other countries are subject to the criminal justice systems and laws of their individual countries.
LEARNING OBJECTIVE 3 List the problems of victimization.	The problems of crime victims can be typified as physical, emotional, family related, economic, or caused by the criminal justice system.
LEARNING OBJECTIVE 4 Tell why the children, the elderly, and the disabled are particularly vulnerable to victimization.	Children, the elderly, and the disabled are especially vulnerable to victimization because they are typically mentally and physically dependent and thus provide easy targets for abuse and financial exploitation by caregivers and strangers.

LEARNING OBJECTIVE 5 Identify the reasons for rendering better assistance to victims.	Reasons for rendering better assistance to victims include improved victim recovery, the need for victims' help in addressing crime, and increased public confidence in the criminal justice system.
LEARNING OBJECTIVE 6 Describe three ways in which the criminal justice system tries to satisfy victims' need for justice.	Punishment, restorative justice, and victim-impact statements are three ways in which the criminal justice system attempts to satisfy victims' need for justice.

Critical Reflections

1. **What is important about the relationship between murder victims and offenders?**
2. **Give several reasons that adult rape victims of both sexes have difficulty being considered as victims.**
3. **Describe some of the problems of victimization.**
4. **What kinds of decisions must victims (or their families) face after an offense?**
5. **Assess the argument that there is a "victim industry."**
6. **Do you agree that some victims precipitate their own victimization? Why or why not?**
7. **Do children, the elderly, and disabled individuals deserve more protections from crime than the rest of us?**
8. **In what ways do victim-impact statements serve the interests of justice and the victim?**
9. **Why are some criminal offenses committed by terrorist organizations considered to be crimes against humanity?**
10. **How do restorative justice programs differ from traditional criminal justice programs in addressing victims' needs?**

Key Terms

arson p. 59
assault p. 58
burglary p. 59
deterrence p. 72
felony p. 63
human trafficking p. 65
larceny/theft p. 59
macro-victimization p. 60
micro-victimization p. 54
murder p. 55
pre-sentence report p. 74
rape p. 56
restitution p. 72
restorative justice p. 72
retribution p. 72
robbery p. 58
situated transaction p. 60
transnational crime p. 65
victim p. 53
victim-impact statement p. 72
victimology p. 53
victim precipitation p. 59

Instant Recall Term

intimate-partner violence (ch. 2)

Notes

1 Nicole Chavez, "What Others Knew: Culture of Denial Protected Nassar for Years," CNN, January 25, 2018, https://www.cnn.com/2018/01/23/us/nassar-sexual-abuse-who-knew/index.html. Accessed April 2018.
2 Carla Correa and Meghan Louttit, "More Than 160 Women Say Larry Nassar Sexually Abused Them. Here Are His Accusers in Their Own Words," *New York Times*, January 24, 2018, https://www.nytimes.com/interactive/2018/01/24/sports/larry-nassar-victims.html. Accessed April 2018.
3 Alice Park, "Aly Raisman Opens Up about Sexual Abuse by USA Gymnastics Doctor Larry Nassar," *TIME*, November 13, 2017, http://time.com/5020885/aly-raisman-sexual-abuse-usa-gymnastics-doctor-larry-nassar. Accessed April 2018.
4 Tim Evans, Mark Alesia, and Marisa Kwiatkowski, "Former USA Gymnastics Doctor Accused of Abuse," *IndyStar*, https://www.indystar.com/story/news/2016/09/12/former-usa-gymnastics-doctor-accused-abuse/89995734. Accessed April 2018.
5 Rachael Denhollander. "Rachael Denhollander: The Price I Paid for Taking on Larry Nassar," *New York Times* January 26, 2018, https://www.nytimes.com/2018/01/26/opinion/sunday/larry-nassar-rachael-denhollander.html?smid=tw-share&mtrref=t.co&assetType=opinion. Evans, Alesia, and Kwiatkowski, "Former USA Gymnastics Doctor Accused of Abuse." Accessed April 2018.
6 Carla Correa and Meghan Louttit, "More Than 160 Women Say Larry Nassar Sexually Abused Them," *New York Times*, January 24, 2018, https://www.nytimes.com/interactive/2018/01/24/sports/larry-nassar-victims.html. Accessed April 2018.
7 Chris Chavez, "Larry Nassar Addresses Victims after 156 Women Share Stories of Abuse," *Sports Illustrated*, January 24, 2018, https://www.si.com/olympics/2018/01/24/larry-nassar-statement-sentencing-156-women-abused-usa-gymnastics-michigan-state. Accessed April 2018.
8 Dan Murphy, "Four New Complaints Filed Against Larry Nassar, Including One Dating to '92," ESPN, April 19, 2017, http://www.espn.com/olympics/story/_/id/19191934/new-complaints-larry-nassar-allege-sexual-abuse-dates-1992. Accessed April 2018.
9 Julie Mack and Emily Lawler, "MSU Doctor's Alleged Victims Talked for 20 Years. Was Anyone Listening?" *MLive*, February 8, 2017, http://www.mlive.com/news/index.ssf/page/msu_doctor_alleged_sexual_assault.html. Kim Kozlowski, "What MSU Knew," *Detroit News*, January 2018, https://www.detroitnews.com/story/tech/2018/01/18/msu-president-told-nassar-complaint-2014/1042071001. Accessed April 2018.
10 Matt Mencarini, "Larry Nassar Indicted on Federal Child Porn Charges," *Lansing State Journal*, December 16, 2016, https://www.lansingstatejournal.com/story/news/local/2016/12/16/attorney-larry-nassar-arrested-federal-officials/95529364. Accessed April 2018.
11 *IndyStar*, "Out of Balance," http://interactives.indystar.com/news/standing/OutOfBalanceSeries/index2.html. Accessed March 2018.
12 Christopher Haxel and Matt Mencarini, "MSU Fires Doctor Facing Sexual Assault Allegations," *Lansing State Journal*, September 20, 2016, https://www.lansingstatejournal.com/story/news/local/2016/09/20/msu-fires-doctor-facing-sexual-assault-allegations/90734818. Accessed April 2018.
13 Ralph Ellis, "Larry Nassar Transferred to Federal Prison in Arizona," CNN, February 10, 2018, https://www.cnn.com/2018/02/10/us/larry-nassar-transferred-to-tucson-prison/index.html. Accessed April 2018.
14 William G. Doerner and Steven P. Lab, *Victimology*, 5th ed. (Newark, N.J.: Matthew Bender & Company, 2008). See Chapter 1.
15 Andrew Karmen, *Crime Victims: An Introduction to Victimology*, 6th ed. (Belmont, Calif.: Thomson Wadsworth, 2007), 12–13.
16 Ibid., 2.
17 Joel Best, "Victimization and the Victim Industry," *Society* 34, no. 4 (May 1997): 9–17.
18 Bureau of Justice Statistics, Data Collection: National Crime Victimization Survey (NCVS), https://www.bjs.gov/index.cfm?ty=dcdetail&iid=245. Accessed February 2018.
19 Rachel E. Morgan and Grace Kena, *Criminal Victimization, 2016* (Washington, D.C.: U.S. Department of Justice Office of Justice Programs Bureau of Justice Statistics, 2017), 1. Available at https://www.bjs.gov/index.cfm?ty=pbdetail&iid=6166. Accessed March 2018.
20 Ibid., 12.
21 Ibid., 12.
22 Ibid., 1.
23 Ibid., 5.
24 U.S. Department of Justice Office of Community Oriented Policing Services, "Bringing Victims into Community Policing," 2002, https://ric-zai-inc.com/ric.php?page=detail&id=COPS-W0016. Accessed March 2018.
25 Doerner and Lab, *Victimology*, 321.
26 Federal Bureau of Investigation, Uniform Crime Reports, *Crime in the United States: 2017*, Murder, https://ucr.fbi.gov/crime-in-the-u.s/2017/crime-in-the-u.s.-2017/topic-pages/murder. Accessed October 2018.
27 Federal Bureau of Investigation, Uniform Crime Reports, *Crime in the United States: 2017,* Table 20: Murder by State, Types of Weapons, https://ucr.fbi.gov/crime-in-the-u.s/2017/crime-in-the-u.s.-2017/topic-pages/tables/table-20. Accessed October 2018.
28 Federal Bureau of Investigation, Uniform Crime Reports, *Crime in the United States: 2017,* Expanded Homicide Data Table 1: Murder Victims by Race, Ethnicity, and Sex, https://ucr.fbi.gov/crime-in-the-u.s/2017/crime-in-the-u.s.-2017/topic-pages/tables/expanded-homicide-data-table-1.xls. Accessed October 2018.
29 Federal Bureau of Investigation, Uniform Crime Reports, *Crime in the United States, 2017,* Expanded Homicide Data Table 3: Murder Offenders by Age, Sex, Race, and Ethnicity, 2017, https://ucr.fbi.gov/crime-in-the-u.s/2017/crime-in-the-u.s.-2017/topic-pages/tables/expanded-homicide-data-table-3.xls. Accessed October 2018.
30 Federal Bureau of Investigation, Uniform Crime Reports, *Crime in the United States: 2017,* Expanded Homicide Data Table 1: Murder Victims by Race, Ethnicity, and Sex, https://ucr.fbi.gov/crime-in-the-u.s/2017/crime-in-the-u.s.-2017/topic-pages/tables/expanded-homicide-data-table-1.xls. Accessed October 2018.
31 Federal Bureau of Investigation, *Crime in the United States: 2010*, "Forcible Rape," https://ucr.fbi.gov/crime-in-the-u.s/2010/crime-in-the-u.s.-2010/violent-crime/rapemain. Accessed March 2018.
32 United States Department of Justice, Attorney General Eric Holder Announces Revisions to the Uniform Crime Reports' Definition of Rape, January 6, 2012, https://www.justice.gov/opa/pr/attorney-general-eric-holder-announces-revisions-uniform-crime-report-s-definition-rape. Accessed March 2018.
33 Federal Bureau of Investigation, *Crime in the United States: 2017,* Rape, https://ucr.fbi.gov/crime-in-the-u.s/2017/crime-in-the-u.s-2017/topic-pages/rape. Accessed October 2018.
34 Morgan and Kena, *Criminal Victimization, 2016*, Table 2, p.5.
35 Federal Bureau of Investigation, Uniform Crime Reports: *Crime in the United States, 2017,* Rape, https://ucr.fbi.gov/crime-in-the-u.s/2017/crime-in-the-u.s.-2017/topic-pages/rape. Accessed October 2018.
36 Susan Brownmiller, *Against Our Will* (New York: Simon and Schuster, 1975), 286.
37 Federal Bureau of Investigation, Uniform Crime Reports: *Crime in the United States: 2007*, Forcible Rape, https://www2.fbi.gov/ucr/cius2007/offenses/violent_crime/forcible_rape.html. Accessed March 2018.

38 Leslee R. Kassing and Loreto R. Prieto, "The Rape Myth and Blame-Based Beliefs of Counselors-in-Training Toward Male Victims of Rape," *Journal of Counseling and Development* 81 no. 4 (Fall 2003): 455–461; "Police Learn Skills in Dealing with Male Rape Victims," *Nursing Standard* 19, no. 6 (October 20, 2004): 9; Sandesh Sivakumaran, "Male/Male Rape and the 'Taint' of Homosexuality," *Human Rights Quarterly* 27, no. 4 (August 2005): 1274–1306.

39 James M. Donovan, "Combating the Sexual Abuse of Children in France, 1825–1913," *Criminal Justice History* 15 (1994): 59–93.

40 American Academy of Child and Adolescent Psychiatry, Child Sexual Abuse, March 2014, http://www.aacap.org/aacap/families_and_youth/facts_for_families/fff-guide/Child-Sexual-Abuse-009.aspx. Accessed March 2018.

41 David Finkelhor, Heather Turner, Richard Ormrod, and Sherry L. Hamby, "Violence, Abuse, and Crime Exposure in a National Sample of Children and Youth," *Pediatrics* 124, no. 5 (2009): 1414. Online at http://pediatrics.aappublications.org/content/124/5/1411. Accessed March 2018.

42 Gabriela Pérez-Fuentes, Mark Olfson, Laura Villegas, Carmen Morcillo, Shuai Wang, and Carlos Blanco, "Prevalence and Correlates of Child Sexual Abuse: A National Study," *Comprehensive Psychiatry* 54, no. 1 (January 2013): 16–27.

43 Faye M. Carlson, Jane Grassley, Janet Reis, and Kelley Davis, "Characteristics of Child Sexual Assault Within a Child Advocacy Center Client Population," *Journal of Forensic Nursing* 11, no. 1 (January 2015): 15–21.

44 Linda Greenhouse, "Justices Bar Death Penalty for the Rape of a Child," *New York Times*, June 26, 2008, A1, late edition; Warren Richey Staff, "Despite Gaffe, Supreme Court Won't Revisit Landmark Child-Rape Ruling," *Christian Science Monitor*, October 2, 2008, 25.

45 Federal Bureau of Investigation, Uniform Crime Reports: *Crime in the United States, 2017,* Table 38: Arrests by Age, https://ucr.fbi.gov/crime-in-the-u.s/2017/crime-in-the-u.s.-2017/topic-pages/tables/table-38. Accessed October 2018.

46 Richard T. Wright and Scott H. Decker, *Armed Robbers in Action: Stickups and Street Culture* (Boston: Northeastern University Press, 1997).

47 Ibid.

48 Marie Rosenkrantz Lindegaard, Wim Bernasco, and Scott Jacques, "Consequences of Expected and Observed Victim Resistance for Offender Violence During Robbery Events," *Journal of Research in Crime and Delinquency* 52, no. 1 (February 2015): 32–61.

49 Catherine A. Bourgeois and Maryanne L. Fisher, "More 'Bros,' More Woes? The Prevalence of Male Coalitions in Crimes of Robbery," *Evolutionary Behavioral Sciences* (December 14, 2017).

50 Marie Skubak Tillyer and Rob Tillyer. "Maybe I Should Do This Alone: A Comparison of Solo and Co-offending Robbery Outcomes," *JQ: Justice Quarterly* 32, no. 6 (December 2015): 1064–1088.

51 Callie Marie Rennison and Chris Melde, "Gender and Robbery: A National Test," *Deviant Behavior*, 35, no. 4 (2014): 275–296.

52 Federal Bureau of Investigation, Uniform Crime Reports, *Crime in the United States: 2017,* Aggravated Assault, https://ucr.fbi.gov/crime-in-the-u.s/2017/crime-in-the-u.s.-2017/topic-pages/aggravated-assault. Accessed October 2018.

53 Federal Bureau of Investigation, Uniform Crime Reports: *Crime in the United States: 2017,* Aggravated Assault, https://ucr.fbi.gov/crime-in-the-u.s/2017/crime-in-the-u.s.-2017/topic-pages/aggravated-assault. Accessed October 2018.

54 Federal Bureau of Investigation, Uniform Crime Reports: *Crime in the United States: 2017,* Table 38: Arrests by Age, https://ucr.fbi.gov/crime-in-the-u.s/2017/crime-in-the-u.s.-2017/topic-pages/tables/table-38. Accessed October 2018.

55 Barbara A. Oudekerk and Rachel E. Morgan, *Co-Offending Among Adolescents in Violent Victimizations, 2004–13* (Washington, D.C.: U.S. Department of Justice Office of Justice Programs Bureau of Justice Statistics, 2016), 6, 9.

56 Federal Bureau of Investigation, Uniform Crime Reports: *Crime in the United States: 2017,* "Expanded Homicide Data Table 10: Murder Circumstances by Relationship," https://ucr.fbi.gov/crime-in-the-u.s/2017/crime-in-the-u.s.-2017/topic-pages/tables/expanded-homicide-data-table-10.xls. Accessed October 2018.

57 M. C. Black, K. C. Basile, M. J. Breiding, S. G. Smith, M. L. Walters, M. T. Merrick, and J. Chen, *The National Intimate Partner and Sexual Violence Survey (NISVS): 2010 Summary Report* (Atlanta, Ga.: National Center for Injury Prevention and Control, Centers for Disease Control and Prevention, 2011), 2. Available at http://www.cdc.gov/violenceprevention/NISVS/index.html. Accessed March 2018.

58 Mary Swanton, "Victims' Rights," *Inside Counsel* 16, no. 178 (September 2006): 2–28.

59 Federal Bureau of Investigation, Uniform *Crime Reports: Crime in the United States: 2017,* Larceny-Theft, https://ucr.fbi.gov/crime-in-the-u.s/2017/crime-in-the-u.s.-2017/topic-pages/larceny-theft. Accessed October 2018.

60 Federal Bureau of Investigation, Uniform Crime Reports: *Crime in the United States: 2017,* Property Crime, https://ucr.fbi.gov/crime-in-the-u.s/2017/crime-in-the-u.s.-2017/topic-pages/property-crime. Accessed October 2018.

61 Federal Bureau of Investigation, Uniform Crime Reports: *Crime in the United States: 2017,* Burglary, https://ucr.fbi.gov/crime-in-the-u.s/2017/crime-in-the-u.s.-2017/topic-pages/burglary; Larceny-Theft, https://ucr.fbi.gov/crime-in-the-u.s/2017/crime-in-the-u.s.-2017/topic-pages/larceny-theft; Motor Vehicle Theft, https://ucr.fbi.gov/crime-in-the-u.s/2017/crime-in-the-u.s.-2017/topic-pages/motor-vehicle-theft. Accessed October 2018.

62 Mark S. Umbreit, Robert B. Coates, and Betty Vos, "Victim-Offender Mediation: Three Decades of Practice and Research," *Conflict Resolution Quarterly* 22, no. 1/2 (Fall/Winter 2004): 279–303.

63 E. A. Fattah, *Understanding Criminal Victimization: An Introduction to Theoretical Victimology* (Englewood Cliffs, N.J.: Prentice Hall, 1991), 291.

64 Lisa R. Muftic, Leana Allen Bouffard, and Jeffrey A. Bouffard, "An Exploratory Analysis of Victim Precipitation among Men and Women Arrested for Intimate Partner Violence," *Feminist Criminology* 2, no. 4 (October 2007): 327–346.

65 Kansas Safe Schools Resource Center, http://community.ksde.org/Default.aspx?tabid=3913. Accessed March 2018.

66 David F. Luckenbill, "Criminal Homicide as a Situated Transaction," *Social Problems* 25, no. 2 (December 1977): 176–186.

67 Doerner and Lab, *Victimology*, 330–31.

68 William Gibson, "Panther Modern's Eyes," October 31, 2004, http://www.williamgibsonbooks.com/blog/2004_10_01_archive.asp. Accessed March 2018.

69 Haya Itzhaky and Rachel Dekel, "Helping Victims of Terrorism: What Makes Social Work Effective?" *Social Work* 50, no. 4 (October 2005): 335–343.

70 Arnold A.P. van Emmerik, Jan H. Kamphuis, Alexander M. Hulsbosch, and Paul M. G. Emmelkamp, "Single Session Debriefing after Psychological Trauma: A Metaanalysis," *Lancet* 360, no. 9335 (September 2002): 766–771.

71 United Nations Office on Drugs and Crime, Good Practices in Supporting Victims of Terrorism Within the Criminal Justice Framework, 2015, https://www.unodc.org/unodc/en/terrorism/news-and-events/victims-of-terrorism.html. Accessed March 2018.

72 U.S. Department of Justice, International Terrorism Victim Expense Reimbursement Program, https://ovc.gov/itverp. Accessed March 2018.

73 Federal Bureau of Investigation, Victim Assistance, https://www.fbi.gov/resources/victim-assistance. Accessed March 2018.

74 United States Victims of State Sponsored Terrorism Fund, http://www.usvsst.com. Accessed March 2018.

75 September 11th Victim Compensation Fund, https://www.vcf.gov/genProgramInfo.html. Accessed March 2018.

76 National Consortium for the Study of Terrorism and Responses to Terrorism, *Annex of Statistical Information: Country Reports on Terrorism 2016*, Incidents of Terrorism Worldwide, Table 1, July

2017, p. 4, http://www.start.umd.edu/publication/annex-statistical-information-country-reports-terrorism-2016. Accessed March 2018.

77 OSCE and Office of Democratic Institutions and Human Rights, "High-Level Meeting on Victims of Terrorism," September 13–14, 2007, Vienna, http://www.osce.org/odihr/30781. Accessed March 2018.

78 Deepwater Horizon Oil Spill, http://response.restoration.noaa.gov/oil-and-chemical-spills/significant-incidents/deepwater-horizon-oil-spill. Accessed August 2018.

79 Ibid. Kim Cross, "The $37 Billion Oil Spill," *Outside*, March 23, 2015, http://www.outsideonline.com/1962276/37-billion-oil-spill. Accessed March 2018.

80 David Barstow, David Rohde, and Stephanie Saul, "Deepwater Horizon's Final Hours," *New York Times*, December 25, 2010, http://www.nytimes.com/2010/12/26/us/26spill.html. Accessed March 2018.

81 Bryce Hall, "Did Fireboats Sink the Oil Rig?," *Slate*, May 6, 2010, http://www.slate.com/articles/health_and_science/green_room/2010/05/did_fireboats_sink_the_oil_rig.html. Accessed March 2018.

82 Cross, "The $37 Billion Oil Spill."

83 Ibid.

84 Ibid.

85 Clifford Krauss, "Judge Accepts BP's $4 Billion Criminal Settlement over Gulf Oil Spill," *New York Times*, January 29, 2013, http://www.nytimes.com/2013/01/30/business/judge-approves-bp-criminal-settlement.html. Accessed March 2018.

86 Campbell Robertson, John Schwartz, and Richard Pérez-Peña, "BP to Pay $18.7 Billion for Deepwater Horizon Oil Spill," *New York Times*, July 2, 2015, http://www.nytimes.com/2015/07/03/us/bp-to-pay-gulf-coast-states-18-7-billion-for-deepwater-horizon-oil-spill.html. Accessed March 2018.

87 Jonathan Stempel, "No Prison Terms for Gulf Spill as Final Defendant Gets Probation," *Reuters*, April 6, 2016, http://www.reuters.com/article/us-bp-spill-sentencing-idUSKCN0X3241. Accessed March 2018. Laura Furr, "Former BP Engineer Receives Probation for Deepwater Horizon Charge," *Houston Business Journal*, April 7, 2016, http://www.bizjournals.com/houston/morning_call/2016/04/former-bp-engineer-receives-probation-for.html. Accessed March 2018.

88 Aruna Viswanatha, "U.S. Bid to Prosecute BP Staff in Gulf Oil Spill Falls Flat," *Wall Street Journal*, February 27, 2016.

89 Krauss, "Halliburton Pleads Guilty to Destroying Evidence after Gulf Spill."

90 John Schwartz, "Rig Owner Will Settle with U.S. in Gulf Spill," *New York Times*, January 3, 2013, http://www.nytimes.com/2013/01/04/business/energy-environment/transocean-settles-with-us-over-oil-spill-in-gulf-of-mexico.html. Accessed March 2018.

91 Russell Hotten, "Volkswagen: The Scandal Explained," BBC, December 10, 2015, http://www.bbc.com/news/business-34324772. Accessed March 2018.

92 Ibid.

93 Ibid.

94 U.S. Department of Justice, Volkswagen AG Sentenced in Connection with Conspiracy to Cheat U.S. Emissions Tests, April 21, 2017, https://www.justice.gov/opa/pr/volkswagen-ag-sentenced-connection-conspiracy-cheat-us-emissions-tests. Accessed March 2018.

95 Allied Control Council, 1945, cited in Daniel Maier-Katkin, Daniel P. Mears, and Thomas J. Bernard, "Towards a Criminology of Crimes against Humanity," *Theoretical Criminology* 13, no. 2 (May 2009): 227–255.

96 Rome Statute, 2002, cited in "Towards a Criminology of Crimes Against Humanity."

97 Ibid.

98 Donald L. Niewyk and Francis R. Nicosia, *The Columbia Guide to the Holocaust* (New York: Columbia University Press, 2000), 45.

99 Douglas O. Linder, "Famous Trials: Nuremberg Trial, 1945–1949," University of Missouri–Kansas City School of Law, http://www.famous-trials.com/Nuremberg. Accessed March 2018.

100 "Swiss Fund to Disburse Millions to Nazi Victims," *New York Times*, July 8, 1997, 6, http://www.nytimes.com/1997/07/08/world/swiss-fund-to-disburse-millions-to-nazi-victims.html. Accessed March 2018.

101 Stephen A. Hart, "Liberation of the Concentration Camps," BBC, http://www.bbc.co.uk/history/worldwars/wwtwo/liberation_camps_01.shtml. Accessed March 2018.

102 United Nations Report of the Independent International Commission of Inquiry on the Syrian Arab Republic, *Rule of Terror: Living under ISIS in Syria*, November 14, 2014, http://www.refworld.org/docid/5469b2e14.html. Accessed August 2018.

103 Jason Burke, "Rise and Fall of Isis: Its Dream of a Caliphate Is Over, So What Now?" *Guardian*, Oct. 21, 2017, https://www.theguardian.com/world/2017/oct/21/isis-caliphate-islamic-state-raqqa-iraq-islamist. Accessed August 2018.

104 United Nations Report of the Independent International Commission of Inquiry on the Syrian Arab Republic.

105 Ibid.

106 Ibid.

107 Ibid.

108 Jo Phoenix, "Sex Traffic: Prostitution, Crime and Exploitation/Human Traffic and Transnational Crime: Eurasian and American Perspectives," *British Journal of Criminology* 47, no. 3 (May 2007): 515–517.

109 Kevonne Small and Bruce Taylor, "State and Local Law Enforcement Response to Transnational Crime," *Trends in Organized Crime* 10, no. 2 (December 2006): 5–17.

110 Lorraine Elliott, "Transnational Environmental Crime in the Asia Pacific: An 'Un(der)securitized' Security Problem?" *Pacific Review* 20, no. 4 (December 2007): 499–522.

111 R. Barry Ruback and Martie P. Thompson, *Social and Psychological Consequences of Violent Victimization* (Thousand Oaks, Calif.: Sage, 2001), vii.

112 U.S. Department of Justice Office of Justice Programs Office for Victims of Crime, First Response to Victims of Crime, 2008, 2, https://www.ncjrs.gov/ovc_archives/reports/firstrep/welcome.html. Accessed March 2018.

113 Luke Broadwater, "Two Boys Carjacked an 80-year-old Baltimore City Councilwoman. Now She's Their Advocate," *Baltimore Sun*, January 3, 2018, http://www.baltimoresun.com/news/maryland/baltimore-city/bs-md-ci-spector-carjacking-mentoring-20171218-story.html. Accessed April 2018.

114 Ibid.

115 UEmpower of Maryland, http://uempowerofmd.org/programs. Accessed March 2018.

116 Broadwater, "Two Boys Carjacked an 80-year-old Baltimore City Councilwoman."

117 Ibid.

118 Ibid.

119 Thomas Simon, James Mercy, and Craig Perkins, *Injuries from Violent Crime, 1992–98*, (Washington, D.C.: Bureau of Justice Statistics, 2001), 1, http://www.bjs.gov/index.cfm?ty=pbdetail&iid=997. Accessed March 2018.

120 Jongyeon Tark and Gary Kleck, "Resisting Crime: The Effects of Victim Action on the Outcomes of Crimes," *Criminology* 42, no. 4 (November 2004): 861–909.

121 U.S. Department of Justice Office of Justice Programs Bureau of Justice Statistics, National Crime Victimization Survey, Criminal Victimization in the United States, 2008 Statistical Tables, Table 70, August 2011, http://www.bjs.gov/index.cfm?ty=pbdetail&iid=2218. Accessed March 2018.

122 Diane L. Green and Naelys Diaz, "Predictors of Emotional Stress in Crime Victims: Implications for Treatment," *Brief Treatment and Crisis Intervention* 7, no. 3 (August 2007): 194.

123 Tracy Sharp, Andrea Shreve-Neiger, William J. Fremouw, and Shawn Hutton, "Exploring the Psychological and Somatic Impact of Identity Theft," *Journal of Forensic Sciences* 49, no. 1 (January 2004): 131–136.

124 Silvia Russo and Michele Roccato, "How Long Does Victimization Foster Fear of Crime? A Longitudinal Study," *Journal of Community Psychology* 38, no. 8 (November 2010): 960–974.

125 Randy Gainey, Mariel Alper, and Allison T. Chappell, "Fear of Crime Revisited: Examining the Direct and Indirect Effects of Disorder, Risk Perception, and Social Capital," *American Journal of Criminal Justice* 36, no. 2 (June 2011): 120–137.
126 Neil Vincent, Joy McCormack, and Susan Johnson, "A Comprehensive Conceptual Program Model for Supporting Families Surviving a Homicide Victim," *Child and Adolescent Social Work Journal* 32, no. 1 (February 2015): 57–64.
127 Laurence Miller, "Family Survivors of Homicide: I. Symptoms, Syndromes, and Reaction Patterns," *The American Journal of Family Therapy* 37 (2009): 67–79.
128 Ibid.
129 Ibid.
130 Gary T. Engel, "Criminal Debt: Court-Ordered Restitution Amounts Far Exceed Likely Collections for the Crime Victims in Selected Financial Fraud Cases: GAO-05-80," GAO Reports (January 2005): 1.
131 David Brietkopf, "State of Va. Creates Special Cards for Crime Victims," *American Banker* 168, no. 222 (November 2003): 21A.
132 George Tita, Tricia Petras, and Robert Greenbaum, "Crime and Residential Choice: A Neighborhood Level Analysis of the Impact of Crime on Housing Prices," *Journal of Quantitative Criminology* 22, no. 4 (December 2006): 299–317.
133 Uli Orth, "Secondary Victimization of Crime Victims by Criminal Proceedings," *Social Justice Research* 15, no. 4 (December 2002): 313–325.
134 Sarah Goodrum, "Victims' Rights, Victims' Expectations, and Law Enforcement Workers' Constraints in Cases of Murder," *Law and Social Inquiry* 32, no. 3 (Summer 2007): 725–757.
135 Doerner and Lab, *Victimology*, 62.
136 R. Barry Ruback and Martie P. Thompson, *Social and Psychological Consequences of Violent Victimization* (Thousand Oaks, Calif.: Sage, 2001), vii.
137 Ibid.
138 Doerner and Lab, *Victimology*, 3.
139 M. Regina Asaro, "Working with Adult Homicide Survivors, Part I: Impact and Sequelae of Murder," *Perspectives in Psychiatric Care* 37, no. 3 (July 2001): 95–101.
140 Ross Macmillan, "Violence and the Life Course: The Consequences of Victimization for Personal and Social Development," *Annual Review of Sociology* 27 (2001): 1–22.
141 Ibid.
142 David Finkelhor, Janis Wolak, and Lucy Berliner, "Police Reporting and Professional Help Seeking for Child Crime Victims: A Review," *Child Maltreatment* 6, no. 1 (February 2001): 17.
143 Katherine J. Bennett, "Legal and Social Issues Surrounding Closed-Circuit Television Testimony of Child Victims and Witnesses," *Journal of Aggression, Maltreatment and Trauma* 8, no. 3 (June 2003): 233–271.
144 Ronet Bachman and Michelle L. Meloy, "The Epidemiology of Violence Against the Elderly: Implications for Primary and Secondary Prevention," *Journal of Contemporary Criminal Justice* 24, no. 2 (May 2008): 186–197.
145 Andrew Karmen, *Crime Victims: An Introduction to Victimology*, 6th ed. (Belmont, Calif.: Thomson Wadsworth, 2007), 236.
146 Donna J. Rabiner, David Brown, and Janet O'Keeffe, "Financial Exploitation of Older Persons: Policy Issues and Recommendations for Addressing Them," *Journal of Elder Abuse & Neglect* 16, no. 1 (January 2004): 65–84.
147 United States Senate Committee on the Judiciary, "Abuse of the Elderly," Congressional Testimony of James Wright, September 23, 2003.
148 Mara H. Gottfried, "Woman, 27, Charged in Forced Prostitution of Half-Sister: Alleged Victim Is Developmentally Disabled," *Saint Paul Pioneer Press*, May 25, 2006.
149 Joan R. Petersilia, "Crime Victims with Developmental Disabilities: A Review Essay," *Criminal Justice and Behavior* 28, no. 6 (December 2001): 655–694.
150 Ibid.
151 I. Hershkowitz, M. E. Lamb, and D. Horowitz, "Victimization of Children with Disabilities," *The American Journal of Orthopsychiatry* 77, no. 4 (October 2007): 629–635.
152 Richard Lucardie and Dick Sobsey, "Homicides of People with Developmental Disabilities: An Analysis of News Stories," *Developmental Disabilities Bulletin* 33, no. 1 (2005): 71–98.
153 Dean G. Kilpatrick, "Interpersonal Violence and Public Policy: What about the Victims?" *Journal of Law, Medicine & Ethics* 32, no. 1 (Spring 2004): 73–81.
154 Executive Office for United States Attorneys, Office of the Victims' Rights Ombudsman, "The Rights Established under the Crime Victims' Rights Act of 2004," https://www.justice.gov/usao/resources/crime-victims-rights-ombudsman/victims-rights. Accessed March 2018.
155 Robert C. Davis and Carrie Mulford, "Victim Rights and New Remedies: Finally Getting Victims Their Due," *Journal of Contemporary Criminal Justice* 24, no. 2 (May 2008): 198–208. National Association of Crime Victim Compensation Boards, http://www.nacvcb.org/index.asp?sid=6. Accessed March 2018.
156 Ibid.
157 Farai Chideya, "What Rights Do Crime Victims Have?" National Public Radio, January 16, 2009, http://www.npr.org/templates/story/story.php?storyId=99466602. Accessed March 2018.
158 Gerry Johnstone, "Review of Repair or Revenge: Victims and Restorative Justice," *International Review of Victimology* 10, no. 2 (2003): 178–180.
159 R. Barry Ruback, "The Imposition of Economic Sanctions in Philadelphia: Costs, Fines, and Restitution," *Federal Probation* 68, no. 1 (June 2004): 21–26.
160 Leo G. Barrile, "I Forgive You, but You Must Die: Murder Victim Family Members, the Death Penalty, and Restorative Justice," *Victims and Offenders* 10, no. 3 (July 2015): 239–269.
161 Marilyn Peterson Amour and Mark S. Umbreit, "Exploring 'Closure' and the Ultimate Penal Sanction for Survivors of Homicide Victims," *Federal Sentencing Reporter* 19, no. 2 (December 2006): 105–112.
162 "Really Really Sorry," *Economist* 368, no. 8335 (August 2, 2003): 54.
163 Roman David and Susanne Y. P. Choi, "Getting Even or Getting Equal? Retributive Desires and Transitional Justice," *Political Psychology* 30, no. 2 (April 2009): 161–192.
164 Ontario, Apology Act, 2009, S.O. 2009, c. 3, https://www.ontario.ca/laws/statute/09a03. Accessed March 2018.
165 Lawrence W. Sherman, Heather Strang, Caroline Angel, Daniel Woods, Geoffrey C. Barnes, and Sarah Bennett, "Effects of Face-to-Face Restorative Justice on Victims of Crime in Four Randomized, Controlled Trials," *Journal of Experimental Criminology* 1, no. 3 (September 2005): 367–395.
166 Carrie J. Petrucci, "Apology in the Criminal Justice Setting: Evidence for Including Apology as an Additional Component in the Legal System," *Behavioral Sciences & the Law* 20, no. 4 (July 2002): 337–362; Jaimie P. Beven, Guy Hall, Irene Froyland, Brian Steels, and Dorothy Goulding, "Restoration or Renovation? Evaluating Restorative Justice Outcomes," *Psychiatry, Psychology and Law* 12, no. 1 (April 2005): 194–206; Umbreit, Coates, and Vos, "Victim-Offender Mediation."
167 Nils Christie, "Conflicts as Property," *British Journal of Criminology* 17, no. 1 (1977): 8.
168 National Center for Victims of Crime, "Victim Impact Statements," http://www.victimsofcrime.org/help-for-crime-victims/get-help-bulletins-for-crime-victims/victim-impact-statements. Accessed March 2018.
169 Ray Paternoster and Jerome Deise, "A Heavy Thumb on the Scale: The Effect of Victim Impact Evidence on Capital Decision Making," *Criminology* 49, no. 1 (February 2011): 129–161.
170 Trina M. Gordon and Stanley L. Brodsky, "The Influence of Victim Impact Statements on Sentencing in Capital Cases," *Journal of Forensic Psychology Practice* 7, no. 2 (April 2007): 45–52.

PART II

Theories of Crime

The Classical and Positivist Schools of Criminology

FEATURES

What was the purpose of punishment before modern criminal justice systems?

Kent Whitaker's attorney reads an email from the Texas Board of Pardons and Paroles, which voted unanimously to recommend clemency for his son, death row inmate Thomas Whitaker. Could you forgive one of your family members who was responsible for killing the rest of your family?

In Sugar Land, Texas, on the evening of December 10, 2003, Thomas "Bart" Whitaker, 24, told his younger brother, Kevin, and his parents, Kent and Patricia, that he would be graduating soon from college. Bart's parents presented him with a Rolex watch, and the family went out to celebrate.[1]

Hours later, when the family arrived home, Bart darted to his car to get his phone. When Kevin opened the door of the house, he was shot, followed by Patricia, then Kent.[2] Bart ran inside and wrestled with the intruder, who shot Bart in the arm before fleeing. Police officers who responded to a neighbor's 911 call found Kevin, 19, killed by a single gunshot. Patricia Whitaker, 51, died soon after arriving at the hospital. Kent Whitaker, 54, survived, as did Bart.[3]

Police realized almost immediately that the incident was not a standard burglary. The house had not been entered forcefully, and nothing had been stolen. The only item missing was Bart's phone. Later, police discovered that Bart was not graduating from college and that he had not been attending at all.[4] They also found out that Bart had cooked up a murder plot with two friends years earlier that was almost exactly like the crime perpetrated against him and his family.

In August 2005, a man named Steven Champagne told police that Bart had planned the crime and had offered to pay "millions of dollars" to him and another friend of Bart's, Chris Brashear, to murder his family. Champagne drove the getaway car, and Brashear pulled the trigger. Bart's fight with Brashear was part of the setup.[5] In March 2007, Bart Whitaker was convicted of capital murder and sentenced to death. Brashear received life in prison without parole, and Champagne received 15 years.[6]

During the trial, the prosecution asserted that Bart's motive was money. Everyone who had plotted with Bart Whitaker to murder his family said Bart wanted to inherit his family's sizeable estate.[7] Champagne told police that just two months after the murders Bart had told him that "the job wasn't finished," and he began discussing ways to kill his father.[8]

In court, Bart said money was not the reason for the murders, but rather his feelings that he could never please his parents. A psychologist who examined Whitaker in 2009 said that he exhibited symptoms similar to Asperger's disorder and had "thin boundaries between fantasy and reality." As a child, he also acted in a feminine manner and had romantic interests in other boys. Bart's father would give him a dollar for every day that he "talked like a boy." Although he was good at school, Bart felt a keen sense of competition with his brother, who was typically masculine and athletic.[9] "In order for me to be that person that my parents would love," said Bart, "I had to be better than I was."[10]

Kent Whitaker, who said he forgave his son, was adamant that Bart be spared and campaigned to save his life. Thirty minutes before Bart's execution in February 2018, the governor of Texas commuted his death sentence to life without parole.[11]

Looking for Explanations of Crime

LEARNING OBJECTIVE | 1

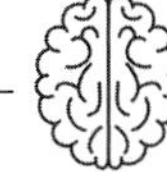

Explain why the supernatural perspective dominated social control for centuries.

LEARNING OBJECTIVE | 2

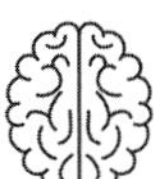

Summarize why contemporary criminologists do not consider the concept of evil as an explanation of crime.

As long as people have collected into societies, they have broken the rules. As societies matured, thinkers and philosophers sought to understand why some people broke the rules in spite of dire punishments that included humiliation, shame, exile, disfigurement, torture, and death. To appreciate criminology, we must understand how certain behaviors became defined as criminal offenses and why people engage in **antisocial** behavior. This chapter will trace the development of explanations of why crime occurs and the role of law from the earliest times to the present day. To accomplish this objective, we will focus on three explanations of crime: one ancient (the supernatural) and two modern (the classical/neoclassical school and the positivist school). The supernatural view looks for explanations of crime that lie beyond the physical world; the classical/neoclassical school seeks explanations within rational thinking; and the positivist school searches for external explanations that affect rational thinking.

Sometimes, the reason for breaking a law seems good enough, such as a man stealing bread to feed his hungry family. But why risk getting caught if the punishment is the amputation of a hand? The thief's motivation is clearly his family, but what factor moves him or her to risk the consequences? Some men with equally starving families would not steal the bread but would find some way to deal with the situation that was within the law. What is the difference between two people in similar situations, then, one of whom obeys the law and the other who breaks it? Was the lawbreaker influenced by a demon and the obedient man by a benevolent spirit? After considering the risks and rewards, did both freely choose their paths under no influence at all but their own? Or did the lawbreaker experience different mental, physical, genetic, or societal influences than the one who obeyed the law? Now consider the case of Bart Whitaker. Why did he arrange the murder of his family? Did he rationally decide that if they were dead, he would inherit a large sum of money and that the risk of getting caught and sentenced to die was worth it? Or is Whitaker a mentally ill man who felt so alienated by his family that he "wanted them dead"?[12] Is it possible that he was affected by an inexplicable, otherworldly force?

Before we explore the modern explanations of crime, the classical/neoclassical and positivist perspectives, we will consider how the causes of crime were perceived in ancient times. Supernatural explanations—which have not been entirely discarded in modern times—look for explanations of crime that lie beyond the physical world.

Supernatural Explanations of Crime

To ensure their survival, early societies structured approved behavior patterns that supported meaningful communities. Societies developed rules to govern the most basic interactions, such as obligations between husband and wife; the discipline of children; and the setting of standards for sexual activity, control of property, and conflict resolution.[13] As societies became more complex, these rules grew into laws and sanctions that defined what individuals were prohibited or encouraged to do. Before the Enlightenment in the 17th and 18th centuries, societies based their standards of behavior on religious doctrine. Religious matters were ingrained not only in the way societies conceived and worshiped their god(s), but also in the laws by which they governed themselves. For example, prior to the Enlightenment, kings were invested with the authority to determine what God intended for the group. This "divine right of kings" specified the king as the sole arbiter of God's law and applied that law to the king's subjects.[14]

DEMONOLOGY

In some societies, it was difficult to tell the difference between religious and secular authority. Church officials and government officials were often the same people. This meant religious doctrine was often the law of the land, and those who engaged in deviant religious behaviors, such as

Instant Recall from Chapter 1 **antisocial** —Following standards of behavior intended to harm society and individuals.

blasphemy (speaking out against God), were punished.[15] It was assumed that crime was motivated by impure thoughts and poor religious instruction, which meant that the church was primarily responsible for the correction of all types of inappropriate behavior. This pre-Enlightenment model for dealing with crime is called **demonology**—a perspective of crime that considers antisocial behavior as caused by an evil entity who lives inside an individual and overtakes his or her personality. The struggle to control antisocial behavior in this model is continually waged between those who are in control and those who are defined as outsiders. Those in control believe the outsiders constitute a threat to the healthy functioning of society, and therefore they must be defined and sanctioned as criminal. Deviance was therefore equated with sin. According to the demonic perspective, deviance is a transgression of the will of the gods that signifies a loss in the supernatural battle between good and evil. Demonic influence can be manifested in one of two ways.

- Temptation. Properly socialized individuals are able to tell the difference between good and evil and make the appropriate choice. However, they will sometimes knowingly make the wrong choice and choose evil not because they do not know better, but because they are tempted by the seductions of deviance. A good example is in the biblical story of Adam and Eve in which Eve succumbs to the temptation of Satan and eats the forbidden fruit. According to the demonic perspective, humankind inherited this weakness for temptation and must continually battle the forces of Satan to make righteous choices.
- Possession. Individuals may be possessed by the devil. In this instance, they do not succumb to temptation of their own free will but rather are subject to antisocial behavior at the instigation of demonic forces. An example of the concept can be seen in occasional news reports in which parents claim their children are possessed by demons and seek exorcism or attempt to exorcise the demons themselves (situations that, unfortunately, can lead to abuse and sometimes the child's death).[16] Modern criminal justice does not generally accept the demonic explanation of possession.[17]

demonology—An ancient perspective of crime that considers antisocial behavior as being caused by an evil entity who lives inside an individual and overtakes his or her personality.

It is difficult to overestimate the influence that religion has had on explanations for antisocial behavior in the past. Religion is a powerful social force that informs the thinking of many people.[18] Many religions exert equally powerful influences on the control of social behavior. We can best understand the demonic perspective by observing how it responded to crime. When a demon was determined to have possessed an individual's body, the response was often to attack that body to drive out the demon. Consequently, a variety of physical punishments were used to exorcise the devil.[19] These punishments had two purposes. First, pain was considered to purge the demon. Second, the public administration of these punishments was believed to restore the community as people witnessed how God, acting through his human agents (the king and the church), maintained social control. Physical punishment thus had a symbolic aspect that encouraged intense, brutal, and painful rituals, such as burning at the stake, that evoked an image of hell. The principle of lex talionis or "an eye for an eye" was used to justify the mutilation and killing of offenders. For example, a thief would have his or her hand cut off, and the tongue of a liar might be mutilated or even removed.[20] All sorts of physical punishments were invented to enable the church to battle the devil by punishing the sinner's body. For instance, the particularly brutal "breaking on the wheel" broke the sinner's bones. It was believed that evil spirits would then have a more difficult time living in the body because the bones were its most enduring part. Similar logic underscored the requirement that the bodies of people who had been hanged had to remain hanging. It was believed that their bodies were full of demons who would endanger the earth's fertility if the bodies were buried. Consequently, until relatively recently, hanged bodies were allowed to dangle from trees until they decomposed.[21]

To the modern mind, the demonic perspective leaves much to be desired. As an explanation for the causes of crime, its emphasis on religion placed too much power in the hands of clergy and kings. Its response to crime focused on purging demons from the body, thus justifying gruesome tortures that elicited confessions and often destroyed the body to such an extent there was little left to bury and little closure for surviving family members.[22]

The demonic perspective gradually gave way to the ideas of the Enlightenment, but we still see its influence in the criminal justice system today. Many mainstream religions have codes such as the biblical Ten Commandments that prescribe religious and social behavior that have made their way into various legal systems. Without a religious basis for social control, many commentators suggest that crime and antisocial behavior are natural outcomes.[23] For the most part, however, contemporary criminologists do not advocate a demonic perspective for the explanation of crime for two reasons. First, from a scientific perspective, it would require the demonstration and measurement of an omniscient "good" pro-human force and a partially omniscient "bad" anti-human force, and evidence that those forces can inhabit human bodies and affect human behavior. Second, the demonic perspective's policies of torture and mutilation are no longer permissible in Western countries.

Torture in the 16th century sometimes involved a procedure called "breaking on the wheel." Torturers would break the limbs of victims in several places, then thread their limbs through the wheel's spokes before hoisting them on a pole to die in the sun. Victims could live as long as four days on the wheel. What was the reasoning behind the breaking on the wheel type of punishment?

EVIL AND IMMORALITY

In recent decades, some social science scholars have proposed to define and study evil. Although not strictly considered demonology, evil is a concept that fits well into the idea of demonology. As a concept, it resists measurement and often definition, but it is one of those concepts that people "know when they see it."

Like a demon, evil is considered to inhabit some people and not others. Some religious people believe it can be exorcised. Modern criminology has no "theory of evil," but the idea that some criminal offenders, murderous political leaders, and terrorists are affected by something terrible but inconceivable still fascinates some scholars. A brief 1999 study that consisted of interviews with forensic psychiatric nurses found that they categorized as "evil" offenders who had committed extreme criminal behavior that seemed deliberate and planned, such as the murder of a child. In this case, then, the nurses defined evil as some component of free will. They did not consider "evil" those offenders who were clearly extremely mentally ill, such as those exhibiting schizophrenia.[24] This agrees with the idea of demonic temptation: The patients who seemed healthy were presented with an evil choice and took it.

Other scholars have sought to typify evil from a biological standpoint. A study on the "neurobiology" of evil distinguished between the ideas of banal evil and sadistic evil: "Whereas banal evil may involve a dissociation of corticostriatal processing from limbic input (reason without passion), sadistic evil may involve a dissociation of limbic processing from frontal controls (passion without reason)." To translate: Banal evil is represented by the bureaucrat who does his or her

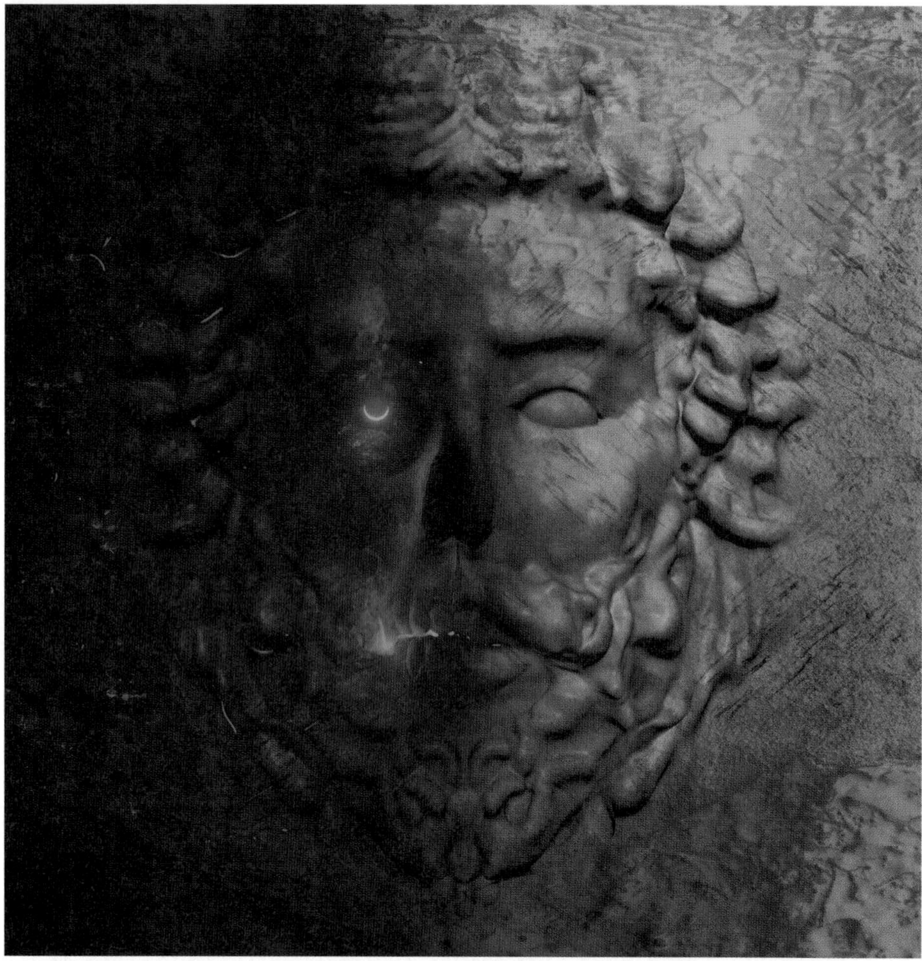
Historically, it was believed that offenders made a choice between good and evil. Why does the contemporary criminal justice system not use the concept of evil?

Bennett and his colleagues adopt a conservative view of society that considers the family and the church as the primary agents of **socialization**; they view crime as the failure of these institutions to instill healthy values in children. They see abuse, neglect, and lack of control of children as the reasons for a diminishing of the moral character of American youth. The culprits, in their view, are the moral relativism of modern American life (the belief that standards of right and wrong are not absolute but vary among individuals); a lax criminal justice system; the values clarification perspective (a technique for encouraging students to relate their thoughts and feelings) that is taught in public schools; gratuitous acts of violence; and the media's portrayal of pro-

job regardless of its horrendous effects—for example, the Nazi clerks who calmly sent millions to their deaths in concentration camps. Sadistic evil is best represented by the serial killer who appears to have little control over the urge to kill and mutilate.[25] This follows the logic of demonology: Banal evil results from the choice to give in to temptation, and sadistic evil represents demonic possession.

Some scholars argue that the cause of crime is a lack of religious-based morality.[26] It may be somewhat of a stretch to attribute the perspective of scholars William Bennett, John DiIulio, and John Walters to supernatural ideas, but their theory of moral poverty and crime echoes some very important aspects of this perspective. Specifically, Bennett and his colleagues decry the permissiveness of contemporary American culture and advocate a return to a period when self-control, good manners, responsibility, and accountability were taught in the family, schools, and church.

miscuity, adultery, and homosexuality. To counteract these negative features of contemporary society, Bennett and his colleagues suggest that

> [t]he flip side of moral poverty is moral health. Being born healthy to or raised by loving biological or adoptive parents or guardians of whatever race, creed, color, social economic status, or demographic description is perhaps the luckiest state that can befall a human being. To be born into or raised by such a family and to grow up surrounded by loving, caring, responsible—parents or guardians, neighbors, teachers, coaches, clergy—is to be raised in moral wealth.[27]

This perspective on moral poverty is an extension of the notion of evil as a cause of crime and antisocial behavior. The notions of moral poverty and evil are vague, difficult to define, and impossible to measure, but they both look to the poor status of individual souls as a cause of problems in society.

PAUSE AND REVIEW

1. Describe the two ways the devil was thought to influence people to break the law.
2. Show how physical punishment was justified as an appropriate way to dispense justice.
3. In early Western culture, why was the church primarily responsible for the correction of all types of inappropriate behavior?

The Classical School of Criminology

LEARNING OBJECTIVE | 3

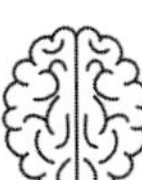

Analyze the classical school of criminology's focus on the offense as opposed to the offender by emphasizing the concept of free will.

LEARNING OBJECTIVE | 4

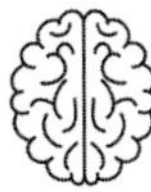

Discuss the Enlightenment's contribution of the social contract to criminology.

LEARNING OBJECTIVE | 5

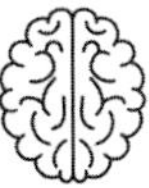

Compare and contrast the ideas of Cesare Beccaria and Jeremy Bentham as the primary architects of the classical school of criminology.

The **classical school of criminology** is a set of ideas that focuses on deterrence and considers crime to be the result of offenders' free will. It represents the most important era in Western legal reform and a major step toward a more humanitarian way of thinking about crime.[28] The classical school is an important prerequisite to the modern criminal justice system, and it would be a mistake to consider it as ancient history because it underlies contemporary justice policies.

Two basic tenets of classical thought are that criminal offenders freely choose to break the law and that punishment should be only as serious as the offense. Before the classical school, no one thought about what motivated offenders beyond supernatural forces. Although classical thinkers aimed to bring humanitarian reform to the legal system, they sought change, not to make life easier for criminal offenders, but to protect society from the harm done by those offenders. From a classical standpoint, overly harsh, arbitrary, and inconsistent punishments harmed society and actually encouraged lawbreaking.

The Enlightenment

In the 17th and 18th centuries, Western societies developed a new understanding of science and the relationship of human beings to the world. During this period, the **Enlightenment**, great strides were made in philosophy and science. The Enlightenment fostered a new "age of reason" that sought to replace religious dogma with intellectual reasoning.[29] The Enlightenment broadened many aspects of learning, including geography, geology, biology, and politics. It changed not only what was known about the world, but also who had the expertise and authority to claim that knowledge. This shift saw the power of the clergy and royalty diminish as the influence of merchants, scientists, and even regular people increased.[30]

Inspired by Enlightenment philosophy, classical school thinkers such as Cesare Beccaria and Jeremy Bentham observed how the legal systems of their countries approached crime and lawbreakers. They did not participate in research studies or interview offenders, victims, and law enforcement. Because the basis of classical thought is not only philosophical, but also centuries old, scientific testing of classical ideas has been carried out only in recent decades.[31] Still, many people today find the idea that offenders freely choose their actions to be simple common sense, especially in a country like the United States where individuals have a wide range of choices about how to live. Why would someone choose the risky offense of robbing a convenience store when he could just get a job? The answer is easy: The robber is too lazy to work, wants fast money, and is sure of getting away with the offense. The robber has chosen the route of robbery. Although this line of thinking seems obvious to us now, it took centuries to develop. However, to understand how the classical school of criminology took shape, we must first understand the philosophical groundwork that was laid during the Enlightenment.

---

socialization—The process of acquiring a personal identity and learning how to live within the culture of one's society.

classical school of criminology—A set of ideas that focuses on deterrence and considers crime to be the result of offenders' free will.

(The) Enlightenment—A period during the 17th and 18th centuries in Europe in which great strides were made in philosophy and science.

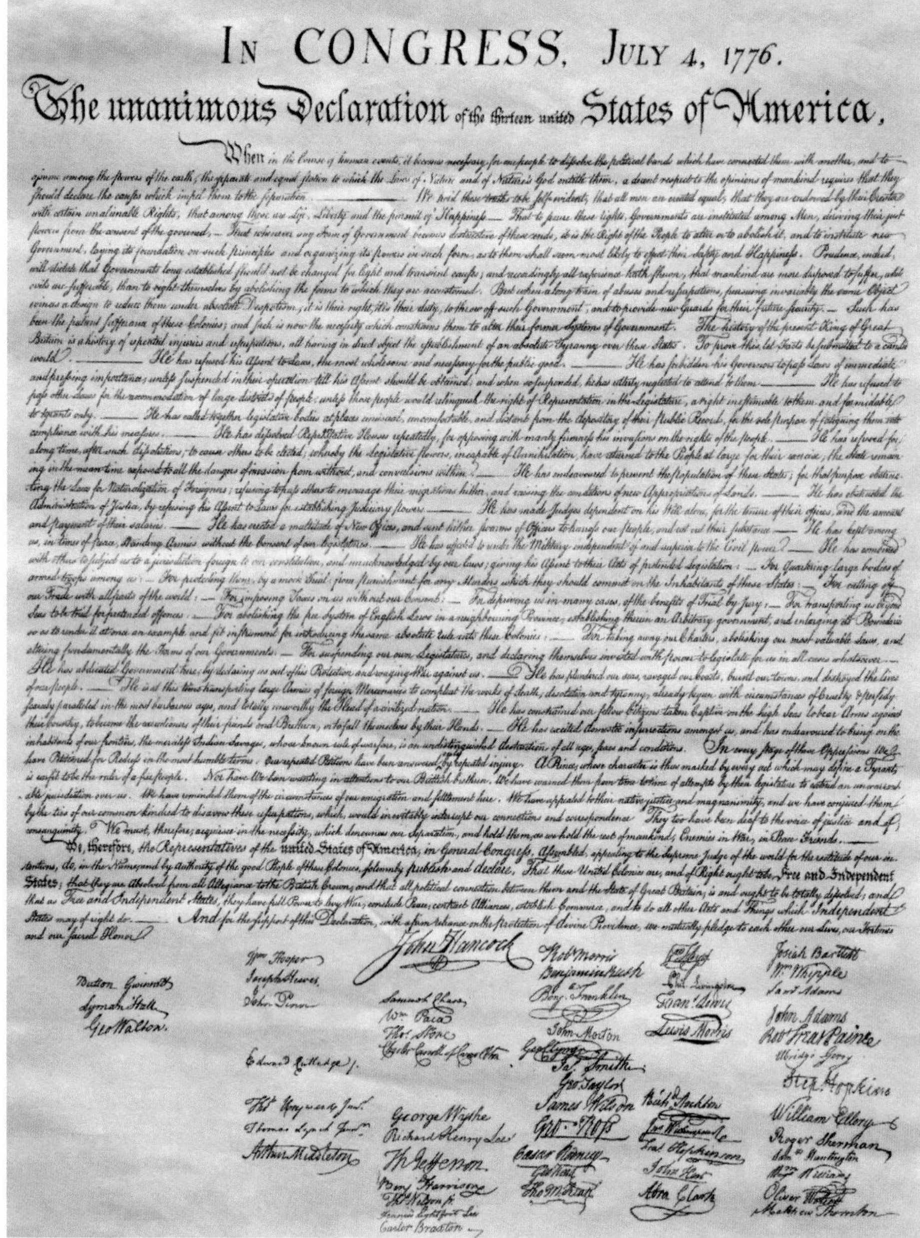
IN CONGRESS, JULY 4, 1776.

The unanimous Declaration of the thirteen united States of America,

The Declaration of Independence of the United States. Why is the Declaration of Independence considered a product of the thinking of the Enlightenment period?

The Reformation's religious upheaval had already stimulated the development of several Protestant sects that challenged the authority of the Roman Catholic Church, and the earlier invention of the printing press made it possible for commoners to acquire knowledge and education and ultimately challenge the status quo.[32] Along with the Enlightenment, these developments set the stage for a new concept of the relationship between human beings and the state, and stimulated thinkers such as Thomas Hobbes, Jean-Jacques Rousseau, and John Locke to question the supremacy of the aristocrats.

This new philosophy profoundly influenced the development of criminological thinking. The supernatural perspective was replaced by a view that emphasized the "natural" rights of human beings—that is, rights that were universal and did not depend on a legal authority for their existence. The key to this new perspective was the idea that individuals were motivated by calculated consideration and the need for rational dealings with others. We find an example of this view at the beginning of one of the foremost products of Enlightenment thinking, the U.S. Declaration of Independence (1776):

> We hold these truths to be self-evident, that all men are created equal, that they are endowed by their Creator with certain unalienable Rights, that among these are Life, Liberty and the pursuit of Happiness. — That to secure these rights, Governments are instituted among Men, deriving their just powers from the consent of the governed. . . .

These few lines contain the ideas that some rights are natural; that they entitle humans to life, liberty, and the pursuit of happiness; and that these rights are secured by some sort of social contract. Let's now explore the relationship between these obligations and classical criminology.

social contract—The idea that individuals in a society are bound by reciprocal obligations.

The Social Contract

According to Enlightenment thinkers, the **social contract**—the idea that individuals in a society are bound by reciprocal obligations—formed the basis for meaningful communities. Instead of envisioning members of society bound by some supernatural spirit, philosophers saw the relationships as being bound by reciprocal obligations based on the idea that each person had to give up some rights and liberties in order to achieve cooperation and safety for all. This social contract also required that individuals respect others' rights and properties in order to receive the same consideration.

Thomas Hobbes (1588–1679) had a pessimistic view of governments based on an even more negative view of human nature. According to Hobbes, individuals concede to the sovereign the right to make the rules of society and to enforce them. By giving up their liberties and freedoms, they are assured safety and uniform enactment and enforcement of laws. Hobbes, famed for his argument that "life is nasty, brutish, and short," viewed the sovereign as having almost universal and complete power over his subjects. Although today this view seems negative and extreme, according to Hobbes, it is necessary in order to control the competing desires and demands of members of society.[33]

English Philosopher John Locke. Why did Locke believe individuals should give up rights and liberties?

At first blush, Hobbes's idea of the social contract may not seem drastically different from the supernatural perspective in that the sovereign or the church has complete power. However, it is significant for distinguishing between the divine right of the sovereign and the willing surrender of liberties by subjects who fear chaos and disorder. In the 21st century, the surrender of liberties can be witnessed by Americans' reaction to the terrorist acts of September 11, 2001. Congress rushed to pass the USA PATRIOT Act apparently without considering how it would affect American rights and freedoms or the conventions of international law, including the Geneva Convention, which specifies how prisoners of war are to be treated.[34]

John Locke (1632–1704) further advanced the idea of a social contract. Like Hobbes, Locke believed that individuals give up rights and liberties in order to live under a sovereign who provides security. However, Locke had a more positive view of this relationship and framed it in a more reciprocal fashion. The power of the sovereign, according to Locke, is not absolute. To receive obedience, the sovereign must respect the rights of the governed; if the sovereign violated the social contract, subjects had a right to rebel.[35] This is a major departure from previous political philosophies that envisioned the sovereign's power as ordained by God and not freely given by society. In Locke's view (also reflected in the Declaration of Independence), the subjects could demand a change in sovereign based on the sovereign's failure to live up to the social contract.

You may notice that Locke's political philosophy, though a departure from the past, falls far short of the expectations we have of the relationship between state and individuals today. Locke, like his contemporaries, was a product of his time and believed that individuals fit into social upper and lower classes that determined their rights and opportunities. In his capacity as commissioner of trade and plantations, he wrote in one report:

> If the causes of this evil be well looked into, we humbly conceive it will be found to have proceeded neither from scarcity of provisions nor from want of employment for the poor, since the goodness of God has blessed these times with plenty no less than the former, and a long peace during those reigns gave us

> as plentiful a trade as ever. The growth of the poor must therefore have some other cause, and it can be nothing else but the relaxation of discipline and corruption of manners; virtue and industry being as constant companions on the one side as vice and idleness are on the other. The first step, therefore, towards the setting of the poor on work, we humbly conceive, ought to be a restraint of their debauchery by a strict execution of the laws provided against it, more particularly by the suppression of superfluous brandy shops and unnecessary ale houses, especially in country parishes not lying upon great roads.[36]

John Locke was very much the aristocrat who, though liberal in his time, would today be considered an elitist. However, we credit him with advancing the social contract by arguing that the sovereign was responsible for the governed.

Jean-Jacques Rousseau (1712–1778) took the idea of the social contract a few steps further. In his book, *The Social Contract* (1762), he formed the idea of extending the opportunity to participate in public affairs to as many people as possible. Furthermore, Rousseau stated that the majority is more often right than wrong. His complex philosophy considers the state as having a personality, which is not simply a mechanism for satisfying human wants but also has a morality that can fulfill the community's will.[37]

Rousseau distinguished between natural law and human-made law. Natural law, the idea promoted by many philosophers including Thomas Aquinas, Thomas Paine, and Thomas Jefferson, postulates that humanity has inalienable natural rights because these rights are inherent in the social contract. With common sense and rationality, we can ascertain that these rights are necessary to the formation of meaningful communities.

In contrast, human-made law is a product of individuals deciding among themselves how to govern themselves. For instance, a major distinction between capitalism and communism is the crucial issue of ownership of property. Under capitalism, the individual ownership of property provides incentives for people to work hard and increase their estates. Conversely, communism specifies that societies function most efficiently and fairly when everyone owns property as a collective.[38] These distinctions are a result of political decisions rather than something we can rationally define from natural law.

Human-made law, according to Enlightenment thinkers, should be a logical extension of natural law. That is, human laws should take advantage of rationality and provide incentives for cooperative behavior that encourages individuals to look beyond their own personal circumstances and consider the community's welfare. By passing laws based on the utilitarian notion of the greatest good for the greatest number of people, these philosophers sought to find a basis of government that everyone could embrace. This period of the Enlightenment greatly affected the origins of classical criminology. As we study the development of classical criminology, with emphasis on Cesare Beccaria and Jeremy Bentham, we will trace the history not only of this perspective but also of those related to contemporary issues of crime and justice.

Cesare Beccaria

Cesare Beccaria (1738–1794), an Italian thinker appalled by the medieval conditions of Italy's prison system, sought to provide the rationale for a more fair and humane system of social control. His 1764 treatise, *On Crimes and Punishments*, presents 41 short chapters on subjects ranging from ways to prevent crime to the origins of punishment and the right to punish. Uncertain political conditions made his harshly critical book an immediate success, but they also meant that initially Beccaria had to remain anonymous as its author. The only book of note Beccaria produced, the volume had a lasting effect on the development of Western law. Thomas Jefferson and John Adams used it partly as the basis for constructing the new government of the United States.

The heart of Beccaria's argument is that punishment should be not "an act of violence," but "essentially public, prompt, necessary, the least possible in the given circumstances, proportionate to the crimes, dictated by the laws."[39] We can distill the most important aspects of Beccaria's ideas into six principles.

1. Rational punishment is necessary to preserve the social contract. Orderly societies would not be possible if each of us were free to punish in our own individualistic and emotional ways. One of the cornerstones of the social contract is that governments are vested with the responsibility for maintaining social order. Citizens cede to the government the authority and ability to respond to transgressions of the law. Rather than lynching a horse thief or castrating a rapist ourselves, we have created courts to rationally determine guilt and correctional systems to

induce punishment. By insisting on a system of rational punishment, society prevents chaos.

2. The legislature makes law, and a judge determines guilt. In order to have a rational system of justice, laws must be written by the legislature and guilt determined by judges. Before the Enlightenment, the despot could make the law up and use torture to coerce a confession from a suspect. Mere charges were considered evidence, and secret accusations and torture were accepted as part of the justice process. Beccaria argued that a rational system of justice invested the legislature with determining both law and punishment and the judge with determining the suspect's guilt. Today, legal codes specify punishments according to the severity of the offense; juries determine guilt, and judges typically determine the sentence. The important advancement of Beccaria's argument is that the law should be transparent, which means not only that it is written but also that evidence is made available to the defense, which has the opportunity to refute it.
3. Individuals act to maximize pleasure and minimize pain. According to classical criminology, individuals perform a moral calculus when deciding whether to break a law. They weigh the rewards of successfully completing an offense against the likelihood of capture and punishment. Government can thus discourage crime by ensuring that antisocial individuals are likely to be discovered, quickly captured, and severely punished.
4. Rationally calculated punishment is a form of social control. If individuals decide to break the law based on rational calculation, it is advisable for the government to set its punishments according to a manageable scale that can inform reasonable people. For instance, a rational person may choose not to commit a capital offense because the death penalty is possible. Instead, this individual might choose to commit a lesser offense in which the penalty is not so severe. By specifying the level of punishment available for each offense, the government can ensure that punishments are sufficiently severe to deter most potential offenders.
5. Deterrence is the object of social control. Deterrence is a very important feature of modern-day criminal justice systems because it prevents a great deal of harm and damage. For deterrence to be effective, justice must be swift, certain, and sufficiently severe. In today's criminal justice system, these principles are sometimes difficult to achieve. For instance, justice is not always swift. Because of a lengthy appeals system, it is often many years before death sentences are carried out. Similarly, justice is not always certain. Many criminal offenders succeed in avoiding detection and capture. In many ways, prisons are full of the unlucky and foolish, while the talented, well connected, and inventive escape detection and punishment.
6. The law should focus on the acts and not the actors. This important principle of classical criminology assumes that all offenders exercise their free will in deciding whether to break the law. Classical criminology does not consider whether a person is impoverished, uneducated, hungry, desperate, or of low intelligence; it does not consider the offender's motivation. By focusing on the act rather than the offender, classical criminology treats similar offenses in a similar way. It ignores offenders' rationalizations and excuses and instead punishes them for their behavior. Consequently, the law considers what has been done rather than who did it.[40]

Beccaria's ideas represented a major departure from the way governments responded to crime. We can readily trace many of the principles of the contemporary criminal justice system to his reforms.[41] In time, other theorists and philosophers, such as Jeremy Bentham, expanded these principles of classical criminology.

Statue of the Italian philosopher and politician Cesare Beccaria in Milan, Italy. How did Beccaria explain why individuals committed crimes?

Jeremy Bentham

An English philosopher and political radical, Jeremy Bentham (1748–1832) sought to reform the archaic British legal system. Like Beccaria, he advocated a new way of dealing with crime based on the concept of utilitarianism. According to **utilitarianism**, individuals should behave according to the principle of "the greatest good for the greatest number of people." This simple idea has far-reaching consequences for determining how individuals ought to behave ethically. For example, the most direct way of acquiring material wealth is to steal it.[42] However, if everyone pursued this line of reasoning, it would become a dog-eat-dog world. Some people would profit from stealing, but others would be harmed, and disorder would prevail. Utilitarian principles argue that ethical behavior allows the greatest number of people to benefit, and society is in much better shape when all benefit than when each individual looks out only for his or her interests.[43]

What is the motivation to engage in this type of utilitarian behavior? According to Bentham, a criminal offender does a **hedonistic calculus** in which he or she calculates the worth of breaking the law by estimating the positive consequences versus the possible negative consequences. In effect, the offender weighs the benefits of a criminal offense against not only the prospect of being caught and punished, but also against the effect it may have on society. For example, many inmates in correctional institutions rationalize or excuse their own behavior and yet believe most of their fellow inmates deserve punishment. Because inmates have family members outside the institution, they support the incarceration of murderers and rapists who might prey on their loved ones.

The execution chamber at the Utah State Prison. What is the principle of reserving capital punishment for the most serious criminal offenses?

utilitarianism—The idea of seeking the greatest good for the most people.

hedonistic calculus—A method proposed by Jeremy Bentham in which criminal offenders calculate the worth of breaking the law by estimating the positive consequences versus the possible negative consequences.

proportionality—The idea that the most serious criminal offenses should have the most severe penalties.

In 1789, Bentham laid out his extensive philosophy in his book, *An Introduction to the Principles of Morals and Legislation*.[44] A major contribution was the suggestion that if potential offenders actually do measure the projected pleasure of breaking the law against the pain of getting caught, then the legislature should take this into consideration and set penalties for each offense at a level designed to deter the unlawful behavior. This is the idea of **proportionality**. It states that the most serious offenses should have the most severe penalties, thus producing a hierarchy of punishments.

Bentham's goal in producing a hierarchy of punishments was to deter crime. He believed that potential offenders freely make complex and what they believe are rational choices in deciding not only what type of offenses to commit but also the severity. To deter these offenses, the legislature must clearly specify the range of penalties. A potential offender cannot do the hedonistic calculus without knowing all the variables. For example, more harm is done to individuals and society in an armed robbery with a gun than in a robbery with a club or a knife. Today, then, many jurisdictions define armed robbery with a firearm as a more egregious offense than robbery without a firearm and allocate a more severe range of punishments for it.

Bentham was a pragmatist who advocated policies he believed would be most effective in deterring crime. One of his ideas was to require citizens to have their names tattooed on their wrists so that they could be identified by police. We would see this practice as intrusive today, but there have been serious proposals to require all U.S. citizens to carry identification cards. Legal and moral concerns surround this type of policy, but from Bentham's pragmatic perspective, many conservative individuals believe it is necessary to alleviate problems inherent in current U.S. immigration policies.[45]

Bentham's ideas for social control have had far-reaching implications. One for which he is still known is his design for a prison based on surveillance. The Panopticon was a circular prison with the cells on the outside and the control station in the middle. This would allow prison staff line-of-sight surveillance of all inmates at all times. The model was not without controversy. Michel Foucault, who saw the Panopticon model as a significant problem because it did not allow inmates privacy or dignity, believed the idea of the Panopticon applied to all of society because individuals are subject to the discipline and surveillance of the state.[46] George Orwell's novel *1984* in which "Big Brother" constantly watches citizens is a fictional but logical extension of the Panopticon.

We can trace to the classical school many of the principles that guide the way social control is exercised over offenders in the criminal justice system today. These principles include a view of human nature based on hedonism, in which individuals are assumed to seek pleasure and avoid pain, as well as the idea of free will, in which individuals are viewed as making rational decisions about whether to break the law, thus allowing governments to set proportional penalties. A third principle is the concept that government is obligated to respect citizens' rights to the degree that is consistent with public safety. This principle of individual rights is always in contention in a democratic society, especially in an age of terrorism in which many are willing to forgo some rights in order to feel safe.[47] Finally, classical criminology emphasizes due-process procedures in the criminal justice system as well as the presumption of innocence and the state's obligation to prove guilt before punishment.

PAUSE AND REVIEW

1. **Who were Cesare Beccaria and Jeremy Bentham? What were their contributions to the classical school of criminology?**
2. **Explain how deterrence is one of the foundations of the classical school.**
3. **Summarize why Cesare Beccaria's work appealed to both conservatives and radicals in the 18th century.**
4. **Assess how the idea of a social contract changed the way people relate to society.**
5. **What are two of the basic tenets of the classical school of criminology?**
6. **What is the Panopticon? How is it related to crime control, and what evidence of it can we see in today's society?**

The Positivist School of Criminology

LEARNING OBJECTIVE | 6

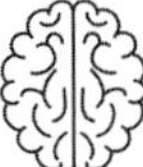

Analyze the positivist school of criminology's assertion that individuals are influenced by external forces.

The 19th century was an exciting time for science. Great strides were made in many fields, and amateur scientists made significant contributions to our understanding of how the world works. For instance, before he went on his historic voyage around the world on the HMS *Beagle*, the young Charles Darwin collected insects.[48] His later books, especially *On the Origin of Species*, laid the groundwork for his theory of natural selection; *The Descent of Man, and Selection in Relation to Sex* extended his ideas to human evolution. Darwin's theory of natural selection is a testament to

Charles Darwin. In what ways did Darwin contribute to the positivist school of criminology?

the practice of making deductions based on observation.[49] His work is widely recognized as fundamental to the development of the **scientific method**—a process of investigation in which phenomena are observed, ideas are tested, and conclusions are drawn—which underlies positivist criminology.

Rather than relying on armchair theorizing about offenders' motivations, as practiced by the classical school of criminology, early contributors to the **positivist school of criminology** instead considered offenders' behavior and attempted to link their explanations of it to external, observable forces that could be measured, such as offenders' biological, psychological, and sociological traits.[50] This significant departure from the classical school relied on a new set of assumptions.

- **Determinism** outweighs free will. The classical school assumes that offenders make rational choices in deciding to break the law. The positivists instead believe that individuals' actions are influenced ("determined") by myriad forces that may be beyond their control and even their consciousness. For instance, for reasons that may be embedded in the biological, psychological, or cultural differences between males and females, each potential offender is affected by his or her sex. This influence can be conscious or unconscious and can be intertwined with other factors such as race or social class. Positivists thus do not consider people to have the broad range of free will that the classical school assumes. The policy implications of these differing assumptions are profound. Whereas the classical school relies on deterrence to alter the moral calculus that offenders do, the positivist school is more concerned with affecting the conditions assumed to cause crime and providing treatment for offenders so that they may avoid **recidivism**.[51]

scientific method—A process of investigation in which phenomena are observed, ideas are tested, and conclusions are drawn.

positivist school of criminology—A set of ideas that considers crime to be the result of external, observable forces that can be measured.

determinism—The idea that everything that occurs, including the choices made by human beings, inevitably follows from previously existing causes.

Instant Recall from Chapter 1 **recidivism** —Repeat offending.

Instant Recall from Chapter 3 **deterrence** —The idea that punishment for an offense will prevent that offender and others from further breaking the law.

- The offender matters more than the offense. Deterrence in the classical school focuses on the penalties for committing the offense, increasing the chances of getting caught, and ensuring timely punishment. In contrast, the positivist school focuses on identifying the social forces that influence offenders and developing treatments to alleviate the underlying problems assumed to cause crime. As we will see in subsequent chapters dealing with biological, psychological, and sociological theories of crime, positivists view offenders as possessing qualities or traits that differ from those of law-abiding people and that are subject to remediation. This difference between focusing on the offense and focusing on the offender has important implications for assigning the responsibility for deviant behavior. For instance, when positivists say that chronic poverty fosters conditions conducive to crime, policy suggests reducing the disparity between the wealthy and the impoverished. Classical theorists would suggest making penalties more severe so that impoverished people would decide not to risk breaking the law.
- Science trumps philosophy. The positivist school attempts to find what *is* rather than what *ought to be*. Positivists use science to attempt to understand why offenders break the law and to prescribe remedies so they do not continue to do so.
- Indeterminate sentencing (a prison sentence that specifies a range of years to be served, with no set date of release) is more effective than determinate sentencing (a prison sentence that specifies an exact number of years to be served). One of the more striking policy implications of the contrast of classical and positivist criminology is the role of punishment and rehabilitation in sentencing. The classical school, with its concentration on the offense, advocates that all offenders receive the same sentence for the same offense. In contrast, the positivist school employs the indeterminate sentence in which the length of incarceration is determined not by the judge but rather by correctional experts, primarily the parole board. The reasoning is that only these experts can ascertain when an offender has been successfully rehabilitated and can be returned to the free world.

This difference in sentencing policy illustrates the competing goals of the criminal justice system. Classical criminology is concerned with deterrence and punishment, whereas positivist criminology is more concerned with the causes of crime and the rehabilitation of offenders. The criminal justice system has aspects of both positivist and classical criminology in its policies, and these philosophies are continually being debated.[52]

In the next four chapters, we will see how the positivist school has contributed most of the theories of contemporary criminology. The development of positivist theory shows how scientific knowledge and cultural pressures affect the way societies respond to crime. The science has not always been good, however, and gross injustices have been visited upon alleged offenders due to misguided assumptions about the nature of human beings.

For instance, in the 19th century, young orphans were taken from the major cities on the East Coast and sent to the developing Midwestern and Western states as part of a plan to rescue them from the problems of urbanization. It was believed that matching these youths with farmers who needed their labor would teach them marketable skills and allow them to grow up in a healthier environment. Many of the young people sent west on these "orphan trains" were placed in situations in which their labor was exploited, and they were subject to physical, psychological, and sexual abuse. The decision-makers were well meaning, but the actual practice had consequences that were often disastrous.[53] In future chapters, we will detail numerous similar examples of how faulty science and the inept implementation of programs based on positivist rehabilitation ideas backfired. The positivist school has greatly increased our understanding of crime and response to unlawful behavior, but it has some issues that require consideration.

1. Positivism accepts the legitimacy of the criminal justice system and its place in the social system. We will see later that critical theories of criminology disapprove of the wholesale acceptance of inequities based on race, sex, gender, and social class. For instance, for decades the only treatment available in women's penal institutions supported traditionally female social roles. Women were not encouraged to challenge the patriarchy, the family, the workplace, or the criminal justice system. Male offenders were trained in automotive technology, carpentry, or other trades in which they might make a living, but women offenders were encouraged to learn to cook, sew, style hair, or pursue other traditionally female occupations. In many ways, then, positivism locked offenders into social inequities.
2. Positivism encourages people to look at the external and internal forces that influence their behavior and seek ways of alleviating their antisocial propensities. Positivism fails to consider the classical school's concept of free will, so it is sometimes viewed as overly deterministic. According to those who subscribe to classical criminology, positivism's focusing of blame outside the offender prevents offenders from taking responsibility for their own behavior.
3. The positivist school envisions offenders as different from law-abiding people and in need of intervention to reform. Positivism has attempted to demonstrate how offenders' biological, psychological, and sociological conditions vary from the norm. Offenders are viewed as "sick or damaged" and in need of drug therapy, psychological counseling, "tough love," or other programs designed to make them healthy, productive citizens. By contrast, the classical school envisions offenders as people who have made bad choices and who can be encouraged, through deterrence and punishment, to make better choices in the future.

This brief introduction to positivism only hints at the contributions this perspective makes to criminology. In subsequent chapters, we will explore several theories that hinge on positivist assumptions. Since criminal justice system reforms come from both the positivist and classical schools of criminology, however, we should not look for which school is correct. Rather, we should appreciate how the development of criminology has benefited from many perspectives and how much theoretical work remains. We will now turn to the resurgence of some of the ideas of classical criminology in neoclassical criminology, which also uses some positivist concepts to define its perspective.

PAUSE AND REVIEW

1. **Discuss some of the major criticisms of the positivist school.**
2. **Compare and contrast the major ideas of the classical school with those of the positivist school.**

3. **The classical school emphasized reason. What is the corresponding basis of the positivist school of criminology?**
4. **The positivist school focuses on the offender rather than on the offense. How does this affect the criminal justice system?**

Neoclassical Criminology

LEARNING OBJECTIVE | 7

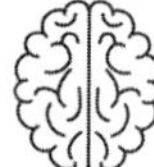

Show how neoclassical criminology recalls the principles of classical criminology.

Developed over the past 40 years, **neoclassical criminology** is a theoretical resurgence in classical criminology that emphasizes free will and deterrence and acknowledges some of the effects of positivism on decision making. It revives some of the principles of classical criminology and combines them with ideas from economic game theory, which argues that people choose their behaviors based on perceived outcomes, with the goal of maximizing their gain while minimizing the resources and output necessary to achieve their goals. This perspective is useful in determining consumers' buying patterns. For instance, a person wanting to buy a fancy, new television will shop around for the best price as well as financing options, installation costs, and warranties. The goal is to make the best purchase for the lowest possible cost. Neoclassical criminologists use this model to explain crime. Just as someone buying a television would investigate all the options and select the best price within the context of other features, neoclassical theory presumes a potential offender will make a choice about what type of offense to commit and when to commit it. Neoclassical criminology has developed several theories, including rational choice theory and routine activities theory, that employ the classical concept of deterrence. Furthermore, neoclassical criminology emphasizes the offender's character and argues that the choice to break the law is contingent upon both opportunity and personal integrity.

If opportunities are limited by deterrence, individuals who are wavering in their decision to break the law may decide that the costs are too high. This deterrent works best for first-time and minor offenders and may not be sufficient for career offenders or those with mental disorders who cannot adequately evaluate the costs and benefits of crime. The neoclassical perspective has been embraced by conservative observers who desire more severe punishments for offenders. It marks a return to emphasis on the offense rather than the offender; however, it recognizes that offenders make choices and that society can influence those choices by limiting opportunities and imposing stiff sanctions. Neoclassical criminology has also been influenced by more recent perspectives, especially positivism. Recall that the positivist school takes issue with the concept of free will and views individuals as influenced by factors that limit their choices. For instance, a young man growing up in a community with substandard schools, prevalent drugs and violence, few jobs, and urban blight does not have the same opportunities for living a lawful life as someone in different circumstances might have.[54]

With this in mind, neoclassical criminology asserts that an element of free will exists even for those in the most difficult social circumstances. It emphasizes individual character and the principle that each of us is responsible for our actions.[55] Rather than considering the behavior of individuals to be determined by economic conditions, socialization, and genetics as the positivist school does, neoclassical criminology argues that deficiencies in these areas can be overcome by rational choices made by individuals who take responsibility for their actions. Therefore, instead of envisioning a choice between hard determinism and free will, neoclassical criminology inserts between them a **soft determinism**—the idea that free will is affected by outside influences. (Go to Figure 4.1 to see how neoclassical criminology fits between classical and positivist criminology.)

The concept of soft determinism allows neoclassical criminology to downplay the social forces that affect individual behavior and reassert some classical ideas. Specifically, neoclassical criminology challenges the positivist emphasis on rehabilitation.[56] More important, the neoclassical school still holds to the concept that free will significantly influences

---

neoclassical criminology—A theoretical resurgence in classical criminology that emphasizes free will and deterrence and acknowledges some of the effects of positivism on decision making.

soft determinism—The idea that free will is affected by outside influences.

premeditation—In reference to crime, the planning of a criminal act.

the reasons that people break the law and should be considered when making law.[57] However, positivism has contributed three limiting factors to the neoclassical idea of free will.

1. Premeditation. **Premeditation** in reference to crime is the planning of a criminal act. It is considered more important for a first-time offender than for a repeat offender because breaking the law has not yet become a habit. Therefore, say neoclassical criminologists, by considering the factors present when first-time offenders decide to break the law, it should be possible to alter their decision-making through deterrence. For the repeat offender, however, laws and punishments are less likely to alter the decision to break the law.[58]
2. Mitigating circumstances. Several circumstances, such as stress, poverty, social pressure, and even the weather, may inhibit the individual's exercise of free choice. By allowing for such mitigating factors, neoclassical criminology moves closer to the idea of determinism. However, it does not go as far as positivist criminology, and it still leaves room for the idea that the decision to break the law is determined not solely by outside forces but also by the individual.
3. Insanity. This third modification of the neoclassical perspective considers how free will may be perverted by mental illness. In the landmark case of Daniel McNaughtan (1843), which underlies the insanity defense, the neoclassical school recognizes that McNaughtan did not have the mental capacity to fully understand the consequences of his actions. McNaughtan believed he had direct communication with God, who informed him that Satan had a plan to establish a reign on earth using the Tory party (Britain's conservative political party) as his instrument. McNaughtan attempted to kill the leader of the Tory party, Sir Robert Peel, but killed his secretary by mistake. According to the courts, McNaughtan did not and could not have full control of his mental facilities because he believed he was doing God's will. Therefore, this case did not meet the standard of accountability necessary for a murder conviction. McNaughtan was declared not guilty by reason of insanity.[59]

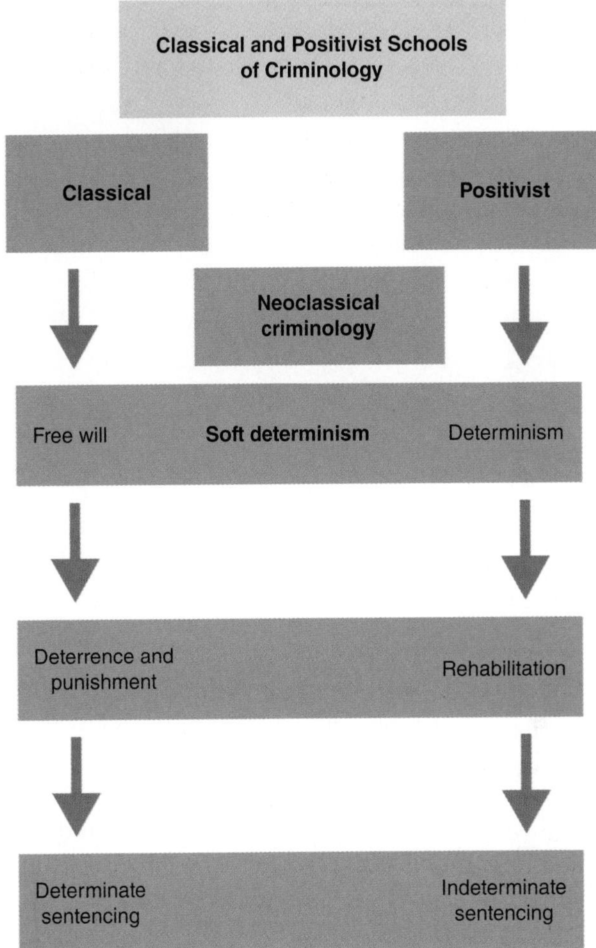

FIGURE 4.1 The gradients between each concept illustrate the major differences between the classical and positivist schools of criminology.

Although the classical school may seem to be as outmoded as the supernatural perspective, many of its principles have been modified by the neoclassical school, and these principles can be seen in contemporary theories that inform public policy. Let's consider a classic study by Marvin Wolfgang and colleagues that shows how public policy may be considered in the sentencing of juvenile delinquents. Wolfgang's study showed that most juvenile delinquents dropped out of a life of crime after one or two offenses. The study concluded that crime tends to be an episodic and situational phase for most young males and that eventually most of them desist. In fact, most delinquents in the study stopped breaking the law by their second offense regardless of how they were treated. The study recommended, therefore, that the full brunt of the law not be brought upon delinquents until their third offense. A small percentage—only 647 of nearly 10,000 individuals—committed five or more offenses, and these youths were responsible for more than half the total number of offenses committed by this cohort.

Jason Dalton, an Uber driver, is accused of shooting eight people randomly, killing six, in a 2016 rampage that occurred even as he picked up and dropped off fares. None of Dalton's friends or family can think of a reason for his actions. An insanity plea is likely in Dalton's trial, although juries rarely accept these pleas. Do you consider Dalton's actions to be a product of free will?

Wolfgang's suggestion was to impose a swift and certain but mild punishment for first and second offenders and to reserve severe punishments for those who continued to break the law. This would accomplish two things. First, most youths would not be subject to the debilitating effects of severe punishment and could get on with their lives. Second, resources would be reserved for the serious delinquents who required incarceration.[60]

Wolfgang and his colleagues can be considered neoclassical scholars because they suggest reserving severe sanctions for serious offenders and because their work laid the foundation for a return to the classical concept of deterrence as a criminal justice goal. Wolfgang's study profoundly affected criminology, appealing to both liberal and conservative thinkers. Treating first- and second-time offenders leniently appeals to liberals' sense that young people should be given the benefit of the doubt because most will not offend again. For conservative thinkers, the policy implications suggest that resources are better spent on chronic offenders, who may be incarcerated for long periods to enhance public safety. Although Wolfgang and his colleagues cannot easily be placed in either the conservative or the liberal camp, and because their ideas straddle the philosophies of the classical and the positivist schools, their viewpoints demonstrate that the neoclassical school has practical implications for modern criminal justice. Now we will consider neoclassical theories based on rational choice.

Deterrence Theory Reconsidered

Long a mainstay of classical criminology, **deterrence theory** is the concept that punishment prevents crime. That is, people will not break the law if the benefits of doing so fall short of the consequences if they are caught (for a look at how deterrence theory is applied in today's courtrooms, see Policy Implications). When considering breaking the law, individuals consider the likelihood that they will succeed and get caught (certainty), the time frame between possibly getting caught and punished (swiftness), and the possible consequences (severity). Historically, deterrence has been envisioned as one of two types: specific and general. **Specific deterrence** is the idea that punishing one person for an offense, usually by incarceration or execution, will prevent that person from committing another offense. It occurs when an offender is caught and punished and decides not to break the law anymore. **General deterrence** is the idea that punishing one person for an offense will provide an example to others not to break the law. It occurs when the rest of society sees what has happened to the offender and decides not to commit similar behavior. General deterrence is thought to be the most important of the two concepts because it affects all of us and not just those who have already broken the law.

Some modern criminologists, however, no longer adhere to the sharp division between these two types of deterrence. Instead, it is argued, most people are likely to have a mixture of direct and indirect experience with punishment and punishment avoidance.[61] They contend that in order to fully appreciate the deterrent effect, researchers should examine four factors that individuals may consider when deciding whether to break the law:

1. Has the individual already been punished for any offenses? This question examines his or her direct experience with punishment.
2. Is the individual aware of others who have been punished? This question examines the individual's indirect experience with punishment.

---

deterrence theory—The concept that punishment prevents more crime from occurring.

specific deterrence—The idea that punishing one person for an offense, usually by incarceration or execution, will prevent that person from committing another offense.

general deterrence—The idea that punishing one person for an offense will provide an example to others not to engage in crime.

POLICY IMPLICATIONS

Let the Penalty Fit the Crime

One of the principles of deterrence theory is that the most serious offenses should have the most serious penalties in order to provide justice and discourage people from breaking the law. Therefore, the federal and state criminal justice systems have created sentencing schedules that specify the type and amount of penalty for each offense level (see the table below for an example of the federal sentencing penalties for marijuana trafficking).

Sentencing schedules are designed for two purposes. First, more serious offenses incur more drastic penalties to discourage people from committing them. This is a relative innovation in the criminal law. There was a time when the death penalty was meted out for many offenses that today we would consider relatively minor. The second purpose of the schedules is to enhance uniformity in sentencing. Offenders who commit similar offenses should receive similar penalties. When judges are permitted to be arbitrary and provide draconian sentences for minor offenses or light penalties for major offenses, the public will quickly lose faith in the fairness of the criminal justice system.

The classical school advocates introducing proportionality and reason into the sentencing process in order to avoid gross injustices. This philosophy is still deeply embedded in the U.S. criminal justice system where offenders are held accountable for their offenses with little regard for their personal attributes.

THINK ABOUT IT

1. Does requiring the severity of penalties to be commensurate with the severity of offenses deter potential offenders? Why or why not?
2. Should judges be allowed to sentence offenders as they see fit without using sentencing schedules?

Federal Trafficking Penalties—Marijuana

DRUG	QUANTITY	1st OFFENSE	2nd OFFENSE*
Marijuana (Schedule 1)	1,000 kg or more marijuana mixture; or 1,000 or more marijuana plants	Not less than 10 yrs. or more than life. If death or serious bodily injury, not less than 20 yrs., or more than life. Fine not more than $10 million if an individual, $50 million if other than an individual.	Not less than 20 yrs. or more than life. If death or serious bodily injury, life imprisonment. Fine not more than $20 million if an individual, $75 million if other than an individual.
Marijuana (Schedule 1)	100 kg to 999 kg marijuana mixture; or 100 to 999 marijuana plants	Not less than 5 yrs. or more than 40 yrs. If death or serious bodily injury, not less than 20 yrs. or more than life. Fine not more than $5 million if an individual, $25 million if other than an individual.	Not less than 10 yrs. or more than life. If death or serious bodily injury, life imprisonment. Fine not more than $20 million if an individual, $75 million if other than an individual.
Marijuana (Schedule 1)	More than 10 kg hashish; 50 to 99 kg marijuana mixture More than 1 kg of hashish oil; 50 to 99 marijuana plants	Not more than 20 yrs. If death or serious bodily injury, not less than 20 yrs. or more than life. Fine $1 million if an individual, $5 million if other than an individual.	Not more than 30 yrs. If death or serious bodily injury, life imprisonment. Fine $2 million if an individual, $10 million if other than an individual.
Marijuana (Schedule 1)	Less than 50 kg marijuana (but does not include 50 or more marijuana plants regardless of weight) 1 to 49 marijuana plants	Not more than 5 yrs. Fine not more than $250,000, $1 million if other than an individual.	Not more than 10 yrs. Fine $500,000 if an individual, $2 million if other than individual.

*The minimum sentence for a violation after two or more prior convictions for a felony drug offense have become final is a mandatory term of life imprisonment without release and a fine up to $20 million if an individual and $75 million if other than an individual.

Source: United States Drug Enforcement Administration, Drugs of Abuse *(Washington, D.C.: U.S. Department of Justice Drug Enforcement Administration, 2017), 31. Available at https://www.dea.gov/pr/legis.shtml. Accessed March 2018.*

3. Has the individual avoided punishment? This question examines the individual's direct experience with punishment avoidance.
4. Is the individual aware of others who have avoided punishment for criminal offenses? This question examines the individual's indirect experience with punishment avoidance.[62]

Looking at both direct and indirect experiences with punishment and avoidance of punishment allows researchers to pick apart the theoretical distinctions between specific and general deterrence. For instance, if a juvenile is arrested and sent to a training school, he or she not only experiences direct punishment, but also interacts with other delinquents and appreciates what happens to them. This indirect experience with punishment influences the delinquent's behavior over and above his or her direct experience. This expanded view of deterrence theory is most evident when we consider people who commit a variety of offenses. Someone who commits a burglary and is caught and punished for it may be specifically deterred from committing burglary again but, in addition, may be generally deterred from committing other types of offenses.[63]

This advancement in deterrence theory calls for research that will likely be complicated. For instance, when we attempt to determine an individual's evaluation of the certainty of being caught and convicted, other theories may come into play. Specifically, self-control and learning ability greatly influence an individual's determination of the certainty of getting caught, so theories that seek to explain self-control and learning (which we will cover in later chapters) would have to be considered.[64]

This extension of deterrence theory demonstrates how neoclassical scholars have adapted classical criminology to contemporary crime and justice issues. However, it is not the only theory that employs classical criminology to explain current criminal justice issues. We turn next to rational choice theory.

Rational Choice Theory

Rational choice theory is the concept that offenders calculate the advantages and disadvantages not only of breaking the law, but also of what type of offenses to commit. The theory has practical implications for criminal justice policies.[65] On the one hand, it is directly linked to classical criminology because it assumes that individuals freely choose whether to break the law. On the other hand, it is neoclassical in that it considers ways in which these choices are bound or limited by circumstance or the offenders' ability. For instance, not every offender has the opportunity to commit certain offenses, such as embezzlement, nor does every offender have the information to make informed choices. Nevertheless, rational choice theory as espoused by neoclassical thinkers assumes that offenders make choices based on their desire to acquire pleasure while avoiding pain.

Derek Cornish and Ronald Clarke developed rational choice theory to capture some of the reasoning behind the decision to break the law. For instance, when considering the costs of breaking the law, the offender looks not just at the expected formal punishment, but also at informal costs such as shame, parental or family disapproval, and feelings of guilt.[66] The theory also considers the difference between criminal involvement and criminal events. Offenders must make two decisions: first, whether to commit an offense (involvement) and, second, what type of offense to commit (event). This is an important distinction. Presumably a motivated potential offender could be deterred from committing one type of offense after calculating the odds of getting away with it and the expected gains. However, having decided to commit an offense, he or she will likely commit a different one if the first looks too dangerous given the expected payoff.[67]

What are the policy implications of rational choice theory? By studying offenders' thinking processes, law enforcement and security experts can take steps to discourage criminal activity. Let's turn now to a perspective derived from rational choice theory called situational crime prevention.

Situational crime prevention considers situational factors that can be modified to discourage crime. The first modification is a reduction in physical opportunities to break the law. This "target hardening" includes using padlocks, security cameras, and increased lighting to protect property. However, the problem of "crime displacement" is always a consideration. When one target appears

---

rational choice theory—The concept that offenders calculate the advantages and disadvantages not only of breaking the law, but also of what type of offense to commit.

situational crime prevention—An extension of rational choice theory that considers situational factors that can be modified to discourage crime.

routine activities theory—The concept that crime occurs when three elements converge: motivated offenders, attractive targets, and the absence of capable guardians.

protected, the potential offender may simply search for a more vulnerable one. Nevertheless, target hardening is a way of affecting the choices that potential offenders make in selecting when and where to break the law.[68]

A second situational modification is to increase the risks of apprehension. A stepped-up police presence is an obvious policy implication. For instance, retail employees can provide a surveillance function in addition to their service and sales functions. By regularly approaching potential shoplifters with offers to help them in their selection of items, employees can reduce the likelihood that they will steal anything. Similarly, research has shown that buildings with doormen have less vandalism and burglary than similar buildings without doormen. The message here is that potential offenders are less likely to strike when an adequate number of employees and security officials are visibly responsible for the establishment.[69]

Further policy implications of situational crime prevention range from reducing the number of guns available to improving the technology designed to prevent drunk driving. For example, some jurisdictions may require the cars of motorists with a history of driving under the influence to be fitted with a device that the driver must blow into to test his or her sobriety. If the driver's blood alcohol level is too high, the device will prevent the car from being started. Situational crime prevention is also at work in airport baggage and passenger screening in which travelers must present photo identification to board the plane. This is not far from Bentham's idea that people should have their names tattooed on their wrist so that they can be readily identified. Classical criminology is constantly being updated by the neoclassical thinkers, who believe it is desirable to focus on crime and its prevention rather than exerting resources on offender rehabilitation or attacking the causes of crime.

Routine Activities Theory

Developed by Lawrence Cohen and Marcus Felson, **routine activities theory** is a neoclassical concept based on the premise that crime occurs when three elements converge: motivated offenders, attractive targets, and the absence of capable guardians.[70] Opportunities for crime are highest, then, when an attractive target has no capable guardians. For example, a bank may be an attractive target for robbers, but if it is protected by security devices and guards and monitored by the FBI as well as local police, it has an abundance of capable guardians that make it less attractive.[71] Routine activities theory is neoclassical because it focuses on the offense rather than the offender. The offenders, who are merely one aspect in the theoretical triangle, freely decide to commit the offense because the other two points in the triangle—attractive targets and the absence of capable guardians—are present.

A ceiling-mounted video surveillance camera is located near a sign alerting commuters of video surveillance at the 34th Street station, in New York. What are some other methods of target hardening that can influence a potential offender's decision to break the law?

According to Cohen and Felson, motivated offenders represent a constant in the routine activities theory equation. This means we can always assume that potential offenders are motivated to break the law, but the theory tells us little about their level of motivation. More important in this theory are the other two conditions: attractive targets and the absence of capable guardians. It is relatively simple to make a target less attractive to would-be thieves. For instance, FedEx has stenciled on its trucks that there is no cash on board, and some convenience

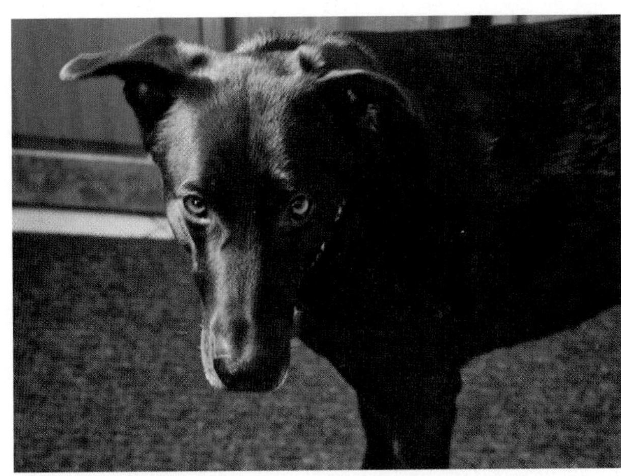
A guard dog can be a capable guardian of private property. Would this dog deter you from approaching an attractive target?

stores have "drop safes" that clerks can deposit cash in but only the manager can open.

The third component of routine activities theory, the absence of capable guardians, is another easy condition to alter in order to discourage crime. Capable guardians include security cameras, private security guards, increased lighting, alarm systems, and guard dogs. Guarding property is a multibillion-dollar business whose products range from steering wheel locks on automobiles to gated communities. When targets are made less attractive and attractive targets are closely watched, routine activities theory postulates that potential offenders will be deterred. This emphasis on deterrence is another hallmark of neoclassical theory.

The fact that Cohen and Felson do not emphasize the first component of their theory, motivated offenders, is both a weakness and a strength.

THEORY TO PRACTICE

Criminological Perspectives in Film

The three schools of criminological thought are often portrayed in films about crime. An entertaining exercise for film buffs and crime scholars is to try to pick out which perspective appears in which film. Often, criminological theory is key to the plot as the filmmakers seek to provide a reason for the lawbreakers' behavior. For practice, let's look at five popular films and the criminological perspectives they employ.

The Supernatural Perspective

- *The Exorcist* (1973). In this classic film, a young girl is possessed by the devil and commits one murder, several assaults, and some household vandalism. This film is one of the best examples of the use of the devil working through human beings to break the law as a major plot device and explanation for crime.

The Classical School

- *Oceans 11* (2001). In this humorous film, a group of thieves decide to rob a casino. The main characters, one of whom lies to his parole officer about his whereabouts, devise an elaborate plan and methodically recruit others to assist. One character is even aware that he will return to prison, but he decides that robbing the casino is worth it. *Oceans 11* is a good example of how offenders may carefully weigh the risk of getting caught against the potential rewards of successfully completing their offenses.
- *No Country for Old Men* (2007). This film is a sobering look at offenders who decide to pursue their criminal offenses, not only for wealth, but also for personal principles. All the offenders in the film are coldly rational, and some are convinced that obtaining a large amount of money makes committing multiple murders and risking their own lives worthwhile. One character's moral calculus, which is based on satisfying his personal principles, requires him to break the law even when nothing is at stake. *No Country for Old Men* is an excellent portrayal of the moral calculus as applied to crime.

The Neoclassical Perspective

- *A Clockwork Orange* (1971). Possibly the best film about criminological theory, *A Clockwork Orange* is director Stanley Kubrick's film adaptation of Anthony Burgess's novel about a young hoodlum, Alex, who is rehabilitated. Alex's antisocial behavior, which appears to be freely chosen, is modified by external forces through rehabilitation.

The Positivist School

- *The Silence of the Lambs* (1991). In this popular thriller, an FBI agent pursues one serial killer with the help of another. Although the film's portrayal of the two serial killers may be exaggerated, it is clear that the source of their antisocial behavior is mental illness, not rational choice.
- *Malcolm X* (1992). This biographical film portrays the life of the social activist *Malcolm X*, who, as a youth, was driven by racism, violence, and poverty to a life of crime. Sent to prison in 1945 for burglary, Malcolm X converted to Islam and renounced the criminal lifestyle. His life meshes neatly with many positivist ideas, especially the notions that antisocial behavior can be brought about by a destructive environment and that offenders can be rehabilitated.

THINK ABOUT IT

1. Are any of these films among your favorites? Do you agree with the explanations of the criminological perspectives given above? Do you see other criminological perspectives in these films?
2. Watch some of your favorite crime films again, and see if you can determine the criminological perspectives they take.

By placing limited importance on motivated offenders, they avoid the difficult task of identifying and measuring motivation, which is not easily discernible. To measure offender motivation, one would have to talk to offenders and attempt to understand why they do what they do. This type of research has substantial obstacles.

Access to offenders is problematic because those who are incarcerated have little to gain by exposing their motivations to researchers, and those who have not been caught are difficult to identify. It is easier for researchers to measure the attractiveness of targets and the presence of capable guardians than it is to determine offender motivation. Thus, treating motivation as a given lets us assume that every offender is motivated by financial gain; therefore, researchers can concentrate on the other two components of rational choice theory.[72]

Ignoring offender motivation is also a weakness of routine activities theory. Even though the theory can explain why targets may be deemed attractive and why guardianship may look inadequate, motivation is difficult to measure. Understanding offender motivation may help in developing crime-prevention techniques. For instance, when dealing with motor vehicle theft, it can make a big difference whether the thief is a teenager intent on joyriding or a professional who plans to dismantle the car and sell its parts.

Finally, understanding offender motivation may provide an opportunity to alter their thinking by providing them with legitimate means of obtaining resources such as job training, education, drug treatment, and other rehabilitative programs. This approach, however, is different from attempting to affect the attractiveness of targets or providing more capable guardianship. By changing offenders' life conditions, we are moving away from classical school principles toward those of the positivist school and its concern with understanding and altering the offender's behavior. As a final exercise to anchor your understanding of the three families of theories, take a look at Theory to Practice to see how criminological perspective is used in film.

PAUSE AND REVIEW

1. **How is the neoclassical perspective distinguished from the classical perspective?**
2. **Describe the reasons that the neoclassical perspective may appeal to modern political conservatives.**
3. **Distinguish between specific and general deterrence.**
4. **Compare the reasons that individuals choose to commit a specific offense according to routine activities theory.**
5. **List the policy implications of situational crime prevention.**

FOCUS ON ETHICS Guns in School

As a high school vice principal, you are in charge of school discipline. You have been at this job for a long time, and you have won the trust of your principal and the school board. The students consider you firm but fair. Now you have a new case that presents you with a dilemma. Do you err on the side of following the rules, or do you do what you think is best for an individual student?

One of your students, Robert, brought a gun to school. The unloaded handgun fell out of his backpack during his honors English class. The school has a strict zero-tolerance policy, and normally the student would be expelled, but because of your long tenure as vice principal you may use your discretion in this case.

Robert is a senior who is a star athlete and an academic All-American who has scholarship offers to play

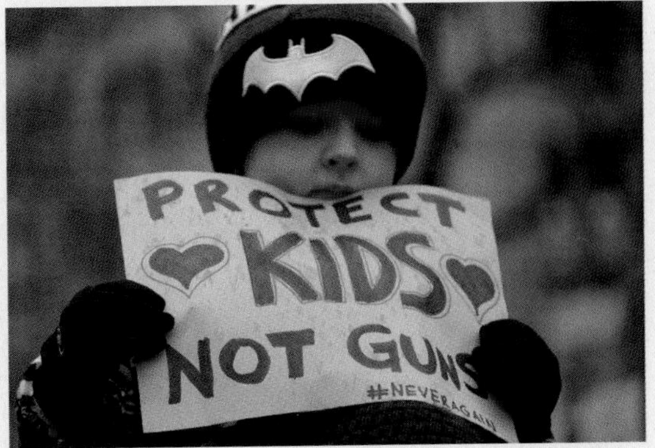

Protesters demonstrate against gun violence in the wake of the 2018 shooting at Marjory Stoneman Douglas High School in Parkland, Florida, where 17 people were killed. Is stricter gun control the answer to school shootings?

football at several big schools. By all indications, he has a bright future, and being expelled from school could jeopardize his athletic and academic prospects. Complicating the situation is the fact that the football team is scheduled to play this weekend in the district championship. Robert is a starting cornerback and wide receiver who is recognized as a team leader. Upon investigating this incident, you learn that Robert has recently broken up with his girlfriend and is depressed. In your opinion, he is a good kid going through a difficult time.

You are getting mixed messages from the school board. One member has indicated that it is important that the school win the district championship, while another member is concerned about student safety. Recent school shootings have made everyone nervous about both school safety and school liability. You recently expelled a white student during deer season for having a loaded hunting rifle in her truck when it was parked in the student parking lot. Last year, you suspended a black student who brought in a BB pistol to show his friends. It would appear discriminatory if Robert, who is white, was allowed to remain in school and play in the championship game.

What Do You Do?

1. Expel Robert. The zero-tolerance policy must be applied consistently if it is to be a deterrent.
2. Suspend Robert from school for two weeks and kick him off the football team. This should be enough to satisfy the zero-tolerance policy.
3. Keep Robert in school, and let him play. It is important to the students and the school board to win the championship.
4. Keep Robert in school, and let him play but insist he surrender all the guns in his home and attend counseling sessions with the school psychologist.
5. Kick Robert off the football team and suspend him for the rest of the school year. He can walk in graduation with his class and make up his credits during summer school. This way he should still be able to go to college on an academic scholarship.

Summary

LEARNING OBJECTIVE 1 Explain why the supernatural perspective dominated social control for centuries.	Before the Enlightenment, religious matters were ingrained in the way that societies conceived and worshiped their god(s), as well as in the laws by which they governed themselves. Religious doctrine was often the law of the land, and those who engaged in deviant religious behaviors were punished.
LEARNING OBJECTIVE 2 Summarize why contemporary criminologists do not consider the concept of evil as an explanation of crime.	Modern criminological perspectives do not accept supernatural reasons for antisocial behavior. As a concept, evil resists measurement and often definition. The notions of moral poverty and evil are vague, difficult to define, and impossible to measure.
LEARNING OBJECTIVE 3 Analyze the classical school of criminology's focus on the offense as opposed to the offender by emphasizing the concept of free will.	The basic tenet of classical thought is that criminal offenders freely choose to break the law. Classical criminology does not consider whether a person is impoverished, uneducated, hungry, desperate, or of low intelligence; it does not consider the offender's motivation. It ignores offenders' rationalizations and excuses and instead punishes them for their behavior. Consequently, the law considers what has been done rather than who did it.
LEARNING OBJECTIVE 4 Discuss the Enlightenment's contribution of the social contract to criminology.	The Enlightenment idea of the social contract requires that individuals respect the rights and properties of others in order to expect that others show them the same consideration.

LEARNING OBJECTIVE 5 — Discuss the ideas of Cesare Beccaria and Jeremy Bentham as the primary architects of the classical school of criminology.	Italian thinker Cesare Beccaria sought to provide the rationale for a more fair and humane system of social control. The most important aspects of Beccaria's ideas are that rational punishment is necessary to preserve the social contract; legislative determination of law; judicial determination of guilt; the hedonistic psychology of deviance: maximizing pleasure and minimizing pain; social control as rationally calculated punishment; deterrence as the object of social control; and the focus on acts and not actors. English philosopher Jeremy Bentham advocated a new way of dealing with criminal behavior based on the concept of utilitarianism, which states that individuals should behave according to the principle of "the greatest good for the greatest number of people."
LEARNING OBJECTIVE 6 — Analyze the positivist school of criminology's assertion that individuals are influenced by external forces.	The positivist school considers the behavior of offenders and attempts to link explanations for this behavior to external, observable forces that can be measured, such as offenders' biological, psychological, and sociological traits. This departure from the classical school relies on a new set of assumptions: that determinism outweighs free will; that the offender matters more than the offense; that science trumps philosophy; and that indeterminate sentencing is more effective than determinate sentencing because the sentence should be tailored to the offender, not the offense.
LEARNING OBJECTIVE 7 — Show how neoclassical criminology recalls the principles of classical criminology.	Neoclassical criminology emphasizes free will and deterrence. It combines some of the principles of classical criminology with ideas from economic game theory, which argues that people make choices based on perceived outcomes with the goal of maximizing gain while minimizing the resources and output necessary to achieve their goals. Neoclassical criminology also emphasizes the offender's character and argues that the choice to break the law is contingent upon both opportunity and personal integrity.

Critical Reflections

1. **What were the implications of the Enlightenment for criminological thought?**
2. **Devise a modern sentencing scheme that incorporates the concept of proportionality into today's moral and political environment.**
3. **Is "evil" a concept that modern criminologists use to explain crime? Why or why not?**
4. **What are the policy implications of the classical school of criminology's focus on the offense rather than the offender?**
5. **What features of deterrence are necessary to make it effective? Why is this often difficult to achieve in the modern criminal justice system?**
6. **What are the modern implications of Bentham's Panopticon model of the prison?**
7. **In what ways is science fundamental to the positivist school of criminology?**

8. The classical school of criminology differs from the positivist school in terms of sentencing policy. One advocates indeterminate sentencing and the other determinate sentencing. Which is which, and what are their implications for offenders?

9. What are the differences between specific deterrence and general deterrence? Which is the most important to the functioning of a healthy society?

10. According to the situational crime prevention theory, what steps can be taken to discourage people from breaking the law?

Key Terms

classical school of criminology p. 89
demonology p. 86
determinism p. 96
deterrence theory p. 100
(The) Enlightenment p. 89
general deterrence p. 100
hedonistic calculus p. 94
neoclassical criminology p. 98
positivist school of criminology p. 96
premeditation p. 99
proportionality p. 94
rational choice theory p. 102
routine activities theory p. 103
scientific method p. 96
situational crime prevention p. 102
social contract p. 91
socialization p. 88
soft determinism p. 98
specific deterrence p. 100
utilitarianism p. 94

Instant Recall Terms

antisocial (ch. 1)
deterrence (ch. 3)
recidivism (ch. 1)

Notes

1 Harry Phillips and Elissa Stohler, "Murder in the Family: 'I Wanted Them Dead'," ABCNews, May 1, 2009, http://abcnews.go.com/2020/story?id=7470379&page=1. Accessed April 2018.
2 Ibid.
3 Ibid.
4 Ibid. Jeff Strange, "A Most Unusual Suspect," *Prosecutor* 37, no. 5, September–October 2007, https://www.tdcaa.com/node/1448. Accessed April 2018.
5 Phillips and Stohler, "Murder in the Family."
6 Ibid.
7 Strange, "A Most Unusual Suspect."
8 Ibid.
9 Kit W. Harrison, report on Thomas Bartlett Whitaker, April 17, 2009, http://www.minutesbeforesix.com/MB6Files/2009/Exhibit 8—Psych Evaluation.pdf. Accessed April 2018.
10 Elissa Stohler and Harry Phillips, "What Would Drive a Young Man to Kill His Family?" ABC News, May 1, 2009, http://abcnews.go.com/2020/story?id=7461122&page=1. Accessed April 2018.
11 Grace White, "Gov. Abbott Commutes Death Sentence of Bart Whitaker," KVUE, February 22, 2018, http://www.kvue.com/article/news/gov-abbott-commutes-death-sentence-of-bart-whitaker/285-521864834. Accessed April 2018.
12 Phillips and Stohler, "Murder in the Family."
13 Daniel J. Boorstin, *The Seekers: The Story of Man's Continuing Quest to Understand His World* (New York: Vintage Books, 1998).
14 D. Alan Orr, "'God's Hangman': James VI, The Divine Right of Kings, and the Devil," *Reformation and Renaissance Review: Journal of the Society for Reformation Studies* 18, no. 2 (July 2016): 137–154.
15 Bassam Tili, "The Challenge of Fundamentalism," in *The Challenge of Fundamentalism: Political Islam and the New World Disorder* (Berkeley: University of California Press, 1998).
16 Jamaal E. O'Neal, "Couple Charged in Death Tried to 'Rid Infant of Demons,'" *Longview News-Journal*, December 4, 2008; Paul James, "Ill Mother Who Killed Sons May Face Execution," *JournalLive*, December 8, 2007, http://www.thejournal.co.uk/news/north-east-news/ill-mother-who-killed-sons-4512842. Accessed April 2018.
17 Stephen Pfohl, *Images of Deviance and Social Control: A Sociological History*, 2nd ed. (New York: McGraw-Hill, 1994), 23.
18 Frank J. Lechner and John Boli, eds., *The Globalization Reader*, 3rd ed. (Malden, Mass.: Blackwell, 2008). See Part VIII, "Cultural Globalization II: The Role of Religions," 343–398.
19 Michel Foucault, *Discipline and Punish: The Origins of the Prison*, trans. Alan Sheridan (New York: Pantheon, 1978).
20 Pfohl, *Images of Deviance and Social Control*, 29.
21 Graeme Newman, *The Punishment Response* (Philadelphia: Lippincott, 1978), 37.
22 Aaron Fichtelberg, *Crime Without Borders: An Introduction to International Criminal Justice* (Upper Saddle River, N.J.: Pearson-Prentice Hall, 2008), 196.
23 William J. Bennett, John J. DiIulio Jr., and John P. Walters, *Body Count: Moral Poverty and How to Win America's War Against Crime and Drugs* (New York: Simon and Schuster, 1996).
24 Joel Richman, Dave Mercer, and Tom Mason, "The Social Construction of Evil in a Forensic Setting," *Journal of Forensic Psychiatry* 10, no. 2 (September 1999): 300–308.
25 Dan J. Stein, "The Neurobiology of Evil: Psychiatric Perspectives on Perpetrators," *Ethnicity and Health* 5, no. 3/4 (August 2000): 303–315.
26 Bennett, DiIulio, and Walters, *Body Count*.
27 William J. Bennett, John J. DiIulio Jr., and John P. Walters, "Moral Poverty and Crime," in *Criminological Theory: Past to Present*, 3rd ed., ed. Francis T. Cullen and Robert Agnew (Los Angeles: Roxbury, 2006), 477.

28 Stephen E. Brown and Fin-Aage Esbensen, "Thoughts of Deterrence: Evolution of a Theoretical Perspective," *International Journal of Offender Therapy and Comparative Criminology* 32, no. 3 (December 1988): 219–232.
29 Crane Brinton, ed., *The Portable Age of Reason Reader* (New York: Viking Press, 1956).
30 Isaiah Berlin, ed., *The Age of Enlightenment: The 18th Century Philosophers* (New York: Meridian, 1984).
31 Brown and Esbensen, "Thoughts of Deterrence," 219–232.
32 Peter Gay, ed., *The Enlightenment: A Comprehensive Anthology* (New York: Simon and Schuster, 1973), 15–25.
33 Thomas Hobbes, "A Tough- Minded View of Power and Nature," in *The Portable Age of Reason Reader*, ed. Crane Brinton (New York: Viking Press, 1956), 137–141.
34 Michael E. Tigar, *Thinking about Terrorism: The Threat to Civil Liberties in Times of National Emergency* (Chicago: American Bar Association, 2007), 160–161.
35 John Locke, "Politics and the State," in *The Portable Enlightenment Reader*, ed. Isaac Krammick (New York: Penguin Books, 1985), 395–404.
36 John Locke, "On the Reform of the Poor Laws," in *The Enlightenment: A Comprehensive Anthology*, ed. Peter Gay (New York: Simon and Schuster, 1973), 100.
37 Jean Jacques Rousseau, *The Social Contract*, trans. Charles Frankel (New York: Hafner Publishing, 1947).
38 Karl Marx and Frederick Engels, *The Communist Manifesto in Selected Works* (New York: International Publishers, 1968).
39 Cesare Beccaria, *On Crimes and Punishments*, trans. Henry Paolucci (Indianapolis, IN: Bobbs-Merrill, 1764/1963), 99.
40 Pfohl, *Images of Deviance and Social Control*, 71–73.
41 Robert J. Mutchnick, Randy Martin, and W. Timothy Austin, *Criminological Thought: Pioneers Past and Present* (Upper Saddle River, N.J.: Prentice Hall, 2009), 1–13.
42 Gilbert Geis, "Jeremy Bentham (1748–1832)," in *Pioneers in Criminology*, ed. Hermann Mannheim (Montclair, N.J.: Patterson Smith, 1972), 15–68.
43 Mark M. Lanier and Stuart Henry, *Essential Criminology* (Boulder, Colo.: Westview Press, 1998), 70–71.
44 Jeremy Bentham, *An Introduction to the Principles of Morals and Legislation* (London: Athlone Press, 1970).
45 David Cole, *Enemy Aliens: Double Standards and Constitutional Freedoms in the War on Terrorism* (New York: The Press, 2003).
46 Foucault, *Discipline and Punish*.
47 Christian Parenti, *The Soft Cage: Surveillance in America from Slavery to the War on Terror* (New York: Basic Books, 2003).
48 Biographers note one humorous incident in which Darwin was collecting beetles and, having one in each hand, spied a third specimen that he wanted. He popped that beetle into his mouth and was promptly rewarded with a foul taste as the beetle excreted a mild poison designed to ward off predators. Janet Browne, *Charles Darwin: Voyaging* (Princeton, N.J.: Princeton University Press, 1995).
49 David Quammen, *The Reluctant Mr. Darwin: An Intimate Portrait of Charles Darwin and the Making of His Theory of Evolution* (New York: W. W. Norton, 2006).
50 Ian Taylor, Paul Wilson, and Jock Young, *The New Criminology: For a Social Theory of Deviance* (New York: Harper and Row, 1973).
51 Ruth Kornhauser, *Social Sources of Delinquency* (Chicago: University of Chicago Press, 1984).
52 Mark M. Lanier and Stuart Henry, *Essential Criminology* (Boulder, Colo.: Westview Press, 1998), 108.
53 Marilyn Irvin Holt, *The Orphan Trains: Placing Out in America* (Lincoln: University of Nebraska Press, 1992).
54 William Julius Wilson, *When Work Disappears: The World of the New Urban Poor* (New York: Alfred A. Knopf, 1996).
55 Derek B. Cornish and Ronald V. Clarke, *The Reasoning Criminal* (New York: Springer, 1986).
56 James Q. Wilson, *Thinking about Crime* (New York: Vintage, 1975).
57 Gregg Pogarsky, "Identifying 'Deterrable' Offenders: Implications for Research on Deterrence," *Justice Quarterly* 19 (2002): 431–452.
58 Daniel S. Nagin and Raymond Paternoster, "Enduring Individual Differences and Rational Choice Theories of Crime," *Law and Society Review* 27 (1993): 467–496.
59 Richard Moran, *Knowing Right from Wrong: The Insanity Defense of Daniel M. Naughter* (New York: The Free Press, 1981).
60 Marvin E. Wolfgang, Robert Figlio, and Thorsten Sellin, *Delinquency in a Birth Cohort* (Chicago: University of Chicago Press, 1972).
61 Ibid.
62 Ibid.
63 Ibid.
64 Alex R. Piquero and Greg Pogarsky, "Beyond Stafford and Warr's Reconceptualization of Deterrence: Personal and Vicarious Experiences, Impulsivity, and Offending Behavior," *Journal of Research in Crime and Delinquency* 39 (2002): 153–186.
65 Kenneth D. Tunnel, *Choosing Crime* (Chicago: Nelson-Hall, 1992).
66 Ronald V. Clarke and Derek B. Cornish, "Rational Choice," in *Explaining Criminals and Crime*, ed. Raymond Paternoster and Rona Bachman (Los Angeles: Roxbury Publishing, 2000), 23–42.
67 Derek B. Cornish and Ronald V. Clarke, *The Reasoning Criminal* (New York: Springer, 1986).
68 Ronald V. Clarke, *Situational Crime Prevention: Successful Case Studies* (Albany, N.Y.: Harrow and Heston, 1997).
69 Bill McCarthy and John Hagan, "Danger and the Decision to Offend," *Social Forces* 83 (2005): 1065–1096.
70 Lawrence E. Cahan and Marcus Felson, "Social Change and Crime Rate Trends: A Routine Activities Approach," *American Sociological Review* 44 (1979): 588–607.
71 John E. Eck, "Preventing Crime at Places," in *Evidence-Based Crime Prevention*, ed. Lawrence W. Sherman, David P. Farrington, Brandon C. Welsh, and Doris Layton MacKenzie (London: Routledge, 2002), 241–294.
72 Pamela Wilcox, Kenneth C. Land, and Scott A. Hunt, *Criminal Circumstance: A Dynamic Multicontextual Criminal Opportunity Theory* (New York: Aldine de Gruyter, 2003).

Biological and Psychological Theories

FEATURES

Individuals are capable of feeling many types of emotions. How can a psychological perspective help explain unlawful behavior?

Sheriff Art Schley escorts Edward Gein (right) into Central State Hospital for the Criminally Insane. Could Gein's diagnosis of schizophrenia explain his gruesome criminal offenses?

One evening in November 1954, Ed Gein visited a tavern in Plainfield, Wisconsin, where 51-year-old Mary Hogan worked. He shot her in the head and dragged her on a sled back to his remote farm where he had lived alone since the deaths of his father, brother, and mother. Three years later, Gein entered a local hardware store where 58-year-old Bernice Worden worked. He loaded a bullet into a rifle that was for sale. While Bernice wrote a receipt for a jug of antifreeze, Gein shot her, put her body into the back of his truck, and drove home.[1]

Worden's son, Frank, who was the deputy sheriff of Plainfield, thought it odd when Gein had questioned him earlier in the week about when he was going hunting. When Worden returned home Saturday afternoon, he found the hardware store locked, blood on the floor, and an unfinished receipt for the antifreeze Gein had said he was going to buy that day.[2]

While Worden arrested Gein at a local restaurant, Sheriff Arthur Schley drove to Gein's farm. Some local residents who knew Schley agree that what he saw there likely contributed to the fatal heart attack he eventually suffered. Ed Gein had not been idle since the death of his imperious mother Augusta in 1945. Although she had abused her two sons, Gein was heartbroken about her passing and had been careful to avoid women because she had warned him that, except for herself, they were all evil and promiscuous. Fascinated with Nazi lore, Gein began exhuming the corpses of women from a local graveyard and used his taxidermy skills to preserve his finds. When Sheriff Schley entered the house, he found Bernice Worden's mutilated body, as well as items crafted from human skin and bones, and human organs in the freezer and on the stove.[3]

Gein, now 51, pleaded not guilty by reason of insanity, was diagnosed with schizophrenia, and sent to a psychiatric institution. After a trial that did not take place until 1968, a judge agreed with Gein's initial plea, and Gein spent the rest of his life in institutions. He died in 1984.[4]

Early Biological Approaches

LEARNING OBJECTIVE | 1

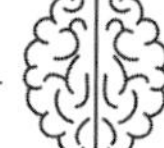

Explain why early biological theories of criminology advance our understanding of criminology.

The introduction of science revolutionized the development of criminological theory. The Enlightenment in the 18th century transformed the way we understand the physical world and began the search for external causes of crime. Rather than relying on religion or philosophy to tell us why and how people break the law, several thinkers cast a scientific eye on a broader range of ideas and possibilities. Consider the opening case of Ed Gein. Prior to the 18th century, an offender like him might have been considered to be possessed by a demon or under the influence of some sort of witchcraft. It is unlikely he would have received any legal proceedings or been housed at the expense of the state in anything resembling a psychiatric institution. He probably would have been tortured and almost certainly killed. It is the positivists of later centuries who would consider Gein to be "sick" and in need of treatment, and they would try to understand from biological or psychological points of view what made him do the things he did.

This chapter highlights the history of the scientific perspective and illustrates some of the limitations and abuses of science that have plagued the criminal justice system. As the quality of science improves, biological and psychological explanations hold great promise for advancing our understanding of crime. By understanding the history of these explanations, not only can we better appreciate their potential for explaining crime and delinquency, but also avoid their possible abuse.

Early biological theories of criminology were limited by the technology and scientific knowledge of their times. They emerged largely from 19th-century Europe, spurred by the publication of Italian physician Cesare Lombroso's work, *L'Uomo delinquente* (1876).[5] The text, which debuted to great criticism and some awe from the scientific community, offered few, if any, new criminological ideas. Instead, it presented some old-fashioned ideas in a **positivist** light—that is, it emphasized observable facts—and placed them in charts and tables, along with a striking collection of ancient representations of "criminal types" and photographs of modern offenders complete with their tattoos, handwriting, and graffiti. It was not Lombroso's content that caught the imaginations of scientists and the public, but his presentation of it in an orderly and documented fashion. It seemed that Lombroso had learned how to measure a soul.[6]

Meanwhile, the United States was experiencing increased industrialization, heavy immigration, urban growth, and the aftermath of a devastating civil war. The first three factors, which intensified until after World War II, contributed to a general increase in the crime rate. At the same time, **physiognomy**, the practice of determining a person's character by facial characteristics, and **phrenology**, the practice of determining a person's character and mental faculties by measuring features of an individual's skull, were both becoming popular. Together with positivism, they provided an attractive way to try to probe criminality. If the nature of a plant or an animal was related to its physical appearance, wouldn't the same hold true for human beings?

The problem with this idea is that our perception of human appearance is greatly affected by our culture and social expectations. As we now understand, what one culture finds beautiful and desirable another finds ugly and undesirable. A face that a 19th-century European would have defined as "criminal" may not have appeared remarkable at all in another part of the world. In fact, recent research has discovered that even some facial expressions, such as fear and disgust, are not universal as was once thought and that people from various cultures interpret some expressions differently.[7] Not understanding this difference, proponents of physiognomy and phrenology continued to measure noses and eyes and bumps on the head well into the 20th century. These forays into measurement are significant, however, because they represented a first attempt in the new pursuit of criminology (which was not yet a science) to measure **antisocial** behavior.

Influence of the morality or immorality of the physiognomy, vintage engraved illustration, 1847. Do you make judgments about people's character based on how they look?

Physiognomy and Phrenology

Physiognomy has been practiced for centuries and likely represents one of the first formalized searches for character and personality within the human body. After all, human emotion shows mainly on the face, so why not look for clues to character there?

Some of the first written references to physiognomy appear in ancient Greek texts. One ancient writer tells of Socrates recognizing Plato's philosophic abilities upon first studying his face. Aristotle wrote extensively about physiognomy, including how to recognize a variety of character dispositions in facial features. An 1836 magazine article that reports this history of physiognomy asserts that the practice was out of style and remained popular only among the "low born, those given to belief in old saws, superstitions, and the marvelous, and as a parlour game."[8] In fact, physiognomy gained in popularity as positivism took root in the late 19th and early 20th centuries, and its criminological adherents were serious about using it to recognize and predict criminality.

---

positivist—An approach that places emphasis on observable facts.

physiognomy—The practice of determining a person's character by facial characteristics.

phrenology—The practice of determining a person's character and mental faculties by measuring bumps and other features of an individual's skull.

Instant Recall from Chapter 1 **antisocial**—Following standards of behavior intended to harm society and individuals.

Phrenology, developed sometime at the turn of the 19th century by Franz Josef Gall, has hung on for a long time, even until the present day. Its official website states that "[p]hrenology is a true science, which is there to benefit humanity" and is a "powerful instrument" for, among other things, law enforcement.[9] An 1849 article describing its merits listed the "fundamental principles" of phrenology as:

1. The brain is the organ of the mind.
2. The mental powers of man can be analyzed into a definite number of independent faculties.
3. These faculties are innate, and each has its seat in a definite region of the brain.
4. The size of each of these regions is the measure of the power manifesting the faculty associated with it.[10]

Phrenology seems to have been more popular than physiognomy both as a parlor game and as a criminological tool. Criminology was never the main concern of phrenology: people visited phrenologists for all sorts of advice about daily living and revelations about their personalities. Some criminologists, however, did try to use it to divine criminality. As with Lombroso's work, the importance of phrenology lies not in any theory it offered, but in the way it approached the study of people. Gall, a medical doctor, practiced in Vienna where he also pursued phrenological research by studying people—alive and dead—in prisons, insane asylums, and royal courts. The Austrian emperor demanded that Gall stop because his efforts located the mind in the physical brain and not in the immortal soul. Gall's radical concept undermined religious teachings, threatened royal authority, and inspired the idea that an individual's actions spring from an organ that can be measured and understood as a product of this world and no other.[11]

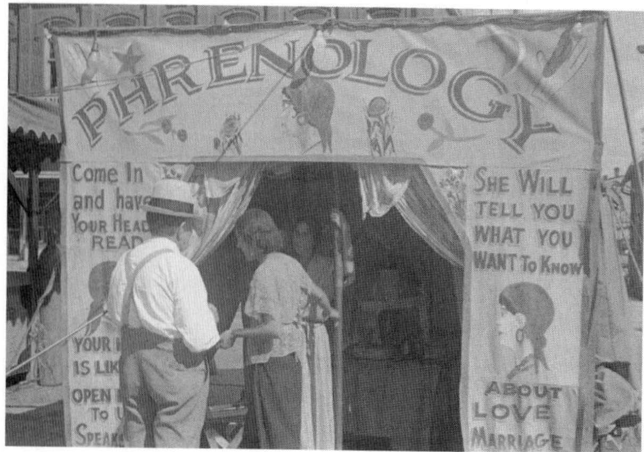

A phrenology reader's carnival attraction in London, Ohio, 1938. Besides being a dubious science, what were some of the other objections to phrenology that were voiced in the 18th century?

Body Types

A 2008 study of Arkansas prison inmates found that an unusually large percentage of those incarcerated for violent offenses were physically fit. The study's authors cautioned that an athletic build does not predict criminality but rather may be tangentially related to it. For example, the drive to stay in shape may be related to aggression, or athletic people may end up in violent situations more often because they feel they can "handle it."[12]

This study is an example of **body-type theory**, a school of thought that developed in criminology in the first half of the 20th century. Although the main thrust of this idea—that the shape of the body directly predicts criminality—has fallen out of favor, it is important because it tried to find some logical basis for criminality and a way to measure it. Popular in the mid-20th century, body-type theory is associated with several well-known criminologists who used aspects of it in their work or were inspired by it. Unfortunately, as we will see when we turn to genetic theories of criminology, early body-type theory influenced and was influenced by racism, fascism, and the idea that breeding could be used to "cleanse" humanity of "impure" types. We now look briefly at the three pioneers of body-type theory: Earnest Hooton, an originator of the theory; William Sheldon, whose ideas are still referenced today; and Sheldon and Eleanor Glueck, whose groundbreaking study of juvenile delinquents utilized some aspects of Sheldon's work.

EARNEST HOOTON AND THE CRIMINALS STUDY

Earnest Hooton, an anthropologist at Harvard University from 1913 to 1954, spent much of his career trying to prove Lombroso's assertion that the body displayed evidence of criminality. In the late 1920s, Hooton embarked on an ambitious, thorough study, gathering data on 17,000 prison inmates from 10 states as well as hundreds of militiamen, hospital patients, and firemen whom he used as control groups.

Hooton determined that each offender type exhibited specific characteristics which he deemed "inferior." First-degree murderers tended to be older, heavier, and taller than other offenders. Hooton also determined that offenders exhibited state-based differences. In his book *Crime and the Man*, Hooton illustrated the differences between the narrow forehead, short ears, and thick lips of a Kentucky offender and the wavy hair, heavy beard, and long earlobes of a Texas inmate.[13] In the end, Hooton came up with so many different types based on such a variety of criteria, such as skin color, state, offense, and country of birth, that his conclusions were useless.

Although Hooton's work saw some popular success, fellow academics and scientists heavily criticized it. The development of sociological theories of crime (covered in Chapter 6) was in full bloom, but Hooton was having none of it. As late as 1939, he insisted that "environment is the universal alibi of human failure," and he continued to pursue the idea that body shape was both source and sign of criminality.[14] His insistence that criminal offenders were "inherently inferior" beings who could not be reformed, should be sent to live on reservations, and should not be allowed to breed marked him as a vocal proponent of **eugenics**, the concept that human beings can degenerate or improve through breeding.

WILLIAM SHELDON AND SOMATOTYPES

William Sheldon was an itinerant scholar who made the study of body shapes and personality his life's work. Although he never earned a permanent appointment at any university and alienated many of his supporters, including Hooton, Sheldon's work is perhaps most associated with body-type theory. His system of **somatotypes**, the practice of determining a person's character by the shape of the body, is based on studies done in the 1920s by German psychiatrist Ernst Kretschmer. It still crops up today in descriptions of various body shapes. Sheldon proposed three basic somatotypes.

1. endomorphs—soft and round, often obese
2. mesomorphs—athletic, muscular, compact
3. ectomorphs—thin, fragile, intelligent

Sheldon's somatotype system was more complicated than simply identifying one of three body types, however. For example, individual physiques displayed some measure of each type, which Sheldon rated on a scale from 1 to 7. An athlete would rate 1-6-3—that is, low on endomorphic qualities, high on mesomorphic qualities, and somewhat less than average on ectomorphic qualities. An obese endomorph would rate 7-1-1. According to Sheldon, the perfect physique rated 4.5-4.5-4.5.

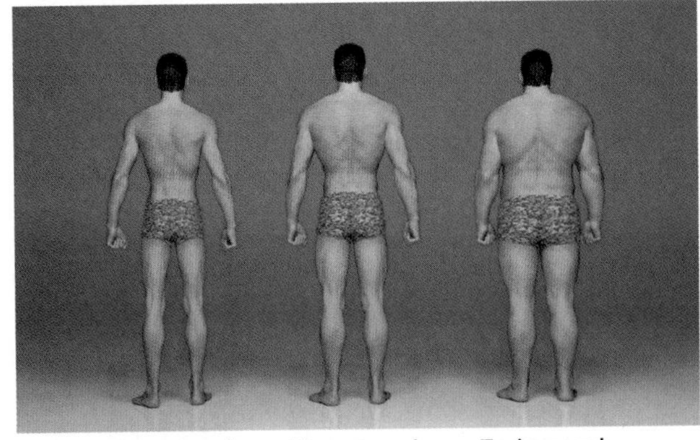

Body type illustration: ectomorph (thin type), mesomorph (muscular type), endomorph (heavy type). Why would determining a person's character based on body types be problematic?

In a later study of juvenile delinquents, Sheldon found that, relative to a control group of college students, the delinquents tended to be mesomorphs. This particular study was based on only 16 cases, however, and even Sheldon suspected that many non-criminal active types, such as athletes, generals, and businessmen, were also mesomorphs. Later criminologists found this result interesting. Recall that in the 2008 Arkansas study, researchers found most of the prison inmates to be physically fit and even used Sheldon's terminology, classifying the inmates as mesomorphs.

Sheldon's critics pointed out that most people did not precisely fit his categories and were more complex than the categories allowed. Although Hooton and Sheldon pursued similar ideas, they arrived at different conclusions. Hooton thought his data proved offenders to be physically inferior. Sheldon's data showed them to be fine physical specimens. Regardless, both thought humanity needed to be saved from its own biology, and the way to do this was through what Sheldon called ""discriminate breeding" or Hooton's outright eugenics.[15]

THE GLUECKS AND JUVENILE DELINQUENCY

The most comprehensive study of juvenile delinquents, *Unraveling Juvenile Delinquency*, was conducted by researchers Sheldon and Eleanor Glueck

---

body-type theory—The idea that the shape of the body directly predicts the propensity for criminal offending.

eugenics—The concept that human beings can degenerate or improve through breeding.

somatotype—The practice of determining a person's character by the shape of the body.

in the 1950s. The Gluecks gathered detailed and wide-ranging data on 500 delinquent boys and 500 non-delinquent boys, including statistics on their families, personal characteristics, intelligence, school performance, friends, church attendance, health, and body type. Although the Gluecks used somatotyping and were inspired and assisted by Hooton and Sheldon, they were careful researchers who gathered valuable data. Their **longitudinal** study was so thorough that in the 1990s criminologists Robert J. Sampson and John H. Laub resurrected it and followed up with many of the subjects.[16]

The Gluecks reported that their study's delinquents tended toward mesomorphic physiques and seemed more virile than the boys from the control group. Does this mean male delinquents and criminal offenders are more athletic and virile than law-abiding males? Probably not. Somatotyping represented only a single aspect of the Gluecks' study, and they were careful to assert that antisocial behavior did not stem from biology alone and that body shape in no way determined propensity for criminality. Like the Arkansas researchers, the Gluecks sought to explain their findings by proposing that people who are more energetic and athletic (especially boys) are more likely to act out because they can. Decades later, Sampson and Laub found that although the Gluecks' delinquents were often mesomorphs, this quality did not affect their likelihood of adult offending. Sampson and Laub proposed that 1950s judges reacted more harshly to athletic boys than to weaker-looking boys; as a result, more mesomorphs were found delinquent than endomorphs or ectomorphs.[17]

Early Biocriminology

Modern biological theories of criminology, or **biocriminology**, represent research that considers the brain and body as a source of antisocial behavior. Since antisocial behavior is an aspect of criminal offending, it is important to stress that biocriminologists look for behaviors, not offenses. No one can look at DNA or a brain scan and tell if that person is a shoplifter, a murderer, or a law-abiding person. Biocriminologists look at physical and mental processes, typically in combination with environmental factors, to understand how they may influence behaviors that influence a person to act contrary to what the law prescribes. Biocriminological factors may be genetic, neurological, hormonal, nutritional, or evolutionary.

The search for the causes of crime and hypotheses about the heritability of behavior has been volatile. Theories about society, culture, environment, and free will have always constituted the basis of criminology, and it is not unusual for theories about the heritability of antisocial tendencies to be dismissed outright. As criminologist Simon A. Cole observed, modern biocriminology is basically ignored by mainstream criminologists, and the work of biocriminologists is "almost never cited by anyone other than the authors themselves."[18] There is good reason for this attitude: The history of biocriminology is not pretty. It involves Nazis, eugenics, racism, classism, misogyny, and the classification as "feebleminded" (a favorite term of eugenicists) whole families whom experts recommended should be prevented from reproducing.

Even as Lombroso was writing his work describing the physical manifestations of the "criminal type," Augustinian monk and father of genetics Gregor Mendel was wrapping up his groundbreaking studies of **heredity**, the biological process in which genetic characteristics are inherited by one generation from the last. Also, Charles Darwin's *On the Origin of Species* (1859) had just been published, demonstrating in the **theory of evolution** that biological forms change over time through genetic inheritance. Neither Darwin nor Mendel directly addressed the subject of crime: Mendel studied pea plants, and Darwin was partial to barnacles and insects. However, many social thinkers were eager to apply Darwin's and Mendel's ideas to human behavior—often with malicious results. The resulting pseudoscience of eugenics (discussed in more detail in the next section) was inspired by ideas about heredity and some early evolutionary theory. Given a mid-18th-century rise in crime, immigration, and general social unrest, eugenics was an explosive philosophy. At its worst, it led to forced sterilization and the Nazis' murder of millions during World War II.

PERSPECTIVES ON HEREDITY, HUMAN EVOLUTION, AND CRIME

The concepts of heredity and the theory of evolution greatly affected criminological thinking in the late 19th and early 20th centuries. Some scholars shifted away from the classical concept that offenders were like anyone else except that they decided to break the law to the positivist idea that lawbreakers were physically or mentally different from law-abiding people. Although they did so with the best intentions, some chilling social attitudes resulted.

Although Darwin's theory of evolution does not specifically address antisocial behavior or crime, some thinkers did not hesitate to try to apply it to criminology. Early criminological thinkers incorrectly interpreted Darwin's theory to mean that lawbreakers were less evolved than the law-abiding. Actually, Darwin's view of evolution was that organisms do not necessarily evolve into something better and that no "arrow" of evolution directs organisms from crude to perfect. Early social thinkers placed lawbreakers at a point on an imaginary line closer to beasts than to human beings.[19]

Darwin did produce some social commentary. His ideas on social and moral evolution in *The Descent of Man* (1871) helped inspire the concept of **social Darwinism**, or the idea that public welfare of any sort only helped the unfit survive to weaken society. Herbert Spencer (1820–1903), the English philosopher who originated social Darwinism, believed that society is literally an organism and crime a disease that had to be "cured." Like germs, lawbreakers had to be eliminated if society were to thrive.[20] At the individual level, the concept of **atavism**, an idea espoused by Lombroso and German morphologist Ernst Haeckel (1834–1919), stated that some people were born before they progressed through all the evolutionary stages to become fully human and were "throwbacks" to an earlier stage of evolution. Although atavism was eventually discredited, it had a profound effect on criminology, as did the idea of devolution, or "backward" evolution.[21]

A related concept, "degeneracy," was considered to be heredity gone wrong. Instead of conferring physical and mental health and intelligence, heredity burdened degenerates with such harmful traits as criminality, mental and physical illness, and impoverishment (typically called "pauperism"). It was not unusual for social theorists to assign a single cause, such as degeneracy, to a host of mental, physical, and social problems and then to decree that the cause was the product of a similar host of social ills. For example, the champion of the degeneracy concept, French physician Bénédict Auguste Morel (1809–1973), determined degeneracy to be caused by moral turpitude; the failure of individuals to educate themselves; wet, marshy environments; alcohol and opium abuse; and poverty, disease, and crowded urban living. Degeneracy could be inherited or acquired, but subsequent generations were susceptible to inheriting it.[22]

In 1877, Richard Dugdale, an employee of the New York State Prison Association, published a landmark eugenics study, *The Jukes: A Study in Crime, Pauperism, Disease and Heredity*. The Jukes were a set of 42 families from upstate New York who boasted an unusual number of criminal offenders, vagrants, ne'er-do-wells, and "feebleminded" persons. After collecting a large amount of data, Dugdale concluded that the Jukes were costing taxpayers a great deal in welfare, incarceration, and social services. However, he did not claim the Jukes' problems were biological. Not only did he point to the families' impoverished circumstances and environment as the root of their behavior, he also called attention to the fact that criminality ran in wealthy and successful families. This part of his work went ignored, however, and *The Jukes* was cited as proof that criminal forebears produced criminal descendants.[23]

Ideas about inheritance, heredity, and degeneracy were thus typically applied only to those who were considered to be weak: immigrants, non-whites, the mentally ill, and the impoverished. The Victorian era was ending, and people accustomed to its strict social mores were aghast at the new century's rising squalor, chaos, social confusion, and crime. It was easy to point to petty lawbreakers and large, impoverished immigrant families and proclaim they must be closer to beast than human. Apparently, it was not so easy, however, to observe the era's robber barons, men responsible for vast financial and criminal offenses, and decry them as degenerates or devolved. As we will see, the eugenicists' prescriptions for social health never applied to the wealthy and upper class. Indeed, they were considered the "breeding stock" that would save American society through "good" marriages.

EUGENICS

Charles Darwin's cousin, British scholar Francis Galton, defined eugenics as "the study of the agencies under social control, that may improve or impair the racial qualities of future generations, either physically or mentally."[24] As discussed earlier, this definition refers to the selective breeding of people

Instant Recall from Chapter 2 **longitudinal**—A type of survey that follows respondents throughout their lives or a significant proportion of their lives.

biocriminology—The search for the causes of antisocial behavior within the brain or body.

heredity—The biological process in which genetic characteristics are inherited by one generation from the last.

theory of evolution—The idea that biological forms change over time through genetic inheritance.

social Darwinism—The idea that public welfare of any sort only helped the unfit survive to weaken society.

atavism—The idea that some people are born before progressing through all the evolutionary stages to become fully human.

In 2002, Oregon governor John Kitzhaber signs a declaration proclaiming December 10 as Human Rights Day in Oregon in 2002 after apologizing for the state's past use of forced sterilization. Girls in reform school, people in mental institutions, and poor women selected by state welfare workers were among the more than 2,500 Oregon citizens reportedly subjected to sterilization under a law that stood from 1917 to 1983. Why was sterilization an accepted practice in the early part of the 20th century?

to include desirable qualities and exclude undesirable ones. In the early 20th century, Galton's work helped replace vague ideas about inheritance with more solid theories about heredity and inspire the search for genetic predispositions to antisocial behavior in individuals.

The eugenics movement grew in popularity from about the turn of the 20th century to World War II. It focused mainly on improving human breeding in the United States partially by sterilizing social undesirables such as the impoverished, the "feebleminded," epileptics, the mentally ill, and so on (see Doubletake). Criminality was one of the undesirable qualities that eugenicists believed children could inherit. "Criminal," in this case, referred to anyone from shoplifters to murderers, and many criminologists believed frequent offenders should be sterilized. In the 1924 edition of his text *Criminology*, eminent criminologist Edwin H. Sutherland wrote: "In so far as it can be determined that criminality is connected with an inherited abnormal trait, it is clearly desirable to stop the reproduction of people who have that trait."[25]

Forced sterilizations, which were particularly easy to carry out on incarcerated offenders and other institutionalized people, continued until the early 1970s. In 1907, Indiana became the first state to legalize the mandatory sterilization of incarcerated offenders as well as those living in poorhouses and mental institutions. As of 1909, Washington and California had ratified their own versions of sterilization laws, followed later by Nevada, Iowa, New Jersey, and New York.[26] In all, 32 states had some sort of mandatory sterilization legislation, with the sterilization of offenders figuring prominently.[27]

Thanks to constitutional restrictions on cruel and unusual punishment, criminal offenders did not suffer the brunt of sterilization laws; instead, this was the sad burden of the intellectually disabled, mentally ill, and "feebleminded." Still, some states did manage to sterilize many offenders. The practice was largely ended in 1942 with the U.S. Supreme Court's decision in *Skinner v. Oklahoma*. In this case, a three-time recidivist successfully challenged Oklahoma's 1935 Habitual Criminal Sterilization Act, which declared that "habitual criminals"—anyone convicted of three offenses of "moral turpitude"—should be sterilized. The case turned on the Constitution's equal protection clause—the sterilization requirement did not apply to violators of the "prohibitory laws, revenue acts, embezzlement, or political offenses"—rather than on the morality of forced sterilization. It effectively halted the states' push to sterilize criminal offenders.[28]

PAUSE AND REVIEW

1. **Analyze how early biological approaches to explaining crime may have been unfair and harmful.**
2. **Differentiate between body types and somatotypes.**
3. **How did Cesare Lombroso attempt to use science to explain antisocial behavior?**
4. **How did physiognomy and phrenology seek to predict antisocial behavior?**
5. **What major criminological theorist used the concept of degeneracy to describe how heredity acted to produce offspring inclined to breaking the law?**

DOUBLETAKE

The Undesirables

Although we associate forced sterilization with totalitarian governments and war crimes, the idea of sterilizing certain people was once openly discussed in the United States. In 1911, a panel of the American Breeders Committee, composed of several of the country's top medical and government professionals, created a list of 10 "antisocial classes" to be eliminated through sterilization. When all the "defectives" were totaled—including institutionalized and noninstitutionalized people, those deemed of "inferior blood," and their apparently normal relatives—the number of people to be sterilized was about 11 million, or what was then 10 percent of the population. The plan was never implemented.

Ten classes were targeted for sterilization:

1. The feebleminded—This blanket term presumably included anyone of low intelligence, the intellectually disabled, and the mildly mentally ill.
2. The pauper class—Impoverished people.
3. The inebriate class—Alcoholics.
4. Criminals—This category included everyone from serious offenders to those jailed for offenses such as non-payment of fines.
5. Epileptics.
6. The insane.
7. The constitutionally weak—This term presumably refers to people who were unhealthy for unspecified reasons.
8. Those predisposed to specific diseases.
9. The deformed.
10. Those who could not see, hear, or speak.[29]

THINK ABOUT IT

1. What gave rise to proposals for forced sterilization?
2. Are you or is anyone you know on the list of "undesirables"?

Modern Biological Perspectives

LEARNING OBJECTIVE | 2

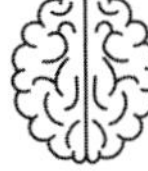

Discuss how genetic and evolutionary perspectives seek to explain antisocial behavior in human beings.

LEARNING OBJECTIVE | 3

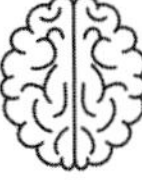

Discuss how neurological perspectives seek to explain antisocial behavior in human beings.

LEARNING OBJECTIVE | 4

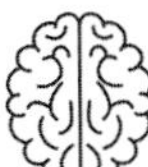

Discuss how environmental perspectives seek to explain antisocial behavior in human beings.

With advances in medicine and genetic science, criminology has returned to the search for a biological component in antisocial behavior. Instead of looking for indistinct markers of criminality and seeking sterilization for recidivists and the mentally ill, however, researchers are now able to look directly at the brain, DNA, and other biological factors that may affect individual antisocial behavior. Many, if not most, researchers theorize that the interplay between biology and environment, often referred to as "nature and nurture," affects antisocial behavior and not one or the other exclusively. Still, academic criminology has not fully accepted biocriminology. Social theories of criminology—which we turn to in Chapter 6—have largely held sway since the 1930s. However, work on finding a link between biology and antisocial behavior continues.[30]

Genetic and Evolutionary Perspectives

Research into the possible effects of genes and evolutionary influences on behavior has surged in recent decades, spurred by the discovery of genes for various ailments and psychological conditions and the use of DNA in investigating criminal offenses and wrongful convictions. Although researchers still arrive at dead ends, such as XYY syndrome (see the next section), other lines of inquiry show promise, including the search for which genes (if any) affect behavior, twin and adoption studies, and hypotheses about the evolution of human behavior.

XYY SYNDROME

Human beings have 23 pairs of chromosomes. Females have two X chromosomes (XX), and males have one X and one Y (XY). **XYY syndrome** occurs when males receive an extra copy of the Y chromosome. They may be taller than average but typically have no other unusual physical features. However, they are usually at increased risk of learning disabilities and delayed speech and language development, delayed motor skills development, weak muscle tone, and sometimes behavioral and emotional issues. Most XYY cases are not inherited.[31]

In 1965, British researchers studying a group of 197 Scottish inmates discovered that seven of them had an extra Y chromosome and calculated that XYY males represented about 3.5 percent of the male prison population. These "supermales" were said to be potentially more violent than normal males.[32] Since then, studies of the possible relationship between XYY syndrome and antisocial behavior have been inconclusive. According to a roundup in 2000 of current hypotheses, scholars are trying to discourage the notion that XYY males are more likely to break the law, and studies showing high rates of XYY males in prison populations have been challenged. There have been few, if any, rigorous criminological studies on XYY and criminality in the past 20 years; with the consensus that "most XYY carriers lead normal, productive lives," this hypothesis appears to be dormant.[33]

GENES AND BEHAVIOR

The suggestion of a straightforward relationship between genes and behavior is perhaps one of the most controversial in biocriminology. As mentioned earlier, biological researchers, including biocriminologists, believe both genes and environment are responsible for behavior rather than genes alone.[34] Criminologist Adrian Raine corrects several other misconceptions about the influence of genes on crime.

- One gene is not responsible for antisocial behavior. There is no "crime gene." A likely scenario for any connection between genes and crime is that a set of genes is responsible for biological processes that make an individual somewhat more likely to break the law.
- Genetics cannot explain antisocial behavior in individuals. Heritability applies to populations, not individuals. It is impossible to pinpoint how much of a criminal offender's behavior is genetic, how much is environmental, and how much is free choice.
- Genetically determined antisocial behavior can be changed. Environmental factors have such a strong effect on behavior that it is impossible to state that any genetic predisposition to antisocial behavior cannot be altered by such things as therapy, rehabilitation, or punishment.
- Genetic study reveals information about more than genetic influences. Such study can, in fact, provide much information about the effects of environment. For example, twin and adoption studies (discussed in detail later in this chapter) provide particularly important data about environmental factors such as home life; nutrition; and sibling, parent, and peer relationships.
- Genes may predict a propensity for antisocial behavior. A common criticism of biocriminology is that the concept of crime exists only as a social construct, so criminality cannot be genetically determined. However, the symptoms of some mental disorders that may lead to antisocial behavior are socially defined. Raine gives the example of schizophrenia. Although the symptoms and effects of this mental illness are socially defined, it has a strong genetic component and has been found to run in families.[35]

So how are researchers studying the genetic aspects of antisocial behavior? It is a challenging task because environmental influences are so pervasive and complex; it is not uncommon for genetic studies to produce inconsistent findings. Samples that appear similar may produce different results simply because they were subjected to different environments. According to some theories, people who are

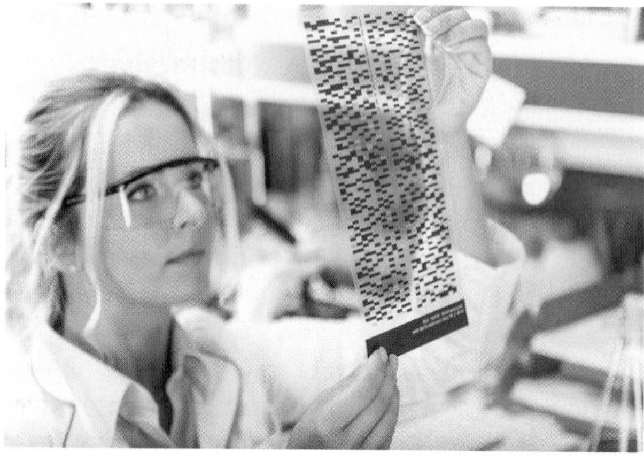

A scientist examines DNA autoradiogram test results in a biochemical laboratory. How has the science of genetics increased our understanding of human behavior?

more likely to break the law lack impulse control and empathy and are more likely to take risks and resort to violence. It is possible that these broad propensities are biological in origin.[36] Other studies claim to have found clear evidence of a genetic basis for personality traits such as novelty-seeking, aggressiveness, and **impulsivity**, or action taken on a whim without consideration of the consequences—all of which are considered to be related to antisocial behavior.[37] At least one study has noted a "robust" relationship between antisocial behavior and brain function.[38]

Here are three examples of the types of studies researchers are pursuing.

- Research on children has found genetic propensities not only for aggressive behavior related to bullying, but also for introverted behavior related to being bullied. That is, both bullies and victims show hereditary personality traits related to their social positions as either bully or victim, or both. One heritable personality trait found to be particularly related to this complex of behavior is "emotional dysregulation," a condition characterized by mood and personality swings. Found in both bullies and victims, it is particularly strong in children who are both.[39]
- An especially important criminological subject is juvenile delinquency. It is rare for a person to go through childhood and adolescence with perfect behavior and then begin serious offending as an adult. Some research has found evidence of genetic determinants for individuals who begin breaking the law as juveniles and continue to do so throughout adulthood. It is possible that these types of offenders may have deficits in brain function. As it is currently estimated that 60 percent of the human genome codes for brain structure and function, faulty brain function, and thus a greater chance of offending, may be genetic.[40] Another study claims to have pinpointed not only three genetic variants for serious and violent delinquency, but also ways the environment affects these variants. One variant is affected by family meals, social services, and the presence of two biological parents; another is affected by school attachment and repeating a grade; yet another is affected by a friend's delinquency. Researchers found that strong family, school, and social networks dampen the delinquency effects of the genetic variants, and weak networks increase them. This, the study explains, is why chaotic environments produce delinquency in some children (who possess the genetic variants) but not in others (who do not possess the variants).[41]
- A controversial line of inquiry is "epigenetics," the study of the biochemical signals that turn genes on or off. When applied to the study of behavior, epigenetics takes the genetic/environment relationship to a new level. For instance, an article from the environment, say a nutritional factor, affects a parent's genes, which then passes that effect to the parents' offspring. An example was found in a study on agouti mice. Under normal circumstances, the fat, yellow agouti mice, which are prone to cancer and diabetes, have offspring just like them. However, if researchers fed the female mice a special diet while they were conceiving their litters, most of the offspring were slim, brown, and healthy. So, although the mothers passed along the agouti gene to their litters, a chemical in their food negated its effects.[42] The application of epigenetic effects to the study of inheritance in human behavior is infinitely more complicated. However, discoveries suggest that the environment of a child's parents or even grandparents may determine aspects of the child's behavior as well as health.[43]

TWIN AND ADOPTION STUDIES

Studies of identical twins and people raised by nonbiological parents are a particularly useful form of research on the effects of genes and environment on behavior. According to researchers Michael Rutter, Terrie E. Moffitt, and Avshalom Caspi, although twin studies have revealed important genetic influences on most types of psychopathology, adoption studies have played the most important role in revealing the influence of genes on behavior.[44]

Produced by the division of a single fertilized egg, identical twins have the same set of genes and thus offer researchers a unique opportunity to study similarities or differences in their reactions to their environments. Using adoption studies, researchers can observe the effects of a familial environment on someone who does not share that family's DNA. Both types of study can separate the effects of genes and environment somewhat.[45] A study of 1,133 twin

---

XYY syndrome—A condition that occurs when males receive an extra copy of the Y chromosome.

impulsivity—Action on a whim without consideration of the consequences.

pairs in Sweden explored the effects of socioeconomic environments on adolescent delinquency. The twins self-reported their antisocial behavior, and their families' socioeconomic status was determined by education and occupation. Researchers assessed neighborhood socioeconomic conditions through ethnic diversity, educational level, unemployment level, purchasing power, and crime rate. They found that genetic influences on antisocial behavior were more apparent in adolescents in wealthier socioeconomic environments, whereas they had diminished influence on the antisocial behavior of adolescents in less-wealthy socioeconomic environments. In other words, a delinquent teen in a wealthy neighborhood is more likely to be influenced by genes, but a delinquent teen in less advantaged surroundings needed less genetic prompting to break the law and was more likely to be influenced by environment.[46]

Research on adopted subjects must use studies in which the subjects' biological parents are known. One database that provides this information is the Danish Adoption Cohort Registry. A 1983 study using this registry concluded that the antisocial tendencies of biological parents were more indicative of an adopted subject's likelihood to break the law than those of the adoptive parents. For example, males whose biological fathers and adoptive parents were criminal offenders were most frequently convicted of breaking the law themselves. Males whose biological fathers were offenders but whose adoptive parents were not were the next most frequent lawbreakers. Females showed these same relationships, though in lower numbers. All the subjects' convictions were for property offenses, not violent offenses, and the researchers found no relationship between parental offending and violent offenses.[47] A later U.S. study supported these findings somewhat, finding that having a biological criminal father was related to psychopathic personality traits in male adoptees, though not in female adoptees.[48]

Twins share the same genetic makeup. How can studying twins inform criminological research?

EVOLUTION, AGGRESSION, AND SURVIVAL

According to some perspectives, antisocial behavior influences human evolution. Behavior considered inappropriate and destructive in our society may once have played a useful role in the development of human beings, and possibly it still does. Hypotheses typically address aggression as related to mate selection, reproduction, survival, and status. Let's look at a few examples of these ideas.

- Rape. Some researchers propose that rather than being a particularly egregious example of antisocial behavior, rape is an adaptation that helps some males better distribute their genes. Biological scholars Randy Thornhill and Craig T. Palmer hypothesize that women are traditionally more physically invested in child-bearing than men due to their role in pregnancy, nursing, and caring for infants. Therefore, women are choosier than men about the quality of their mates. Men, who have little investment in individual children but more interest in increasing the number of offspring who carry their genes, are more interested in quantity of mates. Rape allows them to increase the number of mates and, therefore, the number of possible offspring.[49] A criticism of this hypothesis is that it assumes rape is purely a biological process involving no psychological, cultural, or social processes, such as belief systems or customs and their effects on individual decision-making.[50]
- Aggressive behavior. This perspective views both aggression and aggression-control as having evolutionary advantages. Aggression, in this case, includes a range of behaviors such as self-defense, hunting, athletic competition, occupational competition, children's play behaviors, as well as what we now consider criminal behavior. From an evolutionary standpoint, being aggressive enough to fight off intruders and win competitions but not so aggressive that clan members are constantly fighting each other is advantageous.[51]
- Status-striving. According to evolutionary neuroandrogenic theory, females have evolved to prefer males who strive for status; in response, males spend more time and energy than females trying to attain status. The act of status-striving

is actually a type of aggressive behavior that exists on a continuum from competitive to victimizing.[52] At the competitive end of the continuum, status-striving activities are typically sophisticated and rewarded by society (for example, by attaining a high-paying job or being good at sports). Status-striving behaviors at the victimizing end are those behaviors society punishes (for example, bullying, fighting, and crime). Males begin to display this kind of behavior at puberty when they start to compete for mates. Those with better learning abilities quickly move from victimizing status-striving to competitive status-striving behavior. Males with poor learning abilities move slowly or not at all.[53]

In what ways has aggressive behavior been considered an advantageous type of evolutionary adaptation?

Neurological Perspectives

Some criminologists and behavioral scholars think neurological conditions affect antisocial behavior.[54] These conditions are related to genetic and evolutionary criminological perspectives because, except in the case of injury or some illnesses, they are likely affected to some degree by heredity and adaptation, which affect brain functioning. As in the genetic and evolutionary perspectives, most scholars stress that antisocial behavior is not a product of physical attributes alone but is most likely a function of the interplay between biology and environment. Biological behavioral research is just beginning to understand the relationship between the functioning of the human body and the social environment, so the theory is still developing. With that in mind, we will take a look at three promising areas of research: neurotransmitters, hormones, and the brain itself. This research does not look for direct links to crime but for antisocial behaviors that may lead to crime. See Policy Implications for more insights on the links between the brain and crime.

NEUROTRANSMITTERS

Neurotransmitters are chemicals that transmit messages between nerve cells in the brain. The neurotransmitters most important to the study of behavior are serotonin, norepinephrine, and dopamine, which control mood and feelings such as aggression and pleasure. The amount of neurotransmitters in an individual's brain is determined by genes, which is why genetics is important to the study of neurotransmitters and behavior. The amount of active neurotransmitters is controlled by the brain enzyme monoamine oxidase A (MAOA). Located on the X chromosome, MAOA breaks down neurotransmitters and makes them inactive. Studies have shown that people with low MAOA are more aggressive and react more strongly to stress than those with high MAOA.

A longitudinal study of 442 males from New Zealand followed the male subjects from birth to age 26 and recorded their individual levels of MAOA activity and whether they were abused as children. The researchers were looking for evidence of a relationship between genes and environment—in this case, how an individual's MAOA gene equipped him to react to his environment.[55]

The study found that 36 percent of the men had suffered frequent changes in primary caregivers, rejection by their mothers, or physical or sexual

POLICY IMPLICATIONS

Establishing Links Between the Brain and Crime

Despite the misgivings of some mainstream criminologists, biological research is making inroads into public policy. Technological advances mean that conclusions about behavior are a far cry from the early days of biological theorizing. For instance, brain-imaging evidence showing that adolescents may be unable to exercise mature impulse and emotional control and to properly estimate risk was influential in *Roper v. Simmons* (2005).[56] As far as the determination of individual culpability is concerned, brain imaging is considered to show the most promise so far. One researcher lists the following issues that brain imaging might help resolve:

- Does the defendant have neurological damage?
- Do the brain abnormalities, if any, fit the nature of the offense?
- Is the defendant faking a mental illness or insanity?
- Is the defendant lying?
- If the defendant is guilty, what is the likelihood of recidivism?[57]

Some criminologists suggest that a better understanding of what makes antisocial behavior tick, even if biological influences are slight or are complicated by environment, will lead to more and better rehabilitative treatments of offenders as well as improved public health initiatives.[58]

THINK ABOUT IT

1. Can science provide us with accurate tools to base new techniques to treat or punish offenders?
2. Is it ethically or morally appropriate to examine the brain for evidence of future deviance?

abuse from ages 3 to 11. Men who were abused as children and had the low-activity MAOA gene were nine times as likely as the rest of the **cohort** to fight, bully, lie, steal, and disobey during adolescence. This small subgroup of antisocial males, 12 percent of the cohort, accounted for 44 percent of the group's violent offense convictions. The more serious the childhood abuse, the more violent the low-MAOA males became. The other three subgroups—males with the high-MAOA gene who had been abused, those with the low-MAOA gene who had not been abused, and, of course, those with the high-MAOA gene who had not been abused—were all equally unlikely to engage in antisocial behavior.[59]

An interesting aspect of this study is the experts' estimate that about a third of males carry the low-MAOA gene, which means it probably has a purpose, although no one knows what it is. Finally, this research also offers an explanation of why women are less prone to violent antisocial behavior. The MAOA gene is carried only on the X chromosome, so men, who have one X and one Y chromosome, get only one copy of it. Women, with two X chromosomes, get two MAOA copies, which makes them more likely to receive a high-activity version of MAOA and therefore, some researchers say, makes them more likely to be buffered against a bad environment.[60]

Instant Recall from Chapter 2 **cohort** —A group of people who share statistical or demographic characteristics.

HORMONES

Hormones are chemicals produced by the body that control the activity of cells and organs. The hormones discussed in this section, testosterone and cortisol, affect the brain and behavior, specifically aggression and fear. Nervous, chemical, and perceptual signals stimulate hormone production, which may regulate short-term activities such as a quick response to an external threat or long-term processes such as sex differentiation, maturation, and reproduction.[61] Hormones can both affect and indicate how the brain functions. The study of hormones has practical applications in the criminal justice system because they are easy to measure and target for treatment. Testosterone and cortisol have been associated with antisocial behavior and with some characteristics of psychopathy, such as lower reactions to stress, fearlessness, aggression, and stimulation seeking.[62]

Testosterone, which stimulates the development of male sex characteristics, is produced in significant amounts by the testicles and in small amounts by the ovaries. It is popularly associated with "macho," aggressive behavior, but the relationship is not as simple as "more testosterone equals more machismo." Rather, testosterone is only one factor in a complex of physiological, psychological, and social influences.[63] However, evidence suggests that the aggressive, risk-taking behavior testosterone appears to affect can become antisocial behavior. Men with higher testosterone levels are more likely to be arrested, traffic in stolen property, sustain bad debts, and use a weapon in fights.[64] One study has reported that prenatal exposure to elevated levels of testosterone and other androgens (the class of male sex hormones that includes testosterone) increases the probability of criminal offending later in life.[65] Testosterone levels also peak in young adult males, which coincides with the fact that most criminal offenses are committed by young adult males.

Evolutionary neuroandrogenic theory, discussed above, states that male sex hormones affect the brain to increase the probability of violent criminal offending.[66] A study found positive correlations between self-reported criminal offending and physical characteristics associated with androgens. Self-reported violent offending was correlated with "masculine body appearance, physical strength, strength of sex drive, low or deep voice, upper body strength, lower body strength, and amount of body hair. Among males, even penis size was found to be positively correlated with criminality."[67] According to evolutionary neuroandrogenic theory, testosterone and other androgens are responsible for helping the male brain learn what researchers call "competitive/victimizing behavior." Although males are born with competitive/victimizing tendencies, the rush of testosterone at the onset of puberty further pushes them into this behavior. Young males may manifest these changes with rule-breaking and boundary-testing, including increased aggression and juvenile delinquency.[68]

Cortisol is a hormone released during stress that activates a fear response to mobilize the body's resources and provide energy. It is also believed to help generate sensitivity to punishment and induce individuals to withdraw from difficult situations. High cortisol levels make reaction to stress more likely; low cortisol levels make them less likely. Apparent at an early age, low cortisol might be involved in the development of antisocial behavior. Associated with weak fear reactions in young children and increased sensation-seeking in adult males, low cortisol may decrease sensitivity to punishment and increase dependency on rewards. Several studies have shown low cortisol levels in psychopathic offenders, aggressive children, adolescents with conduct disorder, and violent adults.[69] Finally, research has found that individuals who are the most violent have high levels of testosterone and low levels of cortisol.[70]

Testosterone levels peak in young males. Are increased testosterone levels related to aggressive behavior and crime?

THE BRAIN

Some researchers believe antisocial behavior may be affected by structures within the brain, injury to those structures, or the nature of the brain itself (see Theory to Practice for more on this belief). Two brain regions that researchers think particularly affect behavior are the amygdala and prefrontal cortex, both of which control mood and decision making. A good example of how the brain's condition may affect behavior occurs in the juvenile brain. Many scientists now assert that before the age of 20 and possibly even 25, the brain does not function like the brain of a fully mature adult and that adolescents and children may perform poorly when challenged with situations requiring foresight, judgment, and wise decision-making.[71]

Located in the middle of the brain, the amygdala is an almond-shaped structure that plays a role in initiating emotional memories, rage, fear, aggression, and sexual feelings. It may also influence our awareness of important events and help us separate the significant from the common. Damage to this important structure may cause increased feelings of aggression and fear.[72] One researcher has even stated that diminished amygdala response to emotional stimuli is typical of psychopathic brain activity. That is, people with healthy amygdalas respond to the distress of others with increased amygdala activation. People with low-responding amygdalas show little emotional response to others' distress (or to their own) and therefore have trouble caring about others, which is an important aspect of moral decision-making.[73]

The most infamous example of possible amygdala disruption is the 1966 case of Charles Whitman. After killing his wife and mother, he barricaded himself in a tower at the University of Texas and fatally shot 14 people and wounded 31 others before being killed by police. Whitman, who had been an Eagle Scout, Marine, and university student, had also come from an extremely abusive family. As a young adult, he began having intense headaches and described disturbing thoughts, including the desire to "take a deer rifle and start shooting people." After his behavior began to deteriorate in 1961, he was court-martialed, lost his scholarship, began beating his wife, and in 1964 had his father—the man who beat him as a child—help him procure an honorable discharge from the military. As a University of Texas student, he told a school psychologist that he feared something was wrong with him. Before embarking on the killings, Whitman left notes expressing how much he loved his wife and mother and wondering why he killed them, as well as a note requesting an examination of his brain upon his death.[74]

Although an autopsy revealed a walnut-sized tumor compressing his amygdala, experts still do not agree whether this caused his behavior given his meticulous planning and preparation for the shootings. Still, some researchers point to the disruption of Whitman's amygdala as a likely causative element within a group of factors that included childhood abuse; school, family, and work stress; and the use of pharmaceutical stimulants.[75]

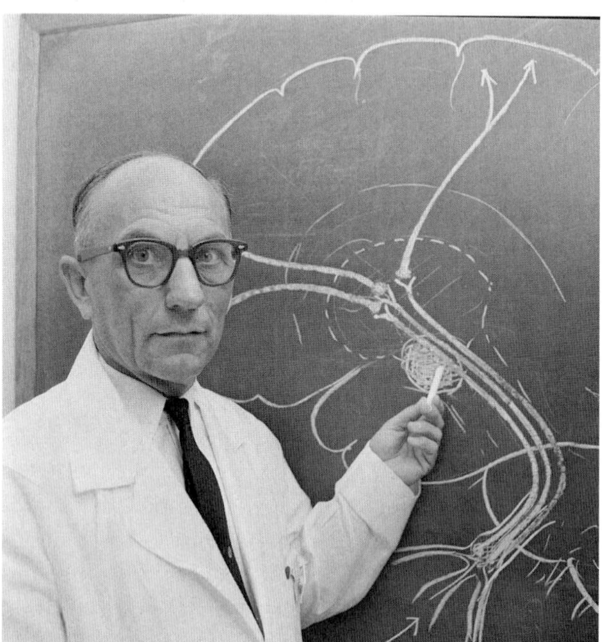

Dr. Coleman de Chenar, who performed the autopsy on Charles J. Whitman, shows the location of the small tumor that he found in Whitman's brain. De Chenar said the pecan-size tumor could have led indirectly to Whitman's actions. Discuss what might have happened to Charles Whitman in court had he been captured alive and tried.

The prefrontal cortex is a frontal lobe structure highly developed in human beings and responsible for problem solving, emotion, and complex thought. Damage to this structure has been reported to impair emotional and social abilities such as empathy, insight, and recognition of emotions in others. Several types of mental illness, such as schizophrenia, bipolar disorder, and attention-deficit/hyperactivity disorder, show abnormal patterns in the prefrontal cortex.[76] Brain-imaging studies have found that low prefrontal cortex volume, as well as abnormal activity and reduced interconnections from the frontal lobes to the rest of the brain, are common in people who are depressed, under constant stress, incarcerated, or have committed suicide.[77] Because the prefrontal cortex integrates information from other parts of the brain to help produce choices and decisions, a severely damaged structure may translate into actions that the thinker, who knows the actions to be wrong or unwise, would typically repress.[78]

In one case, part of the prefrontal cortex of a 35-year-old man was removed due to cancer. Although the surgery did not affect the man's intelligence and memory, it did compromise his ability to act appropriately and morally. Formerly extremely moral and loved by his friends and family, he began to make poor financial decisions that eventually cost him his family and his job, and he later married and quickly divorced a prostitute. Although he could apply moral judgment to ethically problematic situations, he could not act upon this judgment. Despite knowing the best choice, he consistently chose immediate gratification, even though he knew it would lead to a bad outcome for himself and others.[79]

Frontal lobe abnormalities in general seem to be closely associated with violent and criminally offensive behavior. Studies have found that adults with damage in certain frontal lobe areas tend to exhibit impulsive, aggressive behavior. In other studies, subjects with antisocial personality disorder displayed a significantly reduced prefrontal area and diminished prefrontal activity. In short, researchers are finding the frontal cortex regions to be essential to behavioral inhibition, as well as the anticipation of punishment and reward—neurological activities that are critical to successful social function.[80]

Although it had been acknowledged for decades that children's decision-making abilities are less developed than those of adults, no one was sure why.

Now, brain imaging allows us to see exactly how young brains differ from adult brains and to understand how this difference affects information processing, perception, and moral reasoning. Neuroscience is beginning to play an important role in the legal treatment of juveniles.

A brief submitted by the American Medical Association in *Roper v. Simmons* (2005), in which the U.S. Supreme Court considered the constitutionality of the death penalty for offenders who had committed capital offenses before age 18, stated that the incomplete prefrontal development of adolescent brains means that adolescents are less able to control their impulses and cannot be held fully accountable for their actions.[81] In the end, the Court held that the execution of such offenders was unconstitutional.

Exactly what is different about the young brain? Neuroscientists believe the frontal lobe—which, as we discussed, helps restrain impulsive behavior—does not begin to mature until age 17. That means the part of the brain the legal system is most concerned with—the part that controls rational decision-making—is not even fully active until late adolescence. Some neuroscientists believe full maturation does not occur until age 25. So although adults and juveniles have the same basic brain structures, adults process information in a more complex fashion than juveniles. One study found that in decision-making tasks, youths relied mainly on the prefrontal cortex, whereas adults used other parts of the brain as well. Studies that focus on the amygdala, which processes emotional and risk responses, indicate that adolescents act more erratically than adults. Although this finding should not surprise anyone who has raised teenagers, it is remarkable to find evidence for it within the brain.

In the study, researchers had adolescents and adults identify facial displays of emotions in a series of photographs. Brain scans of both young and mature brains showed the amygdala firing upon perceiving a face that showed fear; however, the prefrontal cortex, which became markedly active in adults, showed little response in adolescents. Researchers interpreted this to mean that adolescent brains do not process emotional responses in the same way adult brains do. This dimmer response could also indicate that the adolescents often misidentified fearful faces as angry. Brain researchers agree that adolescents also have trouble with the neurological activity that allows predicting the consequences of risky actions, which means they are likely to take more risks.[82]

Environmental Perspectives: Alcohol and Drugs

Some environmental elements, including nutrition and harmful substances such as lead, are considered to affect antisocial behavior and lawbreaking.[83] Two studies of young adults who grew up in impoverished urban neighborhoods linked childhood lead exposure to a significant loss of brain tissue in the areas responsible for impulse control, emotional regulation, judgment, and anticipation of consequences. The study found that the higher the concentration of lead in the subjects' blood during childhood, the more likely they were to be arrested during adulthood, particularly for violent offenses.[84] Recently, disease and nutrition were cited as elements in a criminal charge against a diabetic woman whose reaction to low blood sugar may have caused a fatal car accident (see Theory to Practice).

Still, the substances most commonly connected to antisocial behavior and criminal offending are drugs, including illegal substances and pharmaceuticals, and alcohol. Whereas statistics on the antisocial effects of nutrition and common chemicals must be gathered through research, the federal government keeps a tally of the effects of drugs and alcohol on crime, which makes them much easier to observe.

Drugs and alcohol are closely associated with crime. According to the Bureau of Justice Statistics study, about 63 percent of jail inmates are habitual drug users, and about 47 percent are habitual alcohol users.[85] Inmates who were substance dependent or substance abusers were more likely than other inmates to have a prior criminal record.[86] During one five-week study, about 25 percent of incidents in which the police were called involved alcohol, whereas only 3 percent involved drugs.[87] Alcohol is implicated in more than 50 percent of violent offenses; the cost of alcohol-related crime is estimated at about $205 billion.[88] Violence between intimates is especially likely to include alcohol abuse.[89] More than a third of state prison inmates serving time for a violent offense said they were under the influence of alcohol at the time of the offense.[90]

ALCOHOL

Alcohol is related to antisocial behavior and crime, though its exact role is unclear. However, criminologists question whether inebriation causes antisocial behavior or crime. Clearly, not everyone who gets drunk breaks the law; indeed, most people who become drunk manage to avoid doing so. Therefore, criminologists seek to understand the relationship

THEORY TO PRACTICE

Low Blood Sugar, Bad Judgment, or Both?

On March 11, 2017, a Chevrolet Equinox sped down Interstate 35 for several miles in the wrong direction. The driver, Lora Walker, 47, was described by a witness as "laughing and waving" as she headed down the wrong exit ramp and drove at speeds of 80 to 90 miles an hour. Motorists honked their horns and attempted to alert Walker as she careened down the highway. Oncoming cars swerved to avoid her, but she smashed head-on into a car driven by 62-year-old Gary Brisky, whose car flipped and caught on fire. Brisky died in the crash. Walker was airlifted from the scene and hospitalized.[91]

Walker, a county commissioner in Chisago County, Minnesota, was not drunk. She was suffering from low blood sugar. She told first responders that she was a diabetic and knew her blood sugar was low. In her car they found glucose tablets, insulin pens, a kit used to check glucose levels, candy bars and cookies, and paperwork indicating that Walker had brittle type 1 diabetes with hypoglycemia unawareness.[92] Patients with this diagnosis have trouble realizing that their blood sugar has dropped because they feel no symptoms.[93]

Walker had a history of difficulty in managing her diabetes. In 2009, her driver's license was revoked after she crashed into a freeway retaining wall. It was reinstated on the condition that she report any diabetes-related loss of consciousness to the Department of Public Safety.[94] However, Walker had at least four episodes— in 2011, 2012, 2014, and 2016—that she failed to report.[95]

On the day of the crash, Walker had been with a home care provider who was monitoring her blood sugar. After the provider left, Walker called her mother, who told police that she had heard her daughter's blood-sugar alarm over the phone. Eleven minutes after the call, Walker was on the highway.[96] Walker has been charged with criminal vehicular homicide and faces a maximum sentence of up to 10 years in prison and/or a $20,000 fine.[97]

THINK ABOUT IT

1. Although the car crash was almost certainly an accident, and Walker's disease is not her fault, she is still criminally charged in the death of Gary Brisky. Why?
2. Can you think of other circumstances in which criminal behavior can be the result of forces outside of one's control? What should the criminal justice system do in these cases?

between alcohol and crime more fully rather than simply pointing to alcohol as causing crime. A better understanding of the inebriation/crime relationship would help lighten the burden on the criminal justice system by improving preventive, therapeutic, and rehabilitative measures for people who commit alcohol-involved offenses or who are at risk of doing so. Researchers seek to understand the effects of alcohol, the characteristics of drinkers, the situations in which alcohol-related crime happens, and the cultural context of alcohol-related antisocial behavior.[98]

One study found that adolescents with no history of conduct problems who drank alcohol early in their teen years were more likely to become substance dependent, contract herpes, have early pregnancies, and be convicted of criminal offenses as adults.[99] Alcohol is also deeply connected to aggressive antisocial behavior. Crime suspects are more likely than crime victims to be intoxicated, and emergency room studies show that patients with violence-related injuries are two to five times more likely to be drunk at the time than people who sustained injuries unrelated to violence.[100] So, although alcohol is not considered to cause crime, it certainly is related to the behaviors most likely to lead to arrest. Why?

- Alcohol is disinhibiting. Its effects on the brain lead to reduced anxiety about the consequences of aggressive behavior while increasing physical reaction to mental perceptions, which thus raises the intensity and level of aggression. Alcohol also affects the balance of serotonin and dopamine in the brain, which reduces impulse control.[101]
- Alcohol reduces sensitivity to pain, which further lessens individual concern about the consequences of aggressive actions.
- Alcohol impairs physical functioning, which increases the likelihood of a drunk individual invading others' physical space.[102]
- The impairment of mental functioning also affects the ability to create nonaggressive solutions to problems, to focus attention, and to restrain emotions. At the same time, inebriation also generates

a form of shortsightedness in which minor incidents are blown out of proportion, which increases the scale of emotional response.[103]

These effects depend not only on individual characteristics, but also on cultural and situational contexts. Inebriation presumably has the same disinhibiting effects on everyone, but only some break the law or engage in violence. However, a disproportionate percentage of those people are affected by alcohol. Criminologists are still trying to clarify this issue.

DRUGS

In the U.S. government's war on drugs, the criminal justice system has defined a category of criminal offense related to the trafficking and possession of non-pharmaceutical and pharmaceutical drugs, although it is not against the law to be addicted to anything. Because this complex topic merits its own text, we will not discuss the war on drugs but will focus instead on the relationship between drugs and antisocial behavior.

Criminologists agree that, as with offending and alcohol, there is a definite empirical relationship between lawbreaking and drugs. What is unknown is the exact nature of that relationship, and there is no agreement that drug use causes crime.[104] There are three models of the drugs–crime connection.

- The enslavement model. Drug addicts and abusers are enslaved by drugs and must commit economic offenses to get the money to support that addiction. Legitimate jobs do not pay enough to support the addiction and/or do not allow the user to take drugs at will. If drug users were not enslaved by drugs, they would not break the law to any great degree. Drug legalization would curtail much drug-related crime because it would allow users to better manage their addictions. Two major assumptions of the enslavement model are that drug users continue their usage to avoid withdrawal symptoms and would be satisfied to maintain their addictions without increasing their usage.[105]
- The predisposition model. It is not drug users but criminal offenders who turn to drugs. Drug users are offenders and delinquents first because they are always seeking novel, risky experiences. Drug addiction is merely part of a criminal lifestyle that many habitual drug users prefer, and they would continue to break the law with or without drugs. Legalization would have no effect on their criminal activities in general.[106]
- The intensification model. This model combines the other two. Drug usage does not cause crime but intensifies it. It is indeed part of a criminal lifestyle that already exists, but it drives addicts and abusers to break the law even more than they normally would. Drug legalization would not end their criminal careers, but it would reduce their offending.[107]

Researchers explore elements of these perspectives when probing the relationship between drugs and crime. For example, the amount of offending may be related to the type of drug. Cocaine and heroin are the two drugs most closely related to crime when volume of consumption is considered.[108] However, a 2005 study still found no direct, causal relationship between heroin and crack cocaine use and theft-related offenses, including shoplifting and street robbery. Such offenses tended to be desperate acts that were sometimes committed only once.[109]

Related to the predisposition model, a 2001 study found that the order in which offenders' drug dependence and criminal career began was important to the type of offending. Those who began offending after becoming drug-dependent were much less likely to commit predatory offenses such as robbery and theft and instead committed victimless offenses such as prostitution. However, those who offended prior to drug dependence were more likely to commit predatory offenses; they also began both criminal careers and drug dependence at earlier ages than people who were drug-dependent first.[110] Risky, sensation-seeking behavior is an element: In nearly every study ever conducted, people who frequently broke the law were more likely to use illegal drugs, drink alcohol, and smoke cigarettes than those who did not.[111]

Critiques

Biological theories of criminology are not popular in mainstream criminology for three principal reasons. First, not only were early theories classist, racist, and sexist, but the search for a way to cure society of crime led to some heinous public policies directed at people who did not fit within a narrow ideal. Realization of these abuses, along with advances in sociological theory, gave mainstream criminology reason enough to abandon biological theories in the latter half of the 20th century. Modern critics of biocriminology worry that renewed interest in biological theories will lead to a 21st-century version of eugenics.[112]

Next, biocriminological research lacks focus and considers an overly broad range of factors. One criminologist stated that even if antisocial behavior does have biological factors, they are so slight that social institutions are better off concentrating on the factors that most certainly contribute to crime, such as social inequality and poverty.[113]

Finally, biocriminological research translates poorly to the criminal justice system. Although biocriminology may shed some light on the biological sources of some antisocial behavior, its conclusions are not strong enough to support public policy, law, or court decisions. In the case of brain imaging, for instance, researchers have warned that jurors are not qualified to accurately assess the significance of brain scans, which often appear more objective than they really are. Other scholars point out that the legal system asks pointed, direct questions about specific individuals, whereas biological research seeks generalizations about groups that share characteristics.[114]

PAUSE AND REVIEW

1. **Outline the evidence that contributed to the development of XYY syndrome as an explanation for aggressive behavior.**
2. **Discuss the connection of drugs and alcohol to criminal offending.**
3. **How have discoveries about brain chemistry and brain structure contributed to our understanding of crime?**
4. **How has the study of twins contributed to the development of genetic theories of crime and delinquency?**

Psychological and Psychiatric Perspectives

LEARNING OBJECTIVE | 5

Describe modern psychological and psychiatric theories of criminal behavior.

Psychological and psychiatric theories consider personality, intelligence, and the mind as factors that can inspire antisocial behavior and criminal offending. The psychological approach focuses on **cognition**—the act of thinking and perceiving—and learned behavior, whereas the psychiatric approach is concerned with neurological processes and illnesses. Throughout this section, you will notice some overlap between the psychological/psychiatric perspectives and the biological perspective. All three share a positivist approach in that they seek the source of antisocial behavior within the brain.

In this section, we will first take a brief look at the traditional psychiatric perspective on antisocial behavior and crime. We will then turn to current psychological and psychiatric perspectives. Before we move on, see Figure 5.1 for a look at where the focal points of the biological, psychological, and psychiatric perspectives correspond to the human body.

Traditional Psychoanalytic Theory

Traditional psychoanalytic theory was less concerned with crime than with explaining behavior—including antisocial behavior—in general. The father of psychoanalytic theory is Sigmund Freud (1856–1939), who sought to explain human behavior as the product of internal motives and drives. According to this perspective, human beings are naturally antisocial and selfish. Without the internal control of conscience and the external control of society, they will do anything to get what they want, including steal, lie, and kill.

The main tenet of the psychoanalytic perspective is that the source of human behavior is located within the individual unconscious, and the environment has only a limited influence on behavior.[115] Criminality is the result of unconscious conflicts. Two other assumptions place the bulk of socialization firmly in childhood. First, socialization depends on the quality and type of childhood experiences; second, a poor parent–child relationship affects the likelihood of delinquency. Although evidence for the first tenet has been hard to pin down, the last two—that adult behavior is rooted in childhood socialization—are the basis of numerous sociological theories of crime. Traditional psychoanalytical theory has not fallen completely out of favor, but scholars do not use it as a sole explanation for antisocial behavior.[116]

Modern Psychological and Psychiatric Perspectives

In this section, we will review a selection of current psychological and psychiatric theories. Although we cannot delve deeply into every theory, these perspectives represent current criminological thinking.

BEHAVIORISM

A psychological perspective concerned with observable human behavior, **behaviorism** states that environment and learning determine how individuals behave. Psychologist B. F. Skinner, the chief 20th-century proponent of behaviorism, held that behavior is the product of the environment and positive and negative reinforcements. This belief is the basis of **operant conditioning**, a form of learning based on the positive or negative consequences of an action, behavior, or activity. Let's look more closely at Skinner's ideas on reinforcement.

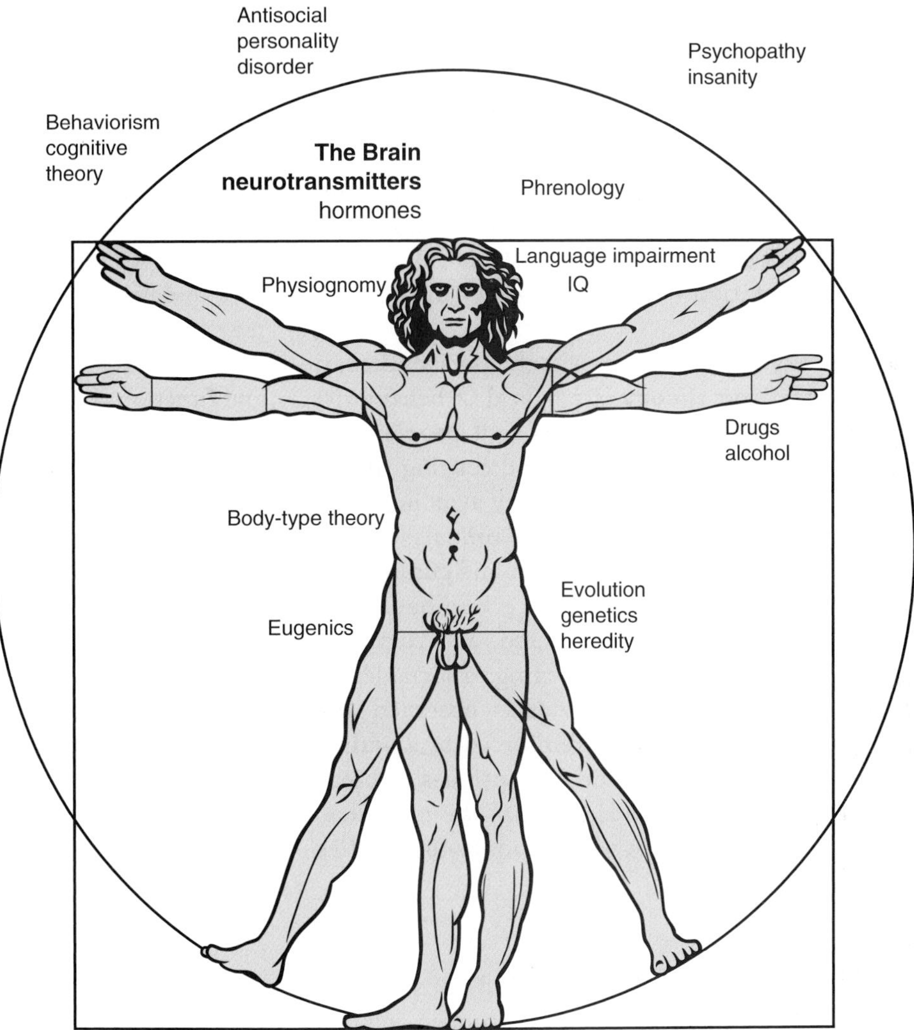

FIGURE 5.1 Biological and Psychological Theories in Relationship to the Human Body

THINK ABOUT IT
Which biological or psychological perspective do you think best describes the reasons for antisocial behavior? Why?

Through **positive reinforcement**, which is the rewarding of a successful action, we engage in behavior designed to gain something we want. Through **negative reinforcement**, which is ending an undesirable consequence as a means of reward, we engage in behavior to avoid something we do not want. An example of positive reinforcement is giving a rat a piece of cheese if it successfully completes a maze. Negative reinforcement is turning off a loud, irritating noise if the rat successfully completes the maze. **Extinction**, according to Skinner, is no reaction to a behavior at all—that is, neither punishment nor reinforcement. Skinner believed punishment to be less effective than extinction because it only temporarily stops a behavior; extinction shows that the behavior brings no reaction. In the case of a misbehaving child, for example, a parent using extinction would not react to the behavior. According to Skinner, the child sees that the behavior brings no reaction and desists.

We can apply Skinner's ideas to operant conditioning and antisocial behavior. According to Skinner, we learn antisocial behavior from the social environment and reinforcements. A financial manager learns from criminal peers that defrauding investors is safe and profitable. The manager's peers have grown wealthy by defrauding investors and have not been caught, so the manager begins her investment scams and becomes wealthy. In this way,

---

cognition—The act of thinking and perceiving.

behaviorism—A perspective stating that environment and learning determine how individuals behave.

operant conditioning—A form of learning based on the positive or negative consequences of an action, behavior, or activity.

positive reinforcement—Rewarding a successful action.

negative reinforcement—Ending an undesirable consequence as a means of reward.

extinction—No reaction to a behavior.

the criminal activity is positively reinforced. This, in a nutshell, is Skinner's behavioral theory. Although his theory inspired current psychological and sociological criminological theories, such as social learning, most criminologists today find his ideas too simplistic on their own. Skinner believed operant conditioning was the key to all human behavior. He saw little effect from genetics and little value in the study of cognition because we cannot directly observe it.[117]

Although considered a behaviorist theory, **social learning theory** is a hybrid of behaviorist and cognitive theories. It holds that people learn how to act by watching others and copying the interactions that are rewarded and by avoiding those that are punished. So, like other animals, human beings are subject to reinforcement and punishment and can be conditioned toward certain behaviors. However, we are also complicated, and cognition affects our behavior, too. According to social learning theory, antisocial behavior is observed and learned from others, then reinforced by criminal activity. Whether an individual continues to break the law, however, depends on what the individual thinks about the activity, which leads us to cognitive theory.

COGNITIVE THEORY

Cognitive psychology is the study of memory, language processing, perception, problem solving, thinking, and other mental processes—in essence, how people think. An area of focus includes the way the mind mediates between an external stimulus and the response to that stimulus. In criminology, we can use cognitive psychology to learn more about the mental processes that precede the decision to break the law. One of the main theories is psychologist Lawrence Kohlberg's stages of moral development, which suggests how we learn to use our minds to negotiate the social world. Let's take a look at this theory and its utility in criminological thought.

According to Kohlberg, children pass through six stages of moral reasoning as they grow up (see Table 5.1). Kohlberg thought the transition to the post-conventional level of moral development ideally occurred during early adulthood, although some people never move past the early stages, which can lead to delinquency and adult offending. For example, some studies of delinquents found that they exhibit a lower stage of behavior than non-delinquents and function as low as level 2.[118]

Although it makes sense that people who break the law must be morally challenged, some theorists caution that Kohlberg's stages measure moral reasoning, not moral behavior. Therefore, discrepancies often turn up between subjects' answers to questions about which stage of moral development they have achieved and the morality of their actual behavior. A white-collar offender may place himself at stage 5 and agree with the ideas at that stage but exhibit stage 1 behavior.

LANGUAGE IMPAIRMENT AND IQ

A psychological perspective related to cognitive theory invokes the roles of IQ and language ability in delinquency and adult crime. Some studies have found low IQ and language impairment, especially in boys, to be solid predictors of delinquency. Some scholars think the connection is indirect, however, with low intelligence and language ability leading to trouble communicating with others, frustration in school, and eventual withdrawal from pro-social activities. Perspectives on intelligence, IQ, and language are considered developmental because they focus on how the process of cognitive development from child to adult may contribute to antisocial behavior and lawbreaking. Learning to think and communicate are integral to the maturation process, and disruptions can lead to social and psychological isolation, which, according to some researchers, can lead to delinquency and adult offending.

A 1993 study found problems speaking and understanding language at age 3 to be a reliable predictor of adult offending.[119] A later study found that boys who were language impaired at age 5 were far more likely to be delinquent at age 19, with higher rates of arrests and convictions, than boys without language impairment. Language impairment in girls, however, was unrelated to delinquency.[120]

---

social learning theory—The idea that people learn how to act by watching others and copying the interactions that are rewarded and avoiding those that are punished.

cognitive psychology—The study of memory, language processing, perception, problem solving, thinking, and other mental processes.

IQ (intelligence quotient)—A measure of intelligence taken by dividing a person's mental age by chronological age, then multiplying by 100.

TABLE 5.1 Kohlberg's Six Stages of Moral Development

	STYLE OF REASONING	IDEAL PERIOD
LEVEL 1	Preconventional level—Moral reasoning is based on obedience and avoidance of punishment	middle childhood
STAGE 1	The rules of others	
	Pursuit of personal interests with the expectation that others will do the same. Exchanges should be equal.	
STAGE 2	Individualism	
	Children obey because they are told to. Moral decisions are based on threat of punishment.	
LEVEL 2	Conventional level—Moral reasoning is based on the expectations of family and significant others.	late childhood
STAGE 3	Relationships and conformity	
	Moral judgments are based on relationships, trust, and emotions.	
STAGE 4	Law and order	
	Belief in and obedience of the social system	
LEVEL 3	Postconventional level—Moral reasoning extends beyond social conventions.	early adulthood
STAGE 5	The social contract	
	Value of the principles behind the law and some that are beyond the law	
STAGE 6	Universal ethics	
	Moral reasoning is based on the idea of equal human rights and following one's individual conscience.	

Source: Lawrence Kohlberg, The Philosophy of Moral Development: Moral Stages and the Idea of Justice, Essays on Moral Development Vol. *1 (San Francisco: Harper & Row, 1981), 17–19.*

A 2008 study found that delinquents in general have trouble understanding others' language and using language to organize their thoughts and express themselves. As a result, they are more likely to use non-verbal communication such as shoulder shrugging and poor eye contact to cover for their poor language skills. Such body language may be interpreted as insolent, rude, and uncooperative, which, according to the authors, can "incur a significant social penalty."[121]

IQ stands for "intelligence quotient," which is simply a measure of intelligence taken by dividing a person's mental age by chronological age, then multiplying by 100. The mental age is determined through testing. It is important to understand the difference between IQ and intelligence: IQ is a score on a test, whereas intelligence is represented by a range of mental abilities and is difficult to define. Many psychologists assert that IQ tests are culturally biased because they are encoded with a set of cultural concepts the test-taker must understand to score well. Regardless, IQ and school performance are closely connected: Children who do well on IQ tests do well in school, and good schools have a good effect on IQ. Just as consistent is the relationship between IQ and delinquency. Lower IQs mean a greater likelihood of delinquency. There is a particularly strong relationship between delinquency and low verbal IQ scores, which recalls our previous discussion about the relationship between language impairment and delinquency. These relationships are true not only for delinquents but also for adult offenders.[122] In the case of delinquency, some researchers look for an indirect effect of IQ. That is, instead of assuming that low IQ leads directly to delinquency, they look for other aspects of the juvenile's life that low IQ may be affecting, such as school performance and peer relationships. It is difficult for the juvenile to adopt pro-social attitudes if these elements are dysfunctional.[123]

ANTISOCIAL PERSONALITY DISORDER, PSYCHOPATHY, AND INSANITY

Antisocial personality disorder (APD) is a mental disorder characterized by a pattern of disregard for the rights of others, as well as impulsive, violent, and aggressive behavior without guilt. **Psychopathy**, a mental disorder that involves a severe lack of empathy, is more difficult to define, although it shares symptoms with APD, specifically the disregard of other people. Psychopathy and APD share so many characteristics that they are often confused, and some professionals believe they are the same condition.[124] Still others consider APD and psychopathy to be similar conditions on the same continuum, with psychopathy being the most severe form of APD-type disorders.[125] For now, the two conditions are generally considered distinct. Another controversial condition is insanity, which has different meanings in legal and medical circles and, like APD and psychopathy, is poorly understood.

About 3 percent of males exhibit APD compared to 1 percent of females. To be diagnosed, the individual must be at least 18 years old and have exhibited conduct disorder before age 15. A diagnosis must also include three of the following behaviors:

- failure to conform to social norms or the criminal law; frequent lawbreaking;
- irritability and unusual aggression; a tendency to get into fights or commit assaults;
- consistent irresponsibility at work and/or with finances;
- impulsivity; a failure to make plans;
- frequent lying or deceiving others for profit or fun;
- disregard for one's own or others' safety; and
- lack of remorse or guilt for wrongdoing.[126]

There are at least two major but not necessarily exclusive perspectives of APD. Both seek to explain why the disorder is so closely associated with offender populations.

- APD commonly occurs within disadvantaged and impoverished populations and is associated with chaotic, dysfunctional households. It is considered to run in families, not because the behavior is biologically inherited, but because children share the same socioeconomic difficulties as their parents.[127]
- Biological in origin, APD is caused by brain abnormalities, possibly dysfunction in the frontal lobe or nervous system. Those with APD display several negative cognitive characteristics, including inflexibility, attention deficits, misunderstanding of contextual cues, and poor behavioral choices.[128]

Although APD is closely associated with crime and antisocial behavior, some scholars and therapists think this association limits the diagnosis to offenders and excludes law-abiding people whose personalities show indications of APD. According to some psychologists, many people with symptoms of APD never enter the criminal justice system and are omitted from the diagnosis because their behavior is largely desirable, such as success in business and politics.[129] This is an intriguing observation, especially given the large number of scandals in business in the late 1990s and early 2000s that bankrupted thousands of people, finished a number of financial institutions, prompted massive government bailouts, and, in 2008, helped bring a recession that some said rivaled the Great Depression.

Recently, the APD diagnosis has fallen out of favor among some criminal justice professionals, who believe it has been overused. More than 50 percent of the correctional population—which includes inmates, probationers, and parolees—has been diagnosed with APD, according to one study.[130] The assignment of APD to such a broad swathe of people has been criticized as being of little practical use.

---

antisocial personality disorder—A mental disorder characterized by a pattern of disregard for the rights of others, as well as impulsive, violent, and aggressive behavior without guilt.

psychopathy—A mental disorder that involves a severe lack of empathy.

not guilty by reason of insanity (NGRI)—Generally, the acquittal of a defendant because he or she is determined to be insane.

A final criticism, also applied to psychopathy, is that the diagnosis is never preemptive and therefore not useful from a criminal justice perspective. Individuals are not tested, found to be symptomatic, and then treated so that they will not break the law. Also, APD and psychopathy cannot be predicted to occur like polio or flu, so they cannot be pre-treated much as those diseases are pre-treated with vaccination. Diagnoses of APD or psychopathy typically occur only after an individual has become a criminal offender. Conceivably, many people who do not commit serious offenses also show APD or psychopathy symptoms but are never diagnosed because their behavior does not result in lawbreaking.

We have said APD and psychopathy share many symptoms, including disregard for truth and the feelings of others. Psychologist Robert Hare has compiled several varieties of his primary psychopathy checklist, the Psychopathy Checklist-Revised (PCL-R), which is probably the most used reference for psychopathic characteristics. The checklist—which contains as symptoms of psychopathy items such as need for stimulation, poor behavioral controls, promiscuous sexual behavior, and irresponsibility—has been criticized.[131] One study concluded that the list can be easily misused in legal systems and forensic psychiatry and that the characteristics are subjective, judgmental, and not measurable.[132]

Some scholars say psychopaths typically show no signs of mental illness, such as hallucinations, excessive anxiety, severe depression, or obvious delusions. Others dispute this assertion and say that psychopaths who are obviously mentally ill can certainly be found in institutions. Also, not all psychopaths are criminal offenders. Many people who exhibit psychopathic symptoms have broken no laws and probably never will. Hare estimated the rate of psychopaths in the general population to be about 1 percent but about 15 to 25 percent in the adult prison population.[133]

Still, psychopathy has a persistent relationship with crime. Studies have found criminal psychopaths to be especially violent, sadistic, and brutal; they tend to murder and rape for fun. Murders by nonpsychopaths are often committed for a reason, however twisted, such as domestic conflict or the heat of argument with a known victim. The murderer will likely feel remorse and never kill again. A criminal psychopath, however, feels nothing for his or her victims. Psychopathic rapists may commit their offenses for non-sexual reasons, such as anger, sadism, malice, or simple opportunity. In all, psychopaths seem to have trouble empathizing with others and comprehending the most basic rules of society because they cannot be aroused to any genuine feelings. Ideally, a child who is corrected for an immoral or improper action feels shame, embarrassment, and the sense that he or she has displeased those who matter the most: parents, siblings, peers, or teachers. The psychopath feels none of these emotions and continues the antisocial behavior because he or she thinks, "Why not?" It is this resistance to remorse or shame that makes psychopaths so difficult to treat or rehabilitate.[134]

Because the term "insanity" is used to describe a state of mind that is connected with criminal offending, we will review it in this section. Insanity is a legal term, not a medical term. No physician, psychologist, or psychiatrist uses the term clinically to describe a person's mental state. Under the law, insanity describes an individual's state of mind only at the time he or she committed an offense.[135]

The insanity defense, **not guilty by reason of insanity** (NGRI), generally means the acquittal of a defendant because he or she is determined to be insane. It has drawn much public criticism and disdain because it appears to give "criminals" a chance to escape justice simply by claiming they were crazy at the time of the offense. This is far from the case. The insanity defense is rarely raised and rarely successful. Juries do not like it.[136] Each state has its own form of insanity defense, which makes it difficult to determine how often it is used, and four states,

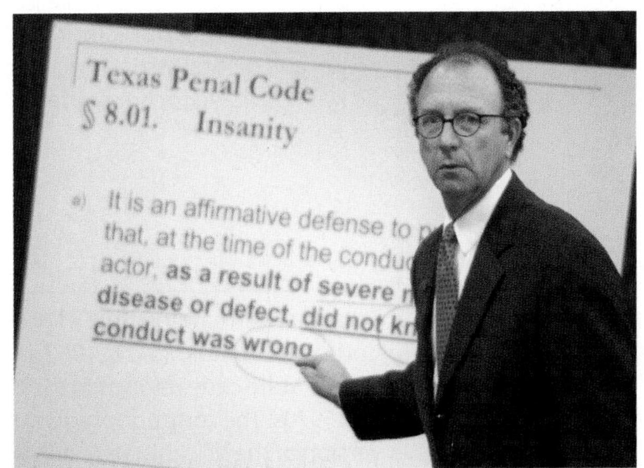

Defense attorney Wendell Odom uses a visual aid as he gives his closing arguments in the capital murder retrial of his client Andrea Yates. Yates, charged with drowning her five children in the bathtub in 2001, pleaded not guilty by reason of insanity but was convicted. The decision was later overturned because of erroneous testimony. In 2006, Yates was found not guilty by reason of insanity and sent to a mental hospital. What should be done with offenders who commit horrible offenses but are judged to be insane?

Kansas, Montana, Idaho, and Utah, do not even allow it.[137] A 1991 study estimated that only 1 percent of felony cases use the insanity defense.[138]

The purpose of deciding whether an offender is insane is to establish responsibility for an offense. Thus far in U.S. criminal law, an offender deemed insane at the time of the offense is not responsible, whereas a sane offender is responsible. A defendant found both to have committed the offense and to be insane is typically confined to a mental health institution. A defendant not found insane is incarcerated. In both cases, the defendant's freedom is curtailed. Andrea Yates, a Texas woman who drowned her five children in the bathtub, was initially found guilty but not insane and sent to prison. This conviction was later overturned, and she was found insane and was confined to an institution.[139] So, contrary to popular belief, defendants ruled not guilty by reason of insanity do not necessarily go free. See Table 5.2 for a look at the current standards of insanity used in U.S. courts.

PAUSE AND REVIEW

1. **Review the current standards of insanity.**
2. **Outline the critiques of the antisocial personality disorder diagnosis.**
3. **Critique the perspective that IQ is related to antisocial behavior.**

TABLE 5.2 Standards for the Insanity Defense

The states and federal government use four major standards of insanity. See FindLaw's Insanity Defense Among the States at http://criminal.findlaw.com/criminal-procedure/the-insanity-defense-among-the-states.html to see how your state interprets the insanity defense.

STANDARD	HISTORY	PRACTICE
M'Naghten rule	In 1843, Daniel McNaughtan tried to kill the British prime minister, but mistakenly shot and killed his secretary instead. As a result of this case, a panel of British judges developed what became known as the M'Naghten standard of insanity.	The defense must prove that the defendant is so delusional, ideally from "disease of the mind," at the time of the offense that he or she does not know right from wrong. This is also called the "right–wrong test."[140]
Durham rule	This rule was represented as an attempt to displace the M'Naghten rule. In 1953, 23-year-old Monte Durham, in and out of prison and mental institutions since he was 17, was convicted for housebreaking.	The appellate judge stated that M'Naghten was based on an "obsolete and misleading conception" of insanity and set forth that a defendant "is not criminally responsible if his unlawful act was the product of mental disease or mental defect." Federal courts later rejected Durham because almost anyone with an irresistible impulse, including alcoholics and compulsive gamblers, could use the rule to win a case.[141]
Model Penal Code	The American Law Institute's Model Penal Code was promulgated in 1962, prompting several state code reforms in the 1960s and 1970s. The code adopted a modified version of the M'Naghten test in which psychiatric experts play a central role in the test's interpretation and application.	The Model Penal Code extends the M'Naghten right–wrong test to defendants who "lack substantial capacity . . . to appreciate the criminality of his conduct." The code also made the insanity defense available to defendants who lacked the ability "to conform his conduct to the requirements of law." After John Hinckley's acquittal in the 1981 shooting of President Ronald Reagan under this part of the Model Code's test, many states and the federal government restricted the insanity defense by removing this test.[142]

Guilty but Mentally Ill (GBMI)	This standard, created in 1975, represents another alternative to the NGRI defense.	This defense holds an offender responsible for the action but recognizes the presence of a mental disorder. This difference is reflected in sentencing, in which the offender is convicted, not acquitted, as he or she would be under the NGRI defense but is also recognized to need medical treatment. Unfortunately, research shows that in states that have adopted this standard, the convicted is no more likely to receive treatment within the prison system than mentally disordered defendants who do not have a GBMI conviction.[143]

FOCUS ON ETHICS Jury Duty

You are on jury duty for the first time in your life. The case that you have been selected for is a sensational one that is the talk of your community. An 18-year-old student who was just about to graduate walked into his high school with a semi-automatic rifle and opened fire. He killed eight students and two teachers and barricaded himself for six hours in a classroom with three female student hostages. He finally gave himself up when one of the students, the captain of the debate team, was able to convince him that he did not want to hurt anyone else.

The student, Roland, was an unlikely candidate to commit such a crime. By all accounts, he was a normal student who played trombone in the marching band and dated a clarinet player. He was tall and gangly, very polite, and was a B-student who had been accepted to the local university and planned to major in accounting.

Upon his arrest, he admitted to having headaches and hearing voices in his head. A thorough medical examination revealed that he had a large brain tumor. This life-threatening situation was corrected by surgery in which the tumor was removed. At the trial, the neurosurgeon contended that the tumor was most likely the cause of Roland's behavior. In the neurosurgeon's opinion, Roland was not responsible for his actions and was no longer a danger to society. She recommended that Roland not be prosecuted.

The prosecutors had a different opinion. They presented evidence that the shooting spree had been planned for months and that Roland had freely decided to enter the school and shoot as many people as possible. Brain tumor or not, they argued, 10 innocent people were dead, and Roland must be held accountable. The victims' families are demanding justice. Roland's parents point out that for 18 years he had been an exemplary child and young man and that he was sick, not bad, when he committed this crime.

Jury duty requires citizens to make important and often life-changing decisions. Could you put your personal feelings aside and determine your vote based on the facts of the case and the law?

What Do You Do?

1. Vote to convict for murder. There is no question that he did it, and he must pay for his crime.
2. Vote to acquit. He killed eight people, but the brain tumor caused this behavior. The tumor has now been removed, so Roland is no longer dangerous.
3. Suggest to the other jury members that they vote to convict on a lesser-included offense, such as involuntary manslaughter. He did kill 10 people, but the tumor is a big mitigating circumstance that must be considered.
4. Decide that you cannot decide and go along with what the other jurors think.

Summary

LEARNING OBJECTIVE 1 Explain why early biological theories of criminology advance our understanding of criminology.	Early biocriminological perspectives sought to measure antisocial behavior and considered it rooted in the physical world. Modern biocriminology considers the brain and body to be a source of antisocial behavior. The history of biological explanations of crime may help us better appreciate their potential for explaining crime and delinquency and avoid their possible abuse.
LEARNING OBJECTIVE 2 Discuss how genetic and evolutionary perspectives seek to explain antisocial behavior in human beings.	Some researchers believe both genes and environment are responsible for behavior rather than genes alone. According to some theories, people who are more likely to break the law lack impulse control and empathy and are more likely to take risks and resort to violence. It is possible that these broad propensities are biological in origin. Other studies claim to have found evidence of a genetic basis for personality traits such as novelty-seeking, aggressiveness, and impulsivity, all of which are considered to be related to antisocial behavior. According to some perspectives, antisocial behavior influences human evolution. Behavior considered inappropriate and destructive in our society may once have played a useful role in the development of human beings, and possibly it still does.
LEARNING OBJECTIVE 3 Discuss how neurological perspectives seek to explain antisocial behavior in human beings.	This research does not look for direct links to crime but for antisocial behaviors that may lead to crime. The neurotransmitters most important to the study of behavior are serotonin, norepinephrine, and dopamine, which control mood and feelings such as aggression and pleasure. The amount of neurotransmitters in an individual's brain is determined by genes, which is why genetics is important to the study of neurotransmitters and behavior. The hormones testosterone and cortisol have been associated with antisocial behavior and with some characteristics of psychopathy, such as lower reactions to stress, fearlessness, aggression, and stimulation seeking. Some researchers believe antisocial behavior may be affected by structures within the brain, injury to those structures, or the nature of the brain itself. Two brain regions that researchers think particularly affect behavior are the amygdala and prefrontal cortex, both of which control mood and decision-making.
LEARNING OBJECTIVE 4 Discuss how environmental perspectives seek to explain antisocial behavior in human beings.	The substances most commonly connected to antisocial behavior and criminal offending are drugs and alcohol. Although alcohol is not considered to cause crime, it is related to the behaviors most likely to lead to arrest because it is disinhibiting, reduces sensitivity to pain, and impairs physical and mental functioning. Crime suspects are more likely than crime victims to be intoxicated. Criminologists also agree that there is a definite relationship between lawbreaking and drugs. Risky, sensation-seeking behavior is an element: In nearly every study ever conducted, people who frequently broke the law were more likely to use illegal drugs, drink alcohol, and smoke cigarettes than those who did not.

LEARNING OBJECTIVE 5	
Describe modern psychological and psychiatric theories of criminal behavior.	Psychological and psychiatric theories consider personality, intelligence, and the mind as factors that can inspire antisocial behavior and criminal offending. The psychological approach focuses on cognition and learned behavior. The psychiatric approach is concerned with neurological processes and illnesses. Behaviorism states that the environment and learning are behavior's main determinants. Social learning theory holds that people learn behavior from watching others, then develop their own thoughts and attitudes. Cognitive psychology is the study of how people think, which can help explain how people decide to break the law. Some studies have found low IQ and language impairment, especially in boys, to predict delinquency. Antisocial personality disorder and psychopathy are closely associated with crime and antisocial behavior. The term "insanity" is used to describe a state of mind that is connected with criminal offending, but it is a legal term, not a medical term.

Critical Reflections

1. **How has the criminal law changed in regard to the psychological concerns of insanity?**
2. **In what ways did some of the early biological theories of crime misuse science?**
3. **Do you think, as some theories claim, that behavior that is considered inappropriate and destructive in our society may have played a useful role in the development of human beings?**
4. **Is it a good idea to control someone's brain with drugs before he or she breaks the law?**
5. **If drug use is related to crime, does that mean it causes crime? Explain the difference.**
6. **In your opinion, is low IQ directly or indirectly related to criminal behavior?**
7. **If you were charged with a crime, which of the following would you like to be used as evidence against you: your body type, your IQ, phrenology, physiognomy, or the XYY syndrome concept?**

Key Terms

antisocial personality disorder p. 134
atavism p. 117
behaviorism p. 130
biocriminology p. 116
body-type theory p. 114
cognition p. 130
cognitive psychology p. 132
eugenics p. 115
extinction p. 131
heredity p. 116
impulsivity p. 121
IQ (intelligence quotient) p. 133
negative reinforcement p. 131
not guilty by reason of insanity (NGRI) p. 135
operant conditioning p. 131
phrenology p. 113
physiognomy p. 113
positive reinforcement p. 131
positivist p. 113
psychopathy p. 134
social Darwinism p. 117
social learning theory p. 132
somatotype p. 115
theory of evolution p. 116
XYY syndrome p. 120

Instant Recall Terms

antisocial (ch. 1)
cohort (ch. 2)
longitudinal (ch. 2)

Notes

1 Mike Mayo, "Whitman, Charles," *American Murder: Criminals, Crime, and the Media* (Canton, Mich.: Visible Ink Press, 2008), 124–126. Harold Schechter, *Deviant: The Shocking True Story of the Original "Psycho"* (New York: Pocket Books, 1989).
2 Ibid.
3 Ibid.
4 Ibid.
5 The title of the work in English is *Criminal Man*.
6 Nicholas Dobelbower, "The Arts and Science of Criminal Man in Fin-de-Siècle France," *Proceedings of the Western Society for French History* 34 (2006): 205–216.
7 Judith Burns, "Facial Expressions 'Not Global,'" BBC, August 14, 2009, http://news.bbc.co.uk/2/hi/8199951.stm. Accessed March 2018.
8 "Musings on Physiognomy," *Britannia Monthly Magazine* 2 (March 1836): 227–230 in *Pioneering Perspectives in Criminology: The Literature of 19th Century Criminological Positivism*, ed. David M. Horton (Incline Village, Nev.: Copperhouse Publishing Company, 2000), 5–8.
9 Phrenology, https://www.phrenology.org. Accessed March 2018.
10 "Phrenology Epitomized," *Continental Repository* 2 (August 1841): 156–159 in *Pioneering Perspectives in Criminology*, 17–24.
11 Stephen M. Soreff and Patricia H. Bazemore, "Examining Phrenology," *Behavioral Healthcare*, January 1, 2007, 14–18.
12 Eric Nagourney, "Exercise Link Is Seen Between Crime and Fitness," *New York Times*, June 17, 2008, late edition, F6; Sean Maddan, Jeffery T. Walker, and J. Mitchell Miller, "Does Size Really Matter? A Reexamination of Sheldon's Somatotypes and Criminal Behavior," *Social Science Journal* 45, no. 2 (June 2008): 330–344.
13 Nicole Rafter, *The Criminal Brain* (New York: New York University Press, 2008). See Chapter 7.
14 Earnest Hooton, *Crime and the Man* (Cambridge, Mass.: Harvard University Press, 1939), 181.
15 Rafter, *The Criminal Brain*, Chapter 7.
16 Ibid.
17 Ibid.
18 Peter Monaghan, "Biocriminology," *Chronicle of Higher Education* 55, no. 32 (April 17, 2009): B4.
19 Rafter, *The Criminal Brain*, 93–94.
20 Ibid., 95.
21 Ibid.
22 Ibid., 98–99.
23 Edwin Black, *War Against the Weak* (New York: Four Walls Eight Windows, 2003), 24.
24 Michael F. Guyer, *Being Well-Born: An Introduction to Eugenics* (Indianapolis, Ind.: Bobbs-Merrill, 1916).
25 Edwin Hardin Sutherland, *Criminology* (Philadelphia: J. B. Lippincott, 1924), 622.
26 Black, *War Against the Weak*, Chapters 6 and 19.
27 Eugenics: Compulsory Sterilization in 50 American States, http://www.uvm.edu/~lkaelber/eugenics. Accessed March 2018.
28 George Hodak, "Eugenics Challenged in Skinner v. Oklahoma," *ABA Journal* 95, no. 6 (June 2009): 72; *Skinner v. State of Okl.* Ex Rel. Williamson, 316 U.S. 535 (1942), 316 U.S. 535; Michael G. Silver, "Eugenics and Compulsory Sterilization Laws: Providing Redress for the Victims of a Shameful Era in United States History," *George Washington Law Review* 72, no. 4 (April 2004): Geo. Wash. L. Rev. 862.
29 Edwin Black, *War Against the Weak* (New York: Four Walls Eight Windows, 2003), 58.
30 Cody Jorgensen, Nathaniel E. Anderson, and J. C. Barnes, "Bad Brains: Crime and Drug Abuse from a Neurocriminological Perspective," *American Journal of Criminal Justice* 41 no. 1 (2016): 47–69. Anna S. Rudo-Hutt, Jill Portnoy, Frances R. Chen, and Adrian Raine, "Biosocial Criminology as a Paradigm Shift," in *The Routledge International Handbook of Biosocial Criminology*, ed. Matt DeLisi and Michael G. Vaughn (New York: Routledge, 2015), 22–31.
31 U.S. National Library of Medicine, Genetics Home Reference, "47, XYY Syndrome," https://ghr.nlm.nih.gov/condition/47xyy-syndrome. Accessed March 2018.
32 Patricia A. Jacobs, Muriel Brunton, Marie M. Melville, R. P. Brittain, and W. F. McClemont, "Aggressive Behaviour, Mental Subnormality and the XYY Male," *Nature* 208 (December 25, 1965): 1351–1352.
33 Nkanginieme Ike, "Current Thinking on XYY Syndrome," *Psychiatric Annals* 30, no. 2 (February 2000): 91–95.
34 Joseph A. Schwartz and Kevin M. Beaver, "Evidence of a Gene × Environment Interaction between Perceived Prejudice and MAOA Genotype in the Prediction of Criminal Arrests," *Journal of Criminal Justice* 39, no. 5 (September 2011): 378–384. Guang Guo, "The Linking of Sociology and Biology," *Social Forces* 85, no. 1 (September 2006): 145–149.
35 Adrian Raine, *The Psychopathology of Crime: Criminal Behavior as a Clinical Disorder* (San Diego, Calif.: Elsevier, 1993), 48–53.
36 Guo, "The Linking of Sociology and Biology," 145–149.
37 Richard P. Ebstein and Robert H. Belmaker, "Genetics of Sensation or Novelty Seeking and Criminal Behavior," in *The Neurobiology of Criminal Behavior*, ed. Joseph Glicksohn (Dordrecht, Netherlands: Kluwer Academic Publishers, 2002), 51–78. L. F. Lowenstein, "The Genetic Aspects of Criminality," *Journal of Human Behavior in the Social Environment* 8, no. 1 (October 2003): 63–78.
38 James M. Ogilvie, Anna L. Stewart, Raymond C. K. Chan, and David H. K. Shum, "Neuropsychological Measures of Executive Function and Antisocial Behavior: A Meta-Analysis," *Criminology* 49, no. 4 (November 2011): 1063–1107.
39 Harriet A. Ball, Louise Arseneault, Alan Taylor, Barbara Maughan, Avshalom Caspi, and Terrie E. Moffitt, "Genetic and Environmental Influences on Victims, Bullies and Bully-Victims in Childhood," *Journal of Child Psychology and Psychiatry* 49, no. 1 (January 1, 2008): 104–112.
40 J. C. Barnes, Kevin M. Beaver, and Brian B. Boutwell, "Examining the Genetic Underpinnings to Moffitt's Developmental Taxonomy: A Behavioral Genetic Analysis," *Criminology* 49, no. 4 (November 2011): 923–954.
41 Guang Guo, Michael E. Roettger, and Tianji Cai, "The Integration of Genetic Propensities into Social-Control Models of Delinquency and Violence Among Male Youths," *American Sociological Review* 73, no. 4 (August 2008): 543–569.
42 Ethan Watters, "DNA Is Not Destiny," *Discover* 27, no. 11 (November 2006): 32–75.
43 Ibid.
44 Michael Rutter, Terrie E. Moffitt, and Avshalom Caspi, "Gene–Environment Interplay and Psychopathology: Multiple Varieties but Real Effects," *Journal of Child Psychology and Psychiatry* 47, no. 3/4 (2006): 226–261.
45 Soo Hyun Rhee and Irwin D. Waldman, "Testing Alternative Hypotheses Regarding the Role of Development on Genetic and Environmental Influences Underlying Antisocial Behavior," in *Causes of Conduct Disorder and Juvenile Delinquency*, ed. Benjamin B. Lahey, Terrie E. Moffitt, and Avshalom Caspi (New York: Guilford Press, 2003), 305–318.
46 Catherine Tuvblad, Martin Grann, and Paul Lichtenstein, "Heritability for Adolescent Antisocial Behavior Differs with Socioeconomic Status: Gene–Environment Interaction," *Journal of Child Psychology and Psychiatry* 47, no. 7 (July 2006): 734–743.
47 Vernon L. Quinsey, Tracey A. Skilling, Martin L. Lalumiere, and Wendy M. Craig, *Juvenile Delinquency: Understanding the Origins of Individual Differences* (Washington, D.C.: American Psychological Association, 2004), 50–51.

48 Kevin M. Beaver, Meghan W. Rowland, Joseph A. Schwartz, and Joseph L. Nedelec, "The Genetic Origins of Psychopathic Personality Traits in Adult Males and Females: Results from an Adoption-based Study," *Journal of Criminal Justice* 39, no. 5 (September 2011): 426–432.
49 Randy Thornhill and Craig T. Palmer, *A Natural History of Rape: Biological Bases of Sexual Coercion* (Cambridge, Mass.: MIT Press, 2000).
50 Elisabeth A. Lloyd, "Violence Against Science: Rape and Evolution," in *Evolution, Gender, and Rape*, ed. Cheryl Brown Travis (Cambridge, Mass.: MIT Press, 2003), 235–261.
51 Christopher J. Ferguson, "An Evolutionary Approach to Understanding Violent Antisocial Behavior: Diagnostic Implications for a Dual-Process Etiology," *Journal of Forensic Psychology Practice* 8, no. 4 (October 2008): 321–343.
52 Anthony W. Hoskin and Lee Ellis, "Fetal Testosterone and Criminality: Test of Evolutionary Neuroandrogenic Theory," *Criminology* 53, no. 1 (2015): 54–73.
53 Lee Ellis, "Sex, Status, and Criminality: A Theoretical Nexus," *Social Biology* 51, no. 3/4 (Fall–Winter 2004): 144–160; Lee Ellis, "Reducing Crime Evolutionarily," in *Evolutionary Forensic Psychology: Darwinian Foundations of Crime and Law*, ed. Joshua D. Duntley and Todd K. Shackelford (New York: Oxford University Press, 2008), 249–267.
54 Jorgensen, Anderson, and Barnes, "Bad Brains."
55 Avshalom Caspi, Joseph McClay, Terrie E. Moffitt, Jonathan Mill1, Judy Martin, Ian W. Craig, Alan Taylor, and Richie Poulton, "Role of Genotype in the Cycle of Violence in Maltreated Children," *Science* 297, no. 5582 (August 2, 2002): 851; *ScienceDaily*, "Gene May Protect Abused Kids Against Behavior Problems," August 5, 2002, www.sciencedaily.com/releases/2002/08/020805075625.htm.
56 Yaling Yang, Andrea L Glenn, and Adrian Raine, "Brain Abnormalities in Antisocial Individuals: Implications for the Law," *Behavioral Sciences and the Law* 26, no. 1 (2008): 65–83.
57 Dean Mobbs, Hakwan C. Lau, Owen D. Jones, and Christopher D. Frith, "Law, Responsibility, and the Brain," *Public Library of Science Biology* 5, no. 4, (2007), https://www.ncbi.nlm.nih.gov/pmc/articles/PMC1852146. Accessed March 2018.
58 Stephen H. Dinwiddie, "Biological Causes of Criminality and Expert Testimony—Some Cautionary Thoughts," in *The Science, Treatment, and Prevention of Antisocial Behaviors: Application to the Criminal Justice System*, ed. Diana H. Fishbein (Kingston, N.J.: Civic Research Institute, 2000), 24.1–24.10.
59 Ibid.
60 Ibid.
61 Alan Booth, Douglas A. Granger, Allan Mazur, and Katie T. Kivlighan, "Testosterone and Social Behavior," *Social Forces* 85, no. 1 (September 2006): 167–191.
62 Andrea L. Glenn, "Neuroendocrine Markers of Psychopathy," in *The Handbook of Neuropsychiatric Biomarkers, Endophenotypes and Genes, Vol. 3: Metabolic and Peripheral Biomarkers* (New York: Springer Science and Business Media, 2009), 59–70.
63 Booth et al., "Testosterone and Social Behavior," 167–191.
64 Alan Booth and D. Wayne Osgood, "The Influence of Testosterone on Deviance in Adulthood: Assessing and Explaining the Relationship," *Criminology* 31, no. 1 (February 1993): 93–117.
65 Hoskin and Ellis, "Fetal Testosterone and Criminality."
66 Lee Ellis, Shyamal Das, and Hasan Buker, "Androgen-Promoted Physiological Traits and Criminality: A Test of the Evolutionary Neuroandrogenic Theory," *Personality and Individual Differences* 44, no. 3 (February 2008): 699–709.
67 Ibid.
68 Ibid.
69 Glenn, "Neuroendocrine Markers of Psychopathy," 61–62.
70 David Terburg, Barak Morgan, and Jack van Honk, "The Testosterone-Cortisol Ratio: A Hormonal Marker for Proneness to Social Aggression," *International Journal of Law and Psychiatry* 32, no. 4 (July 15, 2009): 216–223; Arne Popma, Robert Vermeiren, Charlotte A. M. L. Geluk, Thomas Rinne, Dirk L. Knol, Wim van den Brink, Lucres Jansen, Herman van Engeland, and Theo Ah Doreleijers, "Cortisol Moderates the Relationship Between Testosterone and Aggression in Delinquent Male Adolescents," *Biological Psychiatry* 61, no. 3 (February 2007): 405–411.
71 Timo D. Vloet, Kerstin Konrad, Thomas Hübner, Sabine Herpertz, and Beate Herpertz-Dahlmann, "Structural and Functional MRI-Findings in Children and Adolescents with Antisocial Behavior," *Behavioral Sciences & the Law* 26, no. 1 (January 2008): 99–111.
72 Shelley Batts, "Brain Lesions and Their Implications in Criminal Responsibility," *Behavioral Sciences & the Law* 27, no. 2 (March 2009): 261–272.
73 Elizabeth A. Shirtcliff, Michael J. Vitacco, Alexander R. Graf, Andrew J. Gostisha, Jenna L. Merz, and Carolyn Zahn-Waxler, "Neurobiology of Empathy and Callousness: Implications for the Development of Antisocial Behavior," *Behavioral Sciences & the Law* 27, no. 2 (March 2009): 137–171.
74 Batts, "Brain Lesions and Their Implications in Criminal Responsibility," 261–272. Mike Mayo, "Whitman, Charles," *American Murder: Criminals, Crime, and the Media* (Canton, Mich.: Visible Ink Press, 2008), 372–374.
75 Ibid.
76 Jessica Bramham, Robin Morris, J. Hornak, Peter Bullock, and C. E. Polkey, "Social and Emotional Functioning Following Bilateral and Unilateral Neurosurgical Prefrontal Cortex Lesions," *Journal of Neuropsychology* 3, no. 1 (March 2009): 125–143; D. C. Krawczyk, "Contributions of the Prefrontal Cortex to the Neural Basis of Human Decision Making," *Neuroscience and Biobehavioral Reviews* 26, no. 6 (2002): 631–664.
77 Batts, "Brain Lesions and Their Implications in Criminal Responsibility," 261–272.
78 Ibid.
79 Ibid.
80 Vloet et al., "Structural and Functional MRI-Findings," 99–111.
81 Batts, "Brain Lesions," 261–272.
82 Mary Beckman, "Crime, Culpability, and the Adolescent Brain," *Science* 305, no. 5684 (July 30, 2004): 596–599.
83 Michael Meacher, "Diet Can Make You Nice," *New Statesman*, February 16, 2004, 30.
84 Frank D. Roylance, "Lead Tied to Criminal Behavior: Poisoning Damages Crucial Brain Matter, Studies Find," *Baltimore Sun*, May 28, 2008.
85 Jennifer C. Karberg and Doris J. James, *Substance Dependence, Abuse, and Treatment of Jail Inmates, 2002* (Washington, D.C.: Bureau of Justice Statistics U.S. Department of Justice Office of Justice Programs, 2005), 3, https://www.bjs.gov/index.cfm?ty=pbdetail&iid=1128. Jennifer Bronson and Jessica Stroop, *Drug Use, Dependence, and Abuse Among State Prisoners and Jail Inmates, 2007–2009* (Washington, D.C.: U.S. Department of Justice Office of Justice Programs Bureau of Justice Statistics, 2017), 1. Online at https://www.bjs.gov/index.cfm?ty=pbdetail&iid=5966. Accessed March 2018.
86 Ibid.
87 Gavan Palk, Jeremy Davey, and James Freeman, "Prevalence and Characteristics of Alcohol- Related Incidents Requiring Police Attendance," *Journal of Studies on Alcohol and Drugs* 68, no. 4 (July 2007): 575.
88 Ibid.
89 Lawrence A. Greenfeld, *Alcohol and Crime* (Washington, D.C.: U.S. Department of Justice Office of Justice Programs, 1998), iii, https://www.bjs.gov/index.cfm?ty=pbdetail&iid=385. Accessed March 2018.
90 Bureau of Justice Statistics, Alcohol and Crime: Data from 2002 to 2008, https://www.bjs.gov/content/acf/29_prisoners_and_alcoholuse.cfm. Accessed March 2018.

91 KMSP, "Chisago County Commissioner Charged in Deadly Wrong-Way Crash," March 8, 2018, http://www.fox9.com/news/chisago-county-commissioner-charged-in-deadly-wrong-way-crash.
92 Ibid.
93 American Diabetes Association, Hypoglycemia (Low Blood Glucose), http://www.diabetes.org/living-with-diabetes/treatment-and-care/blood-glucose-control/hypoglycemia-low-blood.html. Accessed March 2018.
94 Karen Zamora, "Driver Charged in I-35 Crash that Killed Douglas County Man," *Duluth News Tribune,* March 10, 2018, http://www.duluthnewstribune.com/news/crime-and-courts/4415967-driver-charged-i-35-crash-killed-douglas-county-man. Accessed August 2018.
95 KMSP, "Chisago County Commissioner Charged in Deadly Wrong-Way Crash."
96 Karen Zamora, "Chisago County Commissioner Charged in Fatal Wrong-Way Crash on I-35," *Star Tribune*, March 9, 2018, http://www.startribune.com/chisago-county-commissioner-charged-in-fatal-crash/476320003. Accessed August 2018.
97 Derrick Knutson, "Chisago County Commissioner Charged with Vehicular Homicide," *Post Review*, March 8, 2018, https://www.hometownsource.com/the_post_review/free/chisago-county-commissioner-charged-with-criminal-vehicular-homicide/article_ff76ebc4-2317-11e8-a5b5-dbce1e724056.html. Accessed August 2018.
98 Susan E. Martin, "The Links Between Alcohol, Crime and the Criminal Justice System: Explanations, Evidence and Interventions," *American Journal on Addictions* 10, no. 2 (April 2001): 136–158.
99 Candice L. Odgers, Avshalom Caspi, Daniel S. Nagin, Alex R. Piquero, Wendy S. Slutske, Barry J. Milne, Nigel Dickson, Richie Poulton, and Terrie E. Moffitt, "Is It Important to Prevent Early Exposure to Drugs and Alcohol Among Adolescents?" *Psychological Science* 19, no. 10 (October 2008): 1037–1044.
100 Gary Michael McClelland and Linda A. Teplin, "Alcohol Intoxication and Violent Crime: Implications for Public Health Policy," *American Journal on Addictions* 10 (January 15, 2001): 70–86; Martin, "Links Between Alcohol, Crime and the Criminal Justice System," 136–158.
101 Martin, "Links Between Alcohol, Crime and the Criminal Justice System," 136–158.
102 Ibid.
103 Ibid.
104 David Farabee, Vandana Joshi, and M Douglas Anglin, "Addiction Careers and Criminal Specialization," *Crime & Delinquency* 47, no. 2 (April 2001): 196–220.
105 Erich Goode, *Drugs in American Society* (New York: McGraw-Hill, 2007). See Chapter 12.
106 Ibid.
107 Ibid.
108 Erich Goode, "Drug Use and Criminal Behavior," in *Out of Control: Assessing the General Theory of Crime*, ed. Erich Goode (Palo Alto, Calif.: Stanford University Press, 2008), 185–199.
109 Chris Allen, "The Links Between Heroin, Crack Cocaine and Crime: Where Does Street Crime Fit In?" *British Journal of Criminology* 45, no. 3 (May 2005): 355–372.
110 David Farabee, Vandana Joshi, and M. Douglas Anglin, "Addiction Careers and Criminal Specialization," *Crime & Delinquency* 47, no. 2 (April 2001): 196–220.
111 Goode, "Drug Use and Criminal Behavior," 185–199.
112 Michael Rocque and Chad Posick, "Paradigm Shift or Normal Science? The Future of (Biosocial) Criminology," *Theoretical Criminology* 21, no. 3 (2017): 288–303.
113 Peter Monaghan, "Biocriminology," *Chronicle of Higher Education* 55, no. 32 (April 17, 2009): B4.
114 Yaling Yang, Andrea L Glenn, and Adrian Raine, "Brain Abnormalities in Antisocial Individuals: Implications for the Law," *Behavioral Sciences & the Law* 26, no. 1 (2008): 65–83.
115 Curt R. Bartol and Anne M. Bartol, *Criminal Behavior: A Psychosocial Approach* (Upper Saddle River, N.J.: Pearson Education, 2008), 9–10.
116 David Putwain and Aidan Sammons, *Psychology and Crime* (New York: Routledge, 2005), 44–45.
117 Bartol and Bartol, *Criminal Behavior*, 115–121.
118 Jack Arbuthnot, Donald A. Gordon, and Gregory Jurkovic, *Handbook of Juvenile Delinquency*, ed. Herbert C. Quay (Chichester, U.K.: Wiley, 1987). See Chapter 6.
119 Håkan Stattin and Ingrid Klackenberg-Larsson, "Early Language and Intelligence Development and Their Relationship to Future Criminal Behavior," *Journal of Abnormal Psychology* 102, no. 3 (August 1993): 369–378.
120 Elizabeth Brownlie, Joseph Beitchman, Michael Escobar, Arlene Young, Leslie Atkinson, Carla Johnson, Beth Wilson, and Lori Douglas, "Early Language Impairment and Young Adult Delinquent and Aggressive Behavior," *Journal of Abnormal Child Psychology* 32, no. 4 (August 2004): 453–467.
121 Pamela C. Snow and Martine B. Powell, "Oral Language Competence, Social Skills and High-Risk Boys: What Are Juvenile Offenders Trying to Tell Us?" *Children & Society* 22, no. 1 (January 1, 2008): 16–28.
122 Bartol and Bartol, *Criminal Behavior*, 54–55.
123 Jean Marie McGloin, Travis C. Pratt, and Jeff Maahs, "Rethinking the IQ–Delinquency Relationship: A Longitudinal Analysis of Multiple Theoretical Models," *Justice Quarterly* 21, no. 3 (September 2004): 603–635.
124 Bartol and Bartol, *Criminal Behavior*, 237.
125 Frederick Rotgers and Michael Maniacci in *Antisocial Personality Disorder: A Practitioner's Guide to Comparative Treatments*, ed. Frederick Rotgers and Michael Maniacci (New York: Springer, 2006). See Chapter 1, "Antisocial Personality Disorder: An Introduction."
126 Bartol and Bartol, *Criminal Behavior*, 235.
127 Ibid., 236.
128 Katherine L. Fitzgerald and George J. Demakis, "The Neuropsychology of Antisocial Personality Disorder," *Disease-A-Month: DM* 53, no. 3 (March 2007): 177–183.
129 Rotgers and Maniacci, *Antisocial Personality Disorder*, Chapter 1.
130 Bartol and Bartol, *Criminal Behavior*, 236.
131 Robert D. Hare, *The Hare Psychopathy Checklist*—Revised 2nd ed. (Toronto, Ont.: Multi-Health Systems, 2003).
132 Willem H. J. Martens, "The Problem with Robert Hare's Psychopathy Checklist: Incorrect Conclusions, High Risk of Misuse, and Lack of Reliability," *Medicine and Law* 27, no. 2 (June 2008): 449–462.
133 Bartol and Bartol, *Criminal Behavior*, 195.
134 Ibid., Chapter 6.
135 Ibid., 241.
136 Jennifer Eno Louden and Jennifer L. Skeem, "Constructing Insanity: Jurors' Prototypes, Attitudes, and Legal Decision-Making," *Behavioral Sciences & the Law* 25, no. 4 (July 2007): 449–470.
137 FindLaw, The Insanity Defense Among the States, http://criminal.findlaw.com/criminal-procedure/the-insanity-defense-among-the-states.html. Accessed March 2018.
138 Lisa A. Callahan, Henry J. Steadman, Margaret A. McGreevy, and Pamela Clark Robbins, "The Volume and Characteristics of Insanity Defense Pleas: An Eight-State Study," *Bulletin of Psychiatry and the Law* 19 (1991): 331–338.
139 Georgia Lee Sims, "The Criminalization of Mental Illness: How Theoretical Failures Create Real Problems in the

Criminal Justice System," *Vanderbilt Law Review* 62, no. 3 (April 1, 2009): 1053–1083.
140 John P. Martin, "The Insanity Defense: A Closer Look," *Washington Post*, February 27, 1998, http://www.washingtonpost.com/wp-srv/local/longterm/aron/qa227.htm. Accessed March 2018.
141 Cornell University Law School, Legal Information Institute, "The 'Insanity Defense' and Diminished Capacity," https://www.law.cornell.edu/background/insane/insanity.html. Accessed March 2018.
142 Paul H. Robinson and Markus Dirk Dubber, *The American Model Penal Code: A Brief Overview*, http://scholarship.law.upenn.edu/faculty_scholarship/131. Accessed March 2018.
143 Bartol and Bartol, *Criminal Behavior*, 248.

Sociological Theories of Crime and Delinquency

FEATURES

Criminologists are interested how individuals interact with others in society. What social factors are related to crime?

About a week before he was to go on a recruiting visit to Eastern Kentucky University, high school football star Caleb Johnson was arrested in the robbery of a phone store. Six other young men were arrested in the heist, but Johnson, 18, was the only adult in the group.[1] Surveillance video showed the teens entering the store wearing masks and carrying guns, some of them automatic rifles. They forced a customer to the ground and ordered workers to open a safe in the back room.[2]

Johnson, who admitted to the robbery, had no juvenile record other than a traffic violation. An aunt of one of the defendants said several of the boys knew each other from playing youth football together. "I think sometimes kids are just looking for acceptance and they look in the wrong place."[3]

About Sociological Theories of Crime

LEARNING OBJECTIVE | 1

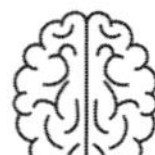

Explain sociological imagination.

The sociological perspective is a robust and exciting lens for viewing crime. Rather than considering crime a problem of the mind, body, or soul, sociological theories of crime observe society and examine how the interaction between people and their social environment produces antisocial behavior. In this chapter and the next, we will examine the major sociological theories of crime and delinquency. These theories provide an insightful tool that sociologist C. Wright Mills called the **sociological imagination**—the idea that we must look beyond our personal experiences to the experiences of others in order to evaluate how social location influences how individuals perceive society. This tool allows people to critique how their social location within society influences their opportunities and choices.[4]

Sociological theories provide a basis for formulating policies to address not only crime, but also the conditions that are considered to cause or contribute to a range of social problems (see Policy Implications). For instance, the effects of racism, sexism, and discrimination based on socioeconomic class have been at the heart of civil rights legislation, poverty programs, and anti-sexual-harassment legislation.[5] Government and social service agencies have been guided by the ideas of scholars who use a sociological lens to focus on society's problems.[6]

We will review the sociological theories of crime and delinquency in the order in which they were developed. The history of social thought is not orderly. Any particular year is filled with competing theories, and long intervals often occur between the introduction of a theory by one scholar and its modification, expansion, or application by another. This quilt-like pattern of sociological and criminological theory makes the study of crime sometimes frustrating and often fascinating. Our study of sociological explanations for crime and delinquency begins with the introduction of sociology in the United States at the University of Chicago in the 1920s and 1930s.

One interesting feature of sociological theories is that many of them were developed to explain juvenile delinquency rather than adult crime. This is not unusual because most adult offenders start breaking the law when they are youths. For example, all of the defendants in the opening scenario are still in high school. A few have juvenile records, and authorities believe all of them have participated in robberies before.[7] Despite their focus on juvenile delinquency, sociological theories can be used to explain both juvenile delinquency and adult crime, so a review of these theories is necessary to obtain a complete understanding of the development of criminological theory.

sociological imagination—The idea that we must look beyond our personal experiences to the experiences of others in order to evaluate how social location influences how individuals perceive society.

POLICY IMPLICATIONS

Sociological Theories

Sociological theories of crime have more policy implications than any other type of criminological theory. This is because, unlike biological theories and psychological theories, sociological theories lend themselves to interventions that can change the way society responds to crime. Briefly, sociological explanations for crime can be used to construct the following interventions.

- Social disorganization theory. If a socially disorganized community has crime problems, the simple answer is to organize community institutions. By providing financial assistance for the impoverished and including citizens in community governance, policymakers attempt to restore the social fabric so that neighbors know and care about each other. Typically, this includes the efforts of local, state, and the federal government, as well as charitable institutions.
- Collective efficacy theory. Like social disorganization theory, collective efficacy theory attempts to develop informal social control in the community by fostering social cohesion and trust. Neighbors who look out for each other can reduce the incidence of crime.
- Differential association theory. Differential association states that crime is learned, particularly from interaction with one's peers. Therefore, policy implications are concerned with the kind of persons children socialize with. Positive opportunities for youths to meet and engage with other children and teenagers help to prevent children from learning delinquent attitudes and techniques.
- Subculture of violence and code of the street. These two theories consider how the culture of disadvantaged neighborhoods may contribute to crime. Often, survival in violent subcultures means that youths must develop defenses that also employ a willingness and ability to use violence. This becomes a vicious cycle that engenders a culture in which the strong dominate and the weak become victims. Policy implications stemming from these theories suggest that the culture of violence must be broken, which is often accomplished by alleviating poverty. Like social disorganization theory, these two theories give credence to the arguments that the culture of the street requires intervention in order for citizens to feel safe.
- Strain theory. The policy implications of strain theory suggest increasing employment and social opportunities so that individuals do not feel strain. Once opportunities for advancement toward culturally desirable goals are no longer blocked, individuals will no longer use crime to achieve their goals.
- Control theories. Those with weak bonds or attachments to family and society are more likely to break the law. The goal is to strengthen the bonds between individuals and society. By developing a sense of community within schools, students can become more committed to their studies and to positive peer relationships. Furthermore, communities that provide adequate recreation facilities and other opportunities for attachment to conventional norms are more likely to prevent crime. To a great extent, all communities do this, but because of limited financial resources, there never seem to be enough programs for all children, especially those whose parents do not have enough money to supplement community involvement.

THINK ABOUT IT

1. Review other sociological theories and see if you can think of or discover real-world applications for them.

Social Disorganization Theories of Crime

LEARNING OBJECTIVE | 2

Discuss the development of social disorganization theories.

The study of crime and delinquency in the United States was greatly influenced by the development of sociology, particularly at the University of Chicago. A unique confluence of factors brought reformist scholars together in a city that was undergoing rapid growth and change. In just 20 years, from 1890 to 1910, Chicago's population doubled in size, an explosive expansion that challenged the city's ability to absorb its growing numbers.[8] The city's relatively organized and homogeneous population became disorganized and heterogeneous as culturally, racially, and linguistically diverse people moved in. The crime rate increased, and the wealthy, the impoverished, and the middle class became more stratified even as their members sought to reorganize themselves and their jobs, living situations, and cultural values and norms.

Social Disorganization Theory

Social disorganization theory was developed to explain the social problems facing Chicago in the first part of the 20th century, but it applies to many cities. One of the cornerstones of social disorganization theory is poverty. Anthropologist Oscar Lewis argued that the effects of poverty are passed down from one generation to the next. Often, people raised in impoverished circumstances do not benefit from available services nor do they take advantage of them. This failure perpetuates a cycle of distrust of government and authority among those who are raised in poverty. The values of this dysfunctional subculture are a major contributing factor to the persistence of crime and delinquency in disadvantaged neighborhoods.[9]

In addition to poverty and delinquency, Chicago's impoverished neighborhoods had high rates of infant mortality, tuberculosis, and dilapidated housing. Some sociologists thought the remedy for crime was not to focus on the individual but rather to organize communities to address the social problems that resulted from a lack of cohesion among neighborhood residents. So, according to **social disorganization theory**, not only do impoverished neighborhoods have a culture of crime, but also the disintegration of social bonds and the failure of social institutions cause crime (see Figure 6.1).

Robert J. Sampson and William Julius Wilson extended social disorganization theory to account for how race and inequality contribute to social disorganization's effect on crime and delinquency. They looked at what they call the "cognitive landscape," which they thought limited the vision of minority people caught in impoverished, transitional neighborhoods. They posited that the residents of some neighborhoods are engulfed in a social isolation that includes going to schools with little socioeconomic diversity, living in segregated housing, and having few experiences outside the neighborhood.[10] Sampson and Wilson then considered the intersection of race, crime, and urban inequality in an effort to delineate how discrimination and lack of opportunity affect community organization to produce the social isolation of youths that results in delinquency.[11]

A group of homeless people sleep in the courtyard of the Midnight Mission in Los Angeles. The mission's courtyard is open to anyone looking for a safe place to spend the night. Why do social disorganization theories of crime focus on poverty?

This isolation differs greatly from the experiences of affluent children, who receive private lessons and are enrolled in summer camps and sports leagues.[12] Many middle-class parents also provide religious instruction or educational support (or both); act as positive role models; and allow their children to see alternatives to a life of crime, poverty, and conflict. An especially attractive feature of social disorganization theory is its public policy implications. Instead of claiming that social isolation is a matter of bad choices or a dysfunctional culture, Sampson and Wilson assert that the social problems of impoverished urban youths are a consequence of persistent racial inequality. By addressing both the policies that allow institutional discrimination—such as banks identifying neighborhoods for higher interest rates for home loans—and dealing with macro-level changes such as the migration of jobs, this theoretical perspective seeks to provide solutions to crime and delinquency.[13]

Concentric Zones

Sociologists from the University of Chicago saw changes in their city as a natural experiment in the spread of dense urbanization and struggled to explain how the social fabric of the community was being altered. One feature they focused on was the lack of stable neighborhood demographics. As the city grew, it expanded from the downtown core and developed zones that formed concentric circles. The outer zones were populated by middle-class and wealthy homeowners, while inner zones included impoverished families and recent immigrants. Immediately outside the city's core were a factory zone and a transitional zone with high rates of crime, alcoholism, and other social problems (see Figure 6.2).

The transitional zone interested sociologist Ernest Burgess, who saw problems that stemmed from the lack of social organization caused by urban expansion and the economic pressure it exerted on residents who were forced out of their neighborhoods by the unattractive aspects of growth. Boarding houses fell into disrepair; people lived in the neighborhood only as long as it took them to find better places; and the social infrastructure crumbled because of the residents' transitory nature.[14] Burgess and other University of Chicago sociologists saw this decline as a sign of social disorganization. They hypothesized that meaningful communities could not be established when neighborhoods had no stability and that in order to reform the citizens, society needed to direct urban renewal and social programs at the impoverished. In many ways, these reformers were victims of their own background. C. Wright Mills contended that the reformers were primarily white, middle-class, Protestant, rural Americans who saw urban dynamics as a symptom of social disorganization that needed to be fixed.[15]

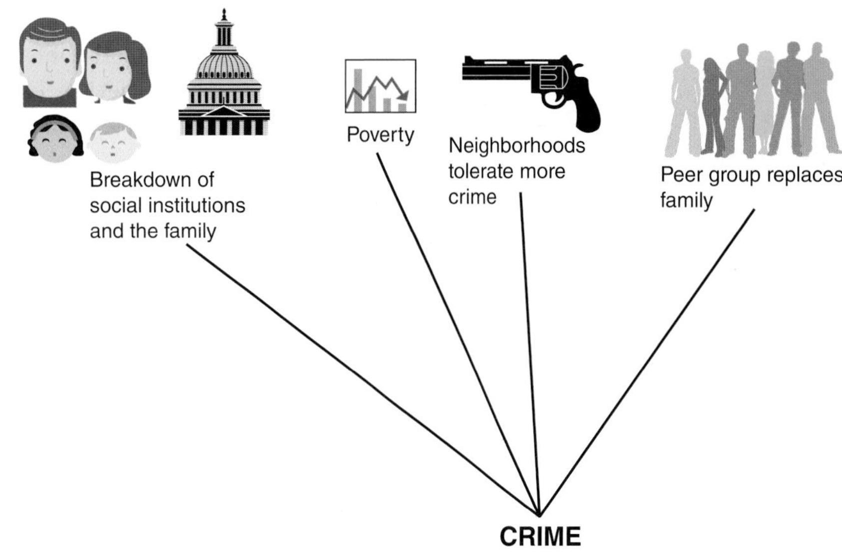

FIGURE 6.1 Social Disorganization Theory

THINK ABOUT IT
What policies can the government develop to counteract the effects of social disorganization?

Clifford R. Shaw and Henry D. McKay conducted studies of **concentric zone theory** to verify that crime would be higher in the transitional zones and lower in affluent and stable areas. This theory posits that geographical areas radiate out from an expanding urban center and that each area has certain dominant social attitudes. How did the theory stack up to reality? According to some scholars, there is substantial support for Shaw and McKay's hypothesis that delinquency flourished in the transition zone and that its prevalence was inversely related to the zone's affluence and distance from the central business district. Using several decades of Chicago court records, one study showed that crime was highest in impoverished, transitional neighborhoods, regardless of which racial or ethnic group resided there, and that as groups moved to other zones, their crime rates decreased.

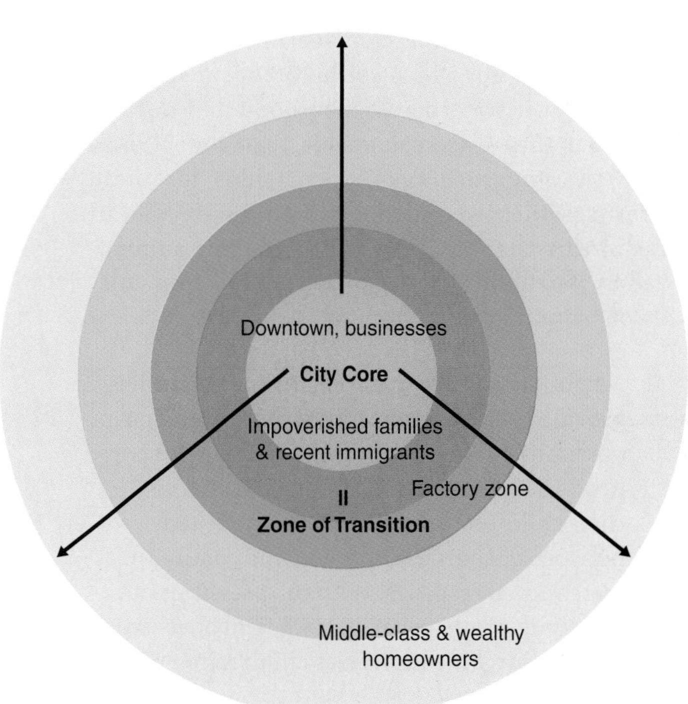

FIGURE 6.2 Concentric Zone Theory

THINK ABOUT IT
Can you detect aspects of concentric zone theory in your city?

This observation led the researchers to conclude that the nature of the neighborhood, not the nature of the individuals within the neighborhood, regulated involvement in crime.[16] It also marked

social disorganization theory—The idea that the breakdown of social bonds and the failure of social institutions cause crime.

concentric zone theory—The idea that geographical areas radiate out from an expanding urban center and that each area has certain dominant social attitudes.

Neighborhoods can go through periods of transition that affect quality of life for their citizens. Why is the economic health of a neighborhood an important factor in its crime rate?

a major shift in criminological theory from the micro-perspective, which looks for deficiencies in individuals, to the macro-perspective, which looks at how groups of people demonstrate similar patterns of crime. But which social forces consistently showed that it was the neighborhood and not the individual that was responsible for crime? Shaw and McKay pursued two explanations for these patterns, which we will look at in greater detail later in this chapter. They can be roughly summarized as neighborhood organization and transmission of criminal values.

1. Neighborhood organization. Affluent families provide their children with structure and opportunities. Families in transitional neighborhoods lack the financial means to supervise their children through a well-established network of churches, schools, and community recreational facilities. With the pressures of rapid migration, urban growth, and poverty, social disorganization frees children to engage in delinquency.[17]
2. Transmission of criminal values. In transitional neighborhoods, children learn negative values from older peers. Even as the racial and ethnic demographics gradually change in the community, life on the street maintains a set of focal concerns that transmits methods of coping with the poverty, lack of legitimate opportunity, and danger that youths must confront. Shaw and McKay developed this perspective from life histories of delinquents based on interviews and autobiographies.[18]

The role of government, as Shaw and McKay saw it, was to provide field workers to act as a catalyst to encourage local democratic participation.[19] In the 1930s, Shaw and McKay, with the help of others, tested their ideas by creating the Chicago Area Project (CAP), which has continued its work for more than 70 years.[20] Shaw's plan was for CAP to discourage community disorganization and encourage social stability through community service, advocacy, and involvement. Programs of the day used punitive methods to discourage crime and delinquency, such as arrest, detention, and incarceration. Shaw, however, directly encouraged gang members to pursue conventional, pro-community lives. CAP developed several strategies, some of which it still uses today.

- "Curbstone counseling" or "street work." CAP workers and former gang members frequented youth hangouts and listened to the youths in a nonjudgmental fashion.
- Individual participation. CAP involved neighborhood residents instead of outside experts and professionals in planning activities and addressing problems.
- Inclusive involvement. A strategy that particularly concerned traditional social workers was the involvement of gang members and other offenders directly in neighborhood planning and decision-making. However, Shaw believed it was better to involve them in planning than to avoid them or work against them.
- Relationships with law enforcement. Local committees and police officers worked together on delinquency problems. Arresting officers might refer delinquent youths to their local committees, and residents would work with probation and parole officers to keep up with delinquents in correctional programs. Parolees often became members of local committees.

Collective Efficacy and Crime

Collective efficacy measures the amount of informal social control and social cohesion, or trust, in a community—that is, how much a community's residents trust and depend on one another. A community in which the residents have little trust in one

collective efficacy—The measure of the amount of informal social control and social cohesion, or trust, in a community.

another, rarely communicate, and do not work together to achieve community goals has low collective efficacy.[21]

The social disorganization theories we have examined so far deal with the structure of societies and are based on census and crime-rate data. Although this broad look at communities can yield valuable insights, it cannot tell us about the social dynamics that influence people to break the law. Francis Cullen and Robert Agnew call structural social disorganization theories "static." That is, the community is considered to be a stable condition that people move into or are born into. However, other social disorganization theories consider the community "dynamic," that is, as a condition that can be changed.[22] Collective efficacy theory, as envisioned by Robert Sampson, Stephen Raudenbush, and Felton Earls, is a dynamic social disorganization theory because it considers the community as a collection of individuals who can change their environment.

In a study called the "Project on Human Development in Chicago Neighborhoods," Sampson and colleagues collected data from 8,782 residents in 343 neighborhoods. They measured the "compositional effects" of each neighborhood by assessing which areas had more people who were prone to lawbreaking. This research allowed them to control for social class, racial diversity, and other variables that might affect crime rates. Then they developed the following two concepts to describe why some areas had higher crime rates than others.

- Informal social control. As a measure of informal social control, residents were asked how likely their neighbors would be to intervene if they witnessed a minor criminal offense. This measure demonstrates how socially committed people believe their neighbors are. It also shows how people envision the overall degree of their neighborhood's social responsibility.
- Social cohesion and trust. Next, residents answered questions that measured how much they trusted their neighbors and how cohesive they believed the neighborhood to be. By measuring how much neighbors trusted each other, Sampson and his colleagues developed an indication of how socially organized the community appeared to be.[23]

Taken together, these measures of informal social control and social cohesion or trust form what the researchers call "collective efficacy." The study showed that a higher collective efficacy meant a lower crime rate. That is, the more that people were willing to step in and, for instance, stop kids who were writing graffiti on the walls (informal social control), and the more they believed their neighbors would be there to help them (trust and social cohesion), the less crime the neighborhood experienced.

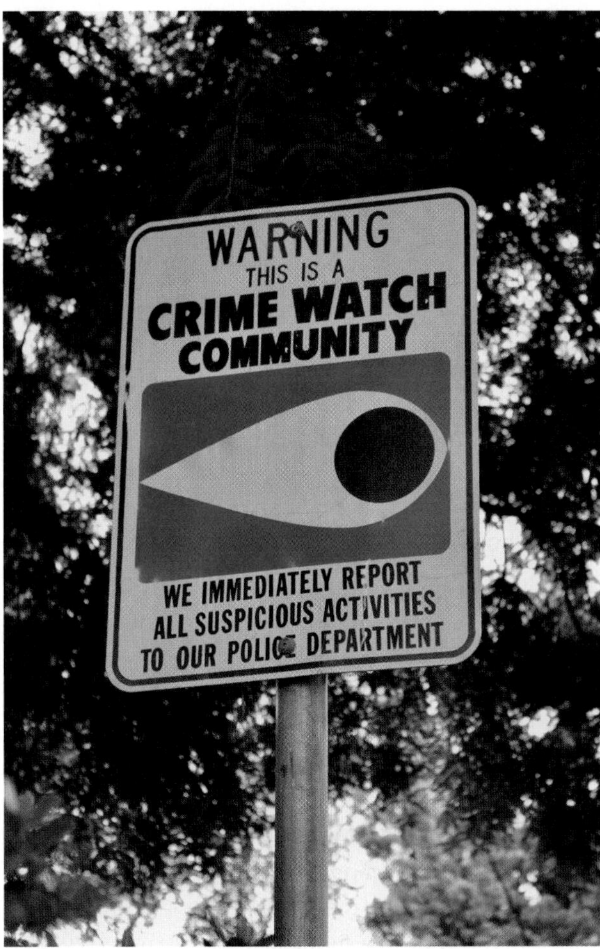

Social cohesion and trust among neighbors is a sign of collective efficacy. How does collective efficacy in a neighborhood affect crime and delinquency?

Although the theory of collective efficacy and crime might seem similar to Shaw and McKay's social disorganization theory in that it measures social organization rather than social disorganization, its appeal lies in the potential it sees for a neighborhood's citizens to do something about crime and delinquency. Rather than merely being a product of the structural makeup of the community, crime in collective efficacy theory is a variable that community action can address by doing such things as conducting neighborhood watches, letting troublemakers know they will be reported to the police, and alerting local politicians that neighborhood residents expect them to provide adequate police patrols and other social services that affect crime and quality-of-life issues.[24]

Social disorganization theories continue to provide interesting explanations of how a community's social structure can contribute to crime and delinquency.[25] As scholars build on Shaw and McKay's social disorganization ideas, it is becoming clear that a neighborhood's physical, social, and economic conditions affect the residents' behavior.[26] But not all residents of high-crime areas break the law. So we must ask, why do certain individuals adopt antisocial behaviors while others do not? One popular explanation is that crime is learned. Let's turn now to **learning theories of crime** to develop an appreciation of how social interaction influences the transmission of antisocial behavior.

PAUSE AND REVIEW

1. **List the reasons why social disorganization theory was developed in Chicago.**
2. **Demonstrate how collective efficacy theory specifies the way society uses informal social control to control crime.**
3. **What are Shaw and McKay's two ideas for concentric zone theory?**
4. **What is the "sociological imagination"?**

Learning Theories of Crime

LEARNING OBJECTIVE | 3

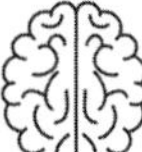

Give some theories of how antisocial behavior is learned.

Learning theories of crime focus on where and how adult offenders and delinquents find the tools, techniques, and expertise to break the law. Many criminologists contend that antisocial behavior is learned from family, peers, and the media, much like any other type of behavior. Children receive messages that it is fun to break the law, which competes with the positive socialization messages that schools, churches, and parents promote. Theorists seek to explain how this learning occurs, while legislators and criminal justice officials try to create public policy that promotes the learning of positive behavior. Learning theories of crime have a good deal of appeal. They appear to be a commonsense explanation and not only to be testable, but also to suggest policies that can be adopted to reduce crime.[27] The first criminologist to suggest a learning theory of crime was Edwin Sutherland. His differential association theory has stimulated others to look at how the techniques and attitudes required to break the law are transmitted.

Differential Association Theory

Edwin Sutherland, who taught at the University of Chicago, developed an appreciation for Shaw and McKay's social disorganization ideas. He was interested in the problems of big cities and how crime seemed to be not a function of an individual's pathology, but rather a product of the social organization in which individuals find themselves.[28] Sutherland developed his theory of **differential association**—the idea that offenders learn crime from each other—to account for how criminal offenders and delinquents learn crime. He believed that crime is learned in the same way that all other learning occurs, and he set out to explain why some people adopt attitudes and behaviors favorable to the violation of the law. Sutherland laid out his theory in nine propositions that attribute the learning of crime to interactions with others, particularly intimate others such as peers and family.

1. Criminal behavior is learned.
2. Criminal behavior is learned by communication.
3. We learn criminal behavior from those closest to us, such as family and friends.
4. Criminal learning includes techniques, motives, rationalizations, and attitudes.
5. We learn either respectful or disdaining attitudes toward laws from others.
6. Delinquency or criminality occurs when we are exposed to more anti-law attitudes than to attitudes that support the law.
7. The quantity and quality of our social interactions affect our attitudes toward the law. Social interactions vary in frequency, duration, priority, and intensity.
8. We learn antisocial or pro-social attitudes in the same way we learn any other skill.
9. Criminal behavior is an expression of needs and values, but it is not explained by those needs and values. For example, the desire to acquire wealth is a normal motive for both working harder at a job and robbing a bank.

A youth's drug and alcohol use can be influenced by peers. Does learning criminal behavior differ from learning other types of behavior?

One of the attractive features of differential association theory is that it lends itself to empirical observation.[29] Since it contends that lawbreakers have learned more attitudes and techniques favorable to lawbreaking than attitudes and techniques favorable to obeying the law, researchers can readily construct studies that look at this learning process.[30] Sutherland identified four factors for researchers to examine.

- Priority. If a youth is exposed early in life to family members or other children who break the law, then he or she will be more likely to adopt criminal attitudes and learn how to commit crime than someone who is not exposed to such associations until later in life. Young children are more receptive to negative messages because they do not have the experience and knowledge to evaluate antisocial behavior.
- Frequency. According to Sutherland, the more you hear a message, the more you are likely to believe it is true. Youths who are surrounded by others who say that breaking the law is fun, noble, or profitable get the message that crime is normal and desirable. If one associates only with youths who promote these views, then repetition of this message overwhelms the pro-social messages of parents and teachers.
- Intensity. We give some messages more credibility because they have a level of volume, sincerity, or passion that we deem more immediate or important. According to Sutherland, the intensity of a message can influence the recipient to adopt a point of view. Just as important, it is something researchers can measure in their study of the learning of criminal attitudes and techniques.
- Duration. If a person is exposed for a long time to others who advocate violating the law, he or she is more likely to adopt this viewpoint than someone who hears the same message for a short period of time. The longer a youth is a member of a delinquent juvenile gang, the more likely he or she will adopt the gang's viewpoint and behaviors.

Differential association theory has stimulated other scholars to extend and refine the processes by which crime is thought to be learned.[31] Ronald Akers's **social learning theory** of crime—the idea that people learn how to act by watching others and copying the interactions that are rewarded and avoiding those that are punished—retains all of Sutherland's ideas but employs the psychological framework of **operant conditioning**, which is a form of learning based on the positive or negative consequences of an action, behavior, or activity. Akers argues that using the concepts of imitation and **differential reinforcement**, or the encouragement of one behavior instead of another, allows

---

learning theories of crime—These theories focus on where and how adult offenders and delinquents find the tools, techniques, and expertise to break the law.

differential association—Sutherland's idea that offenders learn crime from each other.

social learning theory—The idea that people learn how to act by watching others and copying the interactions that are rewarded and by avoiding those that are punished.

operant conditioning—A form of learning based on the positive or negative consequences of an action, behavior, or activity.

differential reinforcement—The encouragement of one behavior instead of another.

social learning theory to explain a greater range of antisocial behavior than differential association. Several studies support social learning theory, and it has become one of the primary theories of why people break the law.[32] For instance, social learning theory has been used to explain why athletes use performance-enhancing drugs, why individuals engage in intimate-partner violence, and why students binge drink.[33] Furthermore, social learning theory better predicts the amount of alcohol consumption among adolescents when compared to social control theory.[34]

Techniques of Neutralization

Some learning theories of crime are concerned with offenders' motives, drives, and rationalizations. With their **techniques of neutralization theory**, Gresham Sykes and David Matza put forth a perspective that refers to the excuses some offenders use to justify breaking the law. They argue that delinquents generally believe in the law and engage in delinquent behavior only after they can rationalize their actions as necessary or unavoidable (see Figure 6.3). Although the theory specifies delinquency, techniques of neutralization can apply to adult offenders as well. Basically, the techniques of neutralization theory tackles the question of how people who break the law deflect the moral blame from themselves and attempt to excuse their behavior by denying that it is their own fault. Sykes and Matza list five ways that unlawful behavior is excused through techniques of neutralization.[35]

- Denial of victim. Offenders may contend that those injured by their actions are not worthy to be considered true victims. In the 1950s, when Sykes and Matza developed this perspective, youths considered attacks on homosexuals, or even on people presumed to be homosexual, to be morally permissible, even though the attacks legally constituted assault. Likewise, attacks on members of minority groups who had "gotten out of hand" were not deemed to be serious transgressions of social norms, even though the attacks were illegal. Today, violent juvenile gangs consider it their duty to injure or kill members of other gangs. By defining victims as enemies or undesirables, offenders are able to attack them without feelings of remorse.
- Denial of injury. Another method offenders use to escape responsibility is denial of injury. For example, they see writing graffiti on walls or engaging in other vandalism in which there is no immediate personal victim as harmless fun. If the victims have insurance or are wealthy, offenders discount the effects of the damage even more. An offender who is in a fight and does not seriously injure the opponent can neutralize culpability by claiming, "I didn't hurt him, I only smacked him around a bit."
- Denial of responsibility. This rationalization allows the offender to blame external forces for inappropriate behavior. According to Sykes and Matza, offenders take the role of a "billiard ball" helplessly propelled into new situations. They blame bad parenting, inadequate schools,

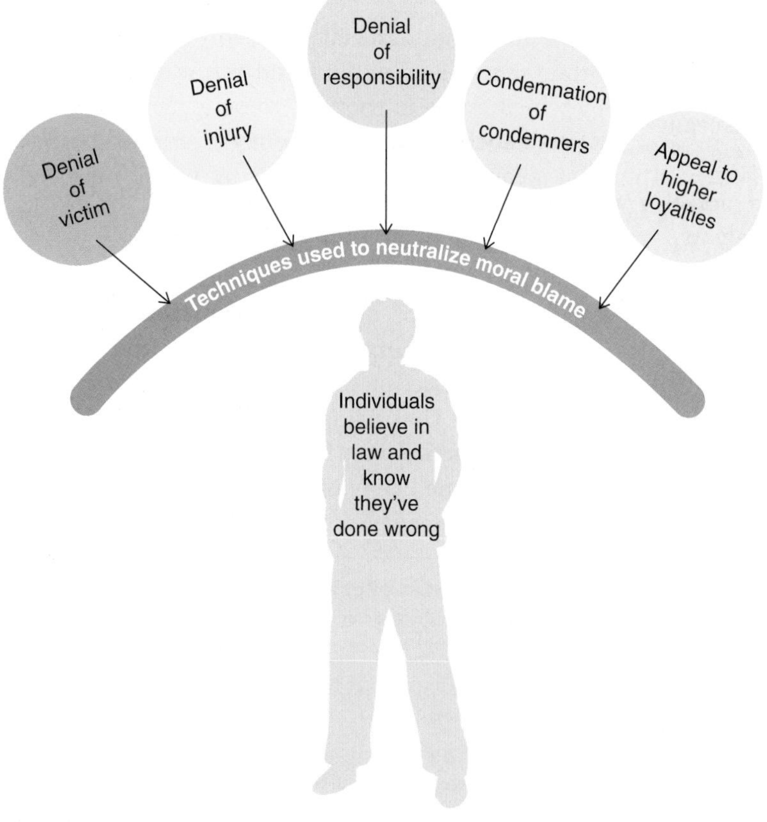

FIGURE 6.3 Techniques of Neutralization

THINK ABOUT IT
Which of these techniques of neutralization do you employ to excuse your own undesirable behavior?

deviant peers, or inescapable situations that lead them into trouble. By denying responsibility for their actions, offenders can escape feelings of guilt and, if they are caught, plead that sanctions are unjustified.

- Condemnation of condemners. Another way to neutralize blame for antisocial behavior is to question the legitimacy, authority, and motives of those who pass judgment. For example, someone given a ticket for speeding might claim that he or she was caught in a "speed trap," and the police, who just want to fill a "quota" of speeders, are not really concerned with public safety and should be out catching "real criminals."
- Appeal to higher loyalties. Often, offenders are not rejecting the norms of the dominant society when they break the law. Rather, they are caught on the horns of a dilemma by competing norms they believe they must satisfy. For instance, the demand to be loyal to friends or a gang might cause a youth to jump into a fight that he or she has no real interest in. An adult arsonist might claim a particular building was dangerous, and he or she had to remove it because no one else would.[36]

Offenders learn these techniques of neutralization at an increasing rate as they delve more deeply into patterns of unlawful behavior. According to Sykes and Matza, this ability to deflect blame is often imperfect, and offenders might feel guilt or shame for some of their actions. However, the more offenders are surrounded by others who share attitudes favoring the violation of the law, the more they internalize and transmit these techniques of neutralization. From a public policy perspective, the way to combat this process of learning and rationalizing crime is to develop programs that allow these offenders, both youth and adult, to interact with others who will provide a different and more positive set of attitudes.

Miller's Focal Concerns of the Lower Class

Subcultures—which are typically (but not always) based on race, religion, socioeconomic class, or education—form when people are separated from the dominant culture through economics, values, or norms. A subculture has its own values and norms, although it does share some values with the dominant culture. According to subcultural theories, adult offenders and delinquents learn the skills, norms, values, and attitudes conducive to lawbreaking from the subcultures in which they live.[37]

Anthropologist Walter B. Miller studied the cultures of lower-class neighborhoods in Boston and concluded that they exhibited value systems different from those of other social classes. Miller's term for "value systems" is **focal concerns**—attitudes that the lower classes perpetuate as a part of the values and norms they believe are necessary for survival in their neighborhoods. He argued that the lower socioeconomic class had focal concerns that encouraged youths to commit delinquent acts.[38]

Miller's analysis is limited to this class, and the way he viewed it is important to any understanding of his theory. According to Miller, although the lower class shares many characteristics and concerns with the middle and upper classes, it is distinct. The U.S. legal system conforms more closely to the standards of middle- and upper-class people than those of lower-class people. Therefore, behaviors that some lower-class subcultures view as appropriate violate moral or legal codes.[39] This means that the types of behaviors required to survive on the street in a lower-class neighborhood are considered inappropriate or even illegal by the greater society. By doing what they need to do in order to participate in their neighborhoods' subcultures, lower-class youths often conflict with the police. The following are the focal concerns of the lower class.

- Trouble. Lower-class youths expect to be in trouble always. Whether in conflict with school authorities, police officers, or parents, lower-class youths believe there is always someone "breathing down their neck" and finding fault with their behavior. Trouble becomes an accepted part of existence, and lower-class youths do not run from it or let it overly concern them. It is just part of life.
- Toughness. Lower-class youths place a high priority on being able to physically defend themselves. Toughness means others cannot take advantage. Fighting hard and losing is preferable to backing down. The youths' self-concept and street credibility are established by toughness.

---

techniques of neutralization theory—A perspective that refers to the excuses some offenders use to justify breaking the law.

focal concerns—Attitudes that the lower classes perpetuate as part of the values and norms they believe are necessary for survival in their neighborhoods.

- Smartness. Smartness is street smarts rather than academic success. A youth is considered smart to the extent that he or she can outwit others, cannot be taken advantage of in economic dealings, and can use cunning to deceive others.
- Excitement. Youths in lower-class neighborhoods crave excitement. They are willing to take risks, get into dangerous situations, and seek thrills. However, this excitement, a product of present-day orientation, can get a youth into long-term trouble.
- Fate. Lower-class youths do not have a great deal of faith in their ability to control their lives. They attribute what happens to them to luck or fate. This allows them to shirk responsibility for their behaviors and justify their negative outcomes as ordained by fate.
- Autonomy. Not having to answer to others is a primary goal. Being able to steal what they want and not depend on parents gives the lower-class youth a sense of autonomy. This attitude also prevents them from engaging in many mainstream activities, like joining a sports team, in which rules and coaches' demands can limit their independence.

It is easy to see how these focal concerns can put youths in danger of running afoul of authorities. In many ways, they reflect the behaviors and attitudes common to all teenagers. The primary difference is that Miller envisions lower-class youths to be immersed in these focal concerns because of their lower-class culture. Middle-class teenagers have many other opportunities and influences, so these concerns are only minor contributors to their behavior.

Physical violence is often a product of young people being denied the American dream of economic and social success. Why do some subcultures experience a high level of violence?

subculture of violence—A culture apart from the main social culture that holds violence to be part of its values, lifestyle, and socialization.

Subculture of Violence

Some groups of people exhibit consistently higher rates of crime and violence than other groups. Shaw and McKay saw this disparity when they observed how particular neighborhoods always seemed to have crime problems, although different groups were constantly moving into and out of the area. Marvin Wolfgang and Franco Ferracuti believe that something about the particular culture of the groups living in these areas nurtures crime. They argue that some neighborhoods have a subculture composed of teenage and young adult males who consider violence to be the appropriate response to a wide range of situations. This **subculture of violence** is a culture apart from the main social culture that holds violence as part of its values, lifestyle, and socialization. Although it believes in the values of the dominant culture, its members also believe violence is necessary to achieve their goals and desires, as well as to protect their masculinity.[40]

The theory was developed more than 30 years ago, but it is still used to understand crime today, including higher rates of violence in urban areas and higher homicide rates in the southern states.[41] Ethnic enclaves in large cities insulate many youths from the values of the dominant culture. Often, these youths band together in gangs to protect themselves from others or to provide the strength in numbers to engage in illegal enterprises such as drug sales, home invasions, or gang warfare.[42]

Countering the negative influences of the subculture of violence is easy to suggest, but difficult to accomplish. It cannot be done one youth at a time; rather, it requires the entire subculture to be assimilated into the dominant culture. This entails providing job opportunities, quality schools, and a realistic chance at the "American Dream" for the entire community. When prejudice and discrimination prevent enclaves of immigrants from assimilating into the dominant culture, their subculture might exhibit levels of violence and gang activity that make their communities dangerous for everyone.[43]

Code of the Street

Sociologist Elijah Anderson extended and updated the subculture of violence thesis with his observations of urban youths in Philadelphia. Anderson contends that urban violence is prompted by a "code of the street" that requires people to quickly resort to violence when they feel they are not getting the proper respect from others.[44] It is difficult to determine where this code originates, but it is a function of several factors, including disadvantaged neighborhoods, racial and ethnic subcultural influences, peer rivalries, and lack of parental supervision.

Anderson distinguishes between "decent families" and "street families." Decent families, according to Anderson, are similar to those found in all neighborhoods in which parents teach their children to respect the law and to work hard. Street families, in contrast, raise children with the "code of the street" perspective in which violence is considered permissible, desirable, and, in many cases, inevitable in order to preserve one's reputation and dignity. Learning antisocial behavior is potentially a problem for children from both types of families. Children from decent families can be sheltered for only so long before they are exposed to street culture. Children from street families see violence being used to settle differences. Anderson provides an excellent view of what it is like to grow up in a family that maintains internal order through violence.

> In these circumstances, a woman—or a man, although men are less consistently present in children's lives—can be quite aggressive with children, yelling at and striking them for the least little infraction of the rules she has set down. Often, little if any serious explanation follows the verbal and physical punishment. This response teaches children a particular lesson. They learn that to solve any kind of interpersonal problem, one must quickly resort to hitting or other violent behavior. Actual peace and quiet, and also the appearance of calm, respectful children conveyed to her neighbors and friends, are often what the young mother most desires, but at times she will be very aggressive in trying to get them. Thus, she may be quick to beat her children, especially if they defy her law, not because she hates them, but because this is the way she knows how to control them. In fact, many street-oriented women love their children dearly.[45]

On the street, this use of violence determines how individuals interact. Children from decent families must quickly decide how they will survive their dealings with street children. Willingness to fight to maintain respect is a pervasive value on the street, and those who are not quick to realize this reality are likely to become victims of those who are. When street children come home crying after an altercation, their parents tell them to go back out and fight to win. Weak or reluctant children learn to fight back, or they lead a miserable life of being bullied. Allowing someone to disrespect you is considered a sign of weakness and is cause for personal devaluation not only from opponents but also from friends. The code of the street requires that youths stand up for themselves even to the point of breaking the law.

Although Anderson studied the code of the street in an urban, black neighborhood, this perspective can be found in varying degrees in many other cultures and is not limited to males. In many circumstances, females must also use verbal and physical violence to maintain their reputations. According to Anderson, the disputes girls engage in are "rooted in assessment of beauty (which girl is the cutest), competition over boyfriends, and attempts to regulate other people's knowledge of and opinions about a girl's behavior or that of someone close to her, especially her mother."[46] The code of the street is difficult to overcome when poverty and racism are pronounced. Anderson contends that it feeds a vicious cycle whereby hopelessness and alienation fuel violence in young people who are trying to maintain respect when legitimate opportunities are lacking.

The code of the street is not limited to males. According to Anderson, what issues underlie female disputes?

PAUSE AND REVIEW

1. List Sutherland's nine propositions of differential association.
2. What are subcultures?
3. Explain Miller's focal concerns of the lower class.
4. What do criminologists use the subculture of violence to explain?
5. What is the code of the street?

Strain Theories of Crime

LEARNING OBJECTIVE | 4

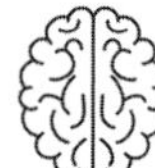

Show how strain theories evolved from the concept of anomie.

People experience strain when their cultures promote a certain way of life but do not provide the means for everyone to achieve that life. In the United States, the way of life that is culturally promoted as the "American Dream" produces strain because it is not equally available to everyone, although most people reach for it. Although it is certainly desirable for people to strive to be economically independent, the intense focus on this goal changes how Americans think about other desirable goals such as civility, cooperation in the community, and the welfare of others. The principle of ensuring the welfare of others is particularly vulnerable in a society that has the American Dream as its driving force.

Anomie

Strain theories of crime evolved from the sociological concept of **anomie**, the erosion of standards resulting from a lack of social control and values that leads to social instability. French sociologist Émile Durkheim observed that when traditional norms are discarded, new norms are slow to emerge. Durkheim's term "anomie" refers to a condition known as structural anomie which is experienced by societies that sustain rapid social change. People experience a sense of individual anomie, or normlessness, and are prone to breaking the law because they feel the old rules no longer constrain them to conforming behavior. Individual anomie, a psychological reaction to rapid social change and its consequences, produces a strain that can result in frustration, desperation, violence, and crime.[47]

Criminologists have used both structural and individual anomie to explain why some countries, such as the United States, have high crime rates. Anomie is manifested in various social problems. For our purposes here, crime is of the most concern. The first sociologist to use the concept of anomie in a criminological theory was Robert Merton in classical strain theory.

Classical Strain Theory

According to strain theorists, Americans strive to achieve economic success. Theorists such as Robert Merton consider this desire to acquire wealth and the status that accompanies financial security to be a cultural goal. In developing **classical strain theory**, Merton argued that people who experience anger and frustration when they cannot achieve cultural goals through legitimate means try to achieve these goals through illegitimate means. According to Merton, Americans are highly committed to the cultural goal of economic success but are less committed to the culturally approved means of achieving that goal, mainly, working hard, deferring gratification, and investing and saving money.[48]

Not everyone has equal access to the culturally approved goal of wealth. Some people who find access to this goal systematically blocked by poverty, racism, or sexism experience strain and therefore must adapt by adjusting their goals or finding new means for achieving them. Merton identifies five adaptations (see Table 6.1) that individuals use to deal with their inability to achieve their goals through culturally approved means.

Merton's adaptations detail how Americans relate to the cultural goals and institutionalized means of achieving those goals.[49] In Table 6.1, a minus sign indicates rejection of the goals or means, and a plus sign indicates acceptance. Following are details of the five types of adaptations.

› Conformity. Most people are conformists. This means that we accept the goal of economic success and are willing to use the culturally approved means (working hard at a conventional

---

anomie—The erosion of standards resulting from a lack of social control and values that leads to social instability.

classical strain theory—The idea that people who experience anger and frustration when they cannot achieve cultural goals through legitimate means try to achieve these goals through illegitimate means.

TABLE 6.1 Merton's Adaptations

ADAPTATION	CULTURALLY ACCEPTED GOALS	CULTURALLY ACCEPTED MEANS
conformity	+	+
innovation	+	-
ritualism	-	+
retreatism	-	-
rebellion	substitution	substitution

Each combination of goals and means has a related adaptation.

job) to achieve this goal. According to Merton, this orientation is absolutely necessary for meaningful communities to exist. Conformity requires that people accept society's rules and laws and not only follow them, but also encourage sanctions for those who violate them.

- Innovation. Those who accept the goal of making a lot of money but are unwilling to work for it in conventional ways might adopt the innovator's adaptation of finding other ways of amassing wealth. For instance, one way of getting money other than working for it is to take it from someone who already has it. Innovators may try to embezzle or steal to meet their goal. Many offenders, in fact, fall into the innovator category.
- Ritualism. Ritualists have given up the pursuit of wealth and accomplishment but continue to participate in the culturally approved means because they derive a certain sense of satisfaction and emotional security from simply going through the motions of work. Ritualists have been socialized to believe that participating in the proper activities is its own reward, even if there is little hope these activities will ever lead to success and accomplishment. Normally, offenders are not ritualists.
- Retreatism. Some individuals are so alienated from conventional society that they simply stop attempting to achieve financial well-being and are not willing to work in a conventional way. In Merton's terms, these individuals reject both the culturally approved goals of society and the culturally approved means of obtaining those goals. Some alcoholics and drug addicts, for instance, consider retreating from society preferable to "playing the game" of seeking conventional success. Predictably, retreatists are often in constant contact with police for various petty and serious infractions.

The hippies of the 1960s are an example of Merton's rebellion adaptation. What new goals and means were the hippies substituting for financial success and hard work?

- Rebellion. Merton's last category of adaptation is rebellion. The rebellionist rejects both the culturally approved goal of financial success and the means of working hard to achieve that success. Unlike the retreatist, who also rejects goals and means, the rebellionist substitutes new goals and means. Hippies in the counterculture of the 1960s rejected the so-called rat race of the corporate world and instituted a new goal of "authentic" interaction characterized by drug experimentation and opposition to the Vietnam War. Without arguing the merits of this perspective, we can recognize that it represented an entirely new way of dealing with the cultural demands of the United States at a time of rapid social change. Young people challenged the conventional wisdom of their elders and substituted a fresh, if naive, philosophy of sex, drugs, and rock-and-roll. Not surprisingly, they clashed with the authority figures of the time and many ended up arrested and incarcerated.

The strength of Merton's strain theory is that it addresses several types of offenses. Most important, it allows other criminologists to envision how strain might affect offenders' reasons for breaking the law. Now, let's turn to more recent developments in strain theory.

Strain and Subculture

Merton contends that we all strive for the goal of economic success and that those who break the law are adapting to the blocked means to achieve their goal (see Figure 6.4). Other theorists have modified strain theory and expanded it to explain why people break the law. Albert Cohen, as a student of Merton, was concerned with how individuals immersed in the subculture of juvenile gangs reacted to the strain of blocked goals.

In his book, *Delinquent Boys: The Subculture of the Gang* (1950), Cohen argued that youths caught up in impoverished and disorganized urban environments are concerned with more than achieving financial success. They also desire middle-class status. The source of strain for these boys is that they do not have a sufficient method for obtaining that status because their means are systematically blocked by poor parenting, bad schools, a juvenile record, and the limitations of growing up in disadvantaged neighborhoods. Although a youth can sell drugs or steal to obtain money, middle-class status cannot be purchased. Therefore, instead of adopting the middle-class value system, delinquent boys reject it and replace it with their own standards of status based on destruction or theft of property, fighting and aggression toward others, and general opposition to conventional standards.[50]

This theory has some limitations that restrict its use. First, it can explain only a small portion of crime because it is applicable to urban, male delinquents. Second, unlike Merton's strain theory, Cohen's theory posits only one type of adaptation: rebellion that rejects conventional values and substitutes a new one (the gang lifestyle). Finally, as we saw in Matza and Sykes's techniques of neutralization, delinquents might not be as opposed to conventional values as Cohen contends. Remember, the idea behind techniques of neutralization is that they allow delinquents to rationalize why it is permissible for them to violate laws in which they believe.

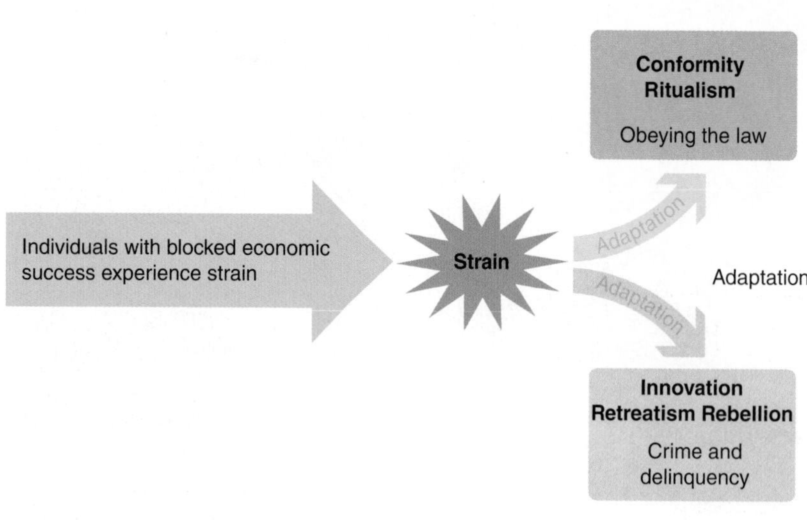

FIGURE 6.4 Merton's Classical Strain Theory

THINK ABOUT IT
Do you use any of these adaptations to cope with your blocked economic success?

Delinquency and Opportunity

Strain theory has progressed through several refinements. Richard Cloward and Lloyd Ohlin extend Cohen's idea that the delinquent subculture is an adjustment to the blocked goals of urban youths by specifying three types of delinquent subcultures. In **differential opportunity theory**, these subcultures provide youths with ways to adapt to the lack of legitimate opportunities, as well as the prospect of developing illegitimate ways of responding to the strain of impoverished and disorganized urban life (see Figure 6.5).[51]

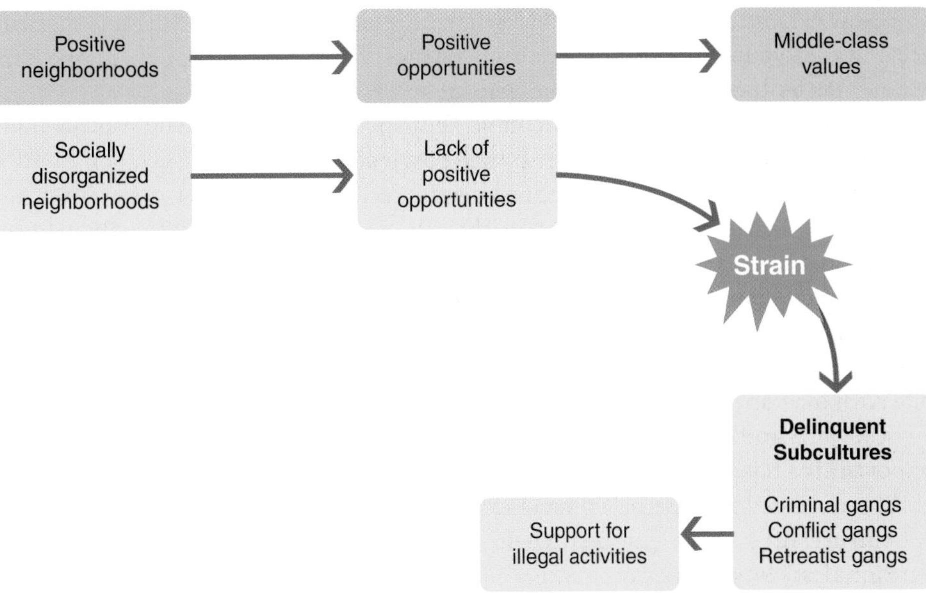

FIGURE 6.5 Differential Opportunity Theory

THINK ABOUT IT
What types of programs can be developed to provide positive opportunists for youth in socially disorganized neighborhoods?

- Criminal gangs. For delinquents to thrive, they must learn illegitimate ways of adapting to strain. One of these ways is to adopt the criminal lifestyle. This type of subculture can develop only in areas with a concentration of disadvantaged youths who can serve as role models and train younger individuals. There must also be environmental supports for this lifestyle, such as bail bondsmen, fences (people who sell stolen goods), and criminal defense lawyers willing to take on petty cases. (Since Cloward and Ohlin developed their theory, the criminal justice and juvenile justice systems have instituted public-defender offices that provide such support.)
- Conflict gangs. Many disorganized neighborhoods have a high degree of residential fluctuation. That is, people tend to move in and out a lot. This damages the stability of community relations; cultural conflict arises because individual youths might come from different racial or ethnic backgrounds. Unlike the criminal subculture that provides a support network for the criminal lifestyle, the conflict subculture does not include ways for youths to achieve financial well-being. Consequently, it can address the status concerns of youths only by rejecting the dominant culture and substituting a deviant way of life dependent on fighting and conflict with other groups.
- Retreatist gangs. For youths who are unsuccessful in developing a criminal subculture based on delinquency or a conflict subculture based on fighting, Cloward and Ohlin identify a third way of adapting to stress called the retreatist subculture. Much like Merton's strain theory, this perspective accommodates individuals who are unable to function adequately in conventional society and fail at traditional criminal or conflict adaptations. The retreatist subculture involves the abuse of alcohol or drugs as a way of escaping the strains of living in disorganized, impoverished neighborhoods.

Street gangs in transitional neighborhoods fight with other groups for dominance. What types of gangs do Cloward and Olin identify?

differential opportunity theory—Cloward and Ohlin's idea that subcultures provide youths with ways to adapt to the lack of legitimate opportunities and with the prospect of developing illegitimate ways of responding to impoverished and disorganized urban life.

Cloward and Ohlin have been criticized for suggesting that youths adopt only one type of lifestyle. Many youths have more than one way to adapt to the strain of not being able to achieve their goals through legitimate means. However, the particular strength of Cloward and Ohlin's theory is the recognition that, in addition to the strain that the individual experiences, both legitimate and illegitimate opportunities must be considered. Only by being aware of the opportunities available to the individual can we appreciate why that person would choose one path over another.

Cloward and Ohlin's theory of delinquency and opportunity has policy implications. Reducing the ability and need for youths to develop an antisocial subculture lifestyle might help them fit into conventional society more successfully. This task can be accomplished in two ways. First, the opportunities for engaging in a criminal, conflict, or retreatist subculture must be reduced. Promoting effective law enforcement and limiting the supply of illegal drugs are two obvious methods. Second, the opportunities for conventional success, such as better schools, after-school activities, and job training, must be increased. Youths would presumably feel less stress if they had more viable chances to compete in law-abiding ways.

Institutional Anomie

Merton's idea that the dominant cultural goal in American society is to acquire wealth as a measure of success might have extensive ramifications for the socialization of young people. Merton believed that having an overarching goal of acquiring wealth in an economic system that does not allow everyone to become equally wealthy results in increased levels of crime as people seek alternative means to get what they are told is desirable. Although this theory seems plausible to many, some theorists contend that it does not go far enough in explaining how strain, which is caused by the values placed on economic success in the United States, plays a role in crime and delinquency.

Specifically, Richard Rosenfeld and Steven Messner argue that focusing on the goal of success is not sufficient and that we must also look at the legitimate means that are available.[52] According to Rosenfeld and Messner, **institutional anomie** occurs when people's commitment to social institutions such as the family, religion, and education becomes subservient to achieving the cultural goal of wealth. This change, in turn, leads to the inability of the neglected institutions to control behavior.[53] Institutional anomie happens for three reasons.

1. Devaluation of non-economic roles and functions. When financial success is the primary goal, other institutions such as the family, religion, and education must play a secondary part. For instance, many students think that the value of education is limited to getting a good job. Other positive aspects, such as self-awareness, appreciation for great music or literature, or understanding how governments and society work, are relegated to secondary status. For example, evidence of the focus on economic roles can be observed in the high enrollments in business schools and low enrollments in anthropology and philosophy programs. Because the criminal justice system employs so many people, criminology programs enjoy robust enrollments.
2. Accommodation to economic roles. Some people pursue their careers to the detriment of other institutions. When a father is "married to his job," he might not participate in the Parent Teachers Association or attend school plays or softball games, or he might not be present when his children are ill, injured, or depressed. A working mother climbing the corporate ladder or holding down two jobs to make ends meet might also sacrifice family events for economic gain. Although this reliance on work is necessary for many families, some parents work excessively to acquire new cars, bigger homes, and country club memberships as symbols of financial success at the expense of their families' overall welfare.
3. Permeation of economic goals. Economic goals can also become the primary focus of other institutions. When churches and universities operate with the ethics, procedures, and bottom-line mentality of businesses, their manifest goals of education and service to parishioners become secondary. We see this imbalance particularly in the move toward accountability in colleges and universities in which enrollment is the driving force behind funding rather than educational quality.[54]

These conditions foster institutional anomie when the messages sent by society reflect the perspective of economic success. Rosenfeld and Messner argue that Americans' over-reliance on the economic dimension in their value systems devalues other institutional support systems, such as education and family. They suggest that we examine how the American Dream undermines our quality of life and the following institutions.[55]

- Education. What is the real value of an education? According to many who pursue the American Dream, a good education is a way to get a high-paying job. Learning for its own sake in order to appreciate art, literature, and history is not highly valued in American society.
- Family. Despite the rhetoric about "family values," we do relatively little compared to other industrialized countries to support families. American families are valued according to how much money their breadwinners provide, and families that deviate from the cultural norm of an intact nuclear family get little cultural support. For instance, many families have a difficult time finding affordable daycare, and children in many states are without health insurance. Women, who still do the most extensive work in maintaining the home, find their activities devalued in relationship to the contributions of those who work outside the home. A stay-at-home father is an oddity and is looked upon as not fully enacting his role as the "man of the house."
- Politics. Rosenfeld and Messner point out that politics in the United States is left to the career politicians and that citizens take only a passing interest in participating in the political process. They argue that an "able-bodied" adult who refuses to work is degraded but that those who do not vote (about half of those eligible) are not. Furthermore, the role of government, according to many Americans, is to provide the economic freedom for corporations to thrive and to allow the economy to provide jobs. Other functions of government, such as providing health care, education, and cultural arts, are viewed as discretionary and more properly the purview of the private sector.[56]

When the economic engine drives our cultural values, other aspects of society are left behind or forced to accommodate themselves to the pursuit of financial success. This creates a sense of institutional anomie in a society where, despite the rhetoric that praises a full and rich life, the American Dream is reduced to making money. This cultural goal of economic success is not only limiting in its own right, but it also subverts the ability of other institutions to fulfill their mandates. When a parent sees his or her worth measured by workplace success, the demands of the family, and especially the children, take a back seat. When schools are measured by how successfully they prepare their students for the workplace, important thinkers and artists get left out of the curriculum.[57]

In many families, the wife is the breadwinner and the husband stays at home to care for the children. What problems might stay-at-home fathers experience?

According to Messner and Rosenfeld, this perverted view of the American Dream is dysfunctional and produces crime and delinquency. Limited reforms in the criminal justice system are unlikely to have a major effect on crime levels. Social reforms that simply allow more people to participate in the dream of economic independence will not solve the problems of crime and delinquency. Rosenfeld and Messner contend that the cultural goal of the American Dream as defined by money must be recast into one that elevates other social institutions, such as the school and the family, to the same level as the economy.[58]

General Strain Theory

As we have seen from Messner and Rosenfeld's work, strain theory is more involved and complicated than Merton first envisioned. Criminologist Robert Agnew's **general strain theory**, a revision of classical strain theory, includes three major

---

institutional anomie—The condition that occurs when people's commitment to societal institutions becomes subservient to achieving the goal of wealth, which leads to the inability of the neglected institutions to control behavior.

general strain theory—Agnew's revision of classical strain theory, which identifies three major types of strain: failure to achieve goals, the loss of positive stimuli, and the gain of negative stimuli.

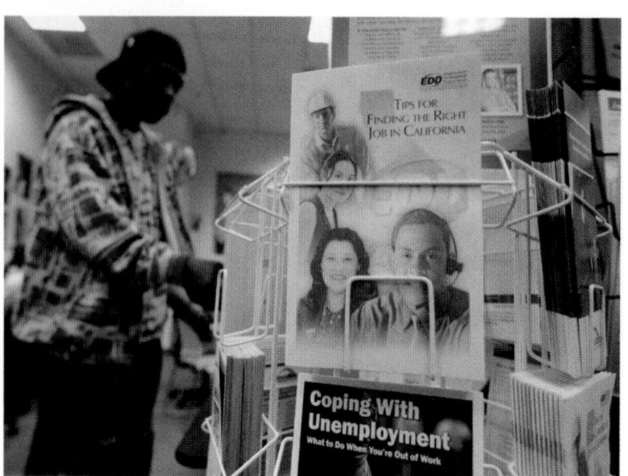

Chronic unemployment is one of the causes of strain for those struggling to avoid breaking the law. What are some other sources of strain that Agnew identifies?

types and levels of strain: failure to achieve goals, the loss of positive stimuli, and the gain of negative stimuli. It explains why some strain is more likely to result in crime and delinquency and shows why some people are more likely to cope with strain through crime.[59]

Agnew presents a comprehensive analysis of strains and stressors experienced by those who might respond by breaking the law. He states that not everyone responds to strain in the same way and that much of what stresses individuals might not be actual strain but merely anticipated strain. He further distinguishes between objective strain and subjective strain. Objective strain is a problem that most people would feel and that we could predict would cause anxiety or pain.[60] For instance, Agnew cites men having their masculinity questioned as an example of objective strain because most males ground their identity in their ideas of manhood.[61] In contrast, Agnew contends that subjective strains are a product of personality traits, goals and values, and prior experiences. He provides the example of divorce as evidence that individuals experience stress differently. For one person, a divorce is traumatic, whereas for another it is liberating.[62]

According to Agnew, the following strains are the most likely to push people into crime:

- parental rejection;
- child abuse and neglect;
- erratic, excessive, or harsh supervision and discipline;
- negative secondary school experiences (low grades, negative relationships with teachers, the experience of school as boring and a waste of time);
- abusive peer relations (insults, threats, physical assaults);
- work in the secondary labor market (low-paying jobs that have few benefits, little opportunity

TABLE 6.2 The Differences Between Classical Strain Theory and General Strain Theory

	MERTON (CLASSICAL)	AGNEW (GENERAL)
Goals	Merton assumed that all Americans are influenced primarily by the capitalist dream of achieving financial success. Although this goal is true for many people, it does not affect everyone in the same way.	Agnew recognized Merton's assumption and expanded the idea of striving for cultural goals beyond that of money.
Means	Merton says crime occurs when means are systematically blocked by such things as poverty and racism.	Agnew argues that the means to achieving cultural goals are also more numerous and varied than Merton suggests and the legitimate and illegitimate means available to potential delinquents more complicated.
Empirical Evidence	Merton's ideas were purely theoretical, although others have tried to test them.	Agnew's research on strain theory is impressive for its increasing sophistication in both statistical technique and the range of populations.

for advancement, and unpleasant working conditions);

- chronic unemployment;
- marital problems;
- failure to achieve selected goals, including thrills/excitement, high levels of autonomy, masculine status, and the desire for much money in a short period of time;
- criminal victimization;
- residence in economically deprived communities;
- homelessness; and
- discrimination based on characteristics such as race/ethnicity and gender.[63]

According to Agnew, some research supports the relationship between these strains and crime.[64] Furthermore, when individuals experience two or more of these conditions, they are even more likely to break the law. These strains accumulate, so that when someone loses a job, there is an increased likelihood that family problems will occur, which can lead to other issues related to delinquency and crime. General strain theory considers how these strains and stressors lead individuals to develop negative emotions such as frustration, anger, depression, jealousy, and fear. Individuals feel bad and are motivated to take corrective action to obtain revenge, acquire valued property, or elevate their status in their own eyes and in the eyes of the community. These strains also reduce the individual's commitment to conventional society and the socially approved means for obtaining success.[65] (See Table 6.2 for the differences between classical strain theory and general strain theory.)

PAUSE AND REVIEW

1. **List the strains that Agnew contends are most likely to lead people to resort to crime.**
2. **Describe the methods youths use to adapt to their failure to achieve culturally desired goals as described by classical strain theory.**
3. **What is anomie? Why is it important to strain theories?**
4. **What are Merton's five adaptations?**
5. **According to Cloward and Ohlin, what do deviant subcultures do?**
6. **According to Agnew, what is the difference between objective strain and subjective strain?**

Control Theories of Crime

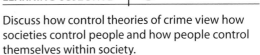

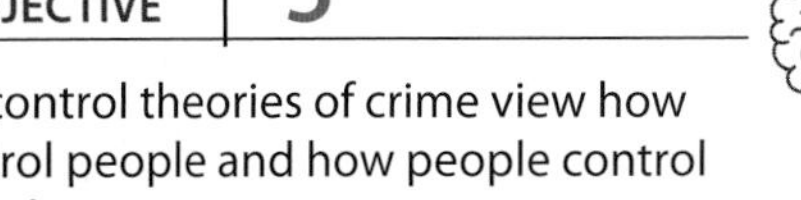

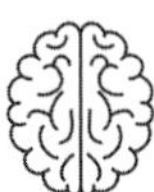

Discuss how control theories of crime view how societies control people and how people control themselves within society.

A perplexing aspect of criminological theory is that the assumptions about human nature on which it rests are often left unstated. Criminologists often take human nature as a given, and the goal of a theory is to explain why some people will violate the law. If we assume that well-adjusted people act in conforming ways, all we have to do is specify how non-conforming individuals have not been adequately socialized. However, another way of looking at human nature assumes that antisocial behavior is not an aberration, but rather that it is to be expected.

Control theories of crime—a perspective that questions why most people do not break the law—have been around for a long time. As we will see with Travis Hirschi's social bond theory, the question of why some people break the law can be reframed to ask why all of us do not break the law.[66]

This reformulation of the assumptions underlying antisocial behavior requires theorists to consider crime in a different way, one that refocuses our attention on how individuals are connected to society. A look at the development and underlying principles of control theories shows us why this perspective is such a popular way to consider crime and delinquency.

Containment Theory

Perhaps the best example of the early control theories is Walter Reckless's **containment theory**, the idea that everyone has internal and external structures that hold them within the larger social structure. It distinguishes between internal factors that "push" people into crime and external factors that "pull" them.[67] According to Reckless, all people have an external structure that "contains" (or restricts) their behavior as well as a protective internal structure. Both structures guard against deviance by securing people within the social structure. Loss or corruption of elements of

---

control theories of crime—A perspective that questions why most people do not break the law.

containment theory—The idea that everyone has internal and external structures that hold them within the larger social structure.

TABLE 6.3 Elements of Containment Theory

ELEMENTS OF EXTERNAL STRUCTURE	ELEMENTS OF INTERNAL STRUCTURE
Roles that guide individual activities	Positive self-concept
Reasonable limits and responsibilities	Self-control
Opportunities for status achievement	Strong ego and conscience
Cohesion among group members	High tolerance for frustration
A sense of belonging and identification with the group	Strong sense of responsibility
Identification with others in the group	
Alternative ways to achieve satisfaction if some ways are closed	

their external structures can "pull" people into law-breaking activities, while internal issues can "push" them. (See Table 6.3 for a look at the elements of containment theory.) Reckless's theory includes many of the ideas covered in social disorganization, differential association, and strain theories. Reckless went one step further, however, and considered the case of the "good boy" in the "bad neighborhood."[68] Why don't all youths exposed to gangs, negative peer pressure, and economic inequality succumb to delinquency?

Reckless's answer is that youths with a healthy self-concept are insulated from the negative effects of a bad neighborhood and antisocial peers.[69] This observation has led a number of scholars to explore how youths bond to society so that they resist the temptations that lead others to delinquency. Foremost among these theorists is Travis Hirschi.

Social Bond Theory

Hirschi's **social bond theory** is the idea that there are forces that keep people connected to social norms and values. It has wide appeal because it specifies how youths are connected to the idea that they should not break the law. Rather than asking about delinquents' motivations to be antisocial, Hirschi considers all youngsters and asks what keeps them from breaking the law. His answer is social control in the form of four elements: attachment, commitment, involvement, and belief. Crime and delinquency occur when these bonds to conventional society are weakened or broken (see Figure 6.6). Let's look at each.

- Attachment. We all have emotional attachments to others. We care about others' opinions of us, and we worry that we might disappoint or hurt them by our actions. Most youths are strongly attached to their parents and strive to live up to their expectations. When teenagers test their freedom by taking the family car out on a Saturday night, they might be tempted to impress their friends by speeding, drinking alcohol, or staying out late. Most teenagers curb these impulses because they are emotionally attached to their parents and do not want to violate their trust. This attachment is a form of indirect parental control that acts to keep children out of trouble. The stronger the attachment, the fewer concrete rules teenagers need. Other teenagers need well-defined rules concerning curfews, where they can go, and whom they may be with. Children who are estranged from their parents may have little consideration for parental approval and feel free to break the law.[70]
- Commitment. Youths who are successful in school, in the community, and among their peers are more likely to stay out of trouble because they develop a commitment to the conventional lifestyle. An old saying points out, "If you've got nothing, you've got nothing to lose." Those who have status, responsibility, and the respect of others have a great deal to lose if they are caught breaking the law; therefore, they are less likely to take chances. From a policy perspective, Hirschi's idea of commitment suggests that parents and communities should find ways to give youths a stake in society, so that they feel they can be successful if they adopt law-abiding behavior.[71]
- Belief. Like other theories such as differential association and techniques of neutralization, Hirschi's social bond theory is concerned with the question of how people who believe in the law can justify breaking it. Most youths obey the law just about all the time. When they do become delinquent, it is because, for some reason, they are able to convince themselves that their behavior is necessary, inevitable, or out of their control. Although differential association argues that some youths hold definitions that

are favorable to the violation of the law, Hirschi's control takes a different tack. Hirschi does not argue that youths believe that lawbreaking is desirable; he contends only that they do not believe it is bad. This is a fine distinction, but it is an important one because it speaks to the strength of youths' beliefs more than to the direction of those beliefs. If the belief that forbids delinquency is weak or absent, then the youth's bond to society is fragile, and the youth will break the law, not because it is considered desirable, but simply because his or her belief that crime is bad is not strong enough.[72]

- Involvement. If "idle hands are the devil's workshop," then one obvious solution to delinquency is to keep youths busy with conventional activities. If youths are involved in recreational programs, music lessons, or soccer camp, they are less likely to find the time to get into trouble. As youths move from being adolescents under their parents' supervision to adults who are fully integrated into society, they have a great deal of leisure time to fill. Those who seek involvement in conventional activities are able to develop a set of values that help them resist the lure of delinquency when they have "too much time on their hands."[73]

Hirschi's social bond theory has received considerable attention from researchers and, for the most part, has withstood their scrutiny. Weak bonds to society do appear to increase the likelihood of being involved in crime, although the quality of the evidence depends on the quality of the research.[74] For a look at how some programs use social bonds to treat drug addiction, rehabilitate offenders and delinquents, and encourage adolescents to conform, see Theory to Practice.

General Theory of Crime

Michael Gottfredson and Travis Hirschi's **general theory of crime** (also called self-control theory) is a logical extension of Hirschi's social bond theory, but it emphasizes the importance of parental influence on children's development of self-control (see Figure 6.7). They assert that the direct control that parents have in monitoring their children's activities and enforcing discipline has a strong influence on how the children develop self-control.[75] Children who learn the consequences of breaking the rules are more successful in limiting their deviant behaviors.[76]

Although this may seem like common sense, it is also important to understand that the way parents supervise their children over a long period of time is crucial to shaping not only their children's ability to resist temporary temptations, but also their personalities. Children who are impulsive, insensitive, and non-verbal are more likely to lack the self-control necessary to avoid the seductions of crime. Those with low self-control will be more likely to engage in delinquent acts such as drinking alcohol, smoking, and skipping school.[77] Related to the failure of youths to develop a strong sense of self-control is the model presented by parents who break the law. Some families demonstrate intergenerational crime in which parents and children have criminal records.

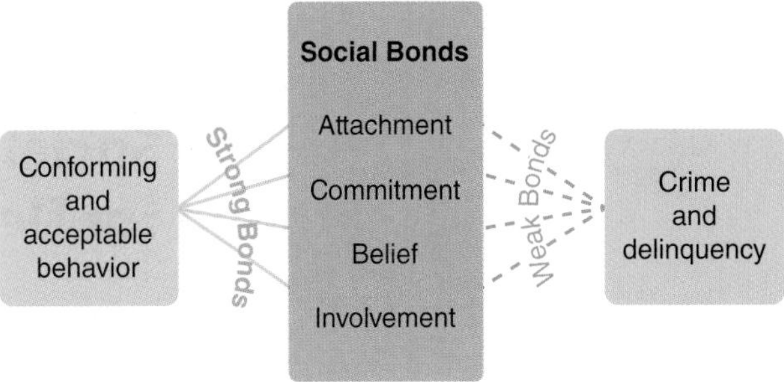

FIGURE 6.6 Social Bond Theory

THINK ABOUT IT
In what ways can social bonds be made stronger in order to promote better behavior?

According to social bond theory, attachment to the family keeps children from adopting deviant lifestyles. What are some other factors that help children avoid breaking the law?

social bond theory—The idea that there are forces that keep people connected to social norms and values.

general theory of crime—Gottfredson and Hirschi's theory emphasizing the importance of parental influence on children's development of self-control.

THEORY TO PRACTICE

Strengthening Social Bonds as Prevention and Treatment for Deviant Behavior

Most prevention and treatment programs can be traced back to sociological criminological theories. The following examples detail how programs have been structured to take advantage of one particular type of theory: Hirschi's social bond perspective. Hirschi identified four ways in which individuals are bonded to conventional society: attachment, commitment, belief, and involvement. These programs, which address the individual's social bonds, have met with mixed success in preventing or treating antisocial behavior.

In programs run by drug courts, a major goal is to address some of the reasons that youths use drugs. By focusing on a youth's links to conventional society, such as parents, peers, school, and religion, the programs can involve them in pro-social activities. Results indicate that social bonds, both positive and negative, play a significant role in whether the youth is successful in desisting from delinquent behavior and completing the program. The effect of juvenile court programs on delinquency and drug use depends largely on their ability to address youths' weak or negative social bonds.[78]

Strengthening social bonds can help treat offenders with drug problems. Getting offenders into treatment quickly can prevent the high failure rate observed during the critical first months that offenders are paroled. It is also possible that attending treatment helps these offenders form stronger social bonds with employers, family, and other conventional institutions.

In attempting to keep adolescents from engaging in premarital sex, some programs ask them to pledge abstinence. This is an attempt to get the youths committed to not having sex until marriage. This strategy has roots in Hirschi's social bond theory, which encourages attachment to parental values, commitment to good behavior, and belief that doing the right thing pays off in the long run. Unfortunately, the success of abstinence programs isn't well established. In one study, 53 percent of youths who took the pledge had sex before marriage. Also, adolescents who pledge abstinence contract sexually transmitted diseases at the same rate as those who do not, and they are less likely to use a condom.[79]

THINK ABOUT IT

1. Come up with an idea for a social program that would use Hirschi's social bond perspective.

These parents tend to be lax in the supervision of their children and inconsistent in their discipline. According to Gottfredson and Hirschi, deviant parents may not even realize they are transmitting negative values to their children.

Finally, it is important to note that lack of parental supervision does not lead directly to crime but rather to a propensity to engage in the sort of deviant behavior that Gottfredson and Hirschi call "criminality." Crime results when criminality meets opportunity. Gottfredson and Hirschi do not elaborate on the concept of opportunity, but contend that low self-control on the part of juvenile delinquents is key to their deviance.[80]

Power-Control Theory

Sociologist John Hagan's **power-control theory of crime** seeks to explain why males commit more offenses and delinquency than females.[81] Hagan considers the family important to the socialization of children. He focuses on the economic inequality that exists between husband and wife and contends that this fosters a condition of patriarchy in which spouses' social roles are determined by gender and are inherently unequal. When this gender inequality is reproduced in the family, the children receive different messages depending on whether they are male or female. Boys are encouraged to take risks and be independent, while girls are socialized into the values of domesticity and are expected to be socially and economically submissive to males.[82]

Recognizing this highly simplified view of the family, Hagan extends the argument to reflect changing family patterns. He envisions the family on a continuum, ranging from the traditional patriarchal family to the egalitarian family. In the egalitarian family, the wife is likely to have a good job and command a share of the family power. Spouses in the egalitarian family are more equal, which results in a different type of gender socialization of the children. This also means that children whose parents have a relationship characterized by equality in decision-making, salary, job benefits, and status are likely to have children whose own behavior is less gender-biased.[83] Among other things, boys and girls will likely both go to college, have skilled jobs outside the home, and engage in similar patterns of delinquency.

An important part of power-control theory has to do with how youths calculate the benefits of delinquent behavior. Those who are highly tolerant of risk are more likely to break the law than those who are willing to risk less. Furthermore, risk tolerance is different for different types of offending. Hagan contends that power-control theory is better suited to explaining minor offenses such as theft, vandalism, and physical aggression than more serious offenses such as homicide, in which calculation of risk is often absent and anger or fear are the motivating factors.[84]

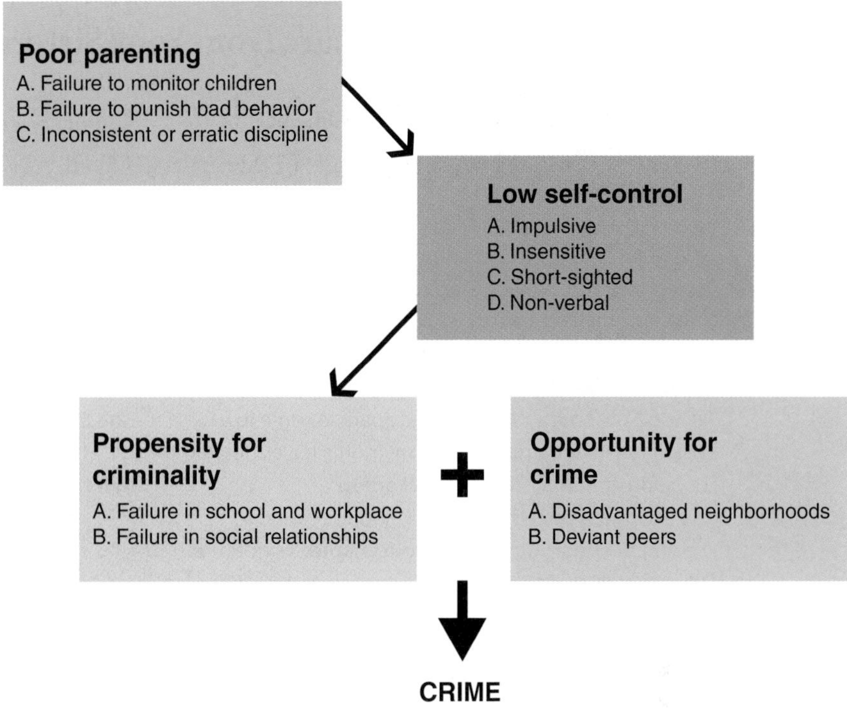

FIGURE 6.7 General Theory of Crime

THINK ABOUT IT
How can youths' self-control be enhanced in order to keep them from breaking the law?

Hagan's power-control theory is important because it shows how the family environment can produce delinquency. He believes that patriarchal families in which gender roles are distinct produce much higher levels of male delinquency than female delinquency. In egalitarian families, the overall level of delinquency will be lower, and the ratio of the misbehavior of boys and girls will be more equal. This has practical applications for family courts, which can look at the dynamics of the families of children in trouble and prescribe family therapy sessions to reduce the level of patriarchy and encourage greater equality in the treatment of boys and girls.

Gender inequality in the family can contribute to delinquency in children, according to Hagan's power-control theory. What are the benefits to children who grow up in families where the power is shared equally by the parents?

PAUSE AND REVIEW

1. **Discuss the attachments to society in Hirschi's social bond theory.**
2. **What are Hirschi's four elements of social control?**
3. **Analyze Hagan's focus on economic inequality within the family as an explanation of why boys break the law more often than girls.**
4. **Explain Reckless's containment theory of "pushes" and "pulls."**

---

power-control theory of crime—A theory that seeks to explain why males commit more offenses and delinquency than females.

Pressure from Your Sisters

You are a junior at a major university and a nursing major. Additionally, you are a member of a sorority and hope to be elected president this year. During rush week, you are in charge of the hazing activities that every new pledge must go through. You were hazed when you were a pledge, and although you found it juvenile and humiliating, you can see how it bonded your sorority sisters to the organization and to each other. Officially, the university prohibits hazing, but all the Greek organizations participate in some low-visibility initiation rites so that members have a feeling of being admitted into a special group.

This year's rush is going well, and everyone is having fun until you come to your chapter's signature rite. After everyone has had too much wasabi vodka to drink (none of the pledges are of legal age to drink alcohol), the pledges must run a gauntlet where members hit them on the buttocks with ceremonial paddles. You endured this same rite when you were a pledge. It smarted a bit, but you felt special and like a full member of the sorority.

After this evening's ritual, however, you notice one of the pledges holding her stomach and complaining of pain. You are concerned. She says she will be all right, but in your experience, prolonged pain is not a common or expected reaction to the activity. You want to take the pledge to the university health center, but she does not want to go. She says she is afraid that everyone will get into trouble and that she would be blackballed from the sorority. Your sisters agree and say that you should wait. They contend that because of the university's alcohol and hazing policies, the sorority could be deactivated, and the sisters (including you) could be subject to criminal charges for providing alcohol to minors.

Nursing training has taught you to take all symptoms seriously, and you are concerned about the possibility of internal bleeding. You are inclined to take the pledge to the health center, but the pledge begs you to give her time to recover. She fears that her strict parents would pull her out of school if they discovered she had been drinking alcohol.

What Do You Do?

1. Tell her to stop drinking and give her an antacid. She will feel better in the morning.
2. Grab a random cell phone and call 911 from the bathroom. Help will arrive, and no one will know it was you who called.
3. Tell everyone that you are washing your hands of the matter. If they do not want you to get the pledge some help, they are responsible for any consequences.
4. Take her to the health center and accompany her when she sees a doctor. You do not want to be part of an organization that is so cavalier about the health of its members. Besides, you need to start acting more like a nurse and less like a college student. Giving young pledges alcohol and hitting them with sticks is a dumb idea anyway.
5. Take her to the health center, but send her inside by herself and tell her to lie about where she has been and what she has been doing. If she cannot learn to protect her sorority sisters, then she should not be in a sorority.

Summary

LEARNING OBJECTIVE 1 Explain sociological imagination.	According to sociologist C. Wright Mills, sociological imagination is the idea that we must look beyond our personal experiences to the experiences of others in order to evaluate how social location influences how individuals perceive society. Sociological imagination allows people to critique how their social location within society influences their opportunities and choices.
LEARNING OBJECTIVE 2 Discuss the development of social disorganization theories.	Social disorganization theory was developed to explain the social problems, such as poverty and delinquency, facing Chicago in the first part of the 20th century, but it applies to many cities. According to social disorganization theory, not only do impoverished neighborhoods have a culture of crime, but also the disintegration of social bonds and the failure of social institutions cause crime.

LEARNING OBJECTIVE 3 Give some theories of how antisocial behavior is learned.	Sutherland's theory of differential association attributes the learning of crime to interactions with others, particularly intimate others such as peers and family. Sykes and Matza's techniques of neutralization theory asserts that delinquents believe in the law and break it only after they can rationalize their actions as necessary or unavoidable. According to subcultural theories, offenders learn the skills, norms, values, and attitudes conducive to lawbreaking from the subcultures in which they live. Wolfgang and Ferracuti argue that some neighborhoods have a subculture of violence in which violence is considered the appropriate response to many situations and is necessary to achieve goals and desires. According to Anderson, urban violence is prompted by a "code of the street" that requires people to quickly resort to violence when they feel others do not respect them.
LEARNING OBJECTIVE 4 Show how strain theories evolved from the concept of anomie.	Durkheim observed that when traditional norms were discarded, new norms are slow to emerge. Durkheim's term "anomie" refers to structural anomie, which is experienced by societies that sustain rapid social change. In individuals, anomie is a psychological reaction to rapid social change and its consequences, and it produces a strain that can result in frustration, desperation, violence, and crime. When people experience anomie, they may break the law because they feel the old rules no longer constrain them to conforming behavior. Strain theories seek to describe how the strain caused by anomie leads to crime.
LEARNING OBJECTIVE 5 Discuss how control theories of crime view how societies control people and how people control themselves within society.	Reckless's containment theory distinguishes between internal factors that "push" people into crime and external factors that "pull" them. Rather than asking why youths break the law, Hirschi's social bond theory asks what keeps youths from violating the law. Gottfredson and Hirschi's general theory of crime (also called self-control theory) asserts that the direct control parents have in monitoring their children's activities and enforcing discipline has a strong influence on how the children develop self-control. Hagan's power-control theory maintains that, in families, boys are encouraged to take risks and be independent, while girls are expected to be socially and economically submissive to males.

Critical Reflections

1. **Examine how the Chicago Area Project applied social disorganization theory to crime problems.**
2. **Evaluate the concentric zone theory's utility in accounting for urban crime.**
3. **How does the theory of collective efficacy and crime differ from Shaw and McKay's social disorganization theory?**
4. **How does the idea of operant conditioning relate to social learning theory?**
5. **Compare and contrast the subcultural theories of Miller, Wolfgang and Ferracuti, and Anderson.**
6. **Categorize Sykes and Matza's techniques of neutralization. Which ones do you use to account for your own behavior?**
7. **What does the American Dream have to do with strain?**
8. **Explain the fundamentally different approach in Hirschi's social bond theory.**

Key Terms

anomie p. 158
classical strain theory p. 158
collective efficacy p. 150
concentric zone theory p. 149
containment theory p. 165
control theories of crime p. 165
differential association p. 152
differential opportunity theory p. 160
differential reinforcement p. 153
focal concerns p. 155
general strain theory p. 163
general theory of crime p. 167
institutional anomie p. 162
learning theories of crime p. 152
operant conditioning p. 153
power-control theory of crime p. 168
social bond theory p. 166
social disorganization theory p. 148
social learning theory p. 153
sociological imagination p. 146
subculture of violence p. 156
techniques of neutralization theory p. 154

Notes

1 Mark Gokavi and Nick Blizzard, "One of 7 Suspects in Huber Heights AT&T Robbery Makes Court Appearance," *Dayton Daily News*, February 2, 2018, https://www.daytondailynews.com/news/local/huber-heights-robbery-juveniles-set-for-afternoon-court-appearances/gSorLOklDT7YpOVnOgO3fP. Accessed February 2018.

2 *Dayton Daily News*, "Community Shows Support for All-State Football Player Accused of Robbery," February 13, 2018, https://www.daytondailynews.com/news/crime—law/community-shows-support-for-all-state-football-player-accused-robbery/g4tXMmqqTXuuDGez0GLokJ. Accessed February 2018.

3 Mark Gokavi, "18-Year-Old Suspect in Huber Heights AT&T Store Robbery Indicted," *Dayton Daily News*, February 9, 2018, https://www.daytondailynews.com/news/crime--law/year-old-suspect-huber-heights-store-robbery-indicted/uvMzZ6EjF7kM5wpPifGgsN. Mark Gokavi, "'Not Going to Sugarcoat': Judge Tells Teens Accused in Huber Robbery They Face Years in Prison," *Dayton Daily News*, February 2, 2018, https://www.mydaytondailynews.com/news/crime--law/not-going-sugarcoat-judge-tells-teens-accused-huber-robbery-they-face-years-prison/2bnnvlfhc6gWYkGI7E5XzL. Accessed February 2018.

4 C. Wright Mills, *The Sociological Imagination* (New York: Oxford University Press, 1959).

5 Claire M. Renzetti, Lynne Goodstein, and Susan L. Miller, eds., *Rethinking Gender, Crime, and Justice* (Los Angeles: Roxbury Publishing Company, 2006).

6 Elliot Currie, *Crime and Punishment in America* (New York: Metropolitan Books, 1998).

7 Gokavi, "18-Year-Old Suspect in Huber Heights AT&T Store Robbery Indicted."

8 Paul Frederick Cressey, "Population Succession in Chicago: 1898–1930," *The American Journal of Sociology* 44, no. 1 (July 1938): 55–69.

9 Oscar Lewis, *Five Families: Mexican Case Studies in the Culture of Poverty* (New York: New American Library, 1965).

10 Douglas S. Massey and Nancy A. Denton, *American Apartheid: Segregation and the Making of the Underclass* (Cambridge, Mass.: Harvard University Press, 1993).

11 Robert J. Sampson and William Julius Wilson, "A Theory of Race, Crime, and Urban Inequality," in *Criminological Theory Past to Present*, 6th ed., ed. Francis T. Cullen, Robert Agnew, and Pamela Wilcox (New York: Oxford University Press, 2018), 576–582.

12 Michael Sokolove, "Constructing a Teen Phenom," *New York Times Magazine* 154, no. 53047 (November 28, 2004): 80–85.

13 Diana M. Pearce, "Black, White, and Many Shades of Gray: Real Estate Brokers and Their Racial Practices" (PhD diss., University of Michigan, 1976).

14 Ernest W. Burgess, "The Growth of the City," in *The City*, ed. R. E. Park, E. W. Burgess, and Roderick D. McKenzie (Chicago: University of Chicago Press, 1925), 47–62.

15 C. Wright Mills, "The Professional Ideology of Social Pathologists," *American Journal of Sociology* 49 (1943): 165–180.

16 J. Robert Lilly, Francis T. Cullen, and Richard A. Ball, *Criminological Theory: Context and Consequences*, 4th ed. (Thousand Oaks, Calif.: Sage, 2007), 38.

17 Jon Snodgrass, "Clifford R. Shaw and Henry D. McKay: Chicago Criminologists," *British Journal of Criminology* 16, no. 1 (1976): 1–19.

18 Clifford R. Shaw, *The Jack-Roller: A Delinquent Boy's Own Story* (Chicago: University of Chicago Press, 1930).

19 Solomon Kobrin, "The Chicago Area Project: A 25-Year Assessment," *Annals of the American Society of Political and Social Science* (March 1959): 19–29.

20 Chicago Area Project Pioneers include Ernest W. Burgess, Tony Sorrentino, Daniel "Moose" Brindisi, Sadie Waterford Jones, Beatrice Caffrey, and E. Toy Fletcher. See Chicago Area Project, http://www.chicagoareaproject.org. Accessed March 2018.

21 John R. Hipp, "Collective Efficacy: How Is It Conceptualized, How Is It Measured, and Does It Really Matter for Understanding Perceived Neighborhood Crime and Disorder?" *Journal of Criminal Justice* 46 (2016): 32–44.

22 Cullen and Agnew, eds., *Criminological Theory: Past to Present*, 92.

23 Robert J. Sampson, Stephen W. Raudenbush, and Felton Sams, "Neighborhoods and Violent Crime: A Multilevel Study of Collective Efficacy," *Science* 227 (August 15, 1997): 918–924.

24 Robert J. Sampson, Stephen W. Raudenbush, and Felton Sams, "Collective Efficacy Theory: Lessons Learned and Directions for Future Inquiry," in *Taking Stock: The Status of Criminological Theory* (Advances in Criminological Theory), ed. Francis T. Cullen, John Paul Wright, and Kristie R. Blevins (New Brunswick, N.J.: Transaction, 2006), 149–167.

25 Tammy Rinehart Kochel, "Police Legitimacy and Resident Cooperation in Crime Hotspots: Effects of Victimisation Risk and Collective Efficacy," *Policing and Society* 28, no. 3 (April 2018): 251–270.

26 Robert J. Bursik Jr. and Harald G. Grasmick, *Neighborhoods and Crime: The Dimensions of Effective Community Control* (New York: Lexington, 1993).

27 John K. Cochran, Jon Maskaly, Shayne Jones, and Christine S. Sellers, "Using Structural Equations to Model Akers' Social Learning Theory with Data on Intimate Partner Violence," *Crime and Delinquency* 63, no. 1 (2017): 39.

28 Gill Geis and Colin Goff , "Edwin H. Sutherland's White-Collar Crime in America: An Essay in Historical Criminology," *Criminal Justice History* 7 (1986): 1–31.

29 Gerben J. N. Bruinsma, "Differential Association Theory Reconsidered: An Extension and Its Empirical Test," *Journal of Quantitative Criminology* 8, no. 1 (March 1992): 29–49.

30 Glenn D. Walters, "Proactive Criminal Thinking and the Transmission of Differential Association," *Criminal Justice and Behavior* 42, no. 11 (November 2015): 1128.

31 Ronald L. Akers, "Is Differential Association/Social Learning Cultural Deviance Theory?" *Criminology* 34 (1996): 229–247.

32 Ronald L. Akers, "A Social Learning Theory of Crime," in *Criminological Theory Past to Present*, 6th ed., ed. Francis T. Cullen, Robert

Agnew, and Pamela Wilcox (New York: Oxford University Press, 2018), 79–92.

33 Saeed Kabiri, John K. Cochran, Bernadette J. Stewart, Mahmoud Sharepour, Mohammad Mahdi Rahmati, and Syede Massomeh Shadmanfaat, "Doping Among Professional Athletes in Iran: A Test of Akers's Social Learning Theory," *International Journal of Offender Therapy and Comparative Criminology* 62, no. 5 (2018): 1384. John K. Cochran, Jon Maskaly, Shayne Jones, and Christine S. Sellers, "Using Structural Equations to model Akers' Social Learning Theory with Data on Intimate Partner Violence," *Crime & Delinquency* 63, no. 1 (2017): 39–60. Michael Capece and Lonn Lanza-Kaduce, "Binge Drinking among College Students: A Partial Test of Akers' Social Structure-Social Learning Theory," *American Journal of Criminal Justice* 38, no. 4 (2013): 503–519.

34 Jeffrey T. Ward, Megan McConaghy, and Juwan Z. Bennett, "Differential Applicability of Criminological Theories to Individuals? The Case of Social Learning vis-à-vis Social Control," *Crime & Delinquency* 64, no. 4 (2018): 510.

35 Shadd Maruna and Heith Copes, "What Have We Learned from Five Decades of Neutralization Research?" in *Crime and Justice* 32: A Review of Research, ed. Michael Tonry (Chicago: University of Chicago Press, 2005), 221–320.

36 Gresham M. Sykes and David Matza, "Techniques of Neutralization," *American Sociological Review* 22 (1957): 664–670.

37 Marvin E. Wolfgang and Franco Ferracuti, *The Subculture of Violence: Towards an Integrated Theory in Criminology* (Beverly Hills, Calif.: Sage, 1982).

38 Walter Miller, "Lower-Class Culture as a Generating Milieu of Gang Delinquency," *Journal of Social Issues* 14 (1958): 5–19.

39 Frank P. Williams, III and Marilyn M. Shane, *Criminological Theory*, 4th ed. (Upper Saddle River, N.J.: Prentice Hall, 2004), 125.

40 Marvin E. Wolfgang and Franco Ferracuti, *The Subculture of Violence* (Beverly Hills, Calif.: Sage, 1982).

41 Karen F. Parker, "A Move Toward Specificity: Examining Urban Disadvantage and Race and Relationship-Specific Homicide Rates," *Journal of Quantitative Criminology* 17 (2001): 89–110.

42 Ramiro Martinez Jr. and Matthew T. Lee, "Comparing the Context of Immigrant Homicides in Miami: Haitians, Jamaicans, and Mariels," *International Migration Review* 34 (2000): 794–812.

43 Elijah Anderson, *Code of the Street: Decency, Violence, and the Moral Life of the Inner City* (New York: W.W. Norton, 1999).

44 Elijah Anderson, "The Code of the Street," in *Criminological Theory: Past to Present*, 6th ed., ed. Francis T. Cullen, Robert Agnew, and Pamela Wilcox (New York: Oxford University Press, 2018), 93–104.

45 Ibid., 97.

46 Anderson, "The Code of the Street," 154.

47 Émile Durkheim, *The Division of Labor in Society*, trans. George Simpson (1893; repr., New York: The Free Press, 1933).

48 Robert K. Merton, "Social Structure and Anomie," *American Sociological Review* 3 (1938): 672–682.

49 Richard Cloward and Lloyd Ohlin, *Delinquency and Opportunity* (Glencoe, Ill.: Free Press, 1960).

50 Albert K. Cohen, *Delinquent Boys: The Subculture of the Gang* (Glencoe, Ill.: Free Press, 1955).

51 Steven F. Messner and Richard Rosenfeld, *Crime and the American Dream*, 3rd ed. (Belmont, Calif.: Wadsworth, 2000).

52 Ibid.

53 Ibid.

54 Ibid.

55 Ibid.

56 Ibid.

57 Ibid.

58 Ibid.

59 Robert Agnew, "Building on the Foundations of General Strain Theory: Specifying the Types of Strain Most Likely to Lead to Crime and Delinquency," *Journal of Research in Crime and Delinquency* 38 (2001): 319–361.

60 Robert Agnew, "Pressured into Crime: General Strain Theory," in *Criminological Theory: Past to Present*, 6th ed., ed. Francis T. Cullen, Robert Agnew, and Pamela Wilcox (New York: Oxford University Press, 2018), 140–149.

61 E. E. Lemasters, *Blue Collar Aristocrats: Lifestyles at a Working Class Tavern* (Madison: University of Wisconsin Press, 1976).

62 Agnew, "Building on the Foundations of General Strain Theory," 206.

63 Robert Agnew, "Pressured into Crime: General Strain Theory," in *Criminological Theory: Past to Present*, 6th ed., ed. Frances T. Cullen, Robert Agnew, and Pamela Wilcox (New York: Oxford University Press, 2018), 140–149.

64 Robert Agnew, "The Origin of Delinquent Events: An Examination of Offender Accounts," *Journal of Research in Crime and Delinquency* 27 (1990): 267–294.

65 Travis Hirschi, *Causes of Delinquency* (Berkeley: University of California Press, 1969).

66 Michael R. Gottfredson, "The Empirical Status of Control Theory in Criminology," in *Taking Stock: The Status of Criminological Theory*, 77–100.

67 Walter C. Reckless, Simon Dinity, and Ellen Murray, "The 'Good Boy' in a High Delinquency Area," *Journal of Criminal Law, Criminology, and Police Science* 48 (1957): 18–25.

68 Walter C. Reckless, Simon Dinity, and Ellen Murray, "Self-Concept as an Insulator Against Delinquency," *American Sociological Review* 21 (1956): 744–756.

69 Stephen A. Cernkovich and Peggy Giordano, "Family Relationships and Delinquency," *Criminology* 25 (1987): 295–321.

70 Eric Poole and Robert Regoli, "The Commitment of Delinquents to Their Misdeeds: A Re-Examination," *Journal of Criminal Justice* 6 (1978): 261–268.

71 Travis Hirschi, "Social Bond Theory," in *Criminological Theory: Past to Present*, 6th ed., ed. Frances T. Cullen, Robert Agnew, and Pamela Wilcox (New York: Oxford University Press, 2018), 169–177.

72 Josine Junger-Tas, "An Empirical Test of Social Control Theory," *Journal of Quantitative Criminology* 8 (1992): 9–28.

73 Hirschi, *Causes of Delinquency*.

74 Michael R. Gottfredson and Travis Hirschi, *A General Theory of Crime* (Stanford, Calif.: Stanford University Press, 1990).

75 Ibid.

76 Michael R. Gottfredson and Travis Hirschi, "A General Theory of Crime," in *Criminological Theory: Past to Present*, 6th ed., ed. Frances T. Cullen, Robert Agnew, and Pamela Wilcox (New York: Oxford University Press, 2018), 178–190.

77 James D. Unnever, Francis T. Cullen, and Robert Agnew, "Why Is 'Bad' Parenting Criminogenic? Implications from Rival Theories," *Youth Violence and Juvenile Justice* 4 (2006): 3–33.

78 Amna Saddik Gilmore, Nancy Rodriguez, and Vincent J. Webb, "Substance Abuse and Drug Courts: The Role of Social Bonds in Juvenile Drug Courts," *Youth Violence and Juvenile Justice* 3, no. 4, (2005): 287–315. Duren Banks and Denise C. Gottfredson, "The Effects of Drug Treatment and Supervision on Time to Rearrest Among Drug Treatment Court Participants," *Journal of Drug Issues* (Spring 2003): 385–412.

79 Sandra G. Boodman, "Virginity Pledges Can't Be Taken on Faith," *Washington Post*, May 16, 2006, p. F04. Janet E. Rosenbaum, "Reborn a Virgin: Adolescents' Retracting of Virginity Pledges and Sexual Histories," *American Journal of Public Health* 96, no. 6 (June 2006):1098–1103.

80 Travis C. Pratt and Francis T. Cullen, "The Empirical Status of Gottfredson and Hirschi's General Theory of Crime: A Meta-Analysis," *Criminology* 37 (2000): 375–404.

81 John Hagan, *Structural Criminology* (New Brunswick, N.J.: Rutgers University Press, 1989).

82 Edem F. Avakame, "Modeling the Patriarchal Factor in Juvenile Delinquency: Is There Room for Peers, Church, and Television?" *Criminal Justice and Behavior* 24 (1991): 477–494.

83 Gary F. Jensen and Kevin Thompson, "What's Class Got to Do with It? A Further Examination of Power Control Theory," *American Journal of Sociology* 95 (1990): 1009–1023.

84 Hagan, *Structural Criminology*.

58
GEOX

Life-Course and Integrated Theories

FEATURES

Life-course-persistent offenders can exhibit antisocial behavior at an early stage. Is there any way to distinguish normal childhood play from an early pattern of aggressive behavior?

Blane Nordahl received an eight-year sentence for stealing the silver from Wilderstein, the home of a relative of Franklin D. Roosevelt, and another nearby mansion in 2002. Nordahl snaked through openings to bypass motion detectors. Why are there not harsher penalties for offenders like Nordahl? Is there a life-course or integrated theory that best explains Nordahl's behavior?

Sometime in the late 1970s, Blane Nordahl dropped out of 11th grade and started getting into trouble with the law. His parents made him join the Navy, and he did well there until he committed his first burglary in 1983. Dishonorably discharged, Nordahl worked with a gang that broke into houses and stole anything that looked valuable. He did this until his first arrest, and his partners informed on him to police. Nordahl worked solo from then on.[1]

Nordahl, the son of renowned artist David Nordahl, began to apply more skill to his technique and his targets. He gave up drugs, alcohol, and caffeine and got into shape. Eventually, he was breaking into wealthy homes with such expertise that the police called him the "burglar to the stars." His booty of choice was sterling silver objects, including antique tableware, art, and historical pieces, such as a 1734 mug that had belonged to King George II.[2] Nordahl was so committed to sterling silver that he would leave all other valuables behind, such as a thousand dollars in cash that was sitting on a table. His proficiency in avoiding alarms grew so masterful that many homeowners did not even realize they had been victimized until they needed their silverware for a party weeks or months later.[3]

Because of the quiet nature of Nordahl's offenses, property crimes without violence, Nordahl never spent a long time behind bars. After getting out of prison, he would move to another part of the country and pick up his profession, although with some refinements to his technique. After being convicted on shoe-print evidence early in his career, Nordahl, on his next series of burglaries, began to wear shoes two sizes too large and discarded all of his clothing after every job.[4]

In 2017, after a series of burglaries in the Southeast, Nordahl, now 55, pleaded guilty to a silver theft he had committed in Georgia. He was sentenced to 11 years in prison and nine years of probation. As of 2018, he also faced charges in Tennessee and South Carolina.[5]

In a 2003 interview Nordahl gave from federal prison in Elkton, Ohio, he said he was thinking of giving up burglary. "I have no visions of being some criminal for my life. That's not cool."[6]

Life-Course Theories

LEARNING OBJECTIVE | 1

State the focus of life-course criminology.

LEARNING OBJECTIVE | 2

Explain when antisocial behavior begins, according to Patterson's developmental perspective, and how long it continues.

LEARNING OBJECTIVE | 3

Identify Moffitt's two categories of youthful offenders.

LEARNING OBJECTIVE | 4

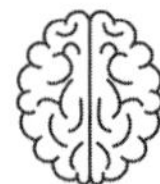

Review Laub and Sampson's focus on the quality of social bonds in persistent offending or desisting from crime.

In this chapter, we consider two types of theories that are of great concern to contemporary criminologists: life-course theories and integrated theories. Both types represent greater sophistication in the level of detail used to explain crime, and both also attempt to expand the range of analysis to include more types of crime.

Life-course and integrated theories build on many of the theories covered in preceding chapters as theorists fine-tune some of the concepts and ideas of other scholars. As new data become available and research techniques more refined, theorists also search for explanations that better reflect the conditions both within society and within individuals that might contribute to crime. Understanding the complexities of life-course and integrated theories is important because, in many ways, contemporary criminological theory increasingly concentrates on these theories. Table 7.1 sets forth the basics of each of the theories discussed in this chapter.

TABLE 7.1 Life-Course and Integrated Theories

This table presents an overview of the theories presented in this chapter, along theorists, strengths, and challenges.

THEORY	THEORIST	STRENGTHS	CHALLENGES
Life-Course Theories *Focus on the development of antisocial behavior, risk factors at different ages, and the effect of life events on individual development*		The behavior of individuals can be examined with respect to aging.	Long periods of study mean that some subjects will be lost. There are more subjects early in the research than in later stages.
Developmental perspective on antisocial behavior *Antisocial behavior begins early in life and often continues through adolescence and adulthood.* *Advocates early intervention to prevent chronic delinquency.*	Gerald R. Patterson Barbara D. DeBaryshe Elizabeth Ramsey	Has been tested in the "real world"	Does not address elements that cause some youths to desist from antisocial behavior.
Pathways to crime *Young offenders are adolescent-limited or life-course persistent.* *Adolescence-limited offenders break the law during youth.* *Life-course-persistent offenders continue antisocial activity into adulthood.*	Terrie Moffitt	Considers biological, psychological, and sociological explanations for delinquency	Divides delinquents into only two groups: adolescent-limited delinquents and life-course-persistent offenders Classifies subjects only after adolescence is over
Persistent offending and desistance from crime *Individuals advance into conventional behavior via turning points and personal agency.*	John Laub Robert Sampson	Based on strong data (the Gluecks' study) Qualitative elements, such as life histories, flesh out the theory	Does not deeply investigate the elements that encourage people to break the law
Integrated Theories *Bring together several theories to explain more types of antisocial behavior*		Seek to provide more detailed explanations for crime	Can be very complicated Currently consider offending at only the individual level

(continued)

TABLE 7.1 Life-Course and Integrated Theories *continued*

THEORY	THEORIST	STRENGTHS	CHALLENGES
Integrated theoretical perspective on delinquent behavior *Everyone is bound to society.* *Strong social bonds produce conventional behavior; weak social bonds produce antisocial behavior.*	Delbert Elliott Suzanne Ageton Rachelle Canter	Combines strain, self-control, and social learning theories Popular among integrated theories	Might try to consider too many variables
Interactional theory of delinquency *Incorporates social learning, social bonds, and life-course theories.* *Considers youths' bonds to parents as particularly important.*	Terence Thornberry	Addresses the reciprocity of social learning, social bonds, and life-course perspectives	Links theories in an "end-to-end" approach, which limits the degree of integration
Control balance theory *Individuals exert control over their lives, and society exerts control over individuals.* *Imbalance in these factors produces antisocial behavior.*	Charles Tittle	Complex, ambitious; seeks to explain not only whether a person will break the law, but also what kind of offense will be committed	Difficult to test and construct research
Social support and crime *Support from society affects individuals and institutions and the likelihood of crime.*	Francis Cullen	Integrates theories in a unique way; accounts for both micro and macro levels "Social support" variable is unique.	Other theories do not employ the concept of social support.
General theory of crime and delinquency *The major causes of crime lie within five life domains.*	Robert Agnew	Links together a broad range of factors that influence crime	It is difficult to test all the variables in such a comprehensive theory.
Integrated cognitive antisocial potential theory *Many factors combine to increase the likelihood of short-term and long-term antisocial behavior.*	David Farrington	Integrates ideas from many classic criminological theories	Focuses on males Does not account for race or crime rates Does not attempt to explain gangs

Life-course theory focuses on three issues: the development of antisocial behavior, risk factors at different ages, and the effect of life events on individual development.[7] Life-course theories are constructed using **longitudinal** data, which means the same individuals are examined at different points in their life course. This dynamic type of theory is significantly different from the static theories that look at the subject at one point in time and do not consider the full context of the person's environment. These "snapshot" theories can neither measure nor explain subsequent changes in behavior.[8] For example, young people account for a large number of arrests.[9] As you can see in Figure 7.1, the number of arrests peaks at age 24. After that, the number of arrests drops off regularly by age group. The major advantage of the longitudinal study methodology used in life-course theories is that it can examine the stability or variability of an individual's behavior as the person ages and matures. The opening scenario depicts Blane Nordahl, who is a life-course offender. Although it is not known if Nordahl ever broke the law during childhood and adolescence, once he started breaking the law as a young adult, he did not stop. Was he simply an antisocial late bloomer? Or were there warning signs early on that went unnoticed? Longitudinal studies allow researchers to observe the behaviors of offenders like Nordahl that are part of the normal maturation process and to determine which factors or conditions contribute to antisocial behavior and crime.

The longitudinal approach has its drawbacks, however. The longer the period under consideration, the greater the likelihood of attrition, or loss, of subjects. That is, as the study continues over a period of years, some subjects might decline to continue to participate in the study, the researchers might be unable to find some of the subjects, or some subjects may die. Thus, there are many more subjects early in the research than in the later stages. The loss of subjects would not be a big problem if we could assume there was no systematic bias between the groups at various stages of the study. However, it is possible that subjects who cannot be found are incarcerated, were killed while breaking the law, or ultimately abandoned the criminal lifestyle and left the jurisdiction. There is no way to be sure that the remaining group of subjects accurately represents the original group. Nevertheless, the longitudinal data used by life-course theorists are useful in developing a more detailed picture of an individual's commitment to a criminal career or the factors that enable a delinquent to adopt a conventional lifestyle. Many social programs that address child development and delinquency focus on the life course.

Child psychologists have long been interested in children's developmental processes and have developed several perspectives that account for many variables. We covered some of these perspectives in Chapter 5. Criminologists are now studying developmental processes to see if this perspective better explains antisocial behavior. Let's turn now to three types of developmental theories of crime and examine how they employ the life-course perspective to better explain antisocial behavior.

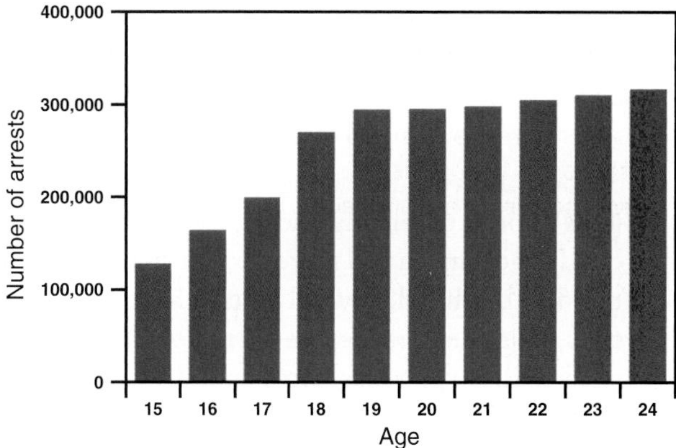

FIGURE 7.1 Arrests by Age

The number of arrests peaks at age 24. In 2016, individuals 18 years of age and over accounted for 91 percent of all arrests.

THINK ABOUT IT

How may life-course theory explain this arrest pattern of young people?

Source: Federal Bureau of Investigation, Uniform Crime Reports: Crime in the United States, *2016, Table 38: Arrests by Age, https://ucr.fbi.gov/crime-in-the-u.s/2016/crime-in-the-u.s.-2016/topic-pages/tables/table-20. Accessed July 2018.*

Developmental Perspective on Antisocial Behavior

According to Gerald Patterson, Barbara DeBaryshe, and Elizabeth Ramsey's developmental perspective on antisocial behavior, antisocial behavior is a developmental trait that begins early and often continues through adolescence and adulthood. These researchers consider a series of predictable steps that lead to chronic delinquency.[10]

- Poor parental discipline and monitoring. The first step in chronic delinquency is poor parenting. Parents who are inconsistent and harsh in their discipline, provide poor role models, and do not adequately supervise their children's activities are more likely to develop offspring who engage in antisocial behavior. Part of this process can be related to Hirschi's control theory, which states that the bond between parent and child is insufficient to promote strong societal values of conformity at work. In addition, a social-interactional perspective suggests that the

Instant Recall from Chapter 2 **longitudinal** —A type of survey that follows respondents throughout their lives or a significant proportion of their lives.

life-course theory—A perspective that focuses on the development of antisocial behavior, risk factors at different ages, and the effect of life events on individual development.

child learns ineffective self-control techniques from parents who are inept at controlling their own emotions or teaching their children positive ways of responding to stress.[11]

- School failure and social rejection. The problems of poor parenting and bad conduct in early childhood can lead to more serious concerns in middle childhood. Several studies have shown that antisocial children perform poorly in school. They spend less time on individual tasks and lack academic survival skills, such as regular attendance and class participation. They may disrupt the classroom and fail to do their homework. Academic failure, as demonstrated by these behaviors, is considered to result directly from antisocial behavior learned in early childhood. Another problem that antisocial children experience is rejection by the normal peer group. Aggressive children are not readily accepted and lack many social cognitive skills. It can be argued that school failure can cause antisocial behavior as much as antisocial behavior can cause school failure. It is a traditional chicken-and-egg problem. However, Patterson and colleagues argue that a stronger case can be made that children demonstrating early antisocial behavior consistently have problems with academic achievement and making friends.[12]
- Commitment to antisocial peer groups. The next step in the developmental process is the formation of an antisocial peer group. Taken from the "birds of a feather flock together" concept, this idea suggests that the developmental process places antisocial youths in groups that reinforce delinquency. The youths provide one another with attitudes and motivations that supply a training ground for antisocial behavior. Because they are placed in the same classrooms, training schools, and treatment programs, they find opportunities to engage in delinquency with one another. Rather than adopting the middle-class values and attitudes of a normal peer group, they continually reinforce and reward their commitment to delinquency and antisocial behavior.[13]
- Delinquency. The preceding developmental processes almost inevitably lead to delinquency. Poor parenting results in early childhood conduct problems that lead to school failure and the inability to develop positive social relationships with peers. These problems in turn lead to a commitment to antisocial peer groups that reinforce delinquency. Commitment to an antisocial peer group consequently results in dropping out of school, unemployment, and substance abuse, which are factors that continue the decline toward delinquency.[14]

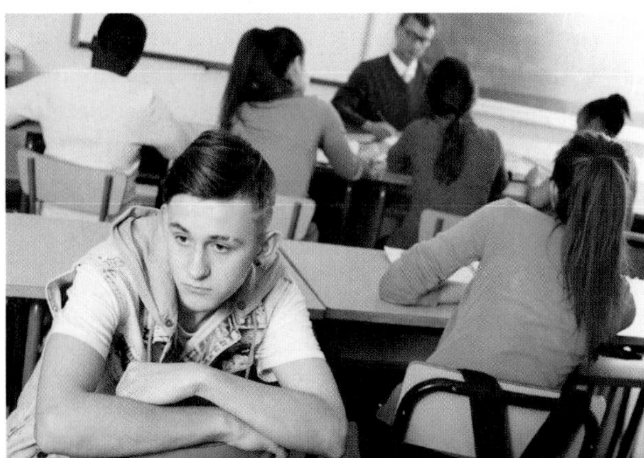

Failure in school can lead to antisocial behavior. Which comes first: the school failure or the antisocial behavior?

Contending that early antisocial behavior can lead to more serious consequences, Patterson, DeBaryshe, and Ramsey advocate early intervention to prevent chronic delinquency. Although their theory is more concerned with what leads a child into antisocial behavior than out of it, their developmental perspective has been used in the field to help troubled families (see Theory to Practice).

The development of antisocial behavior in children can be prevented if it is addressed early. Patterson and his colleagues suggest that providing parents with the skills necessary to develop healthy children is more effective than waiting until middle childhood to address delinquency issues. This developmental perspective argues that the factors that cause delinquency are linked in a way that requires early intervention. The suggested intervention would include not only parent training, but also training children in social skills and providing academic remediation so that they can catch up with their peers.[15]

Pathways to Crime

Criminologist Terrie Moffitt offers another influential developmental theory of crime. According to Moffitt, young offenders fall into one of two categories: delinquents who are **adolescence-limited**—that is, their antisocial behavior is restricted to the teenage years—and **life-course-persistent** offenders, whose antisocial behavior continues throughout adulthood (see Figures 7.2a and 7.2b on pages 182 and 184). The adolescence-limited delinquent breaks the law

THEORY TO PRACTICE

The Oregon Social Learning Center

Located in Eugene, Oregon, the Oregon Social Learning Center (OSLC) researches social and psychological processes related to healthy family functioning. Clinical psychologist Gerald R. Patterson started the OSLC in 1977 from a research group he developed in the late 1950s that focused on developing the theoretical foundation and techniques for parent–management training.[16]

Since the late 1970s, the OSLC has been observing family interactions; interviewing teachers, children, and parents; and collecting school and court records. The center's Multidimensional Treatment Foster Care program, which was originally designed for chronic offending delinquent adolescents, now includes preschool children in the child welfare system. The center's prevention studies also test the effects of parent–management training on various groups, including recently divorced mothers; stepfamilies; the siblings of at-risk youths; parents who are incarcerated, paroled, or on probation; at-risk girls within the child welfare system; and youths at risk for drug and alcohol use. An in-school prevention program called Linking the Interests of Families and Teachers seeks to promote healthy behavior at home, in the classroom, and on the playground.[17]

OSLC's longitudinal Oregon Youth Study, which began in 1983, has been extended to follow its participants' romantic relationships, as well as three generations of their family members. Future research at OSLC will consider biological influences on behavior, examine intervention processes, and develop strategies for implementing evidence-based programs in communities.[18]

THINK ABOUT IT

1. In your opinion, how important is good parenting to preventing delinquency?
2. Relate the work of the Oregon Social Learning Center to Patterson's developmental perspective on antisocial behavior.

only during youth. Life-course-persistent offenders are youths who are unable to break the cycle of crime and maintain that lifestyle into adulthood. Life-course-persistent offenders are what we would call "career criminals" and are never fully integrated into conventional society.[19]

Moffitt's theory has both strengths and weaknesses. Its primary weakness is that it divides delinquents into only two groups. Certainly, antisocial behavior has more variations, and presumably youths flow from one group to the other. The question is, at what point does a youth move from the adolescence-limited category to the life-course-persistent category? If the only way to answer this question is to study individuals after a life of crime, then the theory has limited policy implications.[20] The theory's strength is that it considers biological, psychological, and sociological explanations for juvenile delinquency. By looking at how these factors influence youths over their life-course, Moffitt presents a broad range of explanations that more closely reflect the influences on crime.

LIFE-COURSE-PERSISTENT OFFENDERS

Juvenile delinquents can be responsible for a lot of crime. Some youths are never fully integrated into conventional society, are always at the margins of social institutions, and eventually land in the juvenile justice system.[21] According to Moffitt, the life-course-persistent offender is constantly breaking the law. Moffitt describes life-course-persistent offenders as:

> individuals [who] exhibit changing manifestations of antisocial behavior: biting and hitting at age 4, shoplifting and truancy at age 10, selling drugs and stealing cars at age 16, robbery and rape at age 22, and fraud and child abuse at age 30; the underlying disposition remains the same, but its expression changes form as new social opportunities arise at different points in development. This pattern of continuity across age is matched also by cross-situational consistency: life-course-persistent antisocial persons lie at home, steal from shops, cheat at school, fight in bars, and embezzle at work.[22]

life-course-persistent—Moffitt's term to describe antisocial behavior that continues throughout adulthood.

adolescence-limited—Moffitt's term to describe antisocial behavior that is restricted to the teenage years.

Aggressive behavior can be exhibited throughout a person's life. Why do some individuals seem to exhibit patterns of violence throughout their life-course?

The question of why some people behave this way has no easy answers. According to Moffitt, the answers lie in a complex set of factors that begins with biological considerations. Among these biological influences, Moffitt includes neuropsychological risk factors that contribute to a child's temperament and behavioral problems. Even before a child is born, brain function may be affected by maternal drug abuse, poor prenatal nutrition, or exposure to toxic agents before and after birth.[23] (We should remember, however, that these are merely risk factors and not biological determinants of antisocial behavior.) Along with biological factors, Moffitt adds psychological deficiencies that have also been linked to juvenile delinquency and antisocial behavior. Children who are reared by parents who provide inconsistent discipline tend to develop behavioral problems and have a difficult time distinguishing between appropriate and inappropriate reactions to negative stimuli. Moffitt argues that the transmission of antisocial behavior from parent to child is as much a psychological as a biological factor.[24]

Finally, sociological variables contribute to delinquents' immersion into a life course of crime. Impoverished neighborhoods, antisocial peers, and faulty family structure all contribute to antisocial behavior. This complex of biological, psychological, and sociological factors is persuasive but difficult to measure. Moffitt states that all these factors must be considered when studying the life-course-persistent offender.

The life-course-persistent offender theory may be viewed as a process rather than as a static point. As individuals with negative behavioral traits interact with their negative environment, their negative traits are reinforced, which in turn, leads to antisocial behavior. As Figure 7.2a shows, this process accelerates the youth's immersion into antisocial behavior and a life of crime. A person with a long history of negative behaviors will likely have difficulty breaking the cycle and entering conventional society. Some individuals have very little experience at behaving in socially approved ways and so develop alternative mechanisms such as lying, cheating, and stealing to achieve their goals. Repeated exposure to negative systems exacerbates their antisocial behavior, and the process starts all over again.[25]

Breaking out of this cycle of antisocial behavior becomes more difficult as the delinquents age. They are unable to get off the track of life-course-persistent antisocial behavior for two reasons. The first is the youths' limited behavioral repertoire. Because of their early involvement in the juvenile justice system, they miss out on many opportunities to learn pro-social behaviors. Failing at school, becoming labeled a delinquent, and constantly attempting to solve problems with antisocial behavior combine to produce a cumulative effect that leads to further antisocial behavior. These youths never learn how to act appropriately and successfully engage conventional society. Moffitt contends that "simply put, if social and academic skills are not mastered

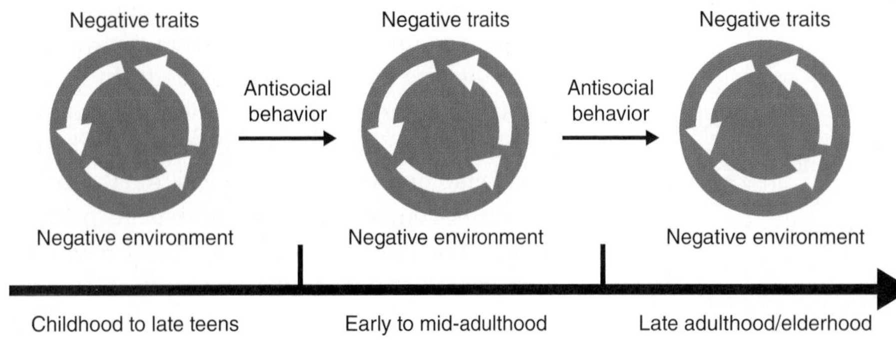

FIGURE 7.2a Moffitt's Pathways to Crime: Life-Course-Persistent Theory

Life-course-persistent offenders are unable to break the cycle of crime and continue to break the law well into adulthood and perhaps for the rest of their lives.

THINK ABOUT IT
List some of Moffitt's personal and environmental influences on life-course-persistent offending.

in childhood, it is very difficult to later recover lost opportunities."[26] The second reason that life-course-persistent offenders have a hard time reentering conventional society is that they become ensnared by the consequences of their antisocial behavior. The decisions they made as adolescent delinquents create a number of disadvantages later in life. Moffitt contends that:

> characteristics such as poor self-control, impulsivity, and inability to delay gratification increase the risk that antisocial youngsters will make irrevocable decisions that close the doors of opportunity. Teenage parenthood, addiction to drugs or alcohol, school dropout, disabling or disfiguring injuries, patchy work histories, and time spent incarcerated are snares that diminish the probabilities of later success by eliminating opportunities for breaking the chain of cumulative continuity.[27]

Moffitt's theory has several policy implications. However, because her theory is so inclusive and complex, these policy implications are complicated, and many of them only indirectly affect antisocial behavior. For instance, children born with neuropsychological problems stemming from poor prenatal nutrition or maternal drug abuse during pregnancy will require extensive attention in order to overcome their difficulties. Similarly, children raised by parents who are poor disciplinarians will require extensive re-education in order to develop the psychological skills necessary to deal with their impulsivity and low regard for others.

Substandard schools, impoverished neighborhoods, and a national economy suffering from the effects of globalization indirectly affect the ability of life-course-persistent offenders to enter mainstream society. Moffitt's theory is powerful because it includes biological, psychological, and sociological factors, but it is also vulnerable to criticism because transforming policies at all these levels is beyond the capabilities and resources of the juvenile justice system.[28] Furthermore, since life-course-persistent offenders have limited opportunities and few social skills, it is unrealistic to think that they will be able to turn over a new leaf without substantial assistance.

ADOLESCENCE-LIMITED DELINQUENTS

Moffitt reports that the second category of juvenile delinquents, adolescence-limited delinquents is much larger than the life-course-persistent group.

Smoking while pregnant can adversely affect infants. In what ways can maternal drug use affect the life-course of a child?

In fact, according to many self-report studies, most youngsters at one time or another are adolescence-limited delinquents.[29] Young people faced with temptations and opportunities will often engage in antisocial behavior or delinquency to meet specific needs and goals. The most curious aspect of these delinquents is that they will participate in antisocial behavior in some contexts while behaving in pro-social ways in other situations. For example, these youths may fight, shoplift, or periodically use drugs while maintaining good grades in school and obeying their parents. Their periods of sporadic lawbreaking punctuate otherwise conforming lifestyles. In addition, most of the delinquents and offenders in this group eventually desist from crime once they age out of their adolescent years and early 20s (see Figure 7.2b). Moffitt finds that the motivations and rewards for adolescence-limited delinquents differ significantly from those of life-course-persistent offenders.

Like life-course-persistent offenders, adolescence-limited delinquents are affected by biological factors related to puberty. Adolescent males are especially affected. Increases in testosterone compel males to engage in riskier behavior and activities aimed at attracting or impressing the opposite sex.[30] In addition to the biological effects of puberty, teenagers' changing status as they enter high school also affects the development of adolescence-limited delinquency. Moffitt uses the term "social mimicry" to describe young teenagers' attempt to control their environment and make a place for themselves in their social hierarchy by copying the behavior of their supposedly more mature older peers. Moffitt suggests that youngsters envy older peers whom they see as having a more mature status that is

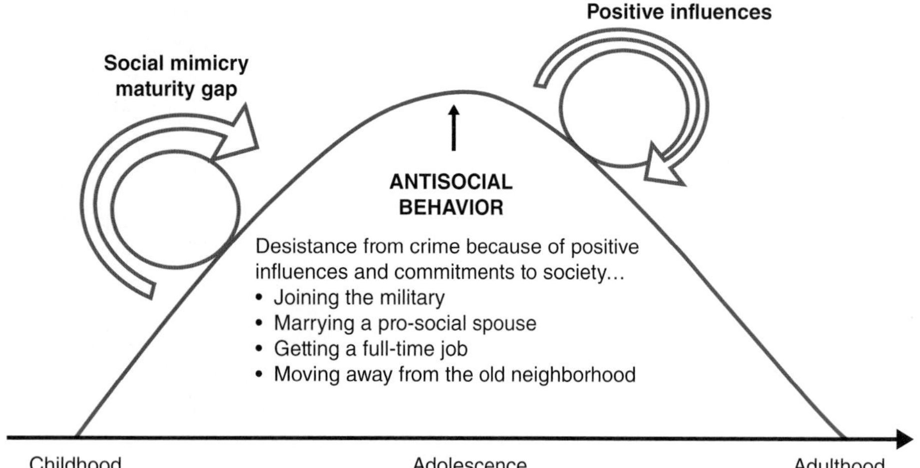

FIGURE 7.2b Moffitt's Pathways to Crime: Adolescence-Limited Delinquency

Moffitt states that adolescent-limited delinquents engage in antisocial behavior as they age into adolescence due to social mimicry (their friends break the law, so they do, too) and low maturity. As these delinquents age out of adolescence, they are eventually deterred from antisocial behavior by positive influences.

THINK ABOUT IT
Give other examples of positive commitments to society.

associated with power and privilege. By attempting to control their own lives, even though doing so might mean engaging in delinquent behavior, these youths seek to develop an independent self-concept that demonstrates to themselves and the rest of the world that they have the power and resources to do what they want. They seek autonomy and self-reliance through delinquency because other, more conventional adaptations require harder work, demand higher social status, or are nonexistent.

Moffitt maintains that a maturity gap is at work in the development of adolescence-limited delinquents. As these youngsters enter high school, they find themselves in the grip of a social institution that greatly limits their freedoms and constrains their choices. In our age-graded society, a person can get a driver's license at 16, vote at 18, and buy alcohol at 21. Young people are encouraged to delay marriage until they are financially stable and often do not start careers until they have completed college. Consequently, between the ages of 12 and 22, these youths experience a decade of dependence in which their bodies are mature, but their parents control many of their decisions. Adolescence-limited delinquents often combat this dependence in several ways:

> For teens who become adolescence-limited delinquents, antisocial behavior is an effective means of knifing-off childhood apron strings and of proving that they can act independently to conquer new challenges. Hypothetical reinforcers for delinquency include damaging the quality of intimacy and communication with parents, provoking responses from adults in positions of authority, finding ways to look older (such as by smoking cigarettes, being tattooed, playing the big spender with ill-gotten gains), and tempting fate (risking pregnancy, driving while intoxicated, or shoplifting under the noses of clerks). None of these putative reinforcers may seem very pleasurable to the middle-aged academic, but each of the aforementioned consequences is a precious resource to the teenager and can serve to reinforce delinquency.[31]

The antisocial and delinquency pattern of adolescence-limited delinquents peaks during late adolescence. As these youths find more opportunities in society and become more bonded to conventional behavior, they begin to desist from breaking the law. They may give up their antisocial behavior as quickly as they began it. In contrast to life-course-persistent offenders, they are not defined by delinquency and easily cast such behavior aside. Moffitt identifies four changes in the life circumstances of adolescence-limited delinquents that inspire desistance from crime.

- Joining the military. Entering the armed forces is a life-altering event for many young people. The military, especially basic training, is similar to a **total institution**, a place in which rigid rules and regulations, such as dress and communication, are clearly defined and strictly enforced (a prison is the best example of a total institution).[32] Those who join the military quickly learn that there is a very particular way of interacting with superiors that is reinforced with punishment for lapses. For many new recruits, the military lifestyle provides a clearly articulated way of being accepted into a

---

total institution—A place in which rigid rules and regulations, such as dress and communication, are clearly defined and strictly enforced.

restricted society in which success is achieved by doing what one is told. Basic training can shock young people out of bad habits and into a conventional lifestyle. Stripped of their ability to interact with family and friends, new recruits are provided new goals, new skills for achieving those goals, and rewards and punishments that reinforce the goals. A period of three to four years in the military can shelter young people from the difficulties of life in the unhealthy environment from which they came. Consequently, they return to civilian life with a positive self-concept, an avenue to escape the dysfunctional community they grew up in, and a vision of the middle-class life to which they aspire. These changes, according to Moffitt, enable adolescence-limited delinquents to desist from antisocial behavior.

- Marrying a pro-social spouse. Marriage is another avenue out of crime for adolescence-limited delinquents. A spouse with middle-class values who is supportive and demands conforming behavior can compel an adolescence-limited delinquent to commit to a pro-social lifestyle. A successful marriage can not only alter self-concept, but also provide a reason to give up behaviors that may lead to prison. Becoming a parent provides further incentive to forgo crime and provides an opportunity for becoming a positive role model. Marriage to a pro-social spouse compels the adolescence-limited delinquent to become more conventional in behavior and establish a longer-term outlook with plans for employment, health care, and pro-social interactions with neighbors and the community.
- Getting a full-time job. Young people who enter the labor market become invested in society. Much like the military, a full-time job requires performance, attendance, and punctuality. Antisocial behavior can jeopardize a person's chances of moving up in the organization or can cause termination. As young people become more invested in their careers, they are more likely to adopt healthier lifestyles in which they are home at a reasonable hour and spend less time in places where antisocial behavior is prevalent. Employment can change the self-concept of marginal youths and give them the confidence to adopt a pro-social lifestyle.
- Moving away from the old neighborhood. The physical and social environment of a disorganized neighborhood is responsible for many of the antisocial motivations of adolescence-limited delinquents. Once removed from this neighborhood, they find it possible to adopt a more positive lifestyle. Separating from other marginal youths, whose response to limited resources is breaking the law, enables many youths to make new friends who have more positive views on life. If the neighborhood is economically distressed, moving to a new neighborhood or new city may also provide a broader array of resources and opportunities to change one's behavior.[33]

Joining the military can be a positive, life-changing event for many people. In what ways can military training alter the attitudes and beliefs of young people?

A happy marriage can encourage individuals to adopt a pro-social lifestyle. How does marriage help one to develop a long-term outlook on the future?

Each of these factors can have a positive effect on an individual's decision to stop breaking the law. They are not mutually exclusive events, however, as a youth could marry, get a new job, and move to a new city, changes that would produce a cumulative effect.

The point is that most adolescence-limited delinquents become motivated to engage in more conventional behavior because of these fundamental changes in their lives.

Moffitt's pathways to crime theory provides an interesting and complex look at how antisocial behavior affects the life course. By developing these two categories of offenders, the life-course-persistent offender and the adolescence-limited delinquent, Moffitt provides an explanation for why some individuals remain mired in crime while others find their way to more socially acceptable lifestyles. She does not neglect the biological and psychological influences that result in crime but rather attempts to integrate them into traditional sociological explanations. Although dividing youthful offenders into only two types is problematic, the categories might be viewed as extreme examples rather than as a comprehensive typology. Often, theoretical explanations must simplify a phenomenon in order to make the theory conceptually manageable.

Persistent Offending and Desistance from Crime

Sociologists John Laub and Robert Sampson have developed a particularly complex and detailed developmental theory of crime and delinquency.[34] Laub and Sampson were graduate students of Travis Hirschi, and their theory has some elements in common with Hirschi's social control theory, which focuses on why people do not break the law. For Laub and Sampson, the element that keeps people from crime is the quality of their social bonds to pro-social peers, spouses, and parents, as well as jobs and schools.[35] The strength of Laub and Sampson's theory is the data on which it is based. Developmental theories of crime depend on following at least one group of offenders throughout their life course. Doing so can be extremely difficult and expensive because researchers typically move on to other subjects or databases or retire from academic life long before life-course offenders progress from juvenile delinquency to adult offending. This logistical problem means that it is almost impossible to keep track of a group of offenders for a period of 40 or more years.[36]

Thanks to some good luck, Laub and Sampson overcame this problem. Laub was doing research in the archives in the basement of the Harvard University Law School library when he stumbled upon the data from a study published in 1950 by Sheldon and Eleanor Glueck.[37] (See Doubletake for the Gluecks' story.) The Gluecks followed the lives of 500 delinquents plus a control group of 500 nondelinquents in the 1930s and 1940s. They collected data on a vast range of variables. Although they did not focus primarily on life-course theories, the Gluecks did lay the groundwork for Laub and Sampson to contact many of these subjects and update their life histories.[38]

Laub and Sampson published two influential books based on the Gluecks' data and their investigations of the research subjects: *Crime in the Making: Pathways and Turning Points Through Life* (1993) and *Shared Beginnings, Divergent Lives: Delinquent Boys to Age 70* (2003). In these two books, which followed the Gluecks' subjects as they grew from young to old men, Laub and Sampson examined the arrest records for the entire sample as well as death certificates.[39] They followed the subjects' involvement in crime and ascertained the points at which the men moved toward more conventional behavior. This alone is a significant accomplishment because for the first time we have an indication of a cohort's involvement in crime throughout a complete lifetime. But Laub and Sampson went one step further. They tracked down 52 individuals from the original sample and did extensive life histories on each.

Laub and Sampson added a new feature to the examination of life-course criminology. Most life-course studies are conducted using quantitative data, particularly arrest records, which yield valuable information about the group in question. However, by adding life histories, Laub and Sampson provided a qualitative element that gave more detailed information about the subjects' lives. Life histories are conducted as extensive interviews in which the researchers ask the subjects not only what happened in their lives, but also why. Life histories also allow researchers to ask follow-up questions and probe for potentially significant details. The life-history methodology is extremely labor intensive and requires the researchers to develop a rapport with the subjects.

Locating 52 individuals from the original 500 delinquents the Gluecks studied was a remarkable feat considering that it had been more than 35 years since the subjects were first interviewed. Given the state of communication in the 1930s and 1940s, it is a wonder any of the men were found. In an age before private telephones were common and long before the Internet, the types of identifying data that would allow for tracing this cohort were greatly limited. Consequently, the data obtained by the Gluecks and the findings of Laub and Sampson are

DOUBLETAKE

The Politics of Theory

Criminological theory informs public policy, so it is useful to look behind the scenes of academia to see how professional rivalries, research strategies, and even the selection of what to study become important factors in how new theories influence the field. John Laub and Robert Sampson analyzed the decade-long debate between Edwin Sutherland, who developed the differential association theory of delinquency, and Sheldon and Eleanor Glueck, who championed the more interdisciplinary approach that informs life-course criminological theory today. Sutherland was a well-known and highly respected sociologist who contended that delinquency should be studied by sociologists. The more interdisciplinary Gluecks, on the other hand, published in leading journals in criminology, social work, psychology, sociology, education, law, and psychiatry.

The debate between Sutherland and the Gluecks can be simplified by looking at the differences in how they conducted their research. Sutherland's differential association is essentially a learning theory of crime; consequently, there was little room for the multiple explanations the Gluecks offered. Sutherland's attack on the Gluecks' work marginalized them even as his own fame in the discipline grew.

The Gluecks were at a disadvantage because they did not hold traditional academic posts. Sheldon Glueck, who had a background in the humanities and law, taught at Harvard Law School. Eleanor Glueck, who never secured a teaching position at Harvard, worked as a research assistant and, according to Laub and Sampson, was somewhat of an outcast at Harvard. Furthermore, the Gluecks did not train PhD students, unlike Sutherland, whose students advanced and popularized his differential association theory.

Sampson and Laub credit the Gluecks with developing the study of crime and delinquency in ways that were ahead of their time and contend that the Gluecks' ideas are central to the development of integrated and life-course theories. They identify four areas in which the Gluecks' work has been especially influential.

- Age and crime. The relationship between age and crime is now well established. Laub and Sampson are building on the Gluecks' data, which remains some of the most important evidence for life-course theory.
- Career criminals and longitudinal research. The Gluecks pioneered the use of longitudinal research to study crime and delinquency. Although some academics dismiss the "career criminal" concept and do not see the utility of longitudinal research, much current research is based on the Gluecks' work.
- Stability of crime and deviance. The Gluecks argued that antisocial behavior and deviance remain remarkably stable across the life course. According to Laub and Sampson, later research has substantiated this idea.
- Social control, family, and delinquency. The Gluecks studied the role of the family, schools, and informal sanctions in an effort to determine the cause of delinquency. Today, many criminologists who consider how the family and other institutions affect juveniles agree that these are significant social relationships.[40]

THINK ABOUT IT

1. How do different academic disciplines provide competing arguments about criminological theory?

extremely valuable contributions to the literature on life-course criminology.

As Moffitt had done, Laub and Sampson found continuities in the life-course behaviors of delinquents. For example, individuals who had difficult childhood and adolescent years were more likely to become involved in crime in their later years. Such individuals are similar to Moffitt's category of life-course-persistent offenders. Laub and Sampson also found changes in the offending patterns of delinquents, and, much like Moffitt's adolescence-limited delinquents, these individuals eventually desisted from breaking the law. But the qualitative nature of Laub and Sampson's theory advanced Moffitt's ideas. An important element in desisting from crime is developing conventional social bonds. As graduate students of Travis Hirschi, Laub and Sampson were especially attuned to the idea that individuals with close ties to families, schools, and communities are invested in good behavior and do not wish to take risks that could put them at a disadvantage in life.[41] Conversely, marginalized individuals have little investment in obeying the law and are much more likely to break it.

These features of social control theory are borne out in the life histories that Laub and Sampson

Laub and Sampson's studies showed that as young men aged, those with close ties to the community were more invested in good behavior. Why are those who are involved in families, schools, and the community less likely to engage in risky behavior?

conducted. However, there is more to life-course criminology than a simple updating of control theory. Laub and Sampson "put meat on the bones" of life-course criminology by providing detailed histories of a set of individuals as they aged. What Sampson and Laub found fits well with what we suspect happens to individuals as they age: They leave antisocial behavior behind and advance into more conventional society. Like Moffitt, Laub and Sampson identified specific events that prompted an individual to desist from crime. These turning points include activities such as joining the military, having a family, and securing a good job. A major feature of these turning points, according to Laub and Sampson, is agency. By "agency," Laub and Sampson mean that individuals make a conscious choice to stop breaking the law. Desisting from crime is not just something that happens automatically when a person marries or joins the military. Rather, the individual decides he or she has too much invested in a new lifestyle to risk any more involvement with the criminal justice system. Laub and Sampson provide an example of a man they call Leon, who was arrested several times as a youth for property offenses, yet grew into a successful adult who had a long and stable marriage. Describing Leon's change of behavior, Laub and Sampson note:

Why does having peers that engage in the same harmful behavior as you prevent you from adopting a more appropriate lifestyle?

> Along with the social support and love that came from this successful marriage, additional factors help explain why Leon was able to desist from crime. First, perhaps a response to his wife's investment in him and vice versa, Leon took his marital responsibilities very seriously. He often worked overtime to support his family. Moreover, later in his career, he turned down a promotion because it would have taken more time away from his wife and children. Second, as a direct result of his marriage, Leon was cut off from his former peer group. These peers were replaced by his wife's friends. At his age 25 interview, Leon disclosed that one of his delinquent friends "went away" for murder. Leon continued, "On the very night of the murder, I had a date with my wife and we went to a dance. If it weren't for my wife, I'd probably be up for murder." Third, Leon spent more time with his wife's family than he did with his own. In fact, the couple moved to get away from his family. They relocated to another part of Boston and his in-laws moved in on the first floor of their two-family home. This action solidified his new family bonds, both practically and symbolically.[42]

Criminologist Mark Warr supports the idea of marriage as a turning point, stating that marriage is associated with desisting from antisocial behavior because it terminates the antisocial spouse's friendships with antisocial peers.[43] Ronald Simons and colleagues add, however, that an antisocial spouse's behavior can be expected to change only if he or she marries a pro-social person. If two antisocial people marry, then both spouses' antisocial behavior can be expected to continue because neither will discourage friendships with antisocial peers.[44]

PAUSE AND REVIEW

1. **List the steps that can lead to chronic delinquency, according to Patterson and colleagues.**
2. **Compare and contrast Moffitt's two categories of young offenders.**
3. **What three issues does life-course criminology focus on?**

4. **Which theory suggests that providing parents with the skills necessary to develop healthy children is more effective than waiting until middle childhood to address delinquency issues?**
5. **What is the difference between Moffitt's adolescence-limited delinquents and life-course-persistent offenders?**
6. **Which theorists based their data on the Gluecks' longitudinal study of 500 delinquents?**

Integrated Theories

LEARNING OBJECTIVE 5

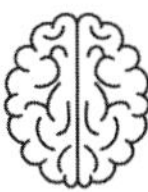

State the emphasis of Thornberry's interactional theory.

LEARNING OBJECTIVE 6

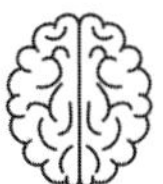

Compare and contrast the concepts of control deficit and control surplus in Tittle's control balance theory.

LEARNING OBJECTIVE 7

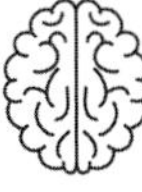

Briefly list the 10 propositions that Cullen uses to explain how social support is related to crime and delinquency.

LEARNING OBJECTIVE 8

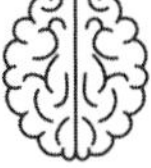

Describe how, according to Agnew, the interaction between five life domains affects the likelihood of antisocial behavior.

LEARNING OBJECTIVE 9

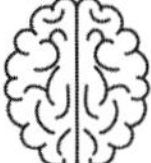

Identify the basis of Farrington's integrated cognitive antisocial potential theory.

Throughout this book we have discussed several major theories that attempt to link crime to a variety of causes. Each of these theories has a certain level of relevance to sociological factors associated with deviance, although none of them can completely explain all types of crime (see Policy Implications). The reason for this is that each of these theories, whether biological, psychological, or sociological, considers the causes of crime to be greatly limited. Few of the theories we have discussed so far try to combine, in an organized way, all the issues that may be responsible for causing people to break the law. We turn now to a discussion of **integrated theories** that attempt to combine several different criminological theories in order to expand the focus on crime.

The life-course theories we have discussed in this chapter are, to a great extent, integrated theories.[45] These theories have limitations, however, in that they focus primarily on the life-course perspective and do not include several other types of explanations. In contrast, integrated theories use several theories to explain more types of antisocial behavior. When considering integrated theories, we must be careful not to use them to explain too much. A grand theory that attempts to explain everything runs the risk of looking at variables in such a superficial manner that they actually explain very little.[46] The integrated theories we examine in this section limit the number of factors or variables they include, while trying to take advantage of how each variable can help explain why people break the law.

Interactional Theory of Delinquency

Terence Thornberry's interactional theory of delinquency incorporates three prominent delinquency perspectives: social learning (particularly from delinquent peers), social bonds (especially as parental bonds weaken), and the life-course perspective. The most important point of Thornberry's theory is the reciprocal nature of these influences, which suggests that once a person is on the path to delinquency, the development of delinquent peers is likely to follow, or vice versa.[47]

Interactional theory considers the social bonds that individuals develop early in life, particularly bonds with parents, as an important influence on delinquency. Youths who bond strongly to parents are less likely to break the law, whereas those with weak bonds are more likely to break the law. Thornberry adds, however, that as individuals progress through their life course, their bonds to parents generally weaken. As youths look to their peers rather than their parents for clues about how to behave, those who become involved with delinquent peers are more likely to break the law.

integrated theories—Perspectives that attempt to combine several different criminological theories in order to expand the focus on crime.

POLICY IMPLICATIONS

Crime Is Complicated

In this chapter, life-course theories of crime present some interesting concerns regarding the development of criminal justice policy. One observation we can take away from these theories is that people break the law for complicated reasons. Dealing with offenders may require more than fixing their diet (biological theories), monitoring their peers (differential association), or providing them with an education so they can compete economically (classical strain theory). It may require most or all of these things.

By understanding the pathways and turning points in a criminal career, it is possible to design programs that take advantage of these observations and intervene in the lives of those who break the law. Sometimes timing is everything. Providing educational opportunities or employment training at critical times can mean the difference in offenders becoming invested in society or turning their back on it. For instance, Cullen's social support theory suggests that families and communities can do much to provide everyone (not just offenders) with the institutional support to prevent potential delinquents and offenders from breaking the law. The key is to provide individuals with enough support to overcome negative peer and neighborhood influences. This integrated theory takes advantage of the principles of numerous sociological and psychological theories and combines them to envision a more comprehensive social support system.

The tough part of selling life-course and integrated theories of crime to criminal justice decision-makers is that the solutions these theories suggest encompass comprehensive programs that are indirectly concerned with crime and delinquency. Therefore, funding for such programs may be difficult to obtain or may require policymakers to have a more expansive view of how to intervene in deviant behavior.

For instance, although a great deal of money is spent on education, less is spent on the education of those caught up in the juvenile and criminal justice systems. It is difficult to get policymakers to allocate additional funds for inmate populations. Similarly, recreational programs designed to keep kids off the street are not considered to be crime-prevention programs and so are not eligible for criminal justice funding. Without adequate funds, the criminal justice and juvenile justice systems cannot always take up the slack. When major institutions such as the family, the schools, and the community fail to integrate youths into conventional society, the justice system must deal with their failures. Life-course and integrated theories argue for greater coordination and cooperation between all institutions.

THINK ABOUT IT

1. Pick a theory from the chapter and come up with a plan to present that theory to a criminal justice official or a legislator so that it will affect real-world criminal justice policy. This may mean designing a program or implementing the theory within a program or criminal justice process already in existence.

Interactional theory particularly emphasizes the reciprocal effects between delinquent behavior and antisocial peers. Specifically, delinquent youths are more likely to associate with antisocial peers, and those whose friends are antisocial are also more likely to break the law. Thornberry sidesteps the chicken-and-egg question of whether delinquent peers cause delinquency or whether initial delinquency brings youths into contact with delinquent peers. Rather, he focuses on how the two interact to produce an "amplifying causal structure" that leads to increasing involvement in delinquency. The reciprocal effects between peers in delinquency can be difficult to unravel, but it is important to understand how the two are intertwined.[48]

Like life-course theory as expounded by Terrie Moffitt, John Laub, and Robert Sampson, interactional theory considers how some people become committed to conventional society and desist from antisocial behavior. Getting married, securing a good job, or joining the military are ways that individuals become invested in conventional behavior and find breaking the law to be no longer beneficial. Thornberry's perspective is not limited to the micro level. Interactional theory also considers structural variables such as sex and class to be important determinants of an individual's initial involvement with delinquency and their ability to control behavior. According to Thornberry, values and behaviors are often part of the structural conditions in which one grows up, and these are determined to a great extent by one's gender socialization and social class.

Control Balance Theory

Charles Tittle developed control balance theory to explain a broad range of antisocial acts. His ambitious theory integrates several perspectives in an effort to provide a comprehensive understanding of why people break the law. This necessarily brief overview of Tittle's complicated theory will demonstrate not only the encompassing range of this theory, but also the degree to which it integrates several other sociological explanations.

Control balance theory rests on the concepts of "control deficit" and "control surplus" (see Figure 7.3).[49] Individuals are constantly seeking to control their lives. All persons experience a control ratio that reflects their status in society, the roles they play, their physical and personal characteristics, their integration with organizations, and the quality of their interpersonal relationships. Tittle's theory states that this control ratio is the starting point for understanding crime and delinquency. Those who have more control exerted on them than they exert are likely to break the law. Those who have a surplus of control are also likely to engage in antisocial behavior.

According to Tittle, people who have a balance of control are constrained by external factors but have sufficient freedom to countermand those factors. Thus, those with a balance of control are less likely to engage in unacceptable or unlawful behavior. According to control balance theory, everyone has a basic impulse to engage in antisocial behavior.[50] This impulse is mediated by control factors outside the individual, such as law enforcement, the rules and regulations of organizations, and lack of opportunity. Individual personality factors, such as a desire for autonomy, motivate people to rebel, but these factors are often checked by external and internal controls. Some factors, such as living in a bad neighborhood or failing in school, encourage antisocial behavior. However, an individual's control surplus or deficit can balance this motivation to break the law. For instance, although an impoverished youth with an inferior education is predisposed toward delinquency, holding a job, even a low-paying job, provides some control. This measure of control can counteract the negative forces exerted by the impoverished neighborhood and failure at school. Tittle lists some of the situations that can provoke an individual to engage in antisocial behavior:

- receiving a harsh, commanding order or sharp, hostile reaction from an authority figure;

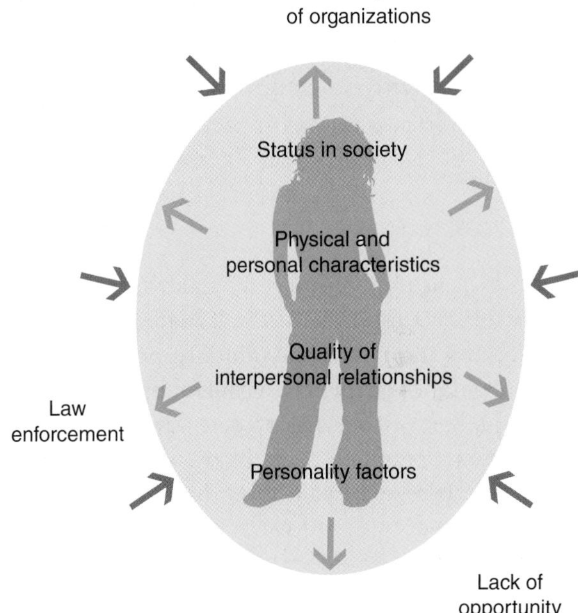
People in control deficit (those with more control exerted on them than they exert) and in control surplus (those who exert more control than they experience) are more likely to break the law. Those in control balance are more likely to be law abiding. The arrows pointing toward the figure represent controls exerted on the subject; arrows pointing away from the figures represent the subject's control.
Rules and regulations of organizations
Status in society
Physical and personal characteristics
Quality of interpersonal relationships
Law enforcement
Personality factors
Lack of opportunity

FIGURE 7.3 Tittle's Control Balance Theory

THINK ABOUT IT
In the control balance figure, the external and internal controls are balanced. According to Tittle, how is this balance achieved?

- breaking up with a romantic partner;
- falling behind in paying debts and bills;
- being questioned about one's authority or rights;
- being pushed while waiting in line;
- being stopped by the police;
- being denied membership in a club; and
- being hungry, with no money to buy food.[51]

Control balance theory considers how such situational provocations can motivate a person to break the law but can be counterbalanced by external constraints. These constraints can be a situational risk, such as store security cameras or police officers patrolling a neighborhood. Another constraint on involvement in delinquency and crime is the seriousness of breaking the law and the punishments associated with it. With this constraint, Tittle integrates the principles of the deterrence perspective into control balance theory.

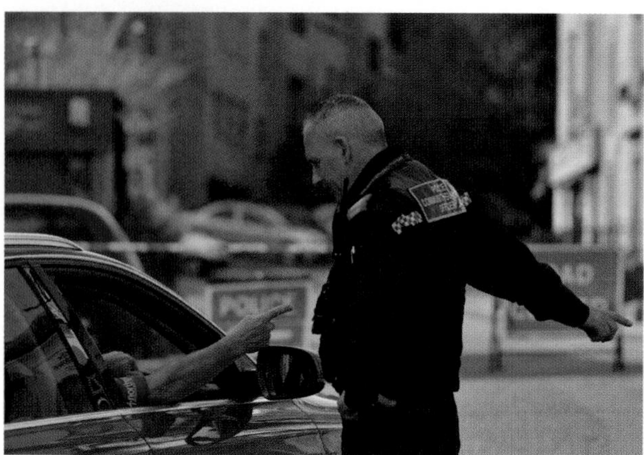

People may feel a lack of control when stopped by the police. What are some other situations where lack of control can cause stress and possibly lead to deviant behavior?

Finally, the opportunity to break the law and the motivation to take risks are weighed against both external and internal constraints to produce either a control balance surplus or a control balance deficit. Those who have either an extreme surplus or an extreme deficit are much more likely to break the law than those who exhibit a more balanced ratio between the freedom they have to affect their behavior versus the constraints exerted on them by the community, schools, and parents.

The crux of control balance theory is the perception of the amount of control individuals have over their lives. Some people bounce like pinballs from one situational provocation to another and are never able to exert agency or direction on their behaviors. Other people have a surplus of control and see this power as an opportunity to take advantage of situations by engaging in antisocial behavior. Although Tittle's theory is complicated, it is useful in encouraging scholars to think about the connections among many of the traditional psychological and sociological theories of crime and deviance. Tittle's integration of theoretical perspectives is difficult to test because it includes so many factors whose relationships to crime are unclear and also because it is hard to construct research designed to investigate how they are related.

Social Support Theory

Francis Cullen has developed a different sort of integrated theory of crime and delinquency. Social support theory shows the advantages of integrating different criminological perspectives into a coherent paradigm that addresses a broad range of crime as well as several motivations and policy implications. Rather than selecting components from other theories, Cullen concentrates on the theme of social support that is implicit in many of the other theories, and he uses 10 propositions to construct an integrated theory around this theme.[52] This unique way of integrating concepts from other theories develops a convincing case for social support at both micro and macro levels (see Figure 7.4). Social support influences not only individuals' decisions (micro level) but also how social institutions (macro level) contribute to the United States' relatively high crime rate. Cullen's concept of social support has four important constructs.[53]

- Social support not only is an objective factor, but is also subject to individual perception. Cullen means that the influence of social support might vary according to how it is perceived. Perception of the influence of social support has important implications for how rehabilitation programs might address the psychological barriers offenders encounter in trying to bond with society. For instance, rehabilitation programs can do a better job of explaining to the offender the importance of the social support system, such as parents, school counselors, and clergy.
- Social support is both instrumental and expressive. Instrumental support can be conceived of as situations in which offenders receive concrete aid in the form of finding a job, being granted a scholarship, or getting a loan. Instrumental support is necessary at a variety of levels for individuals to advance their social situation and integrate into society. Expressive social support deals with the relationships that offenders have with significant others. In interactions with friends and family, frustrations are vented, needs for love and affection are met, and feelings of companionship and belonging are developed.[54]
- Social support at the macro level is the influence of social networks and communities that connect individuals to society. Everyone is attached to larger groups in different ways, and the extent of the connections and commitments to these groups directly influences the propensity to engage in antisocial behavior.
- Social support encompasses both informal and formal relations with others but distinguishes between them. Informal relationships include interactions with friends who have no official role in institutions of social control. Formal

relations include interactions with authority figures, such as teachers and police officers, whose job is to encourage good behavior and sanction bad behavior.

Within this context of social support, Cullen lays out 10 propositions that detail how social support is related to crime and delinquency.

1. The United States has higher rates of serious crime than other industrialized countries because it is a less supportive society. Although this proposition offends some people, it is difficult to argue with Cullen's explanation. Individualism is a core American value. Americans are encouraged to distinguish themselves by accomplishments and behavior, but such individual acts come at the cost of everyone working for the common good. Individuals in more highly integrated countries, such as Japan, are not only subject to more social control, but are also supported by the culture in social and economic ways. Because of the American ideals of individual rights and freedom of action, the United States does not institutionalize social support in the form of health care, welfare, or subsidized schooling to the extent seen in some other countries, such as Canada and Japan. Without this support, Americans all too often decide to turn to crime and delinquency to meet their needs and accomplish their goals. At the informal level, Americans do not feel the social obligation to their fellow citizens that is found in other countries with higher levels of social support.
2. The less social support in a community, the higher the crime rate. Cullen considers several ways that social support in the community reduces crime rates. In these communities, welfare and job programs help buffer the effects of poverty. Cullen contends that although some conservative commentators argue that these types of programs make individuals dependent on government handouts, research demonstrates that this type of social support has a beneficial effect on crime rates. Lack of social support works in other ways to increase crime rates. Communities with a high degree of family dysfunction, weak friendship networks, and low participation and voluntary organizations have more crime.
3. The more support a person's family provides, the less likely that person will break the law.

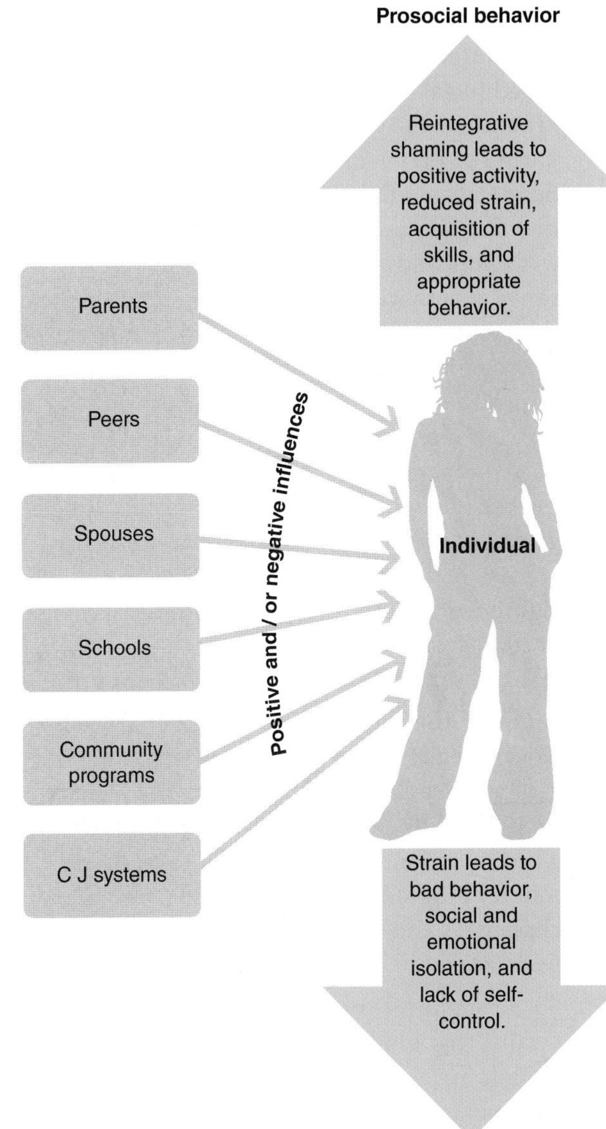

FIGURE 7.4 Cullen's Social Support Theory

The quality of social support affects an individual's behavior to become either pro-social or antisocial. Influence from parents, peers, spouses, schools, community programs, and criminal justice systems can be positive or negative.

THINK ABOUT IT

What leads to pro-social behavior? What leads to antisocial behavior? Why?

Parents provide expressive support by sharing activities, helping with homework, supervising recreational activities with friends, and demonstrating affection. Expressive support is positively related to getting children to conform. Parents provide instrumental support by helping adolescents find jobs and ensuring that they are engaged in healthy after-school programs and are not left to fend for themselves on the street or in front of a television. Cullen points out, however, that family support is subject to broad social forces that can undermine parental attention. One prime example is the changing nature of the evening meal. Today, many families do not share any meals in which all family members are present. Parents who are involved with work and children who are caught up in a range of activities often find it hard to find the time to eat together. Fast-food restaurants and long commutes from work have greatly undermined the traditional evening meal in which families reconnect. Poverty, drugs, and alcohol have further weakened family support. According to Cullen, there is evidence that support given to families in the form of parenting programs, food stamps, and help with day care can significantly supplement the support children need to avoid delinquency.

4. The more social support in a person's social network, the less crime will occur. This proposition draws on strain theory. Social support can help overcome the negative consequences brought on by excessive strain. Adolescents who have friends, family members, and community programs to help them adjust to the challenges and difficulties of their adolescent years are more likely to resist delinquency.
5. Social support lessens the effect of exposure to strains that tend to produce crime. When individuals are enmeshed in support systems, such as a good marriage, loving family, or satisfying job, they are buffered against the strains of temptation to engage in crime or delinquency. The soothing effect of supportive relationships on emotional strains allows people to transform their circumstances so that they become more integrated into conventional society and have less time and fewer opportunities for antisocial behavior.
6. Social support increases the likelihood that offenders will turn away from an antisocial path. People who have positive social support can find ways to desist from crime. When people believe that the "deck is stacked against them," they stop looking for ways to enter conventional society and they experience a sense of isolation and hopelessness.
7. Anticipation of a lack of social support increases criminal involvement. Adolescents who have learned not to expect social support because they have been mistreated, neglected, or abused in the past are more likely to engage in antisocial behavior because they see no reason not to.
8. Social support lessens involvement in crime. Social support is a two-way street. Individuals who receive expressive and instrumental support are likely to behave well. The opportunity to provide that support to others increases their sense of self-esteem, being needed, and having a mission or goal in life. By having socially approved and appropriate roles to perform, individuals reduce the strain in their lives and learn the benefits of supporting others. With the reduction of strain and the opportunity to engage in legitimate behavior, people redefine their identities in more positive ways.
9. Crime is less likely to occur when social support for conformity exceeds social support for crime. Social support can be destructive when it comes from those who view crime and delinquency as desirable and productive. Social support provided by positive peers, law-abiding spouses, or legitimate employment can counteract the support that comes from negative sources. Cullen points out that it is not sufficient to have social support from a spouse if that spouse is also engaged in antisocial activities. The quality of the support is as crucial as its quantity.
10. Social support is often a pre-condition for social control. There are many ways to control antisocial behavior, but several of them can produce negative effects. Cullen cites the work of John Braithwaite on the negative effect of **disintegrative shaming**, or forms of punishment that do not repair the harm

---

disintegrative shaming—Braithwaite's term to describe punishment that does not repair the harm done by the offender and offense and excludes the offender from society.

labeling theory—The idea that society defines an individual, treating him or her differently, and the individual internalizes this definition and acts it out.

reintegrative shaming—Braithwaite's term to describe punishment that seeks to repair the harm done by the offender and offense and draw the offender into society.

Instant Recall from Chapter 6 **social learning theory** — The idea that people learn how to act by watching others and copying the interactions that are rewarded and avoiding those that are punished.

done by the offender and offense and exclude the offender from society. In effect, disintegrative shaming permanently stigmatizes offenders. Individuals who are sanctioned in the juvenile or criminal justice systems often come away with the negative labels of "delinquent," "convict," or "criminal." According to **labeling theory**—the idea that society defines an individual, treating him or her differently, and the individual internalizes this definition and acts it out (we will cover this concept in detail in Chapter 8)—disintegrative shaming can have destructive effects and produce negative self-concepts. Braithwaite, who introduced a more positive way for shaming to be used in social control, uses the term **reintegrative shaming**—or punishment that seeks to repair the harm done by the offender and offense and draw the offender into society—to describe procedures and ceremonies that allow antisocial individuals to express remorse and seek forgiveness. Reintegrative shaming has two important implications for the relationship between social support and crime. First, it helps individuals take responsibility for their behavior, express their regret, and acknowledge their accountability. Second, it provides better opportunities for harm to be repaired. Cullen draws on the theoretical principles of peacemaking criminology and restorative justice to suggest that this form of social control can be directly linked to the advantages of providing social support for those who break the law.

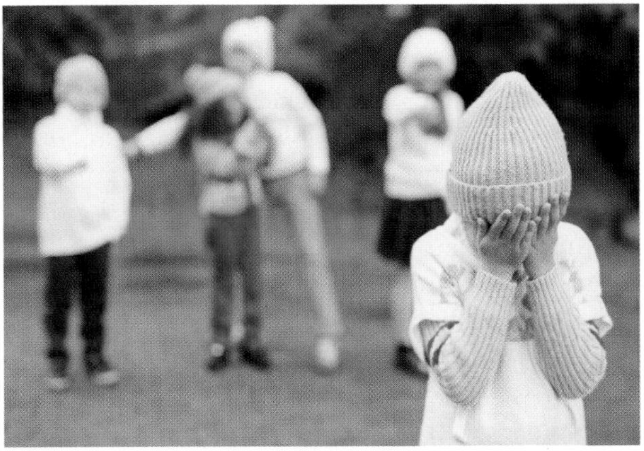

Shame can negatively affect one's self-concept. How can reintegrative shaming repair the harm done by offenders and draw them back into society?

Cullen's social support theory has important implications for criminology. Its focus on the support that individuals give and receive takes advantage of several more traditional criminological theories and places them into a new paradigm. Although Cullen does not specifically borrow the terminology and constructs of many of the theories included in his paradigm, his focus on the theme of social support allows him to link the components of this theory to several other theories. This new paradigm has several advantages.

- Theoretical integration is achieved. Cullen draws widely from a number of traditional theories, but he also looks to some emerging perspectives to construct a comprehensive view of delinquency and crime. His social support theory draws on strain theory, **social learning theory**, and social control theory, as well as newer and more critical theories, such as feminist theory and peacemaking criminology (see Chapter 8 for more on the last two perspectives). In bringing all the theoretical perspectives together under the theme of social support, Cullen's theory demonstrates how this concept has been hinted at previously but now takes a central role in explaining antisocial behavior.
- The theory is empirically informed. Cullen uses empirical studies to construct his theoretical perspective. Social support is based on several respected research studies that Cullen places in the context of social support. The use of empirical studies allows others to evaluate Cullen's perspective and design new studies based on his propositions. An important aspect of any theory is its testability, and Cullen has formulated his perspective in ways that encourage future research efforts.
- The theory has practical implications. It is not difficult to see how social support theory can inform the practices of the criminal justice system. Cullen is a strong advocate of rehabilitation as criminal justice policy, and his social support theory justifies renewed efforts to provide funding and programs to assist offenders in reintegrating into society.[55] Social support may not only reduce the amount of harm done by crime, but also improve the lives of those who have not yet begun to engage in antisocial behaviors. In many ways, social support theory promises to produce a coherent and effective response to crime.

Counseling sessions are good for rehabilitative support. What other types of social support are part of Cullen's theory?

General Theory of Crime and Delinquency

Robert Agnew is best known for his general strain theory in which he expanded on Merton's classic strain theory. Recently, however, Agnew has developed a more ambitious integrated theory that includes not only strain, but also several other theoretical perspectives. His efforts to develop a general theory of crime and delinquency focus on simple relationships between influences that tend to produce crime.[56]

Agnew argues that crime is caused by problems that occur within individuals' five life domains: the self, the family, school, peers, and work. Each domain is important on its own, but, according to Agnew, the interaction between them can accelerate and enhance a person's chances of being drawn into antisocial behavior. The important point in Agnew's theory is that these domains do not act alone or independently; rather, they are interdependent, and negative consequences can have a cumulative effect when problems occur in more than one life domain. These five life domains are related to crime and delinquency in the following ways.

Rock climbing is a positive form of thrill-seeking for many young people. Why is a high degree of thrill-seeking often associated with delinquent behavior?

- The self: irritability/low self-control. Youths are more likely to engage in delinquent behavior when they get upset and are unable to control their emotions and behaviors. These behaviors are often characterized by intense emotional reactions, blame of others for their problems, impulsivity, chronic anger, lack of motivation, thrill-seeking, and an attitude that favors breaking the law. Although this description may fit almost any teenager, it is the degree to which teenagers possess these attributes that makes them potential delinquents.
- The family: poor parenting practices/no marriages or bad marriages. Youths who do not bond to their parents in positive ways are more likely to engage in antisocial behavior. Delinquency is also more likely when parents do not provide adequate supervision and constructive discipline. Parents who are involved in antisocial activities provide poor role models. Families in which there is conflict and abuse as well as families in which the parents are estranged are also linked to delinquency. Parents who are absent or not involved with their children cannot provide the proper supervision and discipline or bond with them in positive ways.
- School: negative school experiences. Schools can play a large part in explaining why youngsters break the law. Negative school experiences, such as poor academic performance and spending little or no time on homework, can be linked to delinquent behavior. In troubled schools, teachers do not provide positive role models and often treat students in negative ways. In addition, those youths who are not intellectually challenged at school are more likely to have limited educational and occupational goals. Those with a limited education find it hard to compete for high-paying jobs and for work they find meaningful and fulfilling.
- Peers: delinquent friends. Adolescents with delinquent friends are more likely to become delinquent themselves. Police often interpret peer conflicts, such as fighting, as delinquency and may detain youths involved in such conflicts. Involvement in the juvenile or criminal justice

system exposes youths to others with a history of delinquency. According to **learning theory**, this exposure can draw a youth deeper into delinquency.

- Work: unemployment/bad jobs. Those who are underemployed or employed at low-paying jobs find little self-esteem in the workplace. Such experiences cause individuals to feel alienated not only from a particular job, but also from positive work habits. Estrangement from work and good work habits can make youths cynical about conventional society.

Individuals' experiences in these five life domains influence whether they choose to conform to conventional society or turn to a delinquent or criminal lifestyle. Good experiences can constrain people against crime by encouraging a high level of self-control and a stake in conformity, as well as by exposing them to interactions with others who share a commitment to law-abiding behavior. Conversely, negative experiences in these life domains can expose individuals to antisocial role models, strain, a belief that crime is beneficial, and a conviction that crime and delinquency can be profitable on a financial or social level. These negative experiences can draw an individual deeper into antisocial behavior.

As noted earlier, Agnew emphasizes the interdependent nature of the five life domains. For instance, a person who is performing poorly in school is likely to seek out peers who share his or her frustration with the educational system. Those already engaged in delinquency might be labeled by teachers as troublemakers, and such labeling can have a negative effect on their performance in school. Negative experiences in several of these life domains increase the chances of an individual turning to criminal and delinquent activities. Agnew brings life-course theory into his perspective by pointing out that the influences of each of the five life domains vary as one ages. These influences are stronger for adolescents than for adults, and the opportunity for commitment to conventional society increases as the individual ages and has opportunities to get well-paying work or enter a satisfying relationship.

Integrated Cognitive Antisocial Potential Theory

David Farrington's integrated cognitive antisocial potential theory (ICAP) integrates ideas from many classic criminological theories, including strain, control, learning, labeling, routine activities, rational choice, and biological theories. The theory is complicated, but the simplified explanation provided here gives a general idea of how ICAP works.

According to ICAP, elements from these theories affect what Farrington calls **antisocial potential**, or an individual's likelihood of breaking the law by engaging in antisocial behavior. A person's antisocial potential is unique, like a fingerprint. Imagine the amount of antisocial potential among all individuals in society as running along a continuum from low to high. At the low end of the continuum are some people who are highly unlikely to engage in antisocial behavior; at the high end are some people who are very likely to do so. The antisocial potential of most people lies between the two extremes, with clustering toward the low end of the continuum. Another continuum describing antisocial potential represents age. The prime antisocial years fall between adolescence and young adulthood, with antisocial potential (and behavior) peaking during the late teens. Most people stop antisocial activities not long after this period; however, some people continue until later into adulthood and others continue throughout their lifetimes (see Figure 7.5). After peaking during adolescence, the amount of antisocial potential remains fairly consistent over the life course.

A person's movement from antisocial potential to antisocial behavior is related to cognitive processes, that is, thinking. Short-term antisocial potential is related to concrete motivations and situations, such as inebriation or anger. In adolescents, these motivations include boredom, peer pressure, or frustration. **Routine activities theory** also plays a part. For example, a good opportunity—say, a busy café, combined with an available victim, such as a woman who is not paying attention and leaves her expensive cell phone on the table to go order coffee—may also inspire short-term high antisocial potential. Long-term antisocial potential is more complicated; in this area, other criminological theories come into play. In adolescence, the motivations that move a person from potential to action are the desire for excitement and consumer goods.

Instant Recall from Chapter 6 **learning theories of crime** —These theories focus on where and how adult offenders and delinquents find the tools, techniques, and expertise to break the law.

Instant Recall from Chapter 4 **routine activities theory** —The concept that three elements are necessary for crime to occur: motivated offenders, attractive targets, and the absence of capable guardians.

antisocial potential—Farrington's term to describe an individual's likelihood of breaking the law by engaging in antisocial behavior.

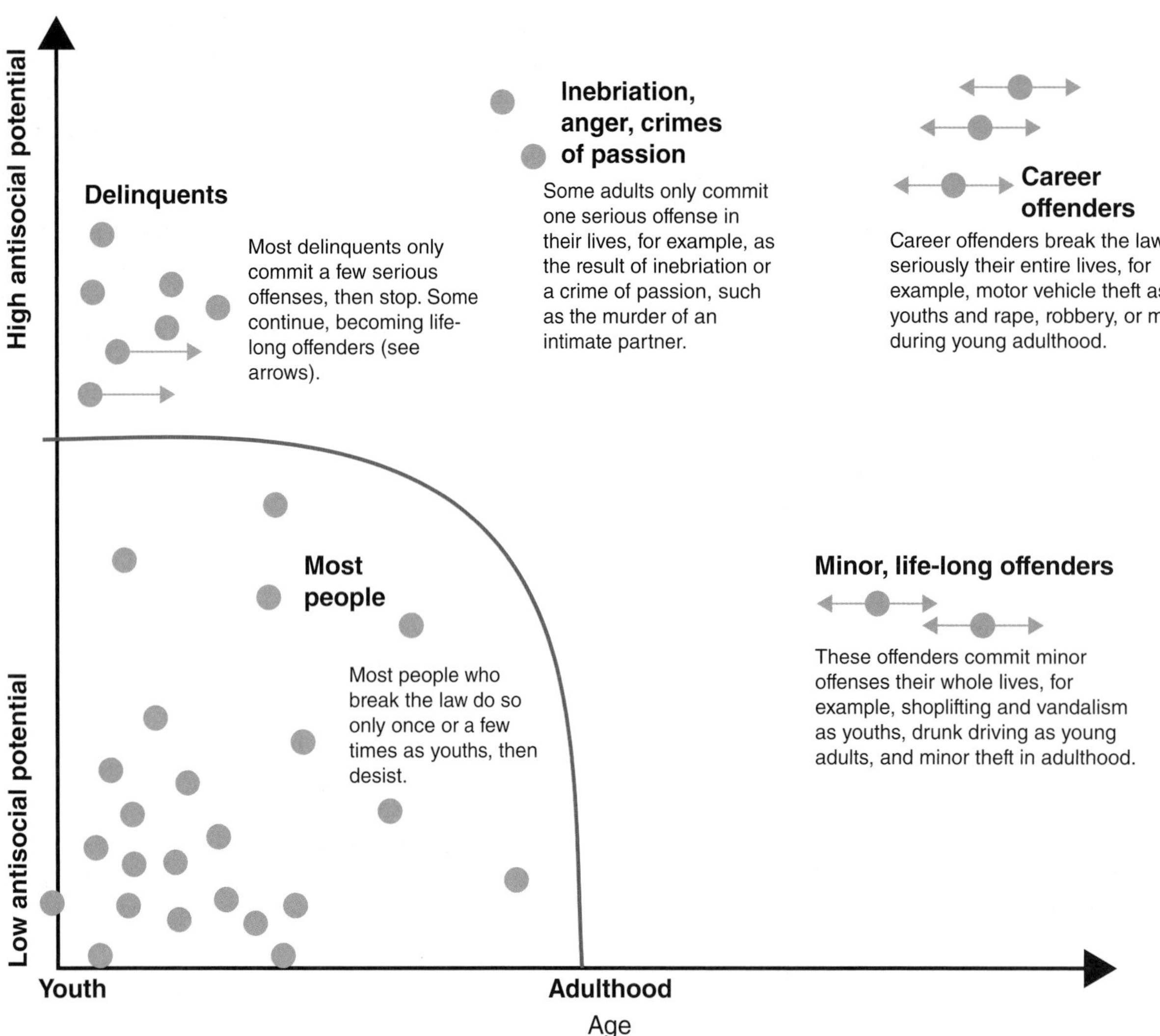

FIGURE 7.5 Integrated Cognitive Antisocial Potential Theory

According to Farrington, antisocial potential lies along an age-related continuum. Most people engage in minor antisocial behavior during youth, then cease as they age. Delinquents engage in high antisocial behavior during youth but cease upon adulthood, although a few continue (see arrows). Some pro-social adults break the law but only under certain conditions, such as inebriation or anger. Career and minor offenders are antisocial their entire lives; it is just a matter of degree.

THINK ABOUT IT
What affects a person's movement from antisocial potential to antisocial behavior?

In adulthood, the motivations are more practical, such as the need for money or drugs. Long-term antisocial potential is related to the following.

- Strain. Strain is brought about by the desire for goods, money, status, excitement, or sex. Those who have difficulty fulfilling these goals, such as the impoverished, the young, and the disadvantaged, tend to choose antisocial methods.
- Modeling and socialization. Consistent parenting, that is, consistent rewards and punishment, leads to low antisocial potential. Inconsistent parenting, such as erratic discipline or frequently absent parents, leads to high antisocial potential. Antisocial peers and models also encourage antisocial potential.
- Life-course events. Antisocial potential tends to decrease after marriage or after a move out of disorganized neighborhoods. It increases after separation from a spouse or significant partner.
- Biological factors. Impulsive people have high antisocial potential; parents with high antisocial potential could transmit that trait to their children. Related biological traits include hormonal issues, low intelligence (which leads to school

failure), and low anxiety (which leads to less worry about the consequences of breaking the law).

- Rational choice. A person with low antisocial potential will not break the law even if it is rational to do so (imagine an impoverished father stealing bread to feed a hungry child). A person with high antisocial potential may break the law even when it is not rational to do so (imagine a wealthy woman stealing jewelry from a department store for excitement). Judgment impairment often plays a role in these situations. For example, people addicted to alcohol or drugs may be motivated to commit offenses that they otherwise would not.
- Labeling. A boy with low antisocial potential might develop long-term antisocial potential if he is caught breaking windows in an old house and is negatively labeled as a vandal for the rest of his youth. Likewise, a middle-aged man being released from prison might discover that he cannot find work because he is a felon. Although his antisocial potential is only moderate, he returns to breaking the law to survive.
- Learning. Peer approval of lawbreaking might increase a youth's antisocial potential, as could the disapproval of authority figures who have become less important to the youth. However, the same parental disapproval of a younger child's antisocial activities might decrease that child's antisocial potential. The strength of ICAP is the number of theories it takes into account. Its disadvantages are that it does not explain variations in crime rates, and although it includes peer influence, it does not explain the development of gangs. In addition, ICAP focuses only on male offending and does not account for gender and race differences. For example, although females are assumed to have antisocial potential, they probably have different risk factors than males, which ICAP does not take into account.[57]

PAUSE AND REVIEW

1. **List the five life domains that Agnew argues are the cause of crime and delinquency.**
2. **Review how social support affects the likelihood of crime according to Cullen.**
3. **Evaluate the relative importance of the imbalance between the amount of control a person has over his or her life and the amount of control exerted by society.**
4. **Briefly explain Tittle's control balance theory.**
5. **Which theory argues that crime is caused by problems that occur within individuals' five life domains?**
6. **What is the basic concept of Farrington's integrated cognitive antisocial potential theory?**

FOCUS ON ETHICS Preventing a Life of Crime

You work in a diversion program for young offenders. You love this job, and you are good at it. You believe you have turned around the lives of several young people who have been entrusted to your care. Now you have a particularly interesting case which requires you to make an important decision

Seventeen-year-old Russell has been under your charge for two years. He was sentenced to your program after his involvement in a gang fight at his high school. At first, he was an argumentative young man given to fits of temper. However, over the past two years, you have developed a working relationship with him, and he has avoided trouble and is working on developing a positive future. His involvement in the diversion program is about to end, but there is a problem.

Russell has beaten up a young man who was aggressively flirting with his girlfriend at a party. The conditions of the diversion program explicitly state that Russell must stay out of trouble, and you should probably report the fight to the judge. It is likely that the judge would revoke Russell's suspended sentence, and he could be incarcerated. Furthermore, he would have an official juvenile record that could hurt his prospects.

You think Russell is at a crossroads in his life. If you do not report this fight, several good things may happen. The first is that Russell would graduate from high school. In Russell's neighborhood, this is not always the case for young males who have been involved with gangs. Russell also wants to marry his girlfriend. She is a positive influence, and her aspirations of becoming a nurse appeared to have motivated him to continue his own education. Finally, Russell intends to join the military. An Air Force recruiter has suggested that Russell could get training in information technology that could greatly improve his employment prospects. You see great benefit in Russell joining the military and leaving his neighborhood. Many of Russell's friends are becoming deeply involved with violent gangs, and if Russell cannot escape the neighborhood, he will most likely be sucked into a criminal lifestyle.

What Do You Do?

1. Report Russell to the judge. He has already been given his chance by having his sentence suspended and placed in the diversion program. He blew it by fighting. Although you can understand his feelings about his girlfriend, he should have handled it differently because he is under court supervision.
2. Say nothing to the judge and hope Russell stays out of further trouble and successfully completes the diversion program.
3. Meet with Russell and his girlfriend and impose some informal conditions. These include a curfew and more frequent reporting. Impress on him that you are sticking your neck out for him and expect a promise from him that he will behave.
4. Include the program director in your meeting with Russell and his girlfriend. Although the director might instruct you to report this fight to the judge, you think you can convince him to go along with your new informal plan. By including the director in this conversation, you are covering yourself in case Russell gets into further trouble.

Summary

LEARNING OBJECTIVE 1 State the focus of life-course criminology.	Life-course criminology focuses on the development of antisocial behavior, risk factors at different ages, and the effect of life events on individual development.
LEARNING OBJECTIVE 2 Explain when antisocial behavior begins, according to Patterson's developmental perspective, and how long it continues.	According to Patterson, DeBaryshe, and Ramsey's developmental perspective on antisocial behavior, antisocial behavior begins early in life and often continues through adolescence and adulthood. Early antisocial behavior can lead to more serious consequences, and early intervention prevents chronic delinquency.
LEARNING OBJECTIVE 3 Identify Moffitt's two categories of youthful offenders.	In her pathways to crime theory, Moffitt considers young offenders as adolescence-limited or life-course-persistent. The adolescence-limited delinquent breaks the law only during youth. Life-course-persistent offenders start to break the law during their youth and continue to do so well into adulthood.
LEARNING OBJECTIVE 4 Review Laub and Sampson's focus on the quality of social bonds in persistent offending or desisting from crime.	Laub and Sampson's theory of persistent offending and desistance from crime, which is based on the Gluecks' data, focuses on what prevents antisocial behavior. For Laub and Sampson, this element is the quality of social bonds to pro-social peers, spouses, and parents, as well as jobs and schools.

Learning Objective	Summary
LEARNING OBJECTIVE 5 State the emphasis of Thornberry's interactional theory.	Thornberry's interactional theory of delinquency incorporates three prominent delinquency perspectives: social learning, social bonds, and the life-course perspective. The most important point is the reciprocal nature of these influences, which suggests that once a person is on the path to delinquency, the development of delinquent peers is likely to follow, or vice versa. The theory considers early social bonds, particularly bonds with parents, as an important influence on delinquency.
LEARNING OBJECTIVE 6 Compare and contrast the concepts of control deficit and control surplus in Tittle's control balance theory.	Tittle's control balance theory focuses on the concept of personal control. People who have more control exerted on them than they exert on others are likely to become antisocial. People who have too much control over others are also likely to engage in antisocial behavior. Those with a balance of control are less likely to engage in unacceptable or unlawful behavior.
LEARNING OBJECTIVE 7 Briefly list the 10 propositions that Cullen uses to explain how social support is related to crime and delinquency.	The United States has higher rates of serious crime than other industrialized countries because it is a less supportive society. The less social support in a community, the higher the crime rate. The more support a person's family provides, the less likely that person will break the law. The more social support in a person's social network, the less crime will occur. Social support lessens the effect of exposure to strains that tend to produce crime. Social support increases the likelihood that offenders will turn away from an antisocial path. Anticipation of a lack of social support increases criminal involvement. Social support lessens involvement in crime. Crime is less likely when social support for conformity exceeds social support for crime. Social support is often a precondition for social control.
LEARNING OBJECTIVE 8 Describe how, according to Agnew, the interaction between five life domains affects the likelihood of antisocial behavior.	Agnew's general theory of crime and delinquency states that the major causes of crime lie within the five life domains—self, family, school, peers, and work—which can accelerate and enhance a person's chances of being drawn into antisocial behavior.
LEARNING OBJECTIVE 9 Identify the basis of Farrington's integrated cognitive antisocial potential theory.	Farrington's integrated cognitive antisocial potential theory (ICAP) is based on strain, control, learning, labeling, routine activities, rational choice, and biological theories. According to ICAP, elements from these theories affect antisocial potential, or a person's likelihood to engage in antisocial behavior.

Critical Reflections

1. Discuss the lengths that Laub and Sampson went to in collecting the data that support their life-course theory.
2. Compare the use of longitudinal data to the use of data that look at individuals at a single point in time.
3. What is the difference between life-course theories and integrated theories?
4. What do integrated theories that use several perspectives contribute to the development of criminological theory?
5. How does Cullen's theory of social support use a comprehensive approach to how individuals are connected to pro-social behavior?
6. Why do some people stop breaking the law as they get older, whereas others persist over their life course?

Key Terms

adolescence-limited p. 180
antisocial potential p. 197
disintegrative shaming p. 194
integrated theories p. 189
labeling theory p. 195
life-course-persistent p. 180
life-course theory p. 178
reintegrative shaming p. 195
total institution p. 184

Instant Recall Terms

learning theories of crime (ch. 6)
longitudinal (ch. 2)
routine activities theory (ch. 4)
social learning theory (ch. 6)

Notes

1 *New Yorker*, "The Thief Who Steals Only Silver," December 22, 2016, https://www.newyorker.com/culture/culture-desk/the-thief-who-steals-only-silver. Stephen J. Dubner, "The Silver Thief," *New Yorker*, May 17, 2004.
2 *New Yorker*, "The 'Thief Who Steals Only Silver."
3 Ibid.
4 Dubner, "The Silver Thief."
5 Terry Dickson, "'Burglar to Stars' Blane Nordahl Pleads Guilty to St. Simons Burglary, Sentenced to 11 Years," *Florida Times-Union*, November 14, 2017, http://www.jacksonville.com/news/georgia/2017-11-14/burglar-stars-blane-nordahl-pleads-guilty-st-simons-burglary-sentenced-11.
6 Dubner, "The Silver Thief."
7 David P. Farrington, "Developmental and Life-Course Criminology: Key Theoretical and Empirical Issues," *Criminology* 41, no. 2 (2003): 221.
8 Michael L. Benson, *Crime and the Life Course: An Introduction* (Los Angeles: Roxbury, 2002).
9 Federal Bureau of Investigation, Uniform Crime Reports: Crime in the United States, 2016, Table 38: Arrests by Age, https://ucr.fbi.gov/crime-in-the-u.s/2016/crime-in-the-u.s.-2016/topic-pages/tables/table-20. Accessed April 2018.
10 Gerald R. Patterson, Barbara D. DeBaryshe, and Elizabeth Ramsey, "A Developmental Perspective on Antisocial Behavior," in *Criminological Theory: Past to Present*, 3rd ed., ed. Francis T. Cullen and Robert Agnew (New York: Oxford University Press, 2006), 495–521.
11 James D. Unnever, Francis T. Cullen, and Robert Agnew, "Why Is 'Bad Parenting' Criminogenic? Implications from Rival Theories," *Youth Violence and Juvenile Justice* 4, no. 1 (2006): 3–33.
12 Anthony Bryk and Barbara Schneider, *Trust in Schools: A Core Resource for Improvement* (New York: Russell Sage Foundation, 2002).
13 Mark Warr, *Companions in Crime: The Social Aspects of Criminal Conduct* (New York: Cambridge University Press, 2002).
14 Alex R. Piquero, Robert Brame, and Donald L. Lynan, "Studying Criminal Career Length Through Early Adulthood Among Serious Offenders," *Crime and Delinquency* 50, no. 3 (2004): 412–435.
15 Patterson, DeBaryshe, and Ramsey, "A Developmental Perspective on Antisocial Behavior," 495–521.
16 Oregon Social Learning Center, http://www.oslc.org.
17 Ibid.
18 Ibid.
19 Terrie E. Moffitt, "Adolescence-Limited and Life-Course-Persistent Antisocial Behavior: A Developmental Taxonomy," *Psychological Review* 4 (1993): 674–701.
20 Amy V. D'Unger, Kenneth C. Land, Patricia L. McCall, and Daniel S. Nagin, "How Many Latent Classes of Delinquent/Criminal Careers? Results from Mixed Poisson Regression Analyses," *American Journal of Sociology* 103, no. 6 (May 1998): 1593–1630.
21 Marvin E. Wolfgang, Robert M. Figlio, and Thorsten Sellin, *Delinquency in a Birth Cohort* (Chicago: University of Chicago Press, 1987).
22 Terrie E. Moffitt, "Pathways in the Lifecourse," in *Criminological Theory: Past to Present*, 504.
23 David C. Rowe, *Biology and Crime* (Los Angeles: Roxbury, 2002).
24 David C. Rowe and David P. Farrington, "The Familial Transmission of Criminal

Convictions," *Criminology* 35, no. 1 (1997): 174–201.
25 Jay Macleod, *Ain't No Making It: Leveled Aspirations in a Low Income Neighborhood* (Boulder, Colo.: Westview Press, 1987).
26 Moffitt, "Pathways in the Lifecourse," 502–521.
27 Ibid., 510–511.
28 Gary LaFree, *Losing Legitimacy: Street Crime and the Decline of Social Institutions in America* (Boulder, Colo.: Westview Press, 1998).
29 Terence Thornberry and Marvin D. Krohn, "The Self-Report Method for Measuring Delinquency and Crime," *Criminal Justice 2000: Measurement and Analysis of Crime and Justice* (Washington, D.C.: U.S. Department of Justice, 2000), 33–83.
30 Diana Fishbein, *Biobehavioral Perspectives in Criminology* (Belmont, Calif.: Wadsworth, 2001), 41–45.
31 Moffitt, "Pathways in the Lifecourse," 517.
32 Erving Goffman, *Asylums: Essays on the Social Situation of Mental Patients and Other Inmates* (Garden City, N.Y.: Anchor Books, 1961).
33 William Julius Wilson, *The Truly Disadvantaged: The Inner City, the Underclass, and Public Policy* (Chicago: University of Chicago Press, 1987).
34 Robert J. Sampson and John H. Laub, *Crime in the Making, Pathways and Turning Points Through Life* (Cambridge, Mass.: Harvard University Press, 1995).
35 Farrington, "Developmental and Life-Course Criminology," 221.
36 Benson, *Crime and the Life Course.*
37 Cullen and Agnew, *Criminological Theory*, 489.
38 Sheldon Glueck and Eleanor Glueck, *Unraveling Juvenile Delinquency* (New York: Commonwealth Fund, 1950).
39 John H. Laub and Robert J. Sampson, *Shared Beginnings, Divergent Lives; Delinquent Boys to Age 70* (Cambridge, MA: Harvard University Press, 2003).
40 John H. Laub and Robert J. Sampson, "The Sutherland-Glueck Debate: On the Sociology of Criminological Knowledge," *American Journal of Sociology* 96, no. 6 (May 1991): 1402–1440.
41 Cullen and Agnew, *Criminological Theory*, 490.
42 Sampson and Laub, *Shared Beginnings, Divergent Lives*, 121.
43 Mark Warr, "Life-Course Transitions and Desistance from Crime," *Criminology* 36 (1998): 183–215.
44 Ronald L. Simons, Eric Stewart, Leslie C. Gordon, Rand D. Conger, and Glen H. Elder, Jr., "A Test of Life-Course Explanations for Stability and Change in Antisocial Behavior from Adolescence to Young Adulthood," *Criminology* 40, no. 2 (May 2002): 426.
45 David P. Farrington, ed., "Integrated Development and Life Course Theories of Offending," *Advances in Criminological Theory* 14 (New Brunswick, N.J.: Transaction, 2005).
46 Robert K. Merton, *Social Theory and Social Structure* (Glencoe, Ill.: Free Press, 1957).
47 Terence P. Thornberry, "Toward an Interactional Theory of Delinquency," *Criminology* 25, no. 4 (2006): 863–892.
48 Ibid.
49 Charles R. Tittle, *Control Balance: Toward a General Theory of Deviance* (Boulder, Colo.: Westview, 1995).
50 Ibid.
51 Charles R. Tittle, "Control Balance Theory," in *Criminological Theory: Past to Present*, 563–581.
52 Actually, Cullen lists 13 propositions, but we have selected 10 here for the sake of clarity.
53 Ibid.
54 John Paul Wright and Francis T. Cullen, "Parental Efficacy and Delinquent Behavior: Do Control and Support Matter?" *Criminology* 39, no. 3 (2006): 677–706.
55 Francis T. Cullen, "The Twelve People Who Saved Rehabilitation: How the Science of Criminology Made a Difference—The American Society of Criminology 2004 Presidential Address," *Criminology* 43, no. 1 (March 2005): 1–42.
56 Robert Agnew, *Why Do Criminals Offend? A General Theory of Crime and Delinquency* (Los Angeles: Roxbury, 2005).
57 David P. Farrington, "Developmental and Life-Course Criminology: Key Theoretical and Empirical Issues—The 2002 Sutherland Award Address," *Criminology* 41, no. 2 (May 2003): 221–255.

RACISM
IS A
WEAPON
OF
MASS
DESTRUCTION

Conflict and Critical Theories of Crime

FEATURES

Marchers raise their signs during the March for Racial Justice from Lincoln Park to the U.S. Capitol in Washington, D.C. Why is race such a controversial topic in the criminal justice system?

In September 1998, Jarrett M. Adams, 17, and two friends traveled from Chicago to the University of Wisconsin-Whitewater to attend a party. During the evening, while in the dorm room of a male student, the three men were invited to another room and took part in what Adams called a "completely consensual" sexual encounter with a white, female student.[1]

Adams and his friends, Dimitri Henley and Rovaughn Hill, were arrested three weeks later after the woman reported that they had raped her. Hill, who was tried separately, had a private attorney who called one of the students as an alibi witness. His case ended in a hung jury, and prosecutors dismissed the charges. Neither Adams nor Henley could afford a private attorney, and at their trial, their court-appointed attorney chose not to offer a defense, explaining that the prosecution could not prove its case. Adams and Henley were convicted by an all-white jury in 2000. Adams was sentenced to 28 years in prison, and Henley to 20.[2]

Adams said he was naive about how the courts really worked. He told NBC News, "My only encounter with the criminal court system was *Law & Order*. [Y]ou don't see guys who are wrongfully convicted go to prison and get sentenced to 28 years."[3]

While in prison, Adams started reading law books in the prison law library and discovered that the Constitution required defendants to be provided effective assistance of counsel. With the help of the Wisconsin Innocence Project, Adams's sentence was overturned, and he was freed in 2007. By 2017, Adams had earned his law degree and became the first Innocence Project exoneree to become an attorney for the organization. Henley was finally freed in 2008.[4]

Understanding Conflict Theory and Critical Theory

LEARNING OBJECTIVE | 1

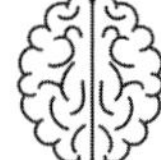

Define primary deviance and secondary deviance and state how these conditions relate to labeling theory.

LEARNING OBJECTIVE | 2

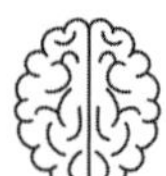

Define social location and discuss its relationship to antisocial behavior.

In the preceding theory chapters, we studied how criminologists look to biological, psychological, and social factors to account for **antisocial** behavior. Theories that consider offenders to be defective, different, or culpable suggest that the remedy for crime is to punish or treat lawbreakers and to deter potential lawbreakers. However, other ways of considering crime and delinquency shift the focus away from the individual offender and toward the role of social institutions and political dynamics. For example, in the case of Jarrett Adams, Dimitri Henley, and Rovaughn Hill, the institution and political dynamics of the court, the ability or inability to afford a private attorney, and each man's understanding (or misunderstanding) of how courts work all played a major role in how they were treated by the court.

These theories are known by several terms, but the most common appellations are "conflict" and "critical." In this chapter, we will study several types of conflict and critical theories that consider the following:

- how the government defines acts as criminal;
- how personal or group power shapes the criminal law and guides the criminal justice system; and
- how an economic system, such as capitalism or communism, can determine what is defined as crime and how punishment is determined and meted out.

Conflict and critical theories may seem much like sociological theories at first, but they are quite different. Sociological theories consider crime to originate with the individual, whereas conflict and critical theories consider crime to be rooted in society itself. Before we move on to traditional conflict and critical theories, however, we should review the theory that bridges the gap between sociological theory and conflict and critical theories. **Labeling theory** does this by shifting the focus on the genesis of crime from individuals—those who are labeled—to those who do the labeling: governments and social institutions such as schools and the family.

When a label is internalized, it becomes a self-fulfilling prophecy. When does a label exert a positive influence on a child?

Labeling Theory

Labeling theory became a popular explanation for crime during the 1960s, although it was created decades earlier. In 1938, criminologist Frank Tannenbaum coined the term "tagging" in his book *Crime and Community* for how individuals are labeled in a negative way that identifies them as deviant.[5] Labels can be positive (good student, star athlete) or negative (delinquent, ex-convict) and eventually become what sociologist Howard Becker called a **master status**—a social standing that takes precedence over all others.[6] Although individuals have many social statuses, a master status overwhelms them all. A negative master status can have a detrimental effect on how a person is treated by parents, teachers, society, and the criminal justice system.

Labeling theory is primarily a theory of delinquency, but it can apply to adult offenders. Basically, labeling theory describes two processes, which sociologist Edwin Lemert identified as **primary deviance** and **secondary deviance**.[7]

Primary deviance occurs when society reacts to an individual's actions, successfully labels that individual, and acts upon that label. This kind of labeling is desirable in many ways. It is useful, for example, to know who the drug addicts, child molesters, and thieves are. However, once this negative label is successfully applied and sticks, labeled individuals are treated as if the label is the only status that matters, and the label becomes the person's master status. Secondary deviance is complete when labeled individuals internalize the label and see themselves as devalued members of society. If you tell a child often enough that he or she is stupid, this label becomes self-fulfilling when the child no longer attempts to excel at school. Once someone starts to live up to a negative label, it becomes part of his or her self-concept, and rehabilitation becomes much more difficult.

Labeling theory has several limitations. The first is that it does not adequately explain the original deviance. It is reasonable to ask where negative labels originated. For example, why did a child labeled as a delinquent first get involved in burglary, drugs, or gang activity? Primary deviance only explains how society treats an individual once the person has been successfully labeled. Another limitation involves secondary deviance. White-collar or corporate offenders do not appear to suffer as much from negative labels as street-crime offenders and do not appear to internalize those labels, instead seeing themselves as shrewd businesspeople. In addition, many violent offenders, such as those who commit spouse abuse or acquaintance rape, have not been previously involved with the criminal justice system and have not suffered primary deviance. Nevertheless, criminologists continue to employ labeling theory to explain repeat offending.

Instant Recall from Chapter 1 **antisocial** —Following standards of behavior intended to harm society and individuals.

Instant Recall from Chapter 7 **labeling theory** —The idea that society defines an individual, treating him or her differently, and that the individual internalizes this definition and acts it out.

master status—A social standing that takes precedence over all others.

primary deviance—A stage that occurs when society reacts to an individual's actions, successfully labels that individual, and acts upon that label.

secondary deviance—A stage that occurs when labeled individuals internalize the label and see themselves as devalued members of society.

First-offender programs in which individuals are diverted from the juvenile or criminal justice systems to rehabilitative programs and/or probation are a good example of the use of labeling theory in criminal justice policy. Many such programs offer to drop the charges—along with the application of the negative label—in exchange for successful completion of the program. The idea is that by limiting an offender's exposure to the criminal justice system and avoiding the labels of "delinquent" or "criminal," society will not treat the individual according to the negative master status, and the individual will not act it out.

Now that we understand how labeling theory locates the origins of crime within social institutions and their definitions of offenders and offenses rather than within offenders' reactions to society (as do sociological theories) or within the offenders themselves (as do biological/psychological and classical theories), we are ready to delve into conflict and critical theory. Conflict and critical theories consider crime to originate within the inequities they consider to be inherent in social institutions.

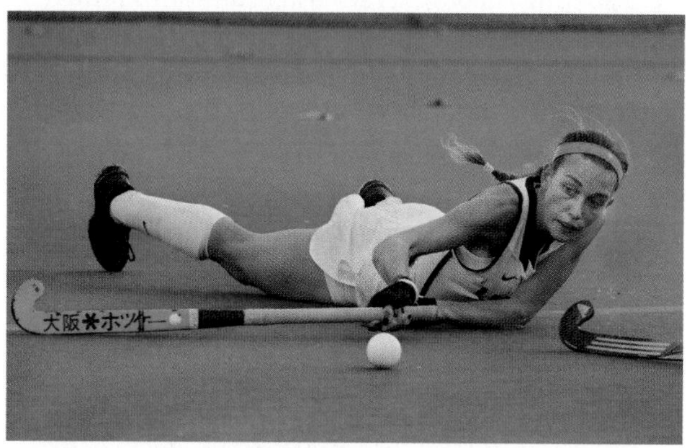

University of Connecticut field hockey player Charlotte Veitner, accused of stealing some makeup from the campus bookstore, applied for a probation program that could clear her record. The program for first-time, peaceful offenders erases charges after a probation period. In what ways does labeling theory underpin this case?

---

social location—The position of an individual within a society according to race, sex, class, geography, and age.

race—The use of certain biological characteristics, such as skin color, to classify human beings into categories.

sex—The biological characteristics that distinguish organisms on the basis of their reproductive ability.

class—A group defined by a particular social, economic, and educational status.

gender—The social concept of how males and females should behave.

political—Referring to the relationships of people in groups and their activities.

conflict theory—A set of criminological propositions based on the philosophy of Karl Marx holding that antisocial behavior stems from class conflict and social and economic inequality.

critical theory—Criminological perspectives that describe and critique the social structure and seek solutions to the problems of crime and criminal justice.

Social Location

Before we get into individual theories, you should become familiar with several terms related to **social location**, or the position of an individual within society according to **race**, **sex**, **class**, **gender**, and, to a lesser extent, age. Sometimes people are identified with antisocial behavior, even if they have broken no laws, because of social location. Social location influences status, opportunities, and obligations. Only by understanding our social location can we appreciate how broad social forces, primarily through social institutions, influence our lives.

Historically, those who were white, male, and economically secure occupied social locations that enabled them to go to the best universities, receive excellent health care, and be welcomed into family businesses. By contrast, people who were female, impoverished, or within minority groups had a much more difficult time. Social location is concerned more with who you are than what you do. The major factors of social location include the following.

- Class. Class refers to a group defined by a particular social, economic, and educational status. Class is not only an organizing factor of society, but also a basis for discrimination. Social class can reflect how power is wielded in society, and some scholars consider the development of the criminal law and the actions of the criminal justice system to be an example of how stronger social classes seek power over weaker ones.
- Race. Race is the use of certain biological characteristics, such as skin color, to classify human beings into categories. Many criminologists believe race is a significant factor in how the criminal justice system creates and applies the law.
- Gender and sex. Gender is the social concept of how male and female persons should behave. The criminal justice system's differential treatment of males and females is based on sex, the biological characteristics that distinguish organisms on the basis of their reproductive ability.
- Age. Many rights and responsibilities are allocated according to age. For example, U.S.

citizens cannot vote until age 18. Many states have mandatory school-attendance policies based on age. People cannot collect social security until age 62. Very young lawbreakers are processed by the juvenile justice system, although some legal rules specify the waiver of some juvenile delinquents to adult courts.

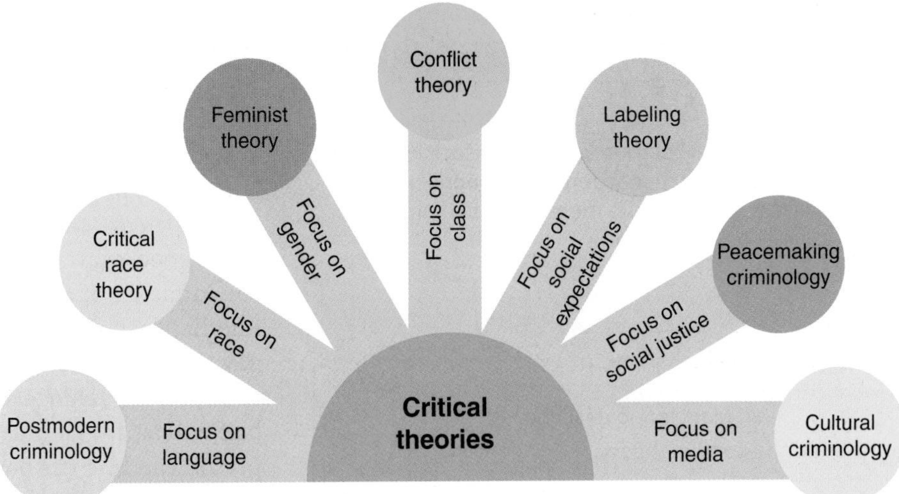

FIGURE 8.1 Critical Theories

Conflict theory spawned critical theory, which eventually became the larger body of theories. Conflict theory is now a part of critical theory, along with several other theories of crime. Note that each theory has a specific means by which it performs its critique. Labeling theory uses social expectations, peacemaking criminology uses social justice, and so on around the circle.

THINK ABOUT IT
Discuss why critical theory become the larger body of theory.

A final key to understanding critical and conflict theories is the proper definition of the word **political**. Although we most often use "political" in relation to government, it also refers to the relationships of people in groups and their activities. The definition and prosecution of crime have political dimensions. That is, people working in groups decide what constitutes crime and how society deals with offenses and offenders. The social identity of these groups affects their decisions about crime. Groups typically tasked with defining crime and how it is dealt with are often wealthy, male, white, and well into adulthood. According to critical and conflict theorists, the political identity of this group affects what it decides to do about crime and whom it classifies as criminals.

There is considerable overlap among the types of theories and heated discussion among criminologists about how they should be categorized.[8] Chronologically, conflict theory came first, and critical theory grew out of conflict theory. However, critical theory is now the larger body of theory and has subsumed conflict theory (see Figure 8.1). Most of the theories in this chapter are critical theories. For the sake of clarity, we will use the following typology which, although not universally accepted, will allow us to differentiate between types of theories.

- **Conflict theory**, a set of criminological concepts based on the philosophy of Karl Marx, holds that antisocial behavior stems from class conflict and social and economic inequality. It considers social class to primarily determine both the type and quality of justice an individual receives and how entangled he or she becomes in the criminal justice system.
- **Critical theory** is a set of criminological theories that describe and critique the social structure and seek solutions to the problems of crime and criminal justice. It uses conflict theory to extend its critiques beyond class to other social locations. Labeling theory focuses on social expectations; feminist criminology focuses on sex and gender; peacemaking criminology on social justice; cultural criminology on media; postmodern criminology on language; and critical race theory on race. Because conflict theory came first and its ideas are important to understanding critical theory, we will begin there.

PAUSE AND REVIEW

1. **Discuss the policy implications of labeling theory.**
2. **Describe how conflict and critical theories are different from traditional sociological theories.**
3. **Define primary deviance and secondary deviance.**
4. **What is the significance of master status to labeling theory?**

Conflict Theory

LEARNING OBJECTIVE | 3

Understand how conflict theory considers social institutions, especially those rooted in economics and social class, to contribute more to crime than individual antisocial behavior.

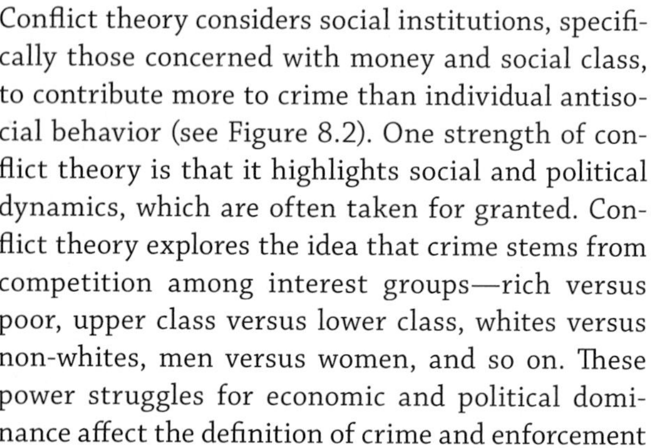

LEARNING OBJECTIVE | 4

Explain who Karl Marx is and describe his contribution to conflict theory.

Conflict theory considers social institutions, specifically those concerned with money and social class, to contribute more to crime than individual antisocial behavior (see Figure 8.2). One strength of conflict theory is that it highlights social and political dynamics, which are often taken for granted. Conflict theory explores the idea that crime stems from competition among interest groups—rich versus poor, upper class versus lower class, whites versus non-whites, men versus women, and so on. These power struggles for economic and political dominance affect the definition of crime and enforcement of the law as dominant interest groups impose their values and judgments through their power to write the criminal law. The uneven distribution of wealth, property, and power leads to want and resentment of the wealthy, which ultimately leads to crime as those without the resources necessary for survival try to acquire them.

A good example is the offense of driving under the influence of drugs or alcohol. A wealthy or even middle-class person arrested for this offense can pay the bail amount and get out of jail before going to court. An impoverished person who cannot pay bail will sit in jail until the court date. The wealthy person can hire the best legal representation, which may seriously affect the sentence. The impoverished person will have to make do with the attorney the state provides, who might not be the best available. According to the Texas Defender Service, death row inmates—who tend to be impoverished and of low social class—have a one-in-three chance of being executed without having claims of innocence or unfairness heard and without a competent attorney investigating their cases.[9]

Social institutions and the resources and ideas for solving problems are largely handed down from the past, especially in the case of criminal justice and criminological theory. To understand our laws and methods of criminal justice and its theoretical critiques, we must first understand where they came from and how they have changed.[10]

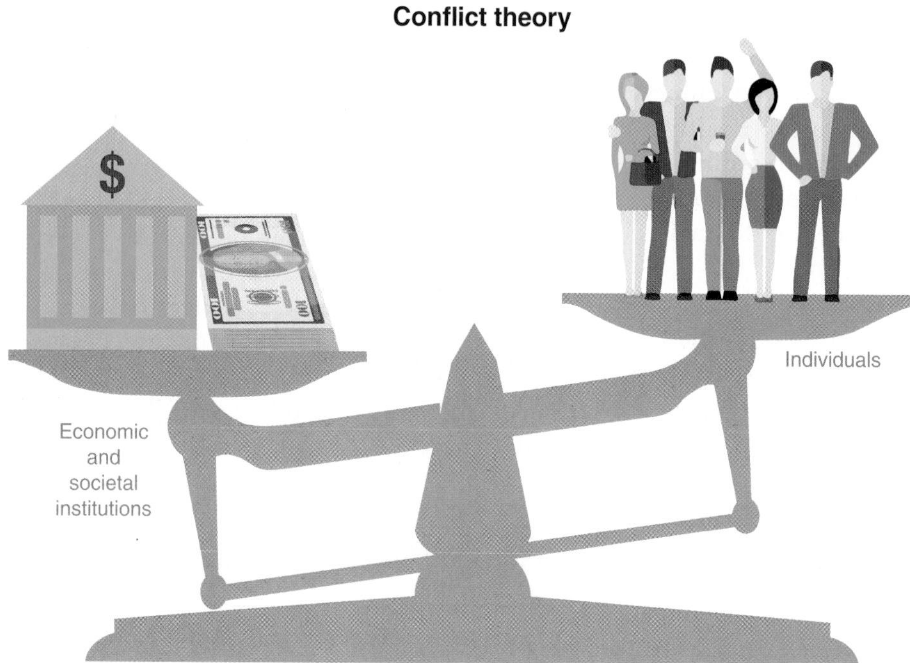

FIGURE 8.2 Social institutions, especially those concerned with money and social class, contribute more to crime than individual antisocial behavior.

THINK ABOUT IT
Discuss why conflict theory asserts that social institutions contribute more to crime than individual behavior.

Marx and Communism

The idea of economics as a primary factor in antisocial behavior can be traced to Karl Marx (1818–1883), a 19th-century German social theorist, philosopher, and economist. Marx did not say much about crime specifically, but his ideas have led other theorists to contemplate the relationship between economic conditions and crime.[11] Popularly known as the "father of communism," Marx is a major intellectual figure and is considered to have provided the foundation for an alternative economic system to capitalism. Although Marx's theories inspired modern communism in China, the former Soviet Union, Vietnam, North Korea, and Cuba, the communism practiced in these countries is not really what Marx envisioned. In order to appreciate his ideas, we must understand the time and context in which he wrote.

In the late 19th century, Europe underwent a radical transformation from an agrarian, rural population to one that is now heavily industrial and urban. As people moved to the city for jobs, they found themselves working hard for low wages. Typically, companies had extensive financial and social relationships with the government that allowed the companies to maximize the value of the workers' labor for a low cost.

Marx was appalled by the effects of this unbridled capitalism on the working class. The owners of the means of production, whom Marx called the **bourgeoisie** (pronounced boor-zhwah-ZEE), paid extremely low wages, maximizing their profits at the workers' expense. Workers were forced to labor in unsafe conditions without any form of safety net for their health or lives. A worker hurt or maimed on the job was out of a job if he or she was unable to continue to work. Companies owed nothing to these workers or to their families, even if company negligence was to blame if the worker was killed. Job security, bonuses, raises, vacations, or clean and safe working conditions were unheard of. Children had to work as hard as adults. Marx believed that a livable wage and decent working conditions were necessary for the **proletariat**, the social class of people who worked for wages.

According to Marx, the proletariat's lack of power caused them to sink into despair, withdraw from society, and depend on fellow workers or turn to crime. Marx called this type of citizen the **lumpenproletariat**, the lowest social class, which was characterized by its disorganization, lack of skill, and impoverishment. Marx's critiques were a wake-up call for industrialized countries as workers around the world began to organize and demand better conditions and wages.

Many of Marx's ideas have been incorporated into modern societies, including the United States. The provision of social security, welfare, aid to families, and other safety-net programs can be partly attributed to Marx's concern for the working class. Still, most members of the working class in the United States today, although they can pay their bills, cannot achieve financial independence. Marx's ideas about property and wealth advocate a more even distribution of these privileges throughout society.

The grave of Karl Marx in Highgate Cemetery, London. What economic system did Marx consistently criticize?

Some countries heavily subsidize education, health care, housing, and child care services, which reduces the need for individuals to have a lot of personal income or inherited wealth. Conceivably, countries with this type of socialist system would have less crime because people would not live in dire need. Friedrich Engels, a 19th-century social philosopher and one of the founders of communism and socialism, speculated on such a society being crime-free. According to Engels, "Crimes against property cease of their own accord where everyone receives what he needs to satisfy his natural and spiritual urges, where social gradations and distinctions cease to exist."[12]

Many people in the United States have a hard time appreciating Marx's ideas. They believe that his ideas are economically naive and that those who espouse Marxism, socialism, or communism are unpatriotic. However, even the U.S. economic system is not purely capitalist. For example, legislation controls how companies conduct business and pursue profit, and regulatory agencies enforce workplace laws. Regardless, conflict theorists still believe that workers are exploited, a condition they assert leads to crime.

---

bourgeoisie—In Marxism, the owners of the means of production.

proletariat—A social class composed of people who work for wages.

lumpenproletariat—In Marxism, the lowest social class, which was characterized by lack of skill, disorganization, and impoverishment.

The extent to which government should regulate the marketplace is often a point of contention, but we need only look at the United States in the late 19th and early 20th centuries, as well as Russia during the 1990s after the Soviet Union disintegrated, to understand how the market can be manipulated. For example, in the United States, in the late 19th century, "robber barons" such as John Jacob Astor, Cornelius Vanderbilt, and John D. Rockefeller took advantage of political corruption, the Industrial Revolution, and nearly non-existent corporate controls to monopolize industries and throttle competition.

- John Jacob Astor monopolized the fur trade and used his political connections to call in the U.S. military against American Indians who complained of being defrauded by Astor's American Fur Company. Astor then speculated in New York City real estate where his tenement housing made him one of the city's foremost slumlords.
- Cornelius Vanderbilt used his influence as a shipbuilder to convince Nicaragua to give his Accessory Transit Company sole access to a passage connecting the Pacific and Atlantic oceans. When the deal soured, Vanderbilt invaded Nicaragua with mercenaries and later persuaded the U.S. government to send in the Marines.
- John D. Rockefeller's Standard Oil Company monopolized the U.S. oil industry by controlling the railroads and charging competitors exorbitant rates to transport their oil. With the help of corrupt officials, Rockefeller controlled 90 percent of U.S. petroleum production by 1890.[13]

U.S. philanthropist John D. Rockefeller gives a dime to a child. What industry did Rockefeller's company dominate?

Much of the same manipulation and corruption are happening in Russia today. Unbridled capitalism has allowed former Communist Party members to amass monopolies on key industries and products. The old Soviet Union's relatively stable, albeit somewhat impoverished, economic system has given way to Russia's incredible inflation, shortages of goods and services, and a dangerous economic system in which power politics and physical force allow some in business to become billionaires while many people starve.

It is probably not fair to compare the emerging Russian economy during the 1990s to other forms of capitalism because it was a time of rapid and overwhelming social change. The discussion we present here simply shows that those who advocate unbridled capitalism may find that its actual practice is devastating in terms of social equality. For example, China has moved toward capitalism more slowly, adopting some capitalist ideas, thus merging aspects of capitalism and communism.[14] The ultimate effect these countries' new policies will have on their crime rates remains to be seen.

Other Conflict Thinkers

Although Marx is the best-known conflict thinker, other theorists have significantly contributed to this line of criminological reasoning. The following brief review of these scholars' ideas will demonstrate how the conflict perspective is grounded in social structure and economic conditions.

MAX WEBER

Max Weber (1864–1930) was a German sociologist who laid the groundwork for analyzing conflict according to three measures of inequality: power, wealth, and prestige. According to Weber, conflict is most likely to occur when an individual or a group possesses all three measures. When this happens, others, who have less or none of the three, feel tension and resentment and are likely to conflict with the privileged.[15] Although Weber did not specifically address crime, his ideas of conflict have been used to explain why economic inequality and imbalances in social power influence individuals and groups to break the law. For example, crime rates are high in Brazil and South Africa, both of which have large impoverished and wealthy populations, deep racial divides, and a relatively small middle class. The gulf between the powerful, prestigious "haves" and the powerless, disrespected "have nots" is striking, and from a Weberian point of view, this gulf is at the root of both countries' crime rates.[16]

RALF DAHRENDORF

German sociologist Ralf Dahrendorf (1929–2009) considered social class to be defined by power rather than property.[17] In his view, groups that desired domination opposed groups that attempted to avoid subjugation, and he considered the interactions of these two groups to be the source of constant social conflict.[18] As each group seeks to legitimize its power over other groups, the political process causes infighting, political maneuvering, and coercion. A contemporary example of these ideas is the controversy over drug laws. Some groups are comfortable with the "war on drugs," whereas others see this policy as contributing more problems than it solves. For example, some organizations are attempting to influence public policy through legitimate ways to decriminalize marijuana, while other groups are pressing hard to not only keep marijuana illegal, but also to maintain severe punishments for users and dealers.

AUSTIN TURK

Sociologist Austin Turk has made a major contribution to conflict theory with his ideas about the interaction of dominant groups and subordinate groups.[19] Turk identified norms of domination and deference whereby the values, standards, and laws of powerful groups must be recognized and respected by subordinate groups. If this recognition does not occur, then the subordinate groups' behaviors and values will be criminalized. Even when subordinate groups adopt the dominant group's worldview, the behaviors of some individuals in the subordinate group will be considered deviant.

Because of the dynamic nature of societies, some groups or individuals will not always be fully invested in the dominant value system and will therefore be considered deviant. Over time, some of this deviance may become normalized. For instance, tattoos were once considered a mark of deviance and rebellion for middle-class people. Today, tattoos have become fashion statements, and such body art no longer has the extremely negative social and political consequences it once had.

CRITIQUES

Conflict theory has spurred many criminal justice system reforms since the 1960s. However, some scholars resist conflict theory because it approaches the problems of crime and delinquency in such a different manner. Some critics of conflict theory consider it to be anti-government because it critiques those who enforce the law.[20] Recall that rather than assuming that offenders are inherently antisocial or that they learn to break the law, conflict criminology examines how societies control their citizens and how this control can sometimes lead to crime. This idea can be uncomfortable for some who want to justify how the criminal justice system operates. Here are some of the critiques of conflict criminology.

- It is more political than scientific. Positivist criminologists emphasize observable facts. They try to use the **scientific method** to show a relationship between offenses and offenders. Conflict theory, however, does not try to be objective; rather, it advocates its position. According to conflict theory, there is no such thing as value-free science, and even the selection of a research topic shows political influence. Conflict theorists believe that explicitly stating a position is desirable; many mainstream criminologists contend that conflict theory studies are unreliable because of political bias.[21]
- It is not measurable. Research in conflict theory is often not subject to measurement. However, conflict theory is largely still in the theoretical stage and is not yet ready to be measured. This does not mean that studies have not looked at the conflict perspective; indeed, many have. However, conflict theory has not advanced as far as **differential association theory** or **strain theory**, both of which have been the subjects of numerous sophisticated studies. Therefore,

Instant Recall from Chapter 4 **scientific method** —A process of investigation in which phenomena are observed, ideas are tested, and conclusions are drawn.

Instant Recall from Chapter 6 **differential association** —Sutherland's idea that offenders learn crime from each other.

Instant Recall from Chapter 6 **strain theory** —The idea that people who experience anger and frustration when they cannot achieve cultural goals through legitimate means try to achieve these goals through illegitimate means.

conflict theory is not as theoretically developed as some other criminological theories.

- It critiques the status quo. Conflict theory requires close observation of how capitalism distributes and maintains wealth. By considering disparities in wealth and income between those who control the means of production and those who do the work, the conflict perspective may be considered to intrude into the affairs of government and business.[22]
- Solutions are financially and politically expensive. Critique of the capitalist system is inherent in conflict theory. This is less of an issue in socialist countries where governments provide such basic needs as food, housing, and health care. Although it can be argued that the United States is becoming increasingly socialist, this journey is incomplete. True socialism would require expensive and politically difficult changes. The United States is deeply committed to capitalism and the idea of the free market. Although communism was popular among some American intellectuals in the 1930s, and some aspects of socialism were introduced during President Franklin D. Roosevelt's administration, both quickly and drastically fell out of favor after World War II. Much of the American public

POLICY IMPLICATIONS

Shifting the Focus

Conflict and critical theories of crime suggest that there is more to deviant behavior than simply an offender's bad decisions. These theories suggest that some of the broad social policies that are the foundation of American society may be partially at fault. This is a sensitive and sometimes uncomfortable issue because it can challenge some of our most deeply held beliefs about human nature, the role of power in society, and the culpability of individuals for the harm they do to others. Nevertheless, by examining some of the policy implications suggested by conflict and critical theories, we can better understand not only how some groups of people are overrepresented in the criminal justice system, but also how inequities might be addressed. The following is a brief list of policy implications that may stem from these theories.

- Conflict theory. This theory addresses how capitalism might be reformed so that individuals are fully compensated for their labor. By looking at the dynamics of capitalism, it is possible to suggest ways that wealth can be spread more evenly across the population rather than having it accrue to only a few. This type of analysis challenges people to think about concerns such as power, entrepreneurship, risk-taking, and economic rewards for creativity.
- Peacemaking criminology. This theory suggests that the "war on crime" is often counterproductive to the goals of the criminal justice system. It argues against making a criminal class out of offenders and suggests that redemption is possible if the criminal justice system is not so focused on deterrence and punishment. Peacemaking criminology observes that most people change their behavior and that policies that accelerate positive change can be developed.
- Feminist theory. This theory suggests that by challenging the patriarchal structure of society, justice can be achieved for everyone, not just the males who have historically had power. By ensuring that everyone is treated equally regardless of their sex, feminist criminology seeks to ensure that females have equal employment opportunities in the criminal justice system; that female offenders are provided with adequate resources for their rehabilitation; and that female crime victims, especially those of domestic assault, are treated with justice and respect.
- Critical race theory. This theory is concerned with developing policies that highlight how race is an important factor in determining who is arrested, sentenced, and punished. Critical race theory looks at issues such as racial profiling and the overrepresentation of minorities in correctional institutions.

The strength of these theories lies in their challenge of the status quo. They require that legislators consider the effect of the laws they enact on disadvantaged groups. An efficient criminal justice system is not necessarily an effective one. To gain the trust of society, the criminal justice system must dispense justice in an even-handed manner. Conflict and critical theories of crime help to analyze the quality of justice.

THINK ABOUT IT

1. What changes in the law do these policy implications of conflict and critical theories suggest?

remains deeply skeptical of any movement toward socialist policies.

- Solutions are culturally unattractive. American culture values creativity and risk-taking, and our capitalist economic system presumably rewards the industrious and visionary. Some critics of conflict theory believe that a socialist economic system discourages people from working hard and creating new services and products. Because the value of products or services does not go directly to the individual but rather to society, it is thought people will do as little as possible and simply collect their government checks.[23]

The solutions that conflict criminology suggests are so sweeping and fundamental that it is unlikely they will be uniformly adopted in the United States in the near future. Still, conflict theory has much to contribute to the examination of crime. The economic gulf between the wealthiest Americans and the most impoverished is so great that many scholars continue to question the legitimacy of the capitalist system when viewed in the light of social justice.[24]

PAUSE AND REVIEW

1. **Describe how the robber barons of the late 19th and 20th centuries manipulated the capitalist system to monopolize industries and throttle competition.**
2. **Summarize Marx's view of the power relationship in 19th-century Europe.**
3. **Critique the argument that conflict theory relies more on political argument than on the scientific method.**

Critical Theory

LEARNING OBJECTIVE | 5 

List and briefly describe at least three critical theories.

According to critical theory, the definitions of crime and justice are located within a social system that is based on and perpetuates social inequality. Although based on conflict theory, critical theories not only describe and critique the social structure, but they also actively seek solutions to the problems of crime and criminal justice.

A historical example of what critical theory would critique is the practice of slavery in the United States prior to the 20th century and the legal apparatus surrounding it. Slave owners were often wealthy and powerful, and, as a result, were often considered to be the backbone of their communities. Today, it is easy to see the paradox of law-abiding, often religious, people perpetuating a deep moral wrong. However, prior to the U.S. Civil War, many people considered slavery to be normal and just. To perpetuate this social order, slave laws defined the rights of the owners and the role of the enslaved, and those who broke these laws often faced criminal penalties. These laws were written by powerful and wealthy slave owners to benefit themselves and control the powerless slaves. If a slave broke a law, the problem was considered to be not with the law but with the slave. Thus, society's idea of justice was deeply rooted in social inequality.

Oluale Kossola (Cudjo Lewis), the last survivor of the Atlantic slave trade, seen here in 1927 during an interview with author Zora Neale Hurston. How were slave owners viewed by the community in the South before the Civil War?

Although laws are generally regarded as desirable and necessary for a working society, slave laws existed to uphold an unjust order that benefited a wealthy few. Slavery was so entrenched in the United States that it was dislodged only by civil war. This is evidence of how difficult it is to alter social paradigms and change individuals' cherished beliefs about their societies. The critical theories we will consider in the rest of this chapter seek to change social paradigms they consider to contribute to social injustice and crime.

Feminist Criminology

Feminist criminology is a set of theories maintaining that gender inequality is at the root of offenses in which female persons are the victims or offenders. It deals with the many issues and problems related to females, crime, and the criminal justice system, including incarcerated females, women in the criminal justice workplace, and gender aspects of victimization.

Crime has traditionally been the province of men.[25] Male persons are arrested more often than female persons, and most crime victims are male (see Figure 8.3).[26] More males are incarcerated, and most criminal justice system workers, especially those in prisons, are male. In a **patriarchal** society—that is, a society that is controlled by men—crime is one of the most patriarchal institutions. However, because of the strides that feminism has made in gender equality, women can now be found at virtually every level of the criminal justice system, from judges to offenders.

A substantial body of literature applies the feminist perspective to issues of crime and justice.[27] Feminist criminology not only critiques male-centric theories, but also creates hypotheses about crime and gender. For example, in the 1970s, Freda Adler and Rita Simons proposed the "liberation hypothesis," which states that the social equalization of females and males means that females will begin committing the same types and numbers of offenses as males.[28] More recent theories also consider the ways in which the criminal justice system manages female persons. The "evil woman" hypothesis, for example, proposes that the criminal justice system treats women and girls who do not meet gender expectations (for example, those who do not act "feminine") differently than it does those who do.[29]

Feminist criminology is also useful for critiquing other theories. Almost all criminological theories have been fashioned to describe and explain the activities of males in the male-dominated world of crime and criminal justice, which, in turn, exists within a male-dominated society. The activities of women and girls as delinquents, offenders, victims, or criminal justice workers have been explained by applying male-centric theories to females and not by doing any in-depth research on female persons. Feminist theory effectively ended this practice by pointing out that female persons are different from male persons.

Not only are females different biologically and psychologically, but they live their lives differently and have different reasons for the things they do because they occupy a different place in society.[30] Feminist theory states that women and girls require their own criminological research and theories to accurately explain their roles in crime and the criminal justice system.[31] In this section, we will review the feminist perspective and consider some of the theories that seek to explain the importance of gender in crime and the criminal justice system. We will also assess the effect of those theories on how crime is addressed, and we will look at their critiques.

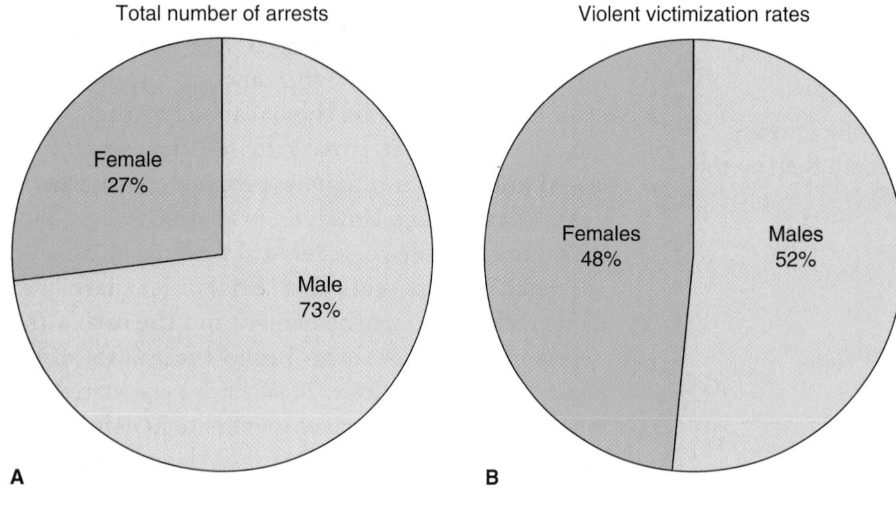

FIGURE 8.3 Sex, Crime, and Victimizations

Crime is traditionally dominated by male persons. Figure A shows the percentage of male and female arrests in 2016, and Figure B shows the percentage of male and female violent crime victimizations.

THINK ABOUT IT

Why are more male persons arrested than female persons? Why are males the most common victims of violence?

Sources: Figure A: Federal Bureau of Investigation, Uniform Crime Reports, Crime in the United States, *2017, Table 42: Arrests by Sex, 2017, https://ucr.fbi.gov/crime-in-the-u.s/2017/crime-in-the-u.s.-2017/topic-pages/tables/table-42. Figure B: Rachel E. Morgan and Grace Kena,* Criminal Victimization, 2016, *Tables 8 and 11, (Washington, D.C.: U.S. Department of Justice Office of Justice Programs Bureau of Justice Statistics, 2006), 9, 13. Online at https://www.bjs.gov/index.cfm?ty=pbdetail&iid=6166. Accessed October 2018.*

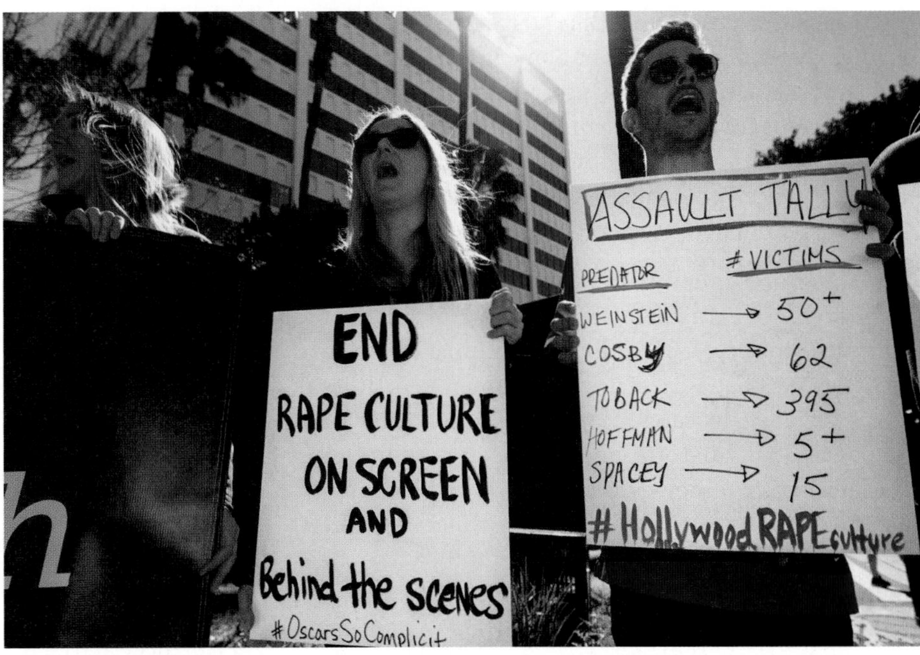

Protesters call for an end to the statutes of limitation on rape and sexual assault. How has the "Me Too" movement changed the way victims of crime respond to their accusers?

To understand the effect of feminism on the criminal justice system, we must briefly review the women's movement. The 1960s saw the beginning of a major feminist initiative in the United States, preceded by a first wave of feminism that came during the late 19th and early 20th centuries as women lobbied for the right to vote.[32] At that time, it was thought (mostly by men) that women were not capable of appreciating the political process and would simply vote as their husbands told them to. Women rejected this perspective and advocated reforms that would allow women to become fully participating citizens. Feminists also fought restrictions that prevented women from owning property in their own name, retaining custody of children after a divorce, and working in many occupations.[33] Although the feminist revolution is largely complete today, women are still treated differently from men in many areas, two of which are crime and criminal justice. Feminist scholars consider women's participation in crime and the criminal justice system in many ways.

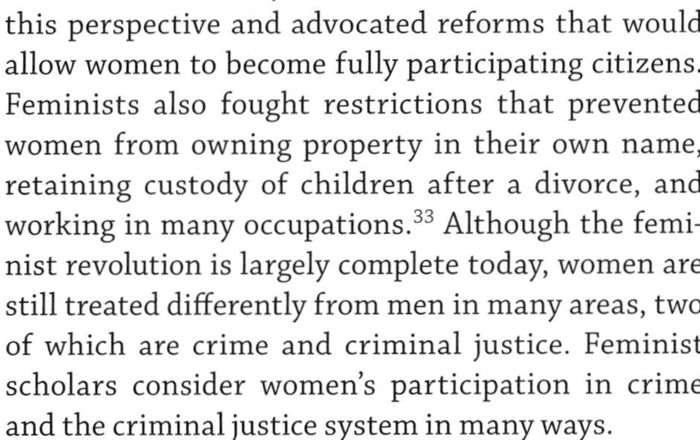

- As offenders. Women and men break the law in different patterns and at different rates. Although women do break the law on their own, they are often ancillaries to male offending. Women are also significantly less violent than men. Feminist scholars consider the experience of women as convicted offenders by comparing their sentencing, rehabilitation, treatment, and incarceration to that of male offenders. Women's issues as inmates include health care (gynecological issues, pregnancy), children, and sexual harassment by other inmates and correctional officers.[34]
- As crime victims. Feminist scholars have made great advances in identifying the special circumstances of female victims.[35] In the case of domestic assault, they have found that the criminal justice system has failed to protect women from violent husbands and boyfriends.[36] In the case of rape, the feminist perspective has helped change some social attitudes, and it is now understood that a rape victim can be further victimized by the criminal justice system's bureaucratic processes.[37]
- As workers. Although more women are working within the criminal justice system than ever, many issues remain, most of which are within law enforcement and corrections. The criticism of women as police officers mirrors that of women serving in the military as soldiers: women cannot do the job because they are not physically strong enough and are too emotional. In corrections, the issues are more focused on females working in all-male environments, especially environments filled with antisocial lawbreakers, many of whom are in prison for violence against women. In this case, federal law that ensures the rights of women to be considered for jobs regardless of their sex runs up against legitimate concerns for their safety in prison environments and for the rights of male inmates, attenuated as they are, to be dealt with

---

feminist criminology—A set of theories holding that gender inequality is at the root of offenses in which women are the victims or offenders.

patriarchal—Referring to a social system that is controlled by males.

in sensitive procedures (like strip searches) by members of their own sex. Some states still restrict the duties of female correctional officers in situations involving personal searches and the transportation of male inmates.[38] Regardless of these concerns, women are serving successfully as correctional officers and as police officers.

According to feminist theory, the criminal justice system's treatment of females mirrors that of the rest of society.[39] Basically, the feminist perspective advocates equal treatment of women and, at its most extreme, advocates a complete reorientation of the power structure of American society. Additionally, feminist criminology is concerned with not only the interactions between males and females, but also the process of constructing masculinity. The socialization of masculinity in many cultures often includes overt messages of support for the exploitation or victimization of women. The way men are socialized into masculine roles that emphasize dominance and toughness has consequences for their involvement in crime.[40]

Feminist theories of crime and delinquency offer an alternative look at how women are motivated to break the law and how the criminal justice system responds to them differently from men. However, they risk minimizing other important factors. For instance, in the victimization of impoverished women, race and social class can be just as important as sex. Although feminist theory may do a good job of explaining female antisocial behavior and victimization, it cannot speak to the antisocial behavior and victimization of men. This is an important point because males commit the most crime, and most crime victims are male.

Feminist theories also tend to consider females who break the law as victims of a patriarchal system and do not give credit to the choices that women make. For example, some women who engage in prostitution might not do so because they are oppressed and have few legitimate opportunities, but rather because they enjoy the power it gives them over men, they prefer the lifestyle, or they want the chance to make a great deal of money quickly. From the **classical criminology** standpoint (see Chapter 4), women who break the law make a rational choice that is not necessarily dictated by economic circumstances or male oppression.

At its broadest level, full implementation of feminist theory would require fundamental changes in the allocation of power and privilege in a patriarchal society. It would require that women receive broader educational opportunities, better enforcement of child-support laws, improved support for child care and dealing with workplace sexual harassment, and stronger measures to alleviate the violence against women that appears to be inherent in patriarchal cultures. As men and women become more aware of the role of gender in culture and crime, improvements will likely be made in the socialization of males and females and in the ways that institutions deal with gender-based prejudice, discrimination, and violence.

Peacemaking Criminology

Peacemaking criminology considers the social and personal effects of crime as a whole, accounting not only for the offender and victim, but also for the social structures that accept, enable, and encourage crime. Criminologist John Randolph Fuller argues that peacemaking criminology should be considered a perspective because it does not yet rise to the level of specificity that theory requires.[41] However, the peacemaking perspective can be applied to problems of crime at the personal, interpersonal, institutional/societal, and global levels (see Figure 8.4).

- The personal level. At the personal level, peacemaking criminology suggests that each of us be gentler on ourselves. Henry David Thoreau wrote in *Walden*, "The mass of men lead lives of quiet desperation." With this observation in mind, peacemaking criminology advocates solving personal, individual problems before developing external solutions to crime. Only when individuals are aware of their own motivations can they effectively deal with their relationships with others.
- The interpersonal level. At the interpersonal level, peacemaking criminology recognizes that manners, politeness, and civility should be used to accomplish goals rather than force, intimidation, and power. Peacemaking criminology guides behavior not only for individuals working within, or caught up in the workings of, the criminal justice system, but also for those who wish for a guide to managing their affairs in all

Instant Recall from Chapter 4 **classical criminology** — Shortened form of "classical school of criminology." A set of ideas that focuses on deterrence and considers crime to be the result of offenders' free will.

peacemaking criminology—Criminological perspective that considers the social and personal effects of crime as a whole.

aspects of life, such as education, family life, and the environment, as well as criminal justice. You might think that the peacemaking perspective risks being so broad that it does not speak specifically to a single issue; however, this would be inaccurate. Peacemaking provides an outline for the conduct of human affairs, and this generalizability makes it an attractive and potentially powerful perspective.[42]

- The institutional/societal level. Peacemaking criminology looks at how the institutions that people develop shape their interactions. For instance, structural issues within American society may contribute to crime and delinquency. Consider, for example, gun control laws. If the legal system interpreted the Second Amendment differently and more tightly restricted the sale and possession of firearms, the United States might have a lower homicide rate.[43] Another example concerns capital punishment. Peacemaking criminology advocates the elimination of the death penalty because it models the very behavior it is supposed to deter.
- The global level. The peacemaking perspective would deal with transnational offenses such as human trafficking, international drug smuggling, and terrorism by trying to solve these problems without violence and in a way that would ensure social justice. For example, when dealing with human trafficking, especially trafficking of young women and children for sexual purposes, peacemaking criminology would not be content to simply catch the smugglers and throw them in prison. Peacemaking criminology would look at the broader social conditions that enable or encourage the practice of human smuggling and advocate improving the economies of developing countries so that selling people for sexual purposes would be unnecessary.[44]

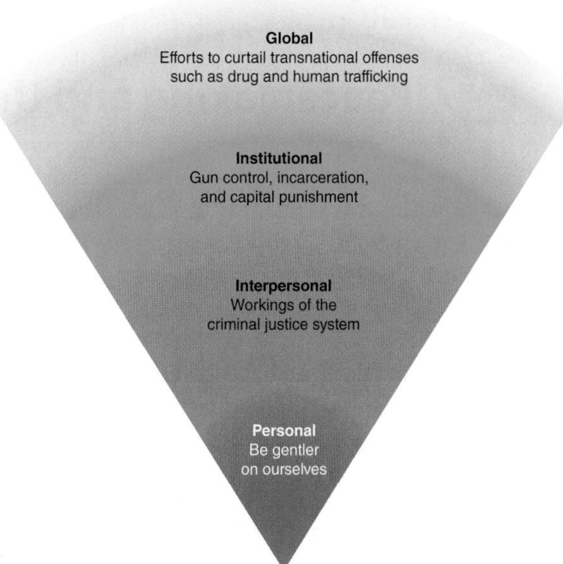

FIGURE 8.4 The peacemaking perspective can be applied to problems of crime at four levels.

THINK ABOUT IT
Discuss how each level contributes to the peacemaking perspective.

Although peacemaking criminology has been around for years, it was not until 1991 when scholars Harold Pepinsky and Richard Quinney published *Criminology as Peacemaking* that the perspective's foundations were defined.[45] Peacemaking criminology derives its ideas and philosophy from the religious and humanist, feminist, and critical traditions. Let's discuss each briefly.

- Religious and humanist traditions. The religious and humanist traditions are responsible for much of what is considered peacemaking criminology. Religious traditions include the world's major religions, such as Buddhism, Christianity, Confucianism, Hinduism, Islam, and Judaism.[46] Each tradition has elements that promote the idea of peace. Although it can be said that religious wars have been responsible for much of the world's sorrow, it can also be contended that sincerely following these religions would lead to a peaceful life rather than one filled with conflict.[47] Several scholars, such as criminologist Michael C. Braswell, have expanded on the idea of religion as a peaceful influence in society, identifying how religion can be applied to the criminal justice system in beneficial ways.[48] Like the religious tradition, the humanist tradition specifies peaceful ways for people to live but asserts that it is possible to be moral without adhering to a specific religion or belief in a supreme being. Humanism contends that people are basically good and will strive toward responsible and ethical behavior if the systems they live in allow it.[49] Religious and humanist traditions, then, give the peacemaking perspective substance and direction in promoting responsible, moral, and healthy behavior. Pepinsky and Quinney do not advocate any specific tradition, but rather assert that any of them can contribute to human moral development.

THEORY TO PRACTICE

Peacemaking and Uncommon Sense

One of the most consistent complaints about the peacemaking perspective is that it is unrealistic and soft on crime. But what does "soft on crime" mean? Those who believe in being "tough on crime" use deterrence theory as one of their underlying theoretical perspectives. Briefly, **deterrence** theory holds that if penalties are certain, swift, and severe, potential lawbreakers will choose not to break the law. The perspective of peacemaking criminology, however, is that deterrence is a fundamentally flawed concept.

Deterrence theory assumes that individuals will weigh the cost of breaking the law against the likelihood of getting caught and punished. However, most people who break the law do not believe they will be caught. Often, they plan the offense and take precautions to escape detection. Even if penalties are substantially increased, potential lawbreakers might not be deterred because they sincerely believe they will not be caught and punished.

Deterrence theory also assumes that lawbreakers can accurately weigh the risk of getting caught against the benefits of succeeding. If this were the case, we would not see so many serious offenses that offer so little reward, such as using a gun to rob a convenience store, which often has little cash. In this scenario, the offender risks an armed-robbery conviction, which carries a hefty penalty that dwarfs the reward for getting away with robbing the store. This is especially true if the store clerk is killed, and capital punishment becomes a possibility.

Rather than attempting to force the offender into lawful behavior, peacemaking criminology seeks to prevent crime by ensuring social justice and providing treatment options for offenders so they can learn the skills to achieve their needs without breaking the law. Peacemaking would address the robber's impoverished neighborhood, disintegrated family, and lack of adequate employment. Sociologist Robert Agnew suggests how we can correct the causes of crime:

> ... traits like impulsivity and low verbal IQ, child abuse, family conflict, poor parenting practices, poor school performance, low commitment to school, association with delinquent peers and gang members, and growing up in poor, disorganized communities. A number of prevention and treatment programs have been developed to address these causes, like pre- and postnatal health care programs, preschool enrichment programs, parent-training programs, and a variety of school-based interventions.[50]

Instead of relying on deterrence to convince potential lawbreakers to obey the law, peacemaking criminology seeks to protect the community by addressing the problems that give rise to antisocial behavior.

THINK ABOUT IT

1. Consider the crime problems in your neighborhood and think of a peacemaking program that might address them.

- Feminist traditions. As explained in the earlier section on feminist criminology, feminism advocates gender equality and the dismantling of patriarchal systems. Gender inequality within the criminal justice system and within crime itself reflects the gender inequality in society.[51] Feminist theorists believe that reforming the criminal justice system will demonstrate how to deal with people who lack power in society and help them to become functioning members of society.[52]
- Critical traditions. The critical traditions include conflict theory, especially a Marxian analysis of the relationship between social structure and crime, as well as some of the newer critical ideas such as postmodern criminology and cultural criminology. All are covered in detail later in this chapter.

A major criticism of peacemaking criminology is that it is naive and utopian (see Theory to Practice for more discussion of that view). Critics contend that peacemaking does not adequately appreciate the danger in the world and takes a simplistic view of human nature. Another criticism is that much of what peacemaking advocates is already part of the criminal justice system and society. For instance, programs for rehabilitating offenders, though limited, have been around for several decades. Finally, peacemaking criminology would require fundamental changes in the way people relate to each other that are beyond the ability of the criminal justice system to effect.

Peacemaking criminology has policy implications for all four levels of analysis. For example, peacemaking can be applied in several ways to reduce crime. At the personal level, many religions and schools of spiritual thought require their adherents to shun violence. At the interpersonal level, methods of conflict resolution are taught in some schools so that children learn how to settle disputes without verbal or physical violence. At the institutional/societal level, the death penalty could be eliminated and the availability of guns greatly curtailed. At the global level, the work of the United Nations in providing a forum for countries to work out their differences without resorting to war is a particularly useful example of the broader implications of peacemaking criminology.

Cultural Criminology

Cultural criminology examines how social ideas, values, and media reflect and produce antisocial behavior. Some of the concerns of cultural criminology are the modeling of police agencies after the military, such as the use of uniforms and ranks, and depictions of crime on television and in film. The images and symbols used by graffiti writers, gang members, and the tattoo and body modification industry are all concerns of the cultural criminologist.[53] Cultural criminology borrows much from media studies and cultural sociology. These disciplines look at how individuals, small groups, and deviant subcultures construct meaning and transmit it to a wider audience.[54] Cultural criminology adopts this perspective to better comprehend how crime is either culturally supported or culturally discouraged by everyday social structures. Here are a few examples.

- Gang apparel and gang signs. Like sports teams, gang members must identify themselves to each other and to rivals, typically with distinctive clothing, special hand gestures, and graffiti.[55] Cultural criminologists consider how these markers symbolize authenticity and power. By understanding how these symbolic behaviors define what is important to gang members, cultural criminologists can better explain why gang conflicts are often more about identity, status, and respect than about disputes over territory or illegal markets. To the broader society, gang activity looks negative, non-utilitarian, and wasteful. However, gang members understand their behavior to be rational and protective of the symbolic meaning of being in a specific gang.
- Media representation of the war on drugs. Cultural criminologists consider how the war on drugs attempts to change not only behavior, but also opinions about certain drugs. In an attempt to decrease the demand for drugs, the government has used the media to demonize some drugs and marginalize the people who sell and buy them. Cultural criminologists study how the government and other social institutions wage this war, as well as how drug sellers and users respond to media influence.[56] The media's role in the war on drugs is important because it has set the political agenda so that politicians cannot afford to be seen as soft on drugs and crime. Therefore, despite conflicting information about the actual harm some drugs cause, drugs such as marijuana are represented as uniformly bad. Nicotine is a good example of the media manipulation of the public perception of drugs. Until the 1970s, the media portrayed the smoking of cigarettes and cigars as sexy and sophisticated. Now that tobacco smoking is considered to be harmful to the health of smokers and those around them, only the "bad guys" smoke in movies and on television.
- Cultural space and crime control. Cultural criminologists study how subcultures and the authorities contest public space. An obvious example of this study is how homeless people are treated throughout the United States. Although homeless people present a significant social problem, in many places they are treated as a public nuisance and embarrassment. Prior to the 1996 Olympics in Atlanta, for example, authorities made a concerted effort to encourage homeless people to leave the city.[57] Similarly, skateboarders are problematic for municipal authorities. Although skateboarding is not illegal, some people consider skateboarders who gather in parking garages, public parks, and malls to be a nuisance.[58] Cultural criminologists look at how authorities attempt to discourage the

Instant Recall from Chapter 3 **deterrence** —The idea that punishment for an offense will prevent that offender and others from further breaking the law

cultural criminology—A concept that examines how social ideas, values, and media reflect and produce antisocial behavior.

congregation of skateboarders, as well as how they define their behavior, communicate their culture, and resist social control.

- Images of authorities. Criminal justice system administrators work hard to manage the impression they give to politicians and the public. One interesting example is the Special Weapons and Tactics (SWAT) teams that have become a fixture in large police agencies. These teams' duties often put them in dangerous situations, and they have structured their image to resemble that of the military. According to criminologist Peter Kraska, SWAT teams' special paramilitary weapons and clothing have gained a unique and highly valued identity within the police organization.[59] The mere presence of SWAT teams can sometimes be enough to resolve a potentially violent situation. However, SWAT weapons and clothing can also be problematic as citizens sometimes think they are under attack. Sometimes SWAT teams make a mistake by entering the wrong residence, frightening and assaulting innocent citizens.[60]

One aspect of cultural criminology that is particularly ripe for research is how some television news programs focus on one particular case and burn it deeply into the public consciousness. Often, these cases involve celebrities or individuals who evoke deep public sympathy or scorn. For example, although the O. J. Simpson murder trial took place in the mid-1990s, it still stands as a landmark case because it set a new standard for crime as cultural spectacle. The case featured a celebrity football star and television personality accused of slaying his attractive white, blonde wife, as well her handsome, young male visitor; an automobile chase; and a televised public trial. The case, however, provided a distorted image of how the criminal justice system operates.[61] Few people can afford Simpson's legal representation or command the constant media coverage and speculation that provided a level of examination virtually no other case has received before or since. Cultural criminologists point out that people who are less interesting to the media because of their minority status or physical appearance are murdered all the time with little coverage of their cases. Still, the effect of such intense media attention is that criminal justice administrators may feel pressured to allocate more resources to a case at the expense of others.

Atlanta, Georgia, SWAT members confer at the scene of a standoff between a barricaded gunman and police. What image of authority does the military attire of SWAT teams portray to the public?

Cultural criminology makes an important contribution to the study of crime and delinquency because it reminds us that we do not know everything about crime and antisocial behavior or about how images of lawbreaking are produced and transmitted to the public. By understanding how the criminal justice system, victims, and offenders attempt to manage their images in the media, cultural criminology reveals that the quality of justice often reflects social standing.[62]

Cultural criminology considers issues far beyond the criminal justice system as it attempts to explain why people break the law and how society reacts. For instance, the use of symbols by street gangs may be interesting to scholars and useful to police, but little can be done to suppress this behavior without violating gang members' rights of free speech. Similarly, although gang graffiti is a problem, law enforcement does not typically handle clearing it from public spaces. Although graffiti may have implications for criminology, it is the responsibility of other social institutions to deal with it.

In another example, although cultural criminology considers the linkage between video games and crime, the criminal justice system can do little to respond to such speculation. Therefore, many of the concerns of cultural criminology, though theoretically interesting, are beyond the purview of the criminal justice system.

The policy implications of cultural criminology include evaluating and examining how the news media report and often sensationalize crime. Cultural criminology examines the role of violence in the media and how it affects its most avid consumers, children and teenagers, as well as society as a whole. Responsible coverage is encouraged rather than the sensationalizing of cases with particularly sexual or emotional aspects. Cultural criminology also proposes finding more positive outlets for the energies and creativity of young people by, for example, supporting sports or music programs in urban areas that have few opportunities for positive or legitimate expression.

Postmodern Criminology

Like cultural criminology, **postmodern criminology** focuses on how language and traditional ideas affect how we define and perceive crime, the law, and society. It offers a unique way of looking at the problems of negotiating the legal world and the criminal justice system. To understand postmodern criminology, we must first briefly explain postmodern thought. Postmodernism explores how language affects the way we construct our perceptions about the world. Language communicates ideas in many ways, not only by words with meanings, but by context, syntax, and even grammar. Language can be used to include group members and alienate outsiders, or it can be used to explain difficult concepts simply. Depending on context, one word can have many different meanings, and the correct use of that word in the correct context can mean inclusion or exclusion from a group. In environments such as a prison or a gang, correct language can mean life or death.

Take, for example, the word "punk." A century ago, you might use a punk, which was another word for kindling, to start a fire. Later, a low-level offender or even a lazy person came to be described as a punk. In the late 1970s, a social movement that was related to a form of popular music was called punk rock. Today, punk is no longer necessarily a pejorative term but rather can be a compliment describing a willingness to be different. However, in prison, a punk is a male inmate who has sex with, and even acts as spouse to, another male inmate. So four contexts involving a simple word emerge: (1) asking someone to start a fire with a punk will probably get you a funny look; (2) calling an elderly person a punk may result in a lecture about respect; (3) calling a youth with a purple mohawk hairstyle a punk will earn you a satisfied sneer; and (4) if you are a prison inmate, carelessly calling another inmate a punk may get you killed.

Of these four contexts, one, the prison, involves a strict and guarded terminology that excludes outsiders and draws insiders closer together by helping them define and understand their context. This, in a nutshell, is the concern of postmodernism: the role of language and ideas in constructing reality.

Postmodern criminology goes beyond that basic example to consider how language and ideas in all aspects of crime and the criminal justice system include and exclude groups of people and how they define the realities of those groups. Postmodern criminology is a critical theory because it examines the status quo and finds it wanting on several fronts. Criminologist Bruce Arrigo identifies three areas of focus in postmodern criminology.[63]

- Language in the criminal justice system. Individuals must negotiate multiple language environments in the criminal justice system, which is crucial to understanding what is happening. Prison can be especially scary for those who are uninitiated and unaware of prison terminology, and the workings of a courtroom often seem foreign to a defendant with little education or experience. When attorneys speak in "legalese," the unsophisticated defendant often cannot understand what is happening and how these proceedings will affect his or her freedom.[64] The legal terminology includes courtroom insiders and excludes just about everyone else, including two of the most important participants: the offender and the victim.
- Partial knowledge. The postmodern perspective calls our attention to the fact that in many encounters between police and citizens, each party is acting on partial knowledge. In this case, misunderstandings can have tragic effects on the police, suspects, and victims. When the police stop a person, they require a certain etiquette that shows the detained person is not violent. When a detained person violates this expected behavior and appears defiant or agitated, the officer might interpret this behavior as aggressive and use inappropriate force.[65] The suspect may have a different idea of what the encounter is about—for example, if the detained person is a victim—and challenge the officer's authority. According to postmodernism, this difference in defining the situation causes many detained people to find themselves subdued, arrested, and hauled before a judge.

---

postmodern criminology—A perspective that focuses on how language and traditional ideas affect how we define and perceive crime, the law, and society.

- Deconstruction. Deconstruction is the examination of rules and regulations by questioning traditional assumptions about certainty, meaning, and truth. Arrigo uses the example of mental treatment for those facing execution.[66] The law states that people who are mentally ill cannot be executed, but it stipulates that once they successfully receive treatment and are healthy, they can be put to death. At issue is the word "treatment" because the term, according to Arrigo, connotes the conferring of a gift or a reward. Postmodernists contend that such terminology does not accurately reflect the situation. In another example, it is the job of medical and legal officials to ascertain whether formerly violent mental patients and inmates can be released. Consequently, many subjects have learned to provide the expected answers to questions and to modify their behavior within the institution. Once released, however, successful institutional adaptation does not necessarily ensure that the subject will successfully adjust to free society. Learning to follow institutional rules does not guarantee that an inmate or patient has been successfully rehabilitated. Life inside and outside the institution is very different, and forcing individuals to adhere to a strict routine, though useful for maintaining control in an institution, leaves them unprepared for life on the outside where the temptations are many and the punishments for not following the rules are extreme.

Through its examination of language, postmodern criminology forces observers to step outside the conventional wisdom and generally accepted assumptions about crime and justice and consider how power is exercised at the expense of marginal groups of people. For critical criminologists, postmodern criminology represents a fresh way of understanding the workings of the criminal justice system and an opportunity to ensure that justice is fully examined for its unintended consequences.[67]

Postmodern criminology suffers from several limitations that have restricted its popularity. The first is language. Critics point to the jargon or parlance of those who engage in postmodern critique and suggest that rather than clarifying things, postmodernists further muddy the waters by providing analyses that are as difficult to understand as the system they critique. Another criticism is the use of models from other disciplines. The models that postmodern theorists use, especially the chaos theorists, require a high level of knowledge of fields that are far removed from criminology, such as physics and mathematics.

Although some consider the use of sophisticated language and complicated models as reflecting the severe limitations of postmodern criminology, these models can also be guides for developing policy. By appreciating how language is used to privilege the wealthy and educated or to confuse those who lack the vocabulary and knowledge of legal procedures, the postmodern critique can show how the criminal justice system can be unfair to those who are at the greatest social disadvantage.

Postmodern critique can illustrate how the knowledge of experts may be used to deny victims and offenders full access to the criminal justice system. For instance, in plea bargaining, the prosecutor must move cases through the system and does not always fully explain to victims why pleas are negotiated. Like many of the critical theories we have discussed in this chapter, postmodern criminology speaks only indirectly to the problems of crime. It is more broadly aimed at cultural influences rather than directly at criminology or the criminal justice system. Nevertheless, it provides a fresh look at how issues of crime and delinquency are resolved in the United States.

Critical Race Theory

Critical race theory is a set of propositions holding that racial inequity is so ingrained in society that it is propagated through legal and social discourse. The development of a theoretical perspective of race is not as advanced as those of class and gender. However, significant scholarship outside criminology details how race is related to many important issues in health care, education, crime, and the criminal justice system.[68] Critical race theory is the most extensive theoretical development of race as a social category that influences power.[69] Critical race theory proposes three basic principles.

- The normality of racism in American culture. The purpose of critical race theory is to eliminate racism by revealing how deeply ingrained it is within American culture.[70]

---

critical race theory—A set of legalistic perspectives holding that racial inequity is so ingrained in society that it is propagated through legal and social discourse.

racial profiling—The disproportionate selection by law enforcement of minority suspects.

- The value of story-telling. Critical race theory uses personal narrative or story-telling to allow oppressed groups to speak from their own experiences and describe their realities.[71]
- The critique of liberalism. Traditional liberal perspectives in terms of historical and current racial reforms are not radical enough to bring about the fundamental changes necessary for equality and justice.[72]

Critical race theory presents important alternative perspectives for looking at how laws are written. Institutional racism has afflicted the United States throughout its history. Even after slavery was abolished, racial minorities continued to be oppressed because of laws that supported the dominant white majority and prohibited minorities from participating in much of society.[73] In the second half of the 20th century, the civil rights movement challenged the status quo and successfully eliminated overt institutional discrimination in state and federal law.[74]

Despite the successes in challenging institutional discrimination, critical race theorists still see disadvantages for people of color. The disadvantages are not as overt as they were in the past, but they can be significant in the lives and careers of those who are subject to even indirect racial discrimination.[75] For example, although affirmative-action policies have brought opportunity and hope to many people of color, critical race theorists have criticized them as limiting rather than emancipating. Sometimes people attribute the success of a person of color to affirmative action rather than to personal ability. Critical race theorists assert that governments have singled out race as an identifying factor in dispensing justice. Examples of how race has been a deciding factor in the dispensation of justice include the resettlement of U.S. citizens of Japanese descent in the United States during World War II, the Jim Crow laws of the South in the early 20th century, and the treatment of American Indians by the U.S. government.[76]

Critical race theorists also call attention to subtle uses of race to assert control. One example is that the media tend to give more extensive coverage to criminal offenses that affect white people than those that affect people of color. (See Doubletake for a discussion of what has been called "missing white woman syndrome.")

Another example, according to law professor Dorothy E. Roberts, is that some drug laws are aimed primarily at people of color and are used to influence reproductive rights. She cites the example of how the state of Florida used a mother's drug addiction as a way to discourage impoverished, black women addicts from caring for their babies. In the case Roberts described, the two babies of a woman who admitted she had smoked crack cocaine shortly before the delivery of both tested positive for traces of cocaine. In Florida, mothers cannot be charged with passing substances to their children while in the womb. So, the prosecutor argued that the mother passed the drug to her children after they were born but before they were detached from the umbilical cord. The mother was then found guilty of giving her children cocaine.[77] Because the effect of this legal precedent fell most heavily on black persons, critical race theorists argue that it was race-based.[78]

Critical race theorists have also scrutinized **racial profiling**, the disproportionate selection by law enforcement of minority suspects. Critics of the criminal justice system have long suspected that people of color are incarcerated at a higher rate because of racism. Studies have shown that when a white person and a person of color are engaged in the same type of behavior, the police are more likely to confront the person of color.[79] Law enforcement officials contend that race is not at issue, but rather the perceptions of experienced police officers that certain people in certain circumstances are more likely to break the law than others.

For example, in March 2018, Cleveland, Ohio, city councilman Kevin Conwell, 58, was walking in his neighborhood. As he cut through the campus of Case Western University, he was stopped by university police officers who asked for his identification.[80] The officers were responding to a call from a student who said that she had seen a black man with missing teeth who was mumbling incoherently and approaching students. This woman did not say that the man had broken any laws but that he was "kind of weird and acting funny." She said the man had a blue hat and a tan coat, which matched what Conwell was wearing. The police did not stop or question anyone else. Conwell suggests that he was stopped for "walking while black." The university later issued an apology.[81]

One concern of critical race theorists in the recent past was the disparity in sentencing for possessing crack cocaine as opposed to powder cocaine.[82] The difference between these substances lies in how they are prepared and consumed: crack cocaine is smoked, whereas powder cocaine is inhaled. These differences led to the creation

DOUBLETAKE

Missing: White Woman

"Missing white woman syndrome" is a colloquial term used to describe media bias toward the coverage of the disappearances and murders of white females.[83] Media experts point out that the U.S. news media have typically given more attention to offenses affecting white persons than offenses affecting people of color. For example, in 1993 in St. Louis, Missouri, Kimbre Young, a 9-year-old black girl, and Cassidy Senter, a 10-year-old white girl, disappeared within months of each other. The *St. Louis Post-Dispatch* ran two stories on Young and at least 23 stories on Senter.[84] One study cross-referenced the coverage of all missing-persons cases from four news organizations with the FBI's missing persons database and found that the coverage of missing white female persons was much greater than their proportions among missing persons. The news media were much more likely to cover cases of missing female persons than missing male persons, and cases of missing white female persons were more likely to get repeat coverage.[85]

A landmark early case was the 1969 Tate–LaBianca murders in which followers of Charles Manson murdered seven people. To this day, the iconic victim is Sharon Tate, an attractive, young, white woman. The other victims, two women and four men, were either male or middle-aged or both. The news media continue to provide deep coverage of murder/missing persons cases involving young, white females, including JonBenet Ramsey, Natalee Holloway, Laci Peterson, Chandra Levy, Polly Klaas, Caylee Anthony, and Kristin Smart. Similar cases involving women and men of color have gone unnoticed. For example, few people have heard of LaToyia Figueroa, Stepha Henry, or Tamika Huston.

1. LaToyia Figueroa, a 24-year-old black and Hispanic Pennsylvania woman who was five months pregnant, went missing in 2005 around the time Natalee Holloway disappeared. After public criticism that her disappearance deserved as much attention as Holloway's, the case got some national coverage. Figueroa's body was found about a month after her disappearance, and the father of her unborn child was charged with her murder.[86]

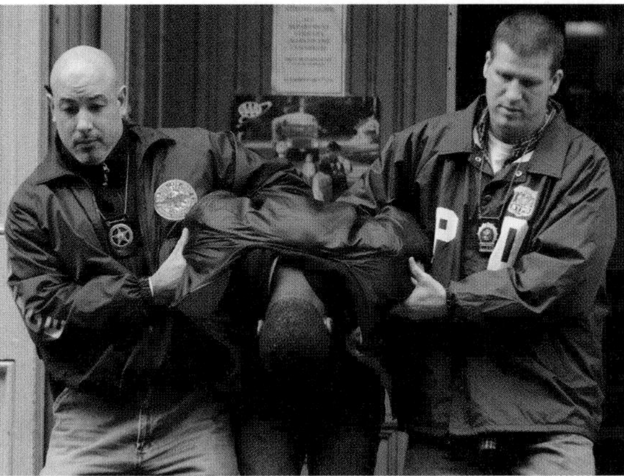

Kendrick Williams, center, is walked out of the 5th Precinct in the Chinatown district of New York. Why do cases concerning white women and girls garner so much attention?

2. Stepha Henry, 23, a black woman from Brooklyn, New York, disappeared in 2007 while vacationing in Florida. The media were criticized for directing most of their coverage at this time to the jail sentence of hotel heiress Paris Hilton.[87] Although Henry's body has not been found, an acquaintance, Kendrick Williams, was charged with her murder in 2008.[88] He has yet to go to trial.[89]
3. In 2004, Tamika Huston, a young black woman, disappeared in Spartanburg, North Carolina. Huston's aunt, a public relations professional, tried to get the national media interested in the case for weeks with little result.[90] Huston's remains were found about a year after her disappearance, and an acquaintance, Christopher Hampton, was convicted of her murder.[91]

THINK ABOUT IT

1. Go to the site Black and Missing (http://blackandmissing.org). Have you heard about any of the cases covered on the site? Choose some cases and see how much news coverage you can find on them.
2. Had you ever heard of the Tate–LaBianca murders? Briefly research the other victims. Give reasons that Sharon Tate became the "face" of the murders.

of the 100-to-1 sentencing disparity for possession of crack versus powder cocaine, which meant that possessing 5 grams of crack cocaine triggered a minimum sentence of five years, although it took 500 grams of powder cocaine to warrant the same sentence. Until 2007, when the sentencing structure was changed to reduce the sentences for crack cocaine possession, black drug users went to prison for minor drug dealing while white drug users escaped incarceration altogether.[92]

In 2010, the U.S. House and Senate approved a measure under the Fair Sentencing Act that reduces the disparity in penalties between the use of crack cocaine and powder cocaine from 100-to-1 to 18-1.[93] The new law drops the five-year minimum sentence for both first-time offenders and repeat offenders who possess less than 28 grams of crack.[94]

A major criticism of critical race theory is that by looking at crime and delinquency through the prism of race, the contributions of other social institutions, such as family, schools, and the media, might be devalued. Sexism, ageism, and social-class bias, in addition to race, provide a more holistic view of inequality. By privileging race as an explanatory factor, critical race theory might discount other equally important factors. Further, the reliance on personal narrative, while purposefully getting away from the scientific method, might disregard other important empirical evidence. Social scientists who depend on sophisticated measuring techniques and statistics are especially suspicious of the narrative form because it is difficult to verify independently.

Critical race theory has some policy implications in the criminal justice system. The first important area to consider is how laws are made. When people are systematically excluded from the lawmaking process, it is almost certain their concerns will be excluded, too. Groups who are able to put their members in positions of power are best able to ensure their value system is encoded into the law. In addition, the wealthy can hire lobbyists and develop educational materials to ensure that their viewpoints are considered in the making of laws.

The challenge, then, is for minorities to see that their values are encoded in the law. This is not as simple as it seems.[95] Take, for instance, the earlier example of crack cocaine. People of color are no more likely than whites to advocate the legalization of crack cocaine. However, they are concerned about the severity of the sentences allocated to crack users and sellers when compared to other substances, especially powder cocaine. When such disparities exist, critical race theorists argue that the law is aimed not at public safety but rather at the social control of marginal groups. Therefore, critical race theorists advocate examining the underlying assumptions behind the law to determine whether a race-related agenda is being implemented throughout the criminal justice system.

Critical race theory recognizes that gains have been made in the legal system regarding racism, but it still considers the task to be incomplete. Structural and sometimes subtle disadvantages based on race are encoded in the law and must be closely examined to see how the criminal justice system can operate more fairly. At one level, this means including minority groups in the criminal justice system at all levels. More important, it means bringing a new awareness to the role of race in the criminal justice system.[96]

This review of conflict and critical theories requires us to consider how the effects of gender, sex, race, color, ethnicity, and sexuality produce offender motivations, as well as reactions by the criminal justice system. The term **intersectionality**

Cleveland, Ohio, city councilman Kevin Conwell (left) with other politicians as Mayor Frank Jackson speaks about a plan to combat gun violence. What is the difference between racial profiling and routine police investigation?

Rep. John Conyers Jr. (left) and Sen. Ben Cardin joined civil rights groups in calling for passage of their legislation, the End Racial Profiling Act. What justification does law enforcement use to explain the over-representation of people of color in the prison system?

intersectionality—A term referring to the intersections of two or more social categorizations such as race, class, color, gender, age, and sex and the added challenges of discrimination faced by individuals at those intersections.

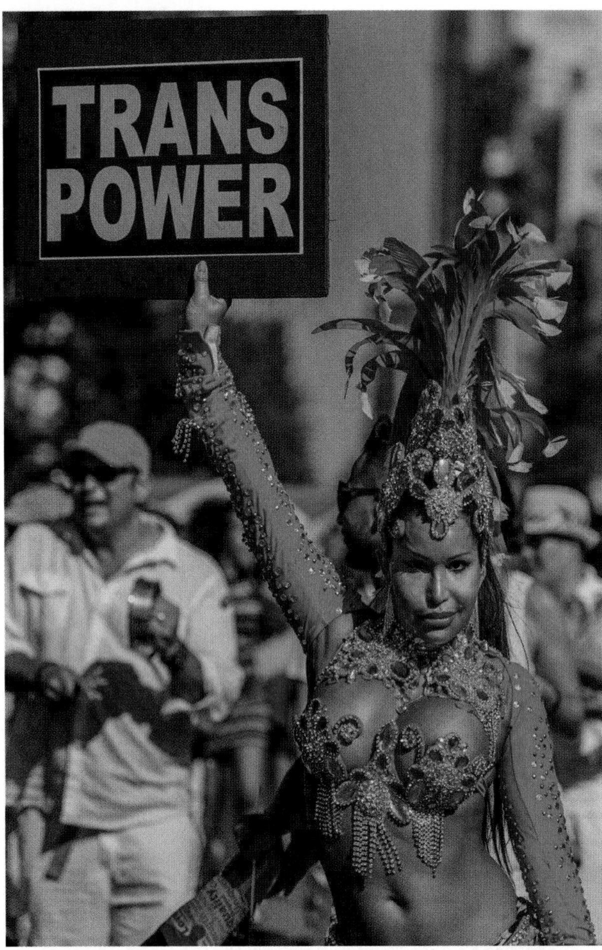

Thousands of people commemorated the 46th anniversary of the first New York City Pride March in 2016 with the largest pride march in the country. How does having more than one minority status compound the challenges a person faces in American society?

encompasses the vulnerabilities of multiple statuses of citizens caught up in the legal system.[97] For example, a woman may be exposed to discrimination within the criminal justice system, but that problem can become more complicated when she is also a racial or ethnic minority, pursues an alternative sexual lifestyle, is impoverished, and/or is considered to be a juvenile.[98]

PAUSE AND REVIEW

1. **What are the four levels to which the peacemaking perspective applies? What traditions does peacemaking draw from?**
2. **Illustrate how feminist criminology approaches women's participation in crime as offenders, victims, and criminal justice practitioners.**
3. **Examine how postmodern criminology uses language to critique how individuals are defined as antisocial.**
4. **Critique the assertion of critical race theory that the criminal justice system and the media are more concerned with offenses against white individuals than those against individuals of color.**
5. **What aspects of culture and the media does cultural criminology critique?**

FOCUS ON ETHICS: An Officer in Field Training

You are a field-training officer for a large police department, and you pride yourself on being a good judge of character. In the past, you have disqualified several potential officers, and history has proven you correct when these individuals got jobs with neighboring police departments and were disciplined or fired for bad behavior. One candidate had a drinking problem. Another had domestic violence issues. And one was just not very bright. The last one resulted in the police department being successfully sued for over $1 million.

Now you have a new recruit who is causing you concern. In many ways, he is an ideal candidate. He has a college education, was a star linebacker in high school, is a military veteran who served with distinction in Afghanistan, and was the top student at the police academy. Now that he is in the patrol car with you on a daily basis, you are seeing a side of him that worries you.

He seems to have a problem with race. When relaxed, he employs racist slurs to refer to every minority group in the city. Additionally, you notice that in encounters with white citizens, he acts with extreme politeness and good humor, whereas with minority citizens he has a cold, official, and sometimes rude or sarcastic tone. You suspect that his military experiences have taught him how to survive in an organization, but you fear that when he is fully certified as a police officer and on the street with minimal supervision, he will be a problem for the department.

He has the demeanor of an adrenaline junkie, and you fear he would use excessive force when dealing with minorities. Also, you suspect he would engage in racial profiling. He has not done anything overtly racist yet, but you have a bad feeling and believe you should do something now to address your concerns before someone is hurt, the department is sued, or he causes a riot.

What Do You Do?

1. Talk to the recruit and tell him you are concerned about his attitudes and behavior and instruct him as to what you expect.
2. Talk to your chief of police and apprise him of your concerns.
3. Declare that the recruit is unfit to become a police officer and fail him on his field training, which would get him fired.
4. Do nothing. The recruit has done nothing illegal, and it is possible that as he becomes a police officer he will become socialized into the proper behavior.

Summary

Learning Objective	Summary
LEARNING OBJECTIVE 1 Define primary deviance and secondary deviance and state how these conditions relate to labeling theory.	Primary deviance occurs when society reacts to an individual's actions, successfully labels that individual, and acts upon that label. Secondary deviance occurs when labeled individuals internalize the label and see themselves as devalued members of society. Labels can become a master status that overwhelms all others. A negative master status can have a detrimental effect on how a person is treated by teachers, parents, society, and the criminal justice system.
LEARNING OBJECTIVE 2 Define social location and discuss its relationship to antisocial behavior.	Social location is the position of an individual within society according to race, sex, class, gender, and age. Individuals may be identified with antisocial behavior, even if they have broken no laws, because of social location. Social location influences status, opportunities, and obligations.
LEARNING OBJECTIVE 3 Understand how conflict theory considers social institutions, especially those rooted in economics and social class, to contribute more to crime than individual antisocial behavior.	Rather than assuming that offenders are inherently antisocial or that they learn to break the law, conflict theory examines how societies control their members and how this may lead to crime. Conflict theory explores the idea that crime stems from competition among interest groups. Power struggles for economic and political dominance affect the definition of crime and enforcement of the law as dominant interest groups impose their values and judgments through their power to write the criminal law.
LEARNING OBJECTIVE 4 Explain who Karl Marx is and describe his contribution to conflict theory.	Karl Marx was a 19th-century German social theorist, philosopher, and economist. According to Marx, unrestricted capitalism causes the lowest social classes to sink into despair, withdraw from society, and depend upon fellow workers or turn to crime. These citizens, called the lumpenproletariat, are characterized by their disorganization, lack of skill, and impoverishment. Conceivably, countries with some form of socialist system would have less crime because people would not live in such dire need.
LEARNING OBJECTIVE 5 List and briefly describe at least three critical theories.	Feminist criminology holds that gender inequality is at the root of offenses in which female persons are the victims or offenders. Peacemaking criminology considers the social and personal effects of crime as a whole, accounting not only for the offender and victim, but also for the social structures that accept, enable, and encourage crime. Cultural criminology examines how social ideas, values, and media reflect and produce antisocial behavior. Like cultural criminology, postmodern criminology focuses on how language and traditional ideas affect how we define and perceive crime, the law, and society. Critical race theory holds that racial inequity is so ingrained in society that it is propagated through legal and social discourse.

Critical Reflections

1. Why is social location important to the perception, legislation, and control of crime?
2. How is critical theory related to conflict theory?
3. Discuss feminist criminology's critique of other criminological theories.
4. How does postmodern criminology critique the use of language in the criminal justice system? How can deconstruction be used to do this?
5. Discuss the limitations and policy implications of peacemaking criminology.
6. Propose a program consistent with cultural criminology that would enable the media to have a greater effect on reducing crime.
7. Explain why racial profiling is a major concern of critical race theory.
8. How is the economic system of capitalism related to crime according to conflict theory?

Key Terms

bourgeoisie p. 211
class p. 208
conflict theory p. 209
critical race theory p. 224
critical theory p. 209
cultural criminology p. 221
feminist criminology p. 216
gender p. 208
intersectionality p. 227
lumpenproletariat p. 211
master status p. 207
patriarchal p. 216
peacemaking criminology p. 218
political p. 209
postmodern criminology p. 223
primary deviance p. 207
proletariat p. 211
race p. 208
racial profiling p. 225
secondary deviance p. 207
sex p. 208
social location p. 208

Instant Recall Terms

antisocial (ch. 1)
classical criminology (ch. 4)
deterrence (ch. 3)
differential association (ch. 6)
labeling theory (ch. 7)
scientific method (ch. 4)
strain theory (ch. 6)

Notes

1 Adrienne Hurst and Camille Darko, "Arbitrary Justice: One Accused Exonerated, the Other Remains Branded," *Injustice Watch*, May 12, 2016, https://www.injusticewatch.org/news/2016/arbitrary-justice-one-accused-exonerated-the-other-remains-branded. The National Registry of Exonerations, Jarrett M. Adams, https://www.law.umich.edu/special/exoneration/Pages/casedetail.aspx?caseid=2980. Elizabeth Chuck and Dan Slepian, "From Defendant to Defender: One Wrongfully Convicted Man Frees Another," NBC News, August 2, 2017, https://www.nbcnews.com/news/us-news/defendant-defender-one-wrongfully-convicted-man-frees-another-n788886. Accessed May 2018.

2 Ibid.

3 Ibid.

4 Ibid.

5 Frank Tannenbaum, *Crime and the Community* (New York: Columbia University Press, 1939), 19.

6 Howard S. Becker, *Outsiders: Studies in the Sociology of Deviance* (New York: Macmillan, 1963).

7 Edwin M. Lemert, *Social Pathology: A Systematic Approach to the Theory of Sociopathic Behavior* (New York: McGraw-Hill, 1951), 17.

8 Thomas J. Bernard, "The Distinction Between Conflict and Radical Criminology," *Journal of Criminal Law and Criminology* 72 (1981): 362–379.

9 Texas Defender Service, *Lethal Indifference: The Fatal Combination of Incompetent Attorneys and Unaccountable Courts* (Austin: Texas Defender Service, 2002), x, http://texasdefender.org/tds-publications. Accessed April 2018.

10 David F. Greenburg, *Crime and Capitalism: Readings in Marxist Criminology* (Palo Alto, CA: Mayfield, 1981), 19.

11 George B. Vold, Thomas J. Bernard, and Jeffrey B. Snipes, *Theoretical Criminology* (New York: Oxford University Press, 2002), 251–252.

12 Friedrich Engles, "Crime in Communist Society" in *Crime and Capitalism: Readings in Marxist Criminology*; Becker, *Outsiders*, 51.

13 Howard Abadinsky, *Organized Crime*, 8th ed. (Belmont, Calif.: Thomson 2007), 35–43.

14 In 1997, I participated in a Fulbright program study tour to China. In one interesting and candid conversation with a Chinese scholar, I asked how long the country could remain communist in light of the pressures of capitalism. The professor told me that although he expected China to continue its rapid move toward capitalism, it was unwise to move too quickly lest the entire system disintegrate as it did in the former Soviet Union. He contended that the only responsible course was to maintain a stable economic system, even as the political system changed.

15 Jonathan H. Turner, *The Structure of Sociological Theory*, 4th ed. (Chicago: Dorsey, 1986).

16 Jack Chang, "Crime Rate Plummets in Brazil's Largest State," *Knight Ridder Tribune*, Washington Bureau (D.C.), December 26, 2007; "Escalating Crime Rate Strangling the Rainbow Ethos," *The Gold Coast Bulletin*, October 7, 2007.

17 William Grimes, "Ralf Dahrendorf, Sociologist, Dies at 80," *New York*

Times, June 22, 2009, https://www.nytimes.com/2009/06/22/world/europe/22dahrendorf.html. Accessed April 2018.

18 Ralf Dahrendorf, *Class and Class Conflict in an Industrial Society* (London: Routledge & Kegan Paul, 1959).

19 Austin T. Turk, *Criminality and the Legal Order* (Chicago: Rand McNally, 1969).

20 David E. Barlow, Melissa H. Barlow, and W. Wesley Johnson, "The Political Economy of Criminal Justice Policy: A Time Series Analysis of Economic Conditions, Crime and Federal Criminal Justice Legislation," *Justice Quarterly* 13 (1996): 223–242.

21 Greenburg, *Crime and Capitalism*; Becker, *Outsiders*, 20.

22 Greenburg, *Crime and Capitalism*, 180.

23 Dragen Milovanovic, "The Political Economy of Liberty and Property Interests," *Legal Studies Forum* 11 (1981): 147–172.

24 Stuart Russell, "The Continuing Relevance of Marxism to Critical Criminology," *Critical Criminology* 11 (2002): 113–135.

25 Mike Callison, "In Search of the High Life: Drugs, Crime, Masculinities and Consumption," *British Journal of Criminology* 36 (1996): 428–444.

26 Federal Bureau of Investigation, Uniform Crime Reports: *Crime in the United States, 2017*, Table 42: Arrests by Sex, 2017, https://ucr.fbi.gov/crime-in-the-u.s/2017/crime-in-the-u.s.-2017/topic-pages/tables/table-42. Rachel E. Morgan and Grace Kena, *Criminal Victimization*, 2016, Table 8, (Washington, D.C.: U.S. Department of Justice Office of Justice Programs Bureau of Justice Statistics, 2006), 9. Online at https://www.bjs.gov/index.cfm?ty=pbdetail&iid=6166. Accessed October 2018.

27 Jody Miller and Christopher W. Mullins, "The Status of Feminist Theories in Criminology," in *Taking Stock: The Status of Criminological Theory*, ed. Francis T. Cullen, John Paul Wright, and Kristie R. Blevins (New Brunswick, N.J.: Transaction Publishers, 2006), 217–249.

28 Alida V. Merlo and Joycelyn M. Pollock, "Sisters in Criminology: The Orgins of Feminist Criminology," in *Sisters in Crime Revisited : Bringing Gender into Criminology*, ed. Francis T. Cullen, Pamela Wilcox, Jennifer L. Lux, and Cheryl Lero Jonson (New York: Oxford University Press, 2015), 17–39.

29 Kevin L. Nadal, Amalia Quintanilla, Ariana Goswick, and Julie Sriken, "Lesbian, Gay, Bisexual, and Queer People's Perceptions of the Criminal Justice System: Implications for Social Services," *Journal of Gay and Lesbian Services* 27, no. 4 (2015): 457–481.

30 Samantha S. Clinkinbeard and Timothy C. Barnum, "Gendered Self-Concepts and Drinking Behavior in a National Sample of Emerging Adults," *Feminist Criminology* 12, no. 2 (2017): 145.

31 Meda Chesney-Lind and Nicholas Chagnon, "Criminology, Gender, and Race: A Case Study of Privilege in the Academy," *Feminist Criminology* 11, no. 4 (October 2016): 311–333.

32 Betty Friedan, *The Feminine Mystique* (New York: W. W. Norton, 2001).

33 Judith Nies, "Elizabeth Cady Stanton," in *Seven Women: Portraits from the American Radical Tradition* (New York: Penguin Books, 1977), 33–61.

34 Candace Kruttschnitt, Rosemary Gartner, and Amy Miller, "Doing Her Own Time? Women's Responses to Prison in the Context of the Old and the New Penology," *Criminology* 38, no. 1 (2000): 681–717.

35 Emma Sleath and Lisa L. Smith, "Understanding the Factors that Predict Victim Retraction in Police Reported Allegations of Intimate Partner Violence," *Psychology of Violence* 7, no. 1 (January 2017): 140–149.

36 Daniel W. Webster, Shannon Frattaroli, Jon S. Vernick, Chris O'Sullivan, Janice Roehl, and Jacquelyn C. Campbell, "Women with Protective Orders Report Failure to Remove Firearms from Their Abusive Partners: Results from an Exploratory Study," *Journal of Women's Health* 19, no. 1 (January 2010): 93–98. Anne O'Dell, "Why Do Police Arrest Victims of Domestic Violence? The Need for Comprehensive Training and Investigative Protocols," *Journal of Aggression, Maltreatment & Trauma* 15, no. 3/4 (December 2007): 53–73. Carolyn M. West, "Sorry, We Have to Take You In: Black Battered Women Arrested for Intimate Partner Violence," *Journal of Aggression, Maltreatment & Trauma* 15, no. 3/4 (December 2007): 95–121. Murray A. Straus, Richard J. Gelles, and Suzanne Steinmetz, *Behind Closed Doors: Violence in the American Family* (Garden City, N.Y.: Anchor Books, 1980).

37 Rosemarie Skaine, *Power and Gender: Issues in Sexual Dominance and Harassment* (Jefferson, N.C.: McFarland & Company, 1996), 91–99. Rebecca Campbell, Sharon M. Wasco, Courtney E. Ahrens, Tracy Sefl, and Holly E. Barnes, "Preventing the Second Rape," *Journal of Interpersonal Violence* 16, no. 12 (2001): 1239–1259. Diana Russell, *The Politics of Rape* (New York: Stein and Day, 1975).

38 U.S. Department of Justice, National Institute of Corrections, Women as Correctional Officers in Men's Maximum Security Facilities: A Survey of the Fifty States, July 1991, https:// static.nicic.gov/Library/009504.pdf. Accessed April 2018.

39 M. Kay Harris, "Moving into the New Millennium: Towards a Feminist Vision of Justice," in *Criminology as Peacemaking*, ed. Harold E. Pepinsky and Richard Quinney (Bloomington: University of Indiana Press, 1991), 83–97.

40 James W. Messerschmidt and Stephen Tomsen, "Masculinities and Crime," in *Sisters in Crime Revisited: Bringing Gender into Criminology*, ed. Francis T. Cullen, Pamela Wilcox, Jennifer L. Lux, and Cheryl Lero Jonson (New York: Oxford University Press, 2015), 281–301.

41 John R. Fuller, *Criminal Justice: A Peacemaking Perspective* (Boston: Allyn & Bacon, 1998).

42 Richard Quinney, *Bearing Witness to Crime and Social Justice* (Albany: State University of New York Press, 2000).

43 U.S. homicide rates are typically higher than those of comparable nations, such as those of western Europe. See "Determining Trends in Global Crime and Justice: An Overview of Results from the United Nations Surveys of Crime Trends and Operations of Criminal Justice Systems," *Forum on Crime and Society* 3, nos. 1–2 (December 2003): 44–45, https://www.ncjrs.gov/App/Publications/abstract.aspx?ID=207372. Accessed April 2018.

44 Christopher Williams, "Toward a Transevaluation of Criminal 'Justice': On Vengeance, Peacemaking, and Punishment," *Humanity and Society* 26 (2002): 101–116.

45 Pepinsky and Quinney, *Criminology as Peacemaking*.

46 Michael Braswell, John Fuller, and Bo Lozoff, *Corrections, Peacemaking, and Restorative Justice: Transforming Individuals and Institutions* (Cincinnati, Ohio: Anderson Publishing, 2001). See especially Chapter 2, "Compassionate Correcting: Contributions of Ancient Wisdom Traditions," 11–27.

47 Kevin Anderson, "Radical Criminology and the Overcoming of Alienation: Perspectives from Marxian and Gandhian Humanism" in *Criminology as Peacemaking*, ed. Pepinsky and Quinney.

48 Bo Lozoff and Michael Braswell, *Inner Corrections* (Cincinnati, Ohio: Anderson Publishers, 1989).

49 Erich Fromm, ed., *Socialist Humanism* (New York: Doubleday, 1965).

50 Robert Agnew, "Society Needs to Get Tough on Causes of Crime, Says Agnew," *Emory Report* 50, no. 28 (April 13, 1998), https://www.emory.edu/EMORY_REPORT/erarchive/1998/April/erapril.13/4_13_98FirstPerson.html. Accessed May 2018.

51 Ngaire Naffine, *Feminism and Criminology* (Philadelphia: Temple University Press, 1996).

52 Christy Vicher, "Gender, Police Arrest Decisions, and Notions of Chivalry," *Criminology* 21 (1983): 5–28.

53 Jeff Farrell and Clinton R. Sanders, "Culture, Crime, and Criminology," in *Cultural Criminology*, ed. Jeff Ferrell and Clinton R. Sanders (Boston: Northeastern University Press, 1995), 3–25.

54 Gregg Barak, "Newsmaking Criminology: Reactions on the Media, Intellectuals, and Crime," *Justice Quarterly* 5 (1988): 573.

55 Louis Kontos and David C. Brotherton, *Encyclopedia of Gangs* (Santa Barbara, Calif.: Greenwood Press, 2007). Jody A. Miller, "Struggles over the Symbolic: Gang Style and the Meanings of Social Control," in *Cultural Criminology*, ed. Ferrell and Sanders, 213–234.

56 Robert Hornik and Lela Jacobsohn, "The Best Laid Plans: Disappointments of the

National Youth Anti-Drug Media Campaign, " *LDI Issue Brief* 14, no. 2 (December 2008): 1–4. Craig Reinarman and Harry G. Levine, "Crack in Context: Politics and Media in the Making of a Drug Scare," *Contemporary Drug Problems* 16 (1989): 535–578.

57 Ronald Smothers, "As Olympics Approach, Homeless Are Not Feeling at Home in Atlanta," *New York Times*, July 1, 1996, A8.

58 Jessica Kartalija, "Skateboarding Banned in Much of Eastern Shore Town," *WJZ*, August 15, 2007, http://wesm913.org/post/skateboarding-banned-much-eastern-shore-town. Accessed April 2018.

59 Peter B. Kraska and Victor E. Kappeler, "Militarizing American Police: The Rise and Normalization of Paramilitary Units," *Social Problems* 1 (1997): 1–17.

60 Peter B. Kraska, "Militarization and Policing: Its Relevance to 21st Century Police," *Policing: A Journal of Policy and Practice* 1, no. 4 (2007): 501–513.

61 Bruce Arrigo, "Media Madness as a Crime in the Making: On O. J. Simpson, Cultural Icons, and Hyper-Reality," in *Representing O. J.: Murder, Criminal Justice, and Mass Culture*, ed. Gregg Barak (New York: Harrow and Heston, 1996), 123–136.

62 Ray Surette, *Media, Crime and Criminal Justice: Images, Realities, and Policies* (Belmont, CA: Wadsworth, 2006).

63 Bruce A. Arrigo, "Postmodern Justice and Critical Criminology: Positional, Relational, and Provisional Science," in *Controversies in Critical Criminology*, ed. Martin D. Schwartz and Suzanne E. Hatty (Cincinnati, Ohio: Anderson, 2003), 43–55.

64 Abraham S. Blumberg, "The Practice of Law as a Confidence Game," *Law and Society Review* (June 1, 1967): 15–39.

65 Jerome Skolnick, *Justice Without Trial: Law Enforcement in a Democratic Society*, 3rd ed. (New York: Macmillan, 1994).

66 Bruce Arrigo, *The Contours of Psychiatric Justice: A Postmodern Critique of Mental Illness, Criminal Insanity, and the Law* (New York: Garland, 1996).

67 Martin D. Schwartz and David O. Friedrichs, "Postmodern Thought and Criminological Discontent: New Metaphors for Understanding Violence," *Criminology* 32 (1994): 221–246.

68 Ebony O. McGee and David Stovall, "Reimagining Critical Race Theory in Education: Mental Health, Healing, and the Pathway to Liberatory Praxis," *Educational Theory* 65, no. 5 (2015): 491–511.

69 Kathryn K. Russell, "Critical Race Theory and Social Justice," in *Social Justice, Criminal Justice*, ed. Bruce Arrigo (Belmont, Calif.: Wadsworth, 1999), 178–188.

70 Richard Delgado and Jean Stefanic, eds., *Critical Race Theory: The Cutting Edge* (Philadelphia: Temple University Press, 1995), xiv.

71 Gloria Ladson-Billings, "Just What Is Critical Race Theory and What's It Doing in a Nice Field Like Education?" *International Journal of Qualitative Studies in Education* 11 (1998): 7–24.

72 Kimberle Williams Crenshaw, "Race, Reform, and Retrenchment: Transformation and Legitimation in Anti-Discrimination Law," *Harvard Law Review* 101, no. 7 (May 1988): 1331–1387.

73 Barbara Jeanne Fields, "Slavery, Race, and Ideology in the United States of America," *New Life Review* 181 (1991): 113–114.

74 Delgado and Stefanic, *Critical Race Theory: The Cutting Edge*.

75 Molly A. Schiffer, "Women of Color and Crime: A Critical Race Theory Perspective to Address Disparate Prosecution," *Arizona Law Review* 56, no. 4 (December 2014): 1203–1225.

76 Patricia Williams, *The Alchemy of Race and Rights* (Cambridge, Mass.: Harvard University Press, 1991).

77 Dorothy Roberts, "Making Reproduction a Crime,"in *The Reproductive Rights Reader: Law, Medicine, and the Construction of Motherhood*, ed. Nancy Ehrenreich (New York: New York University Press, 2008), 374–375.

78 Dorothy E. Roberts, "Punishing Drug Addicts Who Have Babies: Women of Color, Equality, and the Right of Privacy," in *Critical Race Theory: The Key Writings That Formed the Movement*, ed. Kemberle Crenshaw, Neil Gotanda, Gary Peller, and Kendall Thomas (New York: The New Press, 1995), 384–385.

79 Charles R. Epp, Steven Maynard-Moody, and Donald Haider-Markel, "Beyond Profiling: The Institutional Sources of Racial Disparities in Policing," *Public Administration Review* 77, no. 2: (2017): 168–178.

80 Robert Higgs, "Case Western University Apologizes after Officers Demanded Councilman Kevin Conwell Produce ID While He Walked Through Campus," Cleveland.com, March 14, 2018. http://www.cleveland.com/metro/index.ssf/2018/03/case_western_reserve_universit_88.html. Accessed May 2018.

81 Adam Ferrise, "Case Western Reserve Student Called about Panhandler Prior to Officer Stopping Cleveland Councilman Kevin Conwell," Cleveland.com, March 15, 2018, http://www.cleveland.com/metro/index.ssf/2018/03/case_western_reserve_student_c.html. Accessed May 2018.

82 Donna Leinwand, "Lawmakers Consider Lessening Crack Penalties; Federal Guidelines Require Heavier Sentences Than for Powder Cocaine," *USA Today*, March 12, 2007, 4A.

83 This term was coined by PBS news anchor Gwen Ifill at the 2004 Unity: Journalists of Color conference. See the clip at C-SPAN at https://www.c-span.org/video/?c4666788/gwen-ifill-coins-term-missing-white-woman-syndrome. Accessed May 2018.

84 Peter Downs, "Paying More Attention to White Crime Victims," *American Journalism Review*, December 1995, http://ajrarchive.org/Article.asp?id=2016. Accessed May 2018.

85 Zach Sommers, "Missing White Woman Syndrome: An Empirical Analysis of Race and Gender Disparities in Online News Coverage of Missing Persons," *Journal of Criminal Law & Criminology* 106 (2016), https://scholarlycommons.law.northwestern.edu/jclc/vol106/iss2/4. Accessed May 2018.

86 Mark Memmott, "Missing Pregnant Woman Found Dead," *USA Today*, August 22, 2005, 3A.

87 Stephen J. Lee, "Investigator Who Led Search for Dru Sjodin Urges Larger Focus on Victims," *Grand Forks Herald*, June 13, 2007.

88 Christine Hauser, "Suspect Charged in Death of a Woman Who Vanished in Florida," *New York Times*, January 16, 2008, https://www.nytimes.com/2008/01/16/nyregion/16missing.html. Accessed May 2018.

89 David Ovalle, "No Body, but Plenty of Evidence in Miami-Dade Murder Case," *Miami Herald*, November 12, 2015, http://www.miamiherald.com/news/local/crime/article44499969.html. Accessed May 2018.

90 Mark Memmott, "Spotlight Skips Cases of Missing Minorities," *USA Today*, June 16, 2005, final edition, 6A.

91 Alexander Morrison, "Jailhouse Interview: Tamika Huston's Killer: No More Secrets," GoUpstate.com/*Spartanburg Herald-Journal*, March 28, 2017, http://www.goupstate.com/news/20050816/jailhouse-interview-tamika-hustons-killer-no-more-secrets. Accessed May 2018.

92 Alexandra Marks, "More Equity in Cocaine Sentencing," *Christian Science Monitor*, November 2, 2007, https://www.csmonitor.com/2007/1102/p01s02-usju.html. Accessed April 2018.

93 Carol Cratty, "New Rules Slashing Crack Cocaine Sentences Go into Effect," CNN, https://www.cnn.com/2011/11/01/justice/crack-cocaine-sentencing/index.html. Accessed May 2018.

94 Terry Frieden, "House Passes Bill to Reduce Disparity in Cocaine Penalties," CNN, July 28, 2010, http://www.cnn.com/2010/POLITICS/07/28/house.drug.penalties/index.html. Accessed April 2018.

95 Neil Gotanda, "A Critique of Our Constitution Is Color-Blind," in *Critical Race Theory: The Key Writings That Formed the Movement*, ed. Kemberle Crenshaw, Neil Gotanda, Gary Peller, and Kendall Thomas (New York: The New Press, 1995).

96 Barbara Hudson, "Beyond White Man's Justice: Race, Gender, and Justice in Late Modernity," *Theoretical Criminology* 10, no. 1 (February 1, 2006): 29–47.

97 Elizabeth Webster and Jody Miller, "Gendering and Racing Wrongful Conviction: Intersectionality 'Normal Crimes,' and Women's Experiences of Miscarriage of Justice," *Albany Law Review* 78, no. 3 (2015): 973.

98 Stacy De Coster and Karen Heimer, "Choice Within Constraint: An Explanation of Crime at the Intersections," *Theoretical Criminology* 21, no. 1 (2017): 11–22.

PART III

Typologies of Crime

Property Offenses

FEATURES

Edwin Rist stole the skins of birds like this resplendent quetzal. What other rare but valuable commodities are of interest in illegal underground markets?

Edwin Rist, pictured in 2011, admitted stealing rare bird skins from the British Natural History Museum. Rist, then 22, pleaded guilty to burglary and money laundering when he appeared at court. Why did Rist steal these priceless bird skins?

In 2009, a 20-year-old American flute player, Edwin Rist, committed one of the weirdest burglaries ever. Rist broke into the poorly guarded British Natural History Museum and stole the skins of 299 rare birds. The collection that Rist raided, which represented 95 percent of all known living species, contained more than 750,000 bird skins, some collected nearly 350 years ago. Some of the important birds were rather drab, but Rist was not after these. He wanted the rarest and most colorful ones, the ones with feathers that cannot be collected any longer because the birds are endangered. By the time Rist exited the museum, he was carrying $1 million worth of bird skins.[1]

Rist was certainly a connoisseur of feathers, but he was in it for the money, too. The brilliant feathers of rare and endangered birds fetch a high price among expert fly-tyers, people who tie fishing flies. Many fly-tyers have no interest in fishing. They simply want to tie the most elaborate fishing flies they can. Many fly-tyers, if not most, insist that this cannot be done with artificial feathers. They are convinced that they can only achieve the ultimate fishing flies with the feathers of birds so rare that their feathers are nearly unobtainable.[2]

An obsessive fly-tyer himself, Rist began parting out the skins and selling the feathers almost immediately. Before law enforcement caught up with Rist, he apparently managed to destroy about 100 of the irreplaceable skins, making about $166,000 from the sale of feathers. He told authorities he planned to spend the money on himself and buy a better flute. Of the 299 birds stolen, 191 undamaged birds were recovered. Sentenced in Britain, Rist received a 12-month suspended jail sentence, 12 months' probation, and he was ordered to pay back the money.[3]

The Value of Property

LEARNING OBJECTIVE | 1

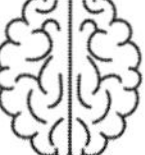

Discuss the major distinction between property offenses and personal violent offenses.

Individuals value their private property and go to great lengths to protect it. The major distinction between property offenses and personal violent offenses has to do with the elements of fear and danger. Property offenders typically do not use intimidation or physical violence as part of their method of breaking the law but, instead, are more concerned about avoiding detection and recognition. Feather-thief Edwin Rist spent months casing the museum and took photographs of the bird skins that he planned to steal.[4]

Most criminal offenses in the United States are **property offenses**, that is, offenses that are perpetrated without personal violence and that are focused on the entering, taking, or destruction of structures, motor vehicles, or goods. In 2016, nearly 8 million property offenses were reported to law enforcement.[5] Although this number seems high, it actually represents a reduction in property offenses over each of the four previous years (see Figure 9.1). Nevertheless, property offenses are frequent enough to be expensive, costing the public an estimated $15 billion in lost property in 2016.[6]

In many ways, the amount of property that Americans possess reflects their social status and

---

property offense—A criminal offense perpetrated without personal violence and focused on the entering, taking, or destruction of structures, motor vehicles, or goods.

TABLE 9.1 Criminological Theory and Property Crime

Classical strain theory	The category of *innovator* in Merton's strain theory captures the motivation of those who have accepted the goal of the American dream of financial gain but have rejected the culturally approved means of hard work. The burglar or the thief aspires to have material goods and money but is not willing to work for either. Therefore, taking the property of others is an alternative means of achieving financial gain.
Critical theory	A number of critical theories can be used to explain property offending. Traditional Marxist theory states that those who control the means of production manipulate the system to increase and extend their wealth. Theft and burglary are two ways that those who do not have power can achieve the means of survival. The theory of left realism explains that impoverished people victimize other impoverished people. Left realism advocates economic policies that alleviate poverty and allow everyone the opportunity to make a legitimate living.
Psychological theory	For some offenders the risk of taking other people's property presents opportunities for thrills. These thrills range from the joyriding of teenagers who steal cars to the deep psychological needs present in kleptomaniacs who steal without understanding exactly why. Many kleptomaniacs take things they do not need despite having enough money to pay for them, risking their reputation and standing in society.

power. Although many people desire financial security, this goal runs a distant second place to what sociologist Thorstein Veblen called "conspicuous consumption."[7] Although comfort and convenience are a couple of reasons that Americans have so much stuff, a more interesting explanation is that the display of property helps to establish social standing in the community. We need only look at the vast quantities of expensive clothing, cars, phones, and a host of other articles and gadgets that people buy not for their utility but, rather, for their display value. It should not surprise us, then, that what people value is coveted by others. When items are conspicuously displayed to establish social standing and identity, those articles become desired by others. Both expensive and inexpensive items are the targets of those who would rather steal than expend their own financial resources or who do not have the financial resources to buy what they want. At least three types of criminological theory can explain why people commit property offenses (see Table 9.1).

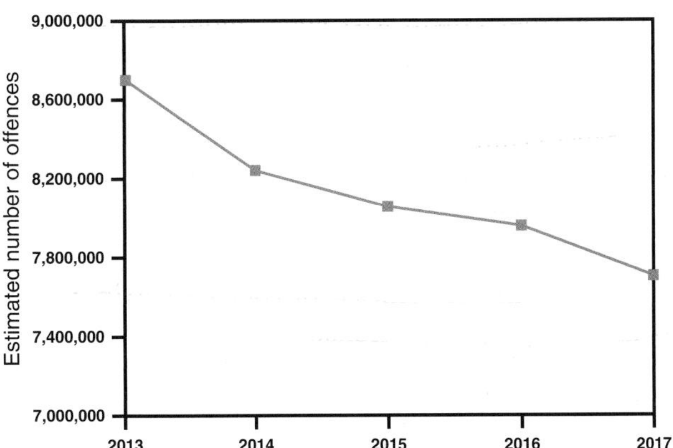

FIGURE 9.1 Property Offenses, 2013–2017

Property offenses have steadily declined for the last five years. Can you think of factors that have caused this decline?

Source: Federal Bureau of Investigation, Uniform Crime Reports, Crime in the United States, 2017, *https://ucr.fbi.gov/crime-in-the-u.s/2017/crime-in-the-u.s.-2017/topic-pages/property-crime. Accessed October 2018.*

PAUSE AND REVIEW

1. **What is it about the American attitude toward property that contributes to property offending?**
2. **What is the major distinction between property offenses and personal violent offenses?**
3. **What criminological theories can be used to explain property crimes?**

Burglary

LEARNING OBJECTIVE | 2

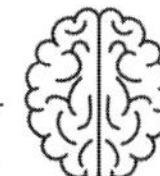

Understand how larceny is different from burglary and robbery.

The FBI defines **burglary** as the unlawful entry of a structure with the intent to commit a felony or theft. For purposes of reporting, the Uniform Crime Reports (UCR) has three subcategories of burglary: forcible entry, unlawful entry in which no force is used, and attempted forcible entry.[8] The UCR defines structures as not only homes, but also apartments, barns, house trailers, houseboats when used as a permanent dwelling, offices, railroad cars, stables, and water-going vessels. The offense of burglary includes not only the unlawful entry of a structure, but also the offender's intent to commit a felony or theft. Recall that because of the FBI's **hierarchy rule**, the UCR only records the most serious offense in a set of offenses. So, if a burglar breaks into a dwelling and commits a rape, the rape is recorded but not the burglary. If a burglary includes a theft, which is lower on the hierarchy, then the burglary is reported. Therefore, the burglaries reported in the UCR represent theft rather than murder, rape, robbery, or aggravated assault. Many of the more serious violent offenses recorded in the UCR also include burglary, but those burglaries were not reported because they are the less serious offense.

Burglary is an offense most individuals fear because it often happens when they are away from their property. To have someone break into your home while you are at work or on vacation is frightening. However, it is even more terrifying if someone breaks into your home at night when you are there asleep. Burglary, therefore, includes three violations of an individual's comfort zone. The first is having someone enter your property without your permission, perhaps by using force to break a window, kick in a door, or destroy a lock. The second violation, if the burglar's intent is theft, is the taking of personal possessions. The taking of an expensive television, jewelry, or intimate personal items is not only an economic loss, but it can also be personally devastating. Finally, if the burglary happens while the resident is home, the potential for other victimizations such as assault, murder, or rape makes it even more serious. Therefore, the analysis of burglary requires us also to consider its emotional and psychological effect on victims.[9]

It should not be surprising that most dwellings are burglarized when the occupants are away. More than half of all residential burglaries for which the time of offense is known, about 51 percent, happen during the day. When we consider the type of building, it is clear that the absence of occupants is even more important. Of non-residential burglaries in which the time of the offense is known, most occurred at night.[10] Therefore, it is clear that burglars are, for the most part, careful to break into buildings when they are reasonably confident that guardians are not present.

As devastating as a burglary can be, it lacks much of the danger and fear that accompany violent personal offenses. The burglar-thief is interested in avoiding confrontation with the victim and will carefully select targets and strike when it appears no one is around. Burglars also may not be carrying weapons, which makes the offense somewhat less problematic for the offender, victim, and criminal justice system than many types of violent personal offenses.

The number of burglaries in the United States is staggering. In 2017, 1.4 million burglaries were reported.[11]

Burglaries are not evenly distributed. They are more likely to happen in large metropolitan areas than in rural or small towns. These distribution patterns can be explained in several ways. First, the anonymity afforded in major metropolitan areas allows burglars not only to find targets of opportunity because of the dense population, but also to escape detection because the large number of people in metropolitan areas makes it easier for burglars to escape recognition. Second, since people can be relatively anonymous in metropolitan areas, the burglar is less likely to have to account for ill-gotten gains to neighbors or police. In small towns, where people live in more intimate settings, a burglar might have a more difficult time explaining or selling stolen property.[12]

Burglars commit their offenses for several reasons. It is important to understand these motivations because burglaries are usually not the result of impulse and opportunity. They are not crimes of passion in which the motivation is spontaneous, based on arguments or on opportunities in which someone has left their property unguarded. Rather, burglaries are usually the result of premeditation and planning.

burglary—The unlawful entry of a structure with the intent to commit a felony or theft.

Instant Recall from Chapter 2 **hierarchy rule** —The Federal Bureau of Investigation's practice of recording in the Uniform Crime Reports only the most serious offense in a set of offenses.

Often, a great deal of effort goes into the selection of targets, including place and time of day, based on the potential for stealing valuable items and the lack of close monitoring in terms of owners being present, security cameras, or police patrols. Malcolm X, the political activist and civil rights leader who led an antisocial lifestyle until his incarceration in 1946 for robbery, provides an interesting look at burglars' attitudes and approaches to their craft in the mid-20th century:

> Burglary, properly executed, though it had its dangers, offered the maximum chances of success with the minimum risk. If you did your job so that you never met any of your victims, it first lessened your chances of having to attack or perhaps kill someone. And if through some slip-up you were caught, later, by the police, there was never a positive eye-witness. It is also important to select an area of burglary and stick to that. There are specific specialities [sic] among burglars. Some work apartments only, others houses only, others stores only, or warehouses; still others will go after only safes or strongboxes. Within the residence burglary category, there are further specialty distinctions. There are the day burglars, the dinner- and theater-time burglars, the night burglars. I think that any city's police will tell you that very rarely do they find one type who will work at another time. For instance Jumpsteady, in Harlem, was a nighttime apartment specialist. It would have been hard to persuade Jumpsteady to work in the daytime if a millionaire had gone out for lunch and left his front door wide open.[13]

Musicians Tariq Trotter (otherwise known as "Black Thought") and Ahmir Thompson (otherwise known as "Questlove") arrive at the Schomberg Center for Research in Black Culture to commemorate the 40th anniversary of Malcolm X's death. Why was burglary the crime of choice for the young Malcolm X?

Although this passage describes incidents that occurred more than 70 years ago, little about successful burglary methods has changed. Sloppy burglars who leave evidence behind or who do not adequately research security systems are soon arrested. However, careful, attentive burglars can ply their trade for years and, if incarcerated, often continue once released from prison. For instance, Blane Nordahl, whose story we read at the beginning of Chapter 7, burglarized only wealthy neighborhoods, stealing only items crafted of sterling silver. Nordahl has given many explanations for why he continues to engage in burglary even after being captured several times.[14] His explanations are reflected in the following reasons burglars commit their offense.

- Financial reward. Burglars break into places mainly to steal money, tools, and other types of valuable property. They may keep the items for themselves, give them to friends and family, or attempt to sell them through a fence (a person who specializes in selling stolen goods). Those who make their living as burglars often have a plan for disposing of the goods in ways that convert them to cash.
- Lack of legitimate opportunities. Some burglars steal to supplement their income because they have low-paying jobs or are unemployed. Some would not engage in this activity if they could meet their needs in more legitimate ways. They see burglary as a part-time and episodic activity that allows them to obtain discretionary funds for parties, gifts, and items that would normally be outside their purchasing range, such as large-screen televisions or expensive jewelry.
- Thrill-seeking. Monetary gain is not the primary motivation for some burglars. Instead, some break into buildings because they can. They get a certain pride of craftsmanship and thrill from overcoming security devices, locks, and other target-hardening efforts. Individuals who identify themselves as professional burglars often see challenges in taking down what guardians consider to be secure buildings. The prospect of getting caught in the act of burglarizing is more of an inducement than a deterrent to thrill-seeking burglars. Thrill-seeking burglars are few, but they can demonstrate an impressive level of skill. In his research on property-crime offenders, sociologist Kenneth Tunnell identifies one motive as "crime is sport." The burglar motivated by this idea considers a successful break-in a form of winning. According to Tunnell, "Successfully completing a crime provided them with a

sense of accomplishment and purpose, and reinforced their belief that they had 'won the game.'" Furthermore, "Whenever they were arrested and convicted, they simply admitted to having lost the game, but only temporarily."[15]

- Sexual deviance. This type of burglar has a fetish for certain objects and breaks into dwellings to steal them. Such burglars are rare, but their motivations make them particularly interesting to the press. The most notable fetish burglars are men who break into women's homes and steal articles of clothing, particularly underwear or shoes, that they keep as part of a trophy collection that constitutes a sexual stimulus.[16]
- Lifestyle. For some burglars, the decision to break the law is part of their street-culture lifestyle. Although they engage in various other offenses, such as larceny and drug dealing, these offenders use burglary as a preferred method of "keeping up appearances" before their peer group. They are heavily active in partying, drug use, alcohol, and sexual exploits. According to researchers Richard Wright and Scott Decker, such burglars treat every night as a Saturday night in which the pursuit of pleasure is paramount. Burglary simply gives them the means to engage in their hedonistic pursuits and provides them with the "street cred" their peer group values. Wright and Decker found that even though the proceeds from burglary were often used for paying bills, they were as likely spent on status symbols such as clothes, cars, and especially drugs. Finally, the influence of peer pressure in a juvenile gang also fits under the lifestyle motivation for committing burglary. Some gangs work as a group in burglarizing homes and businesses, and it is difficult, if not impossible, for a gang member to opt out.[17]
- Revenge. In one study, about 30 percent of the burglars interviewed reported committing their offenses for revenge. These burglars were usually under age 25 and came from dysfunctional homes. Instead of taking the victim's possessions, they vandalized the victim's home to avenge real or imagined slights based on racial discrimination or because someone had "snitched."[18]

Instant Recall from Chapter 3 **deterrence** —The idea that punishment for an offense will prevent that offender and others from further breaking the law.

larceny—The unlawful taking of property from another person.

Not all buildings have an equal chance of being burglarized. A great deal of consideration goes into deciding which buildings, either residential or business, are the best candidates for a burglary. The selection of the target is a good example of the classical school of criminology's focus on **deterrence**. Burglars weigh the risk of getting caught against the potential reward for successfully completing the offense. Therefore, in order to fully understand why burglars select one building over another, we must consider the calculus they use to evaluate potential targets.

Researchers have interviewed professional burglars to determine how they decide which dwellings to burglarize. According to Wright and Decker, burglars consider five characteristics of potential targets.

1. Occupancy. Burglars will determine whether anyone is in the building at the time they wish to break in. As we have learned, most residential burglaries occur in the daytime when no one is home, and most business burglaries occur at night when businesses are closed. One of the hallmarks of a successful burglary is stealth, and the risk of getting caught because someone is present is usually considered too great. Therefore, burglars ascertain that a dwelling is unoccupied before attempting an offense.
2. A location not easily observed. Dwellings that are well off the street or surrounded by trees and bushes are more likely to be broken into than those that are easily seen from the street or neighboring houses. Crime prevention specialists advise homeowners to trim bushes and install motion-detecting lights to deter potential burglars.
3. Location in a neighborhood where the burglar will not stand out. Burglars will bypass neighborhoods where they will stand out because of their race, attire, or car. Police officers look for individuals who do not fit the profile of neighborhood residents. This is especially true in upscale neighborhoods or gated communities where potential burglars would have a hard time explaining their presence.
4. Accessibility. Burglars will evaluate a home or business to determine how easy it would be to break into. Key considerations are the type of locks on the doors and windows, the presence or absence of security systems, and other considerations such as a barking dog. Burglars will

bypass these types of targets in favor of those that appear more accessible.

5. Presence of items worth stealing. The home or business must show the potential to contain items that can be converted into cash. Homes in more prosperous neighborhoods are more attractive targets than run-down homes in disadvantaged areas of the city. Cash, jewelry, electronic items, expensive tools, and silverware are attractive targets for burglars and are more likely to be found in upscale homes. However, there is a delicate balance between the attractiveness of a target and the security with which it is surrounded. Dwellings with items worth stealing are often the least accessible.[19]

Even though this list of target characteristics makes it appear that burglars act rationally and logically, this is not always the case. Often, they spontaneously select homes or businesses for burglary based on many factors. A burglar may make a quick decision to burglarize a dwelling because it is unlocked and unoccupied. With virtually no forethought, the offender may see this target of opportunity and strike quickly.[20] Another reason to break into a dwelling without a plan is that the burglars are under the influence of drugs or alcohol and are incapable of doing the careful calculations they would undertake if they were sober.[21] Sometimes they get lucky and are successful in completing the burglary, but sometimes they are so clumsy and careless they get caught in the act, leave abundant clues that can lead to their detection, or even fall asleep in the middle of the offense.

Criminologists consider several issues when researching burglary in order to detect patterns and develop plans for prevention. One criterion of recent interest to researchers is the distance between a burglar's home and the target. By looking at the distance a burglar travels, the mode of transportation, and the social similarities and differences between the burglar's and victim's neighborhoods, criminologists aim to develop a better understanding of where and how burglaries are committed.

Some intriguing patterns show up when we consider where offenders choose to commit their offenses: various neighborhood characteristics can attract crime.[22] In the case of burglary, some of these characteristics are the number of retail stores in the area, accessibility by public transportation, and similarities in racial and ethnic makeup between neighborhood residents and potential burglars. Burglary can be a simple offense with clear evidence for why it is committed, but it can also be viewed in a much more sophisticated manner that reveals the motivational and logistical factors that make it such a popular offense.[23]

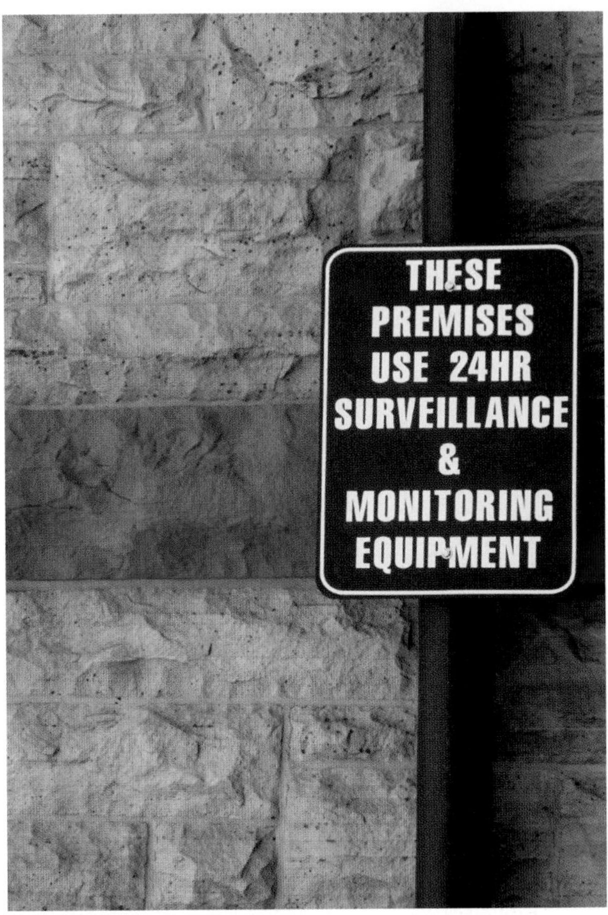

Sign providing a warning to would-be thieves. What other steps can be taken to deter burglars?

PAUSE AND REVIEW

1. **List the three subcategories of burglary.**
2. **Name the five characteristics of potential targets that burglars look for.**

Larceny and Fraud

LEARNING OBJECTIVE | 3

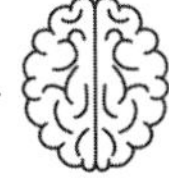

Describe how check fraud and credit card theft are forms of theft.

Larceny is the legal term for theft, which is the unlawful taking of property from another person. The UCR, which refers to the offense as "larceny/theft," defines it as "the unlawful taking, carrying, leading, or riding away of property from the possession or constructive possession of another."[24] Examples are thefts of bicycles, motor vehicle parts, and accessories; shoplifting; pocket-picking; and the stealing of any property or article such as money or jewelry that is not taken by force or fraud. Robbery differs from theft in that it requires the use of or threat of violence. Burglary requires only that a structure be entered with the intent to commit an offense. As we discuss larceny, we will begin to appreciate the many different ways in which people steal and the vast quantities of property they take.

Of all reported offenses, larceny is the most common. More than 5.5 million larcenies were reported in the United States during 2017.[25] Although this statistic is distressing, it is important to realize that there are other offenses much more harmful than larceny. Robbery, rape, and murder are relatively rare compared to larceny and cause injury, death, and fear. This is not to diminish the seriousness of larceny, but only to put it into perspective.

The criminal code recognizes two types of larceny. The first, petit (pronounced petty) larceny, usually includes the theft of items worth $50 or less. The second, grand larceny, has an almost unlimited price tag.[26] There are also two types of thieves: **opportunistic thieves** and **professional thieves.** The opportunistic thief will pick up something that is temporarily left unguarded. Typically, these thieves do not consider themselves as lawbreakers but as simply taking advantage of a situation. Opportunistic thieves tend to take expensive property and often know the people they steal from.

A professional thief is a more serious offender. This person attempts to make a living from larceny and may specialize in a particular form, such as pocket-picking, shoplifting, or breaking into automobiles. The professional thief has honed his or her skills enough to steal on a regular basis without being detected or causing physical harm. Professionals may steal so much merchandise that they must work with another professional in order to fence the goods. Although relatively few in number, professional thieves account for a great deal of the property stolen each year in the United States.

opportunistic thief—Offenders who only steal items that are temporarily left unguarded and who do not consider themselves as lawbreakers.

professional thief—Offenders who attempt to make a living from theft and may specialize in a particular form.

Most people are not victims of professional thieves. Instead, their property is taken by the opportunistic thief.[27] Most common thievery occurs at a lower level, such as the taking of a wallet or purse from a desk drawer or the theft of a child's bicycle from a yard. Often these thieves are juveniles who steal for excitement, to obtain status symbols, or to impress others. They have not entered an antisocial lifestyle but rather are experimenting with deviance, and many quickly outgrow it. There is also a range of vocational offenders that includes adults who shoplift, cheat on their taxes, or steal from their places of employment but do not consider themselves "criminals." These adults have conventional jobs and steal only on an infrequent basis and without a great deal of planning.[28]

On the other hand, professional thieves identify themselves as thieves and attempt to make a living from taking others' property. They have honed their skills to the extent that they can steal on a regular basis without being detected and without causing physical harm. The goal of the professional thief is to work without being noticed. Professionals do not advertise their expertise. Often, they appear to be ordinary or even upstanding citizens and depend on wit and guile to commit theft. The goal is to get in and get out without being discovered and without having to confront victims.

The most extensive, though now dated, picture of this type of offender is in Edwin Sutherland's 1937 book, *The Professional Thief.* The offenders Sutherland studied committed a limited number of offenses and specialized in such activities as stealing jewelry, shoplifting, picking pockets, stealing from offices, and perpetrating confidence games. Sutherland's typology of the professional thief included such terms as "booster" (a shoplifter), "heel" (a thief who steals from stores, banks, and offices), "pennyweighter" (a jewel thief who substitutes fake jewelry for real jewelry), and "cannon" (a pickpocket). The professional thieves of the 1930s took great pride in developing the skill of taking other people's property without attracting attention.[29] They looked down on those who were clumsy and inarticulate and who did not abide by the code of honor that often characterized their attitude toward their illegal activities. In the past, these professional thieves were looked up to in prison culture and were even considered to be role models.[30]

The romantic view of professional thieves as professionals who abide by a code of honor is no longer prevalent, perhaps because thievery has become more widespread since the early 20th century. In fact, one type of thievery, art theft, has become a mainstay for organized crime. Art theft is reported to be the world's third most profitable criminal enterprise, trailing behind only the drugs and weapons trades. Moving money through banking systems or even physically moving cash across borders is often difficult, so art has become useful as a medium of exchange or as a way to launder money. It also has international value; art can be exchanged in any country for any currency or item that the seller requires, often with no questions asked.

Art theft is especially useful for terrorists and gangs. For example, a stolen Picasso worth millions of dollars can be traded for several thousand dollars' worth of automatic weapons. Although the painting is worth more than the weapons, both the buyer and seller are happy with the deal. It is much easier for the seller to steal the Picasso than to come up with cash for the weapons, and the buyer gets a Picasso—although one that can never be publicly displayed or sold—for a bargain.[31] Now let's take a look at some of the techniques professional thieves use.

This work by Picasso, "Nude Before a Mirror," was one of two stolen paintings recovered from a storage locker in a Cleveland suburb in February 1997. Why is rare art such an attractive target for thieves?

Pocket-Picking

Good pickpockets must practice regularly, be proficient at spotting targets that are both potentially lucrative and accessible, and have a cover story or exit strategy that can explain their behavior if they are detected. Some pickpockets work alone, and some work in teams. Teams have highly choreographed strategies in which one pickpocket will distract the victim, while another picks the pocket and passes the booty to a third confederate, who walks away. Even if the victims discover they have had their pocket picked or purse lifted, they have a difficult time ascertaining who did it and even more trouble finding exactly who has their property. It all happens in a matter of seconds, and the victim has little chance of detecting and apprehending the thieves. (See Figure 9.2 for the incidence of pocket-picking.)

The best method for dealing with pickpockets is target-hardening, or making it more difficult for anyone to lift property from your purse or pocket. But even buttons and zippers on pockets and bags may not be enough to deter the professional pickpocket. Professional pickpockets prefer to work in large crowds where there is a lot of jostling and bumping. They may use razor blades to cut through pockets or purses and lift property without exerting any noticeable pressure. The skill they value most highly is called "the light touch," which refers to lifting someone's property without the victim even being aware the thief is near. An accomplished thief can even cut the straps of a purse and steal the whole thing without the victim knowing. Another technique is for the thief to firmly touch the victim on the shoulder with one hand while lifting the wallet from the victim's back pocket with the other.

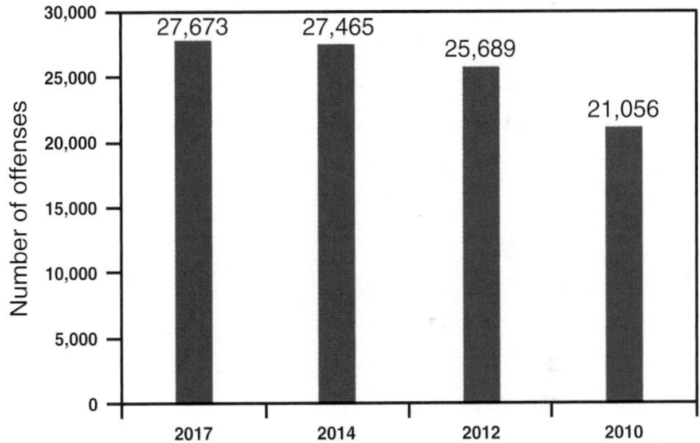

FIGURE 9.2 Pocket-picking

Recorded incidences of pocket-picking tend to rise and fall. How do you protect your pockets or bags from theft?

Source: Federal Bureau of Investigation, Uniform Crime Reports, Crime in the United States, *Table 23: Offense Analysis Number and Percent Change, years 2005–2010. Table 23: Offense Analysis Number and Percent Change, 2011–2012, https://ucr.fbi.gov/crime-in-the-u.s/2012/crime-in-the-u.s.-2012/tables/23tabledatadecoverviewpdfs/table_23_offense_analysis_number_and_percent_change_2011-2012.xls. Table 23: Offense Analysis Number and Percent Change, 2013–2014, https://ucr.fbi.gov/crime-in-the-u.s/2014/crime-in-the-u.s.-2014/tables/table-23. Table 23: Offense Analysis Number and Percent Change, 2016–2017, https://ucr.fbi.gov/crime-in-the-u.s/2017/crime-in-the-u.s.-2017/topic-pages/tables/table-23. Accessed October 2018.*

Picking pockets for a living is risky. It takes a great deal of training and skill to avoid detection, but the thief cannot compensate for all risks. The pickpocket must identify a good target—that is, one who is both vulnerable and likely to have a lot of money—and also be sure the offense is committed in a place that allows a quick escape. Many things could go wrong. The thief might select someone who is keenly aware of his or her surroundings and alert to the possibility of pickpockets lurking about. For instance, a plainclothes police officer may look like a likely target, but it would be a big mistake to attempt to pick the officer's pocket.

Another inherent risk is the possibility of being caught on a security camera. Even though the thief may be successful on one day, returning to the same shopping center or sporting arena can be extremely risky if security personnel are on the lookout for pickpockets and their crews. Video evidence is difficult to explain away in court, and the professional pickpocket can become a marked individual.[32]

Employee theft is one of the biggest problems faced by retailers. How can theft by employees be prevented?

Employee Theft

Sometimes those in the best position to commit larceny are those who are the most trusted. One of the biggest problems retailers face is theft by their employees. According to the National Retail Security Survey, employee theft represents the second largest category of retail losses, accounting for 30 percent of losses by retail stores.[33] This is a staggering amount of money to lose to individuals who are being paid to look out for the retailers' best interests. Let's look at why and how a retail clerk would steal from an employer.

- Large and impersonal stores. Large chain or "big box" stores have become a dominant form of retail enterprise in the United States. Stores such as Best Buy, Walmart, and Target are national brands with thousands of retail outlets across the country. They provide low-cost merchandise to customers but at the same time often pay low wages. Many have policies designed to keep their labor costs down, such as limiting employees' work hours so they do not qualify for health insurance. Although these savings are passed on to customers, employees often find it difficult to make a living wage. High levels of employee theft under these circumstances are hardly surprising.
- Rapid turnover. Retail clerks do not enjoy large salaries and extensive benefit packages, so they are constantly on the lookout for new and better employment. It is difficult to develop a culture of trust and responsibility when there is a high rate of turnover of supervisors and employees. Underqualified employees may be promoted to supervisor positions simply because they have longevity and know the store's policies and products. Supervisors are often conspirators or participants in the largest employee thefts.
- Ineffective inventory control procedures. Retail stores consistently struggle to control their inventory. The use of sensors to stop shoplifters is not effective in deterring employee theft. Employees are not only aware of the various security devices, but they are also often responsible for implementing these safeguards. Therefore, they are in an ideal position to steal from a store because they represent "the fox inside the chicken coop." Although large retail stores go to great lengths to prevent employee theft, they have yet to find effective ways of protecting their inventory from those responsible for pricing, stocking, and selling.

- Organized crime. Various criminal organizations target retail establishments. These range from highly sophisticated crime syndicates that go after numerous retail outlets to small, localized groups that affect only one store. By placing several confederates in a large retail store, organized crime can arrange to have a tractor trailer truck backed up to the loading dock ready to drive away with thousands of dollars' worth of merchandise. A good deal of planning goes into such heists, and by forging documents, using the company's own trucks, and altering the video cameras and tape, thieves are able to accomplish their goals leaving little or no evidence. Some use bribery and corruption to compromise those who should be overseeing the inventory.
- Organized employee theft. There are also less sophisticated forms of organized employee theft. A teenager who works in a store may steal merchandise to sell to friends below cost. By switching price tags and scanning the wrong bar codes, a determined employee can move a great deal of merchandise without being detected. Similarly, a security guard can allow friends to walk out of the store carrying large amounts of merchandise they can later resell.

Retail stores use several strategies to control employee theft. Video technology is particularly popular.[34] Some convenience stores allow managers to keep track of several locations at once via the Internet, either by watching in real time or by checking on previously recorded events, as well as by verifying receipts against stock.[35] Many companies use polygraph (lie detector) examinations, drug testing, and background checks, including researching applicants on the Internet, to attempt to ensure they are hiring honest employees.[36] Most large retail chains have security staff members who specialize in detecting employee theft and shoplifting.[37]

Shoplifting

Shoplifters take millions of dollars' worth of products from stores every year (see Figure 9.3 for the incidence of shoplifting). They range from children experimenting with risky behavior to sophisticated gangs of professional thieves who make their living stealing goods to sell at a discount to their clients.

The National Association of Shoplifting Prevention (NASP) collects information about the frequency and techniques of shoplifting. According to NASP, the primary reason for shoplifting is to "get something for nothing." However, it is not always that simple. Some individuals use shoplifting as a response to other problems. Often, shoplifting is a "substitute for loss" for some who perceive that they were unfairly deprived in some way, such as by divorce, serious illness, death of a loved one, loss of income from a job or investments, or an unexpected expense that makes them feel needy. Stealing a bottle of shampoo, for example, can temporarily help the shoplifter relieve anxiety about his or her financial situation and provide a feeling of control. For other offenders, shoplifting is a sort of "payback" for all they feel they give to others and for which they receive little in return. For still other people, it is about anxiety, frustration, boredom, or depression.

When considered this way, shoplifting becomes a much more complicated and puzzling activity. Because it is such a widespread and expensive offense, it bears scrutiny from a critical perspective so that we can understand not only how it happens, but also how to find better ways to prevent it. Shoplifting is an expensive concern for the retail industry. About $13 billion worth of goods—roughly $35 million per day—is stolen from retailers each year.[38]

Shoplifting is not just about getting something for nothing. For many, it is a means of working out

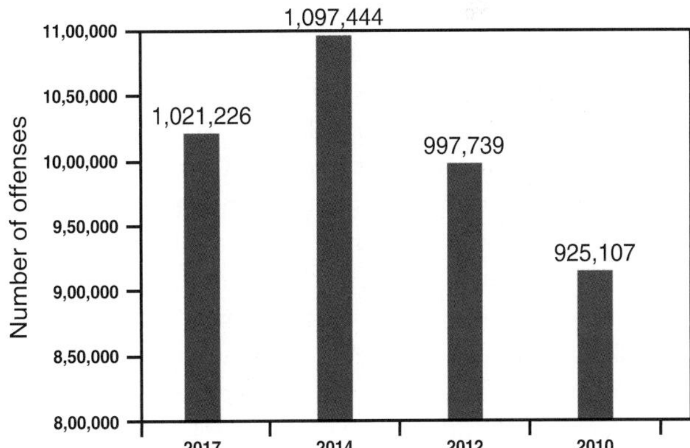

FIGURE 9.3 Shoplifting

Recorded incidences of shoplifting peaked in 2014. Have you ever known anyone who shoplifted? Why did he or she do it?

Source: Table 23: Offense Analysis Number and Percent Change, 2009–2010, https://ucr.fbi.gov/crime-in-the-u.s/2010/crime-in-the-u.s.-2010/tables/10tbl23.xls. Table 23: Offense Analysis Number and Percent Change, years 2012, https://ucr.fbi.gov/crime-in-the-u.s/2012/crime-in-the-u.s.-2012/tables/23tabledatadecoverviewpdfs/table_23_offense_analysis_number_and_percent_change_2011-2012.xls. Table 23: Offense Analysis Number and Percent Change, 2013–2014, https://ucr.fbi.gov/crime-in-the-u.s/2014/crime-in-the-u.s.-2014/tables/table-23. Table 23: Offense Analysis Number and Percent Change, 2016–2017, https://ucr.fbi.gov/crime-in-the-u.s/2017/crime-in-the-u.s.-2017/topic-pages/tables/table-23. Accessed October 2018.

Notorious jewel thief Doris Payne, whose illicit career spans six decades, was caught stealing again in 2017 while wearing an ankle monitoring bracelet from a previous arrest. Payne was charged with misdemeanor theft by shoplifting and later released with credit for time served in jail. Why are some people chronic shoplifters?

deep **antisocial** tendencies. Some shoplifters may not be able to control the urge to steal. They are driven to shoplift by unconscious psychological pressures, and some suffer the same types of conditions as people with severe depression and eating disorders. Their theft is not purpose-driven as it is for normal shoplifters.

For juveniles, shoplifting presents a different set of circumstances. Rather than being a way of acquiring material objects or a result of mental illness, for juveniles shoplifting is often a response to peer pressure. Groups of young people will dare each other to take the risk of getting caught as a method of establishing status and respect. Young shoplifters will often take things they do not need simply to fit into the group or gang. Juvenile shoplifters who are not involved in a group have a different sort of motivation. These lone shoplifters may engage in risky behavior out of a need to feel empowered or to strike back at society. Like other types of shoplifters, they may steal things of little value as a symbolic way of showing the world, their peers, or their parents that they have some sort of power or autonomy. This is especially true when they feel angry, depressed, unattractive, or unworthy.[39]

Shoplifting continues to be a major problem for retailers, and stores have developed ways to protect themselves (see Doubletake). Major retailer Target has its own crime laboratory complete with fingerprint, computer forensic, and video analysis labs, and it even assists the police on some outside cases.[40] Many electronic and other technological devices have

DOUBLETAKE

When Is Shoplifting Not Shoplifting?

On December 26, 2016, Curtis Lawson walked into a Knoxville, Tennessee, Walmart and committed return fraud. Using a receipt for $39.57 in purchases he had made earlier, Lawson picked out the same items that were on the receipt, then brought them to the front and returned the items with the receipt. He took the $39.57 in cash and left the store.[41]

When Lawson was caught by a store loss-prevention officer, he immediately admitted what he had done. After all, Walmart had caught him doing it once before, years earlier, and banned him from its premises. Lawson was later charged with shoplifting and criminal trespass, and thanks to some outstanding warrants, his bail was set at $2,500, and he went to jail. When it was discovered that Walmart had banned him, the misdemeanor shoplifting charge was increased to felony burglary, and his bail was increased to $5,000. In Tennessee, where burglary is defined as "unlawfully and knowingly entering a building without the consent of the owner and committing a theft," the offense is punishable by up to 12 years in prison.[42]

When does shoplifting become burglary? Although some states have decreased the penalties for theft by raising the value thresholds for felony theft (for instance, California raised its threshold so that a theft must total $950 before a felony can be charged), several states use burglary statutes to prosecute some shoplifters as burglars. Because the definition of burglary typically depends on the offender's intent (entering a dwelling or business with intent to commit a crime), prosecutors are using shoplifters' intent as part of the justification to file burglary charges.[43]

Whether burglary laws apply to the entry of stores that are open to the public depends on the state. If a shoplifting suspect has been previously banned, as in Lawson's case, the store's lack of consent may be used to file burglary charges. In another example, Idaho simply does not distinguish between residential burglaries and thefts from open stores. Other states continue to keep "locked building" and/or "forced entry" as part of their burglary definitions. However, as some legislators and retailer associations push for stricter penalties against people who steal from stores, these definitions eventually may be revised to allow shoplifting to be defined as burglary.[44]

been designed to deter or catch shoplifters. However, the loss this illegal activity incurs is still in the billions of dollars a year. Despite efforts by retail associations and organizations such as NASP, it is difficult to determine what has been lost to shoplifters and what has been lost to employees who steal. Merchandise has simply disappeared, and it is often preferable to think it was lost to shoplifters rather than to dishonest employees.

TOR is an anonymity network that allows users to access encrypted websites that are a source of stolen credit card numbers and identity information. What can credit card companies do to make their cards more secure?

Fraud

Fraud is the known misrepresentation or concealment in a transaction made with the intent to deceive another. Two types of fraud related to larceny are credit card theft and check fraud. Although the UCR neither typifies these types of fraud as property offenses nor collects statistics on them, we cover them here because they involve the taking of money with less trickery than other fraud schemes.

CREDIT CARD THEFT

Credit card theft is a billion-dollar industry.[45] Cards and the information on them can be stolen in two primary ways. First, the physical card can be stolen and used. This is perhaps the clumsiest method because once the card owner realizes the card is stolen, the card owner can phone the credit card company and have the card discontinued. The second type of offense is to steal the information on the card and not the card itself. This is a much more subtle way to accomplish credit card theft because it might be days or even weeks before the card owner realizes someone else is using the card number.

Credit card information can be stolen via the Internet—for example, when a card owner enters the card's information to make a purchase from a retail site—or via a method called "skimming." Skimming relies on a device much like the legitimate devices retailers use to read the card's information. The thief's skimmer, however, has a small memory device that records the card's information for later use. These devices are portable and can be worn by the thief—for example, a restaurant worker who accepts a patron's credit card can surreptitiously swipe the card through a skimmer attached to his or her belt before running it through the restaurant's legitimate device—or the device can be attached to ATM machines or gas pumps disguised as legitimate equipment.[46]

The ability of thieves to commit both low-tech and high-tech larceny makes credit card theft a complicated phenomenon. It is a flourishing industry for reasons that have much to do with the credit card companies' desire to make their products easily accessible to users. Credit card companies do not use security measures that would make credit card transactions absolutely safe because they deem them too cumbersome and inconvenient for the public. Therefore, the card companies are willing to accept a certain amount of fraud as a business expense in order to offer their customers greater convenience.

Unfortunately, those who are victimized by credit card thieves have their financial lives severely disrupted. A thief can wreck an individual's credit score, and it can take months or even years for the victim to re-establish good credit. Although credit card companies typically do not hold card users responsible for illegitimate charges, the hassles users experience in dealing with the theft may still be significant.

Instant Recall from Chapter 1 **antisocial**—Following standards of behavior intended to harm society and individuals.

fraud—Known misrepresentation or concealment in a transaction made with the intent to deceive another.

CHECK FRAUD

Another type of offense related to theft is check forgery and the cashing of bad checks. Cashing bad checks is often known as "bouncing a check," "check kiting," or "writing a check with insufficient funds." Let's look at some of the more popular variations.

- Forgery. Criminals who steal wallets and checkbooks will attempt to match the owner's signature in order to write checks out of the account. Vigilant banks and stores try to prevent this type of fraud by insisting that those trying to cash checks provide photo identification. However, sophisticated offenders alter photo identifications by putting their own picture in. It is almost impossible to stop the sophisticated forger at the retail level.
- Counterfeiting and alteration. Making counterfeit checks has become relatively easy to do with computers, scanners, and color copiers. Counterfeiters have access to the same typefaces and fonts that check printers use, so they can produce realistic-looking checks. They can also alter checks that have already been issued by using chemicals to change the payee's name or the amount. This procedure is called "spot alteration" or "check washing" and is relatively easy for the determined forger to accomplish.
- Paperhanging. Paperhanging is the writing of checks on closed accounts. By the time the check makes it to the bank, and it is discovered that the account is closed, the paperhanger is long gone.
- Check kiting. Check kiting involves opening accounts at more than one bank and writing checks that float between them. Because it takes some time for a check to clear from one bank to another, offenders can obtain money before it is discovered that there are insufficient funds in the account upon which the check was written.

Frank Abagnale Jr. (center) testifies to the Senate Commerce subcommittee on consumer protection. Could Abagnale's offenses be committed today?

These techniques have been used for a long time and are becoming more complicated as banks' technological sophistication grows. Both criminal and civil penalties are attached to writing bad checks. Each state has its own laws, but all require the offender to repay the initial amount plus fines and court costs. For instance, the criminal penalty for writing bad checks in the state of Florida can draw up to five years in prison or a $5,000 fine for a felony, or up to $1,000 or one year in jail for a misdemeanor.[47] Still, many states offer a grace period of up to 30 days to allow unintentional bad-check writers to address mistakes and oversights. Many people keep small balances in their checking accounts and inadvertently bounce checks because of math errors. However, many people purposefully attempt fraud by writing checks on accounts with insufficient funds or false accounts.

In a classic study, sociologist Edwin Lemert identified two types of check forgers. The most common is the naive check forger who does not believe his or her actions will hurt anyone. Because retail establishments want to make transactions simple and friendly, the naive check forger seizes the opportunity to obtain quick money with little risk. The problems come later when the police put together the patterns of naive check forgers and make an arrest.

The second type of check forger Lemert identified is the systematic forger who makes a living passing bad checks. The systematic forger has several techniques such as making counterfeits, altering legitimate checks by changing the amount or the name of the payee, writing checks on closed accounts hoping the time required for processing will allow the money to be collected before the check can be canceled, and using someone else's identity to invade their checking account.[48]

It is difficult to separate the systematic forger from the naive forger. The successful systematic forger can pass many checks without being noticed. If apprehended, he or she can appear to be a sloppy and neglectful naive forger, and a pattern of massive check fraud can remain undiscovered. Probably the most infamous check forger is Frank Abagnale Jr. (the subject of the film *Catch Me If You Can*). As a teenager during the 1960s, Abagnale managed to pass $2.5 million in forged checks throughout the United States and 26 other countries, all while impersonating a lawyer, a medical doctor, and an airline pilot. He was so good at forging checks that the FBI hired him to help catch check forgers.[49]

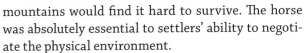

The problem of bad checks may one day become a thing of the past as people stop writing as many checks as they used to. Credit and debit cards and online banking are becoming the new media of financial transactions. This, of course, has led to abuses in these new forms of commerce even as the writing of bad checks decreases.

PAUSE AND REVIEW

1. **Identify the techniques that are involved when a retail clerk steals from his or her employer.**
2. **Describe the differences between opportunistic thieves and professional thieves.**
3. **Determine the best method for dealing with pickpockets.**
4. **What is the most frequent criminal offense?**
5. **Name three types of common larcenies.**
6. **How has technology enabled more credit card theft?**
7. **What are large retail stores now doing to deter shoplifting?**

Motor Vehicle Theft

LEARNING OBJECTIVE | 4

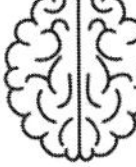

Discuss why motor vehicle theft continues to be a significant problem.

Motor vehicle theft is the stealing or unauthorized taking of an automobile, truck, motorcycle, or any other motorized vehicle allowed on public roads and highways. Motor vehicle thefts are the most likely of all crime types to be reported to police.[50] They continue to be a significant problem that inconveniences thousands of automobile owners each year (see Figure 9.4.). In 2017, more than 700,000 motor vehicles were stolen or were involved in attempted thefts.[51]

In the Old West, horse thieves were hanged. The punishment was harsh for two reasons. First, horses were a major investment, usually representing a person's most expensive possession. Often, having a horse was necessary for a person to work, whether that meant traveling to a job or running a farm. The second reason was that having a horse often meant the difference between life and death. A settler without a horse out on the prairie or in the mountains would find it hard to survive. The horse was absolutely essential to settlers' ability to negotiate the physical environment.

Although we do not execute car thieves, motor vehicle theft is still considered a serious offense for many of the same reasons horse theft was. Cars and trucks represent a significant financial investment for individuals, perhaps the largest aside from the purchase of a home or a college education. Public transportation is not well developed in the United States, making the automobile an often essential mode of transportation. (Another essential mode of transportation, the bicycle, is also a prime target of theft, but, alas, bicycles are not motor vehicles. That does not make their theft any less upsetting to bicycle owners. See Policy Implications for further discussion of this kind of theft.) People depend on their cars to get to work, to help them do their work, and to perform necessary housekeeping duties, such as driving children to school and shopping for groceries. Much as the horse was indispensable in the Old West, the automobile is essential to the American lifestyle.

The theft of a person's car incurs yet another injury for those individuals who look upon their automobile as a special piece of property. Some people go to great lengths to customize their cars and have an intense relationship with their automobile that they do not feel toward other items they own. Therefore, a stolen car can cause intense feelings of loss. Certainly, not all cars elicit this intense response.

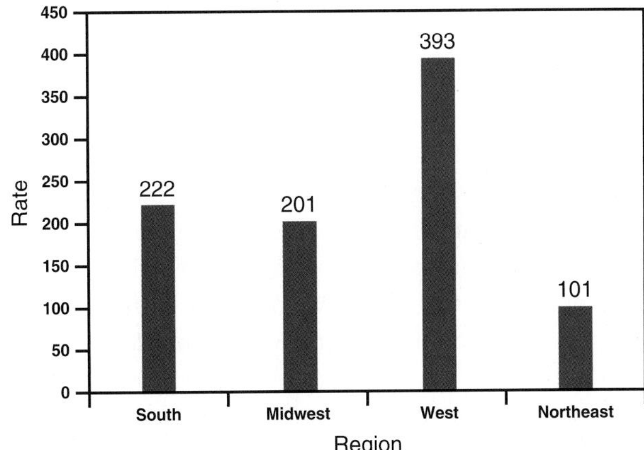

FIGURE 9.4 Vehicle Theft Rate by Region, 2017

Discuss reasons why the rate for motor vehicle theft is so much higher in the West than in other regions.

Source: Federal Bureau of Investigation, Uniform Crime Reports, Crime in the United States, 2017, *Table 4: Crime in the United States by Region, Geographic Division, and State, 2016–2017, https://ucr.fbi.gov/crime-in-the-u.s/2017/crime-in-the-u.s.-2017/topic-pages/tables/table-4. Accessed October 2018.*

POLICY IMPLICATIONS

Bicycles: The New Crime Currency

Larceny/theft is one of the most frequently committed property offenses, according to the FBI, accounting for 72 percent of all property offenses in 2017.[52] Although both professional and non-professional thieves will steal anything, a popular target is bicycles. With more cities installing bike paths (New York City has more than 1,000 miles of bike lanes) and more people in urban areas willing to ride a bicycle to work rather than drive a car, bicycles are an increasingly common sight.[53] Bicycles are also so easy to steal that they—along with cash, sex, and drugs—have become a form of currency in the underground economy.[54] A bicycle is far more likely to be stolen than a car or a motorcycle.[55]

Because of the relatively low cost of most street bikes, most jurisdictions consider bike theft a misdemeanor, except in the case of expensive bikes, when it may be considered a felony. Relative to automobiles, bicycles are difficult to track. They do not have license plates; are not usually registered in any way; and although some are marked with serial numbers, many are not. Even if they are marked, the owner may not remember or take note of the serial number.[56]

A bike theft takes only minutes, and locks and other anti-theft devices are easily defeated. Even when the lock takes some time to break, passers-by rarely report a theft-in-progress, as filmmaker Casey Neistat found out when he did a series of experiments in New York City in which he tried to steal his own bike. Even when using loud power tools, only a couple of onlookers questioned what he was doing.[57]

Although bicycle theft has been around for about as long as bicycles, the offense has quickly become more widespread, yet it is not considered a serious problem. However, stolen bicycles also help fuel the underground economy inhabited by thieves and other lawbreakers. What are the policy implications of this type of offense? Police departments and legislatures have been slow to respond: investigating bike thefts is not a high priority for police, and unlike motor vehicles, bicycles do not have special laws attached to their thefts.[58]

Another policy implication of bicycle theft is that victims and offenders are not necessarily two separate groups. For example, most car owners do not also steal cars or look for stolen cars to purchase. However, it is not uncommon for victims of bicycle theft to either steal a bicycle to make up for the loss or look for a stolen, and therefore inexpensive, bicycle to purchase. This concept is called a "crime multiplier" because one offense may lead to the commission of several others.[59] That is, one stolen bicycle rarely represents one criminal offense.

In the coming years, as urban areas become more bicycle friendly and more people begin riding to work and for recreation, bicycle enthusiasts hope there will be a greater demand for safe places to park their bicycles; harsher penalties for theft (currently, thieves rarely see any time in jail or prison); and more police interest in pursuing thieves and theft rings.

THINK ABOUT IT

1. In what ways does stealing a bicycle differ from stealing a car?

Most car insurance companies cover theft, and some people welcome the opportunity to buy a new car.

Professional automobile thieves are selective about which cars they steal. Often they choose cars based on the market value of their parts. Some garages, called "chop shops," use parts from stolen vehicles so that they do not have to buy new parts. (See Table 9.2 for a list of the most often stolen passenger vehicles.)

Some of these cars are several years old, but they are attractive to thieves because they are best-selling models, and many of their parts are interchangeable. Also, some of the older models do not have the anti-theft technology that is present on newer models. It is simply a matter of volume rather than desirability. However, a chopped car or a car sold as stolen goods may bring only a few thousand dollars.

Another tactic of professional thieves that allows them to get almost the full price for the car is "car cloning." Thieves will steal a desirable, nearly new car and take it across the state line. Then, at a large car dealership, they will find a car identical to the stolen car and copy down the vehicle identification number (VIN). The thieves make a replica of the VIN tag and exchange it for the one in the stolen car. After forging some documents to acquire ownership papers, the thieves can now sell the practically untraceable car to an unsuspecting buyer.[60]

Amateur thieves go about stealing cars in a different way. Rather than looking for automobiles that can be sold as parts or going to the trouble of cloning a car, the amateur thief chooses targets based on status and personal taste. Sports cars and luxury cars are the most likely targets. Or the amateur might be simply looking for a joyride. Many cars are taken and driven extremely fast around the neighborhood and then dumped before the perpetrators can be discovered. Sports cars and

TABLE 9.2

According to the National Insurance Crime Bureau, the 10 most often stolen passenger vehicles in 2016 were:

1.	1997	Honda Accord
2.	1998	Honda Civic
3.	2006	Ford Pickup (Full Size)
4.	2004	Chevrolet Pickup (Full Size)
5.	2016	Toyota Camry
6.	2015	Nissan Altima
7.	2001	Dodge Pickup (Full Size)
8.	2015	Toyota Corolla
9.	2008	Chevrolet Impala
10.	2000	Jeep Cherokee/Grand Cherokee

Source: National Insurance Crime Bureau, https://www.nicb.org/news/news-releases/2016-hot-wheels-report. Accessed May 2018.

An Oxnard, California, police officer talks with a car theft suspect. What are some low-tech ways to protect your car?

luxury cars are also the target of professional thieves who steal to order. Sometimes, these cars are taken to other countries and sold, a type of theft glamorized in the movie *Gone in 60 Seconds*. Tractors and heavy construction equipment are also targets of this kind of theft because they are so expensive.

The prevention of motor vehicle theft relies on many strategies. A combination of new technologies, better-informed law enforcement agencies, and common sense on the part of motorists has reduced the number of stolen cars. Technological efforts to prevent motor vehicle theft include the following.

- Locking devices. The best-known locking device is The Club, a steel bar that clamps onto the steering wheel and makes the car impossible to steer. It is a visual deterrent to automobile thieves because disabling the device requires cutting through steel or picking a secure lock. Either way, this requires more time and effort than thieves are usually willing to devote to the task. They are more likely to move on to another automobile that is not so well protected. Another type of locking device is a hood restraint, which keeps the hood from being opened and prevents "hot wiring" of the car. A third type of device is a steering column collar that protects the ignition from being compromised. Tire and wheel locks wrap around the tire or wheel and immobilize the car. Finally, gearshift locks prevent the transmission from being shifted into gear.
- Cut-off devices. Cut-off devices are switches that either disable the ignition or halt the flow of fuel to the engine. An ingenious protection from all but the most sophisticated thief, they are spliced into the ignition wires or fuel system and are not visible.
- Alarms. Alarms are designed to make a lot of noise so that a potential thief will leave without breaking into the vehicle. Designs include sensors that are connected to the door, windshield, windows, and trunk. Should any of these sensors be disturbed without the alarm being turned off, a loud, irritating noise will be emitted. At a more sophisticated level, alarms that sense motion, vibration, and ultrasonic fields operate in much the same way. One problem with these types of alarm systems is that they might be more irritating to anyone near the car than useful in preventing motor vehicle thefts.
- Tracking devices. The signal emitted by a tracking device allows the car to be located after it is reported stolen. Tracking devices are sold by private companies that coordinate with the police so that cars can be recovered. Perhaps the best-known device is the LoJack, which notifies the monitoring center if the car is started by means other than the use of the ignition key. Some of the more sophisticated tracking devices have the ability to

disable the automobile via satellite if it is reported stolen. This could be very inconvenient for a thief who is attempting to elude police and finds that the car suddenly stops.

PAUSE AND REVIEW

1. **Identify the most common reasons that motor vehicles are stolen.**

Arson

LEARNING OBJECTIVE | 5

Explain why arson is an exception to the FBI's hierarchy rule.

Arson is the deliberate setting of fires. Fewer arsons are committed than other types of property offenses, but arson is still a serious problem (see Figure 9.5 for the incidence of arson). According to the FBI, 41,171 arsons were reported in 2017.[61] The deliberate setting of fires may result not only in financial loss, but also in loss of life. Because arson is such a serious property offense, it is an exception to the FBI's hierarchy rule. If an arson is committed in a set of offenses, both the arson and the most serious offense in that set of offenses (such as murder) are reported.[62]

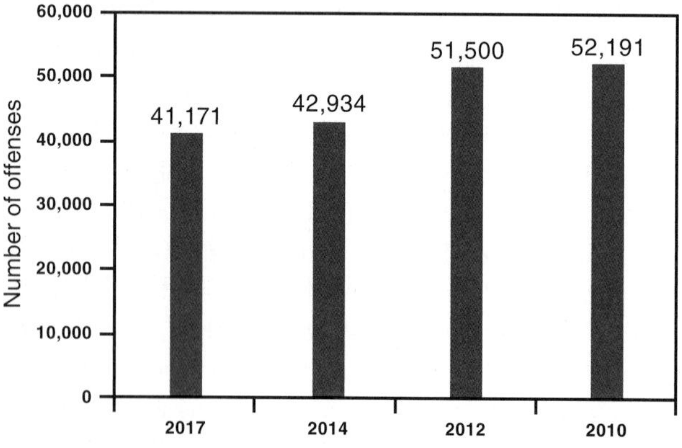

FIGURE 9.5 Arson

Recorded incidences of arson have dropped steadily since 2010. Can you give reasons why?

Source: Federal Bureau of Investigation, Uniform Crime Reports: Crime in the United States, *years 2010–2016, Table 12: Crime Trends by Population Group, 2009–2010, https://ucr.fbi.gov/crime-in-the-u.s/2010/crime-in-the-u.s.-2010/tables/10tbl12.xls. Table 12: Crime Trends by Population Group, 2011–2012, https://ucr.fbi.gov/crime-in-the-u.s/2012/crime-in-the-u.s.-2012/tables/12tabledatadecpdf/table_12_crime_trends_by_population_group_2011_2012.xls. Table 12: Crime Trends by Population Group, 2013–2014, https://ucr.fbi.gov/crime-in-the-u.s/2014/crime-in-the-u.s.-2014/tables/table-12. Table 12: Crime Trends by Population Group, 2016–2017, https://ucr.fbi.gov/crime-in-the-u.s/2017/crime-in-the-u.s.-2017/topic-pages/tables/table-12. Accessed October 2018.*

The problem of fire-setting stretches across time and cultures. Some of the oldest English common laws define arson as the offense of burning another person's dwelling. In 11th-century England, untended fires became such a widespread problem that William the Conqueror banned evening cooking fires with the law of *couvre feu* (cover the fire), which evolved into the modern "curfew," or the banning of any activity after a specified hour.[63]

People deliberately set fires for many reasons, and it is worth exploring these motivations in order to suggest ways that arson can be prevented. Motivations for arson include but are not limited to the following.

- Insurance claims. Many, if not most, structures are insured. In order to get a mortgage for a home, the owners must prove they have insurance that protects against damage, including fire. When individuals get behind on their mortgage payments and are in danger of losing their home, they may be tempted to burn it down in order to recover, through insurance, whatever equity they have in it. In some areas, the home's value may have fallen well below the insurance coverage, and it makes more financial sense to burn the home down than to attempt to sell it. The burning of structures for insurance claims has evolved into such a profitable activity that organized crime has become active in it. Banks are motivated to be complicit in these types of arsons because, like the homeowner, they profit from collecting on inflated insurance coverage of structures that have lost much of their value. The trick to recovering on such claims is to make the fire look accidental. To this end, a person who is a "professional torch" is hired to make the fire look like an accident. It takes an experienced arson investigator to distinguish between accidental fires and arson. One of the primary questions asked is, "Who benefits from this fire?"[64]
- Profit. Fighting fires, and recovering and rebuilding afterward, can provide opportunities for individuals to make money. Those who supply bulldozers, mobile food canteens, and other support mechanisms for firefighters have a vested interest in arson. This is especially true in rural areas with national forests and few employment opportunities. In some areas, volunteer firefighters are paid extra to fight fires and thus are tempted to start them. The millions of dollars brought into an area for fighting large fires can offset much of the financial damage done by fires once insurance

claims are paid out.[65] Thus, arson investigators will consider the possibility of arson for profit.

- Thrill-seeking. Some fires are set for entertainment. Fires can be fascinating to watch as they consume buildings, and some people experience a hypnotic thrill not only from the fire itself, but from the response of fire departments. Sirens and flashing red lights can be stimulating to some arsonists. To experience this thrill, it is necessary to be in the right place at the right time as fires occur. The only way to achieve this excitement consistently is to set the fires.
- Hate crimes. Some fires are set for revenge or intimidation. Individuals in socially marginal groups, such as minorities or those who engage in alternative lifestyles, are sometimes targeted by bigots. One of the more extreme messages socially intolerant people send to those who move into a neighborhood is arson. Although victims may be outraged at the injustice, the need to protect their families can be a powerful motivator to move. In terms of revenge, few activities send a stronger message than burning down the business that laid you off or the apartment building you were evicted from. Such arsons not only do financial damage, but they also put lives at risk.[66]

This list of motivations for arson is not exhaustive. There are many other reasons someone might set a fire to achieve financial or emotional rewards. However, one category of arson deserves greater scrutiny here because it is so different and so prevalent: that of juvenile and young adult fire-starters.

In 2018, five young men in Sharpsburg, Georgia, recorded themselves as they vandalized a vacant home and set it on fire, completely destroying it and endangering the neighborhood. Someone notified police that one of the men had sent videos of the destruction to a friend via social media.[67] This style of offense is not uncommon for young people. In fact, young fire-starters can be divided into four types.

1. Those who play with matches. These children do not necessarily commit arson, but the results can still be disastrous. Children can be warned against playing with matches and learn to use them responsibly. However, many are tempted by the excitement of fire and either intentionally or accidentally set fires that get out of control. One study found that elementary school children through fourth grade who play with matches are more likely to have divorced parents and come from disrupted family backgrounds. For the most part, these are normal children who could be referred to counseling or fire-safety instruction. Without such proper supervision and education, they often become victims of the fires they start.

Plumes of dark smoke rise from a factory fire that was set by two teenagers. Why do some people deliberately start fires?

2. Cry-for-help fire-setters. This type of fire-setter deliberately engages in arson. He or she gets personal satisfaction and pleasure from arson and is more likely to **recidivate**. Often a precipitating event can be identified, such as losing a pet, changing a school or residence, or not being allowed to attend a social function. Fire-setting is a way to deal with the frustration and stress. Cry-for-help fire-setters are also sometimes reacting to physical, psychological, or sexual abuse. The child usually acts alone, setting fire to the bed, the parents' clothes, or something else that symbolizes the child's anger. There is also a relationship between this type of fire-setter and bedwetting (enuresis). These children are psychologically more troubled than those in the playing-with-matches category and require an appreciation for their distress, as well as counseling.
3. Delinquent and criminal fire-setters. Delinquent and criminal fire-setters are often engaging in malicious mischief. Because they deliberately set fires, recidivism is higher than in other categories of arson committed by youths. Motivations include the desire to commit acts of vandalism, the need to cover other offenses for which the evidence is being destroyed, and a search for excitement. Peer influence often contributes to

---

arson—The deliberate setting of fires.

Instant Recall from Chapter 1 **recidivism** —Repeat offending. Also recidivate.

this type of arson. Although younger children in this category set small fires, teenagers and young adults can go to great lengths to set larger fires that do a great deal more damage. One primary target of fire-setters is school buildings. Such fires are usually set on weekends by students who have had negative experiences in the school or by other youths who have a grudge against someone who attends the school.

4. Severely disturbed fire-setters. The severely disturbed fire-setter has deep emotional problems and views fire as a way of rebelling against authority or expressing unresolved psychological issues. There are two types of severely disturbed fire-setters. The first is the impulsive neurotic, who is impatient and reckless and tends to destroy his or her own possessions. The second type is the borderline psychotic, who experiences extreme mood swings, uncontrolled anger, violence, and numerous phobias. This type of fire-setter may also have severe family problems such as parents who use drugs, or other psychological issues such as sleep disorders or severe headaches. The severely disturbed fire-setter is more likely to engage in numerous other forms of delinquency than youths in the other three categories. Treatment can include extensive therapy and sometimes placement in a secure institution. In older teenagers, involvement with the juvenile justice system may become necessary to control this type of destructive behavior.[68]

Although this typology of juvenile fire-setters is not exhaustive, it illustrates important differences in the motivations, behavior patterns, and treatment of youths who commit arson. It is important to note that, without proper treatment, many will graduate into adult fire-setting patterns that can become much more problematic as they become more proficient and aggressive.

PAUSE AND REVIEW

1. **Explain the connection between arson and curfew laws.**
2. **Give reasons why juvenile fire-starters deserve special scrutiny when motivations for arson are considered.**

FOCUS ON ETHICS The Trouble with Amy

The FBI is doing a background investigation on you because you have passed all the hurdles for possible employment as a special agent. You have excellent grades in school, have obtained a master's degree in international relations, are physically fit, and have made the extra effort to become fluent in both Chinese and Russian. The FBI considers you an outstanding candidate and is fast-tracking your application so that you can be eligible for their next academy class starting in a few months.

Being an FBI agent is your life-long dream, and you have been careful to keep your personal conduct pristine. You avoided drinking alcohol underage, and you do not overindulge on the rare occasions that you do drink alcohol. You have never used any illegal drug, and you have picked your friends carefully. You are confident your background investigation will reveal nothing of concern to the FBI except for one small matter: your little sister Amy.

Amy is four years younger than you and a university sophomore. You love her with all your heart, but she has a problem that you are reluctant to reveal to the FBI. Amy likes to steal. When you were younger, Amy would steal your toys. Then she would "borrow" your clothes. Later you noticed she would go into stores and come out wearing clothes or jewelry she was not wearing when she went in. She is a successful and accomplished thief, and she nearly always manages to avoid suspicion and detection. She even tried to steal your girlfriend last year.

Although your parents are somewhat suspicious about Amy's problem, you are the only one who knows the full extent of it. The few times she has been caught, she has talked her way out of it. Sometimes you wonder if her behavior is sociopathic. As a dutiful big sister, you have lectured her about being honest and have exacted a promise from her to correct her behavior before she acquires a criminal record. Two local department stores have already overlooked her deviance but have banned her from entering their premises.

Now you have a decision to make. The FBI investigation is thorough and includes a polygraph examination. You are now filling out an extensive questionnaire that requires a great deal of information about your friends and family. What you put down here will be used by the FBI in an oral examination and the polygraph examination.

What Do You Do?

1. Do not say anything about Amy. She has no official record, and it is possible the FBI will not detect her problem. Besides, she is family, and that is your first loyalty.
2. Tell the FBI everything. They have not caught her doing anything, so she will not get into trouble. It is important that the FBI perceives you as absolutely honest.
3. You have to tell the FBI about Amy. However, you also plan to talk to Amy and try to convince her to get into therapy for her problem. This will show the FBI that you can come up with solutions to problems. It can also help your sister before her problem becomes a crisis.

Summary

Learning Objective	Summary
LEARNING OBJECTIVE 1 Discuss the major distinction between property offenses and personal violent offenses.	The major distinction between property offenses and personal violent offenses has to do with the elements of fear and danger. Property offenders typically do not use intimidation or physical violence as part of their method of breaking the law but, instead, are more concerned with avoiding detection and recognition.
LEARNING OBJECTIVE 2 Understand how larceny is different from burglary and robbery.	Larceny is the legal term for theft. It is different from robbery in that it does not require the use of or threat of violence. Burglary requires only that a structure be entered with the intent to commit an offense.
LEARNING OBJECTIVE 3 Describe how check fraud and credit card theft are forms of theft.	Fraud is a known misrepresentation or concealment in a transaction made with the intent to deceive another. Credit card fraud and check fraud involve the taking of money with less trickery than other fraud schemes.
LEARNING OBJECTIVE 4 Discuss why motor vehicle theft continues to be a significant problem.	Public transportation is not well developed in the United States, so cars and trucks are a significant financial investment for individuals. People depend on cars to get to work, to help them do their work, and to perform necessary housekeeping duties.
LEARNING OBJECTIVE 5 Explain why arson is an exception to the FBI's hierarchy rule.	Because arson is such a serious property offense, it is an exception to the FBI's hierarchy rule. If an arson is committed in a set of offenses, both the arson and the most serious offense in that set of offenses (such as murder) are reported.

Critical Reflections

1. **Think of three offenses that could be committed during a burglary. How would the FBI's hierarchy rule apply to each?**
2. **How does larceny differ from burglary or robbery?**
3. **Why is motor vehicle theft considered such a serious offense?**
4. **Discuss the exception of arson to the FBI's hierarchy rule.**
5. **Why is credit card theft such a difficult offense to prevent?**
6. **In what ways do pickpockets minimize their chances of getting caught?**

Key Terms

arson p. 253
burglary p. 238
fraud p. 247
larceny p. 241
opportunistic thief p. 242
professional thief p. 242
property offense p. 236

Instant Recall Terms

antisocial (ch. 1)
deterrence (ch. 3)
hierarchy rule (ch. 2)
recidivism (ch. 1)

Notes

1 Maggie Fergusson, "The Most Bizarre Museum Heist Ever," *Spectator USA*, April 26, 2018. https://usa.spectator.co.uk/2018/04/the-most-bizarre-museum-heist-ever. Kirk Wallace Johnson, "The Curious Case of the Fly-Fishing Feather Thief," *Outside Online*, April 19, 2018, https://www.outsideonline.com/2298586/feather-thief-excerpt. Accessed July 2018.
2 Ibid.
3 *BBC News*, "Natural History Thief Ordered to Pay Thousands," July 30 2011, http://www.bbc.com/news/uk-england-beds-bucks-herts-14352867. Accessed July 2018.
4 Kirk Wallace Johnson, *The Feather Thief* (New York: Viking, 2018), 90–94. Wildlife Watch, "How an Obsession with Rare Bird Feathers Turned Criminal," April 23, 2018, *National Geographic*, https://news.nationalgeographic.com/2018/04/wildlife-watch-feather-thief-fly-tying-birds. Accessed October 2018.
5 Federal Bureau of Investigation, Uniform Crime Reports, *Crime in the United States, 2017*, Property Crime, https://ucr.fbi.gov/crime-in-the-u.s/2017/crime-in-the-u.s.-2017/topic-pages/property-crime. Accessed October 2018.
6 Ibid.
7 Thorstein Veblen, *The Theory of the Leisure Class: An Economic Study of Institutions* (1912; repr., New York: New American Library, 1953).
8 Federal Bureau of Investigation, Uniform Crime Reports, *Crime in the United States, 2017*, Burglary, https://ucr.fbi.gov/crime-in-the-u.s/2017/crime-in-the-u.s.-2017/topic-pages/burglary. Accessed October 2018.
9 William G. Doerner and Steven P. Lab, *Victimology*, 5th ed. (Cincinnati, Ohio: LexisNexis, 2008). See Chapter 3, "The Costs of Being a Victim."
10 Federal Bureau of Investigation, Uniform Crime Reports, *Crime in the United States, 2017*, Table 23: Offense Analysis Number and Percent Change, 2016–2017, https://ucr.fbi.gov/crime-in-the-u.s/2017/crime-in-the-u.s.-2017/topic-pages/tables/table-23. Accessed October 2018.
11 Federal Bureau of Investigation, Uniform Crime Reports, *Crime in the United States, 2017*, Burglary, https://ucr.fbi.gov/crime-in-the-u.s/2017/crime-in-the-u.s.-2017/topic-pages/burglary. Accessed October 2018.
12 Robert J. Bursik Jr. and Harold G. Grasmick, *Neighborhoods and Crime: The Dimensions of Effective Community Control* (New York: Lexington Books, 1993).
13 Malcolm X, *The Autobiography of Malcolm X: As Told to Alex Haley* (New York: Ballantine), 154.
14 Stephen J. Dubner, "The Silver Thief," *New Yorker* 80, no. 12 (May 17, 2004): 74.
15 Kenneth D. Tunnell, *Choosing Crime: The Criminal Calculus of Property Offenders* (Chicago: Nelson-Hall Publishers, 1992).
16 Eric W. Hickey, ed., *Sex Crimes and Paraphilia* (Upper Saddle River, N.J.: Pearson, 2006).
17 Richard T. Wright and Scott Decker, *Burglars on the Job: Streetlife and Residential Breakins* (Boston: Northeastern University Press, 1994).
18 Paul F. Cromwell, James N. Olson, and D'Aunn W. Avary, *Breaking and Entering: An Ethnographic Analysis of Burglary* (Newbury Park, Calif.: Sage, 1991).
19 Wright and Decker, *Burglars on the Job.*
20 Cromwell and Olson, *Breaking and Entering*, 41.
21 Eric Baumer, Janet L. Lauritsen, Richard Rosenfeld, and Richard Wright, "The Influence of Crack Cocaine on Robbery, Burglary, and Homicide Rates: A Cross City Longitudinal Analysis," *Journal of Research in Crime and Delinquency* 35, no. 3 (1998): 316–340.
22 Wim Bernasco and Richard Block, "Where Offenders Choose to Attack: A Discrete Choice Model of Robberies in Chicago," *Criminology* 47, no. 1 (2009): 93–130.
23 Andy Hochstetler, "Opportunities and Decisions: Interactional Dynamics in Robbery and Burglary Groups," *Criminology* 37, no. 4 (2001): 737–763.
24 Federal Bureau of Investigations, Uniform Crime Reports, *Crime in the United States, 2017*, Larceny-theft, https://ucr.fbi.gov/crime-in-the-u.s/2017/crime-in-the-u.s.-2017/topic-pages/larceny-theft. Accessed October 2018.
25 Ibid.
26 Criminal codes vary across jurisdictions, and the distinction between petit larceny and grand larceny is not as clear-cut as we make it appear here. In fact, the amount of discretion on the part of the prosecutor may have more to do with the charge than the value of the stolen goods.
27 Cromwell and Olson, *Breaking and Entering*, 41.
28 John Hepburn, "Occasional Criminals," in *Major Forms of Crime*, ed. Robert Meier (Beverly Hills, Calif.: Sage, 1984), 73–94.
29 Edwin Sutherland, *The Professional Thief: By a Professional Thief* (Chicago: University of Chicago Press, 1937). This book is the result of collaboration between Sutherland and a professional thief named Chris Cornwell.
30 John Irwin, *The Felon* (Englewood Cliffs, N.J.: Prentice Hall, 1970). Irwin argues that the category of thief is "probably the oldest existing criminal system" (8). He adds: "a thief, to be considered 'all right' by his peers (something which is extremely important to him), must meet his obligations, pay his debts, keep his appointments, and most importantly, never divulge information to anyone which may lead to the arrest of another person" (8).
31 Frank Browning, "Stolen Fine Art: Organized Crime's New Commodity?" All Things Considered (NPR), May 31, 2007, http:// https://www.npr.org/templates/story/story.php?storyId=10588693. Accessed June 2018.
32 Howstuffworks, "How Pickpockets Work," https://money.howstuffworks.com/pickpocket.htm. Accessed June 2018. Many websites give practical advice for avoiding being a victim of pickpockets.
33 National Retail Federation, 2017 National Retail Security Survey, https://nrf.com/resources/retail-library/national-retail-security-survey-2017. Accessed June 2018.
34 "A Dollar Spent Is Money Earned in Loss Prevention," *Security Director's Report* 5, no. 11 (November 2005): 8.
35 Tammy Mastroberte, "An Ounce of Prevention," *Convenience Store News* 42, no. 4 (March 27, 2006): 52–53.
36 Garrett Gleeson, "Keeping an Eye on Shrink," *Dance Retailer News* 7, no. 10 (October 2008): 36–38.

37 Dick Silverman, "With Shoplifting and Employee Theft on the Rise, New Measures Are Being Taken to Stem Losses," *Footwear News*, November 15, 1999.
38 National Association for Shoplifting Prevention, The Shoplifting Problem in the Nation, http://www.shopliftingprevention.org/what-we-do/learning-resource-center. Accessed June 2018.
39 Lloyd W. Klemke, *The Sociology of Shoplifting: Boosters and Smiths Today* (Westport, Conn.: Praeger, 1992).
40 Target, An Unexpected Career: Target's Forensic Services Laboratory, February 15, 2012, https://corporate.target.com/article/2012/02/an-unexpected-career-target-forensic-services-labo?fytdyc. Accessed May 2018.
41 Jessica Pishko, "How Walmart Is Helping Prosecutors Pursue 10-Year Sentences for Shoplifting," *Appeal*, May 8, 2018, https://theappeal.org/how-walmart-is-helping-prosecutors-get-10-year-sentences-for-shoplifting-7d868e8b38b8. Accessed July 2018.
42 Ibid.
43 CBS/AP, "Spike in Shoplifting Blamed on California Prop 47's Reduced Penalties," CBS SF Bay Area, May 14, 2016, http://sanfrancisco.cbslocal.com/2016/05/14/shoplifting-california-prop-47-reduced-penalties. Bill Turner, "Shoplifting Penalties Rarely Benefit Retailers These Days," *LPM Insider*, August 23, 2017, http://losspreventionmedia.com/insider/shoplifting-organized-retail-crime/changes-in-shoplifting-penalties-make-it-tougher-for-retailers. Marella Gayla, "What's the Punishment for Theft? Depends on What State You're In," Marshall Project, August 9, 2017, https://www.themarshallproject.org/2017/08/09/what-s-the-punishment-for-theft-depends-on-what-state-you-re-in. Terri Inefuku, "Expert Says Change in Law Fuels Shoplifters to Steal More, and More Often," September 21, 2017, KHON2, http://www.khon2.com/news/local-news/expert-says-change-in-law-fuels-shoplifters-to-steal-more-and-more-often/901523619. Bob Salsberg, "Felony or Misdemeanor? Massachusetts May Change Larceny Laws," December 2, 2017, *Boston Globe*, https://www.boston.com/news/local-news/2017/12/02/felony-or-misdemeanor-state-may-change-larceny-laws. Betsy Z. Russell, "Idaho SupCourt Upholds Use of Burglary Law Against Wal-Mart Shoplifter," *Spokesman-Review*, December 22, 2015, http://www.spokesman.com/blogs/boise/2015/dec/22/idaho-supcourt-upholds-use-burglary-law-against-wal-mart-shoplifter. Accessed July 2018.
44 Ibid.
45 John Colapinto, "STOP, THIEF!" *New Yorker* 84, no. 26 (September 2008): 74–83.
46 PCMag, "How to Spot and Avoid Credit Card Skimmers," February 15, 2018, https://www.pcmag.com/article2/0,2817,2469560,00.asp. Accessed June 2018.
47 2010 Florida Statutes, Chapter 832, "Violations Involving Checks and Drafts," http://archive.flsenate.gov/Statutes/index.cfm?App_mode=Display_Statute&Search_String=&URL=0800-0899/0832/Sections/0832.05.html. Accessed June 2018.
48 Edwin Lemert, "An Isolation and Closure Theory of Naïve Check Forgery," *Journal of Criminal Law, Criminology, and Police Science* 44 (1953): 297–298.
49 Luke Mullins, "How Frank Abagnale Would Swindle You," *US News & World Report*, May 19, 2008, https://money.usnews.com/money/blogs/the-collar/2008/05/19/how-frank-abagnale-would-swindle-you. Abagnale & Associates, http://www.abagnale.com/index2.asp. Accessed June 2018.
50 Rachel E. Morgan and Grace Kena, *Criminal Victimization, 2016* (U.S. Department of Justice Office of Justice Programs Bureau of Justice Statistics, 2017), 1. Available at https://www.bjs.gov/index.cfm?ty=pbdetail&iid=6166. Accessed June 2018.
51 Federal Bureau of Investigation, Uniform Crime Reports, *Crime in the United States, 2017*, Motor Vehicle Theft, https://ucr.fbi.gov/crime-in-the-u.s/2017/crime-in-the-u.s.-2017/topic-pages/motor-vehicle-theft. Accessed October 2018.
52 Federal Bureau of Investigation, Uniform Crime Reports, *Crime in the United States, 2017,* Larceny-theft, https://ucr.fbi.gov/crime-in-the-u.s/2017/crime-in-the-u.s.-2017/topic-pages/larceny-theft. Accessed October 2018.
53 Winnie Hu, "More New Yorkers Opting for Life in the Bike Lane," *New York Times*, July 30, 2017, https://www.nytimes.com/2017/07/30/nyregion/new-yorkers-bike-lanes-commuting.html. Accessed June 2018.
54 Patrick Symmes, "Who Pinched My Ride," February 2012, *Outside*, https://www.outsideonline.com/1922671/who-pinched-my-ride. Accessed June 2018.
55 Shane D. Johnson, Aiden Sidebottom, and Adam Thorpe, Center for Problem Oriented Policing, Guide No. 52: Bicycle Theft, http://www.popcenter.org/problems/bicycle_theft. Accessed June 2018.
56 Tom Babin, "Why Are Cities Allowing Bicycle Theft to Go Virtually Unpunished?" *Los Angeles Times*, April 21, 2017, http://www.latimes.com/opinion/livable-city/la-ol-bicycle-theft-20170421-story.html. Accessed June 2018.
57 John Metcalfe, "Won't Somebody Please Stop This Guy Stealing Bikes in New York City?," Citylab, March 16, 2012, https://www.citylab.com/equity/2012/03/wont-somebody-please-stop-guy-stealing-bikes-new-york-city/1518. Accessed June 2018.
58 Babin, "Why Are Cities Allowing Bicycle Theft to Go Virtually Unpunished?"
59 Johnson, Sidebottom, and Thorpe, Center for Problem Oriented Policing, Bicycle Theft.
60 CBS, "Authorities Warn about Danger of Buying Used 'VIN Switched' Cars," CBS SF Bay Area, April 14, 2016, http://sanfrancisco.cbslocal.com/2016/04/14/authorities-warn-about-danger-of-buying-used-vin-switched-cars. Scott MacFarlane, Rick Yarborough and Steve Jones, 'Car Cloners' Create Fake VINs to Hide Stolen Vehicles, News4, May 3, 2016, https://www.nbcwashington.com/investigations/Car-Cloners-Create-Fake-VINs-to-Hide-Stolen-Vehicles-377892791.html. Candice Nguyen, People Sell Stolen Cars Through 'Car Cloning': Detectives, 7 San Diego, May 17, 2016, https://www.nbcsandiego.com/news/local/People-Sell-Stolen-Cars-Through-Car-Cloning-Detectives-379743191.html. Accessed May 2018.
61 Federal Bureau of Investigation, Uniform Crime Reports, *Crime in the United States, 2017*, Arson, https://ucr.fbi.gov/crime-in-the-u.s/2017/crime-in-the-u.s.-2017/topic-pages/arson. Accessed October 2018.
62 Federal Bureau of Investigation, *Uniform Crime Reporting Handbook*, 2004, 12. Available at https://ucr.fbi.gov/additional-ucr-publications/ucr_handbook.pdf/view. Accessed June 2018.
63 Technical Working Group on Fire/Arson Scene Investigation, *Fire and Arson Scene Evidence: A Guide for Public Safety Personnel* (Washington, D.C.: U.S. Department of Justice, 2000), 2. Available at https://www.nij.gov/topics/law-enforcement/investigations/crime-scene/guides/pages/twgs.aspx. Accessed June 2018.
64 James Brady, "The Social Economy of Arson: Vandals, Gangsters, Bankers, and Officials in the Making of an Urban Problem," in *Crime and Capitalism: Readings in Marxist Criminology*, ed. David Greenberg (Philadelphia: Temple University Press, 1993), 211–257.
65 Richard Cole, "Arsonists Burning U.S. Forests for Profit on Equipment, Timber," AP/*Austin American-Statesman*, September 4, 1995, A17.
66 Sarah A. Soule and Nella Van Dyke, "Black Church Arson in the United States, 1989–1996," *Ethnic and Racial Studies* 22, no. 4 (1999): 724–742.
67 Raisa Habersham, "Cops: 5 Men Got Drunk, Set Home on Fire, Posted It on Social Media," *Atlanta Journal-Constitution*, May 30, 2018, https://www.ajc.com/news/crime–law/cops-men-got-drunk-set-home-fire-posted-social-media/6XGynmZyk8OilURnc5i06N. Accessed June 2018.
68 Charles T. Putnam and John T. Kirkpatrick, *Juvenile Firesetting: A Research Overview* (Washington, D.C.: U.S. Department of Justice Office of Justice Programs, 2005), 4–5. Wayne S. Wooden and Martha Lou Berkey, *Children and Arson: America's Middle Class Nightmare* (New York: Plenum Press, 1984).

TEACH
Your Son
not to Rape

Criminal Offenses Against People

FEATURES

A woman carries a sign in solidarity for a Stanford rape victim during graduation at Stanford University, in Palo Alto, California. How has the MeToo movement changed the way people think about sexual assault?

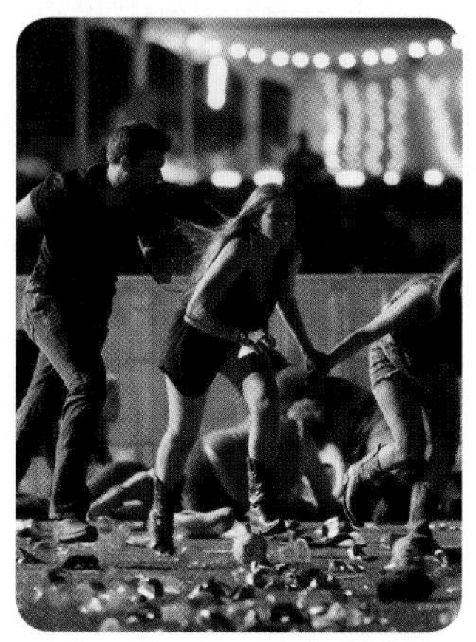

Victims run after hearing gunfire during the Route 91 Harvest Festival. Why were so many people killed or injured in this mass shooting?

On October 1, 2017, the third night of a country music event was in full swing on the Las Vegas strip. At 10:05 PM the Route 91 Harvest Festival was packed with 22,000 people for the outdoor performance of singer Jason Aldean.[1] At first, the crowd thought they heard fireworks, but they were soon shocked as gunfire rained down. Over the next 10 minutes, gunshot victims dropped to the ground as people ran to find safety. When the shooting was over, 58 people were dead and hundreds more were injured.[2]

From the 32nd floor of the Mandalay Bay Resort and Casino, which overlooked the venue, Stephen Paddock, 64, was firing from two adjoining suites where he had stored a small arsenal of weapons. He had 24 guns, including 14 AR-15 rifles, at least one of which had a bump stock, a device that enables a semiautomatic weapon to fire almost as quickly as a machine gun.[3] He ultimately fired more than 1,000 rifle rounds into the crowd, which was constrained by a chain-link fence surrounding the venue.[4]

An hour after the shooting stopped, the police breached Paddock's hotel suites and found him dead of a self-inflicted gunshot wound. Paddock, a retired accountant, had no significant criminal history and no known affiliation with terrorist groups. He was described as an avid gambler.[5]

Sources of Violent Crime

LEARNING OBJECTIVE | 1

Give the common sources of violence.

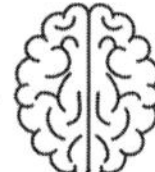

LEARNING OBJECTIVE | 2

Discuss three common physical sources of violent crime.

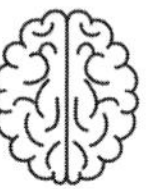

LEARNING OBJECTIVE | 3

Discuss three common social and cultural sources of violent crime.

Aggression is the basic ingredient in violent crime. Why are humans sometimes aggressive? Some scholars believe human **aggression**, an offensive action that is a psychological or physical encroachment without the consent of the other party, is learned. Others believe it is genetic and that human beings, as well as many other types of animals, have evolved to be aggressive in order to survive. From this viewpoint, aggression is not a pathological but a normal, often necessary, response to the world.[6]

Scholars recognize two broad types of aggression: active and passive. Passive aggression manifests itself in the form of refusals: refusal to speak, refusal to move, refusal to perform a task. The passive-aggressive person takes offensive action by not acting. **Violence** is active aggression, that is, physical force with intent to cause fear or to injure, harm, or kill. Psychologist Seymour Feshbach distinguished between two types of aggression: hostile/expressive aggression and instrumental aggression. The purpose of hostile/expressive aggression is to draw attention to oneself or to something else or to make victims suffer for the sake of suffering. Much violent crime, such as the 2017 mass murder in Las Vegas, stems from hostile/expressive aggression. The purpose of instrumental aggression is to attain status or resources that belong to others.[7] The criminal offense of robbery is a kind of instrumental aggression, as is war. As an alternative to Feshbach's dichotomy, psychologists Brad J. Bushman and Craig A. Anderson suggest a continuum of aggression since criminal offenses can have multiple motives. Such a continuum is shown in Figure 10.1.[8]

Aggression, then, is the source of violence, but not all aggression is violence. We can see this difference in the distinction between burglary and robbery. **Burglary** is the illegal entry of a structure with intent to commit a felony or theft. **Robbery** is forcibly taking an item from another person. Burglary, though aggressive, is not violent. Robbery is both aggressive and violent.

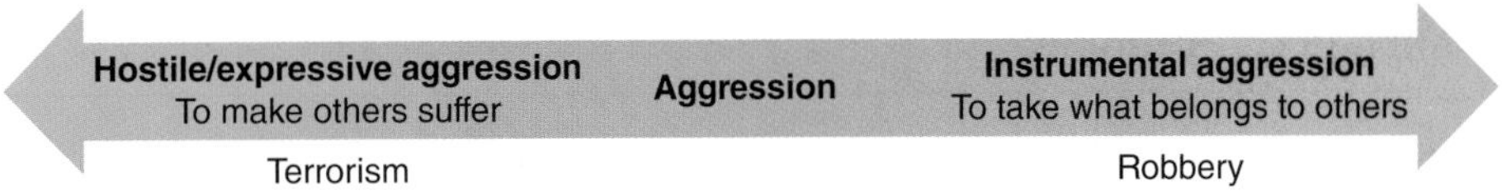

This chapter will focus on criminal offenses that involve violence: murder, **rape**, robbery, and aggravated assault. The perpetrators of these offenses are both aggressive and violent. Although not all aggression is antisocial—imagine an especially exciting football game—acts of violence, except in the case of self-defense and police actions, certainly are.

Hostile/expressive aggression To make others suffer	Aggression	Instrumental aggression To take what belongs to others
Terrorism		Robbery

FIGURE 10.1 The Continuum of Aggression

Hostile/expressive aggression draws attention or makes victims suffer for the sake of suffering. Instrumental aggression seeks to attain status or resources that belong to others. An offense—robbery or murder, for example—may fall anywhere along the continuum.

THINK ABOUT IT
Which type of aggression do you think is more common?

Common sources of violence include psychological abnormality, substance abuse, evolutionary factors, and socialization and cultural values. Some violent crime involves instrumental aggression. A burglar who enters a dwelling intending only to steal a television set might find himself in a fight with the resident who surprises him. In this situation, both combatants are fighting for a reason: The burglar is fighting to get away or to disable the resident in order to steal the television set, and the resident is fighting to disable or frighten away the burglar. Some violent crime, however, includes what we often call "senseless" violence—for example, when a store clerk, a homeowner, or a person walking down the street is attacked or killed for no apparent reason. Is such violence instrumental or hostile/expressive? The shooting, with no apparent motive, of a young man on a street corner seems hostile/expressive to those who learn about it on the nightly newscast. But it makes perfect instrumental sense to the gang member who shot the man to gain status in his gang.

Violent crime has many causes, all of which are located somewhere on the continuum from hostile/expressive to instrumental. See Table 10.1 for a look at three types of criminological theories that address violent crime: subculture of violence theory, feminist theory, and evolutionary theories. Each set of theories contains ideas about the reasons for violent crime that range along the continuum of aggression. For example, some aspects of the subculture of violence theory lie more toward the hostile/expressive end of the continuum (making others suffer to draw attention to oneself), whereas others lie more toward the instrumental end (using violence to achieve status and success).

Please keep in mind that the following typologies are broad and are not meant to explain every possible source of violent crime. The best predictor of whether a person will commit a violent criminal offense is past behavior, regardless of mental or biological state.[9]

Physical Sources of Violent Crime

Physical sources of violent crime can be traced to human biological/psychological processes and events. Three common sources of violent crime that stem from the human body and mind are mental disorder, substance abuse, and evolutionary factors. Let's examine each of these in detail.

MENTAL DISORDER

Mental disorder is a broad term used for various psychological diseases and abnormalities. It is also called mental illness. People with mental disorders have problems coping with daily life and making simple, rational decisions. There are many types and degrees of mental disorder, and some mentally disordered people are more affected by their condition than others. Research has found that individuals within the offender population are three times more likely to have a mental disorder than individuals within the general population, although many

aggression—An offensive action; psychological or physical encroachment without the consent of the other party.

violence—Aggressive physical force with intent to cause fear or to injure, harm, or kill.

Instant Recall from Chapter 3 **burglary**—The unlawful entry of a structure with the intent to commit a felony or theft.

Instant Recall from Chapter 3 **robbery**—The taking or attempting to take anything from another person or persons by violence or the threat of violence.

Instant Recall from Chapter 3 **rape**—"The penetration, no matter how slight, of the vagina or anus with any body part or object, or oral penetration by a sex organ of another person, without the consent of the victim."[10]

mental disorder—Term used for a variety of psychological diseases and abnormalities; mental illness.

TABLE 10.1 Criminological Theory and Offenses Against People

These three sets of theories are examples of how criminological theory can explain violent offending. Other theories discussed in this text may be used the same way, but, for the sake of brevity, these three are discussed here.

Subculture of violence (sociological theory)	Violence is instrumental to achieving status and protecting oneself in a subculture that is not bound by the dominant culture's rules. Subcultures in which violence is common are often rooted in poverty. With an absence of legitimate ways to achieve success and status, violence against other people is highly valued. In addition, the willingness to use violence for self-protection against predators is essential.
Feminist theory (critical theory)	Feminist theories of criminology consider how the patriarchal nature of society encourages men to use violence against women. By having rigid social roles that are determined by gender, the status of women is one of reduced opportunity and service toward men. As women seek greater freedom and control of their own lives, husbands, boyfriends, and fathers often do not easily give up what they believe is their cultural heritage of dominance The resulting physical, psychological, and sexual abuse that women experience has been a focus of feminist theories of violence. In addition, new research on the concept of masculinity sheds light on how men are systematically taught and encouraged to use violence not only in relationship to the women in their lives, but also as a means of establishing their identities with peers.
Evolutionary theories of violence (biological theory)	Violence Is so pervasive in human societies that some criminologists attribute it to heredity. Instead of being maladaptive violence, for example, forced sexual behavior may be conducive to spreading genes. Violence is a reproductive advantage that has allowed aggressive individuals to produce more offspring than those who are less aggressive. These evolutionary theories of crime suggest that violence is deeply embedded in human nature. Critics of evolutionary theories contend that they give too much credit to nature (biological genes) and not enough credit to nurture (social environment).

experts believe this statistic is a better indicator of the poor state of the country's mental health system, which we will discuss later, than it is of the likelihood of the mentally disordered to break the law.[11] Although having a mental disorder is not generally an indicator of violent criminality—that is, mentally disordered people as a group are no more likely to commit violent offenses than those with no mental disorder—people suffering certain severe disorders are more likely to become violent.[12]

The four types of mental disorders most likely to be associated with violent crime are schizophrenic disorders, bipolar disorders, major depressive disorder, and antisocial personality disorder.[13] Although each is briefly described here, it is important to understand that these disorders are complicated, difficult to diagnose, and still not completely understood.

- Schizophrenic disorders. According to the International Classification of Diseases, schizophrenic disorders are characterized by distortions of thinking and perception, including thought echo; thought insertion or withdrawal; thought broadcasting; delusional perception and delusions of control; influence or passivity; and hallucinatory voices commenting or discussing the hearer in the third person.[14] According to mental health scholars, persons diagnosed with **schizophrenia** are at an increased risk to commit violent offenses, especially homicide.[15]
- Bipolar disorder. This disorder is characterized by manic and depressive episodes of behavior. Manic episodes feature euphoria, high energy, and distractibility; depressive episodes are marked by little or no interest in anything and a depressed mood. Bipolar disorder on its own does not usually lead to violent crime, but it may be a factor in risk-taking behavior that leads to crime. The risk of suicide among those with bipolar disorder may be at least 15 times greater than that of the general population.[16]

- Major depressive disorder. The symptoms of major depressive disorder include an exceptionally depressed state that lasts at least two weeks. It is marked by a stagnation of all activity and feelings of despair, worthlessness, and wanting to die. Depression probably plays a significant role in incidents in which a depressed person sets up a situation in which police are forced to shoot (suicide by cop). Depression is also noted in juvenile delinquents, especially girls and young women, although it is unclear whether the depression leads to delinquency or vice versa.[17]
- Antisocial personality disorder. **Antisocial personality disorder**, according to psychologist Robert Hare, is revealed by a person's lack of respect for others, impulsivity, lack of remorse, irresponsibility, disrespect for social norms and the law, irritability, extreme aggression, and inability to hold a job or maintain a relationship. This diagnosis is reserved for adults; children exhibiting these symptoms are considered to have conduct disorder. More males than females are diagnosed with this disorder.[18]

Most mentally disordered offenders are incarcerated for minor and non-aggressive offenses, and many professionals in both criminal justice and psychology have criticized the use of the criminal justice system as a "dumping ground" for mentally disordered people who would be better served by treatment than incarceration. In many major cities, more mentally disordered people can be found in jail than in mental hospitals.[19] Some critics point to cuts in public funding for mental treatment and increases in funding for prisons and jails as part of the reason. Thus, many mentally disordered people who cannot afford treatment go without it until they break the law and wind up within the criminal justice system.[20]

SUBSTANCE ABUSE

The relationship between substance abuse and violent crime is complex. Offenders who use illegal drugs commit robbery and **assault** more frequently than offenders who do not use illegal drugs, although no known substance directly causes people to become violent or break the law.[21] However, there is a relationship between substance abuse and lawbreaking. More than half of state prison inmates and two-thirds of inmates sentenced to jail are considered to be dependent on drugs (excluding alcohol, nicotine, and caffeine).[22] The substances most associated with crime include marijuana, heroin, cocaine, PCP (phencyclidine), amphetamines, methamphetamine, ecstasy (MDMA), rohypnol, alcohol, inhalants (typically, glue and paint solvents), and some pharmaceuticals. Most of these items are illegal (marijuana, heroin, and cocaine); however, some are not (inhalants, pharmaceuticals, and some of the ingredients in methamphetamine). The only listed substance that is legal to buy in every state for the purpose of becoming inebriated is also the one most closely associated with violent crime: alcohol.

Some studies suggest that a reduction in the availability or consumption of alcohol would reduce violent crime.[23] Alcohol has been found to be more closely related to violent crime than drug use.[24] About 37 percent of state inmates serving time for a violent offense have said they were under the influence of alcohol at the time of the offense.[25] In a sample studied by the Panel on the Understanding and Control of Violent Behavior, "alcohol drinking—by the perpetrator of a crime, the victim, or both—has immediately preceded at least half of all violent events, including murders."[26] The reason for these

Mood disorders are difficult to understand and often go undiagnosed. What other types of mental disorders are associated with violent crime?

schizophrenia—A mental disorder that includes delusions, hallucinations, disorganized speech, grossly disorganized behavior, and inappropriate affect.

Instant Recall from Chapter 5 **antisocial personality disorder** —A mental disorder characterized by a pattern of disregard for the rights of others, as well as impulsive, violent, and aggressive behavior without guilt.

Instant Recall from Chapter 3 **assault** —The criminal offense of attempting to inflict immediate bodily harm or making another person fear that such harm is imminent.

relationships is unclear. Is alcohol more likely to cause its users to become violent? Are violent people more attracted to alcohol? Or is alcohol simply the easiest substance to procure and therefore more common?

Alcohol appears to interfere with the brain functions responsible for self-control, although inebriation alone is not responsible for violence.[27] Usually, some other cognitive or situational factor is present—for example, a location where violence is more likely such as a bar or a large party, or the inebriated person's belief that alcohol will make her violent so she becomes violent when drunk.[28] Two factors related to the substance use/violent crime complex are sex and mental disorder. Not only is alcohol inebriation more likely to be associated with violent crime than drug inebriation, this is especially true among female offenders. Women are less likely than men to commit violent offenses but five times more likely to be drunk when they do.[29] Substance abuse is responsible for more violent crime than mental disorder.[30] However, diagnoses of substance abuse often co-occur with diagnoses of mental disorder in offenders.

A study conducted in the San Francisco County jails found that 78 percent of the homeless inmates with a severe mental disorder also had substance-abuse problems. These inmates were also held in jail longer than inmates who had been charged with similar offenses.[31] So, although substance abuse is not a cause of violent crime, it is often one factor among many responsible for violent offending.

EVOLUTIONARY FACTORS

The study of the effect of evolutionary factors on behavior and societies is a relatively new discipline called **sociobiology**. Its premise is that human social behavior, including antisocial tendencies, evolved for specific reasons much as the human body has. According to psychologists Joshua Duntley and Todd Shackelford, "Just as [natural] selection shaped physiological adaptations with specific problem-solving functions, it also shaped the structure of thoughts, preferences, desires, attitudes, and emotions to guide behaviors toward solving historically recurrent problems that affected reproductive fitness."[32]

Generally, the sociobiological approach to explaining crime is that antisocial behavior is not pathological; rather, it exists because humans evolved antisocial tendencies for specific reasons. Exactly what these reasons are—as well as the relationship between the brain, society, behavior, and crime—is currently under research. Here we look at some of the current scholarly approaches to the relationship between human evolution and violent crime.

As an exercise, let's take a sociobiological view of Terrie Moffitt's theory of life-course-persistent and adolescence-limited offenders from Chapter 7. From an evolutionary standpoint, neither type of offending is pathological, but rather each has a biological purpose. Adolescence-limited delinquent males engage in antisocial behavior as a response to competitive mating disadvantages. Their behavior is not genetic but social. For some reason, these young males are having trouble attracting mates, and they engage in antisocial behavior as a way to compete with more successful males. The behavior of life-course-persistent male offenders, however, might have a genetic basis. The strategy is the same, to compete for mates, but the life-course-persistent male offender is genetically obligated to compete for mates in this fashion. The idea is that a society composed primarily of pro-social individuals leaves a niche for the antisocial individual who propagates his genes in an exploitative, non-reciprocating fashion.[33] This very brief, simplified example offers an idea of how sociobiology seeks to explain violent crime. Duntley and Shackelford summarize some sociobiological explanations for violent crime.[34]

- Violence and murder. Violence and murder are ways to take resources or social status from rivals or eliminate rivals altogether. A fit competitor who inflicts more damage on rivals than he or she sustains is considered by others to be difficult to exploit and therefore has better access to resources and mates. The murder of rivals has an evolutionary purpose beyond disposing of them for resources: It eliminates the possibility of the victim's further reproduction, thus preventing the further spread of his or her genes; it hurts the victim's existing offspring by depriving them of parental protection and aid; and it hurts the victim's other close kin by marking them as easy to exploit and depriving them of the victim's social status and aid in group survival. For example, the murder of a kin group's primary hunter would deprive that group of the hunter's food contributions.

sociobiology—The study of evolutionary factors that influence behavior and societies.

- Intimate-partner violence. Both women and men use aggression and sometimes violence to maintain their reproductive relationships. Men tend to hide their partners and use threats and violence against romantic rivals. Women tend to enhance their appearance to demonstrate to their partners their desirability to other men. Although these strategies often resolve conflicts between men and women so they can successfully reproduce, both men and women may use aggression in a bid to defend their relationships when these strategies fail.
- Rape. The idea that rape is an evolutionary reproductive strategy is controversial. The hypothesis is that males use rape to spread their genes frequently and successfully by forcing their offspring upon women of their choosing. This strategy, however, has social and individual costs. It not only damages the women physically and psychologically, but it also prevents them from choosing the mates they believe are most reproductively fit.

Perhaps the most obvious critique of the sociobiological explanation of crime is that it does not explain why, if being antisocial is evolutionarily valuable, humans classify so many antisocial behaviors as criminal offenses. Across generations, countries, and cultures, the same set of violent behaviors—murder, assault, rape, robbery—tend to be classified as crime and bring harsh sanctions. Although these behaviors may benefit individuals from a natural selection standpoint, human societies loathe them if they are unchecked by laws. One reason may be that violent antisocial behavior tends to benefit individuals while harming society. On the one hand, the murder of a good hunter in a small hunter/gatherer tribe may allow the killer to claim the hunter's social and material resources, but the whole tribe is worse off for the loss of a productive member. On the other hand, if the entire tribe is composed of antisocial individuals who cannot cooperate because they are so busy taking advantage of one another, the tribe will be unable to exist for long, and none of its members' genes will survive. Antisocial individuals, then, occupy a survival niche. Like parasites, their success depends on their peers' pro-social abilities. A group can sustain some antisocial behavior from some members, but when the behavior occurs too often (repeated assaults) or is too severe (murder), the group defines the behavior as "crime" and seeks to deal with the offender.

Social and Cultural Sources of Violent Crime

Common social and cultural sources of violent crime include family dysfunction, social disorganization, and some subcultural values. Like biological sources of violent crime, social and cultural sources are contributing factors and are rarely, if ever, the sole sources of violent crime.

FAMILY DYSFUNCTION

Although families are considered the bedrock of American society, sometimes they simply do not work. Family dysfunction can occur for several reasons—poverty, parental abuse, juvenile delinquency, substance abuse, or disagreements among family members—all of which, in some cases, can lead to violence. Although violence within families used to be considered a "family problem" and the business of the family patriarch, it is now usually treated as a public safety issue and falls within the purview of the criminal justice system. Violence that stems from families can strike at two classes of victim: those within the family and those outside it. This type of violence can occur solely against each victim class, which is relatively rare, or, most commonly, against both classes.

- Family victimization only. Family members are victimized by one or more family members. This violence does not extend outside the family. For instance, one spouse beats the other and/or the children. However, neither the victimized spouse nor the children victimize strangers.
- Family victimization leading to extra-family victimization. Family members are victimized by one or more family members. These family members in turn victimize strangers or may become victimized by strangers. For instance, an abused child beats up other children at school or becomes the victim of bullying.[35]
- Extra-family victimization only. Family members are not violent with one another but violently victimize strangers. These cases are rare but have been documented (see Doubletake for the story of a murderous Kansas family). However, chances are, those who are violent outside their families are also violent or have experienced violence within their families.

DOUBLETAKE

The "Bloody Benders"

The Bender family allegedly murdered between 8 and 12 people at their inn on the Osage Trail, near what is now Cherryvale, Kansas, in the early 1870s. Not much is known about the family, which is thought to have immigrated from Germany. The family, John Bender Sr., his wife Kate, and their son John Bender Jr., and their daughter, also named Kate, appeared to have set up their inn and grocery store to attract wealthy travelers, whom they would kill and rob, then bury in their orchard.[36]

In early 1873, local residents noticed that the Benders' inn seemed to be abandoned. By this time, at least 11 people had disappeared. Upon searching the inn and grounds and discovering dead and emaciated livestock and signs of a hurried departure, the townspeople assumed the Benders were victims of the unknown killers thought to be stalking the area. However, a more thorough search revealed not only the bodies buried in the orchard, but a trap door in the house that led to a cellar covered in dried blood.

The Benders' technique was fairly straightforward. The front room—said to be where daughter Kate held séances—was divided by a curtain. The victim would be enticed to sit with his or her back to the curtain, then be distracted, probably by Kate. One of the men hidden on the other side of the curtain would hit the victim on the head with a hammer and drop the body through the trap door to the cellar, where his or her throat would be slit to ensure death.

At least two vigilante groups searched for the family, and the governor of Kansas offered a $2,000 reward. Although sightings of the family were reported for several decades, they were never found.[37]

THINK ABOUT IT

1. Families who work together as serial killers are extremely rare. Think of reasons why this is so.

SOCIAL DISORGANIZATION

According to **social disorganization theory**, disorganized areas, such as impoverished neighborhoods, lack the social controls that prevent violence. These controls include both formal and informal institutions and range from the local government, police, and community organizations, to businesses, schools, and churches to families, informal clubs, and neighborhood groups. The weaker these institutions are, the more disorganized the area. According to some theorists, it is this social disorganization that leads to crime.

Generally, theories of social disorganization and crime state that such attributes as income inequality, trust and involvement among neighbors, and social stability all affect an area's general level of crime as well as its level of violent crime. Social disorganization can affect all types of violence, including stranger violence and acquaintance violence, both hostile/expressive and instrumental. One study even found that any form of social instability in neighborhoods that were becoming wealthier as well as those that were becoming impoverished led to more violent crime simply because of the lack of social stability.[38] Yet another study connected violence to personal income inequality: People who believed they were not making enough money felt shamed and disrespected and denied access to the traditional means of status and respect.[39]

Instant Recall from Chapter 6 **social disorganization theory** —The idea that the breakdown of social bonds and the failure of social institutions cause crime.

Instant Recall from Chapter 6 **focal concerns** —Attitudes that the lower classes perpetuate as part of the values and norms they believe are necessary for survival in their neighborhoods.

SUBCULTURAL VALUES

A final major source of violent crime is found in some of the values held by subcultures. Subcultures can hold the values of the dominant culture as well as some of their own values that defy those of the dominant culture and that the dominant culture would define as negative.

In 1958, criminologist Walter Miller suggested a set of traits he called **focal concerns** that he believed some subcultures perpetuate as a part of their values and norms. These traits include trouble (the ability to get into and out of trouble), toughness, smartness, excitement, fate, and autonomy (independence from authority). Although these are not necessarily violence-prone traits, they are not crime or violence averse. The ability to handle trouble is often the ability to handle breaking the law. Being tough, while also pursuing excitement and thumbing a nose at authority, can lead a person into crime or at least into interpersonal violence.

In some subcultures, the desire to maintain personal honor can also lead to violent crime. Avoiding a physical fight after an insult or a slur may incur unacceptable damage to a person's honor. One study found that, contrary to social disorganization theory, social organization in some cultures, specifically in the South and West, can actually lead to more violence if that social organization is particularly concerned with personal honor. If the culture does not consider violence a deviant response in some situations, then more violence will occur.[40]

PAUSE AND REVIEW

1. **List three physical sources of violent crime.**
2. **Why may a dysfunctional family life lead an individual to violent behavior?**
3. **Summarize the argument that sources of violent crime are embedded in lower-class subcultures.**
4. **Critique the proposal that violent crime may be an evolutionary adaptation.**
5. **What is hostile/expressive aggression? What is instrumental aggression?**
6. **What are common sources of violence?**

Types of Violent Crime

LEARNING OBJECTIVE 4

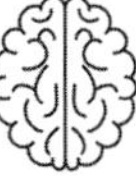

Define violent crime, and state the four violent criminal offenses recognized by the Federal Bureau of Investigation.

LEARNING OBJECTIVE 5

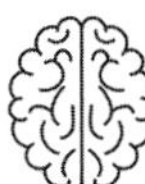

Explain the difference between homicide and murder.

LEARNING OBJECTIVE 6

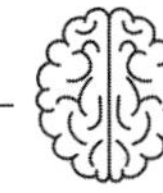

Discuss the traditional and modern defining elements of rape.

LEARNING OBJECTIVE 7

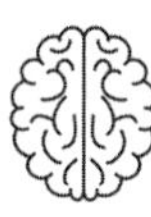

State the primary difference between robbery and other offenses involving theft.

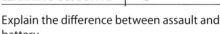

LEARNING OBJECTIVE 8

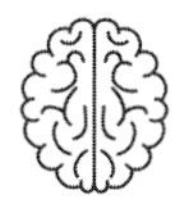

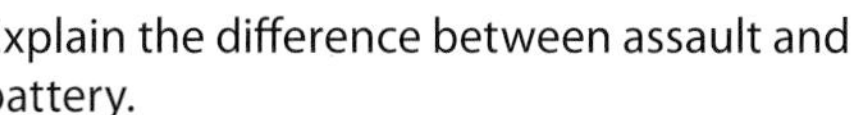

Explain the difference between assault and battery.

The FBI's Uniform Crime Reporting (UCR) program defines violent crime as offenses that include the use of force or threat of force. The FBI recognizes four violent criminal offenses: murder and non-negligent manslaughter, rape, robbery, and aggravated assault. The FBI estimated that 1.2 million violent offenses occurred in 2017, or about 383 violent offenses per 100,000 people. Most were aggravated assault (see Figure 10.2 for a comparison of the number of offenses).[41] The violent crime rate varies by region (see Figure 10.3); it is highest in the South and lowest in the Northeast.[42]

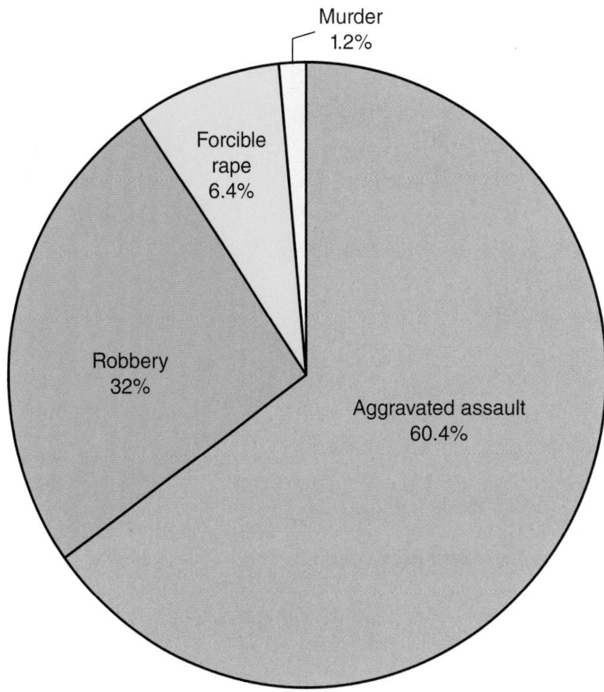

FIGURE 10.2 Comparison of Violent Offenses

THINK ABOUT IT
Discuss reasons why aggravated assault is the most committed violent offense.

Source: Federal Bureau of Investigation, Uniform Crime Reports, Crime in the United States, 2017, *Violent Crime, https://ucr.fbi.gov/crime-in-the-u.s/2017/crime-in-the-u.s.-2017/topic-pages/violent-crime. Accessed October 2018.*

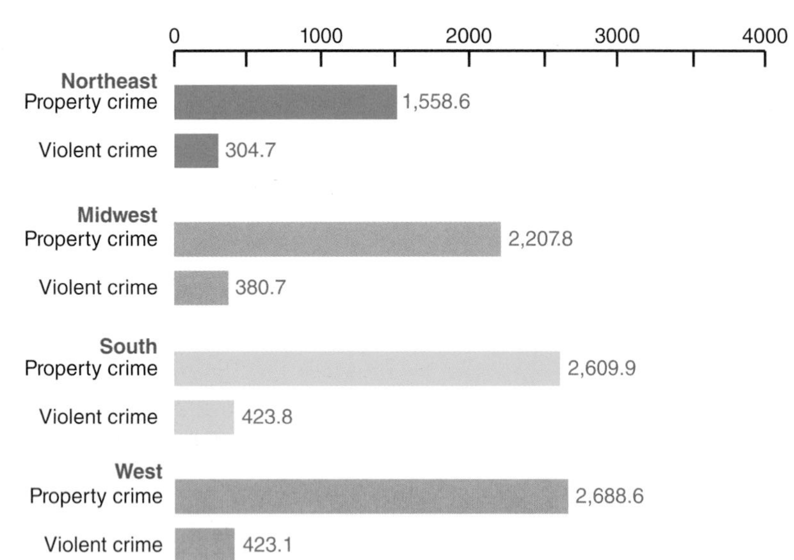

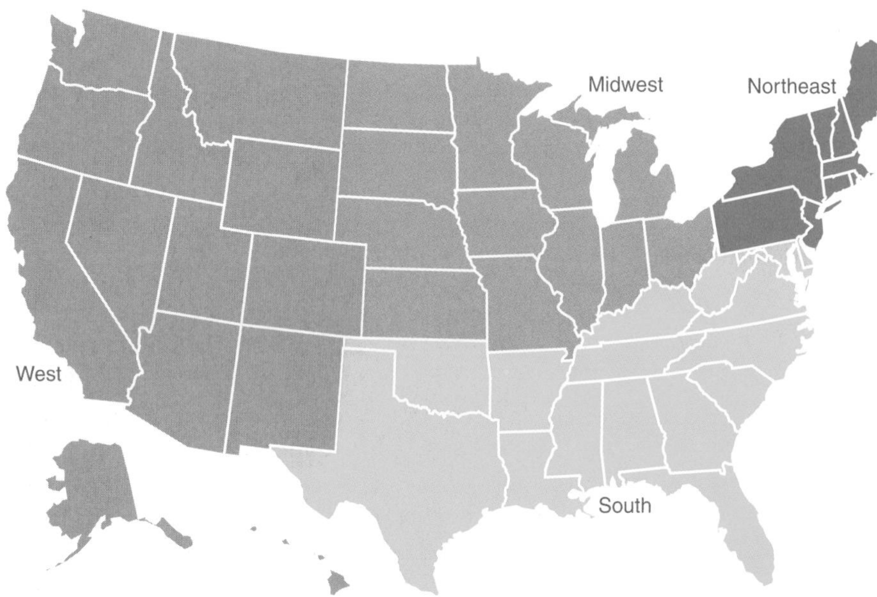

FIGURE 10.3 U.S. Regional Crime Map

The violent and property offense rates are highest in the South and West and lowest in the Northeast.

THINK ABOUT IT

Give possible reasons for the Northeast's relatively low crime rate.

Source: Federal Bureau of Investigation, Crime Map, Uniform Crime Reports, Crime in the United States 2017, *https://ucr.fbi.gov/crime-in-the-u.s/2017/crime-in-the-u.s.-2017/topic-pages/offenses-known-browse-by/region. Accessed October 2018.*

Murder

The FBI defines **murder** and non-negligent manslaughter as the willful killing of one human being by another (for the sake of brevity, we will refer to murder/non-negligent manslaughter as murder).[43] The FBI's classification of an offense as murder for the UCR is based on police investigation only and not on the determination of courts or medical officials. Justifiable homicide—the killing of a felon by a peace officer in the line of duty or the killing of a felon during the commission of a felony by a private citizen—is not counted in these statistics. Therefore, from a statistical standpoint, the number of murders in the United States is determined by the police.

What distinguishes murder from homicide and manslaughter? **Homicide** is simply the killing of one human being by another, regardless of intent.[44] A person can kill another person without meaning to, as in an automobile accident. Therefore, all murders and manslaughters are homicides, but not all homicides are murders or manslaughter. Some homicides are legal, as in the cases of self-defense, war, and execution. Manslaughter is a bit more complicated, and the definition varies from state to state. Generally, **manslaughter** is the unlawful killing of another human being without criminal intent, as in the heat of passion (such as in a bar fight); during the commission of a felony; or by omission of action, such as failing to follow proper safety rules. Vehicular manslaughter falls into this last category. Negligent manslaughter (which the FBI considers as serious as murder) typically involves willful negligence of a duty. For example, a surgeon who performs an operation while inebriated and kills the patient might be charged with negligent manslaughter.

MURDER AND THE LAW

Although the broad definition of murder applies to all states and the federal government, some specific laws differ among the states and federal government. The federal government recognizes two degrees of murder: first and second. Some states recognize a third degree and/or offense called "felony murder."

> **OFFENSE**
>
> Murder is the unlawful killing of a human being with malice aforethought. Every murder perpetrated by poison, lying in wait, or any other kind of willful, deliberate, malicious, and premeditated killing; or committed in the perpetration of, or attempt to perpetrate, any arson, escape, murder, kidnapping, treason, espionage, sabotage, aggravated sexual abuse or sexual abuse, child abuse, burglary, or robbery; or perpetrated as part of a pattern or practice of assault or torture against a child or children; or perpetrated from a premeditated design unlawfully and maliciously to effect the death of any human being other than him who is killed, is murder in the first degree.
>
> Any other murder is murder in the second degree.
>
> **SENTENCING**
>
> Whoever is guilty of murder in the first degree shall be punished by death or by imprisonment for life;
>
> Whoever is guilty of murder in the second degree shall be imprisoned for any term of years or for life.

FIGURE 10.4 U.S. Criminal Code: Murder

THINK ABOUT IT
Can you think of an offense that would constitute second-degree murder?

Source: "Murder." Title 18 US Code, Sec. 1111. Print. http://uscode.house.gov.

- First-degree murder is typically deliberate and premeditated murder planned and carried out in conjunction with felonies such as rape, burglary, or arson. Killing certain people such as children, police officers, and correctional staff can also bring an automatic first-degree murder charge. The specific criteria for first-degree murder differ slightly by state, and the federal government has its own definition. See Figure 10.4 for the federal definitions of first-degree and second-degree murder, as well as sentencing. State laws are usually some variation on this definition.
- Second-degree murder is usually an action in which the victim's death is neither intended nor planned but is a probable result. Imagine, for instance, a bar fight in which one person breaks a beer bottle over another's head, killing the victim. The assailant did not mean to kill the victim but did so in the heat of the moment. State laws vary on the definition of second-degree murder.
- Felony murder and third-degree murder. Some states have special felony murder laws to prosecute murders that happen during the course of a felony, for instance, if a robber accidentally shoots and kills a convenience store clerk. Some states recognize some manslaughter offenses as third-degree murder or may even combine the felony murder and third-degree murder offenses under one definition. The definition of these types of murder, or even their classification as types of murder, varies by state.

Murder sentencing in the states varies greatly depending on the circumstances of the murder and state law. The sentence for first-degree murder in most states and by the federal government is often life in prison or the death penalty. Second-degree murder and some types of manslaughter charges usually bring sentences of many years. According to some research, the offender's sex and race can affect sentencing, as can jurors' sex, race, age, and religion.[45] The victim's sex may also affect sentencing. A 2004 study found a "white, female victim effect" in which defendants in **capital murder** cases—those in which the murder offense, sometimes called a capital offense, is punishable by death—were more likely to receive a death sentence.[46]

Instant Recall from Chapter 3 **murder**—Willful homicide.

homicide—The killing of one human being by another.

manslaughter—The killing of one human being by another without criminal intent.

capital murder—A murder offense that is punishable by death. Sometimes called a "capital offense."

Typically, the severity of sentencing is linked to offender actions that aggravated the murder. Aggravating factors like rape, the victim's status (such as a child or police officer), the use of firearms, and the involvement of illegal substances can push the sentencing from a number of years to the death penalty. A follow-up study to the 2004 research discussed earlier found that female-victim murder cases may be more frequently selected for capital prosecution because female victims are more likely to be considered vulnerable and also seen as not contributing to their murders. Such cases are also more likely to have severe aggravating factors, especially rape.[47] Other factors that bring the death penalty into the picture include multiple victims, presenting a serious risk to others, murder committed during another serious offense, violence in the offender's history, murder committed for the sake of money, and the use of torture.[48] Some factors can mitigate the offense. One study found that jurors in a capital murder case were less likely to sentence an offender to death in the case of:

- unmedicated schizophrenia in which the defendant suffers severe delusions and hallucinations;
- drug addiction and inebriation at the time of the offense;
- a childhood diagnosis of borderline intellectual disability; or
- severe parental physical and verbal abuse during childhood.[49]

Although these mitigating factors were discussed in a single study, they are a good example of the factors the court may consider in a murder case, especially one involving the death penalty.

OFFENDER CHARACTERISTICS

According to the FBI, those most often arrested for murder are black persons between the ages of 9 and 29. After the age of 29, it is white persons who are most often arrested for murder (see Figure 10.5). Most suspects are also male. As you will recall, the police determine these statistics, which represent arrests and not convictions. It is possible that clearances by arrest (clearance occurs when a suspect is arrested, charged, and turned over to the court for prosecution) are significantly affected by police discretion and victim characteristics; that is, the more sympathetic the victim, the harder police work needed to clear the case. One analysis found that murder cases with female or young victims were more likely to be cleared, as well as those including drug- or gang-related activities. However, research has found that the presence and type of physical evidence and witnesses are more important than victim characteristics. Incident characteristics such as inebriated offenders, acquaintance between victims and offenders, weapons, and the number of recent or simultaneous serious violent offenses significantly increased the odds of clearance.[50]

Could violent offenders have a different way of thinking than non-violent offenders or law-abiding people? Some researchers have reported cognitive differences in extremely violent and murder offenders. They find some similarity between these offenders and people with

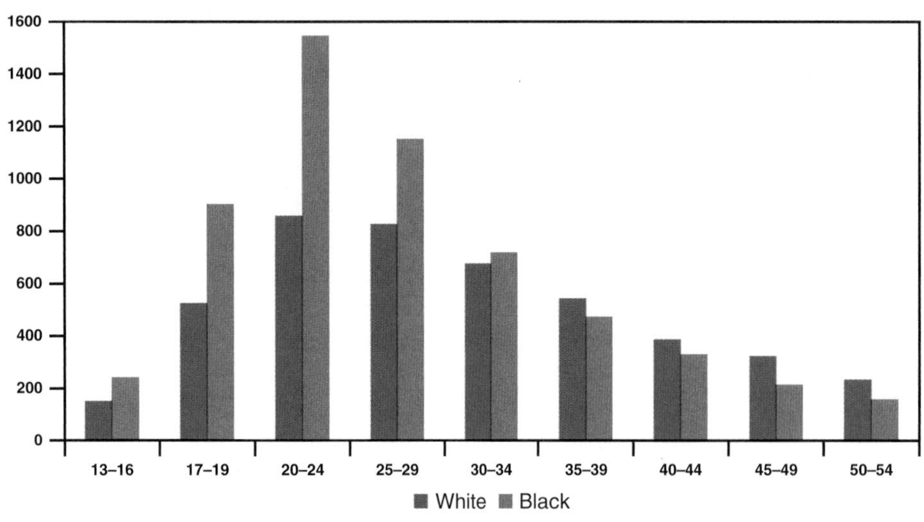

FIGURE 10.5 Murder Arrests by Race and Age

Although more black persons are arrested for murder as teens and young adults, more white persons are arrested as middle age approaches. Also, note that the arrests drop for both categories with the increase in age.

THINK ABOUT IT
Why do arrest rates generally drop with age?

Source: Federal Bureau of Investigation, Uniform Crime Reports, Crime in the United States, 2017, *Expanded Homicide Data Table 3: Murder Offenders by Age, Sex, Race, and Ethnicity 2017, https://ucr.fbi.gov/crime-in-the-u.s/2017/crime-in-the-u.s.-2017/tables/expanded-homicide-data-table-3.xls. Accessed October 2018.*

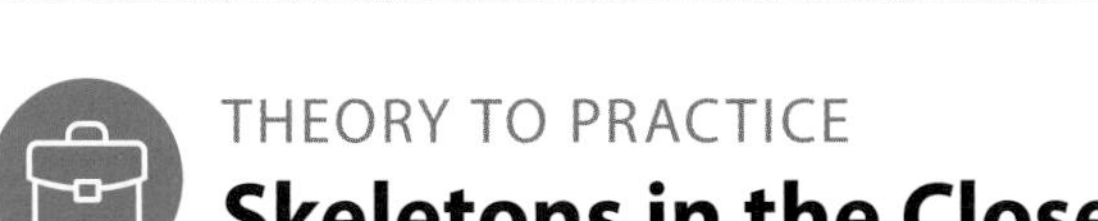

THEORY TO PRACTICE

Skeletons in the Closet

Lizzie Borden took an axe
and gave her mother forty whacks.
When she saw what she had done,
she gave her father forty-one.

In August 1892 in Fall River, Massachusetts, Lizzie Borden called out for help to the family maid, who ran downstairs to discover Lizzie with the body of her father, Andrew, who had been "hacked almost beyond recognition." After the town had been alerted, a neighbor who arrived to comfort Lizzie found the body of her stepmother, Abby Borden, who had also been hacked to death. Lizzie, 33, was tried and acquitted, but not only does she remain the most likely suspect, she was also convicted in the popular imagination.[51] Lizzie's case is not helped by the fact that she was but one descendant in a long line of alleged murderers, including Thomas Cornell who was hanged for the 1673 murder of his mother.[52]

It is tempting to consider such anecdotes as proof that violent behavior is hereditary. However, if violent behavior were found to originate from the body, it is possible that violent tendencies could be inherited much like eye color. As discussed in Chapter 5, researchers think the functioning of the prefrontal cortex and the amygdala may be connected to violent behavior. Other researchers are looking at genetics as an important factor (see the discussion of neurotransmitters in Chapter 5).

Was the family that produced Lizzie Borden and Thomas Cornell itself the victim of a wayward gene or dysfunctional brain structures? What about other members of this family? Were they violent, too, committing deeds that history failed to record?

Enter the Fallon family. A few years ago, the mother of University of California neuroscientist Jim Fallon told him about the possibility of murderous relatives—she had heard some stories about the Fallon side of the family—and asked her son to look into it. After all, Fallon's specialty is the biological basis of antisocial behavior. Was it true that the Fallon branch of the family harbored a lineage of murderers?

When Jim Fallon discovered his family's direct relation to Lizzie Borden, Thomas Cornell, and at least five other alleged murderers, he decided to look a little deeper. Using brain scans and blood samples from himself, his wife, their three children, and his three brothers, Fallon looked for signs of psychopathy and behavioral problems: low activity in the prefrontal cortex and the high-aggression MAOA gene. Everyone's brain scan showed normal activity, and all carried the low-aggression MAOA gene—everyone, that is, except for one person: Fallon himself. His brain scan not only showed abnormally low cortex activity, but also the high-aggression MAOA gene. Fallon told National Public Radio, "If you look at the [brain] scan, I look just like one of those killers."[53]

The research into the effects of brain functioning on antisocial behavior is promising, but much remains to be understood about how nature and nurture interact. Fallon admits that his biological signposts point to a violent, antisocial person. Although Fallon is known in his family for somewhat impulsive, risk-taking behavior—for example, when in Kenya, he took his teenage son fishing in a lion-infested area—he is neither antisocial nor violent. For this, Fallon credits his nurturing: "I had a charmed childhood. If I'd been mistreated as a child, who knows what might have happened?"[54]

It is possible, then, that Fallon's "Cousin Lizzie," as he calls her, got a bum rap. After her trial, Borden and her sister bought a home in Fall River, where Lizzie lived until her death at age 67 in 1927, never harming a soul.[55]

damage in the orbitofrontal region of the brain, which is responsible for memory, reward-pursuit, and decision making.[56] Still, this area of brain study is only just beginning, and researchers are careful about connecting brain activity to antisocial behavior (see Theory to Practice).

MASS AND SERIAL MURDER

The most common definition of **mass murder** is the killing of three or more people in a single incident. Some criminologists recognize a subcategory of mass murder called **spree murder**, in which a killer takes the lives of several victims at successive locations within a longer period of time than a mass

mass murder—The killing of three or more people in a single incident.

spree murder—The killing of several victims at successive locations within a longer period of time than a mass murder.

TABLE 10.2

	MURDERER	YEARS ACTIVE	INCIDENT	OUTCOME
Mass murderers	Charles Whitman	1966	Shot and killed his mother, his wife, and 14 people at the University of Texas.	Suicide at the scene
	Timothy McVeigh	1995	Bombed the Murrah Federal Building in Oklahoma City, Oklahoma, killing 168 people	Execution by lethal injection in 2001
	Nikolas Cruz	2018	Accused of shooting 34 people, killing 17 at Marjory Stoneman Douglas High School in Parkland, Florida	Awaiting trial as of June 2018
Spree murderers	Charles Starkweather and Carol Fugate	1958	Killed 11 people, including Fugate's parents and 2-year-old sister, in Nebraska and Wyoming	Starkweather was executed in Nebraska in 1959; Fugate was sentenced to life in prison but was paroled in 1976
	John Allen Muhammad and Lee Boyd Malvo	2002	Shot and killed 14 people in several states	Muhammad was executed in 2009; Malvo was sentenced to life in prison without parole
	Jason Dalton	2016	Accused of shooting eight people, killing six while picking up and dropping off Uber fares.	As of June 2018, Dalton was still awaiting trial; Dalton's attorney has filed a notice of intent to use an insanity defense
Serial murderers	Ted Bundy	1974–1978	Confessed to 30 murders; possibly committed 34 murders	Executed in 1989
	Dennis Rader	1974–1991	Pleaded guilty to 10 murders	Sentenced to 10 consecutive life sentences without parole
	Karla Homolka and Paul Bernardo	1990–1993	Raped and killed three teenaged girls, including Homolka's 15-year-old sister	Homolka pleaded guilty to manslaughter in exchange for testimony against Bernardo and was released in 2005; Bernardo was sentenced to life without parole for 25 years
	Todd Kohlhepp	2003–2016	Real estate agent from Spartanburg, South Carolina, who killed seven people. Was caught when a woman he kidnapped was found chained by the neck inside a storage container.	Sentenced to seven consecutive life sentences without parole

murder—for example, over a period of a few days or weeks—but a shorter period of time than serial murder. **Serial murder** is the killing of a sequence of victims committed in three or more separate events over an extended period of time. Serial murderers can kill several victims over a long time, decades even, with relatively long periods between each killing. See Table 10.2 for examples of each type of murderer.

Although mass, spree, and serial murderers have long caught the public's imagination and have sold countless novels, films, and other media since the 19th century, such offenders are relatively rare.[57] (However, at least one study says the annual number of serial murders is underestimated because some missing people are never reported as such.)[58] Their rarity is one reason these types of offenses get so much media attention and remain in the public memory long after the killers are locked away or executed. Although the offenders are often romanticized—for example, while in prison, serial killer Ted Bundy received bags of mail from female fans—their activities may be what the public finds most intriguing. The identity of Jack the Ripper, probably the most famous murderer in the Western world, has never been discovered even as his offenses have been repeatedly dissected for clues throughout the decades.

If caught, serial, spree, and mass murderers typically receive either death sentences or life sentences with no chance of parole. A notable exception is Canadian Karla Homolka, who claimed she was abused by her husband and testified against him in exchange for a guilty plea of manslaughter in the killings of three women, including her sister. Her case was particularly controversial because videotapes that portrayed her as having an active and willing role in the killings were not discovered until after she had made her plea deal.[59] Homolka was released from prison in July 2005.[60]

Numerous theories seek to explain, or at least shed some light on, why mass murderers, spree murderers, and especially serial murderers do what they do. Many serial murder theories focus on psychological motivations connected to childhood experiences, particularly animal cruelty, fire-setting, and parental abuse.[61] However, according to a multidisciplinary symposium hosted by the FBI, no single factor causes a person to become a serial killer. It is interesting that the FBI's assembly of academics and criminal justice professionals prefer this classical explanation for serial murder: "The most significant factor [in the development of the serial killer] is the serial killer's personal decision in choosing to pursue their crimes."[62] Theories about mass murder and spree murder often consider mental illness and mental stress as causes, although most mass and spree murderers are not believed to be insane; that is, they know what they are doing.

Rape

The definition of rape as a violent offense against the person is relatively recent and remains controversial.

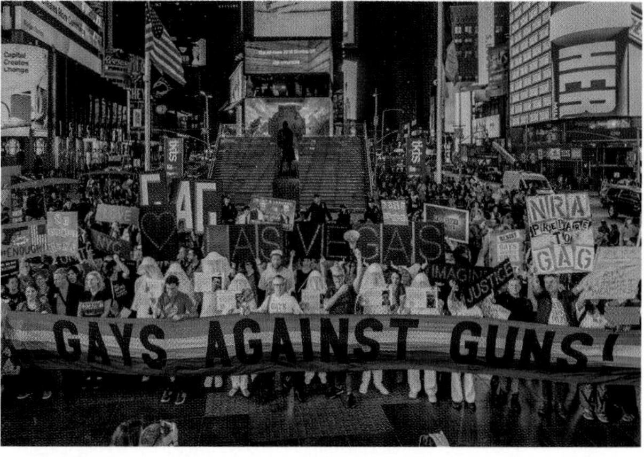

Gays Against Guns organized a rally and a march in New York City in response to the Las Vegas massacre. Why do some people believe gun control legislation is a solution to mass murders?

Rape was once considered an offense involving sex and property and not violence or violation of human rights. In early times, it was an offense against men because it diminished the value of the women who were their property, especially daughters, who could not then be married off.[63] An offender had to make reparations to the primary male relative of the victim and not to the victim herself.

The FBI's old definition of forcible rape, "the carnal knowledge of a female forcibly and against her will," reflected these old norms as it did not include males. A misconception was that it was not possible for males to be raped; they could only be assaulted. The FBI changed its definition of rape in 2013 to the following: "penetration, no matter how slight, of the vagina or anus with any body part or object, or oral penetration by a sex organ of another person, without the consent of the victim."[64] Advances in criminology and gender studies have helped correct these misconceptions to some extent, but rape remains a difficult topic and often turns on the issue of consent. Also, although rape has long been a tactic in war, the strategy of raping and sexually assaulting not only women and children, but also men, has become more common. However, rape happens disproportionately to female persons. In 2016, females reported 272,040 rape victimizations, and males, 51,408.[65] The 25- to 34-year-old age groups, both men (15,951) and women (107,632), reported the largest number of rape victimizations.

---

serial murder—The killing of a sequence of victims committed in three or more separate events over an extended period of time.

A Million Women Rising is a march in London by only women and children to protest the violence against women around the world. Do other countries have rape cultures?

RAPE AND THE LAW

Human beings are not the only animals that have non-consensual copulation. It has been observed among other primates, as well as dolphins, ducks, insects, crabs, seals, and orangutans.[66] However, rape is possible only among human beings because, like other offenses, it is socially defined.

Although rape has always been considered a violation of both the social order and the individual, the nature of that violation has changed throughout the millennia. The Code of Hammurabi, an early legal code, dealt with several types of rape. The rapist of a betrothed virgin was to be killed, but the girl was considered to be without guilt. A father who raped his daughter was thrown out of the city. However, a married woman who was raped was to be thrown in the river along with the rapist because the rape was considered to be adultery and both parties were judged to be at fault. The woman's husband could rescue her if he saw fit, and the king could pardon the rapist. The same was true under early Hebrew law, except that both woman and attacker were stoned to death as adulterers rather than drowned, and neither could be saved by either husband or king.[67]

Gradually, rape became a survivable ordeal for women (that is, if they survived the rape), although it remained a property dispute in many cultures. In early England, men who raped wealthy virgins were killed and dismembered. The female connection to property—females were allowed to inherit their father's property but could not marry without their lords' permission—gave rise to the practice of "heiress theft" in which a knight or other ambitious individual could gain property by stealing and marrying the heiress who owned it.

The treatment of rape as a public safety issue and an affront to the individual rights of women in U.S. law emerged from England's 13th-century Statutes of Westminster. Under these laws, there was no difference between the rape of virgins and that of married women, and children could not give consent at all (which later provided the basis for U.S. **statutory rape** laws). For the first time, the state took an active role in the prosecution of rape on behalf of victims. If the woman or her family failed to institute a civil suit within 40 days, the right to prosecute passed to the state.[68] Although legal action by women was possible in early England, and later in the North American colonies, it was difficult to pursue. The victims, who had to prove their cases to all-male courts, were often intimidated by the family of the accused as well as by the social stigma of the proceedings. For these reasons, rape trials were relatively rare.[69]

A glaring omission from these historical legal treatments of rape is the rape of males by other males. "Male rape," as it is commonly known, is as old as the rape of females, but it occupies a different place in ancient cultures. It was generally not considered an act of sex and adultery but of violence and the assertion of power. In many cultures, including Greek and Roman cultures—both of which include many myths of the rape of men and boys by male gods—defeated soldiers were raped. A raped male soldier was no longer considered able to lead or fight. There appears to be little or no ancient law addressing male rape, possibly because it was carried out as a matter of war and punishment. Although male rape has continued throughout the centuries, the Western view of homosexuality has changed the nature of the stigma somewhat, even as male rape continued to be ignored by the law until recently. We will further explore the modern treatment of male rape victims later in this chapter.

As mentioned earlier, the FBI's old definition of rape specified females, as did other definitions of rape. The English common law definition of rape was "carnal knowledge of a woman forcibly and against her will."[70] Although many states and jurisdictions have dropped the sex/gender requirement from their definitions of rape, the three general elements of the definition are sexual intercourse, force, and, most importantly, the victim's lack of consent. (Modern

---

statutory rape—A criminal offense that takes place when a person has consensual sex with another person who is not old enough to legally consent.

law recognizes the rape of males, but it might be termed "sexual assault" rather than "rape.") Traditionally, the most prominent element has been force. The attacker had to physically force the victim to perform intercourse for a rape to be defined as such. Not many decades ago, a woman who took her alleged attacker to court had to prove she had put up an adequate fight.[71] Also, "intercourse" was narrowly defined as penetration of the vagina by the penis. Any other kind of contact was not considered rape. Today, the basic element in the definition of rape is the victim's lack of consent, regardless of the nature of the victim/attacker relationship.[72]

Although rape laws seem fairly straightforward, often prosecution does not proceed because of the stigma rape carries. It is rare for anyone to think ill of murder or robbery victims, but rape victims are often considered responsible for their victimization, and this presents a problem in the criminal justice system. Rape is the only violent offense whose prosecution depends on proving the lack of something: the victim's consent.[73] A rape trial is sometimes called "the second rape" of the victim because the victim must not only recount the incident, but also prove the case before a jury. (See Policy Implications for changes in the rape laws of some states.)

The type of rape and the type of rapist affect the prosecution of the offense. There are two broad categories of rape: stranger rape and acquaintance rape. Stranger rape has much in common with other street offenses, such as mugging, in that the victim and attacker do not know each other, and the victim was presumably minding his or her own business at the time of the attack. Still, many jurors and even some criminal justice professionals may assume a female victim was "asking for it" by behavior or style of dress, or that a male victim was homosexual and the victimization was simply part of such behavior. Such misconceptions complicate the prosecution of even what appears to be clear-cut stranger victimizations.

POLICY IMPLICATIONS

Changing the Law on Rape

Laws concerning rape and sexual assault are continuously in flux as legislators consider the changing standards as to what constitutes criminal behavior. Here are some examples of new laws, as well as proposals that have yet to be acted upon.

- The North Carolina state supreme court ruled in 1979 that continuing to have sex with someone who at first gave consent, but then changed her or his mind, is not considered rape. Legislation has been introduced to amend the law, but passage appears to be unlikely.[74]
- Maryland has moved aggressively to update its rape laws by passing three bills that support victims of sexual assault. One law states explicitly that a victim of sexual assault does not have to physically resist for the attack to be prosecuted as a criminal offense. Another law stipulates that, like forced intercourse, coerced oral or anal sex is also rape. A third law states that rape kits must be preserved for 20 years instead of discarded after a few months, as has been the practice of some jurisdictions.[75]
- The Kentucky House of Representatives passed a bill that would make someone 28 years of age or older having sex with a 16- or 17-year-old a statutory rape regardless of consent. Violating this law could lead to up to five years in prison. Language in the legislation allows for lack of knowledge of the victim's age on the part of violators to be used as a defense.[76]
- A new Virginia law states that police officers must explain to victims what their rights are concerning rape kits. Victims have the right to see the results of tests on this evidence. Additionally, the law requires police to keep victims updated on their investigations. Rape kits must be sent to the lab within 60 days.[77]
- California has eliminated its statute of limitations for rape and other sexual assaults. Formerly, suspects could not be charged with a criminal offense if the incident happened more than 10 years earlier.[78]
- Oregon passed a law aimed at preventing abuse against women in the janitorial industry. Female janitors work mainly at night and are alone in empty buildings. It is often their supervisors who assault or sexually harass them.[79]

THINK ABOUT IT

1. Do you believe the Me Too Movement will change society's attitude toward rape and sexual assault?
2. What kind of laws would encourage victims to report sexual assault?

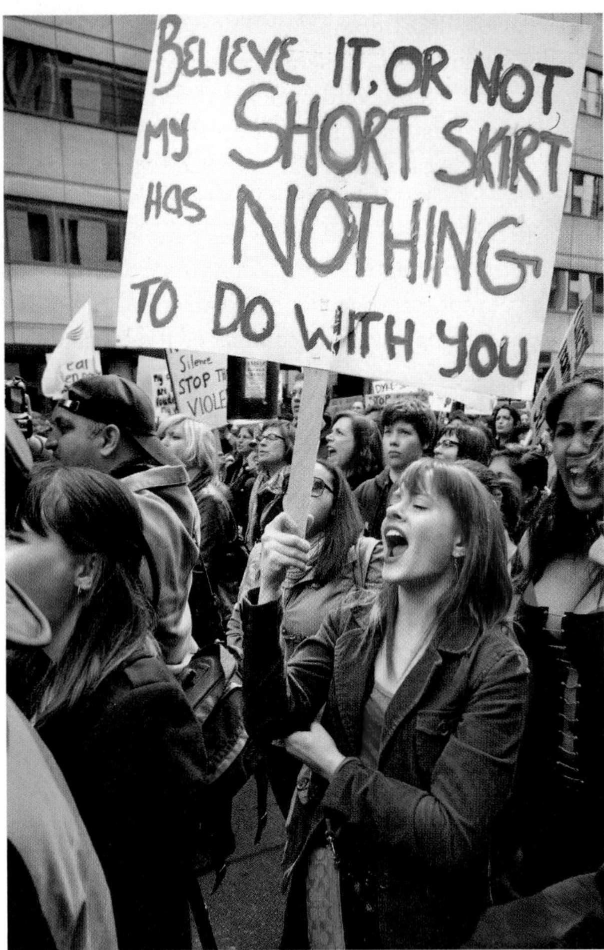

Protestors seek to raise awareness about victim-blaming and rape myths. In what ways does victim-blaming discourage victims from reporting to police?

Acquaintance rape cases are even more difficult to prosecute. If the victim was drugged or inebriated, he or she might be unsure of the circumstances of the rape. If the victim and offender are friends, lovers, or even married, the victim might not know whether the law would even consider the victimization to be rape. Sex workers who are victimized by clients tend to receive even less sympathy. After all, the thinking goes, the sex worker willingly entered the situation, so isn't he or she responsible if things go wrong?[80] Fortunately, these popular attitudes have subsided over the past few decades, and it is now somewhat easier for victims who know their attackers to seek legal redress. Rape shield laws disallow information about an accuser's prior sexual activity from the court case; however, some states' exceptions to these laws allow such information to be heard if it could exonerate a defendant.[81] Until the 1970s, a husband could not be prosecuted for raping his wife because such an offense did not legally exist.[82]

Years of work by feminist activists and criminal justice professionals eventually led to an overhaul of the legal definition of rape. These changes improved the chances that some types of rape victims would find justice, although rape prosecutions remain difficult and rape remains the least-reported violent offense.[83] In 1975, Michigan led the states in rewriting rape laws to include a range of circumstances, as well as male victimization; by 1992, all the states had recast their rape laws to some degree.[84] The most common changes were the following:

- replacing the rape offense with a set of gender-neutral offenses specified by any aggravating circumstances, such as weapon usage, victim injury, or commission of another felony;
- eliminating requirements that the victim physically resist the attacker and that victim testimony be corroborated; and
- introducing rape shield laws.[85]

Since the reform of rape laws, most jurisdictions have recognized a continuum of rape violence. What is often called "simple rape" constitutes a single incident of rape. Additional violence or felonies committed along with the rape increase the seriousness of the rape charge. Co-occurrence of other felonies as well as use of a weapon increases the chances that a rape will be reported to police.[86]

OFFENDER CHARACTERISTICS

Most rapists are male.[87] Typologies of rapists place rapists into categories of behavior. One of the first rapist typologies was published in 1979 by psychologist A. Nicholas Groth.[88] Since then, other researchers have offered their own typologies or have added to Groth's typology. Robert Knight and Raymond Prentky have since come up with a generally accepted four-category typology of rapists that aims to explain what rapists do and why.

- The anger rapist. This rapist uses extreme physical violence—so much, in fact, that the rape is nearly secondary. The anger rapist uses one of two methods to approach his victim: the "blitz style," which is an overwhelming attack and flurry of violence, or the "confidence style" in which the rapist talks his way into the victim's trust and then commits the rape. The motive appears to be a need to express extreme rage, and the offender gets little sexual pleasure from the rape. It is merely one in a set of the worst things that can be done to debase another person.

- The power rapist. The power rapist seeks to control his victims through sexual conquest and be considered by them (and himself) as superior. The power rapist even tends to contact his victims later to ask about them or tell them how much he enjoyed the rape. Power rapists often do not consider their victims as such and even convince themselves that their victims wanted to have sex with them.
- The sadistic rapist. The sadistic rapist is much like the anger rapist in that the motive is to debase the victim in an extreme manner. However, unlike the anger rapist for whom rape is merely a part of the degrading violence, the sadistic rapist is preoccupied with sex that is degrading. The anger rapist uses sex to degrade, whereas the sadistic rapist uses degradation to have sex. The victim's "dread, dependency, and degradation" produces pleasure for the rapist. Pre- and post-rape fantasy is integral to this rapist's motivation.
- The opportunistic rapist. The opportunistic rapist rapes if and when he has a chance, but he does not fantasize about or plan the act. These rapists typically use only as much force as necessary to complete the rape, but otherwise they do not beat or further degrade the victims.[89]

CAUSES OF RAPE

There is probably no single reason for rape; if there were and it could be isolated and addressed, rape would stop. A biological interpretation of rape is that it is a result of natural selection because it assists male reproduction. This view is supported somewhat by the existence of non-consensual copulation among animals. Because it does not involve courtship, rape is an efficient way for males to spread their genetic material and have as many offspring as possible. A social interpretation is that rape is part of general criminality. The rape offense is concentrated among young males, which is the group that commits the greatest proportion of other offenses. Also, the rate of rape rises and falls with the general crime rate as well as with population density. Where there is crime, there will also be rape.[90] These classes of theories seek to explain rape at a group level. Many specific theories and hypotheses address why individual rapists rape. Although we cannot cover all of them here, a couple of ideas address the behavior of individual rapists.

- Immaturity. Behavioral scientist Michael J. Goldstein proposed that in many ways, rapists never grow up. Their attitudes toward sex and female persons remain mired in adolescent or pre-adolescent viewpoints. During adulthood, rapists rely more often on masturbation and erotic media than non-rapist males. However, all types of sex offenders actually have had less contact with erotic media during childhood and adolescence than non-sex offender males, something that often co-occurs with punitive parental attitudes toward sex and sexual issues.[91]
- Attitudes about women and an inability to read negative cues. Some research has found that the beliefs and attitudes of some men about rape contribute largely to the frequency of the offense. Rapists not only believe that men should strive to be controlling and powerful and that women should be submissive and compliant, but they also have difficulty reading women's negative behavioral cues. In one study, rapists in general were significantly less accurate in reading women's negative cues than a control group of non-rapists; among rapists, the ability to read negative cues was less accurate among the more violent rapists than the less violent.[92]

RAPE MYTHS

Although rape is still perpetrated as a way to establish dominance and power and is still used as a weapon in war and as a means of punishment, the feminist, human rights, and anti-prison rape movements have educated the public to some degree about the horrors of rape and its impropriety in all situations. Officially, rape is no longer considered as merely a more forceful means of having sex. The problem of rape in prisons and its prevalence in war is getting some attention, and sexual violence against two groups who were once considered rape-immune, men and wives, is being acknowledged. Myths and misconceptions about rape still abound, however. One consistent finding is that males accept rape myths more readily than females do, which affects how the offense is reported, prosecuted, and punished.[93] Here are the categories of the most common rape myths.[94]

- Victim desire. Victim desire is the myth that victims were "asking for it" by acting in a promiscuous manner or dressing in provocative clothing. Women who have many sexual partners are so often considered to have precipitated their rapes by being "promiscuous" that rape shield laws now prevent courts from exploring victims' sexual relationships during rape trials. The desire myth also perpetuates the idea of "good girls" and "bad girls." "Bad girls" are in danger of being raped, whereas "good girls" never have to worry.[95]

- Fabrication. Victim fabrication is the myth that victims invent or exaggerate their victimization, often because they feel guilty about having sex. Related myths are that the victim is trying to "get back" at the offender for some slight or wrong because he turned down her advances; to deflect blame because she became pregnant during the encounter; or because she is mentally ill.[96]
- Victim masochism. Victim masochism refers to the myth that victims want to be raped. In the masochism myth, women want to be raped so that they can avoid feelings of guilt, or they need men to act aggressively because they are passive and will be considered deviant if they act like they want to have sex.[97]
- Marital rape. The myth that rape cannot occur within marriage is dying hard. It was not until 2006, when the Violence Against Women Act became law, that state laws changed to treat spousal rape as having the same degree of seriousness as stranger rape.[98] Recent research has found, however, that when test subjects are presented with two scenarios, one depicting stranger rape and the other depicting spousal rape, the subjects are less likely to label spousal rape as rape.[99] Marital rape victims are also more likely to be blamed than victims of stranger rape.[100]
- Male rape. The myths about male rape are similar to the myths about female rape, and, because of under-reporting and relatively low awareness, they are probably even more prevalent. Common myths are as follows: (1) Only gay men are sexually assaulted; (2) men cannot have sex unless they are sexually aroused; (3) men are always ready to have sex; and (4) "real" men can defend themselves against sexual assault.[101] As is the case for female rape myths, more men than women believe these fallacies.[102]

RAPE WITHIN ORGANIZATIONS

The frequency of rape and the situational factors differ from culture to culture, but, as stated earlier, there is no "rape-free society." One hallmark of rape is its association with male fraternal groups such as military units; college fraternities; gangs; sports teams; tribal hunter groups; and other small, closely knit male organizations.[103] The common characteristics of these groups include group loyalty; secrecy; competition among group members; and an emphasis on male superiority, commonly accepted notions of masculinity, and hostility toward women. The question is whether these groups foster the characteristics in their members, or whether young men join these groups because they already have the characteristics individually and seek reinforcement from similar males.[104] We do not yet have the answer.

Although the connection between male groups, antagonism toward females, and rape is obvious by now, the prevalence of the rape of males by male groups, specifically of enemy soldiers and prison inmates, emphasizes the importance of dominance, power, control, and social status rather than sex in the rape offense. Let's consider three predominantly male group contexts in which rape is commonly reported: the military, college fraternities, and prisons.

The Military. Rape has always existed in war: Opposing sides rape each other's civilian women and children and captured soldiers as a way to demoralize the enemy and assert power and control. However, what is not expected is the rape of soldiers by fellow soldiers, or what the U.S. Veterans Administration calls "military sexual trauma." Although military sexual trauma has increased as more women have joined the armed forces, male soldiers have reported rape as well.[105]

A RAND study estimated that 20,300 active service members were sexually assaulted during a one-year period, including about 1 percent of men and nearly 5 percent of women. About 116,600 service members were sexually harassed.[106] Between 2002 and 2007, the Pentagon reported nearly 600 sexual assault cases in the U.S. military administrative territory of Afghanistan and Iraq. In the military, rape is possibly even more under-reported than in the civilian world because reporting can end a career.[107] According to a Veteran Affairs Medical Center study, one-fourth of rape victims did not report the rape because the rapist was their ranking officer, and one-third did not report because the rapist was the ranking officer's friend.[108]

What is behind the phenomenon of military rape? The Veteran Affairs Medical Center study found that rape was more likely to occur when a supervisor allowed sexual harassment or had a permissive attitude toward behaviors associated with rape.[109] Another possible explanation is that military bases are a microcosm of American society, with all the problems that occur in any town or small city concentrated within the base. One former Air Force psychologist explained that a military base is much like a college campus with similar factors of physical proximity, youth, and alcohol consumption, and that rape is more likely to occur in this type of setting.[110] In fact, most reported rapes occurred on base and during off-duty periods. Sleeping quarters are particularly high-risk locations.[111] Consistent with other research on rape, alcohol use is a particularly common factor; drinking by offenders or victims occurs in about one-third to two-thirds of military rape offenses.[112]

More women than ever are serving in the U.S. military, which has increased attention to the problem of military sexual trauma. In 2005, the Department of Defense (DOD) established the Sexual Assault Prevention and Response Office as the "single point of accountability" for the military's sexual assault policy and began issuing annual reports. According to the 2017 Annual Report on Sexual Assault in the Military, 5,277 reports of sexual assault involved soldiers as victims.[113] The report details the military's response to alleged sexual assaults, and each military branch has its own program for dealing with reports and offenses.[114] However, considering that the Government Accountability Office (GAO) estimates that rape and sexual assault in the military are underreported by as much as half, this makes the DOD's statistics much more sobering. According to the GAO report, "factors that discourage service members from reporting a sexual assault include the belief that nothing would be done; fear of ostracism, harassment, or ridicule; and concern that peers would gossip." The GAO is also critical of the DOD's sexual assault prevention efforts, stating that, although the DOD succeeds in reporting the number of alleged sexual assaults, there are few or no criteria for measuring its progress in dealing with the problem.[115]

Finally, rape is not confined to the U.S. military. The Israeli military, which, like the United States, allows women in combat, also reports problems with sexual harassment and rape. In 2016, there were 802 reported incidents of sexual assault in the Israeli military.[116] Convicted harassers may be suspended from the Israeli army and relieved of their military degrees; however, according to a report, senior officers accused of harassment are rarely punished, especially if they are highly accomplished.[117]

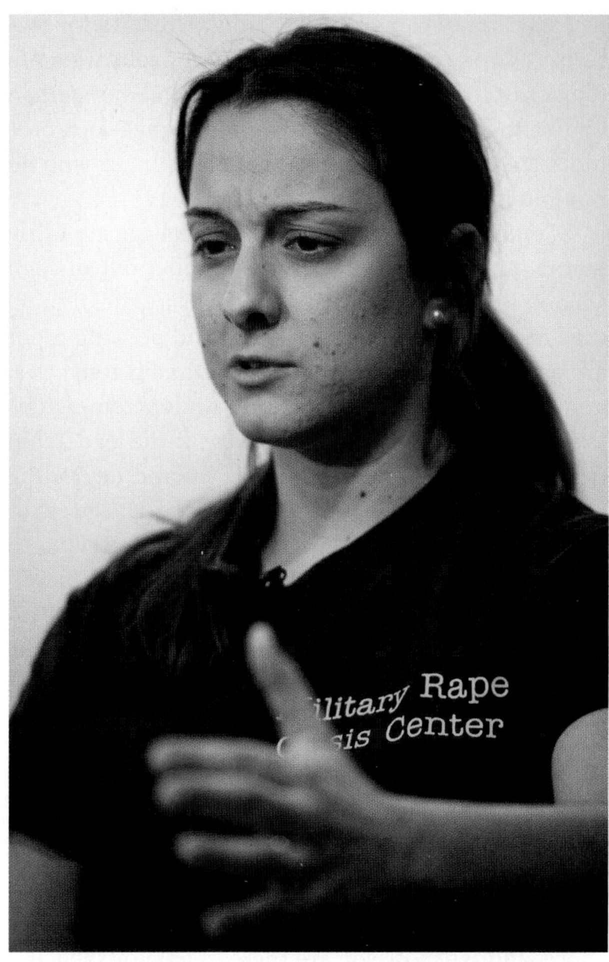

Panayiota Bertzikis, founder of the Military Rape Crisis Center, tells how she was raped while serving in the U.S. Coast Guard. Bertzikis was a plaintiff among 29 men and women who sought change in the military's handling of rape and sexual assault cases. What factors discourage victims from reporting rape while in military service?

College Fraternities. Unfortunately, the college fraternity environment sports almost all the hallmarks of the organizational rape offense: youth, male groups who are antagonistic toward women, alcohol, and proximity. Although fraternities are not the only contexts in which rape occurs at colleges and universities, the fraternity is a common college organization in which rape is known to occur with some regularity.[118]

Like rape in the military, as well as rape in general, rape in fraternities is motivated by males' need to prove their power and secure their status within an all-male group. It often occurs during parties, on dates, and in groups. Research has shown that membership in college fraternities and college sports teams is associated with attitudes related to sexual aggression.[119] In fact, men in these groups score higher on measures of attitudes favorable to sexual aggression than men who are not members.[120]

Another study came up with similar results for fraternities and concluded that those who join are more likely to receive different information about women and sexuality, which tends to encourage and promote the degradation of women, than men who do not join fraternities.[121]

Considering that most males in college are fairly young, typically in their teens and just out of high school, joining a fraternity occurs at a crucial juncture in their development. Status and pecking order are particularly important in teams and fraternities, and members of these groups are under tremendous pressure to fit in. As in the military, if the leadership of the group condones antagonistic and degrading attitudes toward women, that will be the prevailing attitude of the group and of the males trying to achieve status in it. Colleges and universities, as well as student groups, have devoted more attention to the problem of rape by campus groups. For example, the national organization One in Four (the name comes from the statistic that one in four college women has survived rape or attempted rape) seeks to educate college students, particularly male social groups, about rape myths and realities.[122]

Prisons. Rape in prison is a particularly controversial topic, mainly because there is a general attitude that those who are in prison are there to be punished and not protected.[123] Although prisons in recent decades have become more oriented toward punishment than rehabilitation, the government still has a responsibility to see that prison inmates are serving the sentences the state has prescribed and are not being victimized by more aggressive inmates. Unfortunately, preventing such victimization is difficult to do, even in the most secure institutions. In some cases, the prison staff members even allow inmates to be victimized because they feel this is a just punishment.

Lovisa Stannow is executive director of Just Detention International. The Prison Rape Elimination Act created an investigatory commission and established a national zero-tolerance policy for sexual assaults behind bars. Why has prison rape gone largely unacknowledged and unreported?

Rape occurs in any combination across the institutional spectrum. Corrections officers have raped inmates, and inmates have raped corrections officers. But the most common offense is inmates raping other inmates. Inmate/inmate rape does occur in female institutions, but the most common form is male-on-male inmate rape because the vast majority of prison inmates in this country are male. As troubling as it is to contemplate, inmate/inmate rape serves a purpose in prison society: to establish social status and control among inmates. However, attempts are being made to prevent the problem. The Prison Rape Elimination Act has the following provisions:

- to establish a zero-tolerance standard for the incidence of prison rape in prisons in the United States;
- to make the prevention of prison rape a top priority in each prison system;
- to develop and implement national standards for the detection, prevention, reduction, and punishment of prison rape;
- to increase the available data and information on the incidence of prison rape;
- to increase the accountability of prison officials who fail to detect, prevent, reduce, and punish prison rape;
- to protect the Eighth Amendment rights of federal, state, and local inmates.[124]

Although the Prison Rape Elimination Act is a step in the right direction, it came only after decades of rape occurring as a sort of secondary punishment in prisons. One particularly disturbing story is that of Stephen Donaldson, who became known as "Donny the Punk."[125] In 1973, Donaldson, then a Quaker activist, was arrested at a White House protest. As part of the protest, he refused to post his $10 bail. He was held in a cell with other minor offenders, including convicted Watergate offender G. Gordon Liddy (who was awaiting sentencing) until a rumor arose that Donaldson was an undercover reporter trying to get a story on Liddy.[126] Donaldson was then transferred to a cellblock with the jail's most dangerous offenders, where he was raped continuously for two nights by at least 45 inmates. A fellow protester posted Donaldson's bond a couple of days later and sought medical treatment for him. Donaldson's continued activism, combined with the effects of the intense emotional and physical trauma associated with his first rape, landed him in prison four more times.

The prevalence of rape in the country's prisons and jails is unclear, and attempts at accurate record-keeping of incidents have only begun. From 2011 to 2012 (the most recent statistics available), about 29,300 state and federal prison inmates reported an incident involving another inmate; 34,100 reported an incident involving facility staff; and 5,500 reported incidents by both inmates and staff.[127] In 2012, juvenile correctional administrators reported 865 allegations of sexual victimization in state juvenile systems and 613 in local, private, and Indian-country facilities.[128] However, we must take into account the general under-reporting of rape combined with the restrictive and fearful nature of prison life. Doubtless, far more sexual violence is occurring in U.S. prisons and jails than is being reported.

Robbery

The FBI defines robbery as the taking or attempting to take anything of value from the care, custody, or control of a person or persons by force or threat of force or violence and/or by putting the victim in fear. The primary difference between robbery and other offenses in which the object is to obtain money or goods is that robbery includes physical contact (or extreme proximity) with the victim and the use of fear and physical intimidation. In 2017, police recorded 319,356 robberies.[129]

ROBBERY AND THE LAW

Robbery is an old offense. The early English courts defined robbery even before defining larceny.[130] Some states use the simple, common law definition of robbery, which is basically forcible theft, whereas others define degrees of robbery. Each state treats robbery slightly differently, especially if it is combined with other offenses. For example, the state of California defines robbery as a first-degree offense if the offense occurs in a home or inhabited dwelling; if the victim was working as a transit operator or taxi driver; or if the victim was using an automated teller machine. All other robberies are second-degree offenses.[131] In Florida, robbery with a deadly weapon is a first-degree felony, as is a home-invasion robbery with or without a deadly weapon. Robbery without a deadly weapon is a second-degree felony.[132]

TYPES OF ROBBERY

Most reported robberies occur on streets or highways (see Figure 10.6). Other locations classified by the FBI are service stations, convenience stores, residences, banks, and miscellaneous. As you can see in the figure, banks and convenience stores, locations most typically associated with robbery, actually represent a relatively small proportion of robbery locations. Most robberies occur in urban street locations. According to one study, street robbers tend to work socially disorganized neighborhoods close to their residences or places they frequent.[133] Let's take a look at a few of the most common and persistent types of robbery.

- Street robbery. Street robbers are difficult to stop. They are willing to risk committing the offense for the immediate acquisition of small amounts of money or goods; they have a lot of targets; and their offenses do not require much skill or planning.[134] It has been suggested that reforming street robbers is difficult because a lifetime of being able to acquire money quickly

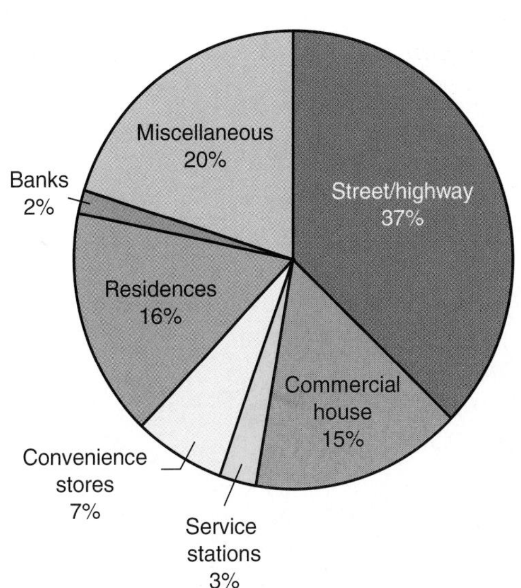

FIGURE 10.6 Percentages of Robberies by Location

Although robbery is typically associated with banks and convenience stores, most take place on streets or highways. (A "commercial house" is any business that is not a bank, service station, or convenience store.)

THINK ABOUT IT

Why do we tend to associate robbery with banks, convenience stores, and gas stations, when the fewest robberies occur there? Is the media is responsible for these perceptions?

Source: U.S. Department of Justice, Federal Bureau of Investigation, Uniform Crime Reports, Crime in the United States, 2017, *Table 23: Offense Analysis, 2016–2017, https://ucr.fbi.gov/crime-in-the-u.s/2017/crime-in-the-u.s.-2017/tables/table-23. Accessed October 2018.*

with little skill or labor, often to support a drug or alcohol habit, is poor preparation for a 9-to-5 job. This is doubtless one reason that street robbery is such a persistent offense.[135]

› Convenience stores. Although convenience stores are not robbed as often as many other locations, convenience store robberies are persistent, and the stores themselves are particularly vulnerable to repeated robberies.[136] Police classify convenience store robberies according to how the robber operates: A "straight robbery" occurs when the offender demands money immediately upon entering the store; in a "customer robbery," the offender spends some time in the store pretending to shop; the least common, "merchandise robbery," includes the taking of goods.[137] Robbers generally commit their offenses at night because they are less likely to be seen. Moreover, the typically late hours convenience stores are open is the strongest factor contributing to robbery.[138] Stores located in high-density commercial settings, such as strip malls, were less likely to be robbed, whereas stores in disorganized neighborhoods or less dense commercial areas were more likely to be robbed.[139] The profile of convenience store robbers matches that of robbers in general: male, usually under age 25, impulsive, opportunistic, and wanting quick cash.[140] Robbers work more often in pairs or groups than alone, although robbers working alone are less likely to be violent to victims.[141] Robbers tend to hit stores in or near their own neighborhoods.[142]

A billboard flashes a wanted poster for a bank robbery suspect in Bridgeton, Missouri. The FBI says the man is also suspected of 20 other bank robberies across the United States. Why is the clearance rate higher for bank robberies than for other types of robbery?

› Bank robbery. Like convenience stores, banks are one of the first locations people associate with robbery, but in fact, less than 2 percent of robberies are of banks.[143] Most bank robberies occur in urban areas and are reported quickly. The likelihood of catching a bank robber at or near the crime scene is higher than for other offenses because most robberies are perpetrated during the day and have several witnesses. Most bank robbers commit their offenses alone, unarmed, and undisguised. The clearance rate for bank robbery is high, nearly 60 percent.[144] Although bank robberies are dangerous for bank personnel and bank customers, the person most often killed in a bank robbery is the robber.[145] Most bank robberies are federal offenses, and suspects are tried in federal courts.[146]

Unlike the motivations for some offenses, especially rape, the motivations for robbery are not particularly deep or mysterious. Robbers rob because they need cash now. The robber lifestyle tends to be carefree, unconventional, and deeply tied to street culture in which image, power, control, a willingness to fight, and a desire for excitement and respect are paramount. Armed robbery provides the cash, excitement, and "street cred" to achieve these goals. Armed robbers, who seem to have little or no future orientation, typically spend their take on clothes, jewelry, gambling, or other superfluous goods and services. This pattern is consistent with the young age of most arrested robbers, whose criminal activity typically peaks under the age of 25 and recedes later into adulthood.[147]

Assault

Assault is the criminal offense of attempting to inflict immediate bodily harm or making another person fear that such harm is imminent. Assault is different from **battery** in that battery is physical contact with the intent to do harm. Assault is the intent and attempt to do another person physical harm; battery is a successful assault. This is why "assault and battery" are often treated as one offense. An assault can exist without a battery, but a battery cannot exist without an assault.[148]

Assault is a challenging topic to define because "assault" is largely a legal term that describes the intent to do harm and not the harm itself. From a theoretical perspective, criminologists deal with the more general issue of violence, of which assault is only one aspect. From a criminal justice standpoint, assault is often charged along with other violent offenses, including battery, robbery, stalking, domestic violence, and child abuse. Any violent offense includes assault, ranging from barroom altercations to murder to the most heinous incidences of terrorism. Of the four categories of violent crime covered by the UCR, the first three—murder, rape, and robbery—necessarily involve the fourth category, aggravated assault. Therefore, it is difficult to discuss assault as separate from other criminal offenses or even as separate from violence in general.

The FBI records statistics on both simple and aggravated assault in the UCR. It keeps more detailed numbers on aggravated assault, which it defines as an "unlawful attack by one person upon another for the purpose of inflicting severe or aggravated bodily injury . . . usually accompanied by the use of a weapon or by other means likely to produce death or great bodily harm." (By comparison, a simple assault does not involve a dangerous weapon, and the victim does not sustain serious or aggravated injuries.)[149] The FBI estimates that about 810,825 aggravated assaults occurred during 2017, with about 1 million arrests for simple assaults.[150] As with other violent offenses, the aggravated assault rate is highest in the South and in metropolitan areas.[151]

ASSAULT AND THE LAW

Assault is a criminal offense in all states. Most states make simple assault a misdemeanor and aggravated assault a felony. Some states, however, classify a simple assault carried out against a police officer or firefighter as a felony.

In many jurisdictions, one of the elements of aggravated assault is the use of a deadly weapon. Exactly what constitutes a "deadly weapon" and its use often turns on the context of the individual case. Common weapons used in aggravated assaults are clubs, sticks, and other blunt instruments.

That blunt objects, guns, and knives are usually considered deadly weapons is no surprise. In some cases, however, hands, feet, and shoes have all been considered deadly weapons because of the way they were used to harm another person. The FBI, in fact, collects statistics on the use of "personal weapons"—that is, hands, feet, and fists—as deadly weapons in aggravated assaults.[152] In a 1982 case, *State v. Zangrilli*, the defendant broke his ex-wife's jaw, strangled her, dragged her through the house, and punched her repeatedly in the face and neck

Verbal arguments can quickly escalate into physical assaults. What is the difference between assault and battery?

before finally shoving her into a bathtub. The courts found that, in this case, the defendant's hands were deadly weapons.[153]

TYPES OF ASSAULT

All violent crime begins with some form of assault. For example, according to the FBI, robbery is assault plus larceny-theft.[154] However, many assaults (or assaults and batteries) are committed solely for the sake of harming another or making that person afraid. Three broad categories of such assaults are stranger assault, intimate-partner violence, and child abuse. Recall the discussion at the beginning of the chapter about Feshbach's differentiation between hostile/expressive aggression and instrumental aggression. Stranger assaults and domestic violence often involve intense emotions as well as the desire for power and control. It is possible, then, that these criminal offenses fall into both of Feshbach's categories: the hostile/expressive, the desire to make the victim suffer for the sake of suffering, as well as the instrumental, the desire to assert personal power and control. In this case, it is probably wiser to plot each case of assault individually along Bushman and Anderson's continuum of aggression.

Stranger Assault. Assault by a stranger is the basis for much fear of crime. However, according to the National Crime Victimization Survey, more aggravated assaults and simple assaults are committed by attackers who know their victims.[155] The risk

---

battery—Physical contact with the intent to do harm.

*Assaults of all kinds have higher percentage of the victim knowing the offender.

of robbery, aggravated assault, and simple assault has declined substantially since the early 1970s.[156] Although the police tend to under-report stranger homicides to statistical agencies such as the FBI's UCR program because of the difficulty of finding the offenders, stranger-committed violence, such as rape, robbery, and assault, is reported more frequently than acquaintance offenses.[157]

Intimate-Partner Violence. Much of the violence between people who know one another occurs between intimate partners, including spouses, ex-spouses, and dating partners.[158] Risk factors for intimate-partner violence include using drugs or alcohol (especially alcohol), being violent or aggressive in the past, witnessing or experiencing violence during childhood, and being unemployed.[159] Most incidences of intimate-partner violence are simple assault; the rest are aggravated assaults and sexual assaults.[160] Although men are affected by intimate-partner violence, women are much more likely to be abused by their intimate partners than men.[161]

One study found that the police are less likely to make an arrest in cases of sexual intimate-partner violence than in other types of intimate-partner violence. The reasons for this finding may be related to the stigma of sexual assault and the types of injuries inflicted. Victims may think that other people may not believe that the assault happened or may believe that the activity was consensual, was the victim's fault, or was inconsequential (or not an assault at all) as compared to an assault in which the victim is beaten. Other beliefs may include that it is not possible to rape an intimate partner, that "decent" women are not victimized, or that the victim is trying to manipulate the perpetrator. Victims may also doubt law enforcement's ability to "do anything" about the case and fear retaliation by the perpetrator.[162]

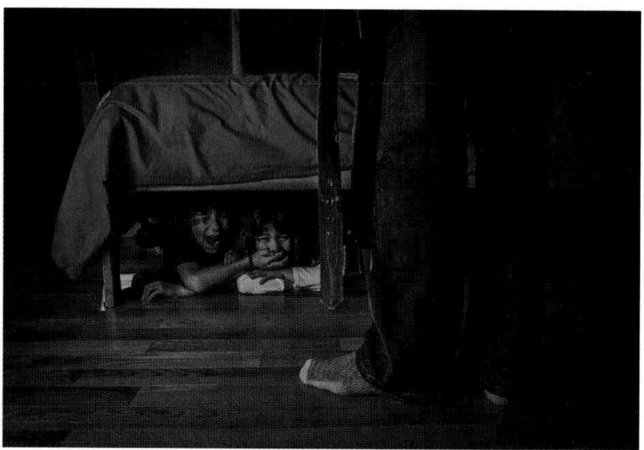

Child abuse often includes physical assault. Why is child abuse so difficult for authorities to detect?

Child Abuse. Child abuse is defined as harming a child or failing to prevent harm. Child abuse, which can be physical, sexual, or emotional, includes neglect, which is not providing for a child's needs. According to the American Academy of Pediatrics, about 3 million cases of child abuse and neglect are reported annually.[163] Although most children are abused by someone they know, physical and sexual child abuse still constitutes assault and battery. Unlike other assault offenders, however, most perpetrators of child abuse are women. As in intimate-partner violence, the reporting of child abuse is often problematic because children who are being abused either cannot or will not tell anyone about it, particularly if the perpetrator is a parent or other beloved relative. Infants are also particularly vulnerable to child abuse.

The prosecution of both intimate-partner violence and child abuse is a relatively new phenomenon in the United States. Until recent decades, family violence was considered a private matter: Parents had the right to treat their children any way they wished, and husbands were considered to have the right to beat both their wives and their children. The criminal justice treatment of family violence has advanced in that the family is no longer treated as a haven for almost any kind of violence that adults wish to perpetrate. Even so, vestiges of this attitude can be observed in the fact that, as we have discussed, stranger assaults are more likely to generate arrests than those committed by intimate partners.

PAUSE AND REVIEW

1. **Give the definition of murder.**
2. **Explain why the offense of rape is rife with so many misconceptions.**
3. **Distinguish between the different types of homicide.**
4. **Differentiate robbery from larceny.**
5. **What are the four violent criminal offenses recorded by the FBI?**
6. **How does murder differ from homicide?**
7. **What is the difference between robbery and other types of larceny/theft?**
8. **What is assault? How does it differ from battery?**

FOCUS ON ETHICS Creepy or Dangerous?

You have always thought that the guy sitting next to you in criminology class is kind of weird. This is the third class you have taken together, and each semester he reveals more about himself that makes you feel uncomfortable. It started last year when he would show up wearing one of his many National Rifle Association t-shirts. He uses racial slurs in private conversations, and he has argued that football players who do not stand for the national anthem should be shot. The opinions that he gives in class make you think he is an extremist. He has stated that he wants to become a law enforcement officer and be on a SWAT team, which does not seem like a reasonable goal given his refusal to get in shape for the physicals he would be required to take to become a police officer.

You have a new concern this semester. Because your state has passed a campus open-carry weapons law, this young man now comes to class with a handgun strapped to his thigh. His new t-shirt announces "good guy with a gun." Other students have dropped the class because they do not want to be around him. They have stated privately to the professor that they do not feel comfortable speaking in class because the student is argumentative and seems to have a quick temper.

This student became even more problematic today. When a writing assignment was returned, you could see that his paper was covered in comments written in red ink and that his grade was a 62. You notice the young man seething in anger and muttering under his breath. You heard him say, "This whole school sucks, and I don't have to take this. I'm going to get that professor." He has not made the threat to anyone other than himself, but you are concerned that between his hostile demeanor and his gun tragedy could happen.

What Do You Do?

1. Say nothing. The law gives him the right to carry a gun in the classroom, and he is understandably upset because of the low grade on his writing assignment.
2. Drop the class like some of your fellow students have. This takes you out of potential danger but means that you will have to repeat the class next semester.
3. Inform your professor, department chair, and campus police about your fear of potential violence. This report may have long-term implications for the prospects of his career as a law enforcement officer.
4. Offer to help him on the next writing assignment. Perhaps by befriending him you can soften his demeanor and help him present himself in a less threatening manner.

Summary

LEARNING OBJECTIVE	
1 Give the common sources of violence.	The common sources of violence include psychological abnormality, substance abuse, evolutionary factors, and socialization and cultural values.
2 Discuss three common physical sources of violent crime.	Biological sources of violent crime include mental disorder, substance abuse, and evolutionary factors. Drugs and alcohol are associated with violent crime, but no known substance directly causes people to become violent or break the law. The sociobiological approach to explaining crime is that humans evolved antisocial tendencies for specific reasons.
3 Discuss three common social and cultural sources of violent crime.	Social and cultural sources of violent crime include family dysfunction, social disorganization, and some subcultural values. Violence that stems from families can strike at victims within the family and victims outside the family. Social disorganization theory asserts that disorganized areas, such as impoverished neighborhoods, lack the social controls that prevent violence. Some values held by subcultures are a major source of violent crime.

LEARNING OBJECTIVE 4 Define violent crime, and state the four violent criminal offenses recognized by the Federal Bureau of Investigation.	The FBI defines violent crime as offenses that include the use of force or threat of force. The FBI recognizes four violent criminal offenses: murder and non-negligent manslaughter, rape, robbery, and aggravated assault.
LEARNING OBJECTIVE 5 Explain the difference between homicide and murder.	The FBI defines murder and non-negligent manslaughter as the willful killing of one human being by another. Homicide is the killing of one human being by another, regardless of criminal intent.
LEARNING OBJECTIVE 6 Discuss the traditional and modern defining elements of rape.	Traditionally, the most prominent element of rape has been force. The attacker had to physically force the victim to perform intercourse for a rape to be defined as such. Today, the basic element in the definition of rape is the victim's lack of consent, regardless of the nature of the victim/attacker relationship.
LEARNING OBJECTIVE 7 State the primary difference between robbery and other offenses involving theft.	The difference between robbery and other offenses in which the object is to obtain money or goods is physical contact (or proximity) with the victim and the use of fear and physical intimidation.
LEARNING OBJECTIVE 8 Explain the difference between assault and battery.	Assault is the criminal offense of attempting to inflict immediate bodily harm or making another person fear that such harm is imminent. Battery is physical contact with the intent to do harm. Assault is the intent and attempt to do another person physical harm; battery is a successful assault. An assault can exist without a battery, but a battery cannot exist without an assault.

Critical Reflections

1. **Why is aggression basic to violent crime?**
2. **What is violence?**
3. **Why might a continuum of violence be more useful in characterizing violent crime than a dichotomy of violence?**

Key Terms

aggression p. 260
battery p. 282
capital murder p. 269
homicide p. 268
manslaughter p. 268
mass murder p. 271
mental disorder p. 261
schizophrenia p. 262
serial murder p. 272
sociobiology p. 264
spree murder p. 271
statutory rape p. 274
violence p. 260

Instant Recall Terms

antisocial personality disorder (ch. 5)
assault (ch. 3)
burglary (ch. 3)
focal concerns (ch. 6)
murder (ch. 3)
rape (ch. 3)
robbery (ch. 3)
social disorganization theory (ch. 6)

Notes

1 *New York Times*, "Multiple Weapons Found in Las Vegas Gunman's Hotel Room," October 2, 2017, https://www.nytimes.com/2017/10/02/us/las-vegas-shooting.html. Accessed June 2018.

2 Lynh Bui, Matt Zapotosky, Devlin Barrett, and Mark Berman, "At Least 59 Killed in Las Vegas Shooting Rampage, More Than 500 Others Injured," *Washington Post*, October 2, 2017, https://www.washingtonpost.com/news/morning-mix/wp/2017/10/02/police-shut-down-part-of-las-vegas-strip-due-to-shooting/?noredirect=on&utm_term=.d5e264086037. Accessed June 2018.

3 Joseph Tanfani, "'Bump Stocks' Allow Rifles to Act a Lot Like Machine Guns." *Los Angeles Times*, October 3, 2017, http://www.latimes.com/nation/la-las-vegas-shooting-live-updates-bump-stocks-allow-rifles-to-act-a-lot-1507074997-htmlstory.html. Accessed June 2018.

4 KTNV Staff, "Las Vegas Shooting: This Is What Investigators Found in Stephen Paddock's Hotel Room," January 20, 2018, https://www.abc15.com/news/las-vegas-shooting/list-guns-and-evidence-from-las-vegas-shooter-stephen-paddock. Accessed June 2018.

5 Bui, Zapotosky, Barrett, and Berman, "At Least 59 Killed in Las Vegas Shooting Rampage."

6 Curt R. Bartol and Anne M. Bartol, *Criminal Behavior: A Psychosocial Approach*, 11th ed. (Boston: Pearson Education, 2017), 113–114.

7 Seymour Feshbach, "The Function of Aggression and the Regulation of Aggressive Drive," *Psychological Review* 71 (1964): 257–272.

8 Brad J. Bushman and Craig A. Anderson, "Is It Time to Pull the Plug on the Hostile Versus Instrumental Aggression Dichotomy?" *Psychological Review* 108 (2001): 273–279.

9 James Bonta, Moira Law, and K. R. Hanson, "The Prediction of Criminal and Violent Recidivism among Mentally Disordered Offenders: A Meta-Analysis," *Psychological Bulletin* 123 (1998): 123–142.

10 United States Department of Justice, "Attorney General Eric Holder Announces Revisions to the Uniform Crime Report's Definition of Rape, January 6, 2012," https://www.justice.gov/opa/pr/attorney-general-eric-holder-announces-revisions-uniform-crime-report-s-definition-rape Accessed June 2018.

11 Jennifer L. Skeem, Paula Emke-Francis, and Jennifer Eno Louden, "Probation, Mental Health, and Mandated Treatment: A National Survey," *Criminal Justice and Behavior* 33, no. 2 (April 2006): 159.

12 Janet Bagnall, "Outcry over Mental Illness—Violence Link; Connection Must Be Admitted and Treated, Montreal Psychologist Says," *Gazette*, February 12, 1996, final edition, A5.

13 Bartol and Bartol, *Criminal Behavior*, 217. Louise Arseneault, Terrie E. Moffitt, Avshalom Caspi, P. J. Taylor, and P. A. Silva, "Mental Disorders and Violence in a Total Birth Cohort: Results from the Dunedin Study," *Archives of General Psychiatry* 57, no. 10 (October 1, 2000): 979–986. Sheilagh Hodgins, "The Major Mental Disorders and Crime: Stop Debating and Start Treating and Preventing," *International Journal of Law and Psychiatry* 24, no. 4 (July 2001): 427–446.

14 World Health Organization, Schizophrenia, Schizotypal and Delusional Disorders, *International Statistical Classification of Diseases and Related Health Problems*, 10th Revision, http://apps.who.int/classifications/icd10/browse/2016/en#/F20-F29. Accessed June 2018.

15 Kris Naudts and Sheilagh Hodgins, "Neurobiological Correlates of Violent Behavior among Persons with Schizophrenia," *Schizophrenia Bulletin*, 32, no. 3 (July 2006): 562–572. Sheilagh Hodgins, "Violent Behaviour among People with Schizophrenia: A Framework for Investigations of Causes, and Effective Treatment, and Prevention," *Philosophical Transactions: Biological Sciences* 363, no. 1503 (August 12, 2008): 2505–2518.

16 Bartol and Bartol, *Criminal Behavior*, 218–219.

17 Ibid., 219.

18 Ibid., 219–221.

19 "Report Finds SMI Persons More Likely to Be in Jails Than Hospitals," *Mental Health Weekly* 20, no. 19 (May 17, 2010): 6. Chris Sigurdson, "The MAD The BAD and The Abandoned: The Mentally Ill in Prisons and Jails," *Corrections Today* 62, no. 7 (December 2000): 70.

20 Philip J. Kinsler and Anna Saxman, "Traumatized Offenders: Don't Look Now, but Your Jail's Also Your Mental Health Center," *Journal of Trauma & Dissociation* 8, no. 2 (June 2007): 81–95.

21 John P. Morgan and Lynn Zimmer, "The Social Pharmacology of Smokeable Cocaine: Not All It's Cracked Up to Be," in *Crack in America*, ed. Craig Reinarman and Harry G. Levine (Berkeley: University of California Press, 1997).

22 This includes marijuana/hashish, cocaine/crack, heroin/opiates, depressants, stimulants, methamphetamine, hallucinogens, and inhalants. Jennifer Bronson, Jessica Stroop, Stephanie Zimmer, Marcus Berzofsky, *Drug Use, Dependence, and Abuse among State Prisoners and Jail Inmates, 2007–2009* (U.S. Department of Justice Office of Justice Programs Bureau of Justice Statistics, 2017), 1. Available at https://www.bjs.gov/index.cfm?ty=pbdetail&iid=5966. Accessed June 2018.

23 Benjamin Hansen and Glen R.Waddell, "Legal Access to Alcohol and Criminality," *Journal of Health Economics* 57 (2018): 277–289. Robert Nash Parker, "Alcohol and Violence: Connections, Evidence and Possibilities for Prevention," *Journal of Psychoactive Drugs* 2 (May 2004): -157–163.

24 Peter Larm, Teresa C. Silva, and Sheilagh Hodgins, "Adolescent Substance Misusers with and without Delinquency: Death, Mental and Physical Disorders, and Criminal Convictions from Age 21 to 45," *Journal of Substance Abuse Treatment* 59 (2015): 1–9. Susan E. Martin and Kendall Bryant, "Gender Differences in the Association of Alcohol Intoxication and Illicit Drug Abuse among Persons Arrested for Violent and Property Offenses," *Journal of Substance Abuse* 13, no. 4 (2001): 563–581.

25 Bureau of Justice Statistics, Alcohol and Crime: Data from 2002 to 2008, https://www.bjs.gov/content/acf/29_prisoners_and_alcoholuse.cfm. Accessed June 2018.

26 Jeffrey A. Roth, *Psychoactive Substances and Violence* (Washington, D.C.: U.S. Department of Justice, 1996), https://www.ncjrs.gov/txtfiles/psycho.txt.

27 Robert O. Pihl, Jordan B. Peterson, and Mark A. Lau, "A Biosocial Model of the Alcohol-Aggression Relationship," *Journal of Studies on Alcohol* 11 (1993): 128–139.

28 Bartol and Bartol, *Criminal Behavior*, 497.

29 Susan E. Martin and Kendall Bryant, "Gender Differences in the Association of Alcohol Intoxication and Illicit Drug Abuse among Persons Arrested for Violent and Property Offenses," *Journal of Substance Abuse* 13, no. 4 (2001): 563–581.

30 Richard A. Friedman, "Violence and Mental Illness—How Strong Is the Link?" *New England Journal of Medicine* 355, no. 20 (November 16, 2006): 2064–2066.

31 Dale E. McNiel, Renée L. Binder, and Jo C. Robinson, "Incarceration Associated with Homelessness, Mental Disorder, and Co-occurring Substance Abuse," *Psychiatric Services* 56, no. 7 (July 2005): 840–846.

32 Joshua D. Duntley and Todd K. Shackelford, "Darwinian Foundations of Crime and Law," *Aggression and Violent Behavior* 13, no. 5 (October 2008): 374.

33 Vernon L. Quinsey, "Evolutionary Theory and Criminal Behaviour," *Legal and Criminological Psychology* 7, no. 1 (February 2002): 1.

34 Duntley and Shackelford, "Darwinian Foundations," 376–377.

35 Kimberly J. Mitchell and David Finkelhor, "Risk of Crime Victimization among

Youth Exposed to Domestic Violence," *Journal of Interpersonal Violence* 16, no. 9 (September 2001): 944.

36 A. N. Glennon, "When the West Was Really Wild," *U.S. Stamp News* 7, no. 2 (March 2001): 30. R. H. Adleman, *The Bloody Benders* (New York: Stein & Day, 1970).

37 Kansas State Historical Society, https://www.kshs.org/kansapedia/bender-knife/10106. Accessed June 2018.

38 Ralph B. Taylor and Jeanette Covington, "Neighborhood Changes in Ecology and Violence," *Criminology* 26, no. 4 (November 1988): 553–589.

39 Richard G. Wilkinson, Ichiro Kawachi, and Bruce P. Kennedy, "Mortality, the Social Environment, Crime and Violence," *Sociology of Health & Illness* 20, no. 5 (September 1998): 578–597.

40 Dov Cohen, "Culture, Social Organization, and Patterns of Violence," *Journal of Personality and Social Psychology* 75, no. 2 (August 1998): 408–419.

41 Federal Bureau of Investigation, Uniform Crime Reports, *Crime in the United States, 2017*, Violent Crime, https://ucr.fbi.gov/crime-in-the-u.s/2017/crime-in-the-u.s.-2017/topic-pages/violent-crime. Accessed October 2018.

42 Federal Bureau of Investigation, Uniform Crime Reports, *Crime in the United States, 2017*, Crime Map, https://ucr.fbi.gov/crime-in-the-u.s/2017/crime-in-the-u.s.-2017/topic-pages/crime-map. Accessed October 2018.

43 Federal Bureau of Investigation, Uniform Crime Reports, *Crime in the United States, 2017*, Murder, https://ucr.fbi.gov/crime-in-the-u.s/2017/crime-in-the-u.s.-2017/topic-pages/murder. Accessed October 2018.

44 John M. Scheb and John M. Scheb II, *Criminal Law* (Belmont, Calif.: Thomson Wadsworth, 2006), 395. Dean J. Champion, *The American Dictionary of Criminal Justice* (Los Angeles: Roxbury, 2001), 64.

45 Monica K. Miller and R. David Hayward, "Religious Characteristics and the Death Penalty," *Law and Human Behavior* 32, no. 2 (April 1, 2008): 113–123. Crystal M. Beckham, Beverly J. Spray, and Christina A. Pietz, "Jurors' Locus of Control and Defendants' Attractiveness in Death Penalty Sentencing," *Journal of Social Psychology* 147, no. 3 (June 1, 2007): 285–298. Christine E. Bergeron and Stuart J. McKelvie, "Effects of Defendant Age on Severity of Punishment for Different Crimes," *Journal of Social Psychology* 144, no. 1 (February 1, 2004): 75–90.

46 Marian R. Williams and Jefferson E. Holcomb, "The Interactive Effects of Victim Race and Gender on Death Sentence Disparity Findings," *Homicide Studies* 8 (2004): 350–376.

47 Amy R. Stauffer, M. Dwayne Smith, John K. Cochran, Sondra J. Fogel, and Beth Bjerregaard, "The Interaction Between Victim Race and Gender on Sentencing Outcomes in Capital Murder Trials: A Further Exploration," *Homicide Studies* 10, no. 2 (May 1, 2006): 98–117.

48 Lucy Adams, "Death by Discretion: Who Decides Who Lives and Dies in the United States of America?" *American Journal of Criminal Law* 32, no. 3 (July 1, 2005): 381–401.

49 Michelle E. Barnett, Stanley L. Brodsky, and Cali Manning Davis, "When Mitigation Evidence Makes a Difference: Effects of Psychological Mitigating Evidence on Sentencing Decisions in Capital Trials," *Behavioral Sciences & the Law* 22, no. 6 (November 1, 2004): 751–770.

50 Aki Roberts, "Predictors of Homicide Clearance by Arrest: An Event History Analysis of NIBRS Incidents," *Homicide Studies* 11, no. 2 (May 1, 2007): 82–93.

51 Doug Linder, "Famous Trials: The Trial of Lizzie Borden," http://famous-trials.com/lizzieborden. Accessed June 2018.

52 Cornell University Press, "Killed Strangely: The Death of Rebecca Cornell," http://www.cornellpress.cornell.edu/book/?GCOI=80140100409080. Accessed June 2018.

53 Barbara Bradley Hagerty, "A Neuroscientist Uncovers a Dark Secret," National Public Radio (NPR), June 29, 2010, http://www.npr.org/templates/story/story.php?storyId=127888976. Accessed June 2018.

54 Gautam Naik, "What's on Jim Fallon's Mind? A Family Secret That Has Been Murder to Figure Out," *Wall Street Journal*, November 30, 2009, http://online.wsj.com/article/SB125745788725531839.html. Accessed June 2018.

55 Linder, "Famous Trials: The Trial of Lizzie Borden."

56 Eldad Yechiam, Jason E. Kanz, Antoine Bechara, Julie C. Stout, Jerome R. Busemeyer, Elizabeth M. Altmaier, and Jane S. Paulsen, "Neurocognitive Deficits Related to Poor Decision Making in People Behind Bars," *Psychonomic Bulletin & Review* 15, no. 1 (February 1, 2008): 44–51. Carmen Cavada and Wolfram Schultz, "The Mysterious Orbitofrontal Cortex," *Cerebral Cortex* 10, no. 3 (March 2000): 205.

57 James Knoll, "Serial Murder: A Forensic Psychiatric Perspective," *Psychiatric Times*, March 1, 2006, pp. 64, 67–68.

58 Kenna Quinet, "The Missing Missing: Toward a Quantification of Serial Murder Victimization in the United States," *Homicide Studies* 11, no. 4 (November 2007): 319–339.

59 Alan Cairns, "Pact Forged in Hell," *Toronto Sun*, June 12, 2005, final edition, 40.

60 Mary Bowerman, "Teen Serial Killer Karla Homolka Volunteered at Montreal Elementary School," *USA Today*, June 1, 2017, https://www.usatoday.com/story/news/nation-now/2017/06/01/teen-serial-killer-karla-homolka-volunteered-montreal-elementary-school/361192001. Accessed June 2018.

61 Zelda G. Knight, "Some Thoughts on the Psychological Roots of the Behavior of Serial Killers as Narcissists: An Object Relations Perspective," *Social Behavior & Personality* 34, no. 10 (December 2006): 1189–1206. Stephen D. Singer and Christopher Hensley, "Applying Social Learning Theory to Childhood and Adolescent Firesetting: Can It Lead to Serial Murder?" *International Journal of Offender Therapy and Comparative Criminology* 48, no. 4 (August 2004): 461–476. James Knoll, "Serial Murder: A Forensic Psychiatric Perspective," *Psychiatric Times* 64 (March 1, 2006): 67–68.

62 Robert J. Morton and Mark A. Hilts, eds., *Serial Murder—Multi-Disciplinary Perspectives for Investigators* (Quantico, Va.: Federal Bureau of Investigation Critical Incident Response Group National Center for the Analysis of Violent Crime Behavioral Analysis Unit-2, 2008), 11. Find online at https://www.ncjrs.gov/App/Publications/abstract.aspx?ID=245787. Accessed June 2018.

63 Susan Brownmiller, *Against Our Will* (New York: Simon & Schuster, 1975), 18.

64 Federal Bureau of Investigation, Uniform Crime Reports, *Crime in the United States, 2017*, Rape, https://ucr.fbi.gov/crime-in-the-u.s/2017/crime-in-the-u.s.-2017/topic-pages/rape. Accessed October 2018.

65 Bureau of Justice Statistics, Number of Rape/sexual Assaults by Sex and Age, 2016, Generated Using the NCVS Victimization Analysis Tool at https://www.bjs.gov. Accessed June 2018.

66 Martin L. Lalumière, Grant T. Harris, Vernon L. Quinsey, and Marnie E. Rice, *The Causes of Rape: Understanding Individual Differences in Male Propensity for Sexual Aggression* (Washington, D.C.: American Psychological Association, 2005). See Chapter 3.

67 Brownmiller, *Against Our Will*. See Chapter 2.

68 Ibid.

69 Sharon Block, "Bringing Rapes to Court," *Common-Place* 3, no. 3 (2003).

70 Catharine A. MacKinnon, *Sex Equality: Rape Law* (Eagan, Minn.: Foundation Press, 2001), 801 (quoting William Blackstone, Commentaries on the Laws of England, 210 [1765]).

71 Matthew R. Lyon, "No Means No? Withdrawal of Consent During Intercourse and the Continuing Evolution of the Definition of Rape," *Journal of Criminal Law and Criminology* 95, no. 1 (Fall 2004): 277–314.
72 Lyon, "No Means No?"
73 Lynn A. Addington and Callie Marie Rennison, "Rape CoOccurrence: Do Additional Crimes Affect Victim Reporting and Police Clearance of Rape?" *Journal of Quantitative Criminology* (February 22, 2008) 24: 205–226.
74 Molly Redden, "'No Doesn't Really Mean No': North Carolina Law Means Women Can't Revoke Consent for Sex," *Guardian*, June 24, 2017, https://www.theguardian.com/us-news/2017/jun/24/north-carolina-rape-legal-loophole-consent-state-v-way. Accessed June 2018.
75 Michael Dresser, "New Maryland Laws Underscore: No Means No, Rape Is Rape," *Baltimore Sun*, September 27, 2017, http://www.baltimoresun.com/news/maryland/politics/bs-md-new-laws-october-20170927-story.html. Accessed June 2018.
76 Ryland Barton, "Kentucky House Approves Measure to Raise Age of Consent," 89.3 WFPL, January 20, 2018, http://wfpl.org/kentucky-house-approves-measure-raise-age-consent. Accessed June 2018.
77 Ellie Romano, "New Virginia Law Changes Rights for Sexual Assault Victims," News 5 WCYB.com, June 30, 2017, http://wcyb.com/news/virginia-news/new-virginia-law-changes-rights-for-sexual-assault-victims. Accessed June 2018.
78 Jazmine Ulloa, "Statute of Limitations for Rape Eliminated in California after Gov. Brown Signs Bill Prompted by Cosby Allegations," *Los Angeles Times*, September 28, 2016, http://www.latimes.com/politics/essential/la-pol-sac-essential-politics-updates-no-more-statute-of-limitations-for-rape-1475096216-htmlstory.html. Accessed June 2018.
79 Nicole Einbinder, "New Oregon Law Addresses Sexual Abuse Against Janitors," *Frontline*. January 16, 2018, https://www.pbs.org/wgbh/frontline/article/new-oregon-law-addresses-sexual-abuse-against-janitors. Accessed June 2018.
80 Michelle J. Anderson, "Prostitution and Trauma in U.S. Rape Law," *Journal of Trauma Practice* 2, no. 3/4 (July 2003): 75–92.
81 "A Turn in the Wrong Direction?" *Economist* 372, no. 8392 (September 11, 2004): 31.
82 Jill Elaine Hasday, "Contest and Consent: A Legal History of Marital Rape," 88 *Calif. L. Rev.* 1373 (2000). Available at https://scholarship.law.berkeley.edu/californialawreview/vol88/iss5/2. Accessed June 2018.
83 Cassia C. Spohn and Julie Horney, "The Impact of Rape Law Reform on the Processing of Simple and Aggravated Rape Cases," *Journal of Criminal Law and Criminology* 86, no. 3 (Spring 1996): 861.
84 Susan Caringella-Macdonald, "An Assessment of Rape Reform: Victim and Case Treatment under Michigan's Model," *International Review of Victimology* 1, no. 4 (1991): 347–361.
85 Spohn and Horney, "The Impact of Rape Law Reform."
86 Timothy C. Hart and Callie Rennison, *Reporting Crime to the Police* (Washington, D.C.: Bureau of Justice Statistics, 2003). Available at https://www.bjs.gov/index.cfm?ty=pbdetail&iid=1142. Accessed June 2018.
87 U.S. Department of Justice Office of Justice Programs Bureau of Justice Statistics, Criminal Victimization in the United States, Statistical Tables Index, "Table 38: Percent Distribution of Single-Offender Victimizations, by Type of Crime and Perceived Gender of Offender," https://www.bjs.gov/content/pub/html/cvus/single_offender_victimizations462.cfm. Accessed June 2018.
88 A. Nicholas Groth, *Men Who Rape: The Psychology of the Offender* (New York: Basic Books, 2001).
89 Ibid. Robert A. Knight and Raymond A. Prentky, "Classifying Sexual Offenders: The Development and Corroboration of Taxonomic Models," in *Handbook of Sexual Assault: Issues, Theories, and Treatment of the Offender*, ed. William Lamont Marshall, D. R. Laws, and Howard Barbaree (New York: Springer, 1990). Henry F. Fradella and Kegan Brown, "The Effects of Using Social Scientific Rape Typologies on Juror Decisions to Convict," *Law and Psychology Review* 31 (March 2007): 1–19.
90 Lalumière et al., *The Causes of Rape*, 29, 62–63.
91 Michael J. Goldstein, "Exposure to Erotic Stimuli and Sexual Deviance," *Journal of Social Issues* 29, no. 3 (1973): 197–219.
92 David N. Lipton, Elizabeth C. McDonel, and Richard M. McFall, "Heterosocial Perception in Rapists," *Journal of Consulting and Clinical Psychology* 55, no. 1 (February 1987): 17–21.
93 Amy M. Buddie and Arthur G. Miller, "Beyond Rape Myths: A More Complex View of Perceptions of Rape Victims," *Sex Roles* 45, nos. 3/4 (August 2001): 139–160.
94 The label "victim masochism" is from Buddie and Miller, "Beyond Rape Myths," 139–160.
95 Ibid
96 Ibid.
97 Tammy Garland, "An Overview of Sexual Assault and Sexual Assault Myths," in *Sexual Assault: The Victims, the Perpetrators, and the Criminal Justice System*, ed. Frances P. Reddington and Betsy Wright Kreisel (Durham, N.C.: Carolina Academic Press, 2005), 16–21.
98 Christine Ferro, Jill Cermele, and Ann Saltzman, "Current Perceptions of Marital Rape: Some Good and Not-So-Good News," *Journal of Interpersonal Violence* 23, no. 6 (June 2008): 764–79.
99 Mary Kay Kirkwood and Dawn K. Cecil, "Marital Rape: A Student Assessment of Rape Laws and the Marital Exemption," *Violence Against Women* 7 (2001): 1235–1253.
100 Candice M. Monson, Jennifer Langhinrichsen-Rohling, and Tisha Binderup, "Does 'No' Really Mean 'No' after You Say 'Yes'"? Attributions about Date and Marital Rape," *Journal of Interpersonal Violence* 15 (2000): 1156–1174.
101 Lana Stermac, Giannetta del Bove, and Mary Addison, "Stranger and Acquaintance Sexual Assault of Adult Males," *Journal of Interpersonal Violence* 19 (2004): 901–915. Ronald E. Smith, Charles J. Pine, and Mark E. Hawley, "Social Cognitions about Adult Male Victims of Female Sexual Assault," *Journal of Sex Research* 24 (1988): 101–112. Michele E. Clements-Schreiber and John K. Rempel, "Women's Acceptance of Stereotypes about Male Sexuality: Correlations with Strategies to Influence Reluctant Partners," *Canadian Journal of Human Sexuality* 4 (1995): 223–231. A. Nicholas Groth and Ann Wolbert Burgess, "Male Rape: Offenders and Victims," *American Journal of Psychiatry* 137 (1980): 806–810.
102 Kristine M. Chapleau, Debra L. Oswald, and Brenda L. Russell, "Male Rape Myths," *Journal of Interpersonal Violence* 23, no. 5 (May 2008): 600–615.
103 Lalumière et al., *The Causes of Rape*, 13.
104 Ibid., 153.
105 Natalie Wilson, "Culture of Rape," *Ms.*, Spring 2010, 32.
106 Andrew R. Morral, Kristie Gore, and Terry L. Schell, eds., *Sexual Assault and Sexual Harassment in the U.S. Military: Volume 2. Estimates for Department of Defense Service Members from the 2014 RAND Military Workplace Study* (Santa Monica, Calif.: RAND Corporation, 2015). Available at https://www.rand.org/pubs/research_reports/RR870z2-1.html. Accessed June 2018.
107 Traci Hukill, "A Peculiar Version of Friendly Fire," *Progressive* 71, no. 1 (January 2007): 17–20, http://www.sharedhost.progressive.org/news/2007/01/4403/peculiar-version-friendly-fire. Accessed June 2018.

108 Anne G. Sadler, Brenda M. Booth, Brian L. Cook, and Bradley N. Doebbeling, "Factors Associated with Women's Risk of Rape in the Military Environment," *American Journal of Industrial Medicine* 43 (2003): 262–273.
109 "Rape and the Military," 8.
110 Diane Richard, "Rape in the Ranks," *Contemporary Sexuality* 37, no. 7 (July 2003): 1.
111 Sadler et al., "Factors Associated with Women's Risk of Rape."
112 Leanne R. Brecklin and Sarah E. Ullman, "The Roles of Victim and Offender Alcohol Use in Sexual Assaults: Results from the National Violence Against Women Survey," *Journal of Studies on Alcohol and Drugs* 63, no. 1 (2002): 57–63.
113 Department of Defense, Fiscal Year 2017 Annual Report on Sexual Assault in the Military, May 2018, p. 3, http://sapr.mil/index.php/reports. Accessed June 2018.
114 Ibid.
115 United States Government Accountability Office, Military Personnel: Preliminary Observations on DOD's and the Coast Guard's Sexual Assault Prevention and Response Programs, July 2008, http://www.gao.gov/new.items/d081013t.pdf. United States Government Accountability Office, Sexual Assault: Better Resource Management Needed to Improve Prevention and Response in the Army National Guard and Army Reserve, February 2017, https://www.gao.gov/products/GAO-17-217. Accessed June 2018.
116 Gili Cohen, "20% Increase in Reported Sexual Assaults in Israeli Army in 2016," *Haaretz*, June 8, 2018, https://www.haaretz.com/israel-news/.premium-20-increase-in-reported-sexual-assaults-in-israeli-army-in-2016-1.5492356. Accessed June 2018.
117 Anat Cohen, "Harassment Complaints Ignored," *Herizons* 19, no. 1 (Summer 2005): 11–12.
118 Patricia Yancey Martin, "The Rape Prone Culture of Academic Contexts: Fraternities and Athletics," *Gender & Society* 30, no. 1 (2016): 30–43.
119 Kaitlin M. Boyle and Lisa Slattery Walker, "The Neutralization and Denial of Sexual Violence in College Party Subcultures," *Deviant Behavior* 37, no. 12 (2016): 1392–1410.
120 Sarah Murnen and Marla Kohlman, "Athletic Participation, Fraternity Membership, and Sexual Aggression among College Men: A Meta-Analytic Review," *Sex Roles* 57, no. 1/2 (July 2007): 145–157.
121 Timothy E. Bleecker and Sarah K. Murnen, "Fraternity Membership, the Display of Degrading Sexual Images of Women, and Rape Myth Acceptance," *Sex Roles* 53, no. 7/8 (October 2005): 487–493.
122 One in Four, http://www.oneinfourusa.org. Accessed June 2018.
123 Cathy Young, "Assault Behind Bars," *Reason*, May 2007, 17–18.
124 Prison Rape Elimination Act of 2003, https://www.bjs.gov/index.cfm?ty=tp&tid=20. Accessed June 2018.
125 Donaldson was born Robert Anthony Martin Jr. but later changed his name.
126 G. Gordon Liddy, *Will: The Autobiography of G. Gordon Liddy* (New York: St. Martin's Press, 1980), 318–321.
127 Allen J. Beck, Marcus Berzofsky, Rachel Caspar, and Christopher Krebs, *Sexual Victimization in Prisons and Jails Reported by Inmates, 2011–12* (U.S. Department of Justice Office of Justice Programs Bureau of Justice Statistics, 2013). 6. Available at https://www.bjs.gov/index.cfm?ty=pbdetail&iid=4654. Accessed June 2018.
128 Allen J. Beck and Romana R. Rantala, *Sexual Victimization Reported by Juvenile Correctional Authorities, 2007–12* (U.S. Department of Justice Office of Justice Programs Bureau of Justice Statistics, 2016), 1. Available https://www.bjs.gov/index.cfm?ty=pbdetail&iid=5560. Accessed June 2018.
129 Federal Bureau of Investigation, Uniform Crime Reports, *Crime in the United States, 2017*, Robbery, https://ucr.fbi.gov/crime-in-the-u.s/2017/crime-in-the-u.s.-2017/topic-pages/robbery. Table 21: Robbery by State, Types of Weapons, 2017, https://ucr.fbi.gov/crime-in-the-u.s/2017/crime-in-the-u.s.-2017/topic-pages/tables/table-21. Accessed October 2018.
130 Thomas J. Gardner and Terry M. Anderson, *Criminal Law* (Belmont, Calif.: Thomson Wadsworth, 2006), 309.
131 Findlaw, California Robbery Laws, https://statelaws.findlaw.com/california-law/california-robbery-laws.html. Accessed June 2018.
132 Findlaw, Florida Robbery Laws, https://statelaws.findlaw.com/florida-law/florida-robbery-laws.html. Accessed June 2018.
133 William R. Smith, Sharon Glave Frazee, and Elizabeth L. Davison, "Furthering the Integration of Routine Activity and Social Disorganization Theories: Small Units of Analysis and the Study of Street Robbery as a Diffusion Process," *Criminology* 38, no. 2 (2000): 489–523.
134 Richard T. Wright and Scott H. Decker, *Armed Robbers in Action: Stickups and Street Culture* (Boston: Northeastern University Press, 1997).
135 Ibid. See Chapter 5.
136 Paul Catalano, Bryan Hill, and Brennan Long, "Geographical Analysis and Serial Crime Investigation: A Case Study of Armed Robbery in Phoenix, Arizona," *Security Journal* 14, no. 3 (2001): 27–41.
137 Kimberly A. Faulkner, Douglas P. Landsittel, and Scott A. Hendricks, "Robbery Characteristics and Employee Injuries in Convenience Stores," *American Journal of Industrial Medicine* 40, no. 6 (2001): 703–709.
138 Natalie Taylor, "Robbery Against Service Stations and Pharmacies: Recent Trends," *Trends & Issues in Crime and Criminal Justice*, no. 223 (Canberra: Australian Institute of Criminology, 2002).
139 Ronald D. Hunter, "Convenience Store Robbery Revisited: A Review of Prevention Results," *Journal of Security Administration* 22, nos. 1 & 2 (1999): 1–13. Scott A. Hendricks, Douglas Landsittel, Harlan Amandus, Jay Malcan, and Jennifer Bell, "A Matched Case-Control Study of Convenience Store Robbery Risk Factors," *Journal of Occupational and Environmental Medicine* 41, no. 11 (1999): 995–1004.
140 Martha J. Smith and Derek B. Cornish, *Theory for Practice in Situational Crime Prevention* 16 (Monsey, N.Y.: Criminal Justice Press, 2003).
141 Catherine A. Bourgeois and Maryanne L. Fisher, *Evolutionary Behavioral Sciences* 12, no. 2 (April 2018): 126-131.
142 Thomas Gabor and Andre Normandeau, "Preventing Armed Robbery Through Opportunity Reduction: A Critical Analysis," *Journal of Security Administration* 12, no. 1 (1989): 3–19.
143 U.S. Department of Justice, Federal Bureau of Investigation, Uniform Crime Reports, *Crime in the United States, 2017*, Table 7: Offense Analysis United States, 2013–2017, https://ucr.fbi.gov/crime-in-the-u.s/2017/crime-in-the-u.s.-2017/topic-pages/tables/table-7. Accessed October 2018.
144 Deborah Lamm Weisel, *The Problem of Bank Robbery*, Guide No. 48, Center for Problem Oriented Policing, http://www.popcenter.org/problems/robbery_banks. Accessed June 2018.
145 Kathleen Maguire and Ann L. Pastore, *Sourcebook of Criminal Justice Statistics 2003* (Washington, D.C.: Office of Justice Programs Bureau of Justice Statistics, 2005).
146 Weisel, *The Problem of Bank Robbery*, 123.
147 Bartol and Bartol, *Criminal Behavior*, 438.
148 Gardner and Anderson, *Criminal Law*, 274.
149 Federal Bureau of Investigation, Uniform Crime Reports, *Crime in the United States*, 2016, Aggravated Assault, https://ucr.fbi.gov/crime-in-the-u.s/2016/crime-in-the-u.s.-2016/topic-pages/aggravated-assault. Accessed June 2018.
150 Federal Bureau of Investigation, Uniform Crime Reports, *Crime in the United States, 2017*, Aggravated Assault, https://ucr.fbi.gov/crime-in-the-u.s/2017/crime-in-the-u.s.-2017/topic-pages/aggravated-assault, Table 29: Estimated Number of Arrests, https://ucr.fbi.gov/crime-in-the-u.s/2017/crime-in-the-u.s.-2017/topic-pages/tables/table-29. Accessed October 2018.
151 Federal Bureau of Investigation, Uniform Crime Reports, *Crime in the United States, 2017*, Table 4: Crime in the United States

by Region, Geographic Division, and State, 2016–2017. Available https://ucr.fbi.gov/crime-in-the-u.s/2017/crime-in-the-u.s.-2017/topic-pages/tables/table-4. Accessed October 2018.

152 Federal Bureau of Investigation, Uniform Crime Reports, *Crime in the United States, 2017*, Table 22: Aggravated Assault by State, Types of Weapons, 2017, https://ucr.fbi.gov/crime-in-the-u.s/2017/crime-in-the-u.s.-2017/topic-pages/tables/table-22. Accessed October 2018.

153 Gardner and Anderson, *Criminal Law*, 275.

154 Federal Bureau of Investigation, Uniform Crime Reports, *Crime in the United States, 2017,* Aggravated Assault, https://ucr.fbi.gov/crime-in-the-u.s/2017/crime-in-the-u.s.-2017/topic-pages/aggravated-assault. Accessed October 2018.

155 Bureau of Justice Statistics, "Number of Aggravated Assaults, and Simple Assaults by Victim-Offender Relationship, 2016." Generated using the NCVS Victimization Analysis Tool at https://www.bjs.gov. Accessed June 2018.

156 Janet L. Lauritsen and Karen Heimer, "The Gender Gap in Violent Victimization, 1973–2004," *Journal of Quantitative Criminology* 24, no. 2 (June 2008): 125–147.

157 Marc Riedel, "Stranger Violence: Perspectives, Issues, and Problems," *Journal of Criminal Law and Criminology* 78, no. 2 (Summer 1987): 223–258.

158 Bureau of Justice Statistics, "Number of Aggravated Assaults, and Simple Assaults by Victim-Offender Relationship, 2016." Generated using the NCVS Victimization Analysis Tool at https://www.bjs.gov. Accessed June 2018.

159 Centers for Disease Control and Prevention, "Understanding Intimate Partner Violence," https://www.cdc.gov/violenceprevention/pub/index.html. Accessed June 2018.

160 Bureau of Justice Statistics, "Number of Aggravated Assaults, and Simple Assaults by Victim-Offender Relationship, 2016." Generated using the NCVS Victimization Analysis Tool at https://www.bjs.gov. Accessed June 2018.

161 Bureau of Justice Statistics, "Number of Rape/Sexual Assaults, Aggravated Assaults, and Simple Assaults by Victim-Offender Relationship and Sex, 2016." Generated using the NCVS Victimization Analysis Tool at https://www.bjs.gov. Accessed June 2018.

162 Alesha Durfee and Matthew D. Fetzer, "Offense Type and the Arrest Decision in Cases of Intimate Partner Violence," *Crime & Delinquency* 62, no. 7 (2016): 954–977.

163 American Academy of Pediatrics, HealthyChildren.org, https://www.healthychildren.org/English/safety-prevention/at-home/Pages/What-to-Know-about-Child-Abuse.aspx. Accessed June 2018.

Organized and White-Collar Crime

FEATURES

White-collar and corporate offenders sometimes go to prison for financial offenses. Why do white-collar and corporate offenders break the law?

"Tell your boy Bouncer that he's the No. 1 on the list for tomorrow."

According to a 47-page affidavit, this is the warning a Glendale, California, police officer allegedly gave to a local gang member wanted on federal racketeering charges about an impending arrest. The gang member fled and was not arrested until a month later.

The police officer named in the affidavit, Detective John Saro Balian, was allegedly involved with both the Mexican Mafia and Armenian organized crime. He has been accused of lying about meeting with gang members, tipping them off about planned searches of marijuana growing sites, and disposing of a firearm used in a shooting that was intended to "scare" a target. Balian also allegedly told a police informant whom to extort and instructed him to "slap around" the targets to convince them to pay. According to the affidavit, Balian allegedly told the informant that Armenians would not respect or pay him if they were not afraid of him.

According to an FBI spokesperson, "Mr. Balian moved in criminal circles and operated as though he was above the law by repeatedly lying to hide his criminal activity and that of others. His alleged actions impeded legitimate investigations into organized violent crime and consequently presented a threat to public safety."

Organized Crime

LEARNING OBJECTIVE | 1

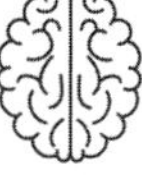

Define organized crime and give examples of its traditional offenses.

LEARNING OBJECTIVE | 2

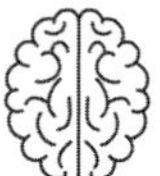

Discuss how differential association theory and classical strain theory are particularly suited to describing the motivations of individuals within crime organizations.

Organized and white-collar crime are criminal offenses typically perpetrated within the context of organizations. The offenses discussed in this chapter are motivated primarily by the desire to amass wealth as well as political or social power or to prevent their loss. As seen in the opening case, these offenses often involve a violation of trust.[1] Although many types of street crime also have a profit or power motive, many of the offenses discussed in this chapter are distinguished by the level of organization, scope, and, in some cases, the otherwise law-abiding nature of those who break the law.[2] Exceptions are white-collar offenses, which are often committed by individuals acting on their own and sometimes acting impulsively. The motivation in these cases is often revenge for real or imagined wrongs to the offender, as well as a desire for money or power.

The three types of crime discussed here overlap to a degree, but we will examine each type separately in order to understand the motives, methods, and harm caused by each. The three types of crime we will discuss are organized crime, white-collar crime, and corporate crime.

1. Organized crime. **Organized crime** is a type of business enterprise involving highly structured or organized groups that break the law and often use violence to achieve goals. Organized crime has traditionally been involved in vice offenses such as gambling, prostitution, and the smuggling of drugs or alcohol. But it also may use the financial proceeds of crime to invest in legitimate enterprises, such as businesses, and financial instruments, such as stocks and bonds. Crime organizations have since expanded the scope of their activities to include trafficking in weapons as well as undocumented immigrants. These organizations are often referred to as "families" because their

participants are often drawn from one ethnic or racial group. Sometimes the members are actually related to one another. In the popular imagination, the typical organized-crime participant is a member of the Italian Mafia (which we will discuss in greater detail later). As we shall see, this stereotype no longer captures the variety and scope of activities now facing law enforcement.[3] Many street gangs that were at one time disorganized bands of juveniles have "grown up" to become effective crime organizations. The FBI and state law enforcement agencies are the main investigators of organized crime.

2. White-collar crime. Although this type of crime takes place within a business or corporate environment, **white-collar crime** refers to the actions of individual employees. A typical white-collar offender might be the bank employee who takes money, the shopkeeper who fails to report income to the Internal Revenue Service (IRS), or the department store clerk who steals merchandise. White-collar crime is perpetrated within the framework of an individual's normal duties and can be difficult to detect.[4] The FBI and state law enforcement agencies are the main investigators into white-collar offenses.
3. Corporate crime. **Corporate crime** consists of offenses committed in the name of a business in the pursuit of money or to prevent losing money. It involves legitimate businesses that engage in unfair business practices, bribe regulators, misrepresent financial assets, or knowingly produce unsafe products or harm the environment. Corporate crime is significantly different from organized crime. The primary purpose of corporations is to make legitimate products, and their criminal offenses are often the result of using shortcuts, taking unfair advantage of other businesses, or being negligent and having poor oversight. Whereas the organized crime network is fundamentally criminal in nature, corporations exist without a criminal intent. Often, the shareholders, board members, and employees have no idea the executives are engaging in illegal practices. Corporations might drift into and out of illegal activities, while always depending on their legitimate concerns to make money for the company.[5] Depending on the size and nature of the offense, several federal and state agencies, including the FBI, the IRS, and the Department of Justice, might have a hand in investigating and prosecuting corporate crime. Organized, white-collar, and corporate crime are becoming a major focus within criminology. The dawn of the 21st century has seen a rash of corporate criminal activity and wrongdoing that has not been witnessed for a century. As we progress through this chapter, the distinctions between these types of offenses will become clearer. We note also that these types of offenses require special skill-sets of law enforcement officers. For instance, to follow the paper trail of corporate, white-collar, and some organized-crime offenders, an investigator needs expertise in financial accounting. Similarly, the law enforcement officer dealing with a toxic waste polluter needs to know something about chemistry and biology.[6]

Organized crime is a global problem that can take many forms. It can be contained within one country, or it can be **transnational crime** and affect several countries.[7] This variety of forms and geographic dispersal makes defining organized crime problematic. Criminologist Howard Abadinsky states that there is no generally accepted definition of organized crime because those who attempt to define the term have occupational or agency agendas that influence their viewpoints. For instance, police officers in a particular city who are responsible for maintaining the peace and arresting offenders see organized crime in a different way than do scholars at the United Nations who must account for various criminal enterprises in different cultures. Instead of defining organized crime, Abadinsky offers a number of attributes that crime organizations tend to have.[8] These

organized crime—A crime organization that breaks the law for money and often uses violence to achieve its goals.

Instant Recall from Chapter 1 **white-collar crime**—Financially motivated criminal offenses committed by way of deceit and without violence, usually involving the offender's place of employment or business.

corporate crime—Offenses committed in the name of a business in the pursuit of money or to prevent losing money.

transnational crime—Criminal offenses that originate in one country and cross one or several national borders.

attributes allow us to consider how crime organizations differ from other types of conventional offenders and terrorist groups.

- No political goals. Unlike a terrorist organization, modern crime organizations are not trying to advance a political agenda. Although the Ku Klux Klan might share some attributes with organized crime, it has an identifiable political purpose of preserving and enhancing white power. Some crime organizations might attempt to influence the political environment in order to make money, but such attempts are generally aimed at gaining protection or immunity for the organization's criminal activities rather than promoting a political cause.[9]
- Hierarchical organization. Crime organizations have a definite chain of command. More extensive than "a leader and followers," this chain of command contains three or more levels of direct authority and, often, staff positions such as legal counselor. Most important, these levels of command do not depend on the personality of any particular individual but are consistent features of the organization, thus making personnel replaceable.[10]
- Limited or exclusive membership. Not just anyone can join a crime organization. Some are limited to persons from particular ethnic backgrounds or with specific criminal experiences. Willingness to put the crime organization as a first priority is paramount, and often an aspiring member must be sponsored by a current member.[11]
- Unique subculture. The members of crime organizations see themselves as distinct from mainstream society. They view the laws and rules of society as meaningless to how they construct their own "underworld" in which honor, loyalty, and secrecy are vital.[12]
- Self-perpetuating. A crime organization has a lifespan greater than that of its individual members. Recruitment and succession of power are important features in maintaining the criminal network over a long period of time.[13]
- Violence and bribery. These are the primary tools of crime organizations, which they use to gain a competitive edge and to protect their interests. **Bribery** involves influencing public officials or employees of businesses with offers of money or valuables. Alternatively, the use of extreme violence can frighten competitors, customers, and even law enforcement officers and government officials into cooperating.[14]
- Specialization or division of labor. Depending on the organization's size, individuals might be assigned specific tasks and responsibilities. Some might physically enforce the group's goals, while others might be responsible for laundering money and investing it in legitimate assets.[15]
- Monopolistic. Crime organizations are not free-market traders. They are concerned with establishing exclusive control over a geographic area or a particular type of business. Much of the violence surrounding organized crime stems from "turf" battles in which one group attempts to encroach on another's business. These disputes can sometimes be negotiated, but more often than not, they are settled by the faction that can muster the most violence.[16]
- Governed by rules or regulations. Order within the crime organization is maintained by rules demanding that participants respect one another's dignity, business, and family. Violation of the rules will result not in a lawsuit, but in violence.

Crime organizations possess these attributes to varying degrees. Although they provide guidelines for recognizing organized crime, the types of structures that engage in organized crime vary greatly. Examination of some specific examples of organized crime will help our understanding of this type of unlawful activity.

The Beginning of Organized Crime in the United States

Organized crime in the United States can be traced back to the **political machines** of large cities in the early 20th century. European immigrants supplied the labor for the emerging industrial growth of the United States. With the immigrants came not only opportunities for their exploitation, but also their own attempts at gaining economic and political power to protect themselves.[17]

The Irish were the first immigrant group to arrive in the United States in large numbers after the original influx of Anglo-Saxon Protestants in

---

bribery—The offense of giving money or valuables to influence public officials or employees of business competitors.

political machine—A type of group in the 19th-century United States that rewarded other powerful individuals, businesses, and organizations who ensured that the machine received votes and administrative control of a jurisdiction.

the 17th and 18th centuries. Fleeing a country ravaged by famine and the exploitive and unfair economic practices of England, the Irish arrived with a political culture that encouraged secrecy, unity, and upward mobility through politics. Irish immigrants settled in the large eastern cities of the United States where they sought to dominate local politics. They found themselves restricted in the educational, economic, and social spheres by the ruling establishment, which looked down on the newcomers as a foreign influence that diminished the cultural heritage of the existing social order.[18]

The political power amassed by the Irish can be attributed to two social institutions: the Catholic Church and the local saloon. Both the Church and the saloon gave the Irish opportunities to build community and establish ethnic identity. The saloon of the late 19th and early 20th centuries is a very different social institution from the bars of the 21st century. Saloons provided the main social base for political activity, neighborhood gossip, and a wide array of services for community social life, including rooms for weddings and union meetings. In cities where power was dispersed to the neighborhoods, saloon keepers were central figures in local political machines. Their ability to deliver votes on election day allowed saloon keepers to influence politics in ways that made them not only politically powerful, but also economically successful.[19]

The degree of organization that evolved from city political machines ensured that certain groups of individuals, often ethnic Irish, Italians, or Germans, had enormous influence on the workings of city government. This influence included many illegal activities that usually involved vices such as gambling, the sale of illicit alcohol, and prostitution. The power of the political machine was all-encompassing. In addition to being able to deliver the vote, the machine could also discourage rivals by denying them parade permits, getting friends and relatives hired and enemies fired from government jobs, and providing the muscle to intimidate those who challenged their power. As city governments and local police departments evolved into less violent forms of graft and political influence, these activities increasingly became the province of a criminal underworld.[20]

The Rise of the Underworld

Powerful political machines and the influential economic leaders of the cities developed a relationship that benefited both parties. The political machine oversaw not only the legitimate businesses run by law-abiding citizens, but also the illegitimate vice activities often used by those same citizens. In order to meet the demand for gambling and other illicit activities, political machines allowed an underworld of criminal activity to exist that helped keep the machine in power and enriched its leaders. Although periodically engaging in the arrest and conviction of underworld figures, the political machine also profited by accepting bribes and services from those same figures.[21] For instance, in 1890, New York state

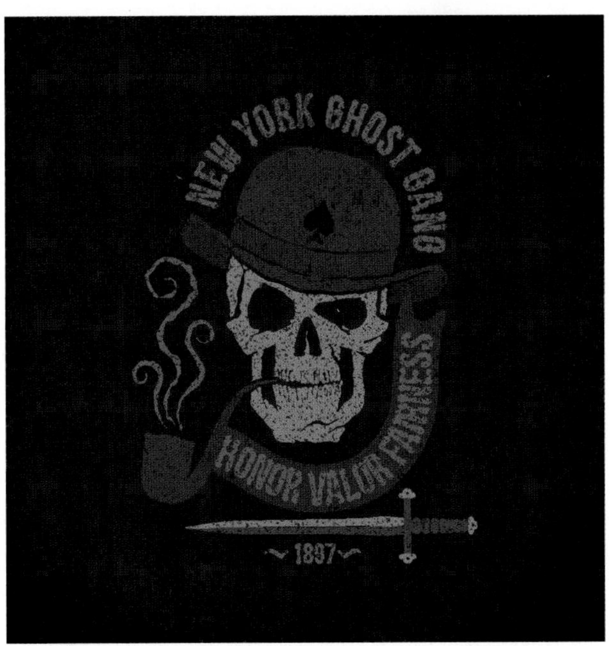

Organized crime in the United States has a long history. What groups of people are stereotypically associated with organized crime? Is this association fair or accurate?

"Who stole the people's money?" What was the relationship between city politicians and crime in the early 19th century?

senator "Big Tim" Sullivan, who was part of the Tammany Hall political machine, was made responsible for Italian and Jewish immigrants to New York City. That is, it was his job to ensure that they voted for politicians approved by Tammany Hall and that those who regularly committed criminal offenses were punctual with their bribes. In return, Sullivan allowed a certain amount of vice in the city.[22]

The best example of how city political machines and the underworld worked in harmony to increase the power and wealth of each is Prohibition, the national ban on the manufacture, transportation, and sale of alcoholic beverages enacted in 1920 by the Eighteenth Amendment to the Constitution. Congress had already passed the Volstead Act in 1919, which created the Prohibition Bureau in the Treasury Department and charged it with the primary responsibility for enforcing Prohibition. However, this bureau turned out to be ineffective and often counterproductive. For instance:

> In addition to being inept and corrupt, Prohibition Bureau agents were a public menace: they ran up a record of being killed (by 1923, 30 had been murdered) and for killing hundreds of civilians, often innocent women and children. The bureau was viewed as a training school for bootleggers, because agents frequently left the service to join their wealthy adversaries.[23]

Local law enforcement agencies often worked in conjunction with bootleggers, speakeasies, and politicians to reap profits from facilitating alcohol sales. Prohibition greatly weakened citizens' trust in law enforcement and contributed to the rise of organized crime. There was simply too much money at stake, and the public's demand for alcohol was so great that the legal institutions of law enforcement, the courts, and city governments were propelled into acquiescence, corruption, and neglect. Prohibition ended in 1933, when ratification of the Twenty-first Amendment to the Constitution repealed the Eighteenth Amendment and nullified the Volstead Act.

The most significant by-product of Prohibition was the shift of power from city bosses to private individuals engaged in organized crime. Rather than being errand boys and thugs at the service of politicians, crime organizations became powerful in their own right. They continued to bribe the city officials who were susceptible, and they intimidated those who were hesitant to be bribed. They turned the immense profits of vice crime to their own ends, thus consolidating their power and wealth. The shift of power to organized crime happened in different ways in different cities. In order to understand the rise of organized crime in the United States, we turn now to an examination of how the insularity and unity of ethnic groups facilitated the consolidation of specific vice markets in the United States.

The American Mafia

When Americans think about organized crime, the first picture that often pops into mind is the Mafia don of Italian descent. The *Godfather* movies, as well as the popular television series *The Sopranos*, provide an entertaining, if distorted, portrayal of organized crime (see Doubletake). Yet there is some truth to this view, and a look at the history of the Mafia in the United States shows how Italians in large cities, particularly New York and Chicago, used violence and intimidation to control their criminal empires.[24]

Italians who emigrated to the United States in large numbers between 1890 and 1920 faced economic and social hardships. They found a society in which Protestant Anglo-Americans dominated the private business sector and a powerful Irish American group had taken over many of the jobs in municipal government. Several factors facilitated the Italian immigrants' entry into organized crime. The Italian immigrants included a sizable number of Sicilians and Neapolitans (immigrants from Naples), who brought with them an organizational model of loosely connected, independent families.

The term "families" requires further explanation. Although actual family relationships were the basis for this type of organizational structure, these business enterprises were composed of groups of families who had some intimate connections and provided a sense of security and protection for one another.[25] In short, there was no ancient, fully formed, tightly organized Mafia that arrived in the United States from Sicily. The modern Mafia, in fact, more closely resembles gangs from 17th-century Naples than the

---

racketeering—The use of extortion and force to engage in illegal business activities.

extortion—The offense of obtaining money, property, or information by threats, intimidation, or false claim to a position of authority.

DOUBLETAKE

Creating the Mafia

Organized crime is a popular subject in entertainment media, and the most popular organized-crime subject is the Mafia. Several Mafia families have reigned since their arrival in the United States in the late 19th century. Today, federal law enforcement efforts have greatly reduced the activities of the New York–based Mafia.[26]

Movies and television, however, have provided us with many more Mafia families: the Corleones of the *Godfather* films, the Sopranos of *The Sopranos*, and the Vittis from *Analyze This*, just to name a few. In one of the most realistic films, *Goodfellas*, which is based on actual Mafia activities, the mobsters engaged in criminal offenses both large and miniscule, as they "stole $6 million from Lufthansa Airlines and sold unstamped cigarettes from the trunk of a car."[27]

Much of what the media present as Mafia reality is not. Like the situations in all fictional media entertainment, some aspects are glorified and dramatized to make the film, novel, or television show more interesting. According to one film critic, this "indulgent, even romantic mythology is a sign that organized crime has never posed a serious threat to the American social order, providing instead a rich trove of tabloid headlines and hard-boiled metaphors."[28] As violent as the Mafia is, few fictional treatments portray mobsters as actually detrimental to the whole of American society. They are portrayed as misunderstood heroes, regular people who just happen to work for the Mafia, or men of honor who live by a code that the outside world just cannot understand.

Other societies have not been so lucky. An Italian film, *Excellent Cadavers* (1999), portrays the Mafia in a far less forgiving light as it tells the true story of the fight against a Mafia-infiltrated government in Sicily. The two Sicilian prosecutors who risked their lives trying to shut down, or at least diminish, Mafia activities were killed by car bombs in 1992, but not before they secured the convictions of hundreds of Mafia soldiers. In the film, the Mafia, which has severely crippled Sicilian civic life, is portrayed not as "the colorful, violent flowering of ancient Mediterranean peasant customs," but as "a thoroughly vicious organization bent on the subversion of democratic norms and the brutal elimination of anyone who dares to oppose its ambitions."[29]

THINK ABOUT IT

1. Why have the media fixated on Italian Americans as representative of organized crime?
2. What social factors might lead the American media to portray Mafia leaders as heroes, while an Italian film portrays them as vicious criminals?

Sicilian bandits, who probably originated as antagonists against the region's Spanish government and later against its Italian government. The Sicilian word "mafioso" described an attitude, which basically meant to be a brave man. The designation "Mafia"—which even in Italy is a blanket term for criminal groups—probably derives from this word.[30]

The range of offenses that involve Italian organized crime families is long and varied. The following criminal activities have been linked to organized crime.

- Racketeering. Although crime organizations are involved in many legitimate industries, they engage in **racketeering**, which is the use of **extortion**—using threats or intimidation to obtain money, property, or information—and

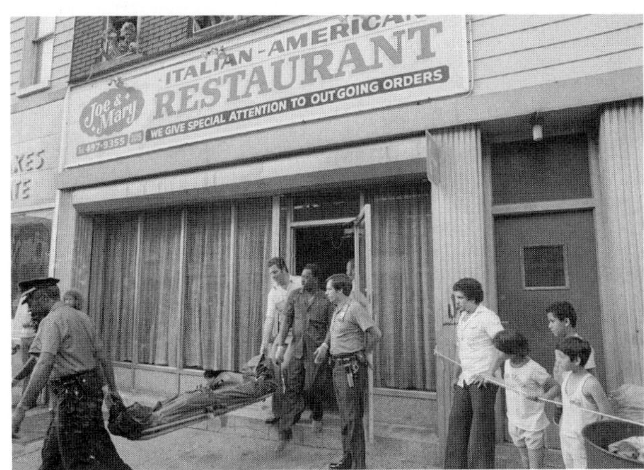

Policemen carry the body of reputed Mafia leader Carmine "Lilo" Galante from the Joe & Mary restaurant in Brooklyn, New York City, in 1979. Galante was shot and killed while lunching in the restaurant's backyard. What is an organized-crime "family"?

force to engage in illegal business activities. Organized crime has been linked to organized labor unions and, through them, to the vending machine, liquor, movie, trucking, and garbage industries.[31] A particularly successful law enforcement tool against organized crime has been the 1970 **Racketeering Influenced and Corrupt Organizations (RICO) Act** (see Theory to Practice).[32]

- Prostitution and pornography. Crime organizations have long been involved in the prostitution trade. Sometimes, involvement has been at the street-level pimping of prostitutes, but more often crime organizations provide protection to brothel owners. The distribution of pornographic materials is another area in which organized crime has traditionally been powerful. Crime organizations owned or controlled theaters that showed X-rated movies and owned or protected stores that sold "adult" books, magazines, or videos. However, the Internet has made the distribution of pornographic materials more difficult for organized crime to control.[33]

Organized crime has traditionally been associated with prostitution. What other illegal enterprises are associated with organized crime?

Instant Recall from Chapter 4 **rational choice theory** —The concept that offenders calculate the advantages and disadvantages not only of breaking the law but of what type of offense to commit.

Racketeering Influenced and Corrupt Organizations (RICO) Act—A federal statute enacted in 1970 to control organized crime.

securities fraud—An offense in which an individual or entity attempts to manipulate the investment market, usually by encouraging investors to purchase securities based on false statements.

- Fraud. Crime organizations have found many activities to be profitable. Credit card fraud is a common offense. Often, crime organizations run up huge amounts of purchases that victims discover only when they receive their credit card statements. Organized crime has also targeted the government in fraudulent endeavors. For example, prior to the 1980s, the method of collecting gasoline taxes was extremely inefficient in several states, and gas stations owned by crime organizations would avoid paying taxes. When finally required to pay, the organizations would simply close the station for a few months, then re-open under a new owner. Local, state, and federal governments could not keep track of who the actual owners were because the businesses were often registered to overseas corporations.[34]
- Securities fraud. **Securities fraud** describes attempts to manipulate the investment market, usually by encouraging investors to purchase securities based on false statements. Organized crime has profited by purchasing securities at low prices, artificially running up the value, and then selling before the deception is detected. As in their other business enterprises, crime organizations use threats and intimidation to raise the price of their securities. They force brokers to convince their clients to buy an overvalued stock, and then they liquidate their own holdings, leaving the client with an investment that quickly loses its value.[35] A typical corporate securities offense is the running of "boiler rooms." These operations, which are usually telemarketing outfits, push nearly worthless, obscure, or fraudulent stocks using dishonest sales tactics.
- Black-market goods. A number of legitimate and illegitimate products are sold outside the bounds of conventional commerce. This means that products sold on the street, in flea markets, and to businesses through the back door or over the Internet are not subjected to taxes. In addition, stolen goods are peddled on the black market, as are prohibited items such as weapons, drugs, and alcohol. Engaging in this type of enterprise is risky, and it is fertile ground for the involvement of crime organizations because they are able to protect themselves, provide protection to those they deal with, and ensure that prices stay high by threatening to harm any competition.

THEORY TO PRACTICE

Racketeering Influenced and Corrupt Organizations (RICO)

The **Racketeering Influenced and Corrupt Organizations (RICO) Act** is a federal statute enacted in 1970 to control organized crime. The purpose of RICO is "the elimination of the infiltration of organized crime and racketeering into legitimate organizations operating in interstate commerce."[36] RICO allows prosecutors to seize criminally gained assets and provide long prison sentences, typically 20 years to life. In the early 1990s, RICO was expanded to target non-traditional crime groups, such as gangs. For example, in 2017 federal agents indicted 30 members and associates of the Nine Trey Gangster Bloods on charges of RICO conspiracy and other charges related to drug distribution and murder in the Atlanta, Georgia, area.[37]

The RICO statutes are based on **rational choice theory**. Crime organizations are motivated by a business ethic aimed at creating a profit. Many have lawyers and accountants to help them determine the potential profit and legal risks for their activities. RICO statutes make offenses that happen across two or more states subject to federal penalties. The intent is to discourage organized crime from expanding its enterprises by increasing the chances that illegal activities will be discovered and to provide severe penalties at the federal level.

The government must prove four conditions to establish violations of the RICO Act.

1. The prosecution must demonstrate that the defendants were associated with an enterprise as defined in the RICO statute. "Enterprise" includes any group of individuals whose association provides for the commission of two or more predicate crimes, or offenses that are included in charging another offense and must be committed in order for the other offenses to be charged. An enterprise must be organized in a way that allows for hierarchic or consensual decision-making (one of the hallmarks of an organization).
2. The government must prove the enterprise engages in, or its activities affect, interstate commerce. An example of interstate commerce would be the use of interstate facilities such as banks, telephones, and wire transfers for drug trafficking.
3. The government must prove that each defendant agreed to participate in the enterprise through a "pattern of racketeering." The "pattern" means the activity requires two or more predicate acts within a decade that must be connected to achieve an illegal end.
4. The government must prove that each defendant agreed to participate in the enterprise's affairs by committing or agreeing to commit at least two predicate offenses.[38] Predicate offenses include but are not limited to counterfeiting, money laundering, drug trafficking, prostitution, murder, kidnapping, gambling, arson, robbery, bribery, and extortion.[39]

THINK ABOUT IT

1. Think of a case that could be prosecuted under RICO.
2. Why did the government deem the RICO statutes necessary?

Ethnically Based Organized Crime in the United States

Not all crime organizations in the United States are set up like the Mafia. Many crime organizations more closely resemble loose networks. Criminologist Jay Albanese cautions against falling into the "ethnicity trap" of assuming that people who share an ethnicity, culture, and language coalesce around a specific criminal element, protect them, and supply them with members.

Some crime organizations operate as fluid networks in which individuals have indirect connections and take on partners only as needed for criminal activity. These networks are not centralized or dominated by a few leaders. Unlike many Mafia groups, no hierarchy exists independent of the criminal offense. One such fluid, organized crime network is that of Russian émigrés in the Brighton Beach area of Brooklyn in New York City.[40] These groups typically have transient members who may be organized around a specific offense, such as the extortion of money from local merchants. There is little or no personal loyalty, and individual group members, even those from common ethnic or cultural backgrounds, typically distrust each other. After the group's criminal objective is attained, say, a successful drug sale, the group may split up or may go on to another criminal enterprise.

Asian gangs exhibit a similar structure. Larger organizations are split into small cells or even partnerships to pursue a single criminal goal, such as the extortion of a particular target. When that goal is complete, the cell or partnership dissolves. Individual members can conduct several criminal enterprises with different groups simultaneously, regardless of ethnic identity.[41] Both the Russian and Asian gangs are only two examples of the variety of ethnic gangs in the United States. Other common gang ethnicities include Dominican, Filipino, Jamaican, Mexican, and Salvadoran.

The network model of organized crime is problematic for both citizens and the criminal justice system. These organizations often do not have a moral code, and the participants have no loyalty either to their ethnic group or to their partners in crime. Criminal groups are loosely organized based on the specific offenses to be committed and are quickly disbanded and reorganized in different ways for future criminal activities. Albanese suggests that instead of thinking of organized crime in ethnic terms, it is more useful to think of it in terms of the types of illicit activities that each group engages in.[42]

GANGS

Some crime organizations started out as street gangs. The difference between crime organizations and street gangs boils down to organization and coherence. For example, when Sicilian bandits began arriving in the United States in the late 19th century, they found street gangs and semi-organized crime groups already operating in cities such as New York, Chicago, and New Orleans. The difference between the Italian bandits and the American gangs was organization. If the head of an American gang was killed or arrested, the gang usually dissipated. Gangs also tended to split into factions. The family structure that the Italian groups brought with them, however, had been forged during hundreds of years of poverty, racism, violence, and political repression. This translated well into the corporate structure later developed by the American Mafia and honed during Prohibition.[43]

Some contemporary gangs have adopted this structure. Six other attributes have been cited as differences and similarities between crime organizations and gangs.

- Corruption. Crime organizations typically make systematic efforts to corrupt public officials, including law enforcement, with large payoffs. Most gangs do not have the relationships with law enforcement and government to engage in these activities.
- Violence. Crime organizations and gangs have in common the use or threat of violence to achieve their goals.
- Continuity. Crime organizations are continuous and persist over years or decades. A few gangs have achieved this as well, but most have not.
- Multiple enterprises. Systematic, continuous engagement in multiple profitable enterprises is a hallmark of crime organizations. The primary profitable enterprise of gangs is selling drugs.
- Legitimate businesses. Regular businesses, such as restaurants, bars, and retail establishments, are just as attractive to crime organizations as illegitimate businesses. Gangs usually do not operate legitimate businesses.
- Sophistication, discipline, and bonding. "Sophistication" refers to the efforts crime organizations employ to hide and advance their businesses, such as the use of paper trails, codes, dummy corporations, lawyers, and accountants. Individual organization members must be disciplined, acting in the organization's interests rather than their own. Finally, crime organizations often use some type of entry ritual to promote bonding among members, much as sports teams or fraternities do. Gangs typically only participate in the latter two of these activities: acting in the organization's interests and entry rituals.[44]

Most gangs do not meet all these requirements for crime organizations (see Policy Implications).[45] This is not to say that some gangs will never rise to this level of sophistication.[46] After all, many crime organizations started out decades ago as gangs. However, as of today, street gangs simply do not meet all the criteria to be crime organizations.

Theories of Organized Crime

Two criminological theories are particularly suited to describing the motivations of individuals within crime organizations: **differential association theory** and **classical strain theory**. According to differential association theory, crime organization members learn crime from each other. This fact is especially relevant because crime organizations are often composed of individuals with social commonalities. In the case of the crime family, some organization members may be related or may be members of several families from the same neighborhood.

POLICY IMPLICATIONS

Unorganized Crime: The Case of MS-13

A gang composed largely of immigrants from El Salvador known as MS-13, or Mara Salvatrucha, has been the target of politicians who use fear of violence to promote anti-immigration policies. To be sure, MS-13 is no mere social club. They have committed gruesome acts of violence in Central America and in the United States. For example, Long Island, New York, police believe that MS-13 is responsible for 25 murders over a two-year period, including one in which a 15-year-old boy was hacked to death with a machete.[47]

MS-13 has been designated as a transnational criminal organization and has been compared to Colombian drug cartels and the Mafia. As reprehensible as the violence of MS-13 is, some scholars are concerned that the rhetoric and response of the U.S. government are not proportional to the actual threat the gang poses. Critics point out that MS-13 is not a network of criminal masterminds, but rather a loosely organized coalition of young men who lack the capability and skill to deal drugs as efficiently as the cartels. Although MS-13 is estimated to have 30,000–50,000 members (8,000–10,000 in the United States), it is basically a bunch of cliques with no central control and no clear leaders.[48]

The genesis of MS-13 is not El Salvador, but rather the streets of Los Angeles. Children of Salvadoran immigrants who fled the 1979–1992 Salvadoran Civil War formed a surrogate family that created a collective identity based on violence and control. In 1996, many of these gang members were deported to El Salvador. This massive influx of established gang members further destabilized a country that was already weakened. According to criminologist Lidia Nuño of California State University, Fullerton:

> One of the dirty little secrets of why we provide so many resources to Central America today is because we know that indirectly—and I will never say that we intended to do this—created a social issue by deporting individuals who only knew how to do crime to a broken country."[49]

MS-13 is prevalent in the United States where El Salvadoran refugees congregate near large cities. The crackdown on MS-13 has produced some unintended consequences as authorities try to determine who are gang members and who are simply refugees.[50]

The policy of focusing on MS-13 may be diverting resources from other, more pressing problems such as the opioid epidemic. Instead of spending so many resources arresting and deporting gang members, some activists suggest strengthening our institutions to keep youngsters from joining gangs, such as afterschool programs, vocational training, educational efforts, and counseling services.[51]

THINK ABOUT IT

1. What other strategies can be used to reduce the influence of criminal gangs such as MS-13?
2. MS-13 has existed for decades. Why is the gang such a political issue now?

In the case of ethnically based organizations, the members may be of the same nationality or ethnicity. In each case, it is likely the members have known each other since childhood and know each other's families. It is especially easy, in this case, to pass on attitudes and techniques for breaking the law. Older members may start their children's criminal education early, for instance, by having them run errands for the organization. The children are further indoctrinated into the organization's goals and methods as they mature.

The second theory that can be applied to crime organizations is classical strain theory. Immigration plays an important role in organized crime. It is difficult to start life over in a new country, and culture and language barriers can be quite difficult. Finding employment, housing, and a welcoming neighborhood to live in can be major challenges. Therefore, some immigrants who find the goals of American life attractive can be discouraged by the socially accepted means to attain them. A few members of immigrant communities may innovate by using the proceeds of crime to attain these

Instant Recall from Chapter 6 **differential association theory** —Sutherland's idea that offenders learn crime from each other.

Instant Recall from Chapter 6 **classical strain theory** —The idea that people who experience anger and frustration when they cannot achieve cultural goals through legitimate means try to achieve these goals through illegitimate means.

goals. Belonging to a crime organization of family, friends, and ethnically similar members makes the innovation that much easier. This innovative attitude can even be passed down through the generations, so that although the members of the crime organization have assimilated into American culture, they continue within the organization because it provides the best means they know of attaining goals.

Organized Crime Offenses

In the following sections, we discuss some of the types of activities crime organizations engage in. Although these organizations might provide services to people of their own ethnicity, their range of activities, customers, and geographic marketplace often extends a great deal further.

ILLEGAL DRUG TRAFFICKING

Organized crime is involved in the manufacture and distribution of illegal drugs, but no single crime organization controls the drug trade. The drug trade is a highly fragmented activity that grows or changes depending on the drug demand, and the degree of organization within crime groups varies depending on the type of drug.[52] One of the most organized groups, the Colombian drug cartels, were especially active in the 1980s and 1990s. When Colombia drove out its major drug cartels in the 1990s, the drug trade moved into Mexico, igniting violent competition for control. The new Mexican cartels, such as La Familia Michoacána, targeted each other with extreme violence. The Mexican government began using the military to capture or kill cartel leaders, splintering the cartels into smaller groups. Because drug trafficking required more resources and infrastructure than the small groups had, many turned to the kidnapping, theft, and extortion of ordinary citizens who were not involved in the drug trade.[53] Today, Mexican crime organizations deliver more drugs to the United States—including cocaine, methamphetamine, heroin, marijuana, and fentanyl—than any other transnational crime organization, including groups from Asia, Colombia, and the Dominican Republic.[54] Although the Mexican organizations are violent in Mexico, their distribution agents in the United States are disciplined and sufficiently quiet that they do not call attention to themselves.[55]

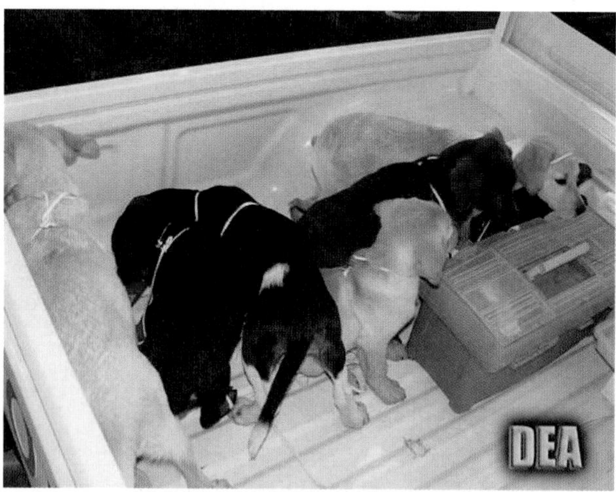

This 2005 photo provided by U.S. Drug Enforcement Administration officials shows puppies rescued from a farm in Colombia destined for a U.S. veterinarian working for a Colombian drug-trafficking ring. The veterinarian used the puppies to smuggle packets of liquid heroin on commercial flights to New York City, where the heroin packets were eventually cut out of the puppies, who died in the process. What punishment should these drug traffickers receive?

PROSTITUTION AND HUMAN TRAFFICKING

Prostitution has long been a primary source of income for crime organizations. Although some prostitutes work only for themselves, others are connected with crime organizations, some of which engage in the transnational smuggling of women and children to be used as sex slaves.[56] These women and children are moved from impoverished countries into tourist areas, large cities, and other places where prostitution flourishes and are psychologically, physically, and economically dominated by crime networks.[57] Unlike the entrepreneurial prostitute who controls his or her working conditions, many of those caught up in international smuggling rings have little or no control of their lives.[58]

A related form of human trafficking involves the trade in human organs. Because human organs are so scarce and the process for getting them is determined by the medical establishment, there is a thriving black market for hearts, livers, and kidneys.[59] At present, this is not a large market primarily because it takes a skilled surgeon to extract the organs and keep them healthy and because the system linking buyers and sellers is inefficient. However, as wealthy Americans and Europeans age and Internet commerce matures, the demand for organs will likely increase, and the prices for them will rise exponentially. This combination of large demand and little supply can produce the types of profits that encourage organized crime.

GAMBLING

Crime organizations are attracted to illegal gambling because the operations require a high degree of cooperation. As legalized gambling has proliferated around the United States in the form of casinos, horse racing, dog racing, and state lotteries, organized crime has lost many of its customers to government-run enterprises.[60] Nevertheless, gamblers have plenty of opportunities to gamble illegally in neighborhood lotteries and poker games, as well as bet on college and professional sports. The activities are popular with some gamblers because they are often able to bet on credit, they find the odds more favorable, and they enjoy the risk of doing something illegal.

The extent to which organized crime is involved in these activities varies by the amount of profit, the nature of the regulatory agency, and the clientele's sophistication. In 2018, Northampton, Massachusetts, police raided a local farm and seized nearly 400 roosters that were allegedly bred for cockfighting, which is banned in every state. The roosters, which are trained to fight with spurs on their feet, can cost as much as $600 on the black market. Animal rights activists say that, although cockfighting is an "underground" activity, it is highly professionalized, which points to a certain level of organization and structure within breeding and fighting networks.[61]

Of great concern currently is the possibility that organized crime will infiltrate legal gambling activities. The legacy of organized crime in Las Vegas, Nevada, has given the public the impression that all modern casino gambling is completely under the control of crime organizations. This is no longer true. Major casinos are typically run by large conglomerates or American Indian tribes. There is a fear that as American Indian reservations and states continue to develop their gambling enterprises, organized crime will once again move into the gambling business unless these operations are closely controlled.

There is also speculation, however, that the immense profits available in gambling have made this enterprise so attractive that crime organizations may be out-competed by non-criminal enterprises. Gambling has become an acceptable way of raising revenue for the state and one that is politically popular with some segments of the population. Although some people oppose gambling on moral grounds, others consider it an acceptable alternative to raising taxes to fund local government activities. Because of the states' inherent advantage, as well as the long odds, state-sponsored gambling has been called "a tax on stupidity." Threats to legal gambling from organized crime include the prospect of some organized criminal group rigging a state lottery.[62]

STOLEN PROPERTY

The market for stolen goods has grown substantially with the increasing globalization of national economies. No longer must goods be fenced locally; now they can be sold to people half a world away. This is especially true of large-ticket items such as automobiles, farm equipment, jewelry, computers, and mobile phones.[63] The cost of stealing and shipping these items to South America, Asia, Africa, Europe, and the Middle East is more than compensated by the prices they fetch at the new destination. The state of California has even developed a problem with the theft of huge shipments of nuts, including almonds, walnuts, and pistachios. There is a thriving international market for nuts, and they are difficult, if not impossible, to track once stolen because nut shipments have no serial numbers, and of course the evidence disappears after the nuts are eaten.[64] Globalization has also affected industrial and intellectual property. Items ranging from computer parts; pharmaceuticals; and automotive, aerospace, rail, and industrial components are regularly stolen, smuggled, and counterfeited.[65]

PAUSE AND REVIEW

1. **How do crime organizations differ from conventional offenders and terrorist groups?**
2. **How has the media distorted our understanding of organized crime?**
3. **How does RICO allow prosecutors to target organized crime?**
4. **In what ways did the prohibition of alcohol in the United States contribute to the rise of organized crime?**

White-Collar Crime

LEARNING OBJECTIVE | 3

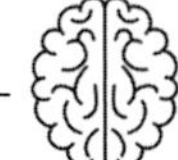

Define white-collar crime.

LEARNING OBJECTIVE | 4

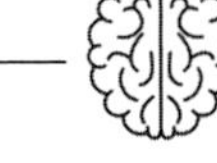

List and explain four theories that can address white-collar crime.

White-collar crime consists of offenses committed by individual employees for their own benefit during the course of legitimate business. Unlike executives who engage in corporate crime, these employees do not seek to lead the company into illegal activities or cover up illegal activities to preserve profit, but merely to enrich themselves. White-collar offenders, who can be difficult to catch, often feel perfectly justified in stealing from a big, bureaucratic company either because they believe that company "owes them" or because the company is so large and complicated that no one will notice the missing funds or items.

Theories of White-Collar Crime

From a theoretical perspective, white-collar crime does not differ substantially from other types of crime, and it can be addressed by at least four criminological theories. The first is Sutherland's differential association theory, which envisions crime as learned. White-collar offenders learn attitudes and techniques from peers and co-workers. If some office workers routinely help themselves to notepads, pens, paper, and the like, then it is more likely that newly hired workers will adopt the same attitudes and learn the techniques for taking the materials out of the office unnoticed.

A second applicable theory is **conflict theory**. Using conflict theory, we can understand how white-collar offenders determine that the corporations and managers exploit workers and thus try to even the score. White-collar crime is a way of ensuring that wealth is spread to the employee. Conflict theory may be paired with a third theory, **techniques of neutralization**. Here, the employee rationalizes that the corporation will not miss the money (denial of injury), that the corporation is overcharging customers and underpaying employees (condemnation of condemners), and that the employee needs the money to provide for his or her family (appeal to higher loyalty). See Table 11.1 for a brief description of how criminological theory can be applied to organized, white-collar, and corporate crime.

Classical strain theory is another applicable theory. Rather than strive for socially accepted goals by socially accepted means, the white-collar offender accepts the goals but has given up on the means to attain them by being a hard-working, honest employee. Instead, the employee "innovates" and seeks the goals through using his or her position as an

TABLE 11.1 Theories of Organized, White-Collar, and Corporate Crime

TYPE OF CRIME	THEORY
Organized crime	**Differential association** Many criminal organizations are set up along family or ethnic lines. Younger members of these groups learn both the attitudes and techniques of committing organized crime from their relatives and peers. **Strain theory** Unable to reach social goals by approved means, members of criminal organizations try to do so by illegal means.
White-collar crime	**Strain theory** Rather than trying to attain success through the generally accepted means of working hard, some employees attempt to reach the goal of financial security by taking advantage of their position of trust within the organization. **Differential association** Employees learn attitudes and techniques for engaging in white-collar crime from peers and coworkers. **Conflict theory** White-collar offenders determine that the corporations and managers exploit workers, and try to even the score. **Techniques of neutralization** White-collar offenders make rationalizations such as denial of injury, condemnation of condemners, and appeal to higher loyalty.
Corporate crime	**Conflict theory** Corporations (the bourgeoisie) attempt to increase their market share, money, and power through illegal activities at the expense of workers, consumers (the proletariat), or the environment.

employee to commit offenses that will provide financial or material reward.

White-Collar Offenses by Employees

The difference between street crime and white-collar crime is not so much the offenders' motivations but rather their techniques. Specifically, white-collar crime does not use violence or the threat of violence and is usually perpetrated with subterfuge. The victims are consumers, clients, the public, or offenders' employers. This type of white-collar offense is extremely difficult to detect and does not inflict great economic hardship on the company or the customer. However, when done hundreds of times, such scams can be a significant source of extra revenue for the employee. Common offenses include the following forms of **fraud** and theft.

- Securities fraud. We discussed securities fraud earlier in the section on corporate crime, but securities fraud can also be committed by individual employees on their own without the employer's knowledge. Typical offenses include churning, insider trading, and stock manipulation. Churning occurs when brokers who earn commissions by buying and selling stocks trade shares frequently to inflate commissions. Insider trading is the use of financial information unavailable to the public to gain an advantage in trading securities. In stock manipulation, or "pump and dump" schemes, a securities professional who owns a particular stock urges clients to purchase it. The stock's price rises as individuals buy in, allowing the securities professional to sell his or her shares at an artificially high price.
- Fraud against the government. A common form of fraud against the government is tax fraud in which individual taxpayers either do not pay their taxes or try to find illegal ways to avoid paying the taxes they owe. Other examples are government contractors who deceive the government about the cost of goods and services.
- Bankruptcy fraud. In this type of fraud, an individual will purposefully overspend on goods and services, then declare bankruptcy to get out of paying bills and/or taxes. Sometimes small businesses engage in this type of fraud when they open a line of credit, order goods they quickly resell on the black market, then close and declare bankruptcy, thus erasing all their debts while keeping the proceeds from the illicit sale of the goods.

Former Turing Pharmaceuticals CEO Martin Shkreli smiles as he exits the United States federal courthouse after day four of deliberations in his 2017 federal securities fraud trial. What are some types of securities fraud?

- Embezzlement. **Embezzlement** is a form of theft in which an employee trusted with funds or goods diverts them to personal use. For example, in 2018 a tax lawyer for Johnson Controls International was convicted for a 15-year embezzlement scheme that cost the company about $4 million. He was sentenced to 32 months in federal prison, fined $90,000, and ordered to pay nearly $3 million in restitution.[66]
- Consumer fraud. This fraud entails some form of theft or deception in the delivery of goods or services to a consumer. For example, an employee may defraud the company by charging the customer extra money for a service or product, which the employee then pockets. This sometimes occurs at drive-through fast-food outlets when the employee slightly overcharges the customer for food and keeps the difference.
- Bribery and kickbacks. One common scheme is for an employee to ask for bribes or kickbacks

Instant Recall from Chapter 8 **conflict theory** —A set of criminological theories based on the philosophy of Karl Marx that holds that antisocial behavior stems from class conflict and social and economic inequality.

Instant Recall from Chapter 6 **techniques of neutralization** —A perspective that refers to the excuses that some offenders use to justify breaking the law.

Instant Recall from Chapter 9 **fraud** —A known misrepresentation or concealment in a transaction made with the intent to deceive another.

embezzlement—The appropriation as one's own, through fraud, money, or property entrusted to one's care.

Kickbacks are one type of white-collar crime. How can law enforcement detect and prosecute this type of offense?

(a payment made to a person who has facilitated a transaction) from his or her company's clients. In one case, a California radiologist paid kickbacks for patient referrals from several clinics and fraudulently billed insurance companies more than $22 million. The doctor was sentenced to 10 years in federal prison and ordered to pay a $250,000 fine.[67]

› Pilfering. **Pilfering** occurs when employees steal money or goods from the employer. It is typically a low-level activity, such as the occasional theft of office supplies. However, it can be a major source of revenue loss when systematically practiced by many employees.

PAUSE AND REVIEW

1. **How does conflict theory explain white-collar crime?**
2. **How are street crime and white-collar crime different?**

Corporate Crime

LEARNING OBJECTIVE | 5

Distinguish corporate crime from white-collar crime and give a theory that addresses corporate crime.

Like organized crime, corporate crime is not committed by isolated individuals. Rather, it occurs within the normal scope of business when corporate executives step over the boundary between aggressive, but legal, business practices and outright cheating.[68] Corporate crime is distinguished from white-collar crime committed by individuals in that corporate officers seek to further their interests by furthering the interests of the company. Through stock options, bonuses, raises, promotions, and other inducements, corporate officers reap the benefits of a successful company. To ensure the company's success, corporate officers will sometimes break the law in the company's name. As with white-collar crime, conflict theory also applies to corporate crime. In this case, corporate officers take advantage of their powerful positions to use the corporation to exploit employees, consumers, and the environment to attain more wealth or power, typically both.

Corporate crime is often difficult to detect because the offenders are the chief officers of the corporation. In their usual occupational duties, these people are considered model citizens who are engaged in a wide variety of social and civic activities. Law enforcement officers are unlikely to suspect someone who is a major fundraiser for the ballet, on the local university's board of directors, and a leader in his or her church. Corporate crime can go undetected for long periods of time because the profits from the illegal enterprises are not always distinguishable from the legitimate profits.[69]

Another reason that corporate crime does not have the visibility of other types of crime is that its victims are often not easy to identify. When a company is involved in a price-fixing scheme, the harm is diffused over a large number of victims, all of whom are injured in relatively minor ways. However, when the harm done to all the victims is totaled, it is clear that corporate crime has a more devastating effect than street crime.[70]

A final reason that corporate crime has such low visibility is that its perpetrators often do not feel the full brunt of the criminal law. Individuals convicted of corporate offenses are often dealt with more leniently, such as being put on probation or being sent to a minimum-security prison, because they are not violent and do not represent an immediate threat to society. Sometimes corporations break obscure business laws, and the harm is unclear, or the activity is legal in one country but illegal in another.

For example, bribery is an accepted way of doing business in many countries. In some countries, it may not even be considered a criminal offense. It is, however, in the United States. Companies that must abide by U.S. business law may have problems competing effectively in countries where bribery is an accepted practice. Nevertheless, the old adage "when in Rome do as the Romans do" is not accepted as a rationalization for bribery.

As we have seen, corporations that are convicted of offenses or cheat the public of millions or billions of dollars are often punished by fines rather than incarceration of their executives.[71] Part of the challenge of bringing a case against a corporation is deciding who to prosecute. As is often the case in corporate crime, the actual offense is perpetrated by a relatively small group of executives at the head of the company, possibly with the collusion of some lower-level employees. However, not every secretary, janitor, intern, middle manager, and part-timer is guilty of a criminal offense; many likely did not even notice their company's involvement in illegal dealings. So who gets prosecuted? Two schools of thought attempt to answer this question.

- Corporate personhood. The concept of **corporate personhood** defines a corporation as an artificial person—although without a mind, body, or soul—who, nevertheless, has a person's rights and responsibilities. Attorneys represent this person in court, and the court treats the corporation as a singular entity.
- Vicarious liability. The idea of **vicarious liability** retains some aspects of corporate personhood in that it still considers the corporation as a legal entity. Although this entity has broken the law, the corporation is not considered responsible. The responsible party consists of those who control the corporation's actions. A good analogy is a small child who breaks a vase in a store. The child has broken the vase, but the parent is considered responsible for the child's actions and must pay the damages.

Currently, the legal system prosecutes corporate offenses using vicarious liability. For example, in the classic early-2000s case of the energy company Enron, company executives were convicted of a range of financial offenses, including the creation of earnings and cash flow and the concealment of debt. The government prosecuted 34 executives, more than 20 of whom went to prison, including former chief financial officer Andrew Fastow and former chief executive officer Jeffrey Skilling.[72]

Offenses Against Consumers

Many schemes, scams, and dishonest activities, including unsafe products, unsafe food, and fraud, are aimed at consumers. These schemes are cloaked in the guise of legitimate business practices and often offer consumers unbelievable deals in conducting business with a company. Often, these schemes prey upon consumers' naiveté and gullibility or the greed of those who want something for nothing.

Schemes and Scams. Auto-repair scams are widespread. Some shops will overestimate the cost of repairs, claim to install new parts, and sometimes even sabotage the car to pad the estimates and make the consumer spend more money. Sometimes it is hard to tell where incompetence stops and criminal activity begins in some of these auto-repair shops. This is one reason why auto insurance companies usually require more than one estimate for damages. Some auto-repair scams are perpetrated against elderly persons or women because they are assumed to know little about cars.

Some scams involve the sale of products that do not work. In 2007, a jury found the owner of a company called Berkeley Premium Nutraceuticals, which sold "Enzyte," an herbal "male enhancement" tablet, guilty of conspiracy to commit mail fraud, bank fraud, and money laundering. The company cheated its customers out of $100 million through deceptive advertising, manipulating credit card transactions, and refusing to accept returns or cancel orders. The company was also accused of creating fictitious doctors to endorse Enzyte, fabricating customer-satisfaction surveys, and making up statistics that supported claims about the supplement's effectiveness.[73]

Consumers are often victimized by false advertising. Grandiose claims are made for a product that promises to produce results that seem incredulous to any rational person but believable to the gullible and desperate. For instance, the Psychic Readers Network collected more than $1 billion from consumers who called the company's television spokesperson, Miss Cleo, a purported psychic, to get advice about their personal lives. As it turned out, Miss Cleo was not a Jamaican fortune-teller as she claimed, but rather an American actress who

---

pilfering—Employee theft of small amounts of money or inexpensive goods from an employer.

corporate personhood—The legal treatment of a corporation as a person.

vicarious liability—When a person or group of people is considered legally responsible for the actions of another person, group of people, or corporation.

affected a Jamaican accent. Eventually, the Federal Trade Commission charged two corporations, Access Resource Services and Psychic Readers Network, with deceptive advertising, billing, and collection practices after the "free calls" promised by Miss Cleo actually resulted in hundreds of dollars in charges for those who called.[74]

Unsafe Products. Sometimes a company manufactures a product that proves to be unsafe, but it does not quickly remove that product from circulation. Companies have a profit motive, and history has shown that many companies are often cavalier about the safety and health of consumers. Nowhere has the disregard for consumers been more apparent than in the tobacco industry. Knowing full well that their product was addictive and contributed to health problems such as cancer, the tobacco industry worked extremely hard to suppress, distort, and explain away tobacco's harmful effects.[75] Until 1997, the U.S. tobacco industry won every lawsuit brought against it. Finally, as part of a lawsuit brought in the 1990s, prosecutors found evidence that cigarette companies knew as early as 1970 that smoking causes lung cancer. In 1998, the industry agreed to pay $368 billion in damages.[76]

Many products are unsafe because of faulty design. Manufacturers have found ways to make their products safer, but doing so is expensive. Automobile manufacturers must make countless decisions about what design elements to put in their vehicles in light of the additional cost. An infamous example of these calculations is the Ford Pinto. During the 1970s, it was discovered that after relatively minor rear-end collisions the car's fuel system ruptured and burst into flames. Ford calculated that it could save more than $87 million by continuing to make the unsafe Pinto, even though it was estimated that 180 people would die in rear-end collisions in these cars. Once several cases involving injuries and fatalities hit the courts, Ford found that its calculations were wrong as a jury awarded more than $120 million to a California teenager who was badly burned in a Pinto that burst into flames after it was hit by a car going only 35 miles per hour.[77]

Workers plant romaine lettuce at a farm. In 2018, there were warnings that romaine lettuce from Yuma, Arizona, apparently had been contaminated with the *E. coli* bacteria. What other types of food have experienced contamination issues?

Unsafe Food. The Food and Drug Administration has established standards for the safety of the country's food supply, and ensuring that food meets these standards requires inspectors to be on-site in food-processing plants. Unlike the toy industry in which the components of a toy determined to be safe stay that way, fresh food that is safe at one time can go bad quickly. Therefore, the food's environment—not only the manufacturing and preparation environment, but also storage and transportation environment—must be considered before food is deemed safe for consumption.[78] Human beings can be healthy only within a narrow range of environmental parameters, and this includes what is consumed.

Globalization has made ensuring the safety of the country's food supply a difficult task. Ingredients come from all over the world, and it is almost impossible to ensure that each product is safe. In 2007, it was discovered that some popular brands of pet food imported into the United States from China contained the industrial chemical melamine. The dangers of the tainted pet food were not immediately apparent because the melamine slowly damaged the kidneys of dogs and cats, resulting in thousands of pet deaths.[79] The use of melamine, which was added to wheat gluten to make the pet food appear to have a higher level of protein, gave rise to concerns about the tainting of processed food for humans, which can also contain wheat gluten. Federal authorities eventually obtained guilty pleas from a U.S. company for importing the tainted ingredients, but they could not pursue the two Chinese companies that exported the ingredients.[80]

There are two basic problems with unadulterated food. One problem is intentional cheating by manufacturers who cut costs by using substandard ingredients, fail to use proper storage and refrigeration equipment, and insert unsafe items into the food. An early example of this type of unsafe practice was detailed in Upton Sinclair's 1906 novel *The Jungle*. In the book, Sinclair described workers falling into the vats of lard and being turned into food sold to consumers. Sinclair's book was influential in the passage of the Pure Food and Drug and the Meat Inspection Acts of 1906.[81]

The second type of problem stems from the attempts of food companies to spend less money producing food. The food industry engages in many practices that are designed to increase profits but have the potential to make people extremely sick or even kill them. For example, the poultry industry uses a technique called forced molting. This practice involves starving hens for a week or more until they begin to lose body weight, stop laying, and lose their feathers. When their feed is returned, the chickens begin laying again and produce more eggs. One report claims that "these molted chickens are 5,000 times more susceptible to salmonella than normally fed birds."[82] Several years ago, the U.S. Department of Agriculture (USDA) ordered the largest beef recall in U.S. history after the Humane Society of the United States released video showing workers at a California slaughterhouse shoving sick or crippled cows with forklifts to get them to stand, and dragging sick cows with chains, shocking them with electric prods, and shooting streams of water in their noses and faces. The lawsuit filed by the Humane Society claimed that the workers were trying to get the animals to stand so they could be considered acceptable for human consumption. Fifty million pounds of meat from that slaughterhouse were sent to school lunch programs nationwide.[83]

Fraud. Unsafe products, such as poorly designed automobiles or tainted meat, can kill, so there is an overwhelming positive value to well-designed automobiles and safe meat. There is, however, another type of corporate crime that does not have such a direct effect. Fraud, which involves intentional deception, might not kill, but it can fundamentally damage the economy, a delicate institution that operates smoothly only when people trust it. Corporations and white-collar offenders violate this trust when they commit fraud. Three types of trust violations that are considered fraud are securities fraud, corporate fraud, and fiduciary fraud.[84]

- Securities fraud. The rules of financial markets are designed to level the playing field so that everyone has an equal opportunity to use their knowledge and judgment to invest wisely and make money. Some people, however, cheat by providing misleading information about their financial products, colluding with others to artificially drive up stock prices, and using insider information in their business dealings.[85]
- Corporate fraud. Corporations are covered by a system of accounting practices that are designed to encourage transparency and honesty. However, occasionally some corporations attempt to mask losses or to inflate their earnings or profits. Sometimes these attempts to manipulate corporation holdings become so convoluted that it is difficult for regulators to ascertain the organization's true value.[86]
- Fiduciary fraud. Fiduciary fraud occurs when individuals and corporations entrust their money and many of their financial dealings to banks, insurance companies, and investment companies, and the companies violate that trust. These institutions, which assure people that their money is safe, sometimes fall victim to unscrupulous employees. Although embezzlement is a potential problem whenever money is controlled by those who do not own it, a new level of fraud has emerged in recent years in which it is not the lowly bank clerk but rather the bank president who violates trust.

There are three types of this form of fraud. The first type is the outright theft of monies from customers' accounts. Bank officials divert money to their own accounts through elaborate schemes designed to launder and hide assets in offshore banks. This form of corporate crime has much in common with white-collar crime because the motivation for it is the bank administration's greed.

In the second type of fiduciary fraud, officials will use funds from one account to cover shortfalls in other accounts. They usually intend to pay back the accounts from which they "borrowed" funds, often by investing in extremely volatile and risky products. The motivation for this type of fraud has to do with bank officials' desire to keep their jobs when economic forces make the markets riskier. At some point, this shell game falls apart, the perpetrators are exposed, and investors lose their money. In the end, because the government guarantees deposits through the Federal Deposit Insurance Corporation (FDIC), it is the taxpayers who are stuck with the tab.[87]

This type of fiduciary fraud can be so widespread that it affects not only individual investors and depositors, but also the entire banking system. Federal bailouts of financial institutions can be done only a few times before they become problematic. This is one reason that the government pursues corporate crime so thoroughly. It is almost impossible for individuals to conduct business without entrusting money to banks and other financial institutions. When the officials of these institutions get greedy or careless, they have the opportunity to divert large sums of money and cover up their misdeeds by "cooking the books."[88]

A third form of fiduciary fraud involves company officials stealing from employee pension funds. In this type of fraud, money set aside for employee retirements is managed and invested by experts to ensure that the pension fund's assets are adequate to pay the promised pensions to employees. Sometimes those entrusted with these pension funds divert the money to their own purposes.[89] For example, federal authorities charged a Tennessee securities broker with embezzling $5.7 million from a Pennsylvania company's employee pension fund. The indictment accused the broker of using money from the fund to make unauthorized loans and investments and to pay off $1.2 million in personal loans and legal expenses.[90] The result of cases like this is that many people who counted on investment managers to make reasonable and safe investments cannot retire because the pension fund no longer has adequate resources. Individual investors cannot foresee these types of fraud because they do not have the opportunity to review the pension fund's financial records. Those covered by the fund rely on laws and honest fund managers to ensure that their investments are properly handled. Greed mixed with bad luck and incompetence has led some pension-fund managers to overstep the law.

Assistant Attorney General John C. Cruden speaks on the sentencing of Duke Energy for Clean Water Act offenses. The subsidiaries of North Carolina-based Duke Energy pleaded guilty to nine criminal violations and agreed to pay a $68 million fine and spend $34 million on environmental projects and land conservation to benefit rivers and wetlands in North Carolina and Virginia. Other than fining corporations, how can environmental damage be addressed?

Offenses Against the Environment

Environmental crime—offenses that manipulate the surroundings to the extent that human beings, animals, or plants that live within it are harmed or unable to survive—can be committed by the government, multinational corporations, small businesses, and individuals. In this section, we will discuss environmental crime as a subset of corporate crime because corporations have committed some of the largest and most visible environmental offenses. Much, if not most, U.S. environmental legislation has been passed to control the environmentally harmful activities of corporate entities rather than those of individuals, although these laws may be applied to individuals in some cases. For example, one of the goals of the 1970 Clean Air Act was for the states to set pollutant standards for "appropriate industrial sources" within each state.[91] As with corporate and white-collar crime, a major motivation for environmental crime is money—typically not to make it but to save it. Following environmental laws, which require treating hazardous waste, recycling some materials and properly disposing of others, and training workers and designing plants and industrial processes to be environmentally safe, can be costly. Unfortunately, many corporations consider these as costs that can be saved.

The damages caused by environmental crime are tricky to assess because they are so long term and wide in scope. In comparison, the damages caused by a single street crime play out over a relatively short period of time and affect only one or a few people, even in the case of murder. This is not to trivialize the effects of serious street crime, but rather only to point out that the effects are relatively narrow. The effects of a major environmental crime, however, can last for generations and directly affect hundreds or even thousands of people. Tainted water, soil, and air can not only be individually fatal, but also cause serious health issues for survivors and birth defects in their children. In developing countries, massive trash dumps can swallow whole villages, destroy forests and wetlands, and leave no room to grow food or raise farm animals.

Environmental legislation and law enforcement are still relatively weak, not necessarily because lawmakers and citizens do not care about the environment, but because pollution often goes hand in hand with economic development. Corporations that pollute the environment through manufacturing processes, the transportation of toxic products, and the manufacture of products that contain toxic materials also happen to be large employers that bring money into their home communities.

Another issue is modern society's limited ability to do without some of these products, such as plastic, computers, and automobiles. The modern Western lifestyle depends on the use of products that are toxic in their manufacture, use, and, often, their disposal. Consequently, the legal system must be careful in its pursuit of corporate polluters. A large fine levied against a polluting corporation might cause the business to raise prices or leave the community and move to a country where environmental laws are more lenient or nonexistent. In the United States, the Environmental Protection Agency (EPA) helps enforce environmental laws by doing research and investigating "negligent, knowing or willful violations of federal environmental law."[92] Environmental offenses are not always massive, headline-grabbing disasters. Here are two examples of typical environmental offenses that the EPA would be responsible for.

- A manager at a metal-finishing company tells employees not to use the company's wastewater treatment unit because the chemicals needed for the unit are expensive. Instead, the company sends untreated wastewater to the sewer system, violating local environmental regulations. In this instance, the plant manager is guilty of a criminal violation of the Clean Water Act.
- To avoid the proper, but expensive, treatment of its hazardous waste, the owner of a cleaning-solvents manufacturer sends dozens of buckets of highly flammable, caustic waste to a local landfill that is not authorized to receive hazardous waste. In this case, the company owner is guilty of a criminal violation of the Resource Conservation and Recovery Act.[93]

Environmental Criminology. Environmental criminology is an emerging field as scholars and activists recognize and evaluate the types of harm done by careless or intentional damage to the environment. Environmental criminology, sometimes called "green" criminology, covers activities and behaviors that have not been within the traditional scope of criminology.[94] The forms of environmental crime are numerous, and their financial costs can be staggering. Environmental offenses range from the everyday to the exceptional, and their legal and political consequences can drag on for decades. The issues that environmental criminology cover include, but are not limited to, the following concerns:

- the abuse and exploitation of ecological systems, including animal life;
- corporate disregard for damage to land, air, and water quality;
- profiteering from practices that destroy lives and leave a legacy of damage for subsequent generations;
- military actions that adversely affect the environment, humans, and animals;
- new challenges to international treaties and to the emerging field of bioethics (the philosophical study of moral values and controversies in biology and medicine);
- illicit markets in nuclear materials;
- legal monopolization of natural resources (e.g., privatization of water, patenting of natural products) leading to divisions between the resource-rich and the resource-impoverished;
- individual acts of cruelty to animals; and
- institutional, socially acceptable human domination of animals in agribusiness, such as in slaughterhouses.[95]

Because of the consequences of damage to the environment, the field of criminology must expand its scope to ensure that it fully considers the direct and indirect harms of environmental crime to the environment, animals, and human beings. A few specific examples illustrate the range of environmental criminology and its potential to expand its mandate.

Animal Rights. The problem of animal exploitation is becoming a concern for criminology. Human concern for animal rights exists on a continuum.

---

environmental crime—An offense that manipulates the surroundings to the extent that human beings, animals, or plants that live within in it are harmed or unable to survive.

At one end of the extreme are those who would knowingly harm no animal, even refusing to use them for food. At the other end are those who believe animals are to be used not only for food, but also for labor, apparel, and sport. They also support the use of animals in medical experimentation to ensure that drugs, surgeries, and other procedures are safe.[96]

Animal rights issues present a "slippery slope" for an ecological debate. One important consideration is that the relationship between humans and animals is culturally and historically bound. For instance, in the move to protect whales from being exterminated by large companies, allowances have been made for indigenous peoples who have historically hunted whales for subsistence. This tension was also apparent in the fox hunts of Great Britain. These hunts, traditionally the purview of aristocrats, were opposed by those who considered the practice immoral. Some people would attempt to sabotage the hunts by laying down artificial scents for the hounds to follow, blowing horns to confuse the hunters, and attempting to physically block access to hunting areas. Fox hunting was banned in England and Wales in 2005, although activists say the sport continues thanks to loopholes in the law.[97]

Nuclear Energy. As oil prices rise, many individuals and corporations have become vocal proponents of revitalizing the nuclear energy business. Environmentalists who claim that nuclear energy is not safe oppose their efforts. The catastrophic damage that can result when a nuclear power plant malfunctions serves as a persuasive argument to be cautious about adopting this source of energy. Although the safety record of nuclear power plants is quite good, these plants present another problem. Nuclear energy produces waste that is not only toxic but also difficult to dispose of safely. Thousands of tons of nuclear waste have been produced, and, for the most part, the waste has been stored on the sites of the nuclear energy facilities.

One federal proposal is to move all this nuclear waste to Nevada to a storage facility at Yucca Mountain.[98] Advocates for this proposal claim that the deep underground storage facility is a safe and viable option for handling nuclear waste. However, many people are concerned about nuclear waste seeping into the environment, as well as the problems of safely transporting this waste across the country. Environmental criminologists question the adequacy of reports on nuclear safety and argue that the construction of nuclear plants will expose large numbers of people to potential harm.[99]

Because of dioxin and PCB contamination in the San Jacinto River in Texas, there are now advisories on the dangers of eating crab and fish from the area. Why is environmental crime so hard to prosecute?

Unsafe Materials. Environmental criminologists are concerned about the harmful ingredients contained in many everyday products. One such product is lead paint, which can affect brain function in children and adults, causing aggressive or violent behavior.[100] Although lead paint is now prohibited in the United States, the 2007 scare over lead paint on toys imported from China demonstrates that the problem of eliminating this unsafe product is still an important consideration.

Disposal is an interesting aspect of the issue of unsafe materials. Although consumers have long used toxic materials, such as lead paint and home pesticides, the use of unsafe materials is reaching record levels because of their ubiquity in consumer electronics. Computers, cell phones, video games, global positioning system (GPS) units, and nearly any other type of consumer electronic contain poisonous substances such as lead, mercury, cadmium, chromium, and materials containing PCBs (polychlorinated biphenyls). These materials, sometimes called "e-waste," are difficult to recycle and tend to pile up in landfills where they might leach toxins and poison the water and soil. Because it is so poisonous, e-waste is often shipped off to developing countries for disposal.[101]

Recyclers and waste contractors in developed countries promise that such refuse will be either thoroughly destroyed or recycled. Unfortunately, this is often not the case. Unscrupulous companies, for example, will label broken computers as "donations" and ship them to countries like Ghana under the guise of charity. When the computers are discovered to be broken, they end up at dump sites like Agbogbloshie, a dumping ground next to a polluted, dead lagoon, which is a common final resting place for such e-waste. Ghanaians who live among the electronic trash pick through it looking for salvageable items, such as working hard drives that they can sell. Broken items are usually burned (releasing even more toxins) to release precious metals such as gold and copper.[102] Environmental watchdog groups estimate that 50 to 80 percent of e-waste collected for recycling is shipped to China, India, Africa, and Pakistan.[103] An international treaty, the 1989 Basel Convention, bans the export of e-waste to less-developed countries; however, the United States has not ratified the treaty.[104]

PAUSE AND REVIEW

1. **How does corporate crime differ from white-collar crime?**
2. **Give examples of corporate crime and white-collar crime.**
3. **What is the typical financial motivation behind environmental crime?**

FOCUS ON ETHICS Insider Trading

You have a big decision to make. Normally, you don't find yourself in ethical dilemmas, but your former spouse, your "ex," has put you in a position where you have to choose between supporting your family and enforcing the law. As a vice detective for a major metropolitan police department, you have earned a reputation after 20 years on the force as an honest and aggressive cop whose ethics cannot be compromised. You have been awarded several department citations for your work, and on one occasion, you played an instrumental role in arresting and convicting five dirty cops who were stealing drugs from the evidence locker. Now you are faced with a decision that has the potential to undo a career's worth of stellar work.

Your ex's younger brother has indirectly placed you in jeopardy. He is a broker for a major Wall Street firm. He advised your ex to invest in a startup biotech firm just before it was given FDA approval for a new cancer drug. It turns out he had insider information that this drug was going to be approved. Your ex invested $10,000, and now those stock shares are worth $50,000 after only three months. You feel guilty about your relationship with your ex because of the divorce, but you could not care less about her brother because he always looked down upon you for being "only a cop." You would have no trouble reporting him, but you do not want to get your ex into trouble as it would affect your 8-year-old twins.

What Do You Do?

1. Do nothing. You need to stay out of your former spouse's life.
2. Tell your ex's brother that you will let this slide, but if you hear that he is engaging in insider trading one more time, you will report him.
3. Report your knowledge of insider trading to the appropriate federal authorities. You are a law enforcement officer, and you cannot allow yourself to be a hypocrite.
4. Be a hypocrite. Tell the brother that you want to be informed of all his insider tips. You can make a lot of money and provide for an Ivy League education for your twins. Wall Street is not your responsibility, and this type of crime does not directly hurt anyone.

Summary

LEARNING OBJECTIVE 1	
Define organized crime and give examples of its traditional offenses.	Organized crime is a type of business enterprise involving highly structured or organized groups that break the law and often use violence to achieve goals. Organized crime has traditionally been involved in vice offenses such as gambling, prostitution, and the smuggling of drugs or alcohol. It also may use the financial proceeds of crime to invest in legitimate enterprises, such as businesses, and financial instruments, such as stocks and bonds.

Learning Objective	Summary
LEARNING OBJECTIVE 2 Discuss how differential association theory and classical strain theory are particularly suited to describing the motivations of individuals within crime organizations.	According to differential association theory, crime organization members learn crime from each other. This is especially relevant because crime organizations are often composed of individuals with social commonalities. According to classical strain theory, immigration plays an important role in organized crime. Some immigrants who find the goals of American life attractive can be discouraged by the socially accepted means to attain them. Some members of immigrant communities may innovate by using the proceeds of crime to attain these goals.
LEARNING OBJECTIVE 3 Define white-collar crime.	White-collar crime consists of offenses committed by individual employees for their own benefit during the course of legitimate business.
LEARNING OBJECTIVE 4 List and explain four theories that can address white-collar crime.	Sutherland's differential association theory envisions crime as learned: white-collar offenders learn attitudes and techniques from peers and coworkers. Conflict theory posits that white-collar offenders determine that corporations and managers exploit workers, and thus they try to even the score. Using techniques of neutralization, the employee rationalizes that the corporation will not miss the money (denial of injury), that the corporation is overcharging customers and underpaying employees (condemnation of condemners), and that the employee needs the money to provide for his or her family (appeal to higher loyalty). Classical strain theory describes how white-collar offenders "innovate" rather than strive for socially accepted goals by socially accepted means, and accept the goals but give up on the means to attain them.
LEARNING OBJECTIVE 5 Distinguish corporate crime from white-collar crime and give a theory that addresses corporate crime.	White-collar crime is committed by individuals. Corporate crime is committed by corporate officers seeking to further their interests by furthering the interests of the company. To ensure the company's success, corporate officers will sometimes break the law in the company's name. Conflict theory applies to corporate crime. In this case, corporate officers take advantage of their powerful positions to use the corporation to exploit employees, consumers, and the environment to attain more wealth or power, and typically both.

Critical Reflections

1. **Trace the development of organized crime in the United States.**
2. **What are typical organized crime activities?**
3. **In what ways can environmental offenses be committed within corporate, white-collar, or organized crime contexts?**
4. **What are the financial and emotional effects of offenses against consumers?**
5. **Discuss why environmental legislation and law enforcement are still relatively weak.**

6. Explain why offenses against animals are a proper focus of criminology.
7. What is corporate personhood? Vicarious liability? What is unusual about these ideas?
8. Should white-collar and environmental crime be prosecuted and punished in the same aggressive manner as street crime?
9. Should white-collar crime by employees be punished by the criminal justice system or by the companies they work for?

Key Terms

Instant Recall Terms

classical strain theory (ch. 6)
conflict theory (ch. 8)
differential association theory (ch. 6)
fraud (ch. 9)
rational choice theory (ch. 4)
techniques of neutralization (ch. 6)
white-collar crime (ch. 1)

Notes

1 President's Commission on Law Enforcement and Administration of Justice, Task Force Report: Organized Crime (Washington, D.C.: U.S. Government Printing Office, 1967).
2 Terry L. Leap, *Dishonest Dollars: The Dynamics of White-Collar Crime* (Ithaca, N.Y.: Cornell University Press, 2007).
3 William Kleinknecht, *The New Ethnic Mobs: The Changing Face of Organized Crime in America* (New York: Free Press, 1996).
4 James W. Coleman, *The Criminal Elite: The Sociology of White Collar Crime* (New York: St. Martin's Press, 1985).
5 Marshall B. Clinard and Peter C. Yeager, *Corporate Crime* (New York: Free Press, 1980).
6 Michael J. Lynch and Paul B. Stretesky, "Conspiracy, Deceit and Misinformation: Standard Operating Procedure in the Chemical Industry," *Critical Criminologist* 4 (1999): 14–18.
7 Sean Grennan and Marjie T. Britz, *Organized Crime: A Worldwide Perspective* (Upper Saddle River, N.J.: Prentice Hall, 2006).
8 Howard Abadinsky, *Organized Crime*, 8th ed. (Belmont, Calif.: Wadsworth, 2007).
9 Gary Potter, *Crime Organizations: Vice, Racketeering and Politics in an American City* (Prospect Heights, Ill.: Waveland, 1994).
10 Joseph F. O'Brien and Andris Kurins, *Boss of Bosses: The FBI and Paul Castellano* (New York: Dell, 1991).
11 Robert M. Lombardo, "The Black Mafia: African American Organized Crime in Chicago, 1890–1960," *Crime, Law, and Social Change* 38 (2002): 33–65.
12 Richard Gambino, *Blood of My Blood: The Dilemmas of the Italian-American* (Garden City, N.J.: Doubleday, 1974).
13 Andrew Martin, "Even with Drug Leaders in Jail, Gang's Drug Business Is Flourishing," *Chicago Tribune*, January 29, 1996, 1.
14 Guy Gugliotta and Jeff Leen, *Kings of Cocaine: Inside the Medellin Cartel: An Astonishing Story of Murder, Money, and International Corruption* (New York: Simon & Schuster, 1989).
15 Mark Motivans, *Money-Laundering Offenders, 1994–2001* (Washington, D.C.: Bureau of Justice Statistics, 2003).
16 Federico Varese, *The Russian Mafia: Private Protection in a New Market Economy* (Oxford: Oxford University Press, 2001).
17 Lincoln Steffens, *The Shame of the Cities* (New York: Hill & Wang, 1957).
18 Lawrence J. McCaffrey, *The Irish Diaspora in America* (Bloomington: Indiana University Press, 1976).
19 Edward M. Levine, *The Irish and Irish Politicians* (Notre Dame, Ind.: University of Notre Dame Press, 1966).
20 Lyle W. Dorsett, *The Pendergast Machine* (New York: Oxford University Press, 1968).
21 Patrick Downey, *Gangster City: The History of the New York Underworld* (Fort Lee, N.J.: Barricade Books, 2004).
22 Thomas Reppetto, *American Mafia: A History of Its Rise to Power* (New York: Henry Holt, 2004), 26–27.
23 Abadinsky, *Organized Crime*.
24 Francis A. Janni, *A Family Business: Kinship and Social Control in Organized Crime* (New York: Russell Sage Foundation, 1972).
25 Gambino, *Blood of My Blood*.
26 "Will the Real Mob Please Stand Up," *New York Times*, March 5, 2006, late edition, East Coast, 4–5. "End of the Gambinos?" *Economist* 386, no. 8567 (February 16, 2008): 41.
27 Ibid.

28 Ibid.

29 A. O. Scott, "A Hard, Unromantic Look at the Mafia's Sicilian Reign," *New York Times*, July 12, 2006, late edition, E1.

30 Reppetto, *American Mafia*, 4.

31 Richard L. Bourgeois, S. P. Hennessey, Jon Moore, and Michael E. Tschupp, "Racketeer Influenced and Corrupt Organizations," *American Criminal Law Review* 37 (2000): 879–891.

32 Martin G. Urbina and Sara Kreitzer, "The Practical Utility and Ramifications of RICO: ThirtyTwo Years after Its Implementation," *Criminal Justice Policy Review* 15, no. 3 (September 2004): 294–323.

33 Charles Winick and Paul M. Kinsie, *The Lively Commerce* (Chicago: Quadrangle, 1971).

34 Richter H. Moore Jr., "Motor Fuel Tax Fraud and Organized Crime: The Russian and Italian-American Mafia," in *Contemporary Issues in Organized Crime*, ed. Jay Albanese (Monsey, N.Y.: Willow Tree Press, 1995), 195.

35 John Sullivan and Alex Berenson, "Dozens Named in Stock Fraud Linked to Mob," *New York Times*, June 15, 2000, late edition, C27.

36 The United States Attorneys, "Organized Crime and Racketeering," in *Criminal Resource Manual,* http://www.usdoj.gov/usao/eousa/foia_reading_room/usam/title9/110mcrm.htm. Accessed June 2018.

37 U.S. Department of Justice, "30 Members and Associates of the 'Nine Trey Gangster Blood' Gang Federally Indicted," October 19, 2017, https://www.justice.gov/usao-ndga/pr/30-members-and-associates-nine-trey-gangster-blood-gang-federally-indicted. Accessed June 2018.

38 U.S. Department of Justice, Offices of the United States Attorneys, 109. RICO Charges, https://www.justice.gov/usam/criminal-resource-manual-109-rico-charges. Accessed June 2018.

39 Kenneth Carlson and Peter Finn, *Prosecuting Criminal Enterprises,* (Washington, D.C.: U.S. Department of Justice Office of Justice Programs Bureau of Justice Statistics, 1993). Available at https://www.ncjrs.gov/App/Publications/abstract.aspx?ID=142524. Accessed June 2018.

40 Jay S. Albanese, *Organized Crime in Our Times*, 5th ed. (Cincinnati, Ohio: Anderson, 2007).

41 Abadinsky, *Organized Crime*, 186–187, 199–200.

42 Ibid., 208.

43 Reppetto, *American Mafia*.

44 Dennis J. Kenney and James O. Finckenauer, *Organized Crime in America* (Belmont, Calif.: Wadsworth, 1995), 286–289.

45 Ibid.

46 Stephen L. Mallory, Michael P. Wigginton Jr., Gregg W. Etter, Sr., Jeffrey M. Johnson, and Sara Thomas, "What Is the Nexus Between Organized Crime and Gangs?" *Journal of Gang Research* 23, no. 1 (2015): 1–21.

47 "MS-13 Gang Members Indicted in Machete Killing of Long Island Boy," *4 New York,* January 11. 2018, https://www.nbcnewyork.com/news/local/MS-13-Gang-Arrests-Long-Island-New-York-NY-Police-Murder-468791273.html. Accessed June 2018.

48 "MS13 in the Americas How the World's Most Notorious Gang Defies Logic, Resists Destruction," *Center for Latin American & Latino Studies, American University,* https://www.american.edu/centers/latin-american-latino-studies/transnational-criminal-capacity-of-ms-13.cfm. Accessed June 2018.

49 Wendy Fawthrop, "Fear over MS-13 Gang Is Overreaction, Says Cal State Fullerton Researcher," *Orange County Register,* March 14, 2018, https://www.ocregister.com/2018/03/14/fear-over-ms-13-gang-is-overreaction-says-cal-state-fullerton-researcher. Accessed June 2018.

50 Ron Nixon, Liz Robbins, and Katie Benner, "Trump Targets MS-13, a Violent Menace, If Not the One He Portrays," *New York Times*, March 1, 2018, https://www.nytimes.com/2018/03/01/us/politics/ms13-gang-threat-trump-policy.html. Accessed June 2018.

51 Jonathan Blitzer, "Former Gang Members Offer Advice on How to Combat MS-13," *New Yorker,* January 30, 2018, https://www.newyorker.com/news/daily-comment/former-gang-members-offer-advice-on-how-to-combat-ms-13. Accessed June 2018.

52 Howard Abadinsky, *Drug Abuse: An Introduction*, 5th ed. (Belmont, Calif.: Wadsworth, 2004).

53 Max Fisher and Amanda Taub, "Mexico's Record Violence Is a Crisis 20 Years in the Making," *New York Times*, October 28, 2017, https://www.nytimes.com/2017/10/28/world/americas/mexico-violence.html. Accessed June 2018.

54 Drug Enforcement Administration Strategic Intelligence Section, *2016 National Drug Threat Assessment Summary* (Washington, D.C.: U.S. Department of Justice Drug Enforcement Administration, 2016), vi. Available at https://www.dea.gov/resource-center/statistics.shtml. Accessed June 2018.

55 Jeremy Kryt, "How Mexican Cartels Prey on Chicago's Chaos," *Daily Beast*, July 29, 2017, https://www.thedailybeast.com/how-mexican-cartels-prey-on-chicagos-chaos. Accessed June 2018.

56 Donna M. Hughes and Tatyana Denisova, "The Transnational Political Nexus of Trafficking in Women from Ukraine," *Trends in Organized Crime* 6 (2001): 43–67.

57 Alexandros Paraskevas, "Nodes, Guardians and Signs: Raising Barriers to Human Trafficking in the Tourism Industry," *Tourism Management* 67 (2018): 147–156.

58 Cathy Zimmerman and Ligia Kiss, "Human Trafficking and Exploitation: A Global Health Concern," *Plos Medicine* 14, no. 11 (2017): 1–11.

59 James Moore, "I"m Not for Sale: Teaching about Human Trafficking," *Social Studies* 109, no. 2 (2018): 74–84.

60 Vicki Abt, James F. Smith, and Eugene Martin Christiansen, *The Business of Risk: Commercial Gambling in Mainstream America* (Lawrence: University Press of Kansas, 1985).

61 Travis Andersen and Jerome Campbell, "Hundreds of Roosters Might Have to Be Euthanized after Northampton Cockfighting Bust," *Boston Globe*, May 29, 2018, https://www.bostonglobe.com/metro/2018/05/29/officials-rescue-nearly-birds-from-cockfighting-pits-northampton-farm-most-will-euthanized/t3UoMBz9bIDWzQ3tAnzxfP/story.html. Accessed June 2018.

62 Florida Department of Criminal Law Enforcement, *The Questions of Casinos in Florida—Increased Crime: Is It Worth It?* (Tallahassee, Fla.: FDCLE, 1994).

63 Robert Salonga, "Thousands of Stolen Laptops, Tablets Recovered in Massive Bay Area Car Burglary Scheme," *Mercury News*, February 1, 2018, https://www.mercurynews.com/2018/01/31/thousands-of-stolen-laptops-recovered-in-massive-bay-area-car-burglary-scheme. Accessed June 2018.

64 *Chicago Tribune*, "International Crime Ring Targeting California Almonds, Walnuts," April 14, 2016, http://www.chicagotribune.com/news/nationworld/ct-california-almonds-walnuts-thefts-20160414-story.html. Peter Vigneron, "The Curious Case of the Disappearing Nuts," *Outside*, May 24, 2017, https://www.outsideonline.com/2186526/nut-job. Accessed June 2018.

65 Federal Bureau of Investigation, "What We Investigate: Intellectual Property Theft/Piracy," https://www.fbi.gov/investigate/white-collar-crime/piracy-ip-theft. Accessed June 2018.

66 Cary Spivak, "Ex-Johnson Controls Executive Sentenced to 32 Months for Masterminding $4 Million Embezzlement," *Journal Sentinel* (Wisconsin), June 15, 2018, https://www.jsonline.com/story/news/crime/2018/06/15/ex-johnson-controls-exec-gets-32-month-running-4-million-scheme/702166002. Accessed June 2018.

67 Alexander Nguyen, "Radiologist Who Paid Kickbacks for Patient Referrals Sentenced to Prison," *Times of San Diego*, June 18, 2018, https://timesofsandiego.com/business/2018/06/18/radiologist-who-paid-kickbacks-for-patient-referrals-sentenced-to-prison. Accessed June 2018.
68 Gilbert Geis and Joseph Dimento, "Should We Prosecute Corporations and/or Individuals?" in *Corporate Crime: Contemporary Debates*, ed. Frank Pearce and Laureen Snider (Toronto: University of Toronto Press, 1995), 72–86.
69 Russell Mokhiber and Robert Weissman, *Corporate Predators: The Hunt for Mega-Profits and the Attack on Democracy* (Monroe, Me.: Common Courage Press, 1999), 8.
70 Jeffrey Reiman, *The Rich Get Richer and the Poor Get Prison: Ideology, Class, and Criminal Justice* (Boston: Allyn & Bacon, 2001).
71 Robert Trigaux, "$1.4-Billion Settlement Just a Slap on Wall Street's Wrist," *St. Petersburg Times*, May 5, 2003, South Pinellas edition, Business section, 1E.
72 Federal Bureau of Investigation, *Financial Crimes Report to the Public*, 7, https://www.fbi.gov/resources/library/financial-crime-reports. Accessed June 2018.
73 Associated Press, "This Is Bob. Bob's Not Doing So Well," *Beaumont Enterprise*, February 23, 2008, D1.
74 Federal Trade Commission, "FTC Charges 'Miss Cleo' with Deceptive Advertising, Billing and Collection Practices," February 14, 2002, https://www.ftc.gov/news-events/press-releases/2002/02/ftc-charges-miss-cleo-promoters-deceptive-advertising-billing-and. Accessed June 2018.
75 Sheryl Stolberg, "Tobacco Exec Lied to Congress about Nicotine, Scientist Charges," *Houston Chronicle*, January 27, 1996, A4.
76 PBS Frontline, "Inside the Tobacco Deal," https://www.pbs.org/wgbh/pages/frontline/shows/settlement/. Accessed June 2018.
77 Francis T. Cullen and William J. Maakestad, *Corporate Crime under Attack: The Ford Pinto Case and Beyond* (Cincinnati, Ohio: Anderson, 1987).
78 Geoffrey Cowley and John McCormick, "How Safe Is Our Food?" *Newsweek* 121 (1993): 7–10.
79 David Barboza and Alexei Barrionuevo, "In China, Additive to Animals' Food Is an Open Secret," *New York Times*, April 30, 2007, section A. Elizabeth Weise, "Lab Says Melamine Not Only Culprit," *USA Today*, May 8, 2007, money, 1B.
80 Tony Rizzo, "2 Plead Guilty in Tainted Pet Food Case," *Kansas City Star*, June 16, 2009.
81 Upton Sinclair, *The Jungle* (New York: Bantam, 1906/1981).
82 Stephen Rostoff , Henry Pontell, and Robert Tillman, *Profit Without Honor: White-Collar Crime and the Looting of America* (Upper Saddle River, N.J.: Prentice Hall, 2007), 121.
83 AP, "Humane Society Sues USDA over Downer Cow Rules," *Bismarck Tribune*, February 28, 2008, 9A.
84 Leap, *Dishonest Dollars*.
85 Mark Stevens, *The Insiders: The Truth Behind the Scandal Rocking Wall Street* (New York: G. P. Putnam's Sons, 1987).
86 Brian Cruver, *Anatomy of Greed: Telling the Unshredded Truth from Inside Enron* (New York: Carroll & Graf, 2003).
87 William K. Black, Kitty Calavita, and Henry N. Pontell, "The Savings and Loan Debacle of the 1980s: White Collar Crime or Risky Business?" *Law and Policy* 17 (1995): 23–55.
88 Kathleen Day and Peter Berg, "Enron Directors Backed Moving Debt Off Books," *Washington Post*, January 31, 2002, A1.
89 Michael A. Hiltzik, "SEC Says First Pension Ran Pyramid Scam," *Los Angeles Times*, May 14, 1994, D1.
90 Wayne Risher, "Memphis Securities Broker John Jumper Accused of $5.7 Million Theft from Pension Fund," *Commercial Appeal* (Tennessee), April 19, 2018, https://www.commercialappeal.com/story/news/crime/2018/04/19/memphis-securities-broker-john-jumper-accused-5-7-million-theft-pension-fund/534397002. Accessed June 2018.
91 U.S. Environmental Protection Agency, Summary of the Clean Air Act, https://www.epa.gov/laws-regulations/summary-clean-air-act. Accessed June 2018.
92 Environmental Protection Agency, Criminal Enforcement, "What Is an Environmental Crime?", https://www.epa.gov/enforcement/criminal-investigations. Accessed June 2018.
93 Ibid.
94 Rob White, "Green Criminology and the Pursuit of Social and Ecological Justice," in *Issues in Green Criminology: Confronting Harms Against Environments, Humanity, and Other Animals*, ed. Piers Beirne and Nigel South (Portland, Ore.: Willan, 2007), 32–54.
95 Piers Beirne and Nigel South, eds., *Issues in Green Criminology*, xiv.
96 Piers Beirne, "Animal Rights, Animal Abuse, and Green Criminology," in *Issues in Green Criminology*, 55–83.
97 Mattha Busby, "Fox Hunting: Activists Claim Trail-Hunts Are a Cover for Continued Bloodsport," *Guardian*, https://www.theguardian.com/uk-news/2017/dec/26/fox-hunting-activists-claim-trail-hunts-are-a-cover-for-continued-bloodsport, December 26, 2017. Accessed June 2018.
98 Rob Nikolewski, "U.S. House Passes Bill to Restart Yucca Mountain and Look for Interim Sites for Nuclear Waste," *San Diego Union-Tribune*, May 10, 2018, http://www.sandiegouniontribune.com/business/energy-green/sd-fi-house-yucca-20180510-story.html. Accessed June 2018.
99 Lawrence Becker and James David Ballard, "Federal Programs and Their Potential to Provoke Political Violence: The Transportation Program for Yucca Mountain and Terrorist Adversaries," in *Terrorism: Research, Readings, and Realities*, ed. Lynne L. Snowden and Bradley C. Whitsel (Upper Saddle River, N.J.: Prentice Hall, 2005), 63–79.
100 Paul B. Stretesky and Michael J. Lynch, "The Relationship Between Lead and Crime," *Journal of Health and Social Behavior* 45 (2004): 214–229.
101 Kat Eschner, "You Could Be Eating a Side of E-waste with Your Takeout," *Popular Science*, May 30, 2018, https://www.popsci.com/e-waste-black-plastic. Accessed June 2018.
102 Adam Minter, "Anatomy of a Myth: The World's Biggest E-Waste Dump Isn't," *Shanghai Scrap* (blog), June 16, 2015, http://shanghaiscrap.com/2015/06/anatomy-of-a-myth-the-worlds-biggest-e-waste-dump-isnt.
103 Michael Hardy, "The Hellish E-Waste Graveyards Where Computers Are Mined for Metal," *Wired*, January 1, 2018, https://www.wired.com/story/international-electronic-waste-photographs. Accessed June 2018.
104 Basel Convention, "Parties to the Basel Convention on the Control of Transboundary Movements of Hazardous Wastes and Their Disposal," http://www.basel.int/Countries/StatusofRatifications/PartiesSignatories/tabid/4499/Default.aspx. Accessed June 2018.

LEGALIZE IT
CANNABIS
SAT

Public-Order Offenses and Values

FEATURES

This brass coin sports a cannabis leaf. Which behaviors should be prohibited by the government?

Hell's Square has a drug problem, and it has to do with dirty cocaine. Any night of the week, the corners of Delancey and Essex to the corners of Bowery and E. Houston on Manhattan's Lower East Side are jammed with people having fun at bars and restaurants.

The problem is that almost none of the cocaine that is so readily available is pure anymore. It has been cut with substances such as baking soda, baby laxatives, ephedrine, fentanyl, and Adderall. Without testing, it is impossible to know what has been mixed into the cocaine even if it is from a trusted dealer.[1] Some cocaine is only 5 percent pure; the rest can be a combination of 40 to 50 different substances, some of them drugs and others just fillers to increase the weight of the cocaine to make it more profitable. By far, the most worrisome additive is fentanyl, a synthetic opioid pain reliever that is typically used for advanced cancer pain and is 50 to 100 times more potent than morphine.[2]

The New York City Department of Health has been trying to deal with the rising rate of fentanyl/cocaine overdoses by educating bartenders to help.[3] New York has Good Samaritan laws that protect those who help victims of drug overdoses.[4] So bartenders, who are trained in how to recognize someone in trouble and how to respond effectively, are given nasal spray kits of naloxone, which blocks the effects of opioids and helps victims to breathe. The average human brain can only be deprived of oxygen for about six minutes, after which it begins to die and a complete recovery becomes less likely. The ambulance response time in New York City is about five minutes. Timely responses by bartenders can make the difference as to whether someone lives or dies.

Crime and Values

LEARNING OBJECTIVE | 1

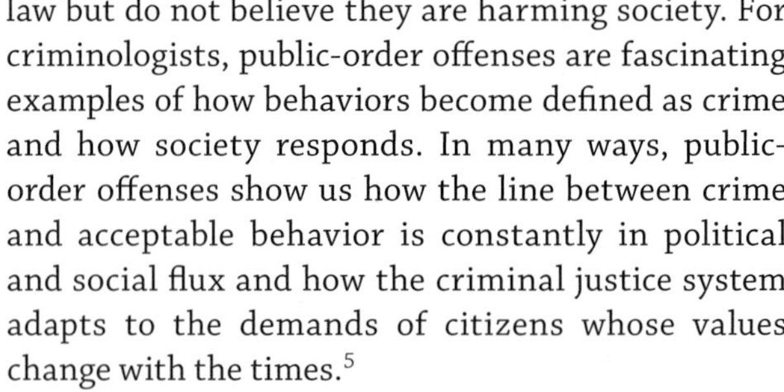

Discuss why public-order offenses present the criminal justice system with perplexing dilemmas in dealing with offenders who have broken the law but do not believe they are harming society.

Many behaviors that offend our sense of right or wrong, morality, or public safety have been made criminal offenses by governing bodies. Other people, who do not consider these behaviors to be wrong or dangerous, attempt to change these laws or violate them on a regular basis—as seen in the opening scenario—without feeling any guilt. These crimes of values, or **public-order offenses**, present the criminal justice system with perplexing dilemmas in arresting, prosecuting, punishing, rehabilitating, and medically treating offenders who have broken the law but do not believe they are harming society. For criminologists, public-order offenses are fascinating examples of how behaviors become defined as crime and how society responds. In many ways, public-order offenses show us how the line between crime and acceptable behavior is constantly in political and social flux and how the criminal justice system adapts to the demands of citizens whose values change with the times.[5]

Ideally, the criminal law reflects the values of the population to which it is applied. Citizens elect representatives to fashion laws that reinforce their sense of fairness, justice, and morality. However, there is always a certain tension between laws and the people, for two reasons. The first is that those who make the laws do not always act in everyone's best interests. In a country where the majority rules, it is inevitable that some people will believe that the law is unfavorable to their concerns. For instance, although slavery was the law of the land for more than a century in the South, it had disastrous consequences for those subjected to it. The second reason for the tension between the law and citizens is that the values of individuals and communities are a moving target. As social and economic conditions change, so do values.

Public-order offenses are often called "victimless crimes."[6] A **victimless crime** offends the values of a segment of society and is against the law but has the willing participation of all parties to the activity and causes no obvious harm to anyone involved. Nevertheless, participants in the activity seek to keep it from becoming known to police. For example, transactions involving drug sales or **prostitution** include a buyer and a seller; as long as each party is satisfied with the exchange, there is no victim. If the deal goes bad and someone gets hurt or killed, then the offense is assault or homicide. However, when the transaction goes smoothly, both the customer and the seller are satisfied. Those who use illegal drugs do not believe that they are crime victims. They have freely chosen to consume these substances.[7] Those who participate in illegal gambling have a similar attitude. They choose to gamble and prefer that the government stay out of that particular area of their lives. Still, society condemns victimless crimes, and the criminal justice system pursues the "offenders" and "victims" who take part.

The work of the criminal justice system would be much easier if it did not have the mandate to enforce public-order laws. If the criminal justice system could concentrate on offenses that have a firm majority consensus, such as murder, larceny, and embezzlement, it could focus its resources more efficiently, enlist the support of citizens more effectively, and limit the numbers of incarcerated people. Some believe that other government agencies or the private sector could better deal with the issues that arise out of the activities of consenting citizens. It is possible that the existence of criminal sanctions for drug use, prostitution, and other public-order offenses does not reduce the amount and severity of these behaviors. In fact, in some ways, criminal sanctions promote the illegal underground economy that arises to supply the demand for these services.

Public-order offenses certainly affect society, but some people wonder if the problems that arise from these offenses are made worse or better by using the criminal justice system to control them. The work of criminologists is important in examining the problems and issues of dealing with offenses against the public order.

General and Indirect Victims

The class of public-order offenses has been created to protect individuals who do not freely engage in these behaviors but might be general or indirect victims. Some people believe that public-order offenses, even when committed by consenting adults in private, affect society in general or family members, neighbors, or the community. Let's briefly consider how three categories of public-order offenses influence the lives of others.

- Substance abuse. The use of and trafficking in illegal drugs affect a variety of people in a number of ways. The drug user might think that no one else is harmed, but drug use can be expensive and addicting. A drug user might use money for rent and food to buy drugs, thus victimizing his or her family by depriving them of a decent standard of living. The effects of drugs can make the user unable to hold down a job, and the drug user must then get money another way, often by stealing or robbery. The danger posed to society can be substantial if violence is used to get or sell the drugs. Drug dealers might use violence

This Ventura County Sheriff's department DUI presentation at a street festival is intended to discourage people from driving under the influence of alcohol. Can driver impairment from drug use be detected as effectively as impairment from alcohol use?

---

public-order offense—An activity that is against the law and offends the values, norms, and/or morals of a dominant sector of society.

victimless crime—An activity that offends the values of a segment of society and is against the law but has the willing participation of all parties to the activity and causes no obvious harm to anyone involved in the activity, who also seek to keep it from becoming known to police.

prostitution—The unlawful promotion of or participation in sexual activities for profit.

to protect their markets, and drug users might use violence to procure the drugs.[8] Finally, those who drive under the influence of illegal drugs can be as dangerous and problematic as those who drive under the influence of alcohol.

- Prostitution. Prostitution affects more than the individuals involved, according to those who believe it should be illegal. Indirect victims of prostitution include loved ones whose trust and commitment are violated, lost tax revenue from the underground-economy transaction, and the social dangers of sexually transmitted disease. In addition, some people believe prostitution threatens the institution of marriage and cheapens the concept of love.[9]
- Gambling. Many states have legalized some form of gambling, but there is a vast underground network of gambling that affects those who do not gamble. Governments might lose tax revenue to illegal gambling, and sometimes those who cannot pay their gambling debts are beaten or killed. Gambling addicts who lose all their assets can become a financial burden on society and on their families.[10] The get-rich-quick lure of gambling is also believed to affect the working habits of children and young adults. Dreaming of cashing in big on a lottery or poker game is not a reasonable substitute for getting an education or learning a marketable skill.

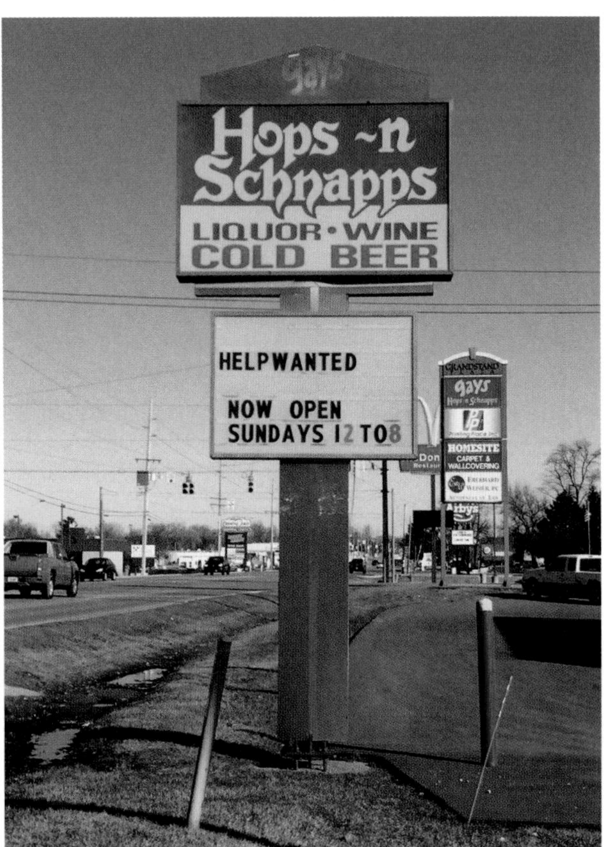

This sign on an Indiana liquor store announces that the store will now be open on Sundays. Why do some local governments prohibit alcohol sales on Sunday?

The victimless nature of public-order offenses is a debatable idea that we will return to often in this chapter. The immediate issue, however, is that many people believe these behaviors are detrimental to society. Therefore, through the democratic process, these behaviors have been deemed to be criminal offenses, and the power of the criminal justice system is brought to bear on those who commit them. The interesting questions that criminologists consider are why certain behaviors are considered public-order offenses and where society draws the line between legal and illegal behavior when morals and values are what is being regulated.[11]

Morality and Crime

Morality is concerned with values. In Western societies with diverse populations, some people must compromise their values in order to function in the public space. For instance, Americans from certain religious backgrounds might find it offensive for women to participate in occupations of responsibility and power such as judge, professor, or police officer. Non-religious Americans might be offended by public displays of religious belief, such as Bible readings or prayer circles. Other Americans might find dancing, alcohol use, and homosexuality offensive and advocate changes in laws to reflect these values. However, personal values are not encoded into law. Therefore, although certain behaviors might offend some people, there is little likelihood that the law will be changed to accommodate their values. If all the behaviors that some groups find objectionable were made illegal, the country would be a very different place than it is now.

The values of some groups, however, are implemented into criminal law through the political process. Political participation allows some groups to have their values supported by legislators who sponsor bills that outlaw or require certain behaviors. The process of making laws is of great interest to criminologists because it is a function of political compromise and a reflection of social attitudes and religious beliefs. In theocratic countries such as Iran, the values of religious leaders are reflected in the law.[12] In the United

States, the law is derived from the will of the people, but the people's will often reflects a variety of historical and religious traditions. Consequently, the law is a tool of the collective morality of some social groups.

Morality and Social Harm

The stated purpose of laws that prohibit public-order offenses is to protect people and society. Actually, when the patterns of laws are examined, it is obvious that some of the most harmful behaviors are legal, while other behaviors that seem to have little potential for significant damage are illegal. For instance, consider the laws concerning drug use in the United States. Tobacco and alcohol are not only legal, but they also constitute billion-dollar industries, whereas marijuana, which has some purported medical uses, remains largely illegal. Similarly, in some states, having a small-stakes poker game in your home can get you arrested, but large-scale gambling is permissible at race tracks, in casinos, and through state lotteries. Social harm, then, is only one imperfect measure of what is judged to be a public-order offense. The other factor that bears consideration is social sensibility. Although some behaviors may not be particularly harmful, they offend some people's sense of decency, morality, and religious sensibilities.[13]

There is a long history of people who have sought to make the world a better place by imposing their moral standards on society. These moral crusaders include those who considered alcohol to be evil and tried to close down saloons in the 19th century and got Prohibition enacted in the 20th century.[14] Today, some jurisdictions still have "blue laws" that restrict the sale of alcohol. For instance, some rural Georgia counties and towns prohibit the sale of all wine and beer on Sundays. However, in urban Atlanta, alcoholic drinks can be purchased in restaurants and bars at nearly any hour on any day.[15]

Why are these laws so different? Part of the answer lies in population size and homogeneity. In less populous jurisdictions, the citizens may share similar sets of values, morals, and norms. If one person thinks that alcohol should not be sold on certain days or at certain times, many others in that jurisdiction—often a majority of others—will likely share that idea. Through the political process, this majority gets its preferences on how, when, and where alcohol should be sold encoded into law, and the businesses of that jurisdiction must follow that law.[16] We will explore these questions in greater detail as we tackle three particularly legally contested areas of public-order offenses: substance abuse, sex offenses, and gambling.

PAUSE AND REVIEW

1. **Why are public-order offenses often called "victimless crimes"?**

Substance Abuse and the Law

LEARNING OBJECTIVE | 2

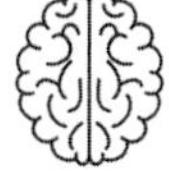

Discuss why the use and abuse of drugs are important to the study of criminology.

The use and abuse of drugs are important to the study of **criminology** for three reasons.

First, drugs and alcohol influence behavior. Although this statement might seem obvious, it lies at the heart of the philosophy behind regulating controlled substances. There is little debate that alcohol and drugs impede the judgment and motor functions of those under their influence.[17] From a strict public-safety perspective, many people accept the government's right and obligation to control the sale and consumption of drugs and alcohol. The public generally agrees that those who are under the influence of drugs or alcohol should not be driving. Likewise, it would be difficult to find someone who would defend the right to sell heroin or methamphetamines to 12-year-old children.

Second, substance abuse is related to other types of crime. The use and sale of alcohol and drugs are not the only ways in which these substances affect the criminal justice system. The illegal drug industry spawns more traditional offenses. For instance, those who have $100-a-day drug habits usually quickly exhaust their discretionary funds and must find money elsewhere if they are to continue the habit. Consequently, those who suffer from drug addiction and lack of financial resources often turn to theft or robbery to obtain the money to buy drugs. As each day demands even more money to finance the habit, the individual gets more desperate and adventurous in victimizing others.[18] For instance, a Wisconsin woman was caught injecting runaway youths with methamphetamine and allowing them to live in her home in exchange for shoplifting

Instant Recall from Chapter 1 **criminology** —The study of the making of laws, the breaking of laws, and the social reaction to the breaking of laws.

People bring flowers to a Medford, New York, pharmacy where four people were shot and killed during a botched painkiller robbery. How can drug-related crime be best addressed?

mobile phones and other items that she would sell to buy more methamphetamine. She was also forcing a "low-functioning adult" to perform sexual acts on men for money.[19] Although it can be claimed that drug use itself is a consensual victimless crime, maintaining the drug habit often results in harm to others' lives through property and personal violent offenses. Criminologists must consider substance abuse as a causative or contributing factor when studying a broad range of offenses from domestic assault and child abuse, to robbery, rape, and burglary.

Third, the war on drugs is difficult, dangerous, and costly. Immense resources are required to combat the illegal sale and use of illegal drugs and underage drinking. Furthermore, the money involved in these illegal activities makes the work of police officers difficult.[20] Those making large sums from the sale of drugs are difficult to deter, are likely to go to great lengths to maintain their cash flow, and are willing to harm others in order to escape detection and punishment. As drug dealers battle over supplies, territory, and customers, they injure or kill not only each other, but also, sometimes, innocent bystanders who are caught in the crossfire. The war on drugs affects not only those actively involved, but also the entire community because in the course of making legitimate arrests, police officers sometimes make terrible mistakes by entering the wrong house or mistaking innocent substances for illegal drugs.[21]

In this illustration of the 1794 Whiskey Rebellion, the rebels escort a tarred-and-feathered tax collector from his burning home. What caused the Whiskey Rebellion?

Drug use and the war on drugs have dominated the activities of the criminal justice system for several decades as society has struggled to deal with the social problem and public-health issues of drug abuse. Criminologists are concerned about these issues, which we will consider next.

A Brief Legal History of Alcohol and Drugs in the United States

The process of restricting drugs and alcohol developed slowly and in a patchwork fashion. After the American Revolution, the new government had no laws that restricted the sale or use of drugs or alcohol. Like many areas of commerce at the time, it was believed that alcohol and drug sales were not the government's business and that individuals should be free to pursue their own recreations as long as they did not adversely affect others. In the country's early years, alcohol was not considered the social problem that it is today. In fact, alcohol was an integral part of the lives of many people.[22] Many of them drank alcohol almost exclusively because it was dangerous to drink the water. We take clean water for granted today, but for much of the country's history, water had to be boiled first to ensure its safety for drinking. Distilled liquor, such as whiskey, provided a safer beverage.[23]

The first U.S. laws restricting the sale of alcohol or drugs were economic and not social. The government did not try to protect people from harmful substances, but rather it wanted to collect the revenue generated from the sale of alcohol. In 1791, Congress passed an excise tax on whiskey. Farmers who made whiskey refused to pay the tax and battled federal tax collectors in states such as Kentucky and Tennessee, where much of the whiskey was made. Tax collectors were tarred and feathered, and the new president, George Washington, had to call in the militia to quell the violence.[24] The Whiskey Rebellion was the first test of the federal government's authority to tax citizens. Had Washington been unsuccessful in putting down the rebellion and compelling the farmers to pay the tax, the failure would have established a precedent that would have greatly limited the federal government's power and authority. Legally, the United States would be a substantially different place today. However, the social harm produced by the consumption of drugs and alcohol was not lost on the early Americans. Many recognized the harmful effects that intoxication had on individuals and the economy, but nearly a century passed before social welfare was considered so urgent that the freedom to consume drugs and alcohol had to be curtailed. Comprehensive drug policy is a recent phenomenon and is still highly contested. The restriction of drugs and alcohol in the United States has had varied success throughout several eras. Let's take a look at some of these attempts.

OPIUM AND MORPHINE

After the Civil War, the country turned its attention to opening up the West, and the expansion of the railroad system brought many Chinese laborers to the United States. These laborers brought opium—the dried excretion from the opium poppy—with them from China. Smoking opium helped the Chinese laborers deal with the physical rigors of railroad work, and railroad administrators found that opium helped keep the laborers docile. Opium use quickly spread from railroad workers to the Chinese populations in large cities like San Francisco and then to the rest of society. As the opium habit bubbled up through the socioeconomic classes and opium-smoking became a trendy recreational pursuit, many people were determined to restrict opium use. San Francisco passed the first law outlawing opium smoking in 1875, followed by New York City in 1882. In 1890, the federal government restricted opium smoking and banned opium imports completely.[25]

As opium became expensive, difficult to find, and risky to use, it was replaced by morphine, which is manufactured from the opium poppy. American soldiers started to use morphine during the Civil War to relieve the pain of wounds and surgery and to alleviate the symptoms of dysentery. Morphine addiction became known as the "soldiers' disease" because so many became addicted. Many doctors became concerned about the addictive effects of morphine and pushed for its control.[26] In fact, an early treatment for morphine addiction was cocaine because its stimulant nature was thought to counteract the depressant effects of morphine.[27]

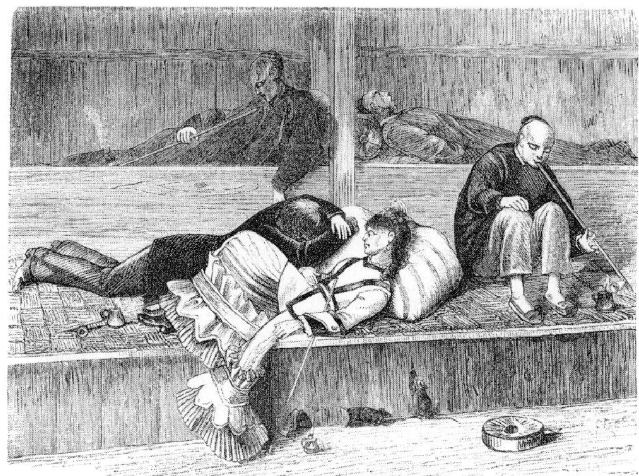

An illustration of an opium den in San Francisco. How did opium first enter the United States?

PATENT MEDICINES

In the late 19th and early 20th centuries, patent medicines were popular concoctions of ingredients that were, in turn, medically benign, useless, harmful, and addictive. Typical ingredients included alcohol, morphine, opium, and cocaine. People would buy something like Dr. Mortimer's Magic Honey Cure-All, which would give its users an immediate feeling of well-being and pain relief. The syrup of the soft drink Coca-Cola, which contained a trace of cocaine until 1929, was first marketed as a patent medicine in 1886.[28]

Unfortunately, many people became addicted to these so-called medicines. By 1904, patent medicines had grown into a $74 million industry and had harmed many people. Unlike the use of alcohol, which was becoming a social stigma, patent medicines could be camouflaged as something beneficial that could be used without guilt or social disapproval, especially since the ingredients were not listed on the labels. Women who would not be found in a local tavern could get quietly drunk at home, and children with a painful toothache could be given a strong dose of morphine or alcohol that had the immediate effect of quelling their pain and discomfort.

1906 PURE FOOD AND DRUGS ACT

Society eventually responded to the problems brought about by the use of unregulated drugs. Spurred in part by Upton Sinclair's *The Jungle*, a book that graphically detailed the unsafe and unsanitary conditions in the country's meatpacking plants, the government passed the 1906 Pure Food and Drugs Act.[29] The law did not prohibit the use of drugs in patent medicines but only required that the amount of each ingredient be specified on the label.[30] The idea was that

Some old patent medicines are still around in collections and antique stores. What ingredients were in patent medicines of the past that would be illegal now?

consumers could make their own judgments about what to consume as long as they had accurate information. The government's goal was to protect people from unscrupulous merchants without restricting their personal freedoms. People were permitted to ingest anything they wanted as far as the law was concerned.

HARRISON ACT OF 1914

The next major impetus toward regulating alcohol and drug use was the Harrison Act of 1914, which was essentially tax legislation. It required those who produced, dispensed, imported, or gave away specified drugs to register with the government and pay a special tax. The goal was not to prevent drug use but to regulate the sale of drugs so that the government would get its cut. In many ways, the Harrison Act did what the Whiskey Act had done many years earlier. Penalties for violating this law were not severe, and those who used drugs not prescribed by licensed dealers were not arrested. Part of the motivation behind the Harrison Act was fear and racism. For example, Dr. Hamilton Wright, one of the primary sponsors of the legislation, gave lectures about the practice of "stuffing" the nose with cocaine. According to Wright, this practice was popular among southern blacks, and he testified before Congress that it led to the rape of white women.[31]

The Harrison Act had another profound influence on the legal treatment of drugs in the United States. Although the medical establishment defined drug addiction as a disease and considered the prescription of drugs to alleviate withdrawal distress as ethical, the act made it illegal for doctors to prescribe narcotics for addicts to maintain their habit and keep them comfortable. The U.S. Supreme Court ruled in two cases in favor of the act, which would stand for more than 80 years.[32] It was not until 2000 that the Drug Addiction Treatment Act allowed doctors to prescribe certain narcotics to help addicts wean themselves from drugs or to maintain their habits.[33]

MARIJUANA AND THE LAW

Marijuana use has an interesting history in the United States. For decades it had a low-profile use among jazz entertainers in New Orleans and Mexican laborers in Texas and the Southwest.[34] With the end of Prohibition in 1933, the Treasury Department, which had regulated alcohol, suddenly found itself with a bloated workforce and a limited mandate. According to some scholars, marijuana was not made illegal because it was a dangerous drug but because it provided the Treasury Department with a new villain. The effect of the Marijuana Tax Act was to make marijuana 10 to 12 times more expensive and to criminalize its use.[35] Following the law's passage, considerable research on the drug questioned the scientific evidence on which the law relied. Two federal laws enacted in the 1950s, the Boggs Act and the Narcotic Control Act, increased criminal penalties and set mandatory-minimum prison sentences for certain drug offenses, including those involving marijuana.[36]

COMPREHENSIVE DRUG ABUSE PREVENTION AND CONTROL ACT OF 1970

The Comprehensive Drug Abuse Prevention and Control Act of 1970 made sweeping changes in the drug laws. First, the law divided responsibilities over drugs between the Department of Justice, which was to enforce drug laws, and the Department of Health and Human Services, which was to evaluate the scientific evidence and make recommendations about which drugs should be controlled. Second, the law established a hierarchy of controlled substances by creating a five-level schedule that classified the drugs according to how dangerous they are, their potential for abuse and addiction, and their legitimate medical value (see Table 12.1). Although some people might debate the wisdom of scheduling particular drugs, the schedule's purpose is to make the most harmful drugs the most difficult to obtain. Third, the law set penalties for the use and sale of these illegal drugs. The level of penalties was adjusted and made more complicated in 1988 when mandatory minimum sentences were added.

OMNIBUS DRUG ACT

In 1988, the Omnibus Drug Act (also called the Anti-Drug Abuse Act) established the Office of National Drug Control Policy and made several important changes to the drug laws.[37] The new legislation included proscriptions against money laundering, the use of airplanes in drug activities, and the sale of firearms to felons. It also restricted certain chemicals used to make some illegal drugs and authorized the death penalty for anyone who killed or ordered the killing of another while committing a drug-related felony. The act also provides for the prevention and treatment of drug abuse.[38] The most interesting part of the law is the way it expands the control of drugs from law enforcement to other areas of government. For example, someone convicted of a drug offense can receive a civil fine, have his or her car or boat confiscated if it was used in the commission of the offense, and lose all federal benefits, including student loans. These additional provisions are meant to deter beyond what the criminal justice system can do. Because prisons and jails are so crowded, individuals may escape incarceration. However, by instituting a financial penalty, the law can punish much

TABLE 12.1 Federal Drug Schedules

Schedule I High potential for abuse. No currently accepted medical use in treatment in the United States. A lack of accepted safety for use of the drug or other substance under medical supervision.	heroin, mescaline, psilocybin, psilocin, LSD, marijuana, hashish, peyote, Ecstasy, Quaalude, synthetic heroin
Schedule II High potential for abuse. Currently accepted medical use in treatment in the United States or a currently accepted medical use with severe restrictions. Abuse may lead to severe psychological or physical dependence.	methadone, morphine, cocaine, amphetamine, methamphetamine, PCP, opium, Ritalin, oxycodone, pentobarbital
Schedule III Potential for abuse less than the drugs or other substances in Schedules I and II. Currently accepted medical use in treatment in the United States. Abuse may lead to moderate or low physical dependence or high psychological dependence.	codeine, anabolic steroids, barbiturates, synthetic THC (Marinol), Vicodin, Ketamine, pentothal
Schedule IV Low potential for abuse relative to the drugs or other substances in Schedule III. Currently accepted medical use in treatment in the United States. Abuse may lead to limited physical dependence or psychological dependence relative to the drugs or other substances in Schedule III.	Xanax, Valium, Darvon, Rohypnol, Halcion, Ativan, Ambien
Schedule V Low potential for abuse relative to the drugs or other substances in Schedule IV. Currently accepted medical use in treatment in the United States. Abuse may lead to limited physical dependence or psychological dependence relative to the drugs or other substances in Schedule IV.	cough syrups, preparations with opium or codeine

Sources: National Criminal Justice Reference Service, https://www.ncjrs.gov/spotlight/club_drugs/legislation.html. U.S. Drug Enforcement Administration, Diversion Control Division, https://www.deadiversion.usdoj.gov/schedules/index.html. Accessed July 2018.

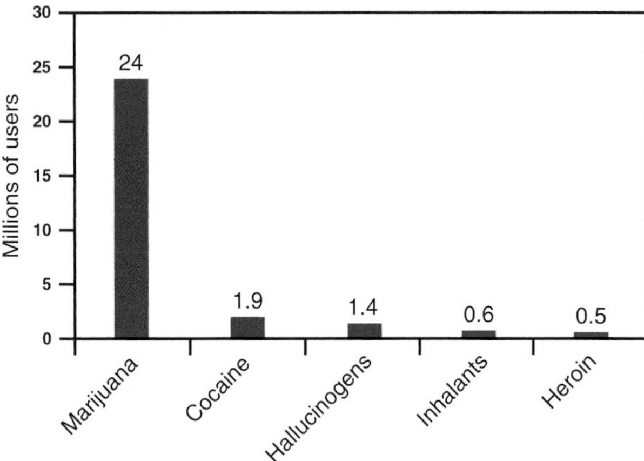

FIGURE 12.1 The National Survey on Drug Use and Health interviews substance users about the type and amount of their drug usage in the past month. The figure compares the frequency of the types of drugs used. Hallucinogens include LSD and Ecstasy. Inhalants include substances such as nitrous oxide, amyl nitrite, cleaning fluids, gasoline, spray paint, certain aerosol sprays, and glue.

THINK ABOUT IT
Are the penalties for drug use in line with the frequency with which people use them?

Source: Substance Abuse and Mental Health Services Administration, Figure 15: Numbers of Past Month Illicit Drug Users among People Aged 12 or Older, Key Substance Use and Mental Health Indicators in the United States: Results from the 2016 National Survey on Drug Use and Health (Rockville, Md.: Center for Behavioral Health Statistics and Quality, Substance Abuse and Mental Health Services Administration, 2017), 14. Online at https://www.samhsa.gov/data. Accessed July 2018.

more efficiently, which will presumably prevent would-be drug sellers and users from risking capture.

This brief history of drug regulation in the United States leaves out the thousands of state and local laws that have been passed over the decades. Most of this legislation is built upon prior legislation. There was never a time when an informed panel of experts got together to decide which drugs should be controlled. The rationales for the early drug laws were primarily financial. The government was not looking to control drug and alcohol use out of concern for public health or safety but simply wanted to generate revenue by taxing its commerce.

Substance Abuse Today

Substance abuse of legal and illegal substances is common in the United States today despite the war on drugs. The most commonly abused substance is alcohol, but this probably has much to do with its legality and availability. Pharmaceuticals such as oxycodone, fentanyl, and other pain-relief medications are also problematic, but these have legal applications, although they are tightly controlled. Common illegal substances include marijuana, cocaine, heroin, methamphetamine, and hallucinogens. Inhalants are a class of drugs that includes many substances not intended for use as drugs, such as glue, spray paint, and compressed air in cans.

The National Survey on Drug Use and Health (NSDUH) is the main source of information on the non-medical use of illicit drugs, alcohol, and tobacco in the United States by the civilian, non-institutionalized population age 12 or older. The survey interviews about 70,000 respondents annually about their substance usage. According to the 2016 survey, 28.6 million people age 12 or older (representing about 10.6 percent of the U.S. population age 12 and older) reported using illegal drugs in the past month.[39] Marijuana was the most commonly used illegal drug with 24 million users. About 1.9 million people reported using cocaine; 667,000 people reported using methamphetamine; and 475,000 people reported using heroin. Finally, 1.4 million people reported using various hallucinogens. (See Figure 12.1 for a visual comparison of the frequency of usage of types of drugs.) Regardless of the age of users, most illicit drug use involves marijuana and the misuse of prescription pain medication.[40]

Theories that explain continued drug usage typically concern biological addiction and psychological dependence. These theories focus on a need to have more of a substance that one has already used for reasons ranging from the desire to be more comfortable socially, the wish or need to be more energetic or creative, or the need to control physical signs of withdrawal. The reasons that people begin using substances are more complicated, but one factor likely involves the young ages at which substance use begins, typically after puberty. This is why the NSDUH begins its study at age 12 and why so much antidrug literature focuses on youths. Theories explaining the young age at which substance usage begins may best be drawn from theories of delinquency (see Chapter 6), which focus on dysfunctional families and antisocial peers. Psychological theories may include the adolescent need to experiment with behaviors, develop individual identity, and integrate socially with peers. Biological theories would point to chemical imbalances in the brain or body that could lead to a need to correct the imbalance with substances. Drug use may turn into abuse when people become addicted or psychologically dependent (see Table 12.2).

legalization—The complete removal of legal proscriptions on acts that were previously illegal.

decriminalization—The lessening or removal of penalties for acts previously subject to criminal prosecution, arrest, and incarceration.

TABLE 12.2 Theoretical Explanations of Substance Abuse

THEORY	EXPLANATION
Biological addiction	Many illegal drugs are highly addictive. Physical addiction results in symptoms of withdrawal when the body does not get enough of a drug it has become accustomed to. These withdrawal symptoms can make the individual extremely uncomfortable and sick and cause such a craving for the drug that he or she will break the law to get it.
Psychological dependence	Individuals may become psychologically dependent on drugs or alcohol. Although the body does not physically crave the substance, the person might use it as a crutch. Psychological dependence is often as difficult to overcome as physical addiction.

Legalization and Decriminalization

If we were to start all over, it is possible that we would construct our drug laws differently. In terms of harm, it is clear that tobacco has killed more people than all the illegal drugs put together. Alcohol continues to be a social problem, yet the government allows it to be easily obtained and collects substantial amounts of money from liquor taxes. Some people advocate a return to the days when all the government required of drug manufacturers was disclosure of their products' contents.

Before we consider the consequences of substance **legalization** and **decriminalization**, we must first differentiate between the terms "legalization" and "decriminalization." Legalization means a given substance is completely legal to consume, just like soft drinks and chocolate are. Cigarettes and alcohol are also considered to be legalized, although there are restrictions on sales to and consumption by minors.

Decriminalization is more of a gray area. Under decriminalization, the substance is not completely legal, but neither is it the subject of a full-scale prohibitive criminal justice effort. For instance, in decriminalizing marijuana, the government might change the offense from a felony to a misdemeanor, thus reducing the drug's stigma. Persons caught with small amounts of a decriminalized substance would be subject to few or no sanctions, while substance abusers would be referred to health or rehabilitative agencies rather than incarcerated or otherwise criminally sanctioned.

Drug legalization probably would not legalize all drugs for everyone.[41] Many proposals to legalize or at least decriminalize drugs stop short of such an extreme scenario. Many of those who wish to legalize drugs believe that even though there may be some increase in the use of drugs, society would be safer.[42] If drugs were to be treated as a medical problem rather than a criminal justice problem, some surmise that much of the violence associated with acquiring money to maintain a drug habit would disappear. Drug dealers would not battle one another over customers and territory, and drug commerce would be governed like the commerce in alcohol and tobacco. Finally, drug users could be confident they would be getting unadulterated drugs, and they would be better able to gauge their potency and prevent the overdoses that are common with illegal drugs.

The legalization or decriminalization of some drugs would carry some risks, however. Although many people can now easily obtain illegal drugs, legalizing them would certainly increase the number of people who would be getting intoxicated.[43] Many would-be drug users today desist from drug use because they do not want to get caught breaking the

Protesters rally in support of marijuana legalization. Are there any drugs other than marijuana that you would consider legalizing?

law. Without the legal sanctions, many would be free to use drugs with impunity; such drug use could affect their productivity and safety at work, their motivation to keep steady employment, and their ability to raise children with the necessary values to be good citizens. We have had enough experience with alcohol abuse to know that being under the influence of behavior-altering substances has consequences for the users.[44]

The question of whether to legalize or decriminalize drugs is difficult to answer. People still use illegal drugs, and the war on drugs has its own consequences in terms of making drug use more dangerous, violent, and expensive. Opinions on what to do about illegal drug use vary widely, ranging from the complete legalization of all drugs to a prohibition on everything, including alcohol. Some people contend that a middle position of decriminalizing some drugs could minimize the harm done by drug use and minimize the war on drugs.[45] Regardless, given the violence currently associated with drug use, the immense resources used by the criminal justice system to stem trafficking, and the high numbers of people in prison for drug-related offenses, it is clear that our present drug policies deserve to be revisited. Other countries, such as Portugal, have been more successful in limiting the violence associated with drug use without spending billions of dollars on incarceration.[46] One approach to preventing drug abuse is harm reduction (see Theory to Practice).

THEORY TO PRACTICE

Harm Reduction as a Drug Strategy

Criminological theory informs efforts to deal with crime and is especially relevant in the area of drug use and abuse. Because the war on drugs has been unsuccessful in halting the flow of drugs and limiting their harm, criminologists have developed other approaches based on harm reduction. These approaches also seek to address several unintended consequences of the war on drugs.

- As the price of illegal drugs rises, addicts sometimes break the law to get the money to pay for their habits.
- Drug users are often at the mercy of sellers who give them adulterated drugs that could be fatal.
- The resources that law enforcement authorities use to fight the war on drugs may be better used in dealing with other types of crime.
- Drug users often do not seek treatment because they are afraid their drug habits will become known to the police and their employers, and they will be arrested or lose their jobs.

Health authorities face the challenge of helping people who are dependent on illegal drugs and who want to be helped without exposing them to the criminal justice system. Rather than treating the drug use as a criminal offense, harm reduction treats it as a medical problem of addiction. Perhaps the best known harm-reduction strategy is methadone maintenance.

Methadone is a drug that prevents the withdrawal symptoms experienced by addicts who stop using heroin. The goal of the methadone program is to wean the addict off all drugs. Methadone is taken orally and its effects last longer than those of heroin, but it is also addictive. Many critics believe methadone maintenance is not useful because the addict is simply trading one addiction for another. Proponents of methadone maintenance point to favorable outcomes in several areas. Those using methadone are reported to reduce their criminal activity, become employed, and generally improve their psychological and social functioning.

Hundreds of programs prescribe methadone or other drugs as substitutes for illegal substances. Methadone maintenance is now so routine that many insurance plans cover treatment. Patients are also protected by the Americans with Disabilities Act as long as they are taking methadone legally and not abusing other drugs.

This harm-reduction strategy shows how criminologists use theory to develop alternative policies to control crime. It is a good example of how the pendulum swings from punishment to rehabilitation and back again as we seek theoretically informed solutions to social problems.

THINK ABOUT IT

1. Apply harm-reduction strategies to the problem of alcoholism.

Sources: Harm Reduction Coalition, http://www.harmreduction.org. Substance Abuse and Mental Health Services Administration, Medication-Assisted Treatment (MAT), https://www.samhsa.gov/medication-assisted-treatment. Accessed July 2018.

PAUSE AND REVIEW

1. Why is substance use and abuse important to the study of criminology?
2. Discuss the history of restricting drugs and alcohol in the United States.
3. What is the difference between substance legalization and decriminalization?

Sex Offenses

LEARNING OBJECTIVE | 3

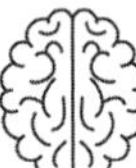

Explain the basis of laws prohibiting prostitution, pornography, and sodomy.

Another class of public-order offense that garners a great deal of attention from criminologists and criminal justice officials is concerned with sexuality, especially prostitution and **pornography**. A third such offense is that of consensual **sodomy**—oral or anal sexual intercourse—which has only recently been legalized. Although both heterosexual and homosexual activities were written into the states' anti-sodomy laws, these laws were directed mainly at homosexual activity, making them especially controversial.[47]

Laws proscribing certain forms of sexual activity have been common throughout history and throughout the world, and the United States is no exception. In the United States, public-order laws dealing with sex largely emerged from a Christian religious philosophy that held that procreation was the only justification for sex. Sex without intention or desire to procreate (adultery and fornication can be assumed here), or any non-procreative form of sex (such as masturbation or sodomy), was considered immoral.[48] Therefore, states inserted laws proscribing such activities into their legal codes early on, and many states never removed them even as times changed.

Today, several states still have laws against adultery (sex with someone other than one's spouse) and fornication (sex without marriage).[49] These laws are rarely, if ever, enforced. The three activities we will consider in detail—prostitution, pornography, and sodomy—were originally proscribed by law because they flouted the prohibition on non-procreative sex. Although Americans' general opinion on the morality of non-procreative sex has long since changed, prostitution remains a criminal offense in 49 states; which types of pornography are illegal is still being debated; and anti-sodomy laws were struck down only recently. Let's take a look at each of these three activities to get an idea of their nature and extent.

Prostitution

People have varying attitudes about the place of sexual behavior in society. Some people consider the purchase of sex to be an issue of personal freedom, whereas others consider it to be immoral, destructive behavior. These differences of opinion can be observed in the terminology used to refer to the sale and purchase of sexual activity. Those who support it and think it should be legalized and regulated refer to the transaction as "sex work." Those who believe that it should remain illegal and that it constitutes immoral activity call it prostitution and define it as unlawfully promoting or participating in sexual activities for profit, including attempts to solicit customers; assisting in or promoting the exchange of sexual activities for money; or owning, managing, or operating an establishment for the purpose of providing a place where sex is exchanged for money. Because the sale and purchase of sex are illegal in every state except Nevada (which we will discuss later), criminal justice agencies refer to the offense as prostitution rather than sex work.

The government's role in regulating sexual behavior between consenting adults is a central issue in prostitution. Some argue that the government has no place in citizens' bedrooms and that prostitution should be regulated by health agencies.[50] However, a brief history of what has been called "the world's oldest profession" reveals why some people have deemed prostitution to be anything but a victimless crime.[51]

It is difficult to estimate how much prostitution exists in the United States because the seller and the customer are usually consenting parties who are satisfied with the transaction and have no motive to report it to the police.[52] Consequently, most prostitution goes unreported. It is difficult to define exactly what constitutes an act of prostitution because prostitutes perform some activities that do not involve sexual intercourse.[53] Prostitution has been described as having the following elements: sexually

---

pornography—Images, sounds, writing, or other communication designed to give sexual pleasure.

sodomy— Oral or anal sexual intercourse.

significant activity for the purchaser; an economic transaction, often in the form of money or other economically significant resources, such as drugs; and emotional indifference on the part of the seller, or both the buyer and seller.[54]

MALE PROSTITUTION

Although most people would probably identify prostitutes as female, many men also engage in prostitution. According to sociologist Robert McNamara, male prostitution has a long history but was relatively understudied in comparison with female prostitution until AIDS (acquired immune deficiency syndrome) and HIV (human immunodeficiency virus), the virus that causes AIDS, became significant social problems in the 1980s. In his work detailing the lives of male hustlers in New York City's Times Square, McNamara contends that male prostitution shares many of the concerns of female prostitution for those who engage in it at the street level.[55]

McNamara's research on male prostitutes in Times Square focused on the community that these men and boys developed within the hustling marketplace and the problems they had with HIV/AIDS. Perhaps the most significant observation from his research is the fact that many of these male prostitutes did not consider themselves to be homosexual. Some were married; many had girlfriends, and they considered hustling an occupation and not a defining parameter of their identity. Because these male prostitutes had unprotected sex with their male clients, unprotected sex with their wives and girlfriends, and tended to be intravenous drug users, they were susceptible to acquiring and transmitting HIV.

Since the advent of the Internet and social media, much male prostitution has moved off the streets and onto websites and mobile phone dating applications (apps). This change has made male prostitution more anonymous and safer. Sex workers are now at less risk of violence and stigma, can work independently, and can extend their careers well into adulthood. The relative ease of sex work via the Internet versus the street means that more male prostitutes only casually participate in sex work to earn extra money or even simply for the excitement. Because Internet prostitutes work alone, they also miss the support and socialization that street prostitutes receive from each other. This means that they have less knowledge when vetting potential clients or negotiating other aspects of the "hook-up" such as price and the usage of condoms.[56]

FEMALE PROSTITUTION

Female prostitution exists in various forms. The market can be highly regulated, with women working for a female madam or a male pimp.[57] These women consider prostitution an occupation and may live an antisocial lifestyle in which others help them deal with police officers, bail them out of jail, or provide them a place to live and help with their medical care. (Several theoretical perspectives can address why women become prostitutes; for an example, see Table 12.3.) Other prostitutes may have lawful occupations and engage in paid sex only sporadically.[58]

The following typology of female prostitutes covers the most prominent forms of prostitution. Although this typology is neither exhaustive (there may be other forms of prostitution) nor exclusive (women may fall into two or more of these categories), it describes the most common forms of this profession.

- Call girls. This type of prostitute occupies the highest rung in the hierarchy of prostitution. Some call girls also act as legitimate escorts in perfectly legal encounters. When a businessman needs a companion for a party or simply a date when out of town, escort and dating services will provide a woman who can act in a respectable and appropriate manner and have

TABLE 12.3 Theoretical Explanations of Prostitution

THEORY	EXPLANATION
Psychological Freudian	Young woman suffers from Electra Complex, always trying to win love of her father. She uses men to achieve affection.
Sociological Critical feminist	Selling her body gives a woman control of her sexuality.
Sociological Differential association	Young girl hangs out with older peers who teach her that prostitution is fun, lucrative, and empowering.

pleasant conversation with the customer. The line between legitimate escort services and prostitution is indistinct, and many of the women are willing to do whatever the customer desires. Escort services cater to people in politics, the movie industry, and big business and can be expensive. Occasionally, scandals occur in which notable figures are linked to call-girl services. These escort services can also be highly organized. For example, one San Francisco ring had 35 phone lines and four people answering the phones dispatching more than 200 call girls. Clients were accepted on a referral basis from trusted clients. The prostitutes in this ring made up to $160 for a one-hour hotel visit. Some call girls, however, can make substantially more.[59]

- Bar girls. Many prostitutes find clients in bars, particularly hotel bars where they are likely to meet out-of-town businessmen. Bar girls will accompany the client back to his room or to a nearby apartment. Some bars employ exotic dancers to attract male customers. These dancers are encouraged to get the men to buy them drinks and will order expensive drinks to get the customers to run up a high bar tab. Some dancers will perform private special shows that include lap dances and more explicit sexual contact. Many bars actively discourage prostitution and report bar girls to the police, but often these women will take the risk in order to meet potential clients who are willing to pay for sex.[60]
- Massage parlors and brothels. Although many businesses provide only clinical massages and legitimate spa services, so-called massage parlors are actually fronts for prostitution. Some openly advertise "body rub" or "body shampoo," but the real service offered is sex for a price. These massage parlors are like brothels where prostitutes sell sex in an establishment run by a madam and pay the establishment part of their earnings. The advantage of brothels (which are legal in Nevada) is that the prostitute does not need to generate customers herself but simply services those who are delivered to her by the madam. The girls have little authority to decide whom they have sex with and must pay a substantial percentage to the house.[61]
- Streetwalkers. Streetwalking can be very dangerous work for very low pay. Streetwalkers will perform various sex acts at whatever price they can negotiate. The streetwalker will often claim a territory on a corner, outside a bar or hotel, or on the sidewalks of a busy street. Customers approach the streetwalking prostitute either on foot or in a car and negotiate a price for a particular service. Because the streetwalker must always be concerned that the potential customer is a police officer, she must quickly evaluate his appearance and be careful with what she says. An elaborate linguistic battle can take place in which the streetwalker tries to avoid being the first one to mention the specific activity or the price. She will often use ambiguous phrases such as "Do you want a date?" so she can later claim she was not hustling in case the client turns out to be an undercover police officer. Streetwalkers live a precarious existence because they are susceptible to being attacked by clients. It is hard for them to control their working environment, and many of them have to work under the protection of pimps to be safe from violent customers or other prostitutes who might dispute the use of a particular corner to ply their trade. Pimps are a separate danger to the streetwalker because they are both their protectors and their exploiters.[62]

As this typology indicates, prostitution can take many forms. Thus, discussing public policies that deal with prostitution is difficult because some types of prostitution may be less objectionable than others. For example, expensive call girls provide services to clients who can afford to pay for sex, and the transactions take place in private to the satisfaction of both parties. In contrast, streetwalkers, who are often controlled by pimps, may be the victims of beatings, drug addiction, and sexually transmitted disease.

The Love Ranch brothel in Crystal, Nevada. A coalition of religious groups and anti-sex trafficking activists have launched referendums to ban brothels in two of Nevada's seven counties where they legally operate. What are the arguments for legalizing prostitution? Against?

LEGALIZED PROSTITUTION

The prospect of legalizing prostitution meets with the same reaction as proposals for legalizing drugs. Many people believe that prostitution and illegal drug use violate community values and are not only socially harmful but also immoral. Many critics also believe legalization would send the wrong message to young people. Some individuals, however, contend that there are good reasons to consider such a policy. Their arguments include the following.

- Legalization of prostitution would make it safer. Currently, much prostitution occurs under dangerous conditions. Drugs and violence are often common in areas where prostitution flourishes. Legalizing prostitution would allow people to engage in this behavior in safer places. There would be no need for pimps, and prostitutes who are assaulted or hassled by customers could turn to the police for help.
- Legalization of prostitution would make it healthier and more fair. At present, prostitutes must hide their activities. Legalizing the practice would subject it to regulation by public health agencies. Prostitutes could get regular checkups and be certified disease-free. They could be educated to use safe-sex techniques and insist to their customers that the government requires condom use. Group health insurance could help improve medical care for prostitutes, and they could also have their interests openly advocated with insurance companies, the community, and state legislatures.
- Legalizing prostitution would allow the government to tax it. Prostitution occurs in an underground economy in which prostitutes do not pay taxes on their earnings and those who run prostitution businesses do not pay taxes on their businesses. Taxation could create new revenue streams for city, county, and state governments, as well as pay for the bureaucracy required for licensing, inspection, and other regulatory controls.[63]

Despite the potential improvements in the public health of the community and the personal health of prostitutes and their customers, many groups and individuals are opposed to legalizing prostitution. They believe it is better to keep this activity against the law and to fine, jail, and otherwise punish both sellers and buyers of sexual services. There is a tension, then, between the freedom of individuals to purchase sex and the community standards of morality. There are three primary reasons for keeping prostitution illegal.

- Some religious moral codes hold that sex between two people is a sacred relationship that should not be bartered or sold. Legal prostitution would cheapen this relationship in society by reducing it to simply another product.
- Prostitution threatens the bonds of marriage. The easy and legal availability of prostitutes may tempt spouses to break their marriage vows.
- Prostitution is responsible for the spread of sexually transmitted diseases. Legalized prostitution would increase the spread of venereal disease because prostitutes would be much easier to access, so diseases would be more easily transmitted.

CHILD PROSTITUTION

The debate on whether to legalize the sale of sex sometimes loses sight of the problem of the exploitation of children. Although prostitution is not a victimless crime when children are involved, child prostitution is still an aspect of the public-order offense category of prostitution. We cover it here not to trivialize the exploitation of children, but to put child prostitution in context to show how public-order offenses can include behaviors that harm vulnerable individuals.

The problems of child prostitution are those of abuse, violence, and exploitation. Children do not have the developmental maturity to enter into such agreements. Even if a child were to say that he or she wanted to be a prostitute, adults and the law generally recognize that children have neither the intellectual nor the emotional capacity to make such a decision. Youth prostitution differs from other types of child sexual exploitation such as incest (sex between blood-related family members) and statutory rape because payment is involved. The payment might be in the form of money, drugs, clothing, jewelry, or other items. The incidence of youth prostitution is staggering. Estimates of the number of adolescent and child prostitutes in the United States range from 500,000 to 3 million. Some child prostitutes are as young as five years old. There are two common scenarios in which these problems of child prostitution may occur.

- Runaway kids. A common scenario involves runaway children who are befriended by pimps who offer them food and shelter in a strange new city. The pimps quickly entangle the runaways in a lifestyle of parties, drugs, and sex. Soon the pimps demand that the youths contribute financially and coerce them into prostitution. Escaping the pimp's grasp is difficult, and some child prostitutes grow into adulthood without acquiring any useful skills or education. The result is a life of violence, poverty, and drug use. Clearly, these youths are victims of exploitation by the pimps and by customers.[64] Children end up in this type of situation for sadly consistent reasons. Often, they are running away from physical and sexual domestic abuse and consider prostitution the only alternative to an intolerable home environment.

- International sex trade. The sexual exploitation of children in other countries is becoming a high-profile political issue. A sex-tourism industry has developed in several Asian and eastern European countries where people from wealthier countries take holidays for the purpose of having inexpensive sex with children. Airlines, hotels, and, in some cases, local governments facilitate sex tourism because it brings millions of dollars. The negative effects of sex tourism, in addition to the exploitation of children, include the spread of HIV and the undermining of the economy with the easy money based on the selling of children. That is, instead of developing legitimate industries, and rather than educating and investing in their young people for the long term, some countries exploit them.[65] Clearly, this type of prostitution is not a victimless crime; we mention it here simply because it is such an integral aspect of worldwide prostitution.

There is considerable debate about the wisdom of making laws that restrict choice in consensual sexual behavior. Much like the debate on drug use, this issue can be considered from two perspectives: the goal of preserving individual choice and the goal of protecting society from those who make poor choices. A third concern of those who question the necessity of outlawing consensual behaviors is pornography, an industry that pits freedom of speech and the press against those concerned with public morality.

Pornography

There is little consensus in the United States on what forms of entertainment should be allowed in the public sphere. The advertising and entertainment industries have long used sex, erotica, and nudity to attract attention and sell their products. Various forms of censorship have been tried over the decades, but there is always a tension between local community standards and the public's desire to be entertained. Pornography is difficult to define. When discussing "hard-core pornography" in *Jacobellis v. Ohio* (1964), U.S. Supreme Court Justice Potter Stewart memorably stated, "I know it when I see it."[66] Although everyone "knows" pornography when they see it, putting that knowledge into a legal definition has been difficult. Basically, pornography refers to "representations designed to arouse, and give sexual pleasure to those who read, see, hear, or handle them."[67] However, this definition is a moving target because the standards of pornography vary across jurisdictions and over time.

Deciding what is pornographic is a personal judgment. Everyone has different standards. As pornography publisher Al Goldstein phrased it, "Eroticism is what turns me on; pornography is what turns you on."[68] Such definitions are not useful guides because we can apply the definition only after experiencing the pornographic material, not before. We have to see the pornographic material first to "know it when we see it." The motion picture and television industries have been legislated to adopt labeling systems that warn potential viewers about the sexual content of their products, but comedy clubs,

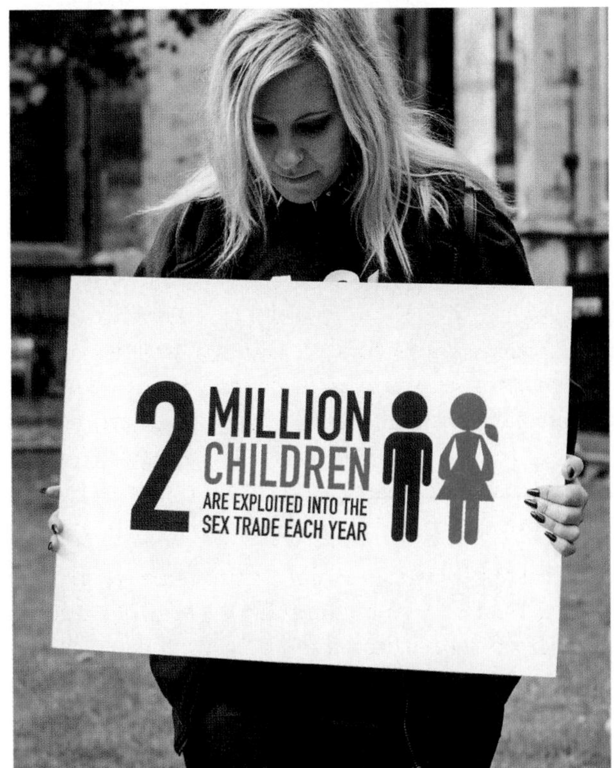

A woman holds a sign at a protest to raise awareness and funds for the fight against human trafficking and slavery. What can be done to combat the international sex trade?

magazines, and the Internet are virtually unregulated and contain something to offend everyone. Discussions of the purported harm of pornography must consider two issues.

- Morality and values. The morality of pornography is a contested and changing issue in American society. Some people believe that pornography weakens moral character. Many who oppose pornography believe that allowing the media to sell material of explicit sexual content makes the general public less respectful of what these opponents consider "decent" behavior. The availability of sexually explicit material on the Internet has prompted many people to urge that the Internet should be subject to the same decency standards required of other media.[69] Yet, no matter what laws might be implemented, there will always be those who argue that the laws do not go far enough.
- Pornography and violence. Many people concerned with women's rights contend that pornographic material dehumanizes women and girls and promotes violence against them. They argue that female pornography treats women's bodies only as objects of sexual desire and portrays women in a submissive and inferior way. Sexist, racist, or homophobic pornography caters to those who are stimulated by subjugation. These aspects of pornography raise questions about the role of pornography in rape, sexual abuse, and domestic violence. Many critics of pornography claim that female pornography is a way for men to maintain power over women and use that power in sexualized ways that demean not only women, but also, through its distorted portrayal of sex, all people.[70]

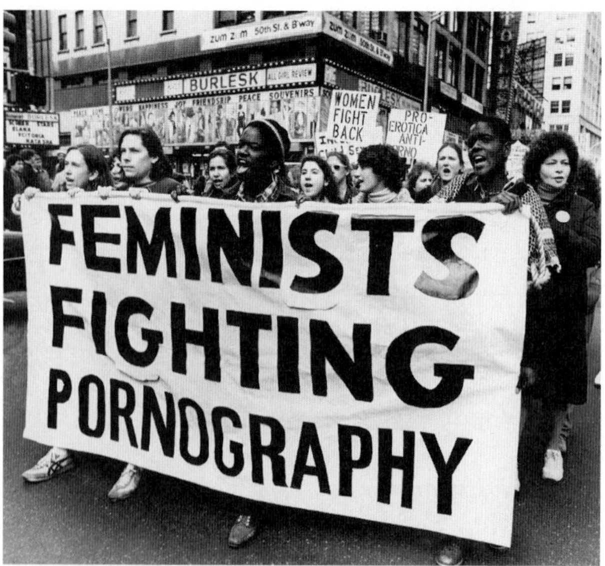

Pornography has been a controversial issue for a long time. These protesters marched through New York City's Times Square area in 1984 protesting pornography. What are the standards for deciding if something constitutes pornography?

At present, pornography is legal in the United States unless it meets the three-part Miller test of obscenity, which was developed in the Supreme Court ruling in *Miller v. California* (1973). According to the Miller test, material is obscene if it meets the following three standards.

- An average person, applying contemporary community standards, must find that the work, taken as a whole, appeals to the prurient (that which arouses sexual desire) interest.
- The work must depict or describe, in a patently offensive way, sexual conduct or excretory functions specifically defined by applicable state law.
- The work, taken as a whole, must lack serious literary and/or artistic, political, or scientific value.[71]

Often, the issue is not whether a work is obscene by *Miller's* standards, but the definition of the standards within the test. Who is an "average person"? What are "contemporary community standards"? Who decides what is "patently offensive"? Who determines whether material has "serious literary and/or artistic, political, or scientific value"?

The courts are still debating these definitions and, so far, have taken a fairly hands-off approach to the control of questionable material. In prior decades, the debate over what is obscene occurred over print material, including novels and magazines, and broadcast material, including film and television. Currently, the contested medium is the Internet. The Supreme Court held that the Communications Decency Act of 1996, which criminalized "certain Internet speech," was unconstitutional because, in part, less restrictive alternatives were available to protect juveniles from questionable Internet content. In *Ashcroft v. American Civil Liberties Union* (2004), a lower court concluded that the Child Online Protection Act (COPA), a federal law enacted to protect juveniles from "exposure to sexually explicit materials on the Internet," was not the least restrictive means required to protect juveniles. The Supreme Court later agreed because COPA "likely" violated the First Amendment.[72]

Sodomy

Until recently, consensual sodomy was illegal in the United States and proscribed by the Uniform Code of Military Justice.[73] Unlike forcible sodomy—a form of forcible rape, a violent criminal offense—consensual sodomy was a public-order offense. Until 1960, all states had anti-sodomy laws that were used mainly to prosecute homosexual sexual activity and, in rare cases, heterosexual activity. Until the U.S. Supreme Court in *Lawrence v. Texas* (2003) struck down a Texas law prohibiting consensual sex between same-sex adults, the states of Kansas, Missouri, Oklahoma, and Texas prohibited sodomy between same-sex couples, and Alabama, Florida, Idaho, Louisiana, Mississippi, North Carolina, South Carolina, Utah, and Virginia prohibited sodomy for all adults. Regardless, consensual sodomy is estimated to be committed rather often, with estimates of about 90 percent of American heterosexual couples regularly engaging in it.[74]

The history of U.S. anti-sodomy laws is often misunderstood. In *Lawrence*, the Supreme Court noted that homosexual sexual activities originally were not criminalized in the United States. The Court stated that early sodomy laws were meant to prevent non-procreative sex and were not "enforced against consenting adults acting in private," but instead against predatory individuals, such as those committing forcible or statutory rape or those engaging in sex with animals. Laws specifically targeting homosexuality did not develop until the mid-20th century.[75]

In *Robinson v. California* (1962), the Supreme Court held that a person could not be prosecuted for having a status or condition, such as homosexuality or drug addiction. But, like drug users, homosexuals were often presumed to be criminal because of the illegality of the private activities in which they were assumed to participate. However, states could prosecute individuals caught in the act of sodomy, just as they could prosecute individuals caught in the act of possessing or using drugs. The *Lawrence* decision lifted this presumption of criminality by decriminalizing an act that became commonly associated with homosexuality.[76]

Recall that criminology is the study of the making of laws, the breaking of laws, and society's reaction to the breaking of laws. In the case of sodomy, the relationship between the breaking of the law and society's reaction to the offense is interesting. Legal authorities admit that the breaking of sodomy laws—even between homosexuals—was rarely prosecuted; even when it was, the punishments were light. The lower court fined the two plaintiffs in *Lawrence v. Texas* $200 each for breaking Texas's anti-sodomy law. Justice Kennedy noted this in giving the Supreme Court's opinion in the case, stating, "[T]here is a pattern of non-enforcement with respect to consenting adults acting in private. The state of Texas admitted in 1994 that as of that date it had not prosecuted anyone under these circumstances."[77] From a social perspective, lack of enforcement could be interpreted to mean that society is perhaps ready for such laws to be changed or removed to reflect new attitudes.

PAUSE AND REVIEW

1. **In the past, how did states criminalize homosexuality?**
2. **Compare the different forms of prostitution in terms of their perceived harms to society.**

Gambling

LEARNING OBJECTIVE | 4

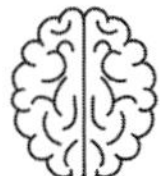

Why do many people wish to keep gambling, or certain forms of gambling, illegal in many jurisdictions?

The United States has an ambivalent attitude toward gambling. Throughout the country's history, gambling has been criminalized, tolerated, and embraced, often all at the same time. Many states that outlawed gambling in the past now use it as a major source of revenue. People who do not approve of casino gambling or going to a horse track might bet on a college basketball tournament in an office pool. There are so many legal and illegal opportunities to gamble in the United States that it can be considered a major form of entertainment, a rich source of government revenue, and a significant law enforcement and social problem.[78] For a look at the theoretical explanations of why people gamble, see Table 12.4.

Gambling includes more than the element of chance, as all forms of human behavior include uncertainty. Inherent in gambling is risk. Another defining feature of gambling is that the results are influenced by chance.[79] Some games are strictly based on chance. Playing a state lottery gives one little opportunity to affect the outcome. Aside from buying multiple lottery tickets, ideally, any person has as good of a chance as anyone else (very little in fact) of becoming a millionaire based on a dollar bet. Other games have an element of skill associated with them. One can improve the chances of winning

TABLE 12.4 Gambling and Criminological Theory

THEORY	EXPLANATION
Psychological Operant conditioning	Gambling works on the behavior principle of intermittent reinforcement. It only pays off some of the time, which makes it exciting, and, to some individuals, addicting. Treatment requires the gambler to understand the psychological principles behind the behavior.
Sociological Strain theory	Merton's strain theory would contend that gamblers are utilizing the adaptation of innovation. They embrace the cultural goal of amassing economic wealth but are unable or unwilling to employ the cultural means of hard work, thrift, and deferred gratification.
Sociological Subcultural theory	Gambling is a cultural norm in various subcultures. Animal fighting is shunned by the dominant culture but is an integral part of some subcultures. Just as gambling on a golf game is considered a way to make the sport more exciting in upper-class subcultures, raising and fighting pit bulls is attractive to others.

at casino blackjack by being aware of the rules of probability. However, casinos attempt to keep too much skill out of the game and do not allow gamblers to count cards to improve their odds of winning. So why does society frown on games of chance, and why is it illegal in many jurisdictions? There are several reasons.

- Gambling can divert people from productive work. When people think they can get rich easily by betting, they are less likely to work hard at getting an education, finding gainful employment, and saving for the future.
- Gambling has often been thought to weaken moral character. Those who gamble are thought to lack the moral fortitude to engage in family, religious, and social affairs in which concern for others and responsibility are important.
- Gambling can divert money from worthy endeavors. Whether it is a mother spending the grocery money on lottery tickets or a local government giving large tax breaks to attract a major casino, money associated with gambling produces little in terms of family security, community infrastructure, or a stable economy. Gambling sells an elusive hope of material gain for little effort and is thought to weaken, not strengthen, the financial conditions of those involved. An economic development consultant who assessed the effect of casinos on the local economies of cities involved in gambling development concluded, "[W]e're just rearranging dollars. . . . And the people who usually win, quite frankly, are the casino operations. The people who lose are the cultural activities in the city, the eating and drinking establishments in other parts of the city. . . . There's absolutely no net gain in terms of the economic impact from gamblers who are located within the immediate trade area of 50 miles."[80]
- Gambling can become addictive. The lure of quick, easy money can cause some people to bet compulsively with money they cannot afford to lose. Problem gamblers can become involved in illegal enterprises to attempt to compensate for their losses.
- Gambling brings unsavory people into the community. The argument can be made that crime follows gambling. Those who exploit gamblers, such as prostitutes, thieves, robbers, and loan sharks, start to appear in communities where there is gambling. The history of illegal gambling in the United States is replete with evidence of the influence of organized crime.[81]

Gambling proponents agree that these concerns are valid when taken to the extreme, but they argue that, for the most part, these claims are exaggerated. For every mother betting with the family's grocery money, there are many more who bet responsibly and for whom gambling is a form of entertainment and relaxation, much like going on a cruise or a vacation at the beach. Furthermore, gambling proponents claim that the jobs and businesses that gambling brings into a community, such as restaurants, gas stations, hotels, and banks, stimulate local economies. Although organized crime was a feature of illegal gambling in the past, it was involved precisely because the activity was illegal. Legalized gambling is a legitimate business, proponents say, and attracts those who employ honest and ethical business practices.

The moral and financial issues of gambling are subject to debate; however, illegal gambling has historically been considered a public-order offense and has been the focus of considerable attention by the criminal justice system. To understand why, we must look at the history of gambling in the United States.

A Brief History of Gambling

Moral objections to gambling are as old as the United States. England has a considerable history of gambling, and many colonists brought the practice with them. However, life in the colonies was precarious and harsh, and it demanded that all colonists carry their weight in being productive workers. In its first year of existence, Massachusetts Bay Colony outlawed dice, cards, and other games thought to produce idleness. The harsh winters and rampant disease made survival a daily battle. Colonists who frittered away their time on games of chance were considered to be a drain on resources.[82]

Other colonies had more liberal attitudes. The Dutch who settled New York saw gambling as commonplace. Gambling was also common in the southern colonies, where newly landed aristocrats owned large plantations worked by slaves. After the American Revolution, the new United States became more hostile toward gambling. In its 1885 ruling in *Irwin v. Williar*, the U.S. Supreme Court declared that debts incurred as part of gambling losses were void because the activity was illegal.[83] This meant that the courts would not enforce gambling laws, and winners had to use threats and violence to get their money. In some states, laws against gambling focused primarily on gambling operations and less heavily on individual gamblers. In other states, an individual gambler might lose the right to hold public office for five years.

Governments did not treat all forms of gambling in the same way. Betting on horse racing was viewed more favorably because the sport had implications for animal husbandry. Gambling encouraged horse breeders to improve equine genetics, which was considered to be beneficial to the horse industry.[84] Gambling gained its strongest toehold in Nevada, where it was legalized in 1869. Gambling licenses were expensive, and regulations prohibited gambling by minors and relegated games to back rooms out of public view. Although Nevada outlawed gambling from 1909 to 1931, it was the only state to allow casinos until New Jersey opened its first casinos in 1976.

Legal Gambling

Today, gambling is a common feature of the economy in many states. Every state except Utah and Hawaii has some form of legal gambling. Why are these two states the exception? First, Utah has a large religious demographic. The Mormons who initially settled in the state are still the state's most populous and most powerful group and have banned gambling for religious reasons. Hawaii has a different reason for not legalizing gambling. Many states have instituted lotteries to generate revenue, but Hawaii's chief form of revenue is tourism. Because Hawaii is such a desirable vacation destination, it has not needed gambling to make money.[85] Other states that once proscribed legalized gambling, such as Mississippi and Georgia, now allow casinos or state lotteries to raise money that may be used for infrastructure and education.

State lotteries are one of the most popular legal forms of gambling. States have relaxed their attitude toward gambling as a revenue source but tightly control who runs the programs. Unlike other forms of gambling in which private businesses can get into the game, state lotteries restrict this benefit to state government. This restriction allows for better regulation and control of legalized gambling and ensures that the state gets its cut because the state government does the actual accounting. State lotteries generate a lot of money, about $70 billion per year. Per capita spending ranged from $36 in North Dakota to $800 in Rhode Island. Although this is a great deal of money for states to take in, less than half actually goes to the states. The rest goes to the cost of running the lotteries and as payouts to the winners.[86]

In 2018, in *Murphy v. National Collegiate Athletic Association*, the Supreme Court overturned the federal prohibition on sports betting, thus allowing the states to offer sports betting much in the way that they offer lotteries.[87] For many people, pro and collegiate baseball, football, and basketball are attractive not so much for the excitement of the game, but for the excitement of betting on it. Major league sports have long had a delicate relationship with gambling. In the 1970s, national sport shows routinely provided viewers with the betting odds on major games. Today, there is still a relationship between these sports and the betting world. For instance, teams are required to report players' injuries or to list them as probable starters so that no inside information can be traded that would give some bettors an advantage.

Criminologists are interested in legal gambling because it demonstrates how public-order offenses reflect individual and community values; the ways that these values change over time; and the economic, social, and political pressures they incur. Legal gambling takes regulation out of the hands of law enforcement and gives that responsibility to administrative agencies. However, in cases of fraud or political corruption connected with legal gambling, law enforcement may once again become involved.[88]

Illegal Gambling

Despite the availability of so much legal gambling, people still risk their money and the possibility of getting arrested by gambling illegally. The reason for this risk has to do primarily with the patchwork availability of legal gambling, which many gamblers find insufficient to meet their desires. A state lottery might be fine for someone who wants a bit of entertainment, but it is purely a game of chance. There is no way for someone to excel at playing the lottery. You pay your money and take your chances. Some gamblers find casinos and traditional games dull and want to wager on something that involves not only chance, but also violence and extreme cruelty. For this reason, dog fighting and cock fighting have seen a resurgence in popularity (see Policy Implications).

Poker games, played for money, are illegal in many states. The game pits players against one another, and those with card skills and the ability to judge others can win. Hence, many people regard poker as more of a skill-based competition than a game of chance. This problem has been compounded by Internet poker in which the players are essentially anonymous and are

POLICY IMPLICATIONS

Dog Fighting and Crime

Gambling on animals is a centuries-old form of entertainment. Some of these sports, such as racing, have become mainstream and have regulatory bodies that ensure the animals' health and safety. Other forms, such as dog fighting, continue in the shadows of society.

According to the Humane Society of the United States, dog fighting is a competition in which dogs are bred, conditioned, and trained to fight each other. Fights can take place in locations from back alleys to specialized arenas. The dogs typically fight in a 14- to 20-square-foot pit and may last a few minutes or several hours. Both dogs may suffer injuries, including puncture wounds, lacerations, blood loss, and broken bones. The dogs usually do not fight to the death, but many dogs die of their injuries. Losing dogs are often discarded, killed, or executed as part of the spectacle.[89]

Dog fighting, which has been popular in the rural South for decades, has recently increased in popularity throughout the United States.[90] The betting pool at some fights can grow to $10,000 or more. A Baltimore, Maryland, animal rescue expert calls dog fighting "big sport, big-money betting."[91]

Dog fights concern law enforcement primarily because they attract a criminal subculture that also tends to be involved in drug-dealing, illegal gun sales, and illegal gambling.[92] A 2001–2004 study by the Chicago Police Department found that in 382 dog fighting cases, 59 percent of the owners were gang members and 86 percent had been arrested at least twice. A local police official in Ohio—who said that in all his department's dog fighting search warrants, drugs were found in every case but one—explained that dog fighting is an expensive activity that requires the kind of disposable income that drug-selling provides.[93]

Dog fighting is a felony in every state. The Animal Fighting Prohibition Enforcement Act of 2007 amended existing federal law to impose a fine and/or prison sentence of up to three years for "(1) sponsoring or exhibiting an animal in an animal fighting venture; (2) buying, selling, transporting, delivering, or receiving for purposes of transportation, in interstate or foreign commerce, any dog or other animal for participation in an animal fighting venture; and (3) using the mails or other instrumentality of interstate commerce to promote or further an animal fighting venture."[94]

THINK ABOUT IT

1. Discuss the reasons why dog fighting is a felony in all states. What is your opinion of the criminalization of dog fighting?

spread across many states and sometimes the world. Internet poker has been difficult to regulate, and minors can play undetected.[95]

The number and variety of illegal gambling opportunities are endless. From country club members betting on a golf game to little old ladies betting on their bridge game to sophisticated urban numbers games (a type of informal neighborhood lottery), illegal gambling is a persistent feature of American society. As law enforcement authorities attempt to police gambling offenses, they encounter an ambivalent attitude from citizens, a lack of resources from the government, and a growing problem with corruption and graft. As a result, law enforcement no longer tries to eliminate illegal gambling but simply seeks to keep it under some control so that it takes place out of public view and, to the extent possible, is unavailable to minors.

PAUSE AND REVIEW

1. **Why do some segments of society question the morality of gambling?**
2. **Why are some forms of gambling legal, whereas others are not?**

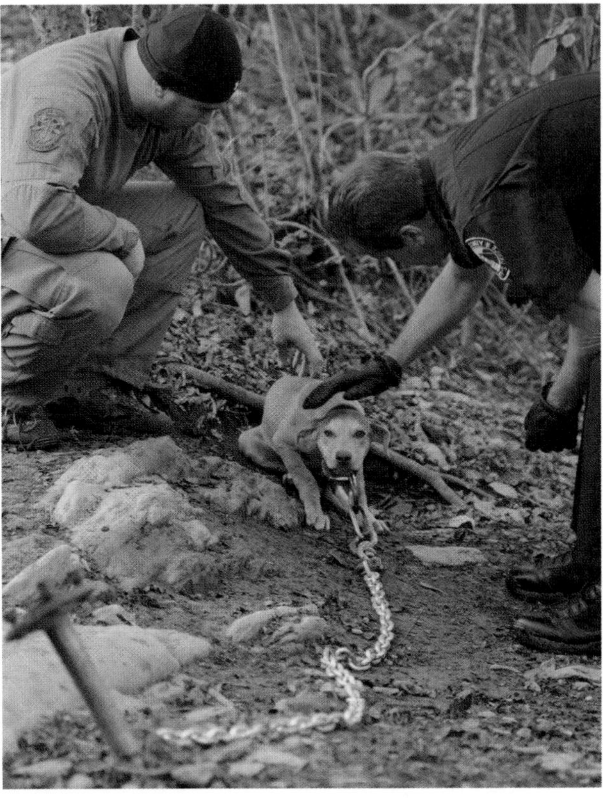

A dog is comforted by authorities after an early morning raid of a breeding operation in Kodak, Tennessee. What other types of gambling feature violence?

FOCUS ON ETHICS Your Little Brother Discovers Sex

You are home for spring break from school, and because you did not want to drag your laptop through the airport, you are using your brother's massive gaming computer to write a paper for your criminology class. This computer setup is fantastic with three large screens, a gaming mouse, and plenty of blinking lights. In fact, the whole computer room is distracting, and you have a hard time concentrating on your paper.

As you explore the software your brother has downloaded, you click on the browser history and discover, to your amazement, that your brother has been viewing pornography sites. When you open one site, the three giant computer screens blast out a video of group sex, graphic nudity, bondage, and sexual violence.

You are appalled by this video. You open several other links from the browser history and see more hardcore pornography. You call your boyfriend who is a psychology graduate student, and he tells you not to worry about it. He says all young boys go through a stage where they explore sex. He confesses that when he was your brother's age, he collected every issue of *Playboy* magazine he could find, and it was not for the articles.

On one hand you can appreciate what your boyfriend is saying, but the videos your brother is watching are not the soft-core variety, but rather violent and probably illegal because some of them feature what appear to be underage girls. You dearly love your little brother, but you fear what kind of man he will become if he continues to consume such pornographic violence.

What Do You Do?

1. Do nothing. Accept your boyfriend's opinion that every young man goes through this stage. Besides, you have snooped on your brother's computer's browsing history and invaded his privacy. To make an issue of this could affect your relationship with your brother forever. Remember, you are not his mom.
2. Tell your parents. Make them promise not to explode and confront your brother, which would expose you as a snitch. Perhaps together you can think of a reasonable way to address this concerning behavior.
3. Talk to your brother. Explain how the pornography he is viewing models violence and dominance. Tell him that if he wants to develop healthy relationships with women as he gets older, he needs to start viewing them as valuable individuals. This conversation could be the first real talk of values you have with him and may deepen your relationship. Or it could make him angry, humiliated, and distrustful of you.

Summary

LEARNING OBJECTIVE 1 Discuss why public-order offenses present the criminal justice system with perplexing dilemmas in dealing with offenders who have broken the law but do not believe they are harming society.	There is always a certain tension between laws and the people for two reasons. The first is that those who make the laws do not always act in everyone's best interests. In a country where the majority rules, it is inevitable that some people will believe that the law is unfavorable to their concerns. The second reason is that the values of individuals and communities are a moving target. As social and economic conditions change, so do values.
LEARNING OBJECTIVE 2 Discuss why the use and abuse of drugs are important to the study of criminology.	The use and abuse of drugs are important to the study of criminology for three reasons: drugs and alcohol influence behavior; substance abuse is related to other types of crime; and the war on drugs is difficult, dangerous, and costly.
LEARNING OBJECTIVE 3 Explain the basis of laws prohibiting prostitution, pornography, and sodomy.	Some people consider the purchase of sex to be an issue of personal freedom, whereas others consider it to be immoral. Currently, pornography is legal in the United States unless it meets the Miller test of obscenity. Sodomy was illegal in the United States until recently. Early sodomy laws were meant to prevent non-procreative sex and target predatory individuals.
LEARNING OBJECTIVE 4 Why do many people wish to keep gambling, or certain forms of gambling, illegal in many jurisdictions?	Gambling can divert people from productive work. Gambling has often been thought to weaken moral character. Gambling can divert money from worthy endeavors. Gambling can become addictive. Gambling brings unsavory people into the community.

Critical Reflections

1. **How can public-order offenses affect the lives of individuals not involved in these offenses?**
2. **Can you defend the principle that religious views of morality should be embedded in the criminal law?**
3. **Can you formulate a plan to legalize certain drugs that will have a good chance of keeping them away from juveniles?**
4. **How have sodomy laws changed to reflect society's evolving view of government control of sexual behaviors?**
5. **How has technology altered both the forms of gambling and the ability of the law to control gambling?**
6. **Why have societies tried to discourage gambling?**
7. **Does the existence of criminal sanctions for drug use, prostitution, and other public-order offenses reduce the amount and severity of these behaviors? Why or why not?**

Key Terms

decriminalization p. 331
legalization p. 331
pornography p. 333
prostitution p. 323
public-order offense p. 322
sodomy p. 333
victimless crime p. 323

Instant Recall Term

criminology (ch. 1)

Notes

1 Laura Klivans, "San Francisco's Newest Tool to Prevent Opioid Overdoses Tests Drugs, Starts Conversations," *KQED Science*, April 18, 2018, https://www.kqed.org/stateofhealth/363143/san-franciscos-newest-tool-to-prevent-opioid-overdoses-tests-drugs-starts-conversations. Accessed July 2018.

2 Centers for Disease Control and Prevention, "What Is Fentanyl?" https://www.cdc.gov/drugoverdose/opioids/fentanyl.html. Accessed July 2018.

3 Julien Levy, "Nightlife Lifeguards: How Your Bartender Is Saving Lives in NYC," *Thrillist New York*, June 28, 2018, https://www.thrillist.com/drink/new-york/fentanyl-laced-cocaine-problem-nyc-bartenders. Accessed July 2018.

4 New York State Department of Health, New York State's 911 Good Samaritan Law Protects You, https://www.health.ny.gov/diseases/aids/general/opioid_overdose_prevention/good_samaritan_law.htm. Accessed July 2018.

5 Bruce A. Jacobs, *Investigating Deviance: An Anthology* (Los Angeles: Roxbury Publishing, 2002). See Introduction, Part 1, "Constructing Deviance."

6 Robert F. Meier and Gilbert Geis, *Victimless Crime? Prostitution, Drugs, Homosexuality and Abortion* (Los Angeles: Roxbury Publishing, 1977).

7 Ethan A. Nadelmann, "The Case for Legalization," *Public Interest*, no. 2 (Summer 1988): 3–32.

8 Duane C. McBride and Clyde B. McCoy, "The Drug-Crime Relationship: An Analytical Framework," *Prison Journal* 73 (1993): 257–278.

9 Marianne Macy, *Working Sex: An Odyssey into Our Cultural Underworld* (New York: Carroll and Graf, 1996).

10 Nancy M. Petry, *Pathological Gambling: Etiology, Comorbidity, and Treatment* (Washington, D.C.: American Psychological Association, 2005).

11 D. Kirk Davidson, *Selling Sin: The Marketing of Socially Unacceptable Products* (Westport, CT: Praeger, 2003).

12 Najati Sayyid Ahmad Sanad, *The Theory of Crime and Criminal Responsibility in Islamic Law: Shari'a* (Chicago: University of Illinois at Chicago, 1991).

13 James Davidson Hunter, *American Evangelicalism: Conservative Religion and the Quandary of Modernity* (New Brunswick, N.J.: Rutgers University Press, 1983).

14 Edward Behr, *Prohibition: Thirteen Years that Changed America* (New York: Arcade Publishing, 1996).

15 LocalAlcoholLaws.com, Alcohol Laws in Atlanta, Georgia, http://localalcohollaws.com/index/1304000/ga/atlanta. Accessed July 2018.

16 Jonathan Finer, "Old Blue Laws Are Hitting Red Lights: Statutes Rolled Back as Anachronisms," *Washington Post*, December 4, 2004, A3.

17 Diana Fishbein, David Lozovsky, and Jerome H. Jaffe, "Impulsivity, Aggression, and Neuroendocrine Responses to Serotonergic Stimulation in Substance Abusers," *Biological Psychiatry* 25, no. 8 (April 15, 1989): 1049–1066.

18 Charles E. Faupel and Carl B. Klockars, "Drugs-Crime Connections: Elaborations from the Life Histories of Hard-Core Heroin Addicts," *Social Problems* 34, no. 1 (February 1987): 54–68.

19 WBAY "Woman Found Guilty in Runaway Meth and Human Trafficking Cases," June 25, 2018. http://www.wbay.com/content/news/Woman-found-guilty-in-runaway-meth-and-human-trafficking-cases-486484921.html.

20 Mark H. Moore and Mark A. R. Kleiman, "The Police and Drugs," *Perspectives on Policing* (Washington, D.C.: National Institute of Justice, Office of Justice Programs, 1989).

21 Radley Balko, "Jury Rules Against Family Subjected to SWAT Raid over Loose-Leaf Tea," *Washington Post*, December 19, 2017, https://www.washingtonpost.com/news/the-watch/wp/2017/12/19/jury-rules-against-family-subjected-to-swat-raid-over-loose-leaf-tea. Accessed July 2018. CNN, "Ex-Atlanta Officers Get Prison Time for Cover-Up in Deadly Raid," February 24, 2009, http://www.cnn.com/2009/CRIME/02/24/atlanta.police. Accessed June 2018.

22 William L. White, *Slaying the Dragon: The History of Addiction Treatment and Recovery in America* (Bloomington, Ind.: Chestnut Health Systems, 1998).

23 H. W. Brands, *The First American: The Life and Times of Benjamin Franklin* (New York: Anchor Books, 2000), 70–71.

24 Oakley Ray and Charles Ksir, *Drugs, Society and Human Behavior* (Boston: McGraw-Hill, 2004).

25 D. T. Courtwright, *Dark Paradise: Opiate Addiction in America Before 1940* (Cambridge, Mass.: Harvard University Press, 1982).

26 Ray and Ksir, *Drugs, Society and Human Behavior*.

27 Howard Wayne Morgan, *Drugs in America: A Social History, 1800–1980* (Syracuse, N.Y.: Syracuse University Press, 1981).

28 Frederick Allen, *Secret Formula: A History of the Coca-Cola Company* (New York: HarperCollins, 1994). James A. Inciardi, *The War on Drugs III* (Boston: Allyn & Bacon, 2002), 21.

29 Upton Sinclair, *The Jungle* (New York: Bantam, 1906/1981).

30 Morgan, *Drugs in America*.

31 Ray and Ksir, *Drugs, Society and Human Behavior*, 91.

32 *Webb v. United States* 249 U.S. 96 (1919); *United States v. Behrman* 258 U.S. 280, 289 (1922); *Linder v. United States*, 286 U.S. 5 (1925).

33 H. Westley Clark, "Office-Based Practice and Opioid-Use Disorders," *New England Journal of Medicine* 349, no. 10 (September 4, 2003): 928–930.

34 Jerome L. Himmelstein, *The Strange Career of Marijuana: Politics and Ideology of Drug Control in America* (Westport, Conn.: Greenwood Press, 1983).

35 Ray and Ksir, *Drugs, Society and Human Behavior*, 458–459.

36 Jennifer M. Cameron and Ronna J. Dillinger, "Narcotic Control Act," in *Encyclopedia of Drug Policy*, ed. James Hawdon and Mark Kleiman (Thousand Oaks, Calif.: Sage Publications, 2011), 543.

37 Jennifer L. Huck, "Omnibus Drug Abuse Act," in *Encyclopedia of Drug Policy*, ed. James Hawdon and Mark Kleiman (Thousand Oaks, Calif.: Sage Publications, 2011), 614.

38 Ray and Ksir, *Drugs, Society and Human Behavior*, 101–102.

39 Substance Abuse and Mental Health Services Administration, *Key Substance Use and Mental Health Indicators in the United States: Results from the 2016 National Survey on Drug Use and Health* (Rockville, Md.: Center for Behavioral Health Statistics and Quality, Substance Abuse and Mental Health Services Administration, 2017), 1. Available at https://www.samhsa.gov/data. Accessed July 2018.

40 Ibid., 15–20.

41 Bruce K. Alexander, "Alternatives to the War on Drugs," *Journal of Drug Issues* (20): 1–27.

42 Randy E. Barnett, "Curing the Drug-Law Addiction: The Harmful Side Effects of Legal Prohibition," in *Dealing with Drugs: Consequences of Government Control*, ed. Ronald Hamowy (Lexington, Mass.: D. C. Heath, 1987), 73–162.

43 Presidents' Commission on Organized Crime, *America's Habit: Drug Abuse, Drug Trafficking, and Organized Crime* (Washington, D.C.: U.S. Government Printing Office, 1986).

44 Rosa Maria Santana, "Drinking Blamed for Teen Death," *Chicago Tribune*, January 3, 1996, metro section.

45 David Corcoran, "Legalizing Drugs: Failures Spur Debate," *New York Times*, November 27, 1989, 9.

46 Susana Ferreira, "Portugal's Radical Drugs Policy Is Working. Why Hasn't the World Copied It?" *Guardian*, December 5, 2017, https://www.theguardian.com/news/2017/dec/05/portugals-radical-drugs-policy-is-working-why-hasnt-the-world-copied-it. Accessed June 2018.
47 Robert P. McNamara, *The Times Square Hustler: Male Prostitution in New York City* (Westport, Conn.: Praeger, 1994).
48 Edward L. Rubin, "Sex, Politics, and Morality," *William & Mary Law Review* 47, no. 1 (October 2005): 1–48.
49 Zoë Heller, "In Defense of Adulterers," *New Yorker*, December 18 and 25, 2017, https://www.newyorker.com/magazine/2017/12/18/in-defense-of-adulterers. Accessed July 2018.
50 Linda M. Rio, "Psychological and Sociological Research and the Decriminalization and Legalization of Prostitution," *Archives of Sexual Behavior* 20 (1991): 205–218.
51 Susan Brownmiller, *Against Our Will: Men, Women, and Rape* (New York: Simon & Schuster, 1975).
52 Harold R. Holzman and Sharon Pines, "Buying Sex: The Phenomenology of Being a John," *Deviant Behavior* 4 (1982): 111.
53 Scott Cunningham and Todd Kendall, "Prostitution, Hours, Job Amenities and Education," *Review of Economics of the Household* 15, no. 4, (2017): 1055–1080.
54 Charles H. McCaghy, Timothy A. Capron, J. D. Jamieson, and Sandra Harley Carey, *Deviant Behavior: Crime, Conflict, and Interest Groups*, 8th ed. (New York: Routledge, 2016), 383.
55 McNamara, *The Times Square Hustler*.
56 Eric W. Schrimshaw, Karolynn Siegel, and Étienne Meunier, "Venues Where Male Sex Workers Meet Partners: The Emergence of Gay Hookup Apps and Web Sites," *American Journal of Public Health* 107, no. 12 (2017): 1866–1867.
57 Julia O'Connell Davidson, *Prostitution, Power, and Freedom* (Ann Arbor: University of Michigan Press, 1998). See pp. 18–21, "Brothels as Business Enterprises."
58 "Police Break Up Prostitution Ring That Employed 200 Housewives, Career Women," *Daily Sentinel-Tribune* (Bowling Green, Ohio), August 23, 1983, 7.
59 McCaghy et al., *Deviant Behavior*, 382.
60 Carol Rambo Ronai and Carolyn Ellis, "Turn-Ons for Money: Interactional Strategies of the Table Dance," in *Investigating Deviance: An Anthology*, ed. Bruce A. Jacobs (Los Angeles: Roxbury Publishing, 2002), 273–288.
61 Paul K. Rasmussen, "Massage Parlors as a Sex-for-Money Game," in *The Sociology of Deviance*, ed. Jack D. Douglas (Boston: Allyn & Bacon, 194), 199–212.
62 Celia Williamson and Terry Cluse-Tolar, "Pimp-Controlled Prostitution: Still an Integral Part of Street Life," *Violence Against Women* 8, no. 9 (2002): 1074–1092.
63 Mary Gibson, "The State and Prostitution: Prohibition, Regulation, or Decriminalization?" in *History and Crime: Implications for Criminal Justice Policy*, ed. James A. Inciardi and Charles E. Faupel (Beverly Hills, Calif.: Sage Publications, 1980), 193–200.
64 R. Barri Flowers, *Runaway Kids and Teenage Prostitution: America's Lost, Abandoned, and Sexually Exploited Children* (Westport, Conn.: Praeger, 2001).
65 Nancy A. Wonders and Raymond Michalowski, "Bodies, Borders, and Sex Tourism in a Globalized World: A Tale of Two Cities—Amsterdam and Havana," *Social Problems* 48 (2001): 545–571.
66 *Jacobellis v. Ohio* 378 US 184 (1964).
67 Joseph W. Slade, *Pornography in America: A Reference Handbook* (Santa Barbara, Calif.: ABC-CLIO, 2000).
68 "Pornography: A Roundtable Discussion," *Harper's* (November 1984): 31–39, 42–45.
69 Ethel Quayle and Max Taylor, "Child Pornography and the Internet: Perpetuating a Cycle of Abuse," *Deviant Behavior* 23 (2002): 331–361.
70 Mimi H. Silbert and Ayala M. Pines, "Pornography and Sexual Abuse of Women," *Sex Roles* 10, nos. 11–12 (June 1984): 857–868.
71 *Miller v. California* 413 U.S. 15 (1973).
72 *Ashcroft v. American Civil Liberties Union* 542 U.S. 656 (2004).
73 In December 2013, President Barack Obama signed into law the National Defense Authorization Act for Fiscal Year 2014, which included a repeal of the ban on consensual sodomy found in Article 125 of the Uniform Code of Military Justice. Congress.gov, H.R.3304 - National Defense Authorization Act for Fiscal Year 2014, https://www.congress.gov/bill/113th-congress/house-bill/3304/text. Accessed June 2018.
74 Henry F. Fradella, "Legal, Moral, and Social Reasons for Decriminalizing Sodomy," *Journal of Contemporary Justice* 18, no. 3 (August 2002): 284.
75 *Lawrence v. Texas*, 539 U.S. 558 (2003).
76 Joseph J. Wardenski, "A Minor Exception? The Impact of *Lawrence v. Texas* on LGBT Youth," *Journal of Criminal Law and Criminology* 95, no. 4 (Summer 2005): 1363–1410.
77 *Lawrence v. Texas*, 539 U.S. 558 (2003).
78 Vicki Abt, James F. Smith, and Eugene Martin Christiansen, *The Business of Risk: Commercial Gambling in Mainstream America* (Lawrence: University Press of Kansas, 1985).
79 Nancy M. Petry, *Pathological Gambling: Etiology, Comorbidity, and Treatment* (Washington, D.C.: American Psychological Association, 2005), 4.
80 Robert Goodman, *The Luck Business* (New York: The Free Press, 1995), 32–33.
81 Davidson, *Selling Sin*, 77–83.
82 Edward A. Morse and Ernest P. Goss, *Governing Fortune: Casino Gambling in America* (Ann Arbor: University of Michigan Press, 2007), 3.
83 *Irwin v. Williar*, 110 U.S. 499 510 (1885).
84 Morse and Goss, *Governing Fortune*, 6.
85 KITV, "HPD Stepping Up Gambling Laws in Hawaii," October 12, 2017, http://www.kitv.com/story/36426584/hpd-stepping-up-gambling-laws-in-hawaii. Accessed June 2018.
86 Derek Thompson, "Lotteries: America's $70 Billion Shame," *Atlantic*, May 11, 2015, https://www.theatlantic.com/business/archive/2015/05/lotteries-americas-70-billion-shame/392870. Accessed June 2018.
87 David Purdum and Ryan Rodenbert, "Can I Gamble Legally on Sports Now?" *ESPN*, May 14, 2018, http://www.espn.com/chalk/story/_/id/22515075/gambling-answers-your-sports-betting-questions-post-supreme-court-ruling. Accessed July 2018.
88 Charles T. Clotfelter and Phillip J. Cook, *Selling Hope: State Lotteries in America* (Cambridge, Mass.: Harvard University Press, 1989).
89 American Society for the Prevention of Cruelty to Animals, Dogfighting, https://www.aspca.org/animal-cruelty/dogfighting. Accessed June 2018. Kathleen Hopkins, "Dog Fighting: Asbury Park Man Who Threw Dog in Trash Sentenced," *app.*, April 18, 2018, https://www.app.com/story/news/local/courts/2018/04/18/prison-asbury-man-who-engaged-dogs-interstate-fighting-ring/527920002. Accessed June 2018.
90 *Spectrum News* (Central, N.C.), "Officials Bust Huge Dog Fighting Operation in Orange County, " April 17, 2018, http://spectrumlocalnews.com/nc/triangle-sandhills/news/2018/04/17/man-charged-with-dog-fighting-in-orange-county. Bill Burke, "Once Limited to the Rural South, Dogfighting Sees a Cultural Shift," *Virginian-Pilot*, June 17, 2007, https://pilotonline.com/news/local/crime/article_e8dfa7d4-619b-5bd7-a10c-39910df01fbe.html. Accessed June 2018.
91 Childs Walker, "Dogfight 'Culture' Reaches to Baltimore," *Baltimore Sun*, June 1, 2007, http://articles.baltimoresun.com/2007-06-01/news/0706010138_1_animal-control-dogfighting-animal-advocates/2. Accessed June 2018.
92 U.S. Department of Justice, "Federal Agents Seize 63 Dogs from Suspected Dog Fighting Ring, " https://www.justice.gov/opa/pr/federal-agents-seize-63-dogs-suspected-dog-fighting-ring. Accessed June 2018.
93 John Futty, "Dogfight Raids Not Just about Animals: Crackdown Turns Up Many Other Crimes," *Columbus Dispatch*, April 2, 2007.
94 Congress.gov, H.R.137—Animal Fighting Prohibition Enforcement Act of 2007, https://www.congress.gov/bill/110th-congress/house-bill/137.
95 Mark Griffiths and Richard T. A. Wood, "Youth and Technology: The Case of Gambling, VideoGame Playing, and the Internet," in *Gambling Problems in Youth: Theoretical and Applied Perspectives*, ed. Jeffrey L. Derevensky and Rina Gupta (New York: Kluwer Academic/Plenum Publishers, 2004), 101–120. Red Chip Poker, When Will Online Poker Be Legal in My State?, https://redchippoker.com/when-will-online-poker-be-legal-in-my-state. Accessed July 2018.

PART IV

Responding to Crime

FOR INFORMATION
The FBI and NYPD are seeking the public's assistance in the investigation into the terrorist act that occurred in Lower Manhattan earlier today. The public is urged to share any images or videos that could assist in the investigation to the FBI link: www.fbi.gov/nyctribeca.

Terrorism and Hate Crime

FEATURES

Society's values are frustrated by hate. How can the criminal justice system counter terrorism and hate crimes?

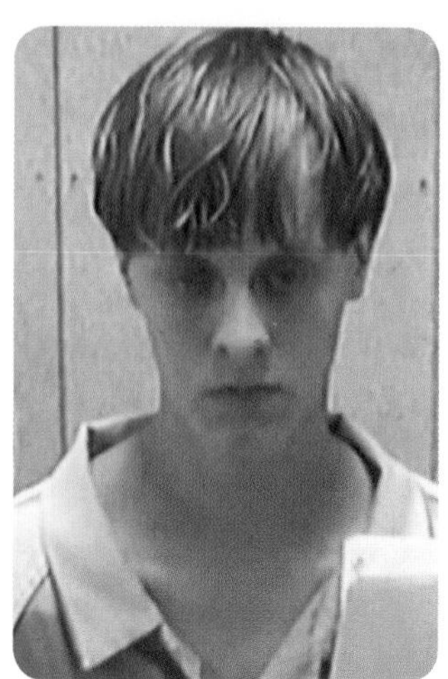

Dylann Roof at his video arraignment. Are Roof's actions a hate crime or terrorism?

On June 17, 2015, a 21-year-old white man attended a Bible study class at the Emanuel African Methodist Episcopal Church in Charleston, South Carolina. After sitting quietly for an hour, he stood up and announced he was there to shoot black people. He pulled out a handgun and shot to death nine worshipers. When one person asked him to stop shooting, the man said, "No, you've raped our women, and you're taking over the country. I have to do what I have to do." The man, Dylann Roof, later told the FBI that his motive was to spark a race war.[1]

On his website, Roof posted pictures of himself posing at sites connected to the Confederacy, armed with a pistol, and standing on and burning an American flag. On his site, he wrote:

> I have no choice. I am not in the position to, alone, go into the ghetto and fight. I chose Charleston because it is the most historic city in my state, and at one time had the highest ratio of blacks to whites in the country. We had no skinheads, no real KKK, no one doing anything but talking on the Internet. Well someone has to have the bravery to take it to the real world, and I guess that has to be me.[2]

Roof, who acted as his own attorney in federal court, was convicted on 33 counts, including two dozen that are federal hate crimes.[3] In January 2017, Roof was sentenced to death, becoming the first person to face execution for a federal hate crime.[4]

Crimes of Fear and Hate

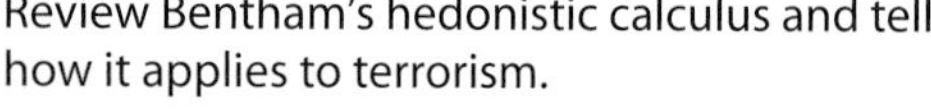

LEARNING OBJECTIVE | 1

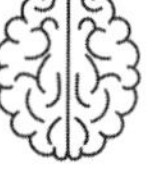

Review Bentham's hedonistic calculus and tell how it applies to terrorism.

Although there is much disagreement on the exact differences between terrorism, both domestic and international, and hate crime, it is easy to see how they are alike. Both terrorism and hate crime rely on the perpetrator's hatred and ability to cause fear.

Many, if not most, criminal offenses are economic in nature.[5] They occur because the offender wants money, resources, or items of value. Some offenses are "crimes of passion." They occur because the offender has lost control of his or her emotions. This is true of many domestic violence offenses and homicides. Other criminal offenses are committed by offenders who are mentally ill or intellectually disabled. Finally, many criminal offenses are designated as such because they disturb other members of society, such as drug usage, prostitution, and gambling. However, terrorism and hate crimes are committed because the perpetrators want to create as much fear as possible or assuage their own fear and hate of others. Perpetrators typically expend wealth, resources, and effort to commit acts of terrorism and hate crime. Other than affecting their targets if they are successful, these perpetrators receive nothing more in return beyond ostracism, imprisonment, and death.

In light of Jeremy Bentham's **hedonistic calculus**, it seems that terrorists and hate-crime perpetrators are not doing the math right. Dylann Roof, from the opening case, had nothing material to gain from murdering nine people. He imagined that he was striking a blow for some racial cause cooked up from various Internet rants. He was also misguided enough to insist that he would be pardoned in a few years when the country was taken over by white nationalists and that he would be made a governor.[6] By Roof's calculus, he was not going to suffer long for his actions. It is tempting to pin Roof's beliefs on mental disability. After all, there was evidence that he suffered from anxiety disorder, depression, and autism. However, Roof showed enough presence of mind that a federal judge allowed him to conduct his own defense at the penalty phase of his trial.[7]

Were Roof's actions terrorism, hate crime, or simply the actions of a deranged person? How is Roof different from someone like Omar Mateen, who in 2016 killed 49 people at an Orlando, Florida, nightclub in the name of the Islamic State terror group (aka ISIL)?[8] How are Roof and Mateen different from James Holmes who killed 12 people in an Aurora, Colorado, theater in 2012 and told police he was the comic book villain The Joker?[9] These are the questions this chapter will try to shed some light on.

Hate Crime

LEARNING OBJECTIVE 2

Define hate crime.

LEARNING OBJECTIVE 3

Briefly review the history of hate-crime legislation.

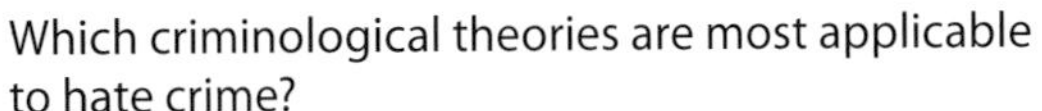

LEARNING OBJECTIVE 4

Which criminological theories are most applicable to hate crime?

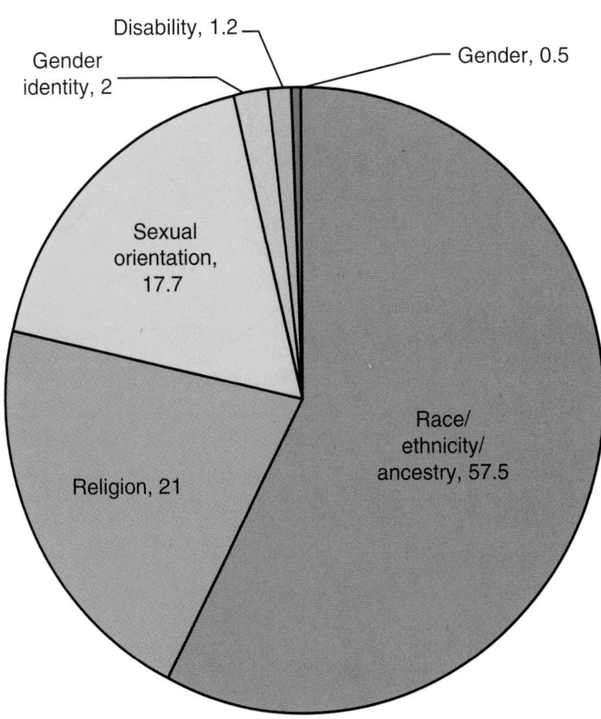

FIGURE 13.1 Motivations for Single-Bias Hate Crime Incidents

In 2016, most of the 6,063 single-bias incidents were motivated by bias against race, ethnicity, or ancestry, with religion and sexual orientation placing a distant second and third, respectively.

THINK ABOUT IT

Give some reasons why most recorded hate-crime incidents are motivated by race, ethnicity, or ancestry.

Source: Federal Bureau of Investigation, 2016 Hate Crime Statistics, Single-bias Incidents, https://ucr.fbi.gov/hate-crime/2016/topic-pages/incidentsandoffenses. Accessed October 2018.

A **hate crime** is a criminal offense like murder or rape, but with an added element of bias (see Figure 13.1 for the most common motivations for some hate crimes). The FBI collects statistics under the definition of hate crime as a "criminal offense against a person or property motivated in whole or in part by an offender's bias against a race, religion, disability, sexual orientation, ethnicity, gender, or gender identity." Although the FBI investigates some hate crimes, most hate-crime cases are investigated at the state and local levels.[10]

Not every criminal offense in which the perpetrator is biased is a hate crime. Motivation is subjective, so it is sometimes difficult to be certain whether a criminal offense resulted from offender bias. Ideally, an agency reports an incident as a hate crime only when an investigation reveals enough evidence to lead "a reasonable and prudent person" to conclude that the offense was motivated by the bias of the offender(s).[11]

Of the 15,254 law enforcement agencies that participated in the FBI's Hate Crime Statistics Program in 2016, 1,776 reported 6,121 hate-crime incidents involving 7,321 offenses.[12] According to the National Crime Victimization Survey (NCVS), the rate of violent hate-crime victimization in 2015 was 0.7 hate crimes per 1,000 persons age 12 or older, a rate that is not significantly different from 2004.[13] However, 2015 marked the first year that more victimizations were reported to police than were not reported to police (see Figure 13.2). The most common reason that victims gave for not reporting was that the victimization was settled another way, such as privately or through a person who was not a member of law enforcement.[14] Finally, according to the NCVS, most violent hate victimizations occurred in the West, whereas the South reported the lowest percentage.[15]

For the NCVS to classify an offense as a hate crime, the victim must report at least one of three types of evidence that the act was motivated by hate: the offender used hate language; the offender left

Instant Recall from Chapter 4 **hedonistic calculus**—A method proposed by Jeremy Bentham in which criminal offenders calculate the worth of breaking the law by estimating the positive consequences versus the possible negative consequences.

hate crime—A criminal offense like murder or rape, but with an added element of bias.

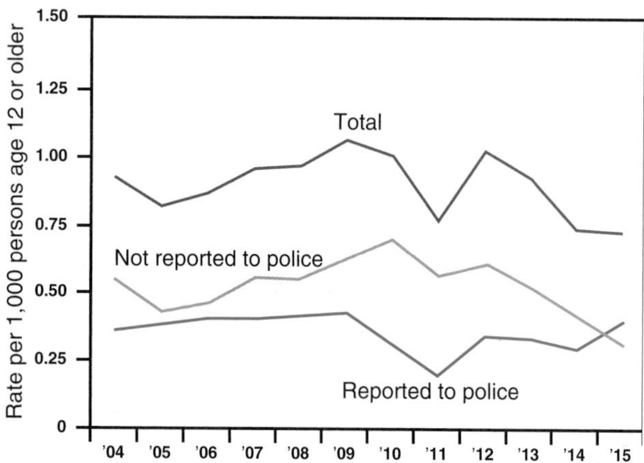

FIGURE 13.2 Violent Hate Crime Victimizations

Until recently, most hate crimes were not reported to police.

THINK ABOUT IT

Why are more people reporting hate crimes to police?

Source: Madeline Masucci and Lynn Langton, Hate Crime Victimization, 2004–2015 *(Washington, D.C.: U.S. Department of Justice Office of Justice Programs Bureau of Justice Statistics, 2017), 1. Available at https://www.bjs.gov/index.cfm?ty=pbdetail&iid=5967. Accessed July 2018. Bureau of Justice Statistics, National Crime Victimization Survey, 2004–2015.*

behind hate symbols; or police investigators confirmed that the incident was hate crime. From 2011 to 2015, most victims have cited the use of hate language as evidence of a hate crime.

About 90 percent of the hate crimes reported in the NCVS involved violence, and about a third of these were serious violent offenses: rape or sexual assault, robbery, and aggravated assault.[16] In contrast, about 45 percent of the hate crimes that were reported to the UCR as crimes against persons were offenses involving intimidation. Another 36 percent were simple assault, and nearly 19 percent were aggravated assault. Only nine hate crimes were murders, and 24 were rapes.[17] A reason for this divergence is that the NCVS only records hate crimes reported by individuals, while the UCR records hate crimes committed against businesses, religious institutions, other organizations, and society. Also, the surveys measure different types of criminal offenses: the UCR records statistics on homicide and vandalism, while the NCVS does not.[18]

Hate Crime and the Law

Early on the morning of November 13, 1988, Ken Mieske, also known as "Ken Death," and two friends, Kyle Brewster and Steve Strasser, were leaving a party in Portland, Oregon. The three men were neo-Nazi Skinheads who spent most of their time handing out racist pamphlets and beating up people.[19]

The three were driving down the street when they spotted Mulugeta Seraw, a young man who had immigrated from Ethiopia to attend graduate school at Portland State University. Seraw had been dropped off at his apartment by two friends, who were also from Africa. He was chatting with them while standing outside his friend's car, which was parked in the middle of the narrow street.[20]

Mieske, Brewster, and Strasser pulled up and screamed at the men to move before leaping from their car to smash the other car's windows with their boots and a baseball bat. During the skirmish, Mieske struck Seraw twice on the head with the bat, toppling Seraw. Seraw was on the ground when Mieske took a final swing, crushing Seraw's head on the pavement.[21]

All three Skinheads pleaded guilty to Seraw's murder. Mieske was sentenced to life in prison. He died in 2011 at the age of 45 from complications of hepatitis C.[22] Kyle Brewster served 20 years in prison.[23] Steve Strasser served six years.[24]

State legislatures began writing hate-crime laws in the 1980s; Oregon was the first state to enact these laws in 1981.[25] The Seraw case helped to galvanize other states and the federal government to begin passing laws to deal with hate crime, and by 1991 at least 32 states had hate-crime laws.[26] (Currently, every state but Georgia, Indiana, Utah, and Wyoming has some form of hate-crime legislation.[27]) The first federal law regarding hate crime was the 1990 Hate Crime Statistics Act, which required the FBI to record hate-crime statistics in the UCR. Hate crime as a criminal act was not specified in the federal law until 2009 with the Matthew Shepard and James Byrd Jr. Hate Crimes Prevention Act (see Table 13.1).[28]

Basically, hate-crime laws criminalize attacks against people or entities (businesses, etc.) because of a "state of being" that falls into a specified category. Depending on the state, these categories may include race, color, religion, national origin, ethnicity, gender, gender identity, sex, disability, and sexual orientation. For a hate crime to be considered as such, the victim must perceive that he or she was targeted for being in one of these categories. It is not enough that the perpetrator has actual or perceived hatred for the victim. In fact, an offender does not even have to hate the victim in the customary sense of the word. More accurate words may be "**prejudice**" or "**bias**," but even those definitions are problematic.[29] Thus, a precise, academic definition of "hate crime" is still being debated, but in popular

TABLE 13.1 Hate-Crime Laws

The Matthew Shepard and James Byrd Jr. Hate Crimes Prevention Act of 2009	The Shepard–Byrd Act makes it a federal crime to willfully cause bodily injury, or attempt to do so using a dangerous weapon, because of the victim's actual or perceived race, color, religion, or national origin. The Act also extends federal hate-crime prohibitions to crimes committed because of the actual or perceived religion, national origin, gender, sexual orientation, gender identity, or disability of any person, only where the crime affected interstate or foreign commerce or occurred within federal special maritime and territorial jurisdiction. The Shepard–Byrd Act is the first statute allowing federal criminal prosecution of hate crimes motivated by the victim's actual or perceived sexual orientation or gender identity.
Criminal Interference with Right to Fair Housing	This statute makes it a crime to use, or threaten to use force to interfere with housing rights because of the victim's race, color, religion, sex, disability, familial status, or national origin.
Damage to Religious Property, Church Arson Prevention Act	This statute prohibits the intentional defacement, damage, or destruction of religious real property because of the religious nature of the property, where the crime affects interstate or foreign commerce, or because of the race, color, or ethnic characteristics of the people associated with the property. The statute also criminalizes the intentional obstruction by force, or threat of force of any person in the enjoyment of that person's free exercise of religious beliefs.
Violent Interference with Federally Protected Rights	This statute makes it a crime to use, or threaten to use force to willfully interfere with any person because of race, color, religion, or national origin and because the person is participating in a federally protected activity, such as public education, employment, jury service, travel, or the enjoyment of public accommodations, or helping another person to do so.
Conspiracy Against Rights	This statute makes it unlawful for two or more persons to conspire to injure, threaten, or intimidate a person in any state, territory, or district in the free exercise or enjoyment of any right or privilege secured to him or her by the Constitution or the laws of the United States.

Source: The United States Department of Justice, Hate Crime Laws, https://www.justice.gov/crt/hate-crime-laws. Accessed July 2018.

discussions of the matter, "hate crime" is the term that has stuck.

For example, imagine a dispute between two neighbors, Smith and Jones. Smith and Jones hate each other. Smith's sprinkler drenched Jones's lawn and muddied the grass. Jones now refuses to clean up after his dog. In a showdown, Jones strikes Smith. When the police show up, both Smith and Jones affirm to the police that they do indeed hate each other, and each wishes the other would just move. Despite all this lurking hate, none of this constitutes a hate crime.

This is an important distinction. An important thing to remember about hate crimes is that by themselves, hate or prejudice is not criminal. A hate crime requires a **predicate offense** that is a crime under any circumstances, such as murder or arson. In the example, Jones did batter Smith, which is a criminal offense. However, no hate crime can be charged because Jones was not motivated to batter Smith for any categorical reason that is specified in their state's hate-crime law.

Hate-crime legislation is often criticized because it is difficult for prosecutors to prove "hateful" motives.[30] Another concern is that hate-crime legislation encourages people to think of themselves as members of specific groups, not as members of a larger society.[31] Hate-crime legislation, in effect, declares that some groups deserve more and better legal protection than others.[32] Another question that is often asked is why are regular criminal statutes not enough to prosecute

---

prejudice—A disparaging opinion that is not based on logic or actual experience with the subject of the disparagement.

bias—Hostile feelings or opinions, usually unreasonable, about a social group or class.

predicate offense—A criminal offense that occurs as part of another criminal offense or complex of offenses.

hateful offenders? After all, for example, a **battery** is a battery. A person who is beaten up because the offender hates homosexuals is in just as much pain as a person who is beaten up in a bar fight because everyone was drunk. A final concern is that hate-crime laws do not deter. In the Mulugeta Seraw case, Oregon's hate-crime legislation had been in effect for seven years. It did not stop Ken Mieske from killing Seraw while screaming racial slurs. (This observation is especially interesting because it is often used as an argument against capital punishment. The death penalty, critics say, is not going to deter anyone who is violent enough or deranged enough to commit a capital offense.)

Proponents of hate-crime laws note that they allow prosecutors to add aggravating factors to a charge. An offender who injures a victim in a bar fight may receive less than a year in jail, if that. An offender who commits battery because he is motivated by hatred of persons in a specified category may spend much longer than a year behind bars. Also, hate-crime legislation typically allows offenders to be sued for civil rights infringements. Mulugeta Seraw's estate won a $12.5 million verdict against infamous Skinhead organizer Tom Metzger, which bankrupted Metzger's White Aryan Resistance organization.[33]

Proponents of hate-crime legislation argue that there is a good reason to toughen the penalties of hate-crime perpetrators. The commission of criminal offenses against categories of people tears society apart in a way that non-hate criminal offenses do not because they target people for a state of being, not just for economic reasons. For example, a victim whose house is burgled can install an alarm system, move to a safer neighborhood, or get a mean dog. Also, chances are, there is only one burglar in the neighborhood, and his motive is probably economic. If he is caught and incarcerated, the burglaries stop.

A person whose home is targeted for vandalism because of her ethnicity, sex, or gender, however, cannot move away from these statuses. A new security system will not make her any safer because she cannot change or shed the attributes that are making her a target. She is likely to be targeted in her home or wherever she goes by any number of people who are motivated to attack her because of her ethnicity, sex, or gender. She is not safe anywhere she goes. The desire to break the law in a way solely to hurt people, even their feelings, is a desire to hurt society. It is a strike at the social order, and in this way it is related to domestic terrorism.[34]

Hate Crime and Criminological Theory

Which criminological theories are most applicable to hate crime? Because the concept of hate crime is so new—there is not even agreement on what hate crime is—few criminological theories have been applied to the concept. From the classical school, there is rational choice theory. Hate-crime perpetrators target certain groups for crime and violence because they want to. They have done some sort of calculus and have come up with an answer that involves attacking a victim for their state of being or membership in some group. Perhaps the violence is thought to achieve a goal, that is, if the perpetrator(s) make(s) enough of "those kind of people" afraid, then they will leave the area or at least be too frightened to be visible. In this way, hate-crime perpetrators have much in common with terrorists in that they are trying to achieve some sort of political goal.

A positivist theory that is applicable to hate crime is **strain theory**.[35] Hate-crime perpetrators may conceive of some social groups as blocking their access to the goals required to be perceived as successful in society. An example would be the complaint that "foreigners" are entering the country and taking away the best jobs and scholarships in the universities. In the mind of the hate-crime perpetrator, she or he is blocked from wealth and education because all the access has been taken away by groups of "others" who are given special privileges solely because of their "otherness." Efforts by employers and higher education to enhance opportunities for women, people of color, people with disabilities, and so on are evidence of this "conspiracy."

Several critical theories of criminology can also be applied to hate crimes. Critical race theory, feminist theory, and theories dealing with alternative lifestyles can help explain why hate crimes happen and what their effect is on victims. Of particular interest in dealing with theories of hate crimes is the concept of **intersectionality**. Individuals who possess multiple attributes that have historically been discriminated against (such as being black and gay) are likely to experience increased victimization.[36] Intersectionality involves not only sex, gender, and race, but also disabilities.[37] For example, disabled women are reported to be up to five times more likely to experience sexual violence than disabled men or women who are not disabled (see Figure 13.3 for a detailed discussion of criminal offenses against persons with disabilities).[38]

Critical theories critique the way dominant power groups (particularly white males) use their privileged status in society to maintain a status quo based on the subjugation of less powerful groups. Critical criminologists have expanded the scope of feminist criminology to reexamine how gender and race have been under-emphasized as significant factors in the relationship between social inequalities and crime.[39] These critical theories play an important role in highlighting the part that hate plays in the victimization of vulnerable groups.

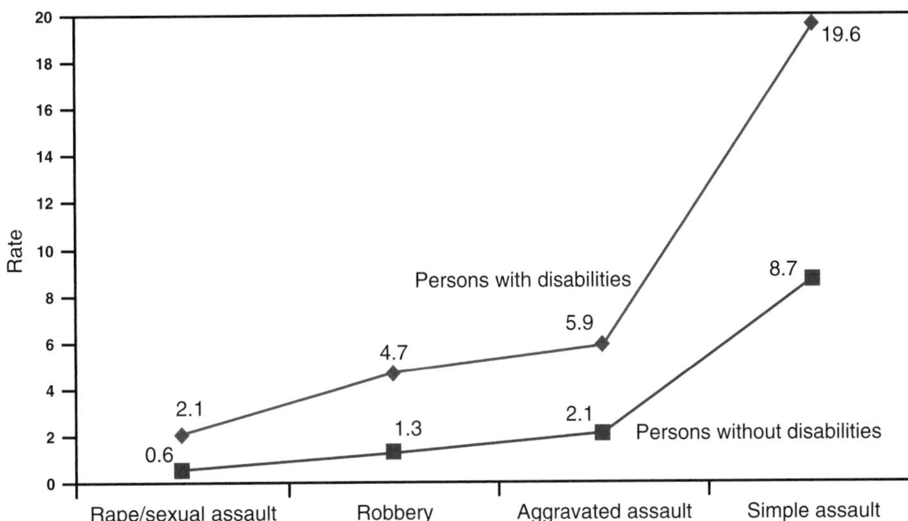

FIGURE 13.3 Rate of Violent Victimization Against Persons With and Without Disabilities

The rate of violent victimization against persons with disabilities is 2.5 times the rate for persons without disabilities.

THINK ABOUT IT

Can you think of reasons that the simple assault rate is so much higher for persons with disabilities than for persons without?

Source: Erika Harrell, Crime Against Persons with Disabilities, 2009–2015—Statistical Tables, *Table 2 (Washington, D.C.: U.S. Department of Justice Office of Justice Programs Bureau of Justice Statistics, 2017), 3. Available at https://www.bjs.gov/index.cfm?ty=pbdetail&iid=5986. Accessed July 2018.*

PAUSE AND REVIEW

1. **When did the states begin writing hate-crime laws? Why?**
2. **What do hate-crime laws do?**
3. **Name some criminological theories that are applicable to hate crime.**

Terrorism

LEARNING OBJECTIVE 5

Give the U.S. government's definition of terrorism. Give the four components of Combs's definition of terrorism.

Defining **terrorism** is difficult because the definition varies depending on who is defining the term. The U.S. government defines terrorism as "premeditated, politically motivated violence perpetrated against non-combatant targets by subnational groups or clandestine agents."[40]

The ambiguity in determining exactly what terrorism is resides in the fact that terrorism is a unique problem because it uses violence or the threat of violence to try to establish control over the lives of others. Depending on one's position and viewpoint, it is possible for reasonable individuals to observe the same behavior and to evaluate it differently. Many people and organizations have developed definitions of terrorism, but in our examination of terrorism, we will use the one created by political scientist Cindy C. Combs because it acknowledges that terrorism must attract attention to be effective. According to Combs, terrorism is "a synthesis of war

Instant Recall from Chapter 10 **battery**—Physical contact with the intent to do harm.

Instant Recall from Chapter 6 **classical strain theory**—The idea that people who experience anger and frustration when they cannot achieve cultural goals through legitimate means try to achieve these goals through illegitimate means.

Instant Recall from Chapter 6 **general strain theory**—Agnew's revision of classical strain theory identifies three major types of strain: failure to achieve goals, the loss of positive stimuli, and the gain of negative stimuli.

Instant Recall from Chapter 8 **intersectionality**—A term referring to the intersections of two or more social categorizations such as race, class, color, gender, age, and sex and the added challenges of discrimination faced by individuals at those intersections.

terrorism—Violence perpetrated against civilians by political groups for the purpose of drawing attention to their cause.

and theater, a dramatization of the most proscribed kind of violence—that which is perpetrated on innocent victims—played before an audience in the hope of creating a mood of fear, for political purposes."[41] Combs's definition has four components.

- The use of violence or the threat of violence. Terrorist activities can range from assassination and bombings to other forms of violence that strike at the state. Once a credible possibility of terrorism has been established, the mere threat of it is enough to frighten people and cause them to change their behavior. Although airplane hijackings are infrequent, countries around the world have instituted elaborate and expensive precautions that inconvenience airline employees and passengers.[42]
- A political dimension. Terrorism can be distinguished from many types of crime because its goal is to change the policies of formal social institutions, such as corporations and governments, as well as informal institutions, such as cultures and norms. The political aims of terrorists who have a religious motivation can range from trying to bring down a government to attempting to enforce specific dress codes, dietary habits, and access to places of worship.[43]
- The killing of innocent people. Terrorists often strike at entire populations rather than just government leaders. People who have little control over the issues that terrorists are concerned with, or even little knowledge of the terrorists' grievances, are targets. For instance, many of the victims of the 1993 bombing of the World Trade Center were completely unaware of the Middle East terrorists' concerns. When Timothy McVeigh set off a truck bomb outside the Murrah Federal Building in Oklahoma City that killed 168 people, including many children in a day-care center located in the building, he referred to the casualties as "collateral damage."[44]
- Symbolic meaning. The targets of the September 11, 2001, attacks were selected because of their symbolic meaning. The World Trade Center represented the global economy, and the Pentagon was a symbol of U.S. military power. The fourth airplane that crashed in a field in Pennsylvania is suspected to have been targeted at either the White House or the U.S. Capitol. Such targets are now protected by multiple layers of security, forcing terrorists to either improve their techniques in delivering their acts of violence or choose more vulnerable targets.

Combs's definition allows us to consider a range of behaviors and to distinguish terrorism from other crime. However, we must always be aware that the term "terrorism" is pejorative. This means that it is loaded with negative and derogatory meanings and that we distinguish between similar behaviors committed by individuals who have different motivations, grievances, or social standing.

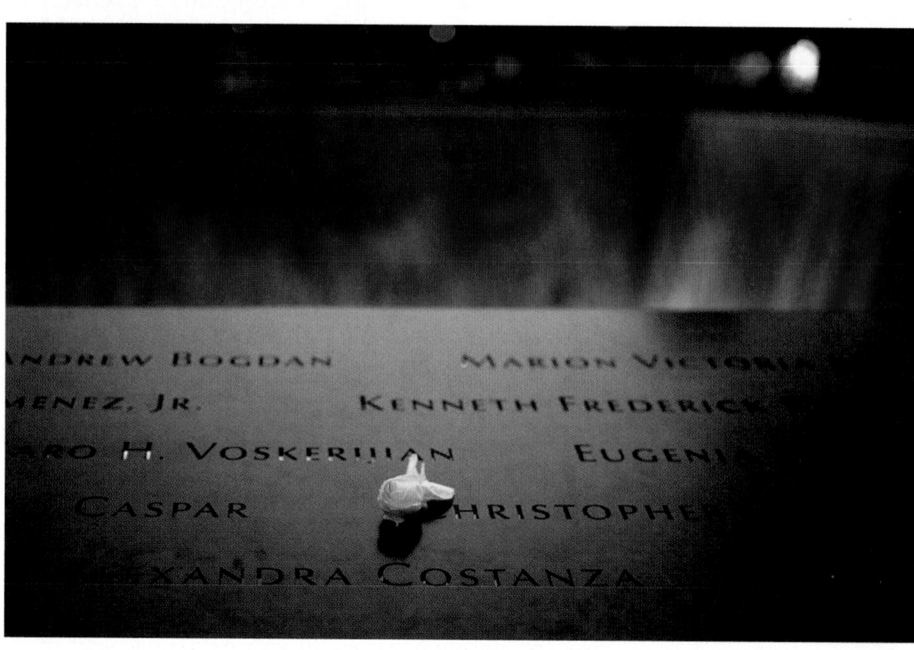

Names of September 11 victims on the World Trade Center memorial. How can terrorism in the United States be prevented?

For example, a government can mistakenly kill people and excuse it as a mistake, whereas the same type of behavior committed by a politically motivated individual would be called terrorism. The 1983 bombing of the U.S. Marine Corps barracks in Beirut, Lebanon, was defined as a terrorist act. In this incident, an Islamist suicide bomber drove a truck loaded with a bomb into a building housing Marines and other military personnel, killing 241 people. (A U.S. judge later declared Iran liable for the attack.)[45] In contrast, in 1999, the

United States mistakenly bombed the Chinese Embassy in Belgrade, Yugoslavia, killing three people. Although the results of these two incidents were similar, the motivations were different. The Marine barracks bombing was intentional. The embassy bombing was not, and the United States apologized and agreed to pay China $4.5 million for its mistake.[46]

The term "terrorism" describes the Marine barracks bombing and is distinguished from the Chinese Embassy tragedy, which is not considered a terrorist act because, as just noted, it was unintentional. Terrorist acts have become an important factor in how governments structure their criminal justice and national defense systems. Although they are relatively infrequent, terrorist acts have come to the forefront in criminology and consume a great deal of governments' attention and resources.[47]

A Short History of Terrorism

Terrorism is an old political weapon that has been used by both the powerful and the powerless throughout history. At any point in human history, groups have perpetrated terrorist attacks to frighten others from continuing to pursue their political goals. Terrorist incidents are recounted in the Bible, and acts of terrorism have been perpetrated just as effectively by governments as by the stateless. The European crusaders and the Spanish Inquisitors acted as extensions of the governments they served as they sowed their share of terror in those whose minds they wanted to change.[48]

In the American Revolution, the British considered the colonial soldiers and militia to be terrorists because they did not abide by the established European standards of warfare. The colonial soldiers were considered cowards because they did not stand in straight rows and trade volleys with the British. Instead, they hid behind trees and rocks and fought only when they had the advantage. To the British, one particularly egregious violation of the rules of war was the colonists' intentional killing of British officers. Today, killing an army's officers might be considered a tactical advantage because doing so would deprive the enemy of leadership and cause confusion. During the American Revolution, however, killing officers was considered a violation of the rules of war.[49]

Although acts of terrorism have been committed throughout history, the word "terrorism," as well as our modern concept of it, did not enter the Western mindset until the end of the 18th century with the French Revolution. During the upheaval, revolutionary leaders were responsible for a "reign of terror" in which thousands of "enemies of the revolution" were beheaded. Modern terrorism can be divided into four waves.[50]

- The first wave. This wave began in 19th-century Russia and ended with the 1914 assassination of Austrian archduke Franz Ferdinand that led to World War I. Terrorism in this era was largely concerned with political reform. In Russia, the terrorist rebel group Narodnaya Volya, or The People's Will, which chose victims for their symbolic importance, assassinated Tsar Alexander II in 1881. The late 19th century saw several other assassinations, with kings, presidents, and prime ministers being killed, many by anarchists, terrorists of the period who had no trouble finding their targets in the low-surveillance 19th-century world. U.S. Presidents Abraham Lincoln, James Garfield, and William McKinley were all assassinated during this period.[51]
- The second wave. This wave, which extended from the 1920s to the early 1960s, was brought on by desires for "national self-determination"

Municipal workers unveil the monument to Czar Alexander II in Moscow. Although his rule was marked by the emancipation of the serfs, and judicial and military reforms, terrorists assassinated Alexander II in 1881. Why did it take so long for the Russian people to commemorate Alexander II?

and the fading of colonial power. Attacking symbolic political figures was not as important, and some terrorist groups even gave advance warnings to minimize harm to civilians. Instead, terrorist groups targeted what they considered to be the "eyes and ears" of their governments, the police. A major development of this era was the terrorist "cell," made up of isolated groups whose members knew little or nothing about other organizational members or leadership. Also, in September 1920, the world was introduced to the vehicular bomb when an Italian anarchist drove a horse and cart packed with a hundred pounds of dynamite down Wall Street in New York City, killing at least 30 people.[52]

- The third wave. In the 1960s, the success of Vietcong guerrillas against the formal military powers of France and the United States inspired the third wave of terrorism as groups saw that by using the right tactics and discipline, they could defeat powerful technology, big budgets, and large standing armies. Several terrorist groups sprang up in the United States as well, including the Weather Underground and the Symbionese Liberation Army. In 1967, the Palestine Liberation Organization continued to fight after Israel's victory in the 1967 Six-Day War. Airline hijacking also became a favorite tactic during this period, with more than 100 carried out annually throughout the 1970s.[53]
- The fourth wave. This wave was fueled by Iran's 1979 Islamic revolution and the Soviet defeat in Afghanistan in 1989, which was assisted by the United States. In this wave, which continues to this day, politics has taken a backseat to religious fundamentalism as a motivating force. The 1991 dissolution of the Soviet Union, a political giant that had kept the lid on centuries of political and religious ill will throughout its 15 separate republics throughout most of the 20th century, set free a torrent of pent-up unrest.[54]

In 1977, members of the Popular Front for the Liberation of Palestine hijacked a Lufthansa airliner. Here, an unidentified man raises his arms to show the hijacker in the door of the plane that he is unarmed. Why were airplanes such a popular target for terrorists?

As the rules of war have changed over the years, so too has the concept of terrorism. This is an especially important distinction because there is a long history of attempting to limit wars to the combat of soldiers, thus sparing civilian populations. However, as mentioned previously, throughout history those who lacked the advantage in weapons or numbers of soldiers have sought ways to equalize their tactical positions. Guerrilla warfare consists of military or paramilitary operations conducted within hostile territory by irregular forces. The term was coined to describe how those who lacked powerful weapons used deceit, diversion, and misdirection to fool or trick their enemies into making poor tactical decisions. Guerrilla fighters strike when least expected, attack government infrastructure, and hide among the people. Once considered to be terrorism, guerrilla warfare is now deemed a legitimate way to fight.[55]

Terrorism and Criminological Theory

Because the terrorist threat to the United States is fairly new and is of such recent concern to the criminal justice system, no traditional criminological theories directly address terrorist activities. However, some theories may indirectly address the reason for terrorist activities. Two prevailing schools of criminological thought that may be used to this end are the classical school and the positivist school.

The classical school states that lawbreaking is the result of a rational choice that offenders make. According to the classical school, then, terrorists make a rational choice to break the law in order to further awareness of themselves and their political causes. Instead of choosing peaceful forms of protest and discourse, they choose violence. Terrorists whose offenses were successful, such as Timothy McVeigh and Osama bin Laden, planned their actions carefully, financed their work, recruited others, and had a logical reasoning for their actions.

The positivist school looks for causes external to the offender to explain crime, such as urban decay, impoverishment, failure within society's institutions, poor nutrition, and disease. According to the positivist school, terrorists would not pursue violence if not for the social disorder and desperate poverty in which many of them live. Many terrorists start out as youths who have nothing but fundamentalist religion to give them hope.

To understand the scope and level of terrorism in the 21st century, we must distinguish between terrorism committed by U.S. citizens and terrorism committed by citizens from other countries, either within the United States or elsewhere. This distinction is required to understand terrorist motivations and tactics and to differentiate between terrorism as a form of war and terrorism as a form of social protest. We will look first at domestic terrorism in the United States as a violent method of protest.

The Ku Klux Klan protested Progressive presidential candidate Henry Wallace at a cross burning in Tennessee in 1948. What groups have replaced the Ku Klux Klan in modern society?

Domestic Terrorism

Terrorism is a tactic, not a cause. Therefore, it is important to recognize that terrorism is not something imported from overseas and committed against Americans, but rather, something that is also homegrown. U.S. citizens have committed acts of terrorism since the birth of the country, and the focus on international terrorism should not blind us to the recognition of terrorist acts committed by U.S. citizens within the country's borders. Incidents of domestic terrorism in the United States have been motivated by racism, fundamentalist religious beliefs, and hatred of the federal government.

The Ku Klux Klan, which emerged shortly after the Civil War, is one example of an early American terrorist group.[56] Southern whites upset by the emancipation of the slaves sought to maintain their social, economic, and political superiority by intimidating black Southerners. The Ku Klux Klan burned homes and churches, committed murder, and conducted numerous highly visible lynchings in an attempt to maintain the social hierarchy in the South. This terrorism was not committed by a few disgruntled people, but rather by some of the most important people within the society, including bankers, merchants, and law enforcement officials. Concealing their identity by wearing robes and hoods, Ku Klux Klan members could engage in terrorist actions without being held personally accountable. In many ways, this was a form of state-sponsored terrorism because the victims were not able to turn to the criminal justice system for relief.

The Ku Klux Klan is still active but no longer advocates violence and has officially moderated its message and tactics to be more socially acceptable. Its members still argue that whites are genetically superior and protest government policies such as affirmative action. However, other extremist white-power groups have arisen to replace the Ku Klux Klan that do engage in terrorist behaviors and sincerely believe that God intended whites to rule over other races.

Modern extremist white-power terrorists can be traced to the Christian Identity movement.[57] This movement advocates the separation of races and inserts its own theology into the ideological underpinnings of the government. Members contend that minorities and liberals have subverted the true intentions of the founders of the United States and that only by revamping the country's political ideology so that it is based on white supremacy can God's true will be accomplished. This movement makes many extreme claims, including the idea that only northern Europeans and their descendants are human because their pale skin makes it possible to see them blush. If a person is not human, then it is all right to kill them, much as one would kill an animal.[58]

One of the best-known branches of the Christian Identity movement is the Aryan Nation. One of its adherents, Robert Matthews, was involved in several violent incidents, including the 1984 assassination of Denver talk-show host Alan Berg. In August 1992, another Aryan Nation adherent, Randy Weaver of Ruby Ridge, Idaho, engaged in a two-week standoff with FBI agents over a weapons charge that resulted in the deaths of three people, including Weaver's wife and young son. This incident fueled the ire of right-wing fundamentalists. Although Weaver was acquitted of murder and conspiracy charges, no federal charges were filed against the FBI agents. (State involuntary manslaughter charges were later filed and then dismissed against

FBI sharpshooter Lon Horiuchi, who killed Weaver's wife.)[59] Several high-level FBI agents were disciplined, and the federal government made a $3.1 million settlement with the Weaver family.[60] The Ruby Ridge incident remains a symbol of the religious right's distrust of the federal government.[61]

Another well-known terrorist connected to the Christian Identity movement is Eric Rudolph, better known as the Centennial Olympic Park bomber. Rudolph was convicted of bombing a gay nightclub in Atlanta, a women's health clinic in Birmingham, Alabama, and Centennial Park during the 1996 Olympics in Atlanta. Rudolph's religious beliefs allowed him to target gay people, abortion clinics, and representatives of the "New World Order" (the Olympics). He hid in the North Carolina mountains until he was captured in 2003 behind a grocery store. Rudolph, who pleaded guilty to the attacks, said the violence was to protest the legalization of abortion and "aberrant sexual behavior."[62] His sister told the Southern Poverty Law Center (see Theory to Practice) that Rudolph's actions were motivated by his belief that white people were becoming an endangered minority; by his discovery that his brother was gay; and by his anger at the government for failing to admit him into the Army Special Forces.[63]

Authorities lead Eric Rudolph from a federal courthouse in Huntsville, Alabama, in 2005. Rudolph is serving a life term for a series of bombings that killed three people in Alabama and Georgia in the 1990s. Who were the targets of Eric Rudolph's violence?

Such religious-based terrorist organizations reject the idea that all people deserve human and civil rights. They are opposed to the government because they believe their religious ideals have been betrayed by a democracy that values everyone. In their opinion, the United States is influenced by those who defy what these organizations believe is God's plan, and they believe the United States has been hijacked by secular groups who allow evil influences.[64] In their quest to return the government to what they see as its rightful Christian foundations, they adopt a warlike attitude that they believe is guided by divine will. They contend that the laws of God supersede the laws of man and that terrorist actions, including murder, are justified.

The best-known example of domestic terrorism by right-wing extremists fueled by their hatred of the federal government is the 1995 bombing of the Murrah Federal Building in Oklahoma City by Timothy McVeigh. McVeigh—whose motivation was not religious but political—used the bombing to express his dissatisfaction with several government policies. Specifically, McVeigh was upset with how federal authorities handled the Ruby Ridge and Waco, Texas, incidents and considered his violent act as both payback and a warning. (In 1993, federal authorities raided the Branch Davidian compound in Waco in connection with an illegal firearms investigation. A shootout ensued, leading to a 51-day standoff, which ended when federal agents overran the compound using tear gas. Seventy-six Branch Davidians died in the resulting conflict.) McVeigh, a veteran of the first Gulf War, used his knowledge of explosives to construct a fertilizer bomb that he delivered in a rented truck. The bomb destroyed the building, killing 168 people, including many children who attended a day-care facility located on the first floor. McVeigh was executed in 2001. His co-defendant, Terry Nichols, who helped build the bomb, was sentenced to life in prison.[65]

When discussing domestic terrorism, it is important to remember that many actions the government defines as criminal offenses are considered by terrorists to be acts of legitimate social protest. Americans have a long history of opposition to the government, which is deemed not only appropriate but desirable in a democracy. However, when social protest becomes violent, it is considered criminal activity. The line between appropriate social protest and crime is indistinct, and those who demonstrate against the authorities often cross this line without believing that what they are doing is wrong. Many

THEORY TO PRACTICE

The Southern Poverty Law Center

Domestic terrorism is often associated with criminal offenses against minorities, women, and homosexuals. It is primarily the purview of white men who see the shift of power in democratic societies moving toward all people and their own influence being diminished. When minorities and women take advantage of laws that provide equal opportunities, supervisory positions and leadership are allocated based on competence rather than tradition. Some neo-Nazi and white supremacist groups resort to domestic terrorism to attempt to keep women and minorities in a subservient status. Consequently, many state legislatures have passed laws with additional penalties for offenses based on race, sex, or gender. These "hate-crime laws" have been instrumental in targeting domestic terrorists.

Several organizations attempt to raise the visibility of racist groups who engage in domestic terrorism. The most successful of these groups is the Southern Poverty Law Center based in Alabama. This group has amassed a database that identifies hate groups active in the United States.[66] These groups include neo-Nazi groups, racist skinheads, the Ku Klux Klan, and black separatist groups. The Southern Poverty Law Center provides several public-education activities aimed at increasing social tolerance and has filed lawsuits that have changed the social landscape and have resulted in many landmark cases. The center's website provides a good deal of information that not only alerts the public to the existence of hate groups, but also promotes a progressive agenda for social justice in the United States.

THINK ABOUT IT

1. Why do some neo-Nazi and white supremacist groups resort to domestic terrorism?

people who engage in social protest believe that it is within their civil rights to criticize the government and resort to extreme measures when they believe that their messages are not being seriously considered. The law recognizes citizens' rights to protest or demonstrate but draws a line at violence.

There is much debate as to whether hate crime is actually a form of domestic terrorism. Proponents of this idea say that because hate crime is a strike against the social order, it is simply domestic terrorism on a smaller scale. For example, Dylann Roof intended to intimidate black people and the government with his attack, and his offense fits the definition of terrorism established by the USA Patriot Act. Thus, Roof is a terrorist and should have been treated as one at his trial.[67]

Although a line may be drawn from hate crime to domestic terrorism, it is important to remember, that acts of domestic terrorism have been committed that have nothing to do with bias against individuals for who they are or what they look like.[68] In the early 1970s, the Weather Underground bombed government buildings to protest the country's involvement in the Vietnam War.[69] The Black Panthers advocated armed resistance and engaged in shootouts with the police in the late 1960s to protest the lack of civil rights for black persons.[70] In the late 1990s, the Earth Liberation Front committed several acts of arson of ski resorts, lumber companies, automobile dealerships, U.S. Forest Service ranger stations, and other businesses in support of environmental causes.[71] However, as the political landscape changes over the coming decades, many people argue that social order depends on the creation of a clearer definition of domestic terrorism as well as criminal statutes that are more streamlined and inclusive.

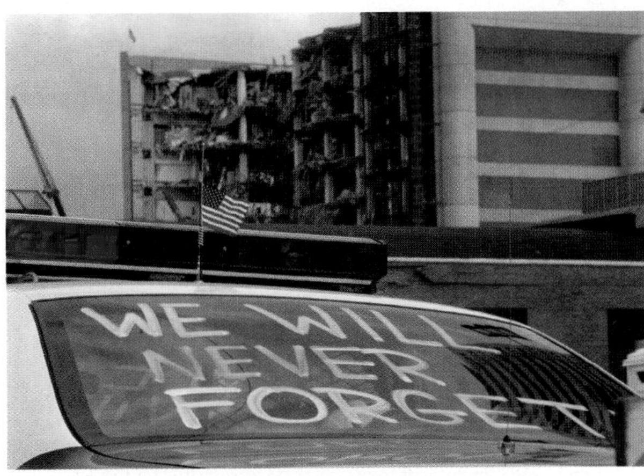

The Alfred P. Murrah Federal Building in Oklahoma City was bombed on April 19, 1995. What was the motivation behind this event?

International Terrorism

When terrorists hijacked four American airliners and flew them into the World Trade Center, the Pentagon, and a field in Pennsylvania on September 11, 2001, the nature of what we consider to be crime changed radically.[72] The lines that separated domestic crime, war, and international law were no longer so clear. Today, criminology has expanded the scope of inquiry from how individuals and institutions contribute and respond to antisocial behavior to broader subjects such as war, international crime, transnational crime, and terrorism, which is politically motivated violence against civilians by political groups for the purpose of drawing attention to their cause. Terrorism and globalization have shrunk the world, so to speak, so that all antisocial behavior is now of concern to the field of criminology.

We will study how Americans have adjusted to this new threat and examine the new agencies that have been created and the new laws that have been enacted to deal with terrorism. The events of September 11, 2001, and the subsequent wars in Iraq and Afghanistan have changed the nature of the U.S. military mandate and domestic law enforcement's mission. For example, the FBI, which once specialized in bank robberies and other types of interstate domestic crime, now plays a major role in dealing with terrorism. This change in mandate has been controversial. Some people believe that terrorism has become more of a media-created crisis and that the government response to terrorism presents the greater threat to individual rights and freedoms. Consequently, we must now view criminology in an entirely different way in order to accommodate this radical shift in the way public order is preserved.[73]

Workmen erect a stone memorial in Lockerbie, Scotland, listing the names of the victims of the Pan Am plane crash that landed on the village in December 1988. Who was determined to be responsible for this terrorist attack?

International terrorist attacks involve a national or a group of nationals from one country crossing international borders and attacking targets in another country.[74] One challenge of international terrorism is that the governments of the affected countries are limited in what they can do to investigate, arrest, and try terrorist suspects. For instance, for attacks in the United States, the U.S. government must cooperate with foreign governments, including their criminal justice systems, to track down terrorist suspects. Sometimes, the U.S. criminal justice system cannot deal with those who attack U.S. citizens or U.S. assets outside the country. For example, 179 Americans died in the 1988 terrorist bombing of Pan Am Flight 103 over Lockerbie, Scotland. However, the trial was held in the Netherlands, and Abdelbaset al-Megrahi, the Libyan man convicted of the bombing, served time in a Scottish prison and was released in 2009 because he was terminally ill with cancer.[75] Because international terrorism can involve several countries, international cooperation is crucial to the control of global terrorism.

In examining international terrorism, it is useful to consider the religious and economic motivations that underlie how and why these offenses are committed. Nearly every region in the world has experienced some degree of international terrorism (see Table 13.2). However, the axiom "One person's terrorist is another person's freedom fighter" makes it clear that terrorism is relative. Terrorism is a political tool, and people can have legitimate differences of opinion about what defines terrorism and what defines self-defense. For instance, insurgents may regard U.S. soldiers with their jet planes, tanks, and other high-technology weapons as terrorists and yet view themselves with their low-tech methods and weapons as freedom fighters battling a superpower. In contrast, U.S. soldiers may believe they are fighting a conventional war against a dishonorable enemy who uses terror as a weapon. Both sides believe they are fighting for values and ideas that are morally correct.[76]

International terrorism has fundamentally altered the mandate of the U.S. legal and criminal justice systems. The country must consider several issues in order to deal with terrorism. Among these concerns are the following.

TABLE 13.2 A Brief Look at International Terrorism

COUNTRY/ REGION	GROUP	YEARS
Spain	The group Basque Homeland and Freedom or Euskadi Ta Askatasuna (ETA) began as a student movement opposed to the oppressive Spanish dictator Francisco Franco. Many Basques living in the Spanish Basque region wanted to separate from Spain because they had their own language and culture and believed that the Spanish government had not allowed them to establish their own identity. Both Spain and France had engaged in periodic attempts to stamp out the Basque culture and language. Lacking new members and unpopular even with Basques, the ETA dissolved in 2018.[77]	1959–2018
Northern Ireland	For hundreds of years, Ireland was a colony ruled by Great Britain. Subjugated by the British, the Irish worked land owned by British royal families. Over the years, Irish peasants protested the poverty in which they were forced to live and their exploitation by the British. A 1921 political settlement split the country, allowing the larger southern part to become an independent country (the Irish Free State, later the Republic of Ireland), while the six northern counties remained part of the British Empire. However, a large contingent of Catholics in the northern counties wanted Ireland to be a single, intact, independent country. As a result, Northern Ireland experienced a continuing wave of terrorist activities and occupation by the British military. The Good Friday Agreement (or Belfast Agreement), a major step in the peace process, was signed in April 1998, marking the end of violence.[78]	1921–1998
Turkey	After the first Persian Gulf War in 1990–1991, the people living in northern Iraq, the Kurds, developed a stable and relatively prosperous government because of the protection they enjoyed from Saddam Hussein. However, the success of the Kurds in northern Iraq greatly concerned the Turkish government because they occupy a territory that includes not only northern Iraq, but also eastern Turkey and western Iran. Militant Kurds in Turkey have developed a political organization called the Kurdistan Workers' Party (PKK). The Kurds at one time wished to develop a Kurdish state in the areas of the three countries they occupy, but an independent country cannot be accomplished without taking land and resources from Iran, Iraq, and Turkey. Recently, the PKK has instead called for more autonomy for the Kurds.[79]	late 1970s–today
Africa	Decades of civil war, poverty, and unrest have opened many African countries to terrorism and have allowed them to serve as places where terrorists from other parts of the world can hide and train. Somalia is particularly vulnerable with its fragile government; violent instability; long and exposed coastline; ill-guarded borders; and proximity to the Arabian Peninsula, which includes Bahrain, Kuwait, Oman, Qatar, the United Arab Emirates, Yemen, and Saudi Arabia. Al-Shabaab poses the most serious threat. Many Somalis protest the group's presence because of its harsh, violent tactics and its adherence to strict Wahhabi Islam rather than the Sufi Islam practiced by many Somalis.[80]	Al-Shabaab 2006–today
	Based in the Nigerian state of Borno, Boko Haram has been active in all countries surrounding the Lake Chad Basin. Recent military operations have liberated several urban areas as well as decreased the land area under Boko Haram control. Following the December 2016 destruction of their headquarters, Boko Haram has declined, but small cells have perpetrated suicide attacks on civilians, often using abducted children to carry explosives.[81]	Boko Haram 2009–today

continued

TABLE 13.2 *continued*

COUNTRY/ REGION	GROUP	YEARS
South Asia	The terror problems in Afghanistan, Pakistan, and India are based in religious and tribal differences, are deep and complicated, and cannot be fully explicated here. As in Africa, several countries in this region are vulnerable because of weak governments and poor security. Because of the relative political and social chaos that has reigned in Afghanistan for so long, the country is an excellent harbor for terror groups. Although a more stable country, Pakistan also presents a safe haven for terrorist organizations, which is especially problematic because it borders Afghanistan. India is plagued by both international and domestic terrorism. A particularly troublesome organization is Lashkar-e-Taiba, whose goal is to unite Kashmir (the region is currently divided between India, Pakistan, and China) under Pakistani jurisdiction.[82]	1985–today
Chechnya	The Russian republic of Chechnya in the Caucasus region of Asia has been in constant conflict with the governments of Imperial Russia, the Soviet Union, and modern Russia. The people of Chechnya are Muslim and have received a lot of attention and support from other Islamic countries. When the Soviet Union disintegrated in 1991 and many of its territories declared independence, Russia rejected the claim of Chechnyan independence, touching off a conflict that continues today.[83]	1991–today
Israel and the Palestinians	After World War II, the Allied victors created several new political configurations. The new political arrangements included providing the Jewish people with the homeland of Israel in the Middle East. Forged from the existing country of Palestine, Israel has, from its inception, experienced conflict, war, and terrorism. The Palestinians and the Israelis do not recognize each other's political legitimacy. Israel has been successful in annexing most of Palestine and has confined the Palestinian people within two areas: the West Bank and the Gaza Strip. Three terrorist organizations have caused particular trouble for Israel, fighting several wars and sponsoring numerous terrorist attacks: the Palestine Liberation Organization (PLO), Hamas, and Hezbollah.	Palestine Liberation Organization, 1964–today Hamas, 1987–today Hezbollah, 1985–today
International	Al Qaeda, under the direction of Osama bin Laden, was responsible for the September 11, 2001, terrorist attacks on the United States. Al Qaeda also orchestrated bombings in Tanzania and Kenya in 1998 and the attack in Yemen on the U.S. Navy destroyer USS *Cole* in 2000. Presently, al Qaeda is likely the most influential terrorist organization in the world, with a global reach from the Middle East to Indonesia. Its organizational structure, lines of communication, and actual number of members are largely unknown.[84]	1988–today
International	The Islamic State (IS)—also known as ISIS, ISIL, or Daesh— was founded when Al Qaeda in Iraq merged with the al-Nusra Front in Syria. IS leader Abu Bakr al-Baghdadi then proclaimed the group a "worldwide caliphate." Shortly thereafter, militant groups around the world swore allegiance, including militants in Libya, Afghanistan, Algeria, Egypt, Pakistan, Yemen, Gaza, India, Russia, Tunisia, Nigeria, the Philippines, and Uzbekistan. Although, after much fighting, the Iraqi and Syrian governments declared the group defeated in their countries, IS continues to be a threat in many regions.[85]	2014–today

- International versus national security. The lines between security abroad and security at home have been blurred. Threats to U.S. citizens in other countries, as well as to those in the United States, are no longer easily separated. The problems of terrorism require more cooperation and coordination among agencies. For example, traditionally there was a distinction between the mandates of the CIA and the FBI. The CIA was designed to gather information on external threats to the United States and was forbidden to engage in espionage within the country. Conversely, the FBI was limited to dealing with threats within the country. Now, these lines of authority have been extended for both agencies as they deal with terrorism.[86]
- The Department of Homeland Security. After September 11, the federal government implemented a major reorganization in an effort to better address terrorism. Several agencies and parts of other agencies were combined into a new Department of Homeland Security (see Figure 13.4).

Included in this department are the U.S. Customs Service (formerly part of the Treasury Department), the U.S. Citizenship and Immigration Services (formerly the Immigration and Naturalization Service within the Department of Justice), and the Federal Emergency Management Agency (FEMA), which used to be an independent agency. The mission of the Department of Homeland Security is to lead and coordinate the effort to secure the country; to prevent and deter terrorist attacks; and to prepare for and respond to all hazards, disasters, and threats to the country. The department is structured to ensure that its component agencies are organized in the most efficient and productive manner (see Policy Implications for more). What is especially interesting about the Department of Homeland Security is not the organizations that were included, but those that were not. One of the indictments of the September 11 Commission, which investigated the terrorist acts, was that there was insufficient coordination between agencies such as the CIA and the FBI. Neither of these agencies is included in the Department of Homeland Security,

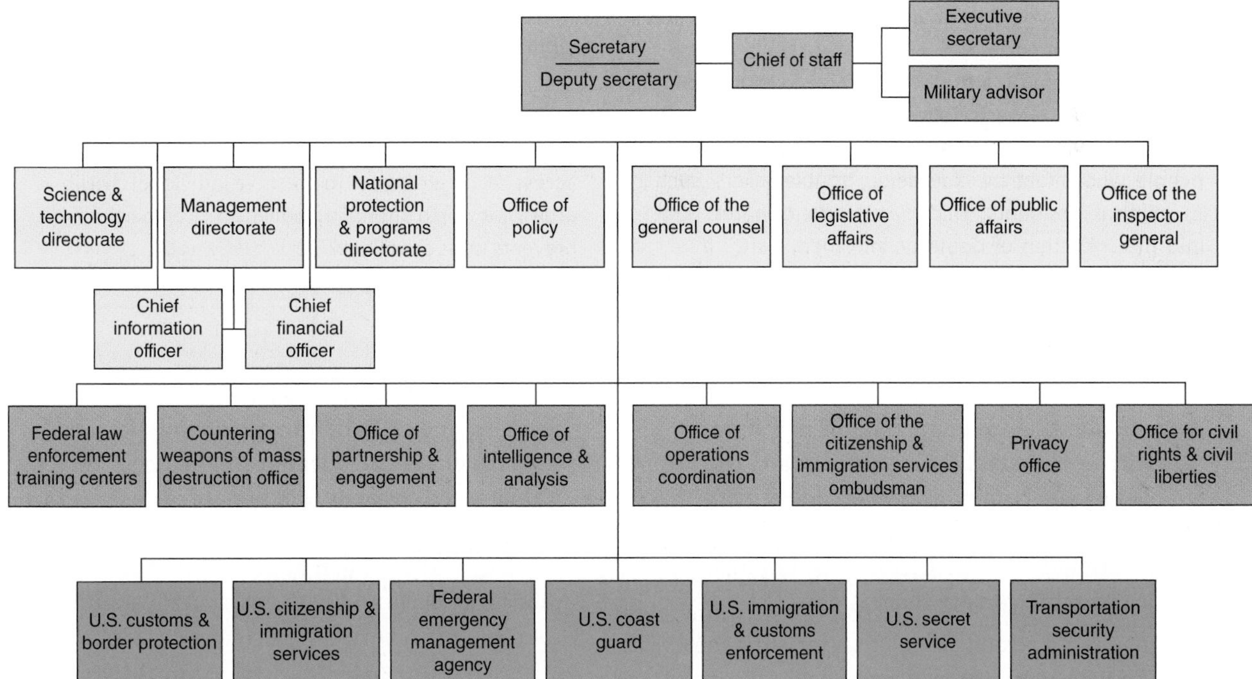

FIGURE 13.4 Department of Homeland Security Organizational Chart

The Department of Homeland Security leads and coordinates the national effort to secure the country, prevents and deters terrorist attacks, and prepares for and responds to all national hazards, disasters, and threats.

THINK ABOUT IT

Study the bottom row of the chart. Why are these agencies included in the Department of Homeland Security? Try to think of the reasoning behind the inclusion of each.

Source: Department of Homeland Security, https://www.dhs.gov/organizational-chart. Accessed July 2018.

POLICY IMPLICATIONS

N-DEx

After September 11, 2001, federal agencies were faulted for not sharing the information they had gathered about foreign terrorists and the possibility that they might attack the United States. Before the attack, distrust and secrecy were the norm among federal law enforcement agencies, state law enforcement agencies, and the military. Each agency or military branch had its own mission, and any intrusion onto another's "turf" was looked upon with suspicion. A congressional report charged that the September 11 attacks might have been prevented had the FBI and Central Intelligence Agency (CIA) shared information about two of the hijackers. The report also found that the National Security Agency (NSA), which monitors foreign electronic communications, acquired information in 1999 about the two hijackers that it did not share with either the FBI or CIA.[87]

In 2008, the Department of Justice announced the formation of the National Data Exchange or N-DEx. Today, N-DEx is a search engine for sensitive criminal justice information about anyone in the United States who has encountered the criminal justice system. The FBI says it keeps records on those who access the data and that source agencies must be notified when arrests are made using that agency's data.

One of the problems with such a system, according to civil liberties experts, is that N-DEx allows the building of files on just about anyone, including law-abiding people who might be considered troublemakers, such as political dissidents. Thirty years ago, Congress limited the collection of domestic intelligence after it was discovered that the FBI, the Army, and some local police agencies had misused their authority to monitor people involved in legal activities. Those reforms separated day-to-day police inquiries from federal national security intelligence-gathering.[88] However, since September 11, laws have been passed to eliminate that separation and to allow databases like N-DEx.

Another problem with N-DEx, and other criminal justice databases like it, is more bureaucratic. On February 28, 2015, Dylann Roof (see the opening scenario of this chapter) was arrested for possession of a medication used to treat opioid addiction without a prescription. On March 2, police in Columbia, South Carolina, uploaded the arrest report to N-DEx. On April 11, Roof applied for a background check so he could buy a .45-caliber Glock. Roof's arrest for illegal drug use would have prevented him from buying the gun. However, FBI examiners doing Roof's background check were not allowed to search N-DEx for the arrest report because of an FBI rule stating that only criminal justice agencies may use N-DEx. Roof was allowed to buy the gun on April 16 because his background check had not been resolved. Two months later, Roof murdered nine people at a Bible study at Emanuel AME Church.[89]

THINK ABOUT IT

1. Presumably the restrictions on which agencies can access N-DEx are meant to preserve individual civil liberties. Is it worth offending individual civil liberties if it prevents mass shootings? Why or why not?

even though their major mandates now are to deal with terrorism. Leaving the CIA and the FBI out of the Department of Homeland Security was more of a political decision than a tactical or organizational one. The CIA and the FBI had the political clout to remain independent.[90]

- Expansion of the definition of terrorism. One of the unanticipated consequences of the war on terror is the way in which traditional criminal offenses are now being defined as terrorism. For instance, there is a relationship between money used in the illegal drug trade and the funding of terrorist activities. Notably, the Taliban in Afghanistan funds itself by taxing farmers who raise heroin-producing poppies.[91] Consequently, drug dealers are being subjected to increased scrutiny and penalties designed to combat terrorism. Although no one defends illegal drug trafficking, it appears that the criminal justice agencies and the legal system are unable to distinguish between normal drug crime and crime that provides financial support for terrorist organizations. Also, some violent individuals are now being charged with offenses under new laws designed to thwart terrorism. In many ways, this overlap has allowed law enforcement agencies to control traditional crime more effectively.[92]

- The increase in anti-terrorism resources. The national focus on terrorism has resulted in the allocation of substantial resources aimed at preventing, detecting, and prosecuting terrorist activities. In tough economic times, Congress has increased the budgets of agencies responsible for addressing terrorism. However, the process used to determine who gets the money has not been without controversy. Members of Congress have added provisions that allocate resources to jurisdictions that have little to fear from terrorists. This sort of "pork-barrel spending" has resulted in public dissatisfaction among those who argue that resources have been diverted from important targets. For example, only a small fraction of the cargo shipped into the United States is ever inspected. If a terrorist wishes to deliver a nuclear weapon to the United States, it would be relatively easy to do so on a container ship in one of the major ports of the east or west coast.[93]
- The Patriot Act. The USA PATRIOT Act (H.R. 3162) was passed on October 24, 2001. President George W. Bush signed it into law two days later. The act's official title is The Uniting and Strengthening America by Providing Appropriate Tools Required to Intercept and Obstruct Terrorism Act of 2001. The act was passed quickly, with little time for public debate and criticism. Few legislators even had time to read the full text of the act before voting on it. Yet only 66 representatives and 1 senator voted against the act, which modified nearly 20 federal statutes.[94] Much of the act provides funds and staff positions to government agencies for anti-terrorism initiatives.[95] According to some critics, the act is problematic because it violates some constitutional rights, including those governing searches and seizures, due process, freedom of speech, and protection against cruel and unusual punishment. In 2007, a federal judge ruled that the act violates the Constitution because it allows the government to conduct surveillance and searches of U.S. citizens without probable cause.[96]

In 2005, Congress made permanent 14 of the USA PATRIOT Act's main provisions and enacted four-year sunset requirements for two other provisions.[97] In March 2010, President Barack Obama extended three controversial sections of the act for one year. The first two provisions allow the government to seize suspects' records without their knowledge and to conduct surveillance of suspects with no known ties to an organized terrorist group. The third allows roving wiretaps or, rather, wiretaps that follow a suspect rather than a communications device. For instance, if the suspect discards a phone in an effort to shake surveillance, the government does not need a new surveillance order on the suspect's new phone; investigators simply transition surveillance to the new phone.[98]

CONTROLLING TERRORISM

Terrorism is difficult to control because it can be extremely hard to identify, locate, and engage the enemy (see Figure 13.5 for a look at international terrorism fatalities and incidents). Dealing with terrorist networks that operate out of many countries and have a decentralized organizational structure makes the problem of controlling terrorism especially difficult. The most important concern in dealing with these types of terrorist organizations is developing actionable intelligence. How intelligence is gathered and the problems of ensuring privacy rights for all citizens are so complex that we will devote the final chapter of this book to these issues. Here we will take a brief look at intelligence-based strategies.

There is a somewhat artificial distinction between the employment of military forces and the dedication of law enforcement and criminal justice resources for dealing with terrorism. For instance, the invasions of Iraq and Afghanistan are military actions that treat terrorism as war rather than as crime. However, the new terrorist threat has deeply altered both the traditional criminal justice response to crime and the military response to war, causing both institutions to adopt some of the other

Demonstrators gather in Durham, North Carolina, to protest provisions of the USA Patriot Act which created the Department of Homeland Security. Why is the Patriot Act unpopular with so many people?

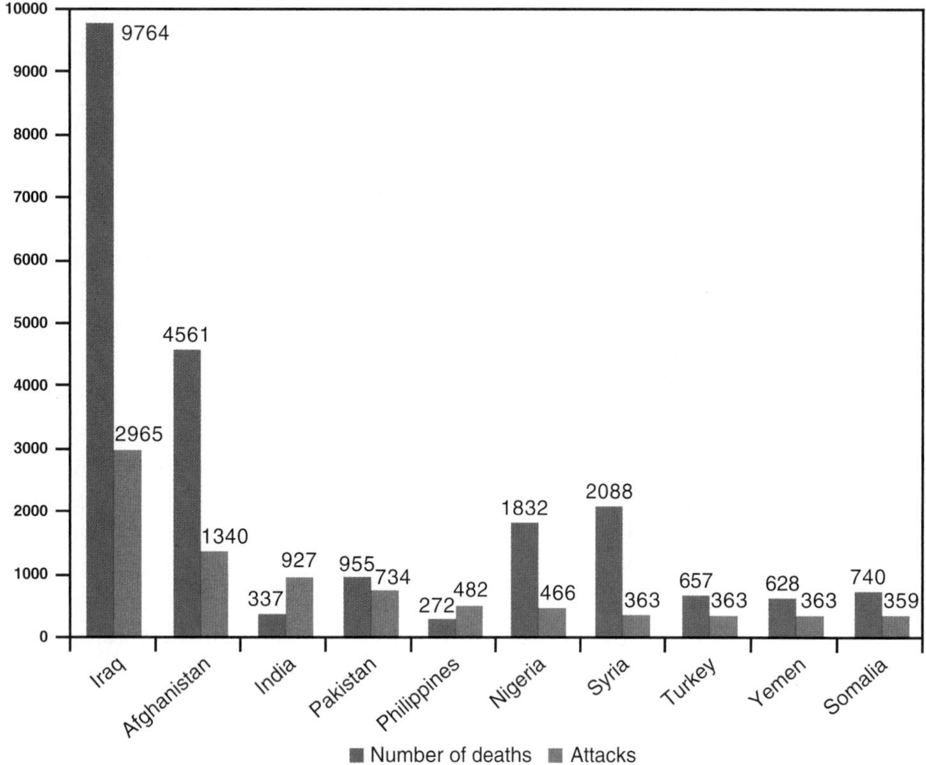

FIGURE 13.5 International Terrorism Fatalities and Incidents by Region

There were terrorist attacks in 104 countries in 2016. Fifty-five percent of all attacks took place in five countries: Iraq, Afghanistan, India, Pakistan, and the Philippines, and 75 percent of all deaths due to terrorist attack occurred in five countries: Iraq, Afghanistan, Syria, Nigeria, and Pakistan.

THINK ABOUT IT
Why were there so many more attacks and deaths in Iraq?

Source: U.S. Department of State, National Consortium for the Study of Terrorism and Responses to Terrorism: Annex of Statistical Information, Location, https://www.state.gov/j/ct/rls/crt/2016/272241.htm. Accessed July 2018.

institution's tactics. For example, in Iraq, the U.S. military has had to adopt some of law enforcement's mandate to preserve social order and deal with civilian issues, such as training police officers. In turn, U.S. law enforcement and emergency response agencies have had to deal with some aspects of global terrorism within the United States.

Only since 2001 has the U.S. criminal justice system become involved in the control of terrorism. Before 2001, terrorism in the United States was generally considered to be an international political issue that had more to do with war than with crime. Only in the past few decades have criminologists begun to take a more analytical look at terrorism and its relationship to crime. Criminology, as you will recall, is the study of the making of laws, the breaking of laws, and society's reaction to these two events. We will consider terrorism within this framework.

It is the third part of the definition of criminology—society's reaction to the making and breaking of laws—that has made terrorism a complicated criminological issue. Society's reaction to "normal" crime is fairly well established. People try to prevent crime in many ways: being alert in public places, locking doors and cars, installing alarm systems, setting up Neighborhood Watch groups, and the like. The police detain criminal suspects, secure arrestees in jails, and begin the first steps of inserting suspects into the criminal justice system. The courts try criminal defendants, and the corrections system deals with the convicted. What is society's reaction to terrorists? So far, it is fear, suspicion, and the scrambling of federal agencies to try to control the problem. Society's reaction to terrorists is not yet well established within any framework of laws.

Terrorists have broken the laws of numerous countries, and terrorist acts certainly qualify as criminal offenses. Murder, assault, kidnapping, vandalism, destruction of property, theft, and illegal weapons-dealing are criminal offenses that occur within the framework of terrorism. However, the definition of terrorists themselves as criminal offenders, rather than as soldiers or political rebels, has proven to be a complicated issue for the world's judicial systems.

Prior to September 11, 2001, terrorists who struck within the United States were treated as criminal defendants. The six foreign-born terrorists who carried out the 1993 bombing of the World Trade Center were tried, convicted, and sentenced to prison with the full complement of constitutional rights extended to any criminal defendant.[99] This was also the case with Timothy McVeigh, the bomber of the Murrah Federal building in Oklahoma City, and his co-conspirator, Terry Nichols.

This situation has changed since the events of September 11, however. Terrorists who attack the

United States in foreign lands pose another problem. To date, the United States has classified these terrorists as "enemy combatants," rather than as soldiers or criminal suspects, and is holding them indefinitely. In 2002, John Walker Lindh, a U.S. citizen who converted to Islam and was caught in Afghanistan fighting with the Taliban, received a trial and a plea deal and was sentenced to 20 years in a U.S. prison.[100] In contrast, Ali Saleh Kahlah al-Marri, a citizen of Qatar attending college in Illinois, was arrested in December 2001 on suspicion of being an Al Qaeda agent. He was held in civilian custody until 2003 when he was transferred to military custody and held as an enemy combatant within the United States. It took another four years for a federal appeals court to decide that al-Marri could not be detained indefinitely without being charged.[101] In 2015, he was released and deported to his home country of Qatar.[102]

PAUSE AND REVIEW

1. **Critique the axiom "one person's terrorist is another person's freedom fighter."**
2. **Discuss how some traditional criminological theories might address terrorism.**
3. **Give reasons why the Ku Klux Klan has been considered a terrorist organization.**

An Army soldier stands guard on a tower at Guantanamo Naval Base in Guantanamo, Cuba. Why does the United States have a military facility in Cuba?

FOCUS ON ETHICS Political Correctness or Political Suicide: You Choose

You are a second-generation Lebanese American who is living the American dream. After graduating from college, you served in Afghanistan with distinction where you were awarded medals for bravery. Upon returning from overseas, you began a law enforcement career and moved up in rank until you became the chief of police for a medium-size southern city. In your desire to continue to serve, you ran for mayor and won.

Now, an issue has come up before the county commission that has divided the city. In front of city hall there is a statue of a Confederate soldier that was placed there 100 years ago. African Americans, who compose about 30 percent of the population, have been agitating to have the statue removed. In their view, it recalls the period of slavery in the United States and should not be displayed in such a prominent

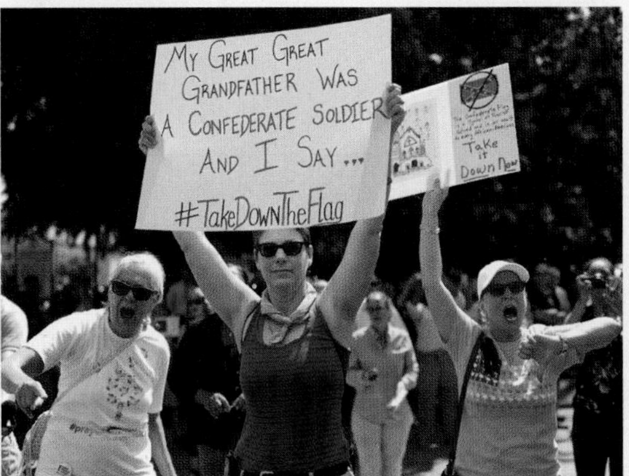

Protesters gather at a rally to take down the Confederate flag at the South Carolina statehouse in Columbia, South Carolina. The shooting deaths of nine people at a church in Charleston reignited calls for the Confederate flag flying on the grounds of the statehouse to come down. Why is the Civil War still so divisive in American culture?

public place. Other citizens object to this proposal. They claim that the Confederacy is part of Southern history and that to remove the statue would be like trying to revise history.

It appears that you must take a stand one way or another. As a child of immigrants, you experienced racial discrimination while growing up in the city, as well as when you were in the military. You are genuinely sympathetic to the proposal to have the statue taken down. However, some of your wife's family is descended from Confederate soldiers, and your father-in-law has strong opinions about this issue. If you support the proposal to remove the statue, it will cause significant conflict within your family. Additionally, your chances of re-election for mayor or election to any other higher office will be greatly jeopardized if you support removing the statue.

What Do You Do?

1. Come out strongly in support of the proposal to remove the statue. You appreciate how celebrating the Confederacy offends many people. This decision may end your political career, but you believe the integrity of your values is at stake here.
2. Vote to keep the statue. The Confederacy is part of the history of the area, and most of the people whom you represent support keeping the statue. This path of action will maintain harmony in your family and not jeopardize your ambitions for higher political office.
3. Try to find a compromise. Some have suggested that the statue could be moved from in front of city hall to a proposed museum that would celebrate all of the history of the area and not just the Confederacy.
4. Try to finesse the issue. Appoint a commission to study it and to delay its findings until you have served your term as mayor. This way you can move on to higher office and leave this difficult decision to your successor.

Summary

Learning Objective	Summary
LEARNING OBJECTIVE 1 Review Bentham's hedonistic calculus and tell how it applies to terrorism.	The hedonistic calculus is a method proposed by Bentham in which criminal offenders calculate the worth of breaking the law by estimating the positive consequences versus the possible negative consequences. Terrorists and offenders who commit hate crime seem to have little to gain from their offenses in return for what they are giving up to commit them.
LEARNING OBJECTIVE 2 Define hate crime.	A hate crime is a criminal offense like murder or rape, but with an added element of bias. The FBI collects statistics under the definition of hate crime as a "criminal offense against a person or property motivated in whole or in part by an offender's bias against a race, religion, disability, sexual orientation, ethnicity, gender, or gender identity."
LEARNING OBJECTIVE 3 Briefly review the history of hate-crime legislation.	State legislatures began writing hate-crime laws in the 1980s. Oregon was the first state to enact hate-crime laws in 1981. By 1991, at least 32 states had hate crime laws. Currently, every state but Georgia, Indiana, Utah, and Wyoming has some form of hate-crime legislation. The first federal law regarding hate crime was the 1990 Hate Crime Statistics Act, which required the FBI to record hate-crime statistics in the UCR. Hate crime as a criminal act was specified in the federal law in 2009 with the Matthew Shepard and James Byrd Jr. Hate Crimes Prevention Act.

LEARNING OBJECTIVE 4 Which criminological theories are most applicable to hate crime?	A classical school theory that applies to hate crime is rational choice theory. Hate-crime perpetrators target certain groups for crime and violence because they want to. Strain theory is an applicable positivist theory. Hate-crime perpetrators may conceive of some social groups as blocking their access to the goals required to be perceived as successful in society. Critical race theory and feminist theory can also be applied. Critical theories critique the way dominant power groups use their privileged social status to maintain a status quo based on the subjugation of less powerful groups.
LEARNING OBJECTIVE 5 Give the U.S. government's definition of terrorism. Give the four components of Combs's definition of terrorism.	The U.S. government defines terrorism as "premeditated, politically motivated violence perpetrated against non-combatant targets by subnational groups or clandestine agents." Combs's definition of terrorism has four components: The use of violence or the threat of violence; a political dimension; the killing of innocent people; and symbolic meaning.

Critical Reflections

1. **What is terrorism? What are four components of terrorism, according to Combs's definition of the term?**
2. **What aspects of terrorism are easily defined as criminal offenses? What aspects of terrorism present problems for the traditional definitions of crime?**
3. **What are the four waves of modern terrorism, and what characterizes each wave?**
4. **How do traditional criminological theories explain terrorist activities?**
5. **What have been motivations behind incidents of domestic terrorism in the United States?**
6. **Which issues must the United States consider in dealing with the problem of terrorism?**

Key Terms

Instant Recall Terms

battery (ch. 10)
classical strain theory (ch. 6)
general strain theory (ch. 6)
hedonistic calculus (ch. 4)
intersectionality (ch. 8)

Notes

1 Ray Sanchez and Ed Payne, "Charleston Church Shooting: Who Is Dylann Roof?" *CNN*, December 16, 2016, https://www.cnn.com/2015/06/19/us/charleston-church-shooting-suspect/index.html. Accessed July 2018.

2 Ibid.

3 Gabe Gutierrez and Corky Siemaszko, "Jury Finds Dylann Roof Guilty of Charleston Church Massacre," *NBC News*, December 15, 2016, https://www.nbcnews.com/news/us-news/jury-finds-roof-guilty-charleston-church-massacre-n696406. Accessed July 2018.

4 *Guardian*, "Dylann Roof Sentenced to Death for the Murders of Nine Black Church Members," January 10, 2017, https://www.theguardian.com/us-news/2017/jan/10/dylann-roof-sentenced-to-death-charleston-church-shooting. Accessed July 2018.

5 Federal Bureau of Investigation, Uniform Crime Reports, 2017 *Crime in the United States*, Table 1: Crime in the United States by Volume and Rate, https://ucr.fbi.gov/crime-in-the-u.s/2017/crime-in-the-u.s.-2017/topic-pages/tables/table-1. Accessed October 2018.

6 Jennifer Berry Hawes and Glenn Smith, "Newly Released Documents Say Dylann Roof Saw His Reputation—Not His Crimes—as 'The Most Important Issue'," *Post and Courier*, May 10, 2017, https://www.postandcourier.com/church_shooting/newly-released-documents-say-dylann-roof-saw-his-reputation-not/article_c25f720a-35b1-11e7-99fb-fbc1a612bf73.html. Accessed July 2018.

7 Kevin Sack and Alan Blinder, "Dylann Roof Himself Rejects Best Defense Against Execution," *New York Times*, January 1,2017, https://www.nytimes.com/2017/01/01/us/dylann-roof-execution-defense-charleston-church-shooting.html. Accessed July 2018.
8 Ralph Ellis, Ashley Fantz, Faith Karimi and Eliott C. McLaughlin, "Orlando Shooting: 49 Killed, Shooter Pledged ISIS Allegiance," *CNN*, June 13, 2016, https://www.cnn.com/2016/06/12/us/orlando-nightclub-shooting/index.html. Accessed July 2018.
9 Richard Esposito, Jack Date, Pierre Thomas, and Lee Ferran, "Aurora 'Dark Knight' Suspect James Holmes Said He 'Was the Joker': Cops," ABCNews, July 20, 2012, https://abcnews.go.com/Blotter/aurora-dark-knight-suspect-joker-cops/story?id=16822251. Accessed July 2018.
10 Federal Bureau of Investigation, "What We Investigate," https://www.fbi.gov/investigate/civil-rights/hate-crimes. Accessed July 2018.
11 Federal Bureau of Investigation, Uniform Crime Reports, 2016 *Hate Crime Statistics,* Methodology, https://ucr.fbi.gov/hate-crime/2016/resource-pages/methodology. Accessed October 2018.
12 Federal Bureau of Investigation, Uniform Crime Reports, 2016 *Hate Crime Statistics,* Incidents and Offenses, https://ucr.fbi.gov/hate-crime/2016/topic-pages/incidentsandoffenses. Accessed October 2018.
13 Madeline Masucci and Lynn Langton, *Hate Crime Victimization, 2004–2015* (Washington, D.C.: U.S. Department of Justice Office of Justice Programs Bureau of Justice Statistics, 2017), 1. Available at https://www.bjs.gov/index.cfm?ty=pbdetail&iid=5967. Accessed July 2018.
14 Ibid., 5.
15 Ibid., 6.
16 Ibid., 3.
17 Federal Bureau of Investigation, Uniform Crime Reports, 2016 *Hate Crime Statistics,* Incidents and Offenses, https://ucr.fbi.gov/hate-crime/2016/topic-pages/incidentsandoffenses. Accessed October 2018.
18 Masucci and Langton, *Hate Crime Victimization*, 8.
19 Bryan Denson, "1998 Story: Legacy of a Hate Crime: Mulugeta Seraw's Death a Decade Ago Avenged," *Oregonian*, November 12, 2014, https://www.oregonlive.com/portland/index.ssf/2014/11/1998_story_legacy_of_a_hate_cr.html. Accessed July 2018.
20 Ibid.
21 Ibid.
22 Bryan Denson, "Notorious Portland Skinhead Kenneth Mieske Dies Serving Life Prison Term in Beating Death of Mulugeta Seraw," July 27, 2011, *Oregonian*, https://www.oregonlive.com/portland/index.ssf/2011/07/notorious_portland_skinhead_ke.html. Accessed July 2018.
23 David Holthouse, "Rude and Crude," *Intelligence Report* (Southern Poverty Law Center), Aug. 8, 2017, https://www.splcenter.org/fighting-hate/intelligence-report/2017/rude-and-crude. Accessed July 2018.
24 Val Zavala, "After the Murder: The Rest of the Story," May 9, 2013, KCET, https://www.kcet.org/socal-cares/southern-poverty-law-center. Accessed July 2018.
25 James Morsch, Comment, "The Problem of Motive in Hate Crimes: The Argument Against Presumptions of Racial Motivation," *Journal of Criminal Law and Criminology* 82 (1991): 659–663.
26 Ibid.
27 NAACP, State-by-State Hate Crime Laws State, https://www.naacp.org/wp-content/uploads/2017/09/Hate-Crimes-laws-by-state.pdf. Accessed July 2018.
28 Gregory M. Herek, "Hate Crimes Against Lesbians and Gay Men: Issues for Research and Policy," *American Psychologist* 44, no. 6 (June 1989): 948–955. Vern E. Smith, "The Vanishing Rainbow: Ethnic Violence on the Rise," *Emerge* 1, no. 9 (1990):56.
29 Mark Austin Walters, "A General Theories of Hate Crime? Strain, Doing Difference and Self Control," *Critical Criminology* (2011) 19: 313–330.
30 James Morsch, "The Problem of Motive in Hate Crimes: The Argument Against Presumptions of Racial Motivation," *Journal of Criminal Law and Criminology* 82, No. 3 (1992): 659–689.
31 Briana Alongi, "The Negative Ramifications of Hate Crime Legislation: It's Time to Reevaluate Whether Hate Crime Laws Are Beneficial to Society," *Pace Law Review* 37, no. 1 (2016): 326–351.
32 Michael Shively, *Study of Literature and Legislation on Hate Crime in America, Final Report* (Washington, D.C.: Department of Justice, 2005).
33 Denson, "1998 Story: Legacy of a Hate Crime."
34 Colleen E. Mills, Joshua D. Freilich, and Steven M. Chermak, "Extreme Hatred: Revisiting the Hate Crime and Terrorism Relationship to Determine Whether They Are 'Close Cousins' or 'Distant Relatives'," *Crime & Delinquency* 63, no. 10 (2017): 1191–1223. Jesse J. Norris, "Why Dylann Roof Is a Terrorist under Federal Law, and Why It Matters," *Harvard Journal on Legislation* 54, no. 1 (January 2017): 501–541.
35 Walters, "A General Theories of Hate Crime?"
36 Deeanna M. Button and Meredith G. F. Worthen, "General Strain Theory for LGBQ and SSB Youth: The Importance of Intersectionality in the Future of Feminist Criminology," *Feminist Criminology* 9, no. 4 (October 2014): 270.
37 Megan Crepeau, "Ringleader Given 8 Years in Prison for Beating Teen with Disability in Attack Livestreamed on Facebook," *Chicago Tribune*, July 5, 2018, http://www.chicagotribune.com/news/local/breaking/ct-met-facebook-live-hate-crime-20180705-story.html. Accessed July 2018.
38 Susie Balderston, "Victimized Again? Intersectionality and Injustice in Disabled Women's Lives after Hate Crime and Rape," *Advances in Gender Research* 18A (December 2013): 17.
39 Kimberly J. Cook, "Has Criminology Awakened from Its 'Androcentric Slumber'?" *Feminist Criminology* 11, no. 4 (October 2016): 334.
40 Central Intelligence Agency, News and Information, "How Do You Define Terrorism," https://www.cia.gov/news-information/cia-the-war-on-terrorism/terrorism-faqs.html. Accessed July 2018.
41 Cindy C. Combs, *Terrorism in the Twenty-First Century*, 4th ed. (Upper Saddle River, N.J.: Prentice Hall, 2006), 11.
42 Edgar O'Ballance, *The Language of Violence: The Blood Politics of Terrorism* (San Rafael, Calif.: Presidio Press, 1979).
43 Mark Juergensmeyer, *Terror in the Mind of Gods: The Global Rise of Religious Violence* (Berkeley: University of California Press, 2000).
44 Morris Dees, *Gathering Storm: America's Militia Threat* (New York: Harper Perennial, 1996).
45 Rick Hampson, "25 Years Later, Bombing in Beirut Still Resonates," *USA Today*, October 16, 2008, p. 1A.
46 James Harding, "US Pays $4.5m for Embassy Bombing," *Financial Times* (London), July 31, 1999, Europe section, 3.
47 Mark S. Hamm, *Terrorism as Crime: From Oklahoma City to Al-Qaeda and Beyond* (New York: New York University Press, 2007).
48 Michael Burleigh, *Blood and Rage: A Cultural History of Terrorism* (London: HarperPress, 2008).
49 John Ferling, *Almost a Miracle: The American Victory in the War of Independence* (New York: Oxford University Press, 2007).
50 David C. Rapoport, "The Fourth Wave: September 11 in the History of Terrorism," *Current History* (December 2001): 419–424.
51 Ibid.
52 Rapoport, "The Fourth Wave: September 11 in the History of Terrorism." Australian Broadcasting Corporation, RadioEye, "A Short History of the Car Bomb," http://www.abc.net.au/rn/radioeye/stories/2008/2141652.htm. Accessed July 2018.
53 Rapoport, "The Fourth Wave."
54 Ibid.
55 Robert B. Asprey, *War in the Shadows: The Guerrilla in History* (Garden City, N.Y.: Doubleday, 1995).
56 Kenneth S. Stern, *A Force upon the Plain: The American Militia Movement and the Politics of Hate* (New York: Simon & Schuster, 1996).
57 Adam L. Silverman, "Zealous Before the Lord: The Construction of Christian Identity Theology," in *Terrorism: Research, Readings, and Realities*, ed. Lynne L. Snowden and

Bradley L. Whitsel (Upper Saddle River, N.J.: Prentice Hall, 2005), 293–302.
58 Ibid., 297.
59 Paul Leavitt, "No Charges in Mountain Assault," *USA Today*, December 9, 1994, 3A. Gary Fields and Kevin Johnson, "FBI Sharpshooter Charged in Ruby Ridge," *USA Today*, August 22, 1997, 1A. Associated Press, "F.B.I. Agent Cleared in Idaho Siege Shooting," *New York Times*, May 15, 1998, late edition, 14A.
60 George Lardner, Jr., and Pierre Thomas, "U.S. to Pay Family in FBI Idaho Raid," *Washington Post*, August 16, 1995, final edition, A1.
61 Catherine Wessinger, *How the Millennium Comes Violently: From Jonestown to Heaven's Gate* (New York: Seven Bridge Press, 2000).
62 CNN, "Rudolph Reveals Motives," April 19, 2005, http://www.cnn.com/2005/LAW/04/13/eric.rudolph. Accessed July 2018.
63 Jack Warner, "Rudolph Indicted in Four Bombings," *Atlanta Journal and Constitution*, November, 16, 2000, 3A.
64 Howard L. Bushart, John R. Craig, and Myra Barnes, *Soldiers of God; White Supremacists and Their Holy War for America* (New York: Kensington Books, 1998).
65 CNN, "Nichols Gets Life for Oklahoma Bombing," June 4, 1998, http://www.cnn.com/US/9806/04/nichols.update.pm/index.html. Accessed July 2018. Lois Romano, "Nichols Is Spared Death Penalty Again," *Washington Post*, June 12, 2004, final edition, A9.
66 The Southern Poverty Law Center, Intelligence Project, https://www.splcenter.org/intelligence-report. Accessed July 2018.
67 Norris, "Why Dylann Roof Is a Terrorist under Federal Law, and Why It Matters.
68 Mills, Freilich, and Chermak, "Extreme Hatred: Revisiting the Hate Crime and Terrorism Relationship to Determine Whether They Are 'Close Cousins' or 'Distant Relatives'."
69 Federal Bureau of Investigation, Weather Underground Bombings, https://www.fbi.gov/history/famous-cases/weather-underground-bombings. Accessed July 2018.
70 James Jeffrey, "Shedding New Light on the (Real) Black Panthers," BBC, April 1, 2018, https://www.bbc.com/news/world-us-canada-43587976. Accessed July 2018.
71 National Public Radio, "If A Tree Falls': The Earth Liberation Front's Rise," February. 21, 2012, https://www.npr.org/2012/02/21/147163544/if-a-tree-falls-explains-earth-liberation-fronts-rise. Accessed July 2018.
72 Strobe Talbott and Nayan Chanda, *The Age of Terror: America and the World After September 11* (New York: Basic Books, 2001).
73 John Mueller, *Overblown: How Politicians and the Terrorism Industry Inflate National Security Threats and Why We Believe Them* (New York: Free Press, 2006).
74 National Counterterrorism Center, 2008 Report on Terrorism, April 30, 2009, https://www.fbi.gov/file-repository/stats-services-publications-terror_08.pdf. Accessed July 2018.
75 Ewen MacAskill, Severin Carrell, and Ian Black, "Lockerbie Row Reignited as Megrahi Exceeds Life Expectancy When Released," *Guardian*, https://www.theguardian.com/world/2009/nov/20/megrahi-health-lockerbie-bomber. Accessed July 2018.
76 Larry Diamond, "What Went Wrong in Iraq," *Foreign Affairs* 83 (2004): 34–56.
77 Goldie Shabad and Francisco José Llera Ramo, "Political Violence in a Democratic State: Basque Terrorism in Spain," in *Terrorism in Context*, ed. Martha Crenshaw (University Park: Pennsylvania State University Press, 1995), 410–472. Raphael Minder, "Basque Group ETA Disbands, after Terrorist Campaign Spanning Generations," *New York Times*, May 2, 2018, https://www.nytimes.com/2018/05/02/world/europe/spain-eta-disbands-basque.html. Accessed July 2018.
78 J. Bowyer Bell, *The Secret Army: A History of the IRA, 1916–1970* (Cambridge, Mass.: MIT Press, 1997).
79 Jerrold M. Post, *The Mind of the Terrorist: The Psychology of Terrorism from the IRA to Al-Qaeda* (New York: Palgrave MacMillan, 2007). BBC, "Who Are Kurdistan Workers' Party (PKK) Rebels?," November 4, 2016, https://www.bbc.com/news/world-europe-20971100. Accessed July 2018.
80 BBC, "Who Are Somalia's al-Shabab?," Dec. 22, 2017, https://www.bbc.com/news/world-africa-15336689. U.S. Department of State, *Country Reports on Terrorism 2008*, "Chapter 2, Country Reports: Africa Overview," https://www.state.gov/j/ct/rls/crt/2008. CNN, "Hundreds Protest Against Al-Shabaab in Somalia," March 29, 2010, http://www.cnn.com/2010/WORLD/africa/03/29/somalia.protest.march/index.html. Accessed July 2018.
81 Armed Conflict Location & Event Data Project, Boko Haram Crisis, https://www.acleddata.com/dashboard. Accessed July 2018.
82 Maria Abi-Habib and Salman Masood, "Pakistan's Shields Suddenly Step Aside, Placing It on Terrorism Listing," *New York Times*, March 1, 2018, https://www.nytimes.com/2018/03/01/world/asia/pakistan-terrorism-china-saudi-arabia.html. U.S. Department of State, *Country Reports on Terrorism 2008*, "Chapter 2, Country Reports: South and Central Asia Overview," https://www.state.gov/j/ct/rls/crt/2008. Accessed July 2018.
83 BBC, Chechnya profile, January 17, 2018, https://www.bbc.com/news/world-europe-18188085. Edward W. Walker, "Roots of Rage: Militant Islam in Central Asia" (paper presented at the University of California, Berkeley, Berkeley, CA, October 29, 2001), https://iseees.berkeley.edu/index.php?q=bps/caucasus/articles.html. Accessed July 2018.
84 Peter Bergen, *Holy War Inc.: Inside the Secret World of Osama Bin Laden* (New York: Touchstone, 2001).
85 Armed Conflict Location & Event Data Project, Islamic State Crisis, https://www.acleddata.com/dashboard. Accessed July 2018.
86 George Tenet, *At the Center of the Storm: My Years at the CIA* (New York: HarperCollins, 2007).
87 David Johnston, "Sept. 11 Laid in Part to CIA and FBI Lapses," *New York Times/International Herald Tribune*, July 25, 2003, news, p. 1.
88 Robert O'Harrow Jr. and Ellen Nakashima, "National Dragnet Is a Click Away: Authorities to Gain Fast and Expansive Access to Records," *Washington Post*, March 6, 2008, A01.
89 Andrew Knapp, "FBI Had Resources to Halt Dylann Roof's Gun Buy, but It Didn't Use Them—and Still Doesn't," *Post and Courier*, February 4, 2018, https://www.postandcourier.com/church_shooting/fbi-had-resources-to-halt-dylann-roof-s-gun-buy/article_452b95ea-0705-11e8-8bc9-8723f84ce9dd.html.
90 Willard M. Oliver, *Homeland Security for Policing* (Upper Saddle River, N.J.: Prentice Hall, 2007).
91 Jon Hemming, "Big Opium Crop Boon to Taliban," Reuters/*Toronto Star*, February 6, 2008, A12.
92 Mueller, *Overblown: How Politicians and the Terrorism Industry Inflate National Security Threats and Why We Believe Them*, 194–195.
93 Philip Shenon and Kevin Flynn, "Mayor Tells Panel 'Pork Barrel Politics' Is Increasing Risk of Terrorism for City," *New York Times*, May 20, 2004, late edition, B9.
94 Walter M. Brasch, *America's Unpatriotic Acts* (New York: Peter Lang, 2005), xi.
95 Ibid., 4.
96 Dan Eggen, "Patriot Act Provisions Voided; Judge Rules Law Gives Executive Branch Too Much Power," *Washington Post*, September 27, 2007, regional edition, A02.
97 *USA Today*, "Wartime Power Grabs Require Beautiful Sunsets," August 7, 2007, final edition, 8A.
98 Michael B. Farrell, "Obama Signs Patriot Act Extension Without Reforms," *Christian Science Monitor*, March 1, 2010, https://www.csmonitor.com/USA/Politics/2010/0301/Obama-signs-Patriot-Act-extension-without-reforms. Accessed July 2018.
99 CNN, "Last World Trade Center Bombing Conspirator Sentenced," April 3, 1998, http://www.cnn.com/US/9804/03/wtc.bombing. Accessed July 2018.
100 Adam Liptak, "A Case of Buyer's Remorse that Could Linger for Years," *New York Times*, April 23, 2007, late edition, A12.
101 Adam Liptak, "Court Takes Second Look at Enemy Combatant Case," *New York Times*, November 1, 2007, late edition, A18.
102 Andy Kravetz, "Former West Peoria Enemy Combatant Ali al-Marri Released from Prison Early, Deported from U.S.," *Journal Star* (Peoria, Ill.), January 17, 2015, http://www.pjstar.com/article/20150117/NEWS/150119312. Accessed July 2018.

Criminology, Technology, and Privacy

FEATURES

Our privacy is something we can no longer take for granted. How have new technologies intruded in our rights to privacy?

Joseph James DeAngelo, 72, during his arraignment in Sacramento County Superior Court in Sacramento, California. How was this suspect finally identified?

Between 1974 and 1986, the Golden State Killer murdered at least 12 people, raped more than 50, and committed 100 burglaries. The perpetrator, variously known as the East Area Rapist, the Original Nightstalker, the Diamond Knot Killer, and the Visalia Ransacker, terrorized 10 California counties with offenses so horrific, frequent, sadistic, and creative that authorities did not immediately realize it was all the work of one person.[1]

The killer was meticulous and crafty. He watched the victims, learning the layout of their homes and their personal routines. He disabled locks and hid weapons. At a 1977 community meeting, a man said a husband would never let his wife be raped by an intruder. Months later, that man's wife was raped while he was home. Said one witness, "I think the rapist was in the meeting that night."[2]

Police continued working the cases long after the attacks stopped but came up with nothing. Only in 2001 was DNA testing able to connect the East Area Rapist cases with those of the Original Nightstalker. Finally, investigator and forensic expert Paul Holes had an idea. In 1980, a pathologist had preserved a duplicate evidence kit of one of the crime scenes. Holes uploaded the DNA to a genealogy website and found distant relatives of the killer, which led to his great-great-great grandparents who lived in the early 1800s.[3]

Of the 25 family trees that investigators created from those grandparents, about 1,000 family members populated the one that included the killer. Other databases the team used contained census data, newspaper obituaries, gravesite locators, and police files. When investigators reached the killer's living relatives, they began looking for suspects who were the right age and had lived in the crime area. Two suspects looked likely. The first was eliminated by a relative's DNA. The other was Joseph James DeAngelo, age 72, of Citrus Heights, California. DeAngelo had served in the Navy in the 1960s and later earned a criminal justice degree. He had been a police officer in the 1970s.[4]

Investigators collected DeAngelo's DNA from his trash and from the handle of his car door. It matched a sample collected from one of the 1980s crime scenes. DeAngelo was arrested in April 2018 and charged with 13 murders.[5]

Criminology and Technology

LEARNING OBJECTIVE | 1

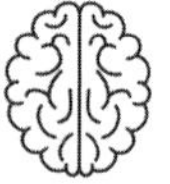

Describe how technology has changed how some lawbreakers break the law.

LEARNING OBJECTIVE | 2

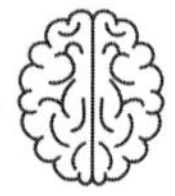

Give examples of how crime is responsible for the advancement of some technologies.

Technology has always been an element of crime prevention. Today's criminology student must have a greater appreciation of the role of technology in preventing and controlling crime and develop skills that did not even exist a generation ago. There were no leads in the Golden State Killer case until 30 years after the last offense had been committed, and those leads could only be followed using a technology few had dreamed would ever be available.

This chapter will provide a broad overview of the technological issues of working in the criminal justice system and suggest some emerging concerns. This final chapter will begin with a short history of technology and crime, then concentrate on three effects of technology on the criminal justice system that have made the study of criminology more interesting and more complex.

1. Technology gives lawbreakers more opportunities. As society becomes more dependent on technology, lawbreakers with knowledge

of how to use and manipulate sophisticated electronic systems have more opportunities to break the law. In this section of the chapter, we will look at how some offenders use technology to break the law in ways that were not possible in decades past.

2. The criminal justice system employs technology to discover, apprehend, process, and incarcerate offenders. Criminal justice officials employ technology to counter the technological expertise of lawbreakers and make the criminal justice system more efficient and less costly. Here, we will concentrate on how the criminal justice system uses technology to prevent crime and dispense justice.
3. Technology alters our concepts of privacy. Technology allows law enforcement to keep better track of offenders and protect life and property, and it also allows for the surveillance of ordinary law-abiding citizens in ways that challenge our concepts of privacy. This section of the chapter will examine the delicate balance between individual rights and public security and suggest that this balance will take a long time to achieve because of the rapidly changing nature of technology.

A Short History of Technology and Crime

The use of technology to break the law is not new. The cat-and-mouse game between lawbreakers and those who wish to protect themselves and their property has always existed. Bars on windows, deadbolt locks, safety deposit boxes in banks, and countless other examples of technology are a testament to how hard lawbreakers are willing to work to get something for "free" (see Theory to Practice).

In some ways, computers and security technology have greatly increased the level of sophistication required to commit such offenses as larceny, theft, robbery, and most property offenses. However, we should realize that these "technological" offenses are mostly an extension of street crime. The theft of an identity using computers is still theft. The use of a denial-of-service (DoS) attack to disable an Internet server is still vandalism, malicious mischief, or a prelude to theft. The Internet has simply made it easier to break the law on a large scale as well as in a more comprehensive and nearly anonymous manner.

The use of technology to break the law has caused major concerns among law enforcement agencies and financial institutions, as well as the general public. These concerns have jump-started a computer-security industry that requires workers with a high level of technological expertise, and law enforcement agencies have had to develop new protocols for investigating offenses committed with computers. Criminology students looking for a rewarding career in the criminal justice system must now learn electronic and computer skills and develop a level of technological sophistication that will enable them to step outside the traditional bounds of criminology.

There is a case to be made that crime, in many ways, is responsible for the advancement of some technologies. Although we must be careful not to overstate this point because some people will always seek opportunities to break the law, society must set up safeguards to protect property, information, and public safety. For instance, many homes now have Internet-connected security systems that are integrated with systems that control lighting, heating, and air conditioning, home entertainment centers, and other appliances. Without the advances in private security–system technology, many of these other systems would not have been developed in such advanced ways. Fear of crime has created a profit motive for manufacturers of these systems not only to develop technology to provide security, but also to tack on other features to make their systems more marketable.

Advanced crime-scene investigation technologies and techniques have inspired a new interest in chemistry, biology, and computer science. Many students are drawn to criminology because they want to become crime-scene technicians or work in crime labs. The attractiveness of crime-scene investigation derives in part from the answers that science can provide to help solve cases.

Finally, crime has pushed technological advances in the area of security of money and identity. The Treasury Department has continuously battled counterfeiters by making money distinctive and difficult to replicate. These efforts have led to advances in special inks, optical effects, and technologies such as holograms to thwart counterfeiters. Security concerns in protecting identity have prompted the development of fingerprint and handprint scanners, voice recognition software, and technology that scans human irises to validate identity.

We must be careful not to overstate the idea that crime is responsible for advances in technology. However, in a capitalist society, the profit motive is crucial to developing practical applications for technological innovations. The disruption that crime causes in society creates markets for technological products that prevent criminal offending or help solve cases.

THEORY TO PRACTICE

Because That's Where the Money Is

When asked why he robbed banks, Willie Sutton replied, "Because that's where the money is." Individuals have long sought to protect their money from the likes of Willie Sutton and have gone to great extremes to make it more difficult for thieves to take it. A great lesson in technology can be learned from the efforts to protect banks, which are attempts at **situational crime prevention**, an extension of **rational choice theory**.

Author Robert Letkemann traced the evolution of bank security in his book *Crime and Work* in which he interviewed bank robbers and safe crackers to find out how they learned their trade. According to Letkemann, today's bank security is a result of the success of thieves and safe crackers in penetrating the defenses designed to secure the bank's contents. These advances included vault design, security cards, cameras, infrared sensors, and other technological mechanisms. Bank robbers still found a way around these innovations. For example:

- When banks found that thieves were able to penetrate their safes, they designed stronger safes with more sophisticated locks. The response from bank robbers was to remove the safe to a place where the robbers had the time and tools to crack the safe.
- Banks responded by making the safes bigger, heavier, and bolting them to the floor. Robbers began using dynamite to blow the safes open.
- Banks used stronger metals that dynamite could not penetrate. Bank robbers responded by using nitroglycerin and other more powerful explosives.
- Banks designed safes with circular doors so that the nitroglycerin would drain to the bottom of the door, rendering the explosive ineffective. So thieves kidnapped bank managers and forced them to open the safes.
- Banks then developed safes with timers that prevented employees from opening them during non-banking hours.

You get the idea. As a result of trying to make banks a harder target for thieves to penetrate, bank officials have essentially given up on many of the target-hardening aspects of situational crime prevention and now instead try to limit their losses. Today, bank employees cooperate with robbers and hand over the cash. However, each teller has a limited amount of cash, and each bank has a limited total amount of cash. Cameras also photograph or record the likenesses and activities of everyone at the bank, both inside and out.

Because so much banking is now done electronically, physically robbing a bank is no longer considered a big score. Although bank robbers sometimes get away with their offenses, they must rob many banks to make a living, increasing the likelihood of capture.

THINK ABOUT IT

1. How does situational crime prevention describe the efforts to physically secure banks?

Making counterfeit money on a home ink jet printer. What steps has the government taken to make counterfeiting money more difficult?

One of the most momentous technological innovations of the last 50 years is that of information technology, a general term used to describe devices and software that transmit, receive, and store data. Information technology includes any device that provides information about another person, including tracking, identification, and surveillance devices, as well as computer **databases**. Although information technology was not developed primarily in response to crime, one of its uses has been to establish the security of governments, corporations, and individuals through the movement and restriction of information. Currently, the star application of information technology systems is the Internet, which was, in its early stages, intended to provide secure communications for the U.S. government.

THE BEGINNINGS OF THE INTERNET

The Internet grew out of various government projects that began at the end of World War II and the start of the Cold War. The reasons for developing a decentralized national computer network were military and scientific. One of the first projects, Whirlwind, at the Massachusetts Institute of Technology, monitored and coordinated radars that tracked the movement of Russian aircraft. The U.S. government also wanted a system that could provide multiple routes for electronic communication in the aftermath of a nuclear conflict. In the 1960s, the Advanced Research Projects Agency (ARPA) initiated a project that would allow computers at the nation's science labs, government agencies, and universities to communicate with one another.[6] ARPANET officially went online in October 1969 with a test message sent from UCLA to the Stanford Research Institute. In 1987, the National Science Foundation (NSF) took over responsibility for ARPANET's civilian nodes. Initially called NSFnet, the NSF's system eventually became known as the Internet. ARPANET was discontinued in 1990; in 1991, the NSF lifted the restrictions on the commercial use of its network. (The government had allowed no commercial activity on ARPANET.)[7] From that date, civilian use of the Internet took off, and, presumably, the first laws were broken with its help shortly thereafter.

THE INTERNET AND CRIME

Crime is socially defined. In other words, it takes a society, a network of people, to define the rules of behavior, decide how they are applied, determine when they are broken, and assess the consequences of their breakage. Crime cannot exist in a society of one (imagine a person marooned on a deserted island). The formation of a human network of any sort means that rules will be made and broken, and the breakage of some of these rules will be regarded as crime. The Internet is a tool for communication; like any tool, it is not a source of crime, but it does offer unscrupulous people new and creative ways to break the law. The Internet also offers unprecedented anonymity (although probably not as much as some people think). As with any network, the larger and more open to new membership it is, the more crime will occur. Probably little to no crime occurred on ARPANET because it was a tightly controlled network of individuals from the closed communities of science and the military.

Perhaps the most interesting and serious consequence the Internet has had for traditional criminal justice is its effect on **jurisdiction**, or legal authority. In the United States, as throughout much of the world, legal jurisdiction is one of the cornerstones of criminal justice. Jurisdiction can be established politically (federal, state, and local jurisdictions), geographically, or by the nature of the offense. For example, an offense that takes place within a state is handled by that state's criminal justice agencies, depending on the seriousness of the offense. Local law enforcement deals with drunk drivers. A serial murderer who does not cross state lines will be pursued by the state's major law enforcement agency. A serial murderer who does cross state lines involves the FBI. A person who commits tax fraud is pursued by the Internal Revenue Service (IRS). Someone who commits an offense involving the postal service is investigated by that agency's law enforcement bureau. All these cases flow through the criminal justice system in order of jurisdiction.

This way of allotting criminal justice resources worked just fine until the Internet. Today, a major financial offense that involves both copyright and illegal pornography can be committed by a group of people distributed throughout one country, via servers in a second country, against victims located in yet a third country, for clients in a fourth country. Where is the jurisdiction? Who investigates the case, arrests the suspects, tries the defendants, and punishes the convicted? The Internet has set up these questions, and criminal justice systems across the globe are trying to come up with an answer. (See Table 14.1 for a list of federal agencies that investigate computer-related crime.) To understand crime on the Internet, we must first understand how it began.

THE WHISTLER, CAP'N CRUNCH, AND THE EVOLUTION OF COMPUTER NETWORK CRIME

The use of a technological network to break the law did not start with the Internet. Undoubtedly, the law had been broken with the use of radios early in

Instant Recall from Chapter 4 **situational crime prevention** —An offshoot of rational choice theory that considers direct factors that can be modified to discourage crime.

Instant Recall from Chapter 4 **rational choice theory** — The concept that offenders calculate the advantages and disadvantages not only of breaking the law, but of what type of offense to commit.

database—An organized set of information.

jurisdiction—Legal authority.

TABLE 14.1 Federal Computer Crime Investigation Agencies and Divisions

These agencies investigate offenses that are perpetrated via computer networks.

AGENCY OR DIVISION	TASK
National Cyber Security Division	The task of the National Cybersecurity Division is to collaborate with public, private, and international entities to build and maintain an effective national Internet response system and to implement a risk management program to protect critical national infrastructure.
US-CERT	The United States Computer Emergency Readiness Team (US-CERT) is a partnership between the Department of Homeland Security and the public and private sectors. Established in 2003 to protect the nation's Internet infrastructure, US-CERT coordinates responses to computer-based attacks in the United States.
FBI Cyber Investigations	The mission of the FBI Cyber Investigations unit is to stop those behind the most serious computer intrusions and the spread of malicious code; to identify and thwart sexual predators who use the Internet to meet and exploit children and to produce, possess, or share child pornography; to counteract operations that target U.S. intellectual property; and to dismantle national and transnational organized criminal enterprises that engage in Internet fraud.
Internet Crime Complaint Center (IC3)	The Internet Crime Complaint Center (IC3), a partnership between the FBI and the National White Collar Crime Center, receives, tracks, analyzes, and organizes Internet crime complaints and refers the complaints to the appropriate federal, state, local, or international law enforcement agency or regulatory agency for investigation.
Department of Justice Computer Crime and Intellectual Property Section	The Computer Crime and Intellectual Property Section implements national strategies in combating computer and intellectual property offenses throughout the world.

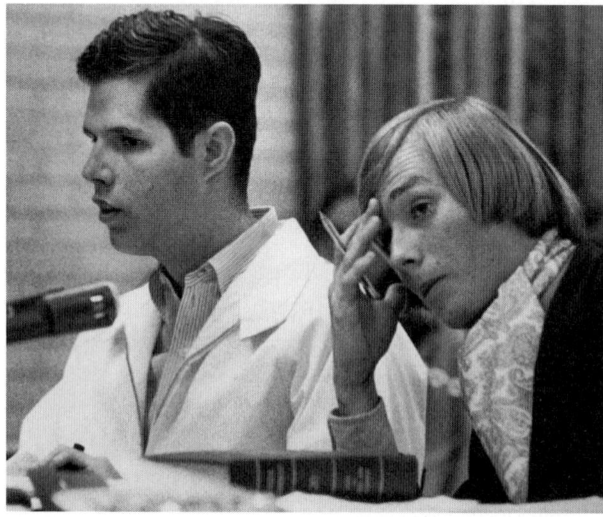

Joe Engressia, left, who placed free telephone calls by whistling into the receiver, at a disciplinary hearing in 1968. University of South Florida officials put Engressia on probation and directed him to make restitution to the phone company. Is this type of hacking still possible today?

hacking—The unauthorized use of an information system or network.

the 20th century, but the modern era of **hacking**—the unauthorized use of an information system or network—emerged with Joe Engressia in the 1950s. Also known as "The Whistler," Engressia (who in 1991 changed his name to Joybubbles) was born blind but gifted with excellent hearing and perfect pitch. As a child in the 1950s, Engressia learned to manipulate the telephone system, which, at the time, was based on tones.

While still a toddler, Engressia discovered he could dial a telephone by tapping the hookswitch like a telegraph key. At the age of seven, he whistled a sound he heard on a long-distance phone call and discovered that it disconnected the call. Engressia later began to whistle the telephone company's tones to manipulate the phone system and make free calls. Years later, the University of South Florida expelled Engressia for making free long-distance phone calls for his friends. In 1971, Engressia was convicted of telephone fraud, but his skills were so rare that by 1975 Mountain Bell had hired him to diagnose its network problems. As the first "phone phreak"

DOUBLETAKE

Phun with Fonics

Students of Internet crime will notice that some of the offenses—the ones that begin with an "f" sound—have odd spellings. The reason for this is most likely connected to the word "phone," short for "telephone," which was probably the first public network to be hacked. Early telephone network hackers substituted "ph" for "f" in creating a moniker for themselves: "freaks." Thus, "freaks" became "phreaks," and telephone hackers became known as "phone phreaks" and telephone hacking as "phreaking." Now, nearly anytime the letter "f" appears at the beginning of a word associated with hacking or Internet crime, that "f" is replaced with a "ph." For example, an identity thief's "fishing" for information is often spelled "phishing."

THINK ABOUT IT

1. Subcultures, such as street gangs and hackers, often use alternative spellings and clever wordplay to describe themselves and their activities. Discuss possible reasons for this.

(see Doubletake for why the term is spelled that way), Engressia became legendary and developed a following that included such computing pioneers as Steve Jobs and Steve Wozniak of Apple Computer. In one stunt, Engressia whistled his way through telephone systems around the globe so that he could talk into one phone and listen to himself on another.[8]

Computer pioneer John Draper expanded on Engressia's methods by using a toy whistle from a box of Cap'n Crunch cereal to make the same tone. Draper, now known as "Cap'n Crunch," was arrested several times throughout the 1970s for stealing long-distance phone calls (he graduated to other methods to make his phone calls when the telephone company dropped the tone system in 1971). Draper went to prison for telephone fraud even as he was writing groundbreaking software for the fledgling computer industry.[9]

For the most part, the perpetrators of this early form of technology-based crime broke the law in pursuit of knowledge rather than money. They wanted to learn more about how the telephone system, then the primary communications system in the United States, worked. Also, it was not unusual for phone phreaks and other early hackers to work on both sides of the law. Some began their careers breaking the law to learn more about computer and telephone networks, then were later employed by the very companies they had victimized. Others, like John Draper, continued their unlawful activities while working legitimate jobs in the same industry.

Since the early 1980s, computer and network crime has been increasingly pursued for profit, and it has more in common with street crime in terms of the perpetrators' intent. In 1995, Kevin Mitnick was arrested and sentenced to five years in prison for breaking into the systems of Motorola, Novell, Fujitsu, Sun Microsystems, and Nokia to steal software code. Active for 15 years, Mitnick spent two years on the run from the FBI; however, he appears never to have used or sold his stolen goods, which consisted of corporate intellectual properties.[10] Today the valuable items are personal information such as names, social security numbers, and credit card numbers, which are often sold on Internet "dark markets." (See more on dark markets in the section "The Dark Web.")

PAUSE AND REVIEW

1. **What is hacking?**
2. **What are the origins of the Internet?**
3. **What makes crime on the Internet different from street crime?**

Types of Computer Network Crime

LEARNING OBJECTIVE 3

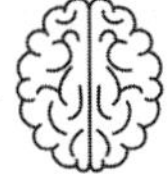

Show why the Internet provides a nearly ideal network for crime.

Today, most people equate the Internet with the World Wide Web, but other basic applications include e-mail, FTP (file transfer protocol), and telnet (a protocol to run a remote computer). These Internet applications can be used in various ways to break the law. Internet crime is actually street and white-collar crime perpetrated with a different sort of human network. Most Internet crime involves fraud, larceny-theft, vandalism, and copyright violation, offenses that existed long before the Internet.[11] Networks on which crime is common share some characteristics.

- They are large.
- They offer some degree of anonymity.
- They offer something of economic value or access to it.
- They are easy to access and use.
- They are versatile.

We can use these characteristics to trace the development and likelihood of crime on technology-based networks. ARPANET offered none of these characteristics and so was virtually crime-free. (Rules were still broken, however; see the next section, "The Computer Crime Toolbox"). The U.S. phone system offers some of these characteristics: It is large; it can be anonymous, though less so today than in decades past; it offers economic value (phone service) and access to something of economic value (other people); and it is easy to access and use. Although a great deal of fraud occurs over the phone, phone service does not offer the versatility that the Internet does.[12] If some technological network were to be developed that was better than the Internet on these five characteristics, even more crime would likely occur on that network. In fact, a lot of crime is already occurring with the use of other networked devices, such as cell phones and credit card readers. See Table 14.2 for theories about Internet crime. Keep these theories in mind as we discuss various types of Internet-based offenses.

The Computer Crime Toolbox

The programs and methods used to break the law through the computer include viruses, worms, Trojan horses, spam, and malware. The names of these programs and methods succinctly describe

TABLE 14.2 Theories of Internet Crime

THEORY	EXPLANATION
Space transition theory	People behave differently in different spaces. "Space transition" describes the movement of people from one space to another. Space transition theory holds that people engage in illegal behavior online that they would avoid in physical space. Space transition theory seeks to explain only offenses committed via computer, not those committed in physical space.[1]
Neutralization theory	The neutralization techniques that computer network offenders use most often to justify their activities are denial of injury, denial of victim, condemnation of the condemners appeal to higher loyalties, and self-fulfillment. They rarely use denial of responsibility or the "sad tale."[2]
Routine activities theory	For the law to be broken, three things must happen simultaneously: A suitable target must be present; there must be no suitable guardian to prevent the offense; a motivated offender must be present.[3] Deterrence occurs when any one of these elements is shifted. However, such shifting is difficult on the Internet: Suitable guardians are rare, and motivated offenders are present everywhere, as are suitable targets. A motivated offender might be presented with a suitable target at any time. Therefore, the Internet is a more likely place for some laws to be broken than physical space.
Opportunity theory	Opportunity must exist for a criminal offense to occur. If an offense cannot be committed in one place, it will be committed in another. The opportunity for crime on the Internet is increased because it is no longer bound by physical place.[4]

1. K. Jaishankar, "Space Transition Theory of Cyber Crimes," in *Crimes of the Internet*, ed. Frank Schmalleger and Michael Pittaro (Upper Saddle River, N.J.: Pearson Prentice Hall, 2009), 292.
2. Orly Turgeman-Goldschmidt, "The Rhetoric of Hackers' Neutralizations," in *Crimes of the Internet*, 317–332.
3. Raymond W. Cox III, Terrance A. Johnson, and George E. Richards, "Routine Activity Theory and Internet Crime," in *Crimes of the Internet*, 302–315.
4. Ibid., 302–315.

what they do and how they work. Most of the offenses committed using these tools involve theft and vandalism. The list of methods used to commit computer network crime presented here is not exhaustive, for new and increasingly technical methods are being invented every day. However, most of the common computer network offenses and the tools used to commit these offenses fall within the broad categories discussed here.

THE DARK WEB

Sometimes called the "darknet," the dark web is a part of the World Wide Web that is accessible only with certain types of software or authorization. Probably the most common way to get to the dark web is through a Web browser called "Tor," which is short for its original name "The Onion Router." Tor assists anonymous communication between users and is used to provide gateways to dark websites that cannot be accessed through other browsers.

Although Tor advocates say that the browser is indispensable for political dissidents, journalists, law enforcement officers, and business professionals who require security and anonymity, Tor and the dark web are often used for illegal activities. These activities typically entail the exchange of illegal information, such as stolen identities, false identities, and stolen credit card numbers; certain types of pornography; or goods and services such as weapons, drugs, and computer hacking. There is even a market for "likes" and "dislikes" to drive up the popularity (or unpopularity) of social media content. Payment for such information, goods, and services is rendered in a cryptocurrency—a type of digital "money" that uses cryptography to secure financial transactions—such as Bitcoin.

Because the dark web is so notorious, law enforcement watches it closely. In 2013, the FBI shut down the first, and probably most infamous, dark web market, Silk Road. Its creator and manager, Ross Ulbricht (known as Dread Pirate Roberts), was convicted of money laundering, computer hacking, conspiracy to traffic fraudulent identity documents, and conspiracy to traffic narcotics via the Internet. Ulbricht is serving two life sentences plus 40 years without the possibility of parole.[13] In 2016, an international law enforcement effort, Operation Hyperion, took down many of the dark markets that sprang up to replace Silk Road.[14] Despite all this law enforcement attention, dark markets continue to pop up before being inevitably shut down.[15]

This sign shows that this business accepts bitcoin as payment. Are cryptocurrencies such as bitcoin here to stay? Why or why not?

SOCIAL ENGINEERING

Social engineering—manipulating individuals so that they give away information or perform actions—is one of the oldest tools used in breaking into computer networks. However, social engineering takes advantage of the human network rather than a computer network and has much in common with con games. Many of the most infamous network break-ins involved not cracking a system's passwords but merely inventing a story, then asking someone in charge to reveal the passwords. This particular form of social engineering is called "pretexting."

Recall the earlier account in this chapter of how Kevin Mitnick broke into the systems of several companies to steal software code. Mitnick posed as an employee of software maker Novell, Inc., and called the company's systems administrator late at night to request access to Novell's network. Mitnick explained that he was out of town and needed to connect to the network to work on a project. As a security check, the systems administrator called the employee's voice mail to make sure the voice that answered matched the voice that he had heard on the phone. The voices matched, and the systems administrator let Mitnick access the system. However, earlier Mitnick had called another Novell technician and convinced that technician to give him access to the employee's voice mail account. Mitnick recorded a new answering message using his voice, so when the systems administrator called to check if the

---

social engineering—The manipulation of individuals so that they divulge information or perform actions.

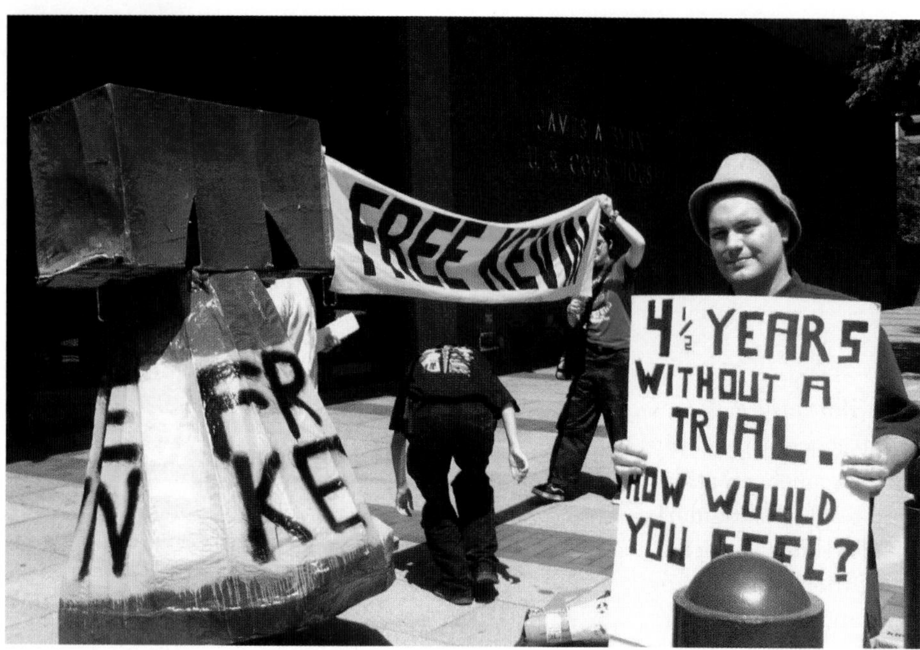

A small group of supporters of Kevin Mitnick demonstrates outside a federal courthouse. Was Mitnick a successful hacker?

voices matched, they did. Once inside Novell's systems, Mitnick copied the code for Novell's most important product, NetWare.[16]

Companies are a bit wiser to social engineering attempts now than they were in 1994, but social engineering and pretexting are still regularly attempted. A popular target is financial information. The 1999 Gramm–Leach–Bliley Act specifically prohibits pretexting to obtain consumers' personal financial information, such as bank balances, from financial institutions. Enforced primarily by the Federal Trade Commission (FTC), the law prescribes fines and imprisonment for violators, with enhanced penalties for aggravated cases. The 2006 Telephone Records and Privacy Protection Act makes it a federal offense to use pretexting to obtain telephone records, with penalties of up to 10 years in prison.[17]

Other forms of social engineering rely more specifically on the use of computers to acquire information.

- Phishing. Phishing involves the use of an e-mail that resembles an important communication from a bank or other trusted institution. The e-mail asks recipients for sensitive account information or refers recipients to a false website that resembles the institution's website in order to trick them into entering their passwords and account numbers. Often, the website will respond with a "bad password" message to get victims to enter their information repeatedly. Thieves then collect this information into a database and sell or use it to victimize the person immediately. A "spear phishing" attack is more focused, with the e-mail being personalized to the receiver, often by information picked from a social media site. Although only a small percentage of victims will respond to these e-mails, enough people usually respond to make the phishing expedition worthwhile.
- Trojan horses. These usually arrive in the form of e-mail attachments that appear interesting to recipients, promising exciting pictures, screensavers, music, software, or other goodies. Clicking on the attachment releases a hidden program that allows control of the computer by a third party, downloads sensitive information from the computer, destroys data on the computer, or otherwise vandalizes the system.

SPAM

Spam, or unsolicited e-mail advertising a product or service that is sent in bulk to large numbers of people, was invented in 1978 by Gary Thuerk of the Digital Equipment Corporation. Thuerk decided to advertise the company's new computer system by sending an e-mail to 600 people on ARPANET. Because ARPANET was not supposed to be used for commercial advertising, Thuerk was reprimanded, and the academic debate about network usage and free speech began.[18]

Unfortunately, spam is now more than a debate topic for university network administrators. Spam clogs servers, overloads individual e-mail accounts, and delivers inappropriate and pornographic messages, as well as malware. Spam is more problematic than unsolicited bulk postal mail because of the low costs associated with sending spam. Bulk mail sent through the postal system incurs printing and postage costs as well as the costs of storing, sorting, and sending the mail. Because spam is electronic, however, it requires little more than an Internet account and a list of e-mail addresses, which is inexpensive and easily purchased. Because of the low overhead costs, enough spam can be sent to overload Internet servers and e-mail accounts, costing individuals and businesses millions in time and money to deal with it.

In an effort to control spam, the U.S. Congress passed the Controlling the Assault of Non-Solicited Pornography and Marketing Act (CAN-SPAM Act) in 2003. The first application of CAN-SPAM occurred in 2007, when two men, Jeffrey A. Kilbride and James R. Schaffer, were sentenced to more than five years in prison for sending pornographic spam. Kilbride and Schaffer were fined $100,000 and ordered to pay $77,500 in restitution to AOL Inc., as well as forfeit more than $1.1 million in profits from their spamming operation.[19]

DENIAL-OF-SERVICE ATTACKS

Denial-of-service (DoS) attacks are a form of computer network crime that is often combined with worms, viruses, Trojans, and spam as their "payload." A DoS attack is an attempt to make a computer or server so busy with meaningless activity that it is unavailable for anything else. The typical target for a DoS attack is any website that attracts a lot of traffic such as bank or credit card payment sites, or gaming servers. A DoS attack makes the servers so busy that they cannot deal with the thousands of legitimate requests from the site's users.

Often, the purpose of such an attack is extortion. The perpetrators contact the site's owners and demand money in exchange for leaving the site alone. If the site owners do not pay, then the site is attacked. In what has been called the "street crime of the Internet," DoS extortionists prefer to target smaller sites, whose owners are turning a profit, but not so much that they can afford to hire the best computer security or lawyers. Other likely targets are site owners who are involved in questionable activities themselves, making them unlikely to go to authorities. Such sites would include gambling and pornography websites. These site owners simply pay off the extortionists in order to stay online and avoid involving the police.[20] These kinds of targets make DoS extortionists very difficult to track down and prosecute.

VIRUSES, WORMS, AND OTHER MALWARE

Malware is software that purposefully damages, disables, or steals information from computers and computer systems. Both viruses and worms are malware. A computer virus is a program that is attached to another file or program. When the file or program is run, the virus runs too. A virus can copy and attach itself to other programs and files. When these files are sent to another computer, either over a network or by media (such as a USB drive), the virus goes, too, and infects the new system. A worm is much like a virus, but it is not attached to another file or program. Once resident on a computer, worms scan the network for specific types of security holes that they can move through to infect new machines.[21]

Before computer networks were common, early viruses were transmitted via floppy disks. The virus would save itself to a floppy disk inserted into an infected computer, then install itself on the next computer the disk was inserted into. The first computer virus, called Creeper, appeared in the early 1970s on ARPANET. Computers infected with Creeper would display the message: "I'M THE CREEPER: CATCH ME IF YOU CAN." Shortly after Creeper came the virus Reaper, which apparently had the task of deleting the Creeper virus. The authors of these two viruses are unknown. The first virus to spread among common computer users was Elk Cloner, which was transmitted between Apple II computers via floppy disks in the early to mid-1980s. Like the Creeper and Reaper viruses, Elk Cloner was not written with criminal or destructive intent and only displayed a string of rhyming verses.[22]

Since then, computer viruses have become steadily more destructive and more easily spread. Destructive viruses typically damage computers by deleting data and interfering with the computer's operation, such as causing the computer to turn itself off or causing the hard drive to reformat itself, or by using up computer memory and processing speed. One of the most problematic viruses was the Melissa virus of 1999, a Microsoft Word 2000 macro virus that propagated via e-mail attachments. Several companies, including Microsoft, had to shut down their e-mail systems until Melissa could be brought under control.[23]

Unlike viruses, worms were first created by professional programmers to assist computer systems. In 1978, Xerox PARC (Palo Alto Research Center) researchers John Shoch and Jon Hupp designed a worm that would find idle computers on the network and put them to work on specific tasks, thus

---

spam—Unsolicited e-mail advertising a product or service that is sent in bulk to large numbers of people.

increasing computing efficiency. Although the worm was beneficial and designed to expire after a certain period, it was difficult to control and crashed several computers.[24] Since then, worms have grown increasingly destructive, with the main goal of worm writers apparently being to control computers and harvest data. For example, the Storm Worm, which became active in 2007, added infected computers to a botnet (private computers that have been harnessed into a network without their owners' knowledge and used for criminal purposes), which was then used to spread spam, steal identities, and shut down computer networks.

Many virus and worm writers have emphasized that the purpose of their activities is to exploit security holes in software and operating systems so that they can be patched. However, in recent years, the profit motive behind these activities has become clear. For example, ransomware is a form of malware that takes over an individual's computer and encrypts its data, promising to restore access for payment.

Because the Internet has connected so many computers around the world, including critical public systems, virus protection is not only big business, but also a major concern of government authorities. A particularly devious virus or worm could do immense damage to government and military computers, putting public safety and security at risk.

In 2018, computing experts warned that the Russian government had infected more than 500,000 routers in 54 countries with malware. (A router is the equipment in many homes and businesses that directs Internet traffic to multiple computers.) The malware, called VPNFilter, was so robust it could survive a reboot of the router and other efforts to remove malware. Among the many capabilities of this malware was that it could exploit specific devices connected to an infected network; look for passwords in Web traffic so they could be copied; and covertly relay and alter the communication between two parties who think they are directly communicating with each other. According to one expert, "[The perpetrators] can modify your bank account balance so that it looks normal while at the same time they're siphoning off money. . . . They can manipulate everything going in and out of the [router]."[25]

The Most Serious Offenses

Every day, hundreds, if not thousands, of serious criminal offenses are perpetrated via the Internet. These include copyright infringement, child pornography, identity theft, and e-mail scams. Although this list does not include every possible form of criminal offense that occurs online, they do represent the most common types of offenses. Because the Internet is not limited by geography, investigation and prosecution of nearly all online offenses require cooperation among several jurisdictions and types of law enforcement agencies, including those located outside the United States.

COPYRIGHT INFRINGEMENT

Copyright infringement is the duplication of information without permission from the copyright's owner. Copyright is a legal concept that makes information, such as that in the form of media or ideas, profitable. Only the entity that owns the copyright to a piece of information can reproduce that information, usually for the purpose of sale. Copyrights have economic value and can be bought, sold, or otherwise transferred. Restricting the public's ability to reproduce copyrighted information protects that information's economic value for the copyright owner. For example, a piece of music can legally be reproduced only by the copyright owner, who may then sell those reproductions. However, if listeners reproduce that music on their own without permission from the copyright holder, theoretically they do not need to purchase that music. The music then loses its economic value for the copyright holder, who has also lost control of the copies because it has become free of charge.

Prior to the Internet, copyright infringement was not a great problem for copyright holders, and few cases were pursued in the courts. Copies made by amateurs were of low quality and often required special equipment, so it made more sense for consumers to purchase the item. However, the Internet and digitalization have changed those circumstances for media producers, especially those who specialize in recorded music, film, and software. These items have proven particularly, even disastrously, suitable for digitalization, copying, and transmission over the Internet. For instance, prior to digitalization, a person could make an audio tape of a song from the radio or a vinyl album. However, doing so was not a serious problem for the music companies because the copies were of relatively low quality as compared to the originals. Furthermore, the copies could not be transmitted electronically (at least not easily). Now, it is easy to copy and transmit digital media, and the copies are, in the case of music and film, nearly as good as the originals. In the case of software, the copies are an exact match.

Since the early 1990s, when Internet file-trading became popular enough to cause concern in the media and software industries, several legal bouts took place between corporate interests and the public. For example, for several years, modified peer-to-peer networks, of which Napster was the most popular, were the target of corporate music interests. Later, file-trading moved to a true peer-to-peer model, the most popular of which is BitTorrent. This protocol allows individuals to trade small pieces of files until all users have the whole file. This is a much more difficult protocol for copyright holders to control than the modified peer-to-peer models because most users have only pieces of files. Presumably, once users collect a whole file, they log off the system. The tug of war over copyright infringement is likely to continue for years to come.

CHILD PORNOGRAPHY

The Internet has made child pornography easier to distribute and obtain and more difficult to control. In the mid-1980s, before Internet usage became common, law enforcement felt confident that child pornography had almost been stamped out. Because the child pornography trade involved the use of tangible photographs, magazines, and videotapes, it was fairly easy to trace the source of the pornographic materials, which were expensive to produce and distribute. The Internet made the transmission of electronic material simple, fast, and anonymous, reviving what had been a fading criminal offense.

Like other computer network offenses, the distribution of child pornography is an old offense. Although the Internet augmented the trade in child pornography, this offense was not invented on the Internet. The Internet is simply a tool that child pornographers use to further their antisocial behavior, much as photography was used in the 19th century.[26] More than 200 child pornography magazines were being sold in the United States by 1977.[27]

However, because the idea of children as a protected class with its own rights and justice system is a relatively modern American concept, the offense of exploiting children sexually is also relatively new. Until the 1880s in the United States, girls as young as 10 years old could consent to sexual activity.[28] As late as 1977, only two states specifically banned the use of children in obscene material, and the first federal child pornography law was passed in 1978. Laws specifying computers and child pornography were not passed in the United States until 1988.[29] Because of the international nature of the Internet, the trade in pornographic material crosses jurisdictions as well as international boundaries. It is a problem many countries must deal with. To help define the scope of online child pornography, the Australian government has compiled a useful typology of pornographers.

- Browser. This Internet user happens upon pornography accidentally but decides to keep the material.
- Private fantasy. A computer user creates pornographic material for private use and stores the material on electronic media but does not distribute the material via a computer network.
- Trawler. This person actively seeks child pornography using openly available Web browsers using little to no security.
- Non-secure collector. This person actively seeks material through peer-to-peer networks, which are somewhat more secure.
- Secure collector. This individual actively seeks material through secure networks only. Some networks require that members submit a certain number of images to join. In this way, all the network's members take responsibility for the network's activities.
- Groomer. A groomer pursues online relationships with children with the intent to establish either a virtual or physical sexual relationship.
- Physical abuser. This person physically abuses a child, with pornography being used to augment the abuse in some way (possibly by frightening or trying to seduce the child). The abuse might be recorded for the personal use of the abuser.
- Producer. A producer physically abuses a child, records the abuse, and then distributes the material.
- Distributor. This person may be more interested in the business of child pornography than in the material or actual activity. In that case, the distribution of pornographic material is solely an avenue to make money. However, this does not preclude some distributors from being in any of the above categories as well.[30]

Most major investigations of Internet child pornography require the cooperation of law enforcement agencies in multiple countries or jurisdictions. In one incident, Christopher Neil, a Canadian man living in South Korea, posted on the Internet photographs of himself sexually abusing several Vietnamese and

Cambodian children. Neil had digitally scrambled his face in the photos to hide his identity. German police discovered the photos and unscrambled them to reveal Neil's face. Interpol issued a bulletin asking anyone who knew the man to come forward. According to Interpol, 350 people responded, with five sources from three continents identifying Neil, who was then arrested in Thailand.[31]

As is the case with many types of crime, large law enforcement agencies will have specialized departments, whereas small agencies will not. In small agencies, responsibility for investigating Internet child pornography often falls to officers who do not specialize in this type of crime. However, one study found that more than half of all Internet child pornography arrests were made by agencies that did not specialize in such investigations.[32] Although several federal law enforcement and legal agencies prosecute child pornography, the FBI's Innocent Images National Initiative focuses specifically on electronic exploitation through investigation, enforcement of child pornography laws, and the search for and rescue of child victims.[33]

U.S. law treats child pornography much more stringently than it does adult pornography. Currently, the following standards apply to all forms of child pornography.

State Senator Ralph Shortey, R-Oklahoma City, who was indicted by a federal grand jury on child pornography and child sex trafficking charges, pleaded guilty to child sex trafficking and was sentenced to 15 years in prison. Why is child pornography treated more stringently than adult pornography?

---

identity theft—The taking of critical personal information that comprises an individual's legal person.

- A child is anyone under the age of 18.
- The definition of child pornography includes any sexually explicit behavior, not just obscene behavior or nudity. In *United States v. Knox* (1993), a man was convicted for possessing images that focused on the clothed genital areas of young girls.[34]
- Possession, production, and distribution of child pornography are criminal offenses. Electronic images have only to be accessed, not necessarily printed, saved to digital media, or otherwise retained to be considered a criminal offense.[35]

The Internet has introduced several new challenges to the control of child pornography. According to the Department of Justice, these include the following.

- The Internet's decentralized structure, which makes it difficult to track offenders.
- International jurisdictional issues that require cooperation between the criminal justice systems of several countries, as well as some countries' lack of regulation or vastly different legislation. For example, the age of consent in some countries might be far lower than 18 or even non-existent.
- The advanced computer skills of some offenders, which can make them very difficult to catch and prosecute, as well as the increasing sophistication of Internet applications and security.
- The high volume of Internet traffic, which decreases the chance of any individual offender being caught.[36]

IDENTITY THEFT

In 2017, hackers broke into the computer systems of the credit bureau Equifax and stole data belonging to more than 147 million people in the United States. The thieves made off with social security numbers, dates of birth, home addresses, driver's license numbers, and credit card numbers. The breach is considered to be one of the worst ever in the United States.[37]

Identity theft, one of the fastest growing offenses in the United States, occurs when one party steals the information required to legally pose as another party.[38] This information typically includes full names, home addresses, telephone numbers, financial account numbers, and social security numbers. Like the Internet-based offenses we have discussed, identity theft is an old offense, but the Internet and other devices have made it much easier to do. For example, a thief can attach a card skimmer to a gas pump or ATM card reader to steal users' financial information. In fact, most identity theft is via credit cards (see Figure 14.1).

Increasingly, social security numbers are required for people to participate in anything connected to the public network—that is, to get a job, enroll in college, collect benefits, open bank accounts, get a loan, apply for a credit card, and so on. In the United States, a social security number has become as necessary as a name. Thieves are especially attracted to social security numbers because any institution that deals with money requires them to establish individual identity. With a social security number, a person can set up accounts, move money, receive money, and spend money. Using the Internet, the person can do all of these tasks without leaving home.

Using a sketchy set of personal information, a skilled identity thief can steal thousands of dollars before a victim even knows what has happened. Although it can be easy for the thief to steal an identity, it can be difficult for the victim to get that identity back. According to the National Crime Victimization Survey, 52 percent of victims spent several hours or a whole day resolving the issue, and about 9 percent of victims spent more than a month.[39]

The FTC and the FBI typically handle identity theft complaints, although 92 percent of victims do not report the offense to police.[40] The Identity Theft and Assumption Deterrence Act of 1998 makes identity theft a federal offense. The Identity Theft Penalty Enhancement Act of 2004 established for aggravated identity theft a mandatory two-year minimum sentence to be served in addition to any other sentence.[41]

Finally, a twist on identity theft must be considered: the harvesting of Internet users' private information by companies. Instead of a perpetrator breaking into a company's computer network to steal clients' information to sell, a company acquires and sells its clients' information. For example, in 2014, the British data analysis firm Cambridge Analytica harvested the private information of more than 50 million Facebook users without their permission. Cambridge Analytica said it used the data to develop tools that could ascertain the personalities of U.S. voters and influence their actions.[42] Because data-harvesting is not like stealing information from a company's network, such activities currently do not expressly violate U.S. criminal law. Facebook was not hacked—the users whose information was harvested voluntarily participated in a personality quiz—and as of 2018, no party to Cambridge Analytica's data-harvesting had been prosecuted. It is not unusual for technology to be several years ahead of the law.[43] It is possible that eventually criminal legislation prohibiting such activities will be enacted.

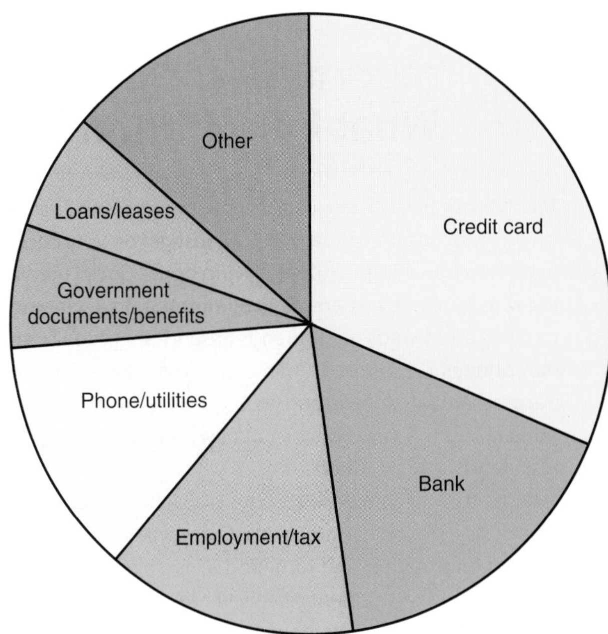

FIGURE 14.1 Types of Identity Theft

In 2017, most identity theft occurred by credit card fraud.

THINK ABOUT IT

Give reasons why most identity theft occurs via credit card.

Source: Federal Trade Commission, Consumer Sentinel Network Data Book 2017, *March 2018, p. 18,* https://www.ftc.gov/policy/reports/policy-reports/commission-staff-reports/consumer-sentinel-network-data-book-2017/main.

Sergey Medvedev, 31, is arrested outside his Bangkok apartment for his alleged role in an international identity theft ring that sold stolen credit card information on the dark web. How is it possible for someone overseas to be successful at identity theft in the United States?

POLICY IMPLICATIONS

What Information Should You Share?

Technology has greatly simplified our lives. Instead of going to the shopping mall, you can just get on your computer and buy things without leaving home. Social media allow us to share vast amounts of information, including pictures and videos, with friends around the globe from our phones. Technology has expanded our ability to become global citizens and to acquire information and goods from the vast universe of news agencies, marketers, friends, and strangers.

Yet there is a downside to the global reach that technology has provided each of us. Companies are collecting this information and targeting us in specific ways to ensure the advertisements we view are related to the information we provide to them. On the same pathways we use to reach out to the world, the world can reach back and take our money, ruin our reputations, or threaten the well-being of our families. As a matter of policy, everyone must be mindful of the information they share with the world. Thoughtful consideration should be used to evaluate the fine line between taking advantage of convenience and exposing ourselves to predators who seek to exploit our private data for any number of reasons.

Recently, the European Union enacted a set of privacy protections called the General Data Protection Regulation (GDPR) to give European citizens more control over the information that Internet services collect. Basically, the GDPR requires companies to clearly seek consent from consumers before collecting their personal information.[44]

Once you release data about yourself, it has the potential to be sold or stolen. For many people, the lure of the Internet affords them the opportunity to extend their visibility, marketing range, and friendship networks. Social media can be instrumental in keeping in touch with friends and pursuing commerce opportunities. However, there are risks involved that are to be considered. We should be aware that:

- Shopping online can be problematic. Not all online sites are what they purport to be. Many are outright scams.
- Internet connections are not always secure. This is especially true when you are using wireless computers or phones. Giving out credit card numbers or any other personal information on wireless devices is risky.
- Be careful about what you share on social media sites. A good thing to remember is that if the social media service is free, then you are the product.

THINK ABOUT IT

1. What steps do you take to protect yourself from online predators?

E-MAIL SCAMS

Like street con games, e-mail scams often rely on personal contact with victims to convince them to hand over money or personal information. Like identity theft scams, the perpetrators only have to fool a small percentage of the thousands of people they target with messages. Many e-mail scams are actually old street scams. According to the United States Computer Emergency Readiness Team, the most common ones include bogus business opportunities, communications from false IRS and bank officials, health and diet scams, and discount software offers. As with identity theft, investigations, depending on the exact type of offense, often involve the Internet Crime Complaint Center, Department of Justice, the FBI, the U.S. Postal Inspection Service, the U.S. Secret Service, the FTC, and state and local agencies.

Cambridge Analytica harvested data from 50 million Facebook profiles to target U.S. voters in 2016. Should such data harvesting be illegal? Why or why not?

PAUSE AND REVIEW

1. **What do networks on which crime occurs have in common?**
2. **What technological networks besides the Internet have been used to break the law?**
3. **What are some of the most serious offenses that occur on the Internet?**

Information Technology in the Criminal Justice System

LEARNING OBJECTIVE | 4

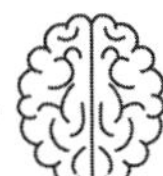

Give examples of how the criminal justice system uses technology.

Like many other aspects of society, the criminal justice system is saturated with technology. Sophisticated lethal and less-than-lethal weapons, armor, computers, and tracking and communications devices are now used routinely by law enforcement, the courts, and correctional facilities. The type of technology that arguably has advanced criminal justice work the most—and is also the most controversial in terms of personal privacy—is information technology. Because information technology has such profound implications for the criminal justice system and its relationship with the rest of society, we will concentrate our discussion on this form of technology.

The criminal justice system uses information technology to collect and share information on criminal offenders. For instance, the purpose of closed-circuit cameras is to catch lawbreakers in the act with the greater purpose of discouraging them from breaking the law at all, thus making everyone more secure. The same philosophy lies behind other forms of information technology: if people know they are being watched, that their movements are being tracked, and that every transgression of the law will be entered into a "permanent record" of sorts, then they will be less likely to break the law. Of course, this means that a lot of information is being recorded about a lot of citizens, from litterbugs to serial killers, and that many people who have broken no law are being watched without their knowledge or consent.

Technology for Surveillance and Short-Term Tracking

Surveillance is systematic, institutionalized encroachment into individual privacy that is often done in secret.[45] Surveillance technology includes cameras, electronic monitoring via ankle bracelets, radio frequency identification tags, and the relatively low-tech telephone. Cameras and telephones are probably the devices used most often, followed by ankle bracelets. In the future, advances in technology may produce even smaller devices feasible for keeping up with probationers, parolees, and offenders who are deemed to be more appropriate candidates for house arrest than incarceration.

CAMERAS

Cameras were first used as surveillance devices in 1942 when German engineer Walter Bruch designed a system to monitor missile launches.[46] Since then, various types of cameras have been developed to keep an eye on both people and things. The high cost of the technology and the low quality of the images kept the use of surveillance cameras relatively rare until the 1980s when the price of electronics began to drop and their sophistication began to rise.[47] Surveillance cameras became commonplace in the 1990s to watch not only retail and industrial situations, but also convenience stores, local banks, street corners, school buses, and automobile traffic.[48] By 2000, high-quality security cameras were being trained on anything by just about anybody and the images sent to the Internet.

Although those concerned about privacy and civil liberties continue to question the use of surveillance cameras in public places, the general public seems to have accepted their use and even welcome it in some situations. Much of the funding for surveillance cameras comes from the Department of Homeland Security for the purpose of spotting potential terrorist activity. For example, in 2008, surveillance cameras were part of a $4.6 million federal grant that went to nine Boston, Massachusetts, communities.[49]

A variety of surveillance cameras are displayed at the New England Cannabis Convention in Boston. With the use of cameras so pervasive, can we be certain we still have the right to privacy?

surveillance—Systematic, institutionalized, usually secret encroachment into individual privacy.

Law enforcement credits surveillance footage for helping to secure the conviction of 2013 Boston Marathon bomber Dzhokhar Tsarnaev.[50]

Britain has more than 5.9 million surveillance cameras, or one camera for every 11 people.[51] New York City, Chicago, Los Angeles, and Washington, D.C., have installed thousands of public surveillance cameras. The debate about whether surveillance cameras reduce crime continues, with few conclusions apparent. Some police studies report that the cameras reduce crime, whereas other critical studies claim that they do not.[52] However, with terrorism still a national threat and the federal government continuing to provide millions of dollars in funding for surveillance systems, jurisdictions will probably continue to install surveillance camera networks.

ELECTRONIC MONITORING

Electronic monitoring refers to the surveillance of individuals by electronic means. The first personal electronic monitoring device was developed in the 1960s by Dr. Ralph Schwitzgebel and other researchers at Harvard's Science Committee on Psychological Experimentation. Schwitzgebel's experimental device, tested on offenders, mental patients, and other researchers between 1964 and 1970, worked by sending signals to "repeater stations" installed throughout the community. Although the device was patented in 1969, the expense of electronic monitoring discouraged its use in tracking offenders until the 1980s.[53]

A probation and parole team supervisor shows off an ankle monitor. The number of offenders being monitored with electronic bracelets is rising, but experts warn that the tracking system is far from a panacea for criminal activity. What types of offenders are appropriate for release with ankle monitors?

Currently, the most common method of electronically monitoring parolees and probationers is by way of an electronic "ankle bracelet." This device sends signals that identify the individual wearer and alert the monitoring center if it is tampered with or removed. Offenders usually pay the costs of their monitoring, which can be from $5 to $15 a day. The most common use of electronic monitoring is by states for offenders on probation.[54]

Although electronic monitoring has its critics, one four-year study of nearly 75,000 offenders on home confinement found that it "significantly reduce[d] the likelihood of technical violations, re-offending, and absconding."[55] Critics of electronic monitoring say that it does nothing to rehabilitate offenders, assist their socialization, or facilitate their return to society. However, proponents of electronic monitoring say that its purpose is punitive and designed to be harsher than traditional parole/probation, yet less restrictive than incarceration. The inventor of electronic monitoring, Ralph Schwitzgebel, also criticizes its widespread use for offenders. He states that the relatively low recidivism rate of those on electronic monitoring can be attributed to the likelihood that offenders deemed safe enough to live outside prison walls are less likely to break the law again. Schwitzgebel and other critics of electronic monitoring also question the electronic devices' net-widening effect, measures that draw more offenders and individuals in the criminal justice system or more deeply involve those within the system, claiming that devices are being used for low-risk offenders who otherwise would have been placed on regular probation.[56]

RFID TAGS

One of the latest technological additions to the criminal justice system, **radio frequency identification (RFID) tags**, are devices that transmit information embedded in the tag via radio to a special receiver or reader. Retailers have used RFID tags for years to monitor inventory. Although RFID tags are a common sight—they are usually found in the form of a thick, plastic tag on a piece of merchandise—many people do not know exactly what they are. RFID tags are also used on "contactless" credit cards, which users wave over a card reader to pay for a purchase. RFID chips have been implanted in pets for several years, and the employees of some companies have had chips implanted to make it easier to log in to devices, open doors, and pay for food in the company cafeteria.[57]

Prisons throughout the world, including the United States, use RFID tags for inmates and guards. For example, in 2007, the Minnesota Department of Corrections began using a system that detects such activities as when an inmate ventures too close to a fence or when two gang leaders get too close to each other. Prison administrators know exactly who is doing what because the tags also transmit the complete histories and identities of the inmates. The guards also have RFID devices that signal their exact location and identities; if trouble breaks out, administrators can locate the guards and direct their activities accordingly.[58]

Technology for Identification and Long-Term Tracking

Although some devices described in the preceding section could also be listed here, technology for identification and long-term tracking focuses on identifying people and tracking them throughout their lives rather than just a short period of time, such as a few months or years on parole or probation. Technologies for these purposes include computer databases and biometrics, both of which are used in sectors other than the criminal justice system, such as private security, marketing, and retail. This variety of uses heightens concerns about privacy and information sharing. For example, there are concerns that biometrics information, such as fingerprints taken by private companies for security purposes, could be used by the state in criminal investigations. Because these technologies are so new, few laws, if any, specify the handling and jurisdiction of this information.

DATABASES

A computer database is an organized set of information that is kept on computer. The concept of the database is decades old—library card catalogs were databases, as are telephone books and other organized repositories of information. The advantages of a computer database are the volume of information that it can hold and the ease with which users can search and collate that information. Although we are accustomed to the idea of vast computer databases, it is important to understand the implications they have not only for the criminal justice system, but also for individual privacy.

Before computer databases were developed, the ease of organizing and accessing information was linked to its volume. Because information was usually recorded in writing on paper, it was easier to access a small amount of information than a large amount. Imagine wading through the New York City telephone book looking for someone named "Smith." Computer databases solved this problem. Typing the name "Smith" into a digitized New York City phonebook, along with a few other details, makes it a lot easier to find the Smith you are looking for. The same goes for criminal offenders, inmates, suspects, and arrestees. Information that is recorded about these individuals is not only far more easily accessed than it was a few decades ago, it is also accessed by more people. As an exercise, find the website for your state's department of corrections. Chances are that website has an "inmate search" or an "inmate locator" that provides personal details about specific prison inmates, their offenses, and often even their photographs. There are also several online databases designed to search only for sex offenders. Before computer databases and the Internet, this information was not easily available to the public. Now, anyone with an Internet-connected device can find it.

Some of the most controversial types of crime-related databases are those that contain samples of human DNA. **DNA (deoxyribonucleic acid)**, the molecule that transmits genetic information, is present in all human tissue, including blood, bone, hair, and saliva. Human beings differ by only one-tenth of a single percent of DNA, so forensic scientists use those specific bits of DNA to create genetic profiles of individuals. DNA databases contain this information and make it easily searchable.

The country's premier criminal DNA databases are the FBI's CODIS (Combined DNA Index System) and NDIS (National DNA Index System). NDIS is a database of DNA profile records provided by state criminal justice agencies, and CODIS is the information-processing and telecommunication system that supports NDIS.[59] CODIS comprises the entire system of DNA databases:

---

electronic monitoring—The surveillance of individuals via electronic means.

radio frequency identification (RFID) tags—Devices that transmit information embedded in the tag via radio to a special receiver or reader.

DNA (deoxyribonucleic acid)—The molecule that provides the genetic design for the physical characteristics of all living things.

the National DNA Index System, the State DNA Index System, and the Local DNA Index System.[60] NDIS contains more than 13,413,029 offender profiles and 864,128 forensic profiles.[61] The larger CODIS contains DNA profiles of convicted offenders, arrestees, missing persons, unidentified human remains, and biological relatives of missing persons, as well as DNA collected from crime scenes.[62]

DNA databases are controversial because of concerns about accuracy and privacy. Critics of DNA collection fear that the information might eventually be used for something other than its original purpose of identifying criminal offenders or victims. Others fear that the DNA of people who have broken no laws might be collected and permanently retained. Britain has been collecting DNA on its citizens, some of whom have broken no laws, for years. Currently, Great Britain has one of the largest DNA databases, with more than 5 million genetic profiles.[63]

Another criticism is that working with DNA evidence is not as flawless as was once thought. In an fascinating case, 26-year-old Lukis Anderson, homeless, alcoholic, and mentally ill, was charged with the murder of Raveesh Kumra, 66, in his home in Monte Sereno, California. Anderson's DNA, along with that of other attackers, had been found on Kumra's fingernails. Because of Anderson's alcoholism and mental condition, he said he could not remember where he was during the murder, telling his public defender, "Maybe I did do it." However, an investigation proved that Anderson was actually in a hospital at the time of Kumra's murder. Early that evening, he had been picked up by paramedics after getting drunk and collapsing in a convenience store. Hours later, those same paramedics had treated Kumra. It is speculated that they had gotten some of Anderson's DNA on their hands earlier in the evening and deposited it on Kumra while checking his vital signs.[64]

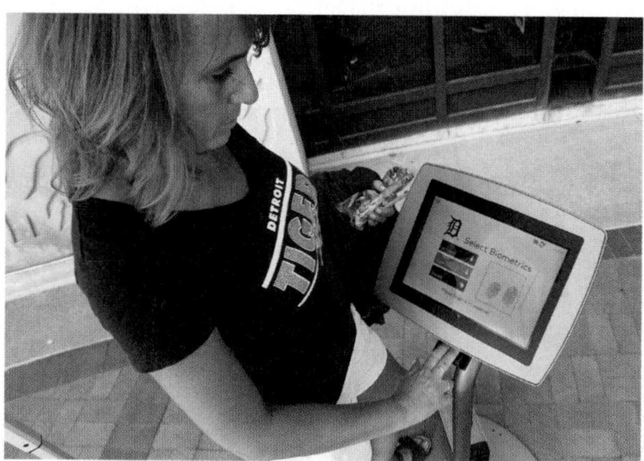

A woman scans her fingerprints at a biometric system before going in to a baseball game. How are biometrics used in the criminal justice system?

BIOMETRICS

Biometrics are methods used to verify identity based on physiological or behavioral characteristics, such as iris or retinal scans, facial recognition, hand/finger characteristics, voice identification, or signatures. The National Institute of Justice and the Department of Defense began developing biometrics for criminal justice purposes in 2000; however, like other methods of surveillance and identification, biometrics is older than you might think.[65] In 1879, French police inspector Alphonse Bertillon proposed a system of body measurements to identify repeat offenders. By 1896, British scholars began the development of the fingerprint classification system, an early form of biometrics.[66]

Currently, the primary criminal justice use for biometrics is to maintain security in prisons and jails. The use of biometrics identification for criminal justice purposes is still under development. It is likely that biometrics will be combined with other technologies, such as databases and electronic monitoring, to identify and track offenders inside institutions and out. Currently, the FBI's Next Generation Identification system is the world's largest biometric database of criminal offenders.[67]

PAUSE AND REVIEW

1. **What types of technologies does the criminal justice system use and for what purposes?**
2. **What is surveillance?**

Privacy, Security, and the Future

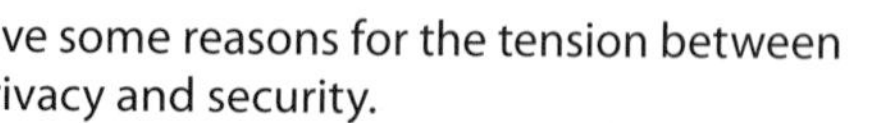

LEARNING OBJECTIVE | 5

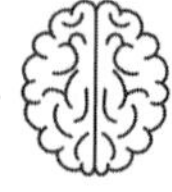

Give some reasons for the tension between privacy and security.

The most common form of government surveillance is something that has been called dataveillance, or "the systematic use of personal data systems in the investigation or monitoring of the actions or communications of one or more persons."[68]

---

biometrics—The methods used to verify identity based on physiological or behavioral characteristics, such as iris or retinal scans, facial recognition, hand/finger characteristics, voice identification, or signatures.

Governments—which have always conducted dataveillance, collecting information on births, deaths, and marriages, as well as data for taxes, voter registration, social services, and education—are increasingly conducting dataveillance via information technology.[69] Although many Americans, maybe even most, expect the government to collect such information, there is concern about the government's ability to keep it safe and private, as well as about how the government will use such information. For example, such data, when combined with other forms of surveillance and dataveillance, such as criminal records, video surveillance, and communications surveillance, could be used to build a comprehensive database on U.S. residents. However, many people may not even know their information has been collected.

A current example of this data collection involves the use of wireless devices, specifically cell phones, which may be used to establish their users' locations. In *Carpenter v. United States* (2018), the U.S. Supreme Court affirmed that the police need a search warrant to collect information about where suspects have used their cell phones.[70] Governments will continue to use technology to investigate and watch criminal suspects, and, since the law cannot keep up with the capabilities of technology, the way that governments are allowed to use technology to conduct surveillance will continue to be tested in the courts. The important questions are: How much information can the government collect? How can it be legally collected? Whose information can we collect?

These are important questions. Unfortunately, since suspects look a lot like non-suspects, watching suspects means watching everyone else, too. To date, there is no technology that conducts surveillance only on lawbreakers or on those who seek to break the law. It is becoming apparent that personal privacy and security are in a delicate balance in which having more of one means having less of the other. It is up to the citizens to decide which they prefer.

The tension between privacy and security has always been with us, and it is difficult to predict how the relationship between these two areas will change. There are several key issues.

- Privacy is not what it used to be. Americans have voluntarily given up much of what they used to consider private in order to do many things on the Internet, such as purchasing items, banking and investing, and keeping up with family and friends through social media. Much information about individual citizens is now stored on databases. Although these databases are supposedly secure, they are shared by many organizations and government agencies. In many ways, we have sacrificed our privacy and financial security to ease commerce.
- Technology changes everything. While our concept of privacy was developing over the course of several decades, technology was changing as well. The technology in use today is different from what it was in the past or will be tomorrow. Today's rapidly changing technology forces us to reconsider our laws, habits, and ideas of privacy. Technology has become so sophisticated that it has outstripped our ability to control what information about us remains private and secure.
- Security is a global concern. Not only must we be concerned about thieves taking our mail from our mailboxes, but we now are faced with the prospect of individuals in distant countries stealing our identities and spending our money without our being able to seek legal recourse in U.S. courts. In addition, governments routinely read our e-mails and use networked databases to monitor our travels, financial dealings, correspondence, and medical records.
- Things will continue to change. We cannot predict the future relationship between privacy and security. As governments and corporations develop new ways to track citizens and target consumers, more and more information about each of us will be available to a wider variety of people, agencies, and corporations that we would prefer not know much about us.
- Young people have different ideas about privacy. Many teenagers and young adults who grew up with the Internet and social media are quite comfortable with the technology, to the point that they give little thought to how their private information is viewed or by whom. Many young people place their personal information on social networking websites and expect that information to be available only to their friends and families. The problem is that many of the personal items young people post online are likely to remain there practically forever. Even if the social networking website is taken offline, information that was posted to the site is likely to remain in a database that may be searched and accessed from the Internet, possibly for decades to come. Some of these young people who apply for jobs at age 40 might be surprised to discover that a photograph of them doing a keg-stand (or something more embarrassing) at age 19 might be readily available online.

We must now reconcile the gap between privacy and security so that we can enjoy our freedoms and liberties and still protect ourselves from those who would harm us. This tenuous balancing act can be accomplished only by recognizing that the relationship between individuals, corporations, and governments is changing and by requiring that those who make our laws consider the values and ideals that the United States was founded on.

PAUSE AND REVIEW

1. **What is dataveillance?**
2. **What happened in *Carpenter v. United States*?**

FOCUS ON ETHICS Peeping Drones

You have a part-time job in a big electronics store. Most of the time, you are assigned to the part of the store that features computers. You like your job, and it is essential to your finances and allows you to attend college and pursue your criminal justice degree.

Because a fellow employee has gone on maternity leave, you have been reassigned to a section of the store that sells drones. Although you have heard of drones, you have never given them much thought. Now you are amazed at what these little flying machines can do and are even thinking about buying one for yourself.

As you become more familiar with drones, you discover there is a small subculture of drone enthusiasts who frequent your store. It is almost exclusively made up of males ranging in age from 17 to 55. Two of your coworkers are at the center of this group because of their experience with drones, and they have started a club called "Eye in the Sky." Your store has allowed this group to use one of its backrooms for monthly meetings, and now this group is rapidly expanding and is responsible for generating thousands of dollars in drone sales. The manager is delighted at the way your two co-workers have used the group to market drones.

Yesterday, you heard some disturbing news. A young customer said he was buying a drone because he heard the group had a list of addresses where "interesting" people lived. Without saying directly, he gave you the impression that club members were using drones to record people through their bedroom windows. You decided to investigate. By striking up a conversation with several club members, you discover that there was much more to this customer's story.

Club members are not only filming people in their private moments in their private spaces, but they also post these videos online. This local group is part of a much larger, nationwide group that uses the sites to post a variety of inappropriate content, including child pornography. You know you should do something, but you are conflicted as to what your responsibilities are. You like your job and the money you make from it. You like your coworkers, and your store manager is happy because of the booming business selling drones.

What Do You Do?

1. Do nothing. Your job is to sell drones, not morality. What customers do with the drones is their business, and you have no obligation to snitch.
2. Report your observations to your manager. He should be made aware that the store's backroom is being used for meetings that support behavior that could result in a lawsuit.
3. Report your observations to your local police. Let them decide which laws are being violated and what charges, if any, to bring.
4. Report your findings to the media. If a television station did an exposé on the issues, potential victims would be alerted and could take precautionary steps.

Summary

LEARNING OBJECTIVE 1	
Describe how technology has changed how some lawbreakers break the law.	Computers and security technology have greatly increased the level of sophistication required to commit larceny, theft, robbery, and most property offenses. These "technological" offenses are mostly an extension of street crime. The Internet has made it easier to break the law on a large scale as well as in a more comprehensive and nearly anonymous manner.

LEARNING OBJECTIVE 2 Give examples of how crime is responsible for the advancement of some technologies.	Society must set up safeguards to protect property, information, and public safety. Many homes now have Internet-connected private security systems. Advanced crime-scene investigation technologies and techniques have inspired a new interest in chemistry, biology, and computer science. Security concerns in protecting identity have prompted the development of fingerprint and handprint scanners, voice recognition software, and technology that scans human irises to validate identity. A major use of information technology has been to establish the security of governments, corporations, and individuals through the movement and restriction of information.
LEARNING OBJECTIVE 3 Show why the Internet provides a nearly ideal network for crime.	Internet crime is actually street and white-collar crime perpetrated with a different sort of human network. Networks on which crime is common, such as the Internet, share some characteristics: they are large; they afford some degree of anonymity; they offer something of economic value or access to it; they are easy to access and use; and they are versatile.
LEARNING OBJECTIVE 4 Give examples of how the criminal justice system uses technology.	The criminal justice system uses information technology to collect and share information on criminal offenders. These technologies include cameras, electronic monitoring (ankle bracelets), and RFID tags. Information technology is also used for identifying people and tracking them throughout their lives rather than just a short period of time, such as during parole or probation. Technologies for these purposes include computer databases and biometrics.
LEARNING OBJECTIVE 5 Give some reasons for the tension between privacy and security.	Governments will continue to use technology to investigate and watch criminal suspects. Having more personal privacy may mean having less security, and vice versa. The law cannot keep up with the capabilities of technology, so the way that governments are allowed to use technology to conduct surveillance will continue to be tested in the courts. There is concern about the government's ability to keep personal information safe and private, as well as about how the government will use such information. Data when combined with other forms of surveillance and dataveillance may be used to build a comprehensive database on U.S. residents. Many people may not even know the information has been collected.

Critical Reflections

1. **What effects has technology had on criminology and the criminal justice system?**
2. **How has crime helped advance technology?**
3. **What effect has the Internet had on jurisdiction?**
4. **In what ways has the introduction of new technology altered the delicate balance between privacy and security?**
5. **What risks do social media sites pose to your privacy?**
6. **What types of Internet crime are you the most susceptible to?**
7. **Have advances in technology favored lawbreakers or law enforcement agencies?**
8. **What information about yourself are you willing to provide to the government or to corporations in order to be protected from hackers, scammers, and lawbreakers?**

Key Terms

biometrics p. 394
database p. 379
DNA (deoxyribonucleic acid) p. 393
electronic monitoring p. 392
hacking p. 380
identity theft p. 388
jurisdiction p. 379
radio frequency identification (RFID) tags p. 392
social engineering p. 383
spam p. 384
surveillance p. 391

Instant Recall Terms

rational choice theory (ch. 4)
situational crime prevention (ch. 4)

Notes

1 Justin Jouvenal, "To Find Alleged Golden State Killer, Investigators First Found His Great-Great-Great-Grandparents," *Washington Post*, April 30, 2018, https://www.washingtonpost.com/local/public-safety/to-find-alleged-golden-state-killer-investigators-first-found-his-great-great-great-grandparents/2018/04/30/3c865fe7-dfcc-4a0e-b6b2-0bec548d501f_story.html. Corky Siemaszko, "Golden State Killer Suspect Charged with 13th Murder—Possibly His First," *NBCNews*, August 13, 2018, https://www.nbcnews.com/news/us-news/police-pin-13th-murder-accused-golden-state-killer-n900266. Avi Selk, "All We Know about Joseph DeAngelo, the Golden State Killer Suspect Who Became a Suburban Grandfather," *Washington Post*, April 26, 2018, https://www.washingtonpost.com/news/post-nation/wp/2018/04/26/joseph-deangelo-golden-state-killer-suspect-was-normal-grandpa-according-to-teen. T.J. Ortenzi, "Hunt for Golden State Killer Led Detectives to Hobby Lobby for DNA Sample," *Washington Post*, June 2, 2018, https://www.washingtonpost.com/news/post-nation/wp/2018/06/02/hunt-for-golden-state-killer-led-detectives-to-hobby-lobby-for-dna-sample. Accessed August 2018.
2 Ibid.
3 Ibid.
4 Ibid.
5 Ibid.
6 Public Broadcasting Service, *Nerds 2.0.1: A Brief History of the Internet* (1998).
7 Alison Hewitt, "Internet Pioneer Wins Highest Science Honor in U.S.," UCLA Newsroom, August 25, 2008, http://newsroom.ucla.edu/stories/080825_kleinrock-medal-science. Accessed August 2018.
8 Douglas Martin, "Joybubbles, 58, Peter Pan of Phone Hackers, Dies," *New York Times*, August 20, 2007, http://www.nytimes.com/2007/08/20/us/20engressia.html.
9 Chris Rhoads, "The Twilight Years of Cap'n Crunch," *Wall Street Journal*, January 13, 2007, A1.
10 Arlene Weintraub and Jim Kerstetter, "Cyber Alert: Portrait of an Ex-Hacker," *Bloomberg Businessweek*, June 9, 2003, https://www.bloomberg.com/news/articles/2003-06-08/cyber-alert-portrait-of-an-ex-hacker. Accessed August 2018.
11 Federal Bureau of Investigation, Internet Crime Complaint Center, *2017 Internet Crime Report*, 2017 Crime Types, p. 20. Available at https://www.ic3.gov. Accessed August 2018.
12 Federal Trade Commission, *Consumer Sentinel Network Data Book 2017*, March 2018, p. 12, https://www.ftc.gov/policy/reports/policy-reports/commission-staff-reports/consumer-sentinel-network-data-book-2017/main. Accessed August 2018.
13 Nick Marinoff, "Ross Ulbricht Is Denied Prison Sentence Review by Supreme Court," *Bitcoin Magazine*, June 29, 2018, https://bitcoinmagazine.com/articles/ross-ulbricht-denied-prison-sentence-review-supreme-court. Accessed August 2018.
14 U.S. Immigration and Customs Enforcement, "Law Enforcement Agencies Around the World Collaborate on International Darknet Marketplace Enforcement Operation," October 31, 2016, https://www.ice.gov/news/releases/law-enforcement-agencies-around-world-collaborate-international-darknet-marketplace. Accessed August 2018.
15 Chris Baraniuk, "AlphaBay and Hansa Dark Web Markets Shut Down," *BBC*, July 20, 2017, https://www.bbc.com/news/technology-40670010. Accessed August 2018.
16 Weintraub and Kerstetter, "Cyber Alert: Portrait of an Ex-Hacker."
17 Anne Broache, "President Signs Pretexting Bill into Law," CNET News, January 16, 2007, https://www.cnet.com/news/president-signs-pretexting-bill-into-law. Accessed August 2018.
18 Michael Specter, "Damn Spam: The Losing War on Junk E-mail," *New Yorker* 83, no. 22 (August 6, 2007): 36.
19 Mike Sakal, "P.V. Man Sentenced in Porn Spam Case," *East Valley Tribune*, October 12, 2007, http://www.eastvalleytribune.com/news/p-v-man-sentenced-in-porn-spam-case/article_59cd1647-f25f-5d4d-ab73-53d8471506d1.html. Accessed August 2018.
20 Jim Giles, "The Street Crime of the Internet," *New Scientist* 194, no. 2607 (June 9, 2007): 30–31.
21 Marshall Brain and Wesley Fenlon, "How Computer Viruses Work," howstuffworks, https://computer.howstuffworks.com/virus.htm. Accessed August 2018.
22 John Leyden, "Computer Virus Turns 25," *Register*, July 13, 2007, https://www.theregister.co.uk/2007/07/13/virus_silver_jubilee. Accessed August 2018.
23 Brain and Fenlon, "How Computer Viruses Work."
24 John Shoch and Jon Hupp, "The 'Worm' Programs—Early Experience with a Distributed Computation," Communications of the Association for Computing Machinery 25 (March 1982): 172–180.
25 Dan Goodin, "VPNFilter Malware Infecting 500,000 Devices Is Worse Than We Thought," *Ars Technica*, June 5, 2018, https://arstechnica.com/information-technology/2018/06/vpnfilter-malware-infecting-50000-devices-is-worse-than-we-thought. Accessed August 2018.
26 Tim Tate, *Child Pornography: An Investigation* (London: Methuen, 1990).
27 John Crewdson, *By Silence Betrayed: Sexual Abuse of Children in America* (Boston: Little, Brown, 1998).
28 Philip Jenkins, *Beyond Tolerance: Child Pornography on the Internet* (New York: New York University Press, 2001).
29 Richard Wortley and Stephen Smallbone, *Child Pornography on the Internet* (Washington, D.C.: U.S. Department of Justice, Community Oriented Policing Services, May 2006), p. 4, https://ccoso.org/library/child-pornography-internet-richard-wortley-and-stephen-smallbone-published-2006-department. Accessed August 2018.
30 Tony Krone, *Trends and Issues in Crime and Justice: A Typology of Online Child Pornography Offending* (Canberra, Australia: Australian Institute of Technology, 2004), 4. Available

online at https://aic.gov.au/publications/tandi/tandi279. Accessed August 2018.

31 Almas Meherally and Lora Grindlay, "Convicted 'Swirl Face' Sex Offender Christopher Neil to Live in Vancouver," *Vancouver Sun*, March 26, 2017, https://vancouversun.com/news/local-news/convicted-swirl-face-sex-offender-christopher-neil-to-live-in-vancouver. Accessed August 2018.

32 Janis Wolak, Kimberly J. Mitchell, and David Finkelhor, "Escaping or Connecting? Characteristics of Youth Who Form Close Online Relationships," *Journal of Adolescence* 26 (2003): 105–119.

33 General Accounting Office, *Combating Child Pornography* (Washington, D.C.: Government Printing Office, 2011), 2. Available online at https://www.gao.gov/products/GAO-11-334. Accessed August 2018.

34 *United States v. Knox*, 32 F.3d 733 (3d Cir. 1994), cert denied, 513 U.S. 1109 (1995). Philip Jenkins, *Beyond Tolerance: Child Pornography on the Internet* (New York: New York University Press, 2001).

35 Wortley and Smallbone, *Child Pornography on the Internet*.

36 Ibid.

37 Lily Hay Newman, "Equifax's Security Overhaul, a Year after Its Epic Breach," *Wired*, July 25, 2018, https://www.wired.com/story/equifax-security-overhaul-year-after-breach. Accessed August 2018.

38 The Internet Crime Complaint Center, *2007 Internet Crime Report*, p. 18. Available at https://www.ic3.gov/media/annualreports.aspx. Accessed August 2018.

39 Erika Harrell, *Victims of Identity Theft, 2014* (Washington, D.C.: U.S. Department of Justice Office of Justice Programs Bureau of Justice Statistics, 2015), 10. Available at https://www.bjs.gov/index.cfm?ty=pbdetail&iid=5408. Accessed August 2018.

40 Ibid., 11.

41 Congress.gov, H.R.1731—Identity Theft Penalty Enhancement Act, https://www.congress.gov/bill/108th-congress/house-bill/1731. Accessed August 2018.

42 Matthew Rosenberg, "Professor Apologizes for Helping Cambridge Analytica Harvest Facebook Data," *New York Times*, April 22, 2018, https://www.nytimes.com/2018/04/22/business/media/cambridge-analytica-aleksandr-kogan.html. Accessed August 2018.

43 Ibid.

44 Brian Fung, "Why You're Getting Flooded with Privacy Notifications in Your Email," *Washington Post*, May 25, 2018, https://www.washingtonpost.com/news/the-switch/wp/2018/05/25/why-youre-getting-flooded-with-privacy-notifications-in-your-email. Accessed August 2018.

45 Sun Sun Lim, Hichang Cho, and Milagros Rivera Sanchez, "Online Privacy, Government Surveillance and National ID Cards," *Communications of the ACM* 52, no. 12 (December 2009): 116–120.

46 Jay Ankeney, "Videoconferencing Systems," *Sound & Video Contractor* 26, no. 4 (April 2008): 34–42.

47 Martha M. Hamilton, "Waging War on the Shoplifter," *Washington Post*, July 14, 1977, DC1.

48 Louise Sweeney, "School Bus Surveillance Increases," *Christian Science Monitor*, September 1, 1992, 6.

49 Richard Thompson, "Focus Is on Safety vs. Privacy," *Boston Globe*, August 24, 2008, 3rd edition, 6.

50 Curt Nickisch, "Boston Marathon Surveillance Raises Privacy Concerns Long after Bombing," *National Public Radio*, April 17, 2015, https://www.npr.org/2015/04/17/400164221/boston-marathon-surveillance-raises-privacy-concerns-long-after-bombing. Accessed August 2018.

51 David Barrett, "One Surveillance Camera for Every 11 People in Britain, Says CCTV Survey," *Telegraph*, July 10, 2013, https://www.telegraph.co.uk/technology/10172298/One-surveillance-camera-for-every-11-people-in-Britain-says-CCTV-survey.html. Accessed August 2018.

52 Timothy Williams, "Can 30,000 Cameras Help Solve Chicago's Crime Problem? " *New York Times*, May 26, 2018, https://www.nytimes.com/2018/05/26/us/chicago-police-surveillance.html. American Civil Liberties Union, What's Wrong with Public Video Surveillance?, https://www.aclu.org/other/whats-wrong-public-video-surveillance. Accessed August 2018.

53 U.S. Congress, Office of Technology Assessment, *Criminal Justice, New Technologies, and the Constitution*, OTA-CIT-366 (Washington, D.C.: U.S. Government Printing Office, May 1988), p. 33, https://www.hsdl.org/?abstract&did=728554. Accessed August 2018. Ralph Schwitzgebel, "Electronic Innovation in the Behavioral Sciences: A Call to Responsibility," *American Psychologist* 22, no. 5 (May 1967): 364–370.

54 Lauren E. Glaze and Thomas P. Bonczar, *Parole in 2006 (Appendix Tables)*, Table 9, (Washington D.C.: Bureau of Justice Statistics, 2008), https://www.bjs.gov/index.cfm?ty=pbdetail&iid=1106. Accessed August 2018.

55 Kathy G. Padgett, William D. Bales, and Thomas G. Blomberg, "Under Surveillance: An Empirical Test of the Effectiveness and Consequences of Electronic Monitoring," *Criminology and Public Policy* 5, no. 1 (February 1, 2006): 61–91.

56 Ralph Kirkland Gable and Robert S. Gable, "Electronic Monitoring: Positive Intervention Strategies," *Federal Probation* 69, no.1 (January/December 2005), http://www.uscourts.gov/federal-probation-journal/2005/06/electronic-monitoring-positive-intervention-strategies. (The authors changed their names from Schwitzgebel.) Accessed August 2018.

57 Yael Grauer, "A Practical Guide to Microchip Implants," *Ars Technica*, January 3, 2018, https://arstechnica.com/features/2018/01/a-practical-guide-to-microchip-implants. Accessed August 2018.

58 Marc L. Songini, "Minnesota Turns to RFID to Monitor Inmates," *Computerworld*, June 18, 2007, https://www.computerworld.com/article/2541908/mobile-apps/minnesota-turns-to-rfid-to-monitor-inmates.html. Accessed August 2018.

59 Federal Bureau of Investigation, Freedom of Information/Privacy Act, http://foia.fbi.gov/ndispia.htm. Accessed August 2018.

60 The No Suspect Casework DNA Backlog Reduction Program, "Glossary of Terms and Acronyms," http://www.usdoj.gov/oig/reports/OJP/a0502/app2.htm. Accessed August 2018.

61 Federal Bureau of Investigation, CODIS-NDIS Statistics, https://www.fbi.gov/services/laboratory/biometric-analysis/codis/ndis-statistics. Accessed August 2018.

62 Federal Bureau of Investigation, Combined DNA Index System (CODIS), https://www.fbi.gov/services/laboratory/biometric-analysis/codis. Accessed August 2018.

63 Vickie Oliphant, "Big Brother Britain: Government Accused of Trying to 'Expand DNA Database,'" March 7, 2017, https://www.express.co.uk/news/uk/759572/DNA-database-expanded-government-paternity-fraud-police-crime. Accessed August 2018.

64 Katie Worth, "Framed for Murder by His Own DNA," *Wired*, April 19, 2018, https://www.wired.com/story/dna-transfer-framed-murder. Accessed August 2018.

65 Christopher A. Miles and Jeffrey P. Cohn, "Tracking Prisoners in Jail with Biometrics: An Experiment in a Navy Brig," *NIJ Journal* 253, https://www.nij.gov/journals/253/pages/tracking.aspx. Accessed August 2018.

66 Anil K. Jain and Sharath Pankanti, "Beyond Fingerprinting," *Scientific American* 299, no. 3 (September 2008): 78–81.

67 Federal Bureau of Investigation, Next Generation Identification, https://www.fbi.gov/services/cjis/fingerprints-and-other-biometrics/ngi. Accessed August 2018.

68 Roger Clarke, "Information Technology and Dataveillance," *Communications of the ACM* 31, no. 5 (May 1988): 498–512.

69 Lim, Cho, and Sanchez, "Online Privacy, Government Surveillance and National ID Cards," 116–120.

70 *Carpenter v. United States*, SCOTUSblog, http://www.scotusblog.com/case-files/cases/carpenter-v-united-states-2. Accessed August 2018.

Glossary

A

adolescence-limited Moffitt's term to describe antisocial behavior that is restricted to the teenage years.

aggression An offensive action; psychological or physical encroachment without the consent of the other party.

anomie The erosion of standards resulting from a lack of social control and values that leads to social instability.

antisocial Following standards of behavior intended to harm society and individuals.

antisocial personality disorder A mental disorder characterized by a pattern of disregard for the rights of others, as well as impulsive, violent, and aggressive behavior without guilt.

antisocial potential Farrington's term to describe an individual's likelihood of breaking the law by engaging in antisocial behavior.

arson The deliberate setting of fires.

assault The criminal offense of attempting to inflict immediate bodily harm or making another person fear that such harm is imminent.

atavism The idea that some people are born before progressing through all the evolutionary stages to become fully human.

B

battery Physical contact with the intent to do harm.

behaviorism A perspective stating that environment and learning determine how individuals behave.

bias Hostile feelings or opinions, usually unreasonable, about a social group or class.

biocriminology The search for the causes of antisocial behavior within the brain or body.

biometrics The methods used to verify identity based on physiological or behavioral characteristics, such as iris or retinal scans, facial recognition, hand/finger characteristics, voice identification, or signatures.

body-type theory The idea that the shape of the body directly predicts the propensity for criminal offending.

bourgeoisie In Marxism, the owners of the means of production.

bribery The offense of giving money or valuables to influence public officials or employees of business competitors.

burglary The unlawful entry of a structure with the intent to commit a felony or theft.

C

capital murder A murder offense that is punishable by death. Sometimes called a "capital offense."

civil law Law that is related to private rights and disputes between citizens.

class A group defined by a particular social, economic, and educational status.

classical school of criminology A set of ideas that focuses on deterrence and considers crime to be the result of offenders' free will.

classical strain theory The idea that people who experience anger and frustration when they cannot achieve cultural goals through legitimate means try to achieve these goals through illegitimate means.

clearance The closure of an offense by arrest or other means.

cognition The act of thinking and perceiving.

cognitive psychology The study of memory, language processing, perception, problem solving, thinking, and other mental processes.

cohort A group of people who share statistical or demographic characteristics.

collective efficacy The measure of the amount of informal social control and social cohesion, or trust, in a community.

concentric zone theory The idea that geographical areas radiate out from an expanding urban center and that each area has certain dominant social attitudes.

conflict theory A set of criminological propositions based on the philosophy of Karl Marx holding that antisocial behavior stems from class conflict and social and economic inequality.

containment theory The idea that everyone has internal and external structures that hold them within the larger social structure.

control theories of crime A perspective that questions why most people do not break the law.

corporate crime Offenses committed in the name of a business in the pursuit of money or to prevent losing money.

corporate personhood The legal treatment of a corporation as a person.

crime Behavior that is prohibited by laws and has prescribed punishments.

crime rate The number of offenses divided by the population, usually expressed as a rate of offenses per 100,000 people.

criminal law Law that deals with the prosecution and definition of crime.
criminology The study of the making of laws, the breaking of laws, and the social reaction to the breaking of laws.
critical race theory A set of legalistic perspectives holding that racial inequity is so ingrained in society that it is propagated through legal and social discourse.
critical theory Criminological perspectives that describe and critique the social structure and seek solutions to the problems of crime and criminal justice.
cross-sectional survey Research in which different individuals are studied during each research period.
cultural criminology A concept that examines how social ideas, values, and media reflect and produce antisocial behavior.

D

dark figure of crime A term that describes criminal offenses that are unreported to law enforcement officials and never recorded.
database An organized set of information.
decriminalization The lessening or removal of penalties for acts previously subject to criminal prosecution, arrest, and incarceration.
demonology An ancient perspective of crime that considers antisocial behavior as being caused by an evil entity who lives inside an individual and overtakes his or her personality.
determinism The idea that everything that occurs, including the choices made by human beings, inevitably follows from previously existing causes.
deterrence The idea that punishment for an offense will prevent that offender and others from further breaking the law.
deterrence theory The concept that punishment prevents more crime from occurring.
deviance Behaviors that violate cultural norms, rules, or laws.
differential association Sutherland's idea that offenders learn crime from each other.
differential opportunity theory Cloward and Ohlin's idea that subcultures provide youths with ways to adapt to the lack of legitimate opportunities and with the prospect of developing illegitimate ways of responding to impoverished and disorganized urban life.
differential reinforcement The encouragement of one behavior instead of another.
disintegrative shaming Braithwaite's term to describe punishment that does not repair the harm done by the offender and offense and excludes the offender from society.
DNA (deoxyribonucleic acid) The molecule that provides the genetic design for the physical characteristics of all living things.

E

electronic monitoring The surveillance of individuals via electronic means.
embezzlement The appropriation as one's own, through fraud, money, or property entrusted to one's care.
(The) Enlightenment A period during the 17th and 18th centuries in Europe in which great strides were made in philosophy and science.
environmental crime An offense that manipulates the surroundings to the extent that human beings, animals, or plants that live within in it are harmed or unable to survive.
eugenics The concept that human beings can degenerate or improve through breeding.
extinction No reaction to a behavior.
extortion The offense of obtaining money, property, or information by threats, intimidation, or false claim to a position of authority.

F

felony A serious offense usually punishable by a prison sentence of more than one year or sometimes by life imprisonment or death.
feminist criminology A set of theories holding that gender inequality is at the root of offenses in which women are the victims or offenders.
focal concerns Attitudes that the lower classes perpetuate as part of the values and norms they believe are necessary for survival in their neighborhoods.
fraud Known misrepresentation or concealment in a transaction made with the intent to deceive another.

G

gender The social concept of how males and females should behave.
general deterrence The idea that punishing one person for an offense will provide an example to others not to engage in crime.
general strain theory Agnew's revision of classical strain theory, which identifies three major types of strain: failure to achieve goals, the loss of positive stimuli, and the gain of negative stimuli.
general theory of crime Gottfredson and Hirschi's theory emphasizing the importance of parental influence on children's development of self-control.

H

hacking The unauthorized use of an information system or network.
hate crime A criminal offense like murder or rape, but with an added element of bias.
hedonistic calculus A method proposed by Jeremy Bentham in which criminal offenders calculate the worth of breaking the law by estimating the positive consequences versus the possible negative consequences.

heredity The biological process in which genetic characteristics are inherited by one generation from the last.
hierarchy rule The Federal Bureau of Investigation's practice of recording in the Uniform Crime Reports only the most serious offense in a set of offenses.
homicide The killing of one human being by another.
human trafficking The buying and selling of human beings.

I
identity theft The taking of critical personal information that comprises an individual's legal person.
impulsivity Action on a whim without consideration of the consequences.
institutional anomie The condition that occurs when people's commitment to societal institutions becomes subservient to achieving the goal of wealth, which leads to the inability of the neglected institutions to control behavior.
integrated theories Perspectives that attempt to combine several different criminological theories in order to expand the focus on crime.
intersectionality A term referring to the intersections of two or more social categorizations such as race, class, color, gender, age, and sex and the added challenges of discrimination faced by individuals at those intersections.
intimate-partner violence Abuse that occurs between two people in a spousal, domestic, or romantic relationship.
IQ (intelligence quotient) A measure of intelligence taken by dividing a person's mental age by chronological age, then multiplying by 100.

J
jurisdiction Legal authority.

L
labeling theory The idea that society defines an individual, treating him or her differently, and the individual internalizes this definition and acts it out.
larceny/theft The unlawful taking of property from another person.
learning theories of crime These theories focus on where and how adult offenders and delinquents find the tools, techniques, and expertise to break the law.
legalization The complete removal of legal proscriptions on acts that were previously illegal.
life-course-persistent Moffitt's term to describe antisocial behavior that continues throughout adulthood.
life-course theory A perspective that focuses on the development of antisocial behavior, risk factors at different ages, and the effect of life events on individual development.
longitudinal A type of survey that follows respondents throughout their lives or a significant proportion of their lives.
lumpenproletariat In Marxism, the lowest social class, which was characterized by lack of skill, disorganization, and impoverishment.

M
macro-victimization The harm caused to masses of people by large-scale criminal offenses.
manslaughter The killing of one human being by another without criminal intent.
mass murder The killing of three or more people in a single incident.
master status A social standing that takes precedence over all others.
mental disorder Term used for a variety of psychological diseases and abnormalities; mental illness.
methodology The rules and principles that govern how research is performed.
micro-victimization The harm caused to small groups of people or individuals by small-scale criminal offenses.
murder Willful homicide.

N
National Incident-Based Reporting System (NIBRS) The Federal Bureau of Investigation's incident-based reporting system in which data are collected on every single offense.
National Crime Victimization Survey (NCVS) A survey of a nationally representative sample of residences that collects information about crime from victims.
negative reinforcement Ending an undesirable consequence as a means of reward.
neoclassical criminology A theoretical resurgence in classical criminology that emphasizes free will and deterrence and acknowledges some of the effects of positivism on decision making.
net-widening Measures that draw more offenders and individuals in the criminal justice system or more deeply involve those within the system.
not guilty by reason of insanity (NGRI) Generally, the acquittal of a defendant because he or she is determined to be insane.

O
operant conditioning A form of learning based on the positive or negative consequences of an action, behavior, or activity.
opportunistic thief Offenders who only steal items that are temporarily left unguarded and who do not consider themselves as lawbreakers.
organized crime A crime organization that breaks the law for money and often uses violence to achieve its goals.

P
patriarchal Referring to a social system that is controlled by males.
peacemaking criminology Criminological perspective that considers the social and personal effects of crime as a whole.

phrenology The practice of determining a person's character and mental faculties by measuring bumps and other features of an individual's skull.
physiognomy The practice of determining a person's character by facial characteristics.
pilfering Employee theft of small amounts of money or inexpensive goods from an employer.
political Referring to the relationships of people in groups and their activities.
political machine A type of group in the 19th-century United States that rewarded other powerful individuals, businesses, and organizations who ensured that the machine received votes and administrative control of a jurisdiction.
pornography Images, sounds, writing or other communication designed to give sexual pleasure.
positive reinforcement Rewarding a successful action.
positivist An approach that places emphasis on observable facts.
positivist school of criminology A set of ideas that considers crime to be the result of external, observable forces that can be measured.
postmodern criminology A perspective that focuses on how language and traditional ideas affect how we define and perceive crime, the law, and society.
power-control theory of crime A theory that seeks to explain why males commit more offenses and delinquency than females.
predicate offense A criminal offense that occurs as part of another criminal offense or complex of offenses.
prejudice A disparaging opinion that is not based on logic or actual experience with the subject of the disparagement.
premeditation In reference to crime, the planning of a criminal act.
pre-sentence report A report about an offender's personal details and history that is prepared by a probation officer to assist a judge in sentencing.
primary deviance A stage that occurs when society reacts to an individual's actions, successfully labels that individual, and acts upon that label.
professional thief Offenders who attempt to make a living from theft and may specialize in a particular form.
proletariat A social class composed of people who work for wages.
property offense A criminal offense perpetrated without personal violence and focused on the entering, taking, or destruction of structures, motor vehicles, or goods.
proportionality The idea that the most serious criminal offenses should have the most severe penalties.
pro-social Following standards of behavior intended to facilitate society and individuals.
prostitution The unlawful promotion of or participation in sexual activities for profit.
psychopathy A mental disorder that involves a severe lack of empathy.
public-order offense An activity that is against the law and offends the values, norms, and/or morals of a dominant sector of society.

R

race The use of certain biological characteristics, such as skin color, to classify human beings into categories.
racial profiling The disproportionate selection by law enforcement of minority suspects.
racketeering The use of extortion and force to engage in illegal business activities.
Racketeering Influenced and Corrupt Organizations (RICO) Act A federal statute enacted in 1970 to control organized crime.
radio frequency identification (RFID) tags Devices that transmit information embedded in the tag via radio to a special receiver or reader.
rape As defined in the Uniform Crime Reports, "The penetration, no matter how slight, of the vagina or anus with any body part or object, or oral penetration by a sex organ of another person, without the consent of the victim."
rational choice theory The concept that offenders calculate the advantages and disadvantages not only of breaking the law, but also of what type of offense to commit.
recidivism Repeat offending. *Also* recidivate.
reintegrative shaming Braithwaite's term to describe punishment that seeks to repair the harm done by the offender and offense and draw the offender into society.
reliability The ability of research to be successfully repeated and to provide similar results.
restitution Money paid to compensate for loss or injury.
restorative justice A form of resolving offenses that emphasizes repairing the harm done by crime through cooperation of the victim, offender, and justice system.
robbery The taking or attempting to take anything from another person or persons by violence or the threat of violence.
routine activities theory The concept that crime occurs when three elements converge: motivated offenders, attractive targets, and the absence of capable guardians.

S

schizophrenia A mental disorder that includes delusions, hallucinations, disorganized speech, grossly disorganized behavior, and inappropriate affect.
scientific method A process of investigation in which phenomena are observed; ideas are tested, and conclusions are drawn.
secondary deviance A stage that occurs when labeled individuals internalize the label and see themselves as devalued members of society.

securities fraud An offense in which an individual or entity attempts to manipulate the investment market, usually by encouraging investors to purchase securities based on false statements.

self-report study Research based on data offered by respondents about themselves.

serial murder The killing of a sequence of victims committed in three or more separate events over an extended period of time.

sex The biological characteristics that distinguish organisms on the basis of their reproductive ability.

situated transaction The idea that a scenario is the result of agreed-upon norms, interactions, and roles played by those involved.

situational crime prevention An extension of rational choice theory that considers situational factors that can be modified to discourage crime.

social bond theory The idea that there are forces that keep people connected to social norms and values.

social contract The idea that individuals in a society are bound by reciprocal obligations.

social Darwinism The idea that public welfare of any sort only helped the unfit survive to weaken society.

social disorganization theory The idea that the breakdown of social bonds and the failure of social institutions cause crime.

social engineering The manipulation of individuals so that they divulge information or perform actions.

social learning theory The idea that people learn how to act by watching others and copying the interactions that are rewarded and avoiding those that are punished.

social location The position of an individual within a society according to race, sex, class, geography, and age.

socialization The process of acquiring a personal identity and learning how to live within the culture of one's society.

sociobiology The study of evolutionary factors that influence behavior and societies.

sociological imagination The idea that we must look beyond our personal experiences to the experiences of others in order to evaluate how social location influences how individuals perceive society.

sodomy Oral or anal sexual intercourse.

soft determinism The idea that free will is affected by outside influences.

somatotype The practice of determining a person's character by the shape of the body.

spam Unsolicited e-mail advertising a product or service that is sent in bulk to large numbers of people.

specific deterrence The idea that punishing one person for an offense, usually by incarceration or execution, will prevent that person from committing another offense.

spree murder The killing of several victims at successive locations within a longer period of time than a mass murder.

statutory rape A criminal offense that takes place when a person has consensual sex with another person who is not old enough to legally consent.

street crime Materially destructive or violent criminal offenses that are often interpersonal and represent those for which the police are most often called.

subculture of violence A culture apart from the main social culture that holds violence to be part of its values, lifestyle, and socialization.

surveillance Systematic, institutionalized, usually secret encroachment into individual privacy.

T

techniques of neutralization theory A perspective that refers to the excuses some offenders use to justify breaking the law.

terrorism Violence perpetrated against civilians by political groups for the purpose of drawing attention to their cause.

theory A statement or set of statements that explains a concept and that has withstood repeated tests and can be used to make inferences about other concepts.

theory of evolution The idea that biological forms change over time through genetic inheritance.

total institution A place in which rigid rules and regulations, such as dress and communication, are clearly defined and strictly enforced.

transnational crime Criminal offenses that originate in one country and cross one or many several national borders.

U

Uniform Crime Reports A Federal Bureau of Investigation program that collects law enforcement statistics from voluntarily participating agencies throughout the United States.

utilitarianism The idea of seeking the greatest good for the most people.

V

validity A statistical property that describes how well a study is measuring what it is designed to measure.

vicarious liability When a person or group of people is considered legally responsible for the actions of another person, group of people, or corporation.

victim In criminology, a person who suffers a criminal offense.

victim-impact statement A communication by those directly affected by an offense to the court stating the personal effects of the offense.

victimless crime An activity that offends the values of a segment of society and is against the law but has the willing participation of all parties to the activity and causes no obvious harm to anyone involved in the activity, who also seek to keep it from becoming known to police.

victimology The study of the harm that people suffer as a result of crime.

victim precipitation An offense in which the victim plays an active role in initiating or escalating the offense.

violence Aggressive physical force with intent to cause fear or to injure, harm, or kill.

W

white-collar crime Financially motivated criminal offenses committed by way of deceit and without violence, usually involving the offender's place of employment or business.

X

XYY syndrome A condition that occurs when males receive an extra copy of the Y chromosome.

Credits

Part I Opener
p. 1: © iStock/francescoch

Chapter 1
p. 2: © iStock/wildpixel; p. 3: Cleveland Police via AP, File; p. 6: Kyodo via AP Images; p. 7: AP Photo/Jim Mone; p. 8 (left) AP Photo/The Hutchinson News, Tim Goessman; p. 8 (right) Texas Department of Criminal Justice via AP; p. 10: Isaac Hale/The Daily Herald via AP; p. 11: AP Photo/Rick Bowmer; p. 13: AP Photo/Mark Faram; p. 15: AP Photo/Ann Heisenfelt; p. 16: AP Photo/Charles Edouard Jottras; p. 18: Photo by Alex Milan Tracy/Sipa via AP Images

Chapter 2
p. 22: © Richard Cavalleri/Shutterstock.com; p. 24: AP Photo/Salt Lake Tribune, Al Hartmann, Pool; p. 27 (top): AP Photo/Damian Dovarganes; p. 27 (bottom): AP Photo/Jeff Roberson, File; p. 30: ©iStock/carrollphoto; p. 31: Toshi Sasak/Getty Images; p. 32: Ty Milford/Getty Images; p. 34: Paul Morigi/AP Images for Human Rights Campaign; p. 36: ©pixs4u/Shutterstock.com; p. 38: ©guruXOX/Shutterstock.com; p. 39: ©majo1122331/Shutterstock.com; p. 41: ©wavebreakmedia/Shutterstock.com

Chapter 3
p. 50: © iStock/wildpixel; p. 52: ©Leonard Zhukovsky/Shutterstock.com; p. 53: ©sirtravelalot/Shutterstock.com; p. 54: AP Photo/Chris Carlson; p. 56: Photo by Bastiaan Slabbers/NurPhoto/Sipa via AP Images; p. 57: Clatsop County Jail via AP; p. 58: AP Photo/News-Herald, Megan McCormick; p. 59: AP Photo/The Evansville Courier & Press, Molly Bartels; p. 61: AP Photo/Amy Sancetta; p. 63: AP Photo/Gerald Herbert, File; p. 67: Oliver Morrison/The Wichita Eagle via AP; p. 69: AP Photo/Nanine Hartzenbusch; p. 74: Jeff Gritchen/The Orange County Register via AP

Part II Opener
p. 81: © iStock/bowie15

Chapter 4
p. 82: ©Melkor3D/Shutterstock.com; p. 84: Ralph Barrera/Austin American-Statesman via AP; p. 87: Photo by Archiv Gerstenberg/ullstein bild via Getty Images; p. 88: © breakermaximus/Shutterstock.com; p. 90: © Susan Law Cain/Shutterstock.com; p. 91: ©iStock/Nastasic; p. 93: ©Annavee/Shutterstock.com; p. 94: AP Photo/Trent Nelson, Pool; p. 95: Messers. Elliot and Fry; p. 100: Mark Bugnaski/Kalamazoo Gazette, Live Media Group via AP, File; p. 103 (top): AP Photo/Stephen Chernin; p. 103 (bottom): ©iStock/Shelly Bychowski; p. 105: Photo by Alex Milan Tracy/Sipa via AP Images

Chapter 5
p. 110: © iStock/Skapl; p. 112: AP Photo/Stephen Chernin; p. 113: ©Morphart Creation/Shutterstock.com; p. 114: ©Everett Historical/Shutterstock.com; p. 115: ©TreesTons/Shutterstock.com; p. 118: AP Photo/Don Ryan; p. 120: ©Scanrail1/Shutterstock.com; p. 122: ©iStock/RichardUpshur; p. 123: Photo by Time Life Pictures/Mansell/The LIFE Picture Collection/Getty Images; p. 125: John Woods/The Canadian Press via AP; p. 126: AP Photo; p. 135: AP Photo/Brett Coomer, Pool; p. 137: ©iStock/Image Source

Chapter 6
p. 144: © iStock/DigtialStorm; p. 148: AP Photo/Jae C. Hong; p. 150: ©iStock/Richard Wellenberger; p. 151: ©Nikimlc/Shutterstock.com; p. 152: © Monkey Business Images/Shutterstock.com; p. 156: ©Frenzel/Shutterstock.com; p. 157: ©iStock/GeorgiaCourt; p. 159: Photo by Rolls Press/Popperfoto/Getty Images; p. 161: ©iStock/shironosov; p. 163: Ariel Skelley/Getty Images; p. 164: AP Photo/Paul Sakuma; p. 167: © Monkey Business Images/Shutterstock.com; p. 169: ©wavebreakmedia/Shutterstock.com

Chapter 7
p. 174: Mayte Torres/Getty Images; p. 176: AP Photo/Jim McKnight; p. 180: Iakov Filimonov/Shutterstock; p. 182: iStock/Getty Images Plus/mrohana; p. 183: Photo illustration by Daniel Berehulak/Getty Images; p. 185 (top): ©wavebreakmedia/Shutterstock.com; p. 185 (bottom): ©Rawpixel.com/Shutterstock.com; p. 188 (top): ©Rawpixel.com/Shutterstock.com; p. 188 (bottom): ©Axente Vlad/Shutterstock.com; p. 192: ©1000 Words/Shutterstock.com; p. 195: ©Pressmaster/Shutterstock.com; p. 196 (top): By Photographee.eu; p. 196 (bottom): ©Photobac/Shutterstock.com

Chapter 8

p. 204: Cal Sport Media via AP Images; p. 207: jeffbergen/Getty Images; p. 208: Melanie Stengel/Hartford Courant via AP; p. 211: ©iStock/Lwilk; p. 212: AP Photo; p. 215: Erik Overbey Collection, The Doy Leale McCall Library, University of South Alabama; p. 217: Photo by Ronen Tivony/NurPhoto/Sipa via AP Images; p. 222: John Spink/Atlanta Journal-Constitution via AP; p. 226: Photo/The Plain Dealer, Tracy Boulian; p. 227 (top): Photo by Douglas Graham/CQ Roll Call via AP Images; p. 227 (bottom): Photo by Erik McGregor/Pacific Press; p. 228: AP Photo/Henny Ray Abrams

Part III Opener

p. 233: ©MARCO SOLBIATI/Shutterstrock.com

Chapter 9

p. 234: ©Juan Carlos Vindas/Getty Images; p. 236: Press Association via AP Images; p. 239: Press Association via AP Images; p. 241: ©iStock/sassy1902; p. 243: AP Photo/Plain Dealer, Phaedra Singelis; p. 244: Getty images/iStock; p. 246: AP Photo/John Bazemore, File; p. 247: © iStock/NoDerog; p. 248: Photo by Olivier Douliery/Abaca, Sipa via AP Images; p. 251: Photo by Stephen Osman/Los Angeles Times via Getty Images; p. 253: James Neiss/The Niagara Gazette via AP

Chapter 10

p. 258: GABRIELLE LURIE/AFP/Getty Images; p. 260: Photo by David Becker/Getty Images; p. 263: ©iStock/kieferpix; p. 273: Photo by Erik McGregor/Pacific Press/LightRocket via Getty Images; p. 274: ©Ms Jane Campbell; p. 276: ©Anton Bielousov/Shutterstock.com; p. 279: AP Photo/Cliff Owen; p. 280: AP Photo/Reed Saxon; p. 282: AP Photo/Jeff Roberson; p. 283: Blend Images/Alamy Stock Photo; p. 284: ©iStock/marcduf

Chapter 11

p. 292: ©Skyward Kick Productions/Shutterstock.com; p. 297 (top): ©iStock/Agor2012; p. 297 (bottom): North Wind Picture Archives via AP Images; p. 299: AP Photo; p. 300: AP Photo; p. 304: US Drug Enforcement Administration via AP; p. 307: Dennis Van Tine/MediaPunch/IPX via AP; p. 308: © iStock/PeopleImages; p. 310: AP Photo/Ted S. Warren; p. 312: Rhett Butler/The Daily Reflector via AP; p. 314: Melissa Phillip/Houston Chronicle via AP

Chapter 12

p. 320: ©Adrian Today/Shutterstock.com; p. 323: ©Michael Gordon/Shutterstock; p. 324: Mike Marturello/ The Herald Republican via AP; p. 326 (top): AP Photo/Kathy Kmonicek, File; p. 326 (bottom): Everett Historical/Shutterstock.com©; p. 327: ©Stocksnapper/Shutterstock; p. 328: AP Photo/Richmond Times-Dispatch, Bob Brown; p. 331: AP Photo/Richmond Times-Dispatch, Bob Brown; p. 335: AP Photo/John Locher; p. 337: ©John Gomez/Shutterstock; p. 338: AP Photo/Nancy Kaye; p. 343: AP Photo/The Mountain Press, Curt Habraken

Part IV Opener

p. 347: ©Leonard Zhukovsky/Shutterstock.com

Chapter 13

p. 348: ©iStock/stillburning; p. 350: Centralized Bond Hearing Court, of Charleston, S.C. via AP; p. 356: iStock Editorial/Getty Images Plus; p. 357: AP Photo/Alexander Zemlianichenko; p. 358: AP Photo; p. 359: ©Everett Historical/Shutterstock.com; p. 360: AP Photo/Huntsville Times, Dave Dieter; p. 361: AP Photo/Rick Bowmer; p. 362: AP Photo; p. 367: AP Photo/Karl DeBlaker; p. 369 (top): AP Photo/pool, Mark Wilson/Getty; p. 369 (bottom): AP Photo/Rainier Ehrhardt

Chapter 14

p. 374: ©MikhailSh/Shutterstock.com; p. 376: AP Photo/Rich Pedroncelli; p. 378: ©digitalreflections/Shutterstock.com; p. 380: AP Photo/Tampa Bay Times; p. 383: AP Photo/Gillian Flaccus, File; p. 384: AP Photo/Rusty Kennedy; p. 388: AP Photo/Sue Ogrocki, File; p. 389: Crime Suppression Division of the Thailand via AP; p. 390: Photo by Alex Milan/ Sipa via AP Images; p. 391: AP Photo/Steven Senne; p. 392: AP Photo/Sue Ogrocki; p. 394: AP Photo/Paul San

Index

A reference that includes *d* indicates that the term is defined on the page. A *t* indicates that the information may be found in a table; *f* indicates that the information is located within a figure; *b* indicates that the information is located within a feature box; *p* indicates that the information is located in a photograph caption.

CHAPTER 6: Sociological Theories of Crime and Delinquency

THEORY	MAJOR THEORISTS	WHAT THE THEORY EXPLAINS	POLICY IMPLICATIONS	INFLUENTIAL ACTORS
SOCIAL DISORGANIZATION THEORY	Robert J. Sampson, William Julius Wilson		Urban renewal, neighborhood programs, planned communities, law-enforcement programs.	legislators, activists, neighborhood organizers, social workers, developers
Concentric zones	Ernest Burgess, Clifford R. Shaw, Henry D. McKay	Geographical areas radiate from an expanding urban center; each area has specific social attitudes.		
Collective efficacy	Robert Sampson, Stephen Raudenbush, Felton Earls	Measures the amount of informal social control and social cohesion in a community.		
LEARNING THEORIES		Focus on where and how offenders and delinquents find the tools, techniques, and expertise to break the law.	Parents and other authority figures should monitor children's friends and ensure they are enrolled in programs that provide pro-social activities and messages.	parents, teachers, coaches, clergy, law enforcement, social workers
Differential association	Edwin Sutherland	Crime is learned through interactions with antisocial peers.		
Techniques of neutralization	Gresham Sykes, David Matza	Delinquents generally believe in the law and break it only after they can rationalize their actions as necessary or unavoidable.		
Focal concerns of the lower class	Walter B. Miller	The lower socioeconomic class has focal concerns that encourage youths to break the law.		
Subculture of violence	Marvin Wolfgang, Franco Ferracuti	Describes how cultures apart from the main culture hold violence as part of their values, lifestyle, and socialization.		
Code of the street	Elijah Anderson	Requires people to quickly resort to violence when they feel they are not getting proper respect.		

CHAPTER 6: (Continued)

THEORY	MAJOR THEORISTS	WHAT THE THEORY EXPLAINS	POLICY IMPLICATIONS	INFLUENTIAL ACTORS
STRAIN THEORY	Robert Merton, Robert Agnew	Blocked opportunities cause strain within individuals which propels them toward unlawful behavior.	Increasing opportunities so strain does not build up to the point that individuals select crime as a way to release it; increasing quality of housing, jobs, relationships.	job coaches, employers, employment counselors, developers, clergy
Anomie	Emile Durkheim, Albert Cohen	Erosion of standards resulting from a lack of social control and values that leads to social instability.		
Deviant subcultures	Richard Cloward, Lloyd Ohlin	Deviant subcultures allow youths to adapt to the lack of legitimate opportunities to develop illegitimate ways of responding to the strain of impoverished and disorganized urban life.		
Institutional anomie	Richard Rosenfeld, Steven Messner	Institutional anomie occurs when commitment to social institutions such as family, religion, and education becomes subservient to achieving the goal of wealth.		
CONTROL THEORIES		Looks at why people do not break the law rather than why they do.	Develop more programs and support services so they do not resort to crime to fulfill their needs.	parents, teachers, counselors, recreational directors, clergy
Containment theory	Walter Reckless	Internal factors "push" people into crime and external factors "pull" them.		
Social bond theory	Travis Hirschi	Asks what factors keep juveniles law-abiding.		
Power-control theory	John Hagan	Seeks to explain why males commit more offenses and delinquency than females; focus on familial patriarchy.		

CHAPTER 7: Life-Course and Integrated Theories

THEORY	MAJOR THEORISTS	WHAT THE THEORY EXPLAINS	POLICY IMPLICATIONS	INFLUENTIAL ACTORS
LIFE-COURSE THEORIES		Focuses on the development of antisocial behavior, age-related risk factors, and the effect of life events on development.	Early intervention to prevent chronic delinquency, rehabilitation programs, employment, higher education.	coaches, teachers, spouses, military, employers
Developmental perspective on antisocial behavior	G. R. Patterson, Barbara D. DeBaryshe, Elizabeth Ramsey	Antisocial behavior begins early in life and often continues through adolescence and adulthood.		
Pathways to crime	Terrie Moffitt	Adolescent-limited offenders break the law during youth; life-course-persistent offenders continue into adulthood.		
Persistent offending and desistance from crime	John Laub, Robert Sampson	Individuals advance into conventional behavior via turning points and personal agency.		
INTEGRATED THEORIES		Combines theories to explain antisocial behavior.	Crime is explained in a more comprehensive manner, so policy implications are numerous.	Integrated theories use some or all of the actors already mentioned.
Interactional theory of delinquency	Terence Thornberry	Combines social learning, social bonds, and life-course theories; parent-youth bonds are important.		
Control balance theory	Charles Tittle	Individuals control their lives and society controls individuals; imbalance produces antisocial behavior.		
Social support theory	Francis Cullen	Social society affects individuals and institutions and the likelihood of crime.		
General theory of crime and delinquency	Robert Agnew	The major causes of crime lie within five life domains.		
Integrated cognitive antisocial potential theory	David Farrington	Factors combine to increase the likelihood of short-term and long-term antisocial behavior.		